BASEBALLHQ.COM'S **2014**

MINOR LEAGUE
BASEBALL
ANALYST

ROB GORDON AND JEREMY DELONEY | BRENT HERSHEY, EDITOR | NINTH EDITION

TRIUMPH
BOOKS

This book is available in quantity at special discounts for your group or organization. For further information, contact:

Triumph Books LLC
814 North Franklin Street
Chicago, Illinois 60610
(312) 337-0747
www.triumphbooks.com

Printed in U.S.A.
ISBN: 978-1-60078-842-0

Cover design by Brent Hershey
Front cover photograph by Kim Klement/USA TODAY Sports Images

Acknowledgments

Jeremy Deloney:

This is my fifth time around with the *Minor League Baseball Analyst* (MLBA) and I'd like to think that it gets easier each subsequent year, but it doesn't. Each year brings about different challenges and this year has been no exception. I am very honored to be part of the BaseballHQ.com team and I owe plenty of gratitude to many people.

My wife Amy is unbelievably supportive in whatever passion I pursue. She is the most selfless person I know and she sacrifices so much in order to make other people happy. She is a phenomenal wife, friend, mother, and overall human being. My kids and I are incredibly lucky to have her with us every single day.

My children—Owen, Ethan, and Madeline—are absolute treasures. Raising children is a thankless endeavor, but I wouldn't trade it for a Honus Wagner rookie card. Each of my kids is unique and I am very proud to be their father. I look forward to seeing them learn and grow as I encourage them to follow their passions, whether it is sports, music, dance, or electronics. I have great kids.

My parents—Bill and Nancy—and my brothers—BJ and Andy—have all helped make me the person I am today. I have a little bit of all of them in my personality and, unfortunately for them, they may have a little bit of me in them.

The terrific people at BaseballHQ.com have been instrumental in helping me pursue this passion. Deric McKamey helped get me started in this industry and I am forever grateful. Rob Gordon has been my partner in this book for the past five years and I've learned a great deal from him. Brent Hershey and Ray Murphy provide excellent leadership and organization and this book wouldn't be the success that it has become without their tireless efforts.

Lastly, I want to thank the readers and supporters of the MLBA. I appreciate your support and hope to see you again next year.

Rob Gordon:

In 2003 Ron Shandler gave me the opportunity to do something I'd wanted to do all of my life—write about baseball. Ron is one of the smartest baseball people I've ever had the pleasure of meeting and I owe him a huge thank you.

Deric McKamey took me under his wing and spent countless hours explaining what scouts look for. Deric's total recall of the most obscure minor league players still amazes me. Deric has moved on to bigger and better things in professional baseball, but his imprint on the structure and content of this book lives.

Jeremy Deloney and I are now in our fifth edition of the MLBA and each year I'm more and more impressed with his comprehensive and astute knowledge of the minor leagues. Jeremy sees tons of games in the MWL and elsewhere and is able to quickly and concisely analyze a player's potential.

I would also think to thank Brent Hershey. Brent served as our editor at BaseballHQ.com throughout the year and throughout the production of this book. Brent stuck by me in what was a challenging year—Thank you!

Many other baseball people provided invaluable support and encouragement over the years. They include Jeff Barton, Jim Callis, John Sickels, Ray Murphy, Rick Wilton, Patrick Davitt, Todd Zola, Jason Grey, Joe Sheehan, Jeff Erickson, Lawr Michaels, Mark Murray, Brian Walton, Jason Collette, Kimball Crossley, Steve Moyer, Phil Hertz, Jock Thompson, and Doug Dennis.

Some day someone will write a story about Baseball Unlimited. Until then I'll just have to thank the boys—Michael Hartman, Steve Hartman, Michael Cooney, Bob Hathaway, Doug Hathaway, Raj Patel, Derald Cook, Todd Hooper, Dave Dannemiller, Ted Maizes, Nick Gleckman, Greg Murrey, Randy Jones, and John Mundelius. You guys rock and may BU live forever!

My oldest son Bobby is in his second year of travel baseball. His Head Coach Brad Ebben took the team to another level. All of them improved and learned good sportsmanship along the way. I'd also like to thank Assistant Coaches Rob Stockman and Rob Curtis.

I would especially like to thank my family. My two boys—Bobby and Jimmy—make the sky bluer, the sun brighter, and the crack of the bat all the more sweet. My mother Sandra Gordon took me on an annual birthday trip to see the Cubs play and drove me to countless baseball practices. My father Robert W. Gordon III took me to Chicago to see the great Roberto Clemente play in his last season and has shared my passion for the game of baseball. My sister Susan Arntson helped raised me and tried to keep me out of trouble. Thank you! Her husband Jeff and kids Rachael, Josh, Marrisa, and Jake seem like more than just family.

Finally—a huge thank you to my amazing and beautiful wife Paula Gordon. This may sound like a cliché, but I really would not have been able to do this without her in my life.

TABLE OF CONTENTS

by Jeremy Deloney

Welcome to the *2014 Minor League Baseball Analyst*, the ninth edition of BaseballHQ.com's annual prospect book. Deric McKamey, now a scout with the St. Louis Cardinals, started the tradition several years ago and many elements of the 2014 book remain intact due to his invaluable insight and vision. We've expanded the minor league group at BHQ with knowledgeable writers and they've made significant contributions for this edition. Rob Gordon and I took the reins from Deric five years ago and while we've enjoyed putting this together, we wanted to bring more insights into the fold. Colby Garrapy and Chris Mallonee have unique perspectives while Brent Hershey continues to be at the top of his game. We know that you demand excellence and we strive to put a quality product in your hands. We hope you enjoy the contents as much as we do.

We understand that the universe of minor league baseball has grown exponentially. Doing a simple search on the Internet for minor league prospects will bring a voluminous amount of information, probably much more than necessary. It used to be difficult to keep tabs on your favorite minor leaguers. Now, several websites focus on this great game.

We truly appreciate the thirst for prospect information and there are several other qualified prospect sites and outlets available to you. Rob and I have done this for a long time and have connections within the game. We don't simply regurgitate information from other outlets and present it as our own. We spend a lot of time at minor league ballparks every summer and think it shows. We encourage you to make the MLBA a staple of your annual routine, whether it be taking it with you to a minor league game this summer, or enjoying the daily and weekly analysis via BaseballHQ.com.

The general format of the book has generally been constant over the years with a few wrinkles here and there. Some of the essays may appear to be similar to themes from years past and that is by design. We will continue to provide prospect assessments on over 1,000 players along with a vast amount of statistical analysis. It seems everybody loves lists and we've got more lists for your enjoyment. As always, we aren't looking for you to agree with everything the BHQ team brings to you, but our goal is to provide different perspectives and opinions that may challenge you to look a little closer. There aren't many things more enjoyable than a healthy debate—we have our own internal ones as well.

Writing this book is essentially a year-round process. We don't simply take last year's ratings, rankings, and grades and slightly modify them the way that college football pollsters adjust their weekly rankings. Watching games is an absolute must. Just as important is having contacts who can provide relatively insider information and scouting tips on various players. Even as a lifelong Midwesterner, I'd like to think I have a very solid knowledge base of the California League even though I have never attended a game in that circuit. The point is to compile and gather as much information and data as possible. Then, and only then, can we put pen to paper and write this book.

Due to the number of contributors to this edition, we split up the duties more equitably this time around. I still have the entire American League under my domain, along with San Diego. The National League was split between Rob (Atlanta, Chicago, Pittsburgh, St. Louis, Arizona and Colorado organizations), Colby (Miami, Milwaukee, Los Angeles, San Francisco), Chris (New York, Washington, and Cincinnati), and Brent (Philadelphia). Future editions will likely see even more diversification. There are many benefits to this approach, including offering different perspectives and areas of expertise. It is very evident that after editing and proofing the contents that these talented gentlemen know their stuff.

BaseballHQ.com's rating system has generated several questions and comments since it was introduced in 2007. The Potential Ratings is a two-part system in which a player is assigned a number rating based on his upside potential (1-10) and a letter rating based on the probability of reaching that potential (A-E). A 10 implies a Hall of Fame potential whereas a 1 is a minor league roster filler. Certainly you will not find a player less than 5 in the 2014 MLBA. The MLBA is filled with prospects of varying probability ratings, however.

The rating system is not an "end all, be all" system; there are times in which the argument could be made that an 8A player may actually be a 9D player. We rate players first by the upside potential. If a position player offers five tools or the potential for five tools, that player will receive a high number. If that same player has a history of poor performance or is in the lower depths of the minors, he may be assigned a low letter rating. Our goal isn't to squelch debate; rather it is to shed light on a player's ultimate potential.

What is the difference between an 8A and a 9D? It's a good question, and one that is difficult to answer. This depends on such factors including, but not limited to his athleticism, tools, ability to improve, and historical performance. Ratings can and will change, depending on the aforementioned factors. Our goal is to give you a snapshot of a player's ultimate upside and likelihood of success.

You may strongly agree with some of the ratings, rankings, and grades within the book. You may vehemently disagree with others. I have no problem if you disagree—offer me your evaluation and your reasons behind that assessment. I'd like to think that constructive criticism is healthy and necessary in order to grow as a talent evaluator.

Don't think of this book as just about stats. While there are a ton of numbers to enjoy, the defining aspects are the essays and prospect profiles. This is what we hope sets us apart from other baseball annuals. The essays and profiles attempt to add a little color to the black-and-white statistics and answer "why" or "how" those stats came to be. Additionally, analyzing minor league prospects is all about projection several years down the road.

The meat and potatoes of the book continue to be the hitter and pitcher profiles. We bring you expanded stats, tool assessments, expected arrival dates, draft info, potential roles, and their ultimate rating. While a player's skills may improve or regress from year to year, our goal is to qualify/quantify and measure a player at one certain point in time. Equally important as the statistical tables is the tool analysis. Over-analysis of statistics in the minor leagues can be a dangerous proposition. Not only are there severe hitters/pitchers environments, but these are mostly still young players who are developing their bodies and their games. Don't get too caught up in a hitter's BA or a pitcher's ERA—look deeper at their skills and how their tools project. That's where the BHQ team comes into play. It's one thing to look at an OBP and draw conclusions. It's another thing to provide reasons why the OBP is at a certain level and why it may get better or get worse.

Evaluating a hitter is based on several factors, including but not limited to bat speed, pitch recognition, plate discipline, power, and the ability to use the entire field. These factors can be evident in a player's stats, but some cannot. How does a player make adjustments? Does he have a loose swing with projection? Is he solely a fastball hitter who struggles with breaking stuff? There can be a lot of noise in statistical evaluation of a hitter. Park factors, age vs. level, hidden injuries, and a player's makeup can be such distractions. The job of a scout is to filter out the noise and gauge a player's future worth. Of course, we expect some disagreement from time to time. But isn't that part of the fun?

Pitching assessment also has its challenges. Certain statistics paint a colorful picture. ERA, Dom, Ctl, HR per game, and Cmd are very valuable. But how does an ERA in the hitter-friendly California League compare to an ERA in the spacious ballparks of the Florida State League? The pitcher profiles in the MLBA attempt to paint a picture beyond what the stats may say. Take a look at the types of pitches and their velocities that are provided in the book. Evaluating pitching can be much more difficult than hitters. Often times, a pitcher's command simply clicks and the prospect sees his status rise considerably. Sometimes, a pitcher

loses his pitchability and can't throw strikes. We attempt to determine if those skills can return.

We've kept the same format of the HQ100 as the 2013 edition. Prior to 2013, the Top 100 list was solely a combination of my and Rob's individual Top 100 lists. This year's HQ100 is the by-product of five individuals. It continues to be an interesting exercise to see how similar—and different—each list can be from one another. None of us looked at any other list prior to formulating our own. We'll again share both my list and Rob's list in this year's book.

Nothing seems to get more looks or debate than a Top 100 list. Many of our loyal readers know that I don't put too much stock into lists. Is there really that much of a difference between #25 and #100? Not really. Of course, personal biases come into play with any list and those are difficult to separate from the process. I can say that I considered about 170 players for my Top 100. I'd bet that if I put together a Top 100 from scratch tomorrow, it would likely look slightly different from the one that is in the book.

The Top Prospects By Position coordinate directly to the HQ100. The Top Prospects By Organization continue to be the individual lists of whichever BHQ writer covered that organization. That's why you may see a prospect that is ranked higher than another in their organization, but not in the HQ100. We all have our individual lists and we certainly don't practice groupthink.

We hope you enjoy the ninth edition of the MLBA. We work very hard all year to bring you the best product we can provide. Whether you are a fantasy baseball fanatic or simply a baseball fan, we welcome any opinions, ideas, constructive criticisms, or feedback. Read our essays, give our lists some thoughts, assess a prospect's statistical lines, and uncover something new you didn't know previous to opening the book. Enjoy the contents and the 2014 baseball season!

Poor Performers from the 2012 Draft

by Brent Hershey

Well, maybe 2011 wasn't that unique after all.

Last year in this space, we lauded the first round of 2011 MLB draft as an outlier, as so many of the picks started out well in pro ball. Looking back at 2012, it's much the same; the poor performers are more difficult to spot than the ones that hit the ground running. Perhaps it's a function of teams drafting better—weeding out the potential draftees with question marks, and spending their bonus money more wisely. Heck, maybe by next year, we won't even need this column.

But back to the present—there *are* enough first-round slow starters when we use last year's approach and extend our pool to the supplemental round. The quest is for players who have underperformed in their initial exposure to professional ball. The answer we seek: Do these players still have the goods to rebound and regain top-prospect status? Or are they on their irreversible path to "bust"?

In past years, we've identified some players who have gone on to re-gain their prospect status after a sluggish start to their professional career. Only time will tell us if any of these following players will follow:

Courtney Hawkins (OF, CHW) might be a bit of a stretch in the "poor performer" category. After all, he does have 27 home runs in his 612 professional at bats since being taken 13th overall in 2012. But it's the mind-boggling accumulation of strikeouts from 2013—160 in 103 games—that led to a .178 BA that rightfully have some worried. In retrospect, he was pushed to high-A before he was really ready, as he was one of the youngest players in the league. But the club also kept him there the whole season, choosing not to demote him in an attempt to re-establish his confidence. This case reminds us how much we, as outsiders, don't know about front offices and the choices they make regarding player development. The Sox must have thought either he would turn it around, or that he was strong enough to endure this failure. How Hawkins recovers, both statistically and mentally, from such a disastrous season will say a lot about his future potential—and Chicago's ability to judge what's best for one of their high draft picks.

D.J. Davis (OF, TOR) was selected #17 overall, but languished along in his second short-season assignment, hitting just .240 with very little power in 225 AB in the Appalachian League. Still a teenager, Davis did have 13 stolen bases, but was also caught eight times, which is curious given his top-grade speed. He'll have to improve on recognizing breaking pitches to get back on track to fulfill his potential as a MLB lead-off hitter. Some scouts even think he'll develop some power as he fills out.

Clint Coulter (C, MIL) started out in full-season Low-A ball in the Midwest League, but after he was clearly overmatched in his first 116 AB (.207/.299/.345), he logged time for two short-season affiliates. He had some success in the Arizona Rookie League, but it was more of the same in the Pioneer League (.573 OPS). Coulter was drafted with a considerable offensive upside, and while he showed some power in 2013 (7 HR over 250 combined AB), it's not what the Brewers were hoping for with the #27 pick. Still a physical specimen (6'3", 210), Coulter is from Washington state and it's likely that he needs is more baseball reps. He still has potential with the bat and will likely give the Midwest League another try in 2014.

Shane Watson (RHP, PHI) didn't have an awful season, but it was cut short by a shoulder issue that was still bothering him in the offseason. At 6'4" and 200 lbs., Watson has a classic power pitcher's build, but in 2013 his k/9 didn't reflect it—Dom fell to 6.6 and he walked more than usual. With a 92-94 fastball that he's not afraid to bring inside, a big-breaking curveball and a show-me change-up, the stuff is there when he's healthy. As long as the shoulder doesn't require surgery, Watson is a good bounceback candidate.

Matt Smoral (LHP, TOR) didn't pitch professionally in 2012 due to a foot injury, and the southpaw didn't fare well in short-season ball in 2013 (20 ER in 25.2 IP). He struggled mightily with control, walking 26 in those 25.2 IP, though he did strike out 27. Smoral is a huge 20-year-old at 6-8, 200 lbs., so it's perfectly understandable that there would be some rust to shake off. He gets a tough angle on his mid-90s fastball, and has a plus slider as well. Look for the Jays to take it slow with Smoral, but if he returns to throwing strikes, a big upside remains.

Mitch Gueller (PHI) is the second Phillie on this list; both he and Watson have had tough beginnings. Gueller made 14 starts at short-season Williamsport in 2013, but walked 4.0 batters per nine and only struck out 5.4 per nine. Supremely athletic and well-proportioned at 6'3", 210 lbs., Gueller had problems locating his breaking pitch and opponents banged out 83 hits in just 58.1 IP, along with a 5.89 ERA. The battering seemed to affect his confidence a bit, something he'll need to recover to renew his prospect status.

Walker Weickel (RHP, SD) is a case where it's best to set the ugly 5.04 ERA and 1.52 WHIP from 2013 aside. Tall and lanky (6'6", 195 lbs.), he has three potential average-to-plus pitches and pitched in a full-season league at 19 years old. There's some physical projection in his profile, he had some good stretches through the season, and has been lauded for his pitching instincts. It might take some time and he likely isn't top-of-the-rotation material, but the ingredients are in place for a 2014 rebound.

Steve Bean (C, STL) is generally seen as the organization's best defensive catcher in the minors. But outside of 50 AB in the Gulf Coast League, Bean's bat has had a tough time in two stops in Rookie-level Johnson City. In 2013 he hit just .229 with just six extra-base hits in 188 AB. The Cardinals still believe there's enough pop in his bat to succeed, but the lefty swinger has had trouble smoothing out his mechanics and putting the ball in play (44 Ks in 2013). Given the demands of catching, he might take additional development time than first anticipated.

2013 First-Year Player Draft Recap

by Jeremy Deloney

AMERICAN LEAGUE

BALTIMORE ORIOLES

The Orioles haven't been among the deeper farm systems in baseball, but they did well in stockpiling high school and junior college players at the top of the draft. These prospects, highlighted by RHP Hunter Harvey (1st) and OF Josh Hart (supplemental 1st), were chosen with Baltimore's first seven selections. They felt a strong need to bolster their catching depth by drafting and signing three prep catchers in the first six rounds. C Chance Sisco (2nd) has the potential to become a do-everything backstop, though will likely need time to develop. While the Orioles didn't focus on pitching, they nabbed a high upside arm in LHP Stephen Tarpley (3rd) who feasted on rookie-level hitting by posting a 2.14 ERA, 1.3 Ctl, and 10.7 Dom in 21 innings in his debut. Baltimore signed 17 of their first 18 selections.
Sleeper: LHP Steven Brault (11th) used his precise fastball location to succeed at short-season Aberdeen with a 2.09 ERA and 8.0 Dom in 12 starts. His stuff isn't overwhelming by any means, but he knows how to pitch and keep hitters off-guard.
Grade: B

BOSTON RED SOX

The Red Sox benefited from a rare early pick in the first round and selected high-upside LHP Trey Ball (1st) out of an Indiana high school. He has an incredibly high ceiling and Boston is excited to bring him into the fold. They also were able to select a slew of pitchers with strong arms and excellent velocity. RHP Teddy Stankiewicz (2nd) and RHP Myles Smith (4th) have solid potential whether as a starter or reliever. Not many position players were selected early, though C Jonathan Denney (3rd) gives the Red Sox another potential stud backstop. He is big and strong with excellent raw power. This class may take time to develop, but there is intriguing upside here.
Sleeper: RHP Joe Gunkel (18th) was absolutely terrific after his selection out of small West Chester (PA) University. He throws from a low ¾ slot and gets good pitch movement to deceive hitters. He was 3-0 with a 1.29 ERA and 14.1 Dom in 21 innings between the rookie-level Red Sox and short-season Lowell.
Grade: B+

CHICAGO WHITE SOX

The White Sox quietly put together a robust draft class with a terrific mix of position players and pitchers. Further, they were able to sign their first 32 picks, including a handful of quality high schoolers. Top pick SS Tim Anderson (1st) was among the more athletic players in the draft and could evolve into a quality offensive infielder. The biggest surprise of the draft class was OF Adam Engel (19th) who dominated the short-season Appalachian League and is already one of their better prospects. An intriguing selection, RHP Tyler Danish (2nd), is as advanced as any high school pitcher in the draft and he could ascend the ladder quickly with an impressive mix of command and arm action.

Sleeper: 3B Trey Michalczewski (7th) was selected out of an Oklahoma high school and has excellent raw power from both sides of the plate. He'll need to work on his defense as well as his pitch selectivity, but he could become an ideal 3B with good power and arm strength.
Grade: B+

CLEVELAND INDIANS

One organization who made it a point to bolster their pitching depth was Cleveland. After nabbing high school OF Clint Frazier in the first round, the Indians went with pitchers with their next seven picks. Though much of their bonus pool was allocated to the high upside Frazier, they were able to sign a few terrific pitching prospects in the 3rd through 5th rounds. LHP Kyle Crockett (4th) could be the first college arm to reach the majors, and he has the look of a lefty specialist in the bullpen. He has solid, present command and a good breaking ball. RHP Dace Kime (3rd) is a college pitcher with a deep repertoire, but needs to throw more consistent strikes. LHP Sean Brady (5th) was a high school selection who merits a long look with his advanced feel and clean delivery. The position players were scant, but Frazier has the talent to carry the torch of this draft class.
Sleeper: OF Silento Sayles (14th) is far from a polished product, but the prepster has unbelievable speed and athleticism. He has surprising pop in his 5'9" frame, but his speed is what sets him apart.
Grade: B-

DETROIT TIGERS

It could be argued that the Tigers played it the safest of any organization in baseball by selecting college pitchers with their first seven picks. Their first high school selection was in the 23rd round, though he didn't sign. There also weren't many position players who exhibit great upside. The pitching prospects were led by Florida RHP Jonathon Crawford (1st). He's been inconsistent, but has a great arm and the ability to register Ks. He could move quickly if converted to a reliever. RHP Corey Knebel (supplemental 1st) pitched out of the bullpen and could move to the rotation, but he can dominate in short stints. The Tigers like college arms from major programs to stockpile the lower minors and the 2014 campaign will be no different.
Sleeper: RHP Calvin Drummond (6th) is already 24, but he has a strong, raw arm that produces easy mid-90s velocity. He also mixes in a hard slider. At Low-A West Michigan, he pitched 40 innings and posted a 2.23 ERA and 10.5 Dom out of the pen.
Grade: C

HOUSTON ASTROS

With the first overall pick in the draft, the Astros opted for Stanford RHP Mark Appel (1st) who not only has a high ceiling, but he has an elevated floor. The organization did a solid job in scouring the college ranks for arms and position players. Pitchers were also selected in the next two rounds with college RHP Andrew Thurman (2nd) and LHP Kent Emanuel (3rd). Thurman has the more polished skill set and simply knows how to pitch. The Astros really like Emanuel who may lack ideal velocity and projection, but he throws strikes from a good angle to the plate.

The position players aren't thought of as highly, but there are some good ones here. 1B Conrad Gregor (4th) has the ingredients to become a terrific pro hitter, but may need to change his approach to realize his power potential.

Sleeper: 2B/OF Tony Kemp (5th) has a small (5'6") frame, but is an amazing athlete with top-of-the-line speed. He plays small ball well and knows the value of getting on base consistently so he can wreak havoc on the basepaths.

Grade: B+

KANSAS CITY ROYALS

It was considered a surprise when the Royals selected college SS Hunter Dozier (1st) with the #8 overall pick, but they were able to sign him for less than slot and use the extra amount on Indiana State LHP Sean Manaea (supplemental 1st). They also signed junior college LHP Cody Reed (2nd) to a seven figure bonus. All in all, the Royals had quite a haul in a top-heavy draft. Manaea didn't pitch upon signing, rather he underwent hip surgery to repair a torn labrum. For the most part, Kansas City chose a nice variety of players and could have a steal in Georgia Tech C Zane Evans (4th). He quieted his doubters by destroying the Pioneer League upon signing. The success of the draft will be predicated on the success of the top three guys, but there is a lot to like.

Sleeper:1B Brandon Dulin (12th) has a big frame and exciting power potential. He has some tweaks to work out with his hitting mechanics, but he has value outside of his bat. He runs well and could potentially move to the outfield.

Grade: B+

LOS ANGELES ANGELS

They didn't have a first round pick—again—but did add depth to their scant pitching ranks by selecting 10 arms with their first 11 picks. The Angels weren't afforded the luxury of a high bonus pool, but they still managed to sign all but one of their draftees. High school LHP Hunter Green (2nd) was the only big name popped in this draft class. He has an athletic delivery, but doesn't have a plus fastball quite yet. There are other pitchers who could turn into good picks. RHP Elliot Morris (4th) uses a lively fastball and athletic, durable build. RHP Harrison Cooney (6th) also has some giddyup with his fastball, though he doesn't have great upside. Position players were relatively scarce, though 3B Cal Towey (17th) and OF Michael Fish (32nd) enjoyed impressive pro debuts.

Sleeper: LHP Cole Swanson (19th) pitched at a small college in California, but he knows how to pitch with limited stuff. He is tough to make hard contact against with a deceptive delivery and a slider that can miss bats. He could become a lefty specialist.

Grade: D

MINNESOTA TWINS

Looking at the draft class for the Twins, it was obvious they wanted to stockpile pitchers and catchers. Four of their first five picks were arms while three catchers were selected in the first nine rounds. Outside of prep RHP Kohl Stewart (1st), Minnesota chose relatively safe picks, though some have the potential to do more than expected. Stewart is clearly the jewel of the selections, but college RHP Ryan Eades (2nd) continues to tease with

his impressive arsenal. The Twins are high on college C Stuart Turner (3rd) who should reach the big leagues based upon his glove alone. He surpassed expectations with his bat upon signing. The most intriguing pitcher chosen could be high school LHP Stephen Gonsalves (4th) who has significant projection and could become a rare power arm in the system.

Sleeper: RHP Brian Gilbert (7th), a college draftee, has a big fastball out of the bullpen and could move quickly. He sits in the low-to-mid 90s and is only a more polished breaking ball away from becoming a high K pitcher in the minors.

Grade: B-

NEW YORK YANKEES

Blessed with three first round picks, the Yankees jumped all over the available talent and signed each of the three for at least $1.65 million. 3B Eric Jagielo (1st) is a pure hitter who makes easy contact with a smooth stroke. Big and very athletic OF Aaron Judge (1st) was the second first-rounder and he brings power potential to the organization. LHP Ian Clarkin (1st), a high school pitcher, has good velocity to go along with a terrific curveball. They selected a good mix of players with a wide variety of skills—power, athleticism, natural hitters. They went with position players with five of their first six picks and later focused on building depth within the college ranks.

Sleeper: SS Tyler Wade (4th) wasn't ranked very highly entering the season, but the high school selection showed excellent defensive skills with good hands and range while also exhibiting the potential to become an average hitter down the road.

Grade: A-

OAKLAND ATHLETICS

The Athletics may have the most balanced draft class with a nice mix of position players and solid arms. They also injected some youth into the system with a handful of high school players. Prep OF Billy McKinney (1st) was the highlight of their selections, but Oakland was able to nab quality pitchers as well. LHP Dillon Overton (2nd) likely won't pitch until late 2014 due to Tommy John surgery, but he combines deception with the ability to sequence and change speeds. Their best drafted pitcher may be RHP Bobby Wahl (5th) who has a first round arm. He immediately becomes one of their better prospects. Another well-known pitcher selected was RHP Dylan Covey (4th) who was a first round pick by Milwaukee in 2010.

Sleeper: OF Justin Higley (13th) is all about tools and projection. He has a very athletic build at 6'4" and has the power-speed combination that the Athletics covet. He needs significant polish, but he fared well in Rookie ball upon signing.

Grade: A-

SEATTLE MARINERS

Many organizations focused on pitching, but the Mariners had other ideas by selecting position players with five of their first six picks, including the first three. They opted for several college players while also mixing in some nice middle infielders as they always do. The trio of 3B D.J. Peterson (1st), OF Austin Wilson (2nd), and OF Tyler O'Neill (3rd) is as good as any three round haul in this overall draft. Peterson is a natural hitter who should be able to hit for both BA and power. Wilson has excellent athleticism and impact tools while O'Neill complements the other two with a solid all-around game. There aren't too many arms to get overly excited about, though LHP Ryan Horstman brings athleticism and pure arm strength to the mound.

Sleeper: SS Jack Reinheimer (5th) has the natural athleticism and quickness to profile as a big league shortstop. He may not have much of a power profile, but he puts the ball in play with a patient, contact-oriented approach.

Grade: A-

TAMPA BAY RAYS

This is an organization with the reputation for selecting quality high school athletes and this draft didn't do anything to change that perception. The Rays had two first round picks and selected high school C Nick Ciuffo (1st) and Arkansas RHP Ryne Stanek (1st), two players who could become standouts at the big league level. The draft class was littered with athletic position players, several of whom have good speed and terrific defensive ability. SS Riley Unroe (2nd) should be able to stick at shortstop and OF Thomas Milone (3rd) has excellent potential in CF. The Rays didn't opt for many arms, though Stanek is good enough to carry the class on his shoulders with a fastball that touches the high-90s.

Sleeper: 2B Kean Wong (4th) is the brother of Cardinals 2B Kolten and has similar tools and skills. He batted .328/.377/.390 with a nifty approach and solid contact ability. He won't hit for plus power, but is a relatively safe bet to reach the big leagues.

Grade: B

TEXAS RANGERS

The Rangers inevitably changed course this year and added a number of quality arms to the organization after focusing on position players the previous two seasons. Simply put, this was an outstanding draft with a combination of high upside prospects and safe, secure bets. They really like the power arms possessed by RHP Alex Gonzalez (1st) and RHP Akeem Bostic (2nd). Both had success upon signing and could appear on several top prospect lists at any time, especially Gonzalez. RHP David Ledbetter (3rd) was chosen from a small Ohio college, but has the goods to be an asset at the middle or back-end of the rotation. High school SS Travis Demeritte (1st) could eventually become an impact bat, but needs to work on his defense. This may be the best draft class of any in baseball.

Sleeper: RHP Sam Wolff (6th) owns a huge fastball that reaches the upper-90s, though he generates velocity despite a small frame. He simply dominated pro ball at short-season Spokane and Low-A Hickory, posting a 0.60 ERA and 13.2 Dom in 30 innings.

Grade: A

TORONTO BLUE JAYS

They focused on pitching by selecting arms with their first nine picks, though the Blue Jays were unable to ink high school RHP Phil Bickford (1st) to a contract. The lack of a first round signing has a devastating impact on the upside potential of the draft class, but there are reasons to be excited. They were able to sign high school LHP Jake Brentz (11th) and power-hitting prep 1B Rowdy Tellez (30th) in later rounds with well over-slot bonuses. The best

of the signed pitchers is RHP Clint Hollon (2nd) who can hit the mid-90s with his fastball while mixing in a good breaking ball. As they didn't draft a position player until the 10th round, the Blue Jays are pinning their hopes on Tellez.

Sleeper: LHP Matt Boyd (6th) was selected from Oregon State and immediately assigned to Low-A Lansing upon signing a contract. He fared well on two levels, including High-A Dunedin, by posting a 2.63 ERA, 1.5 Ctl, and 8.6 Dom. He won't wow with a great pitch mix, though his offerings are sufficient to succeed, especially with solid command.

Grade: C

NATIONAL LEAGUE

ARIZONA DIAMONDBACKS

The Diamondbacks used their top two picks in the draft to add pitching depth, taking college right-handers Braden Shipley (Nevada) and Aaron Blair (Marshall) with the 15th and 41st picks. Shipley has a plus 93-96 mph fastball that tops out at 99 mph. He's a bit raw on the mound and had mixed results in his pro debut, but has the velocity and secondary offerings to be a legit #2 starter. Blair doesn't have the same long-term potential, but is a bit more polished and both should move up quickly. The trade of Matt Davidson, leaves the organization a bit thin of high-end position prospects, but they did add two interesting prospects in OF Justin Williams (2nd round) and 2B Jamie Westbrook (4th round). Williams is somewhat of a project, but has as much raw power as any player in the draft.

Sleeper: Jimmy Sherfy (RHP) was one of the better college closers for the University of Oregon. Sherfy has a good 94-96 mph fastball and a swing-and-miss slider. He had an impressive pro debut, going 1-1 with a 1.04 ERA, 4 BB/29 K in 17.1 IP. Given his plus two-pitch mix and collegiate experience, he could advance quickly.

Grade: A- *(Rob Gordon)*

ATLANTA BRAVES

The Braves had to wait until the 31st pick before they made their first selection in the 2013 draft and not surprisingly they took a starting pitcher. Oklahoma State right-hander Jason Hursh made it four years in a row that the Braves have taken a pitcher with their first pick. Hursh has a plus fastball that sits at 93-96 mph and has been clocked as high as 99 mph. He had Tommy John surgery in 2011, but was fully recovered leading up to the draft. Hursh also has a good slider and a decent change-up, but needs to be more consistent. The Braves also added a nice power bat in Victor Caratini and they will attempt to move him behind the plate during instructional play. If that experiment works, the quality of their draft improves greatly. They also added speedy OF Kyle Wren (8th), son of General Manager Frank Wren, who hit .328 with 35 SB at Low-A and RHP Carlos Salazar who features a plus upper-90s heater.

Sleeper: Michael Swanner (RHP) was taken in the 16th round after serving as Pepperdine's closer. Swanner has a good low-90s sinking fastball. He throws strikes and has some nice deception. He looked impressive in his debut, posting a 1.99 ERA with 6 BB/20 K in 22.2 IP for Danville.

Grade: B- *(Rob Gordon)*

CHICAGO CUBS

3B Kris Bryant (1st) and OF Jacob Hannemann (3rd) were the only position players selected in the first eight rounds, but the Cubs needed to stockpile their organization with arms. They handed out three seven-figure bonuses and weren't shy about aggressively going after players who fell due to signability concerns. RHP Trevor Clifton (12th) falls into that category. LHP Rob Zastryzny (2nd) is a college pitcher who should get to the majors fairly quickly. He can locate his fastball impeccably and has good enough secondary offerings to stick in the rotation. RHP Trey Masek (5th) has a deep arsenal and could eventually become a late-innings reliever with a solid, lively fastball. The goal was to add pitching and the Cubs did just that while picking a terrific prospect in Bryant with the second overall pick.

Sleeper: RHP Scott Frazier (6th) has the kind of arm that scouts crave and he can pepper the strike zone with mid-90s heat. He also has a nice breaking ball and average change-up. The hope is that professional coaching will help iron out his delivery and allow him to throw consistent strikes.

Grade: A-

CINCINNATI REDS

With two of the first 38 picks, the Reds were able to secure the services of two terrific college players, OF Phillip Ervin (1st) and RHP Michael Lorenzen (supplemental 1st). Both enjoyed success immediately upon signing and could sniff the big leagues within 2 seasons, if not sooner. The Reds signed their first 14 picks and were able to sprinkle in a handful of high school players who could pay long-term dividends. The focus was on pitching and the best of the lot after Lorenzen could be college RHP Ben Lively (4th) who registers strikeouts with a combination of deception and good stuff. He could join Lorenzen on the fast track. The highest upside among high school hitters belongs to 3B K.J. Franklin (2nd) who brings plenty of raw power to the table, but he swings and misses quite a bit.

Sleeper: SS Cory Thompson (5th) has positive tools and could grow into a legitimate big league shortstop. He possesses athleticism, good hands, and a strong arm. As a hitter, he has some power, but focuses on contact with a repeatable stroke.

Grade: B+

COLORADO ROCKIES

The Rockies had one of the better draft classes and focused on college players, both pitchers and position guys. They were delighted to see RHP Jonathan Gray (1st) fall to them at #3 and he could turn out to have the best career out of anybody in this draft. He dominated upon signing and posted a 0.75 ERA, 2.3 Ctl, and 13.5 Dom in five starts at High-A Modesto. 3B Ryan McMahon (2nd) was one of only three high school players selected in the first 19 rounds, but the Rockies are counting on him to be a cornerstone type of player. The Rockies used some of their bonus pool to draft and sign INF Dom Nunez (6th) for an $800,000 bonus and he could be a steal given his instincts and power potential. Gray could make or break this draft on his own accord, but they could use depth with pitchers like RHP Alex Balog (supplemental 2nd) and LHP Sam Moll (3rd).

Sleeper: OF Terry McClure (8th) was a pick out of high school and is best known for his plus speed. He has a ways to go to become a polished hitter, but there are intriguing tools with his average power potential and ability to be a very good CF.

Grade: A-

LOS ANGELES DODGERS

After taking college performers in the first three rounds—including pitchers with the first two picks—the Dodgers went the high school and junior college route for the next three. The standouts of the class were clearly RHP Chris Anderson (1st) and LHP Tom Windle (2nd), the top two selections. Both were immediately successful in Low-A and have the potential to ascend the minor league ladder very quickly. With strong fastballs and very good breaking balls, they could become top prospects in the near-term. The selected position players don't carry nearly as much upside, though the Dodgers like the potential of 1B Cody Bellinger (4th) who has good hitting acumen and solid defensive ability. A few catchers—Kyle Farmer (8th) and Spencer Navin (11th)—have major league ability as well.

Sleeper: RHP Jacob Rhame (6th) has the pitch mix of a reliever at this point, but he brings a fastball that tops out in the mid-90s. He can be tough to hit, but needs polish to his secondary offerings to have a greater role.

Grade: B

MIAMI MARLINS

The depth of the draft class is challenged after the Marlins failed to sign two of their top five selections, including high upside LHP Mark Krook in the supplemental first round. All hope isn't lost, however, as they were able to ink their first round pick 3B Colin Moran, a smooth-swinging infielder who has as good of an approach as any. After Moran, they also chose several position players, including OF K.J. Woods (4th) who has excellent power to all fields, but may spend quite a few years in the minors. Of the first eleven draftees who signed, only two were pitchers. RHP Trevor Williams (2nd) and RHP Colby Suggs (supplemental 2nd) both have excellent velocity, though Suggs has a reliever profile. The Marlins really didn't go too much above slot to sign players and the lack of depth is concerning.

Sleeper: SS Justin Bohn (7th) is a sound defender who can play multiple positions, including 3B. His glove is ahead of his bat at this stage of the game, but he offers a simple approach and has some punch in his quick bat.

Grade: D

MILWAUKEE BREWERS

They were another organization without a first round selection, but drew rave reviews with their first two picks out of high school. RHP Devin Williams (2nd) and SS/3B Tucker Neuhaus (supplemental 1st) were both potential first rounders. Williams has very high upside predicated on his strong arm and athleticism. He could soon find himself as the Brewers top prospect if he continues his success in 2014. They also popped several strong arms to go along with a number of pure hitters. There is evidence of nice balance between college and high school as well as pitching and position players. The lack of a first rounder may hurt the ceiling of this draft class, but there were enough selections to give the Brewers hope for the future.

Sleeper: RHP Andy Hillis (11th) dominated the Pioneer League upon signing, posting a 0.44 ERA, 5.2 Ctl, and 10.0 Dom in 20.2 innings out of the bullpen. He mostly works with a high-90s fastball and uses his size (6'7") as leverage. With a more consistent slider could come closing opportunities.

Grade: C

NEW YORK METS

The Mets were focused on upside as they took high school players with their first four picks in the draft. After that, they essentially focused on filling the system with college selections. All in all, this was a fairly balanced draft. 1B Dominic Smith (1st) highlights the class and he has a chance to be a special player. He found pro ball to his liking and could move quickly for a prep player. OF Ivan Wilson (3rd) brings heavy lumber to the lineup, though he has the profile to spend another year in short-season ball. He could also stick in CF and possesses above average speed. The Mets like the raw arm strength of RHP Andrew Church (2nd) and believe he has the pitchability to be a vital part of the future rotation. Projection is the name of the game for RHP Casey Meisner (3rd) who stands 6'7", but needs to find consistency with his mechanics.

Sleeper: OF Jared King (5th) has an all-around skill-set and has solid athleticism to match his offensive prowess. There are varying opinions on his power potential, but he is a good hitter from both sides with bat speed and strength.

Grade: C+

PITTSBURGH PIRATES

The Pirates could arguably have the best draft haul after having two first round picks and the wherewithal to ink their first twenty selections. They nabbed two high school players in OF Austin Meadows and C Reese McGuire in the first 14 overall picks and could team them with OF JaCoby Jones to provide outstanding upside with three bats. The pitching selections may not have the same upside, but there are a handful who could be useful in a variety of roles. LHP Blake Taylor (2nd) could be a steal due to his athleticism and projection while LHP Cody Dickson (4th), a college arm, has the potential to become even better with professional coaching. There isn't much to scoff at with this draft class and while they had the bonus pool to get high profile guys, they also spent wisely in the later rounds.

Sleeper: SS Adam Frazier (6th) has an innate feel for the game to enhance his average tools. Don't expect much pop from his bat, but he uses the entire field with his line drive approach and gets on base at a consistent clip.

Grade: A

PHILADELPHIA PHILLIES

The Phillies eschewed pitching in favor of position players and they picked quite a haul. They chose position players with their first five selections, including four from high school. RHP Shane Martin (9th) was the first pitcher to be drafted and signed. The class is clearly highlighted by exciting SS J.P. Crawford (1st) who is ultra-athletic and has above average defensive abilities. He's also a solid hitter with excellent speed. OF Cord Sandberg (3rd) signed

despite his commitment to Mississippi State for football. Now that he'll focus on baseball, he's sure to iron out the wrinkles in his game. C Andrew Knapp (2nd) has the power that the Phillies covet, but he needs work behind the plate. Additionally, he underwent Tommy John surgery in the fall.

Sleeper: RHP Dan Child (18th) is a reliever with a ton of effort in his delivery, but that effort also enhances his stuff. He can fire fastballs into the mid-90s while mixing in a solid-average slider. He could move quickly as he reached High-A at the end of the season.

Grade: B

ST. LOUIS CARDINALS

The Cardinals put a premium on pitching and they loaded up with two lefties with their two first round picks. Overall, they signed their first 29 selections and were able to lure three players in the last six rounds with six-figure bonuses. The Cardinals spent quite a bit of coin on this class, but it was money well spent. LHP Marco Gonzales (1st) may not have great velocity, but he has a plus-plus change-up and simply knows how to attack hitters. LHP Rob Kaminsky (1st) was a high school pitcher with an advanced arsenal for his age. RHP Mike Mayers (3rd) wasn't considered a great prospect entering the draft, but he works with a nice repertoire and could get better with a more polished delivery. There aren't many position players that stand out, but SS Oscar Mercado (2nd) has the glove and footwork to be an outstanding shortstop some day.

Sleeper: RHP Nick Petree (9th) has a well above average feel for pitching and commands his pitches extremely well. He doesn't light up the radar guns with a high-80s fastball, but he can cut and sink while mixing in a big-bending curveball.

Grade: B-

SAN DIEGO PADRES

The Padres did a spectacular job of mixing things up with this draft class, choosing a wide range of players. They chose position players with six of the first eight selections—including the first three—but also selected high upside pitchers down the line. The biggest surprise in the first handful of rounds was RHP Bryan Verbitsky (3rd). The Padres were intrigued with his pure arm strength and will give him time to develop now that he will concentrate on pitching. OF Hunter Renfroe (1st) brings a classic RF profile to the organization and should evolve into a power hitter. 3B Dustin Peterson (2nd) has a nice approach at the plate and pure hitting skills to hit for BA. Two high school hitters with upside—OF Jordan Paroubeck (supplemental 2nd) and 1B Mason Smith (4th)—could be the jewels of the class if they develop as hoped.

Sleeper: RHP Trevor Gott (6th) is a smallish reliever, but owns a big arm that produces a low-to-mid 90s fastball with plenty of late action. There is some deception in his delivery that enhances his arsenal, especially his breaking ball that befuddled hitters in Low-A.

Grade: A-

SAN FRANCISCO GIANTS

After taking two prep hitters with their first two picks, the Giants selected college players with the next eight. They raised eyebrows when they popped SS Christian Arroyo (1st) with the 25th overall pick and then reaching for 3B Ryder Jones (2nd) in the second round. Both justified their high spots with terrific debuts in Rookie ball. Jones has a bit more pop whereas Arroyo has natural hitting skills with better defensive chops. College RHPs Chase Johnson (3rd), Dan Slania (5th) and Nick Vander Tuig (6th) are ideal for development and could pitch in a number of roles. Johnson has the most upside of any pitcher in the class. C John Riley (31st) could be a steal in the later rounds and the Giants inked him to a $450,000 bonus. He was considered a tough sign and fell in the draft as a result.

Sleeper: RHP Pat Young (13th) pitched out of the bullpen upon signing and was quite good with two pitches. He stands 6'5" and throws from a low ¾ slot, but gets heavy action on his low-to-mid 90s fastball. He threw strikes in his pro debut and could grow into a solid setup man.

Grade: B

WASHINGTON NATIONALS

They didn't have a first round selection and didn't pick until #68 when they popped RHP Jake Johansen (2nd) from Dallas Baptist. The Nationals like the pitchers they selected in the early rounds, though only Johansen as intriguing upside. RHP Austin Voth (5th) started 11 games between 3 levels and posted a 1.2 Ctl and 10.7 Dom along with a 1.75 ERA. There weren't many position players to get overly excited about, though high school 3B Drew Ward (3rd) showed polish and pure hitting ability in his pro debut. The success of this draft class will be almost entirely dependent on how the pitchers turn out. RHP Nic Pivetta (4th) could be one who flies under the radar, but he needs more experience.

Sleeper: SS David Masters (14th) is a sure-handed infielder who oozes athleticism. He is a pure shortstop with enough range and arm to be a standout with the glove. He may not profile well with the bat, though he owns a decent approach and some wiry strength.

Grade: C

Top 20 International Prospects for 2014

by Rob Gordon

Jose Abreu (1B, CHW)

Abreu is a 26-year-old who defected from Cuba in August of 2012. At 6-3, 250 pounds, he has plus raw power and a good approach. There are concerns about his bat speed and ability to handle quality fastballs, especially on the inside half. He moves reasonably well at 1B, but overall has below-average athleticism and speed. The White Sox made a substantial investment and Abreu will be expected to contribute right away. In 2010-11, Abreu hit an amazing .453/.597/.986 with 33 HR in 66 games.
Signing bonus/status: Signed a six-year, $68 million deal
MLB Debut: 2014

Erisbel Arruebarruena (SS, Cuba)

Arruebarruena was 23 when he defected from Cuba in November 2013. He is a slick defender in the mold of the Tigers Jose Iglesias with a Gold Glove ceiling. He has great range, soft hands, and a strong arm. Scouts are mixed on his ability to hit for average due to a long swing, limited bat speed, and ability to hit off-speed offerings.
Signing bonus/status: Remains a free agent
MLB debut: 2015

Rusney Castillo (2B/OF, Cuba)

In December, Castillo became the latest player to defect from Cuba. The 26-year-old was considered one of the country's better players and has seen action at 2B, 3B, and CF. At 5-9, 185 he has nice pop for his size, but is more of a gap hitter, despite 18 HR in 2010-11 and 16 the following year. He is a plus runner and can create havoc on the bases. Defensively he uses his speed competently at multiple positions. He can be overly aggressive at bat, but his versatility, experience, and speed should have plenty of value.
Signing bonus/status: Castillo remains a free agent
MLB debut: 2014

Rafael Devers (3B, BOS)

Devers was one of the more polished hitters in this year's Latin American pool. He has an exaggerated leg kick that might need adjustment, but once under way he has a smooth left-handed stroke. He shows good bat speed and projectable power as he loads well and explodes through the ball. His defense is average, but he moves well at 3B, has good hands, and a strong arm. Devers is more advanced and doesn't have as much projection as some of the other international prospects.
Signing bonus/status: Signed for $1.5 million
MLB debut: 2017

Marcos Diplan (RHP, TEX)

Diplan is a short, skinny right-hander from the Dominican Republic. He has a quick arm and comes after hitters with a good 90-93 mph fastball that tops out at 94 mph. He also shows the making of a good power curveball and a seldom used change-up. He locates all three offerings well and has some nice deception in his delivery and is aggressive on the mound.
Signing bonus/status: Signed for $1.3 million
MLB debut: 2018

Shintaro Fujinama (RHP, Japan)
The 19-year-old right-hander had a solid rookie season for the Hanshin Tigers, going 10-6 with a 2.75 ERA. He struck out 126 and walked 44 in 137.2 IP. Fujinama has a good 90-94 mph fastball with late life. He also features a potentially plus hard slider, a splitter, and a decent change-up. Shintaro showed solid command in high school and posted a respectable 2.8 Ctl ratio in his debut. Like his countryman Shohei Otani, Fujinama is years away from being posted, but remains an excellent long-term talent.
Signing bonus/status: Fujinama remains in Japan and is unsigned.
MLB debut: ?

Miguel Alfredo Gonzalez (RHP, PHI)
Lean, athletic right-hander defected from Cuba and signed with the Phillies. At 6-3, the 26-year-old Gonzalez has good size and features a good 90-94 mph fastball that tops out a 96 mph with good arm-side run. His secondary pitches include a splitter, change-up, and curveball. The change and splitter show solid potential, but the curve is below-average. Gonzalez has an outside chance to make the Phillies opening day roster, but might need some time in the minors.
Signing bonus/status: Signed for three years/$12 million
MLB debut: 2014

Alexander Guerrero (2B, LA)
Guerrero is 27 years old and defected from Cuba. He has been one of the most consistent hitters in Cuba over the last several years. At 5-10, 205 he's a short, muscular 2B with good bat speed and above-average power (21 HR in 2012). Guerrero moves well, has good hands, and a strong arm. He's played SS in the past, but projects as a 2B in the majors and the Dodgers will give him a look at the position in the spring.
Signing bonus/status: Signed for four years, $28 million
MLB debut: 2014

Yeltsin Gudino (SS, TOR)
Gudino is a solid defender from Venezuela who moves well, has good hands, and enough arm strength to stick at the position as he moves up. He has decent speed and projects as a good 1-2 hitter. At 6-0, 150 he doesn't project to have power, but shows a quick line-drive stroke and a good understanding of the strike zone.
Signing bonus/status: Signed by Toronto for $1.29 million
MLB debut: 2018

Jose Herrera (C, ARI)
The switch-hitting Herrera is the top catching prospect in 2013's international class. The 17-year-old Venezuelan backstop is just 5-9, 180, but moves well behind the plate, has a good feel for signal calling, and has a strong, accurate arm. At the plate, he has good pop for his size and makes consistent, hard contact, especially as a right-handed hitter, but he does have some swing-and-miss issues.
Signing bonus/status: Signed for $1.06 million
MLB debut: 2019

Raisel Iglesias (RHP, Cuba)
The 23-year-old left Cuba in September 2013. At 5-11, 165 Iglesias is small in stature, but features a plus 92-95 mph fastball. He also has the makings of an above-average slurvy curveball and an inconsistent change-up. Iglesias varies his arm slot and will sometimes come after hitters from a low ¾ slot that gives him good movement. Unfortunately it also leads to inconsistent mechanics and struggles with control. In 2011-12, he worked mostly in relief, posting a 3.29 ERA with 54 BB/53 K in 76.2 IP, but showed better control in 2012-13, striking out 74 while walking 30.
Signing bonus/status: Iglesias remains a free agent
MLB debut: 2015

Eloy Jimenez (OF, CHC)
Lean, projectable OF with good speed and above-average raw power. Currently his swing is more conducive to hitting line drives, but at 6-4 he has the size to develop above-average power down the road. His swing can get long and tends to have a flat plane and scouts are mixed on whether he will hit for average, but he has plus bat speed and makes good contact. He has good athleticism, covers ground well in the OF, and has enough arm strength to play either corner in the majors. Raw, but very projectable.
Signing bonus/status: Signed for $2.8 million
MLB debut: 2018

Kenta Maeda (RHP, Japan)
Maeda is one of the better pitchers in Japan. The 25-year-old righty has said he would like to be posted and pitch in the U.S. in 2014. Maeda was 15-7 with a 2.10 ERA, 40 BB/158 K in 175.2 IP. Maeda isn't overpowering with a fastball that sits in the 88-93 mph range, but he does get good late action. None of his secondary offerings stand out and he profiles more as a back-end starter.
Signing bonus/status: Maeda remains in Japan
MLB debut: 2014

Leonardo Molina (OF, NYY)
Molina is a tall, athletic OF from the Dominican Republic. He has some of the best speed in this year's pool of Latin American players and is already an above-average defender in CF. He has a quick bat and the potential to hit for moderate power, but he's unrefined in his approach at the plate and has a slight hitch before making contact. Long-term, he has the size and athleticism to be an impact player, but has more questions about his ability to hit than others on this list.
Signing bonus/status: Signed for $1.4 million
MLB debut: 2018

Shohei Otani (RHP/OF, Japan)
Remains one of the top pitching prospects in Japan. Strong, physical right-hander has a plus 92-96 mph fastball that can occasionally go as high at 100 mph. He also throws a good low-80s hard slider, a splitter, and an under-developed big-breaking curveball. He gets good movement on all, but struggles to find the strike zone consistently. Otani is only 19 years old, so is likely years away from being posted. In his rookie season, Otani has both pitched and played in the field where he showed impressive potential.
Signing bonus/status: Remains in Japan and is unsigned.
MLB debut: ?

Mayky Perez (RHP, SD)
Perez is a tall 17-year-old from the Dominican Republic. At 6-5, 195 he has good size and is physically mature for his age. His fastball sits 88-93 mph with room for a bit of projection. He gets some

decent arm-side run on his heater and does a good job of keep the ball down in the zone. He mixes in a slider that shows potential and a change-up that needs work. Perez has decent mechanics but struggles maintaining consistency and varies his release point. If correctible, he has the size and arm strength to develop into a solid mid-rotation starter.

Signing bonus/status: Signed for $634,000
MLB debut: 2019

Masahiro Tanaka (RHP, Japan)
Tanaka is the top Japanese prospect and was posted to the U.S. in December. The 25 year-old right-hander has a good, firm low-90s fastball that gets a small amount of arm-side run, but is fairly straight. He mixes in a good splitter that dives in on right-handed batters, a good slider, and a useable curveball. At 6-2, 205 Tanaka is on the smallish side and that is one reason why his fastball tends to be flat. He has excellent control and profiles as a solid #3 starter.

Signing bonus/status: Not signed at press time, but will pitch in U.S. in 2014.
MLB debut: 2014

Gleyber Torres (SS, CHC)
Polished SS prospect widely viewed as the 2nd ranked international prospect and the top-ranked player from Venezuela. He has five above-average tools. He has a good approach at the plate with good bat speed, nice pop for his size, and makes consistent contact. He has decent range, soft hands, and a strong, accurate arm, though some scouts question whether he has the speed to stick at SS. He isn't a burner, but shows solid instincts on the bases. If his power develops as anticipated, he has the tools to be an impact middle infielder. Jimenez will likely make his pro debut along-side Eloy Jimenez in Rookie ball with Boise.

Signing bonus/status: Signed for $1.7 million
MLB debut: 2018

Yeson Yrizarri (SS, TEX)
Yrizarri is a projectable 17-year-old SS from Venezuela. He has a quick right-handed stroke and an upright stance. He has a good understanding of the strike zone for a young player and is willing to use the whole field. He projects to have gap power, but at 6-0, 175 has the size to develop average power once he matures. He moves well defensively with a decent arm, but doesn't have plus range and might not stick at SS long-term.

Signing bonus/status: Signed for $1.3 million
MLB debut: 2018

Micker Adolfo Zapata (OF, CHW)
Tall, physically mature OF from the Dominican Republic. Zapata is one of the top five prospects from this year's Latin American pool. At 6-3, 225, Zapata has plus raw power from the right-hand side. He uses a small leg kick and good extension to generate plus bat speed and is quick through the hitting zone. He tends to pull the ball too much in game action, gets off-balance, and swings and misses to the point where some scouts are concerned about his ability to hit for average. He has good speed for his size and a strong arm so profiles well in RF.

Signing bonus/status: Signed for $1.6 million
MLB debut: 2018

Sleepers Outside the HQ100

by Jeremy Deloney

Every season, there are several unheralded players who enjoy breakout campaigns and thrust themselves into the mainstream discussion on prospects. Some of these players were high draft picks and only needed more professional experience whereas others have flown under the radar for a few seasons and have slowly emerged as top prospects. Compiling a Top 100 list isn't easy. Of course, most top prospect lists have similar names among the top 25 or 50. After that, things get a little murkier. This essay will focus on ten minor league prospects who you likely won't locate on any Top 100 list. These ten prospects not only have relatively high ceilings, but they could appear on future Top 100 lists. For fantasy leaguers with deep farm systems, these names should be kept in the forefront when prospecting for such players.

The Giants selected 23-year-old **Ty Blach** (LHP, SF) in the 5th round of the 2012 draft and he didn't make his pro debut until 2013. As a command-oriented pitcher, he bypassed Low-A and began the year at High-A San Jose. He found that level much to his liking, winning the league's Pitcher of the Year award while leading the circuit in ERA. For the year, the 6'1" 200 pounder was 12-4 with a 2.90 ERA, 1.2 Ctl, and 8.1 Dom in 20 starts covering 130.1 innings. He also held hitters to a .248 oppBA. With a successful first season such as that, expectations have been raised. The Giants have stockpiled an impressive arsenal of young arms and Blach is right there in the conversation as one of the better ones.

His upside may be limited due to the lack of premium velocity and a knockout breaking ball, but he works all quadrants of the strike zone with impeccable precision. His repertoire consists of four pitches that are at least average to above average. The effectiveness of Blach's offerings play up due to the deception in his delivery. His fastball generally sits in the low 90s, but touches 94 on occasion, but it is his command of the pitch that sets him apart. Blach uses two breaking balls in his slow curve and big-breaking slider and he will miss some bats with the latter. His best secondary offering is his change-up that is thrown with the same arm speed as his fastball. Rarely does he allow HR and he thrives with excellent pitch movement. He'll likely make the jump to Double-A for 2014 and could continue his progression to the big leagues by early 2015.

With a large, athletic frame, 19-year-old **Dylan Cozens** (OF, PHI) looks the part of an NFL player. He stands 6'6", 235 pounds and exhibits natural athleticism. His strength hasn't yet translated to extreme success as a baseball player, but he has lots of potential. He began the 2013 campaign in extended spring training and was assigned to short-season Williamsport in the New York-Penn League in June. There, the left-handed hitter batted .265/.343/.469 with 19 doubles, 9 HR, and 11 SB. The raw numbers were impressive for such a raw player, though he'll need to make better contact as evidenced by his 64 K in 245 AB. As a 2nd round pick in the '12 draft out of an Arizona high school, the Phillies have big plans for him.

Cozens has outstanding raw power that is starting to emerge in game situations. He swings a lightning-fast bat with plenty of loft and leverage. Combining his bat speed with his strength gives him that plus-plus pop potential. His stroke can get long at times and he can be beaten inside with quality stuff, but he is showing improvement with his approach and pitch selectivity. Cozens has sufficient secondary skills and only needs more game action and repetitions to get better. He runs quite well for his size and he has average defensive potential. While some scouts see him as a future 1B, the consensus seems to be that he could become a solid RF with a strong arm and passable range. Cozens is far from a finished product and has plenty of work to do, but he could eventually evolve into a .275+ hitter with 30 HR at maturity.

The White Sox were more than thrilled when **Tyler Danish** (RHP, CHW) fell to them at pick #55 in the second round of the 2013 draft. He immediately went to work and showed why he could have—or should have—been selected much higher than that. Chicago handled him cautiously as he mostly pitched out of the bullpen in his pro debut at Rookie-level Bristol in the Appalachian League. At that level, the 19-year-old posted a 1.38 ERA, 1.7 Ctl, and 7.6 Dom. He was later promoted to Low-A Kannapolis where he pitched four scoreless innings with six strikeouts. Between the two levels, Danish held the opposition to a .162 oppBA. Because of his quick success, he will likely begin the 2014 season with Kannapolis.

The 6'2" 190 pound righty exhibits both pure stuff and feel for pitching. He pitches aggressively with a plus 90-94 mph fastball that features natural sink and late life. As a result, he induces a large number of groundballs. He doesn't allow many HR and he uses his arm slot to pitch downhill. He pitches off his fastball and establishes command of the plate immediately before mixing in a power slider that sits in the high 80s. His breaking ball is particularly tough against right-handed hitters, though he can miss bats against lefties as well. Danish has outstanding arm speed for his developing change-up and he'll need to refine that pitch in order to succeed at the upper levels. Given his feel for changing speeds, that should happen sooner rather than later. The only concern at present is the effort in his delivery, but he has natural athleticism and should be able to smooth it out in the near-term.

Michael Feliz (RHP, HOU) has spent his first three pro seasons in Rookie and short-season ball, but that doesn't tell the story of his true upside potential. The 20-year-old took a big step forward in 2013 with a dominating campaign with Tri-City in the short-season New York-Penn League. He was 4-2 with a 1.96 ERA, 1.7 Ctl, and 10.2 Dom while holding hitters to a .209 oppBA. He showed vast improvement in each facet of the game and that fact was evident in his stats. He's always shown pure arm strength, but his overall game is starting to emerge. The Astros have outstanding depth in the minor league pitching ranks and Feliz has nearly as high of a ceiling as any arm in the system.

The 6'4" 210 pound right-hander leverages his arm strength and athletic frame to pump a 91-97 mph fastball into the strike zone. His heater is a true power pitch that can be located in the lower half. While he can blow balls by hitters up in the zone, he can take a little off and get batters to bury the ball into the ground. He generates his velocity with loose arm action which also gives him a hint of projection. His strikeout rate elevated due in part to

an improving power slider that has plus potential. It can get a little slurvy at times and he needs to throw it with more conviction. His third offering is a below-average change-up that he doesn't trust enough yet. The combination of velocity and control could make for an ideal late-innings reliever if his offspeed pitch doesn't get refined. Nevertheless, he'll take the next step to Low-A in 2014 and he could dominate that level.

The Nationals knew what they were getting when they selected **Jake Johansen** (RHP, WAS) in the second round of the 2013 draft from Dallas Baptist. He's always had incredible arm strength that resulted in radar gun readings in the high 90s. The Nationals weren't expecting, however, for him to show rapid improvement across the board in his pro debut. He was initially assigned to short-season Auburn upon signing, but finished the year at Low-A Hagerstown. Between the two levels, the 22-year-old had an impressive 1.92 ERA, 4.0 Ctl, and 8.9 Dom in 51.2 innings. He only allowed 2 HR and held hitters to a .183 oppBA. That performance is noticeably better than his college numbers.

Johansen is all about velocity and power. He has a long and tall frame—6'6" 235 pounds—and uses a downward angle to the plate that gives him some deception. His 92-97 mph fastball is leaps and bounds above his other offerings at the present, though it can be flat at higher velocities. He's learning to change speeds with it and move the ball around the plate more effectively. He has shown better pitchability than expected and his heater could turn into a legitimate plus-plus offering that either misses bats or results in groundballs. Johansen uses two breaking balls in his curveball and slider, though both are slightly below average. The curveball has a touch more potential and could evolve into a swing-and-miss offering. His change-up is mostly a show-me pitch at the moment. Because of his size and velocity, he could easily convert to a reliever if starting doesn't work for him. The Nationals are not contemplating that conversion quite yet.

There aren't many high school draftees who immediately succeed in pro ball as they aren't used to training and playing every day while moving away from home for the first time. That wasn't the case with **Gosuke Katoh** (2B, NYY) a second round pick who absolutely stood out in his pro debut in the Rookie-level Gulf Coast League. The 18-year-old had a sterling line of .310/.402/.522 with 11 doubles, 5 triples, and 6 HR in 184 AB. He showed a disciplined approach at the plate while walking 27 times versus 44 strikeouts. He was one of the league's better players and showed remarkable polish for such a young player. He could easily make the jump to Low-A Charleston to begin the 2014 season.

The Yankees are enthralled with Katoh's natural tools. The tall and thin infielder has surprising strength in his lean frame and has enough punch to make loud, hard contact and occasional long ball power. He has a discerning eye at the plate and can work counts to his advantage and be a tough out. With a quick stroke and ideal bat control, Katoh should be able to sustain a high BA while mixing in average pop. He is an excellent athlete with above average speed and quickness. As he gets on base at a consistent clip, he has stolen base potential. He's still a bit raw as a baserunner and it could take some time for him to post above average stolen base outputs. As a defender, he exhibits all positive attributes with the exception of a fringy arm. He has the range, hands, and quickness to play either middle infield spot. The Yankees may move him to SS for 2014, though most see his long-term position at 2B.

First round draft picks become immediately known as the media generally focuses their attention on such picks. Second rounders have similar pedigrees and some of those players fall in the draft because of expected exorbitant bonus demands. **Ryan McMahon** (3B, COL) seemingly fell because he was a star football player and had scholarship offers to play quarterback in college. The Rockies enticed him with a $1.3 million bonus and he tore up the Rookie-level Pioneer League. With Grand Junction, the 18-year-old hit .321/.402/.583 with 18 doubles and 11 HR in 218 AB.

McMahon has a tall and lean, yet strong frame that is ideal for above average power potential. He has better natural hitting skills than expected and he's realizing his power earlier than anticipated. The 6'2" 185 pound left-handed hitter needs to add more strength and he likely will as he continues to grow. He has plenty of leverage in his swing to generate good power at present and he makes easy, hard contact. McMahon also has shown the ability to hang in against left-handed pitchers by hitting .311 against them in his pro debut. There's more to his game than just offense. He has excellent athleticism that allows him to possess natural quickness at 3B. He possesses clean hands along with a strong arm. He sometimes has sloppy footwork which limits the accuracy of his throws and he needs to clean up the careless errors. Regardless, he should become a middle-of-the-order hitter who plays average defense at 3B.

It would've been expected had **Mitch Nay** (3B, TOR) showed rust after delaying his pro debut until 2013 after he broke his foot shortly after signing as a supplemental first round pick in the 2012 draft out of an Arizona high school. Not only did he shake off the cobwebs quickly, but he was one of the better players in the Rookie-level Appalachian League as a 19-year-old. After a successful campaign, he's turned himself into one of the Blue Jays better prospects. The right-handed hitter batted .300/.364/.426 with 11 doubles and 6 HR while striking out only 35 times against 25 walks. Nay should be able to sustain that success with Low-A Lansing in 2014.

With a projectable and strong frame, Nay has well above average power potential from the right side of the plate. He stands 6'3" and has a powerful, quick stroke. He has ideal swing mechanics which is quite rare for someone with such little professional experience. He has strong forearms and quick wrists to generate his plus-plus power to all fields. Not only can he put a charge into the ball, but he possesses natural hitting instincts with improved pitch recognition. He can identify breaking balls and shorten his swing when necessary. Because he puts bat to ball so easily, Nay should hit for both BA and power at his peak. The remainder of his game is still in the development phase. He's not a particulary fast runner and he didn't steal a base in 2013. While he should be able to stick at 3B, he lacks the quickness to become above average. Nay exhibits a strong arm and acceptable range and could eventually move to an outfield corner.

Entering the 2013 college season, many assumed that **Austin Wilson** (OF, SEA) was going to be a sure-fire first round pick, possibly among the top ten picks. He then incurred an injury to his throwing elbow and missed a bit of the season. Regardless, he offers above average physical tools and Seattle popped him in the second round. The 21-year-old right-handed hitter was assigned to short-season Everett in the Northwest League and was among the better prospects at that level. In 203 at bats, he hit .241/.319/.414 with 11 doubles and 6 HR. Wilson expanded the strike zone and was subject to strikeouts as he fanned 42 times against only 17 walks.

He is a physical specimen who has significant upside because of his big, strong frame and above average tools. The only thing holding him back at this point is an inconsistent swing that can be exploited. He'll need to refine his pitch recognition and develop a sound two-strike approach, but he has a chance to become a pure power hitter in the big leagues. Wilson swings the bat with authority and gives the ball a long ride. He has a tendency to be pull-conscious, but has the strength and hitting acumen to hit to all fields. With good speed, he has stolen base potential and needs experience in reading pitchers. Wilson fits the RF profile and he has a chance to turn into a plus defender because of his instincts and above average arm strength. The elbow injury is in the past and he's fully healthy. He'll test his skills in Low-A to begin the season and could reach High-A if all things go according to plan.

The Reds aren't exactly known for developing pure hitters, but when they do, they turn into good ones. One farmhand who has a skill set similar to the homegrown Joey Votto is 20-year-old **Jesse Winker** (OF, CIN). After hitting .338/.443/.500 with Rookie-level Billings in 2012 upon his selection in the supplemental first round, he feasted on Low-A pitching in the Midwest League. He batted .281/.379/.463 with 18 doubles and 16 HR in 417 AB. Adding to his positives was 63 walks while striking out only 75 times. With pure hitting skills, he has evolved into one of the better prospects in the system.

It is curious as to why Winker doesn't get more love on prospect lists. He has the natural hitting instincts that scouts crave while satisfying the analytical community with his ability to draw walks and get on base. A further analysis, however, shows that his secondary skills are a bit limited. Nevertheless, the left-handed hitting Winker can hit and hit with authority. He offers natural strength in his 6'2" 210 pound frame and has the ability to hit left-handed pitching. He recognizes pitches very well and can modify his swing with two strikes. With a patient approach and compact stroke, he offers significant value with his on base skills and bat-to-ball ability. Though he may not project to 30+ HR, he should reach 20+ while having seasons of .300+. The downside to his prospect status is he is relegated to LF because of his lack of speed and weak arm. He's not a particularly seasoned defender and he could eventually move to 1B. With Votto entrenched at that position, Winker will stick in LF in the hopes that he improves.

2014 College Names to Know

by Chris Lee

As fantasy leagues become more generous in allowing owners to stash minor leaguers on rosters for years before they become big-leaguers, the serious fantasy baseball player must now become familiar with the next crop of up-and-coming stars before they even hit professional ball. Just following the draft isn't enough, as a player's MLB and fantasy value aren't always the same. With that, here's a good look at some of 2014's top collegiate players who have a good shot to become fantasy-relevant one day.

1. Trea Turner, SS

North Carolina State … R/R … junior … 6-1, 171

Turner's not big, but there may not be a more complete offensive player in the draft for fantasy purposes. He was a nobody until his senior year of high school, where he passed on an offer from the Pirates to go to the Atlantic Coast Conference. That was a great move: as a freshman he led the nation with 57 steals in 61 tries to go with a .432 on-base average, five homers and 13 doubles in 255 at-bats. An ankle injury held Turner down a bit last season, but he's got 80 speed on the scouting scale. He won't be a huge power threat in the professional ranks, but that dimension of his game has developed nicely since high school.

The bottom line: When someone's this fast, you take note. When he can also get on base, has good strike zone judgment and a little bit of pop, you put him on a prospect list. When he's got the ability to do all that plus play shortstop at the MLB level, you seek him out for your fantasy farm team.

2. Carlos Rodon, LHP

North Carolina State … junior … 6-3, 234

If the draft were held today, Rodon would be the first pick. The lefty was a nice prospect out of high school, where he was a 16th-round pick of the Brewers, but he hit the weight room hard, bumped his velocity up into the upper-90s, and became one of college baseball's best player. As a freshman, he posted a 1.57 ERA with 135 strikeouts and 41 walks in 114.2 innings. Rodon has a good slider that he complements somewhat with a curve and a change, and he has the competitiveness and mental approach to succeed at any level.

The bottom line: Rodon is considered the best collegiate lefty since David Price, and he could have the same type of early MLB success. He's probably also the least-risky college pitcher given the way he's dominated in both his collegiate seasons.

3. Tyler Beede, RHP

Vanderbilt … junior … 6-4, 215

Beede was the only first-rounder from the 2011 draft not to sign, turning down $2.3 million from the Blue Jays to attend Vanderbilt. Blessed with electric stuff, the sophomore was downright unhittable most of the 2013 season due to a combination of a fastball that touches the mid-90s, a nice 12-to-6 curve and a change-up that some think is his best pitch. Beede was dominating the Southeastern Conference until too much nibbling resulted in

control problems. He let it affect him and completely fell apart in the NCAA Tournament, where he lasted 6.2 innings combined in two starts. Vanderbilt tinkered with Beede's mechanics and release point in tge fall and it appeared to work: he walked none and struck out 16 in VU's fall inter-squad series. If that holds, his best work is ahead.

The bottom line: Beede's got the frame, the stuff and the work ethic and attitude to succeed. Since 2007, Vanderbilt has sent David Price, Mike Minor and Sonny Gray to the majors and Beede's upside at this stage of his career ranks just behind Price's.

4. Kyle Schwarber, C/IB/OF

Indiana … L/R … junior … 6-0, 235

After a .300/.390/.513 freshman season that included eight homers in 230 at-bats, Schwarber took another leap up as he helped the Hoosiers advance to the College World Series. The doubts about Schwarber center around his defense. He's primarily a catcher at IU, but no one really thinks he's a catcher at the next level. That will probably keep him from rising to the very top of draft boards, but it's hard to find anyone saying negative things about his bat. In fact, some think he's the best pure power prospect in the college ranks after he ranked third in the NCAA in homers. The Big Ten is not a good baseball league, but the cold weather makes just about every park in the league a pitchers' park, meaning that Schwarber's power is legit. He also led Team USA with seven doubles in 18 games last summer.

The bottom line: Schwarber might be a better fantasy player than an MLB player because of the defensive issues. There may not be a better combination of power and batting eye among college players in the draft, and being a lefty is a bonus.

5. Aaron Nola, RHP

LSU … junior … 6-1, 183

It's rare that a freshman demonstrates the kind of polish that Nola did, posting a 3.61 ERA with 89 strikeouts and just seven walks in 89.1 IP. He followed that up with a similar sophomore campaign in which he was a first team All-American and the Southeastern Conference Pitcher of the Year. Nola, who has a three-quarters delivery, throws a low-to-mid-90s fastball with some sink, complemented with a nice curve and an above-average change-up.

The bottom line: Between his command and his success at the highest level of college baseball, he's one of the lower-risk pitchers around. He's a better collegiate hurler than Beede, but lacks his MLB upside.

6. Mike Papi, OF/IB

Virginia … L/R … junior … 6-3, 210

If you like late bloomers, here's one to watch. A 30th-round pick of the Angels out of high school, Papi was a part-time player who got hurt in late- pril of his freshman season and didn't become a starter until the 11th game of his sophomore year. But he wound up leading the Atlantic Coast Conference in hitting and the country in on-base percentage in 2013 despite playing most of his games in a pronounced pitcher's park. CollegeSplits.com, a great site to use when trying to make sense of college numbers due to the vast differences in parks and levels of competition, normalized his 2013 stat line to .409/.542/.653.

The bottom line: Papi's a late-first-rounder at best heading into the 2013 season, and the limited body of work makes him a little tougher to evaluate. However, he's got enough athleticism that he played center field in summer ball, and has a frame that seems to be filling out. Not every high-OBP, high-average college guy is able to translate that to next-level success, but watch him closely in the spring—it helps that he plays in one of college baseball's best leagues.

7. Michael Conforto, OF
Oregon State … L/R … junior … 6-1, 215

A two-time All-American, Conforto's numbers slipped a bit from his .349/.438/.601 line as a freshman, but they were still good enough to tie for the PAC 12 lead in homers and win the league's Player of the Year. Even with the slight dip elsewhere, his Eye did improve from his first season. Scouts like his bat speed and while he's not an outstanding athlete, his nine outfield assists last year suggests he can play right field in the majors. Everybody seems to think that the power projects to the professional level, and the fact that the PAC 12 is full of pitcher's parks (including Conforto's home park at OSU) isn't damaging that notion.

The bottom line: Conforto isn't going to steal bases or win batting titles, but he's one of the more solid power prospects in the draft. Given the track record of consistency his first two years, it's hard to see him not getting a big-league shot at some point. Being left-handed doesn't hurt, either.

8. Derek Fisher, OF
Virginia … L/R … junior … 6-3, 210

Fisher was easily the more heralded of the two UVA outfielders mentioned here coming into 2013, and his stat line was a mild disappointment after he'd been a Freshman All-American. Another big kid with big-time power, Fisher was a top prospect out of high school and should be a first-rounder this June. His plate judgment (25 walks, 19 Ks) took a big step forward in the Cape Cod League, where he hit .333 with six doubles, 13 steals. He's played center field in college and has athleticism, but scouts knock his instincts and think he'll fit better in right.

The bottom line: Some think he's the best pure hitter in the draft, but there's been a disconnect between the tools and the production. Watch his spring carefully.

9. Jeff Hoffman, RHP
East Carolina … junior … 6-4, 192

Hoffman is similar to former Stanford hurler Mark Appel in that the scouting love at this stage of his career is ahead of his production. The Cape Cod League's No. 1 prospect last summer sports a fastball that sits in the mid-90s with great movement, and two good off-speed pitches. He gets lots of ground balls, and does a

nice job of working different parts of the zone from his three-quarters arm slot.

The bottom line: Back-to-back great summers in the Cape have some whispering that Hoffman could challenge Rodon for the No. 1 pick as some think his stuff rivals the N.C. State ace, though the odds are against that. Hoffman's certainly a prospect to watch, but it would be unwise to get carried away and elevate him over others on the list until the stats catch up with the stuff.

More to watch:

Nick Burdi, Jr., RHP, Louisville: If there was a guy in college baseball that you didn't want to see for an inning at a time in 2013, it was certainly Burdi. As a sophomore, Burdi sometimes hit triple digits on the radar gun and posted absurd numbers: an 0.76 ERA with 62 strikeouts in 35.2 innings (15.6 K/9). Burdi's a two-pitch reliever, and projecting what a college closer is going to do at the next level is incredibly difficult. But he's too good to ignore and may be a high first-rounder. Being 6-foot-4 and 215 pounds doesn't hurt, either, and if he could still become a starter if he could ever come up with a third pitch.

Michael Cederoth, Jr., RHP, San Diego State: Cederoth was a reliever to start his career, but had become the Aztecs' No. 1 starter by the end of 2012. He posted a 4.25 ERA in 2013 and walked 48 in 95.1 innings, but also struck out 109. The 6-foot-6, 210-pounder has also touched triple digits and should be one of the top five college hurlers taken.

Austin Cousino, Jr., CF, Kentucky: Cousino was one of the SEC's best players as a freshman (.319/.408/.515, with nine homers and 15-26 SBs) before falling off to a .249/.383/.402 line in 2013 with six homers in 209 ABs. The undersized lefty (5-foot-10, 180 lbs.) needs to improve his strike-zone judgment (0.50 Eye) but if the bat gets better, he's got the defensive ability to stick in the majors.

Joey Pankake, Jr., SS, South Carolina: The 6-foot-1, 200-pound Pankake was an immediate starter for one of college baseball's best programs as a freshman and helped the Gamecocks get to the College World Series finals. You could see the power potential then, and sure enough, Pankake jumped from two homers as a freshman to 11 last year and complied a .311/.387/.496 stat line with 29 walks to 29 strikeouts in 238 ABs. There are warts—he won't steal a lot of bases and it's unlikely he has the defensive chops to stay at SS as a pro— but just watch him play before you write him off.

Brad Zimmer, Jr., OF, San Francisco: At 6-foot-4 and 195 pounds, Zimmer's a pure hitter (.320/.437/.512, 7 HR and 0.9 Eye in 203 ABs) with power potential. Zimmer's not great at any one thing, but does not have a glaring weakness, either.

ORGANIZATION RATINGS/RANKINGS

Each organization is graded on a standard A-F scale in four separate categories, and then after weighing the categories and adding some subjectivity, a final grade and ranking are determined. The four categories are the following:

Hitting: The quality and quantity of hitting prospects, the balance between athleticism, power, speed, and defense, and the quality of player development.

Pitching: The quality and quantity of pitching prospects and the quality of player development.

Top-End Talent: The quality of the top players within the organization. Successful teams are ones that have the most star-quality players. These are the players who are a teams' above average regulars, front-end starters, and closers.

Depth: The depth of both hitting and pitching prospects within the organization.

Overall Grade: The four categories are weighted, with top-end talent being the most important and depth being the least.

TEAM	Hitting	Pitching	Top-End Talent	Depth	Overall
Houston	A-	A-	A	A	A
Pittsburgh	A	B+	A	A	A
Boston	B+	B+	A-	A-	A-
Chicago (N)	A	B-	A	B+	A-
Minnesota	A-	B+	A	B+	A-
St. Louis	A	B-	A	B	A-
San Diego	B+	A	B+	A-	A-
Los Angeles (N)	B+	A-	A-	B+	B+
Kansas City	B+	B+	A	B	B+
Miami	B	A-	B	B+	B+
San Francisco	B-	A	B+	B+	B+
Tampa Bay	B	B+	B+	B+	B+
Texas	B+	B	B+	B	B+
Seattle	B	B	B+	B	B
Colorado	B-	B+	B	B	B
Arizona	C	A-	B-	B-	B
New York (A)	B	B-	B	B	B
Cleveland	B-	C+	B+	B-	B-
New York (N)	C	B	B+	B-	B-
Milwaukee	B-	B-	B-	C+	B-
Washington	B-	B	C	B-	B-
Cincinnati	C	B-	B	C+	C+
Oakland	C+	C	C+	C-	C
Philadelphia	C	C-	C	C+	C
Toronto	D	B-	C	D	C-
Atlanta	D	B	C-	C-	C-
Baltimore	D	B	C-	C-	C-
Chicago (A)	C+	D	C-	C	C-
Los Angeles (A)	C-	D	D	D	D
Detroit	D	D+	D	D	D

POSITIONS: Up to four positions are listed for each batter and represent those for which he appeared (in order) the most games at in 2011. Positions are shown with their numeric designation (2=CA, 3=1B, 7=LF, 0=DH, etc.)

BATS: Shows which side of the plate he bats from—right (R), left (L) or switch-hitter (S).

AGE: Player's age, as of April 1, 2014.

DRAFTED: The year, round, and school that the player performed at as an amateur if drafted, or where the player was signed from, if a free agent.

EXP MLB DEBUT: The year a player is expected to debut in the major leagues.

PROJ ROLE: The role that the batter is expected to have for the majority of his major league career, not necessarily his greatest upside.

SKILLS: Each skill a player possesses is graded and designated with a "+", indicating the quality of the skills, taking into context the batter's age and level played. An average skill will receive three "+" marks.

- **PWR:** Measures the player's ability to drive the ball and hit for power.
- **BAVG:** Measures the player's ability to hit for batting average and judge the strike zone.
- **SPD:** Measures the player's raw speed and base-running ability.
- **DEF:** Measures the player's overall defense, which includes arm strength, arm accuracy, range, agility, hands, and defensive instincts.

PLAYER STAT LINES: Player statistics for the last five teams that he played for (if applicable), including college and the major leagues.

TEAM DESIGNATIONS: Each team that the player performed for during a given year is included.

LEVEL DESIGNATIONS: The level for each team a player performed is included. "AAA" means Triple-A, "AA" means Double-A, "A+" means high Class-A, "A-" means low Class-A, and "Rk" means rookie level.

SABERMETRIC CATEGORIES: Descriptions of all the sabermetric categories appear in the glossary.

CAPSULE COMMENTARIES: For each player, a brief analysis of their skills/statistics, and their future potential is provided.

ELIGIBILITY: Eligibility for inclusion is the standard for which Major League Baseball adheres to; 130 at-bats or 45 days on the 25-man roster, not including the month of September.

POTENTIAL RATINGS: The Potential Ratings are a two-part system in which a player is assigned a number rating based on his upside potential (1-10) and a letter rating based on the probability of reaching that potential (A-E).

Potential

10:	Hall of Famer	5:	MLB reserve
9:	Elite player	4:	Top minor leaguer
8:	Solid regular	3:	Average minor leaguer
7:	Average regular	2:	Minor league reserve
6:	Platoon player	1:	Minor league roster filler

Probability Rating

- A: 90% probability of reaching potential
- B: 70% probability of reaching potential
- C: 50% probability of reaching potential
- D: 30% probability of reaching potential
- E: 10% probability of reaching potential

SKILLS: Scouts usually grade a player's skills on the 20-80 scale, and while most of the grades are subjective, there are grades that can be given to represent a certain hitting statistic or running speed. These are indicated on this chart:

Scout Grade	HR	BA	Speed (L)	Speed (R)
80	39+	.320+	3.9	4.0
70	32-38	.300-.319	4.0	4.1
60	25-31	.286-.299	4.1	4.2
50 (avg)	17-24	.270-.285	4.2	4.3
40	11-16	.250-.269	4.3	4.4
30	6-10	.220-.249	4.4	4.5
20	0-5	.219-	4.5	4.6

CATCHER POP TIMES: Catchers are timed (in seconds) from the moment the pitch reaches the catcher's mitt until the time that the middle infielder receives the baseball at second base. This number assists both teams in assessing whether a base-runner should steal second base or not.

1.85	+
1.95	MLB average
2.05	–

Abreu,Jose — 3 — Chicago (A)
EXP MLB DEBUT: 2014 | POTENTIAL: Starting 1B | 8B

Bats R Age 27 | 2013 FA (Cuba) | Pwr ++++ | BAvg +++ | Spd ++ | Def ++

Year	Lev	Team	AB	R	H	HR	RBI	Avg	OB	Slg	OPS	bb%	ct%	Eye	SB	CS	x/h%	Iso	RC/G
2009	FOR	Cuba	289	60	100	19	32	346	386	623	1009	6	76	0.28	0	0	41	277	7.89
2010	FOR	Cuba	304	83	118	30	76	388	508	786	1294	20	82	1.35	2	1	49	398	11.98
2011	FOR	Cuba	252	93	113	37	98	448	563	952	1515	21	85	1.78	2	1	47	504	14.29
2012	FOR	Cuba	297	74	117	37	103	394	523	835	1358	21	86	1.86	1	0	48	441	12.49
2013	FOR	Cuba	285	61	98	19	60	344	455	604	1058	17	85	1.35	2	6	37	260	8.85

Big, powerful slugger who signed huge contract in Oct and expected to play prominent role with CHW. Value is tied to bat as he has exceptional raw power to all fields and keen instincts. Has shown moderate bat speed, but pure strength with plenty of leverage in stroke. Lacks athleticism and speed and relegated to 1B.

Adames,Cristhian — 6 — Colorado
EXP MLB DEBUT: 2015 | POTENTIAL: Utility INF | 6C

Bats B Age 22 | 2007 FA (DR) | Pwr ++ | BAvg +++ | Spd +++ | Def ++++

Year	Lev	Team	AB	R	H	HR	RBI	Avg	OB	Slg	OPS	bb%	ct%	Eye	SB	CS	x/h%	Iso	RC/G
2010	Rk	Casper	145	30	42	1	15	290	352	372	725	9	83	0.58	4	5	24	83	4.58
2011	A	Asheville	399	63	109	8	44	273	342	386	728	10	81	0.57	2	0	25	113	4.58
2012	A+	Modesto	418	59	117	2	54	280	353	378	731	10	80	0.57	4	2	26	98	4.75
2013	AA	Tulsa	389	45	104	3	36	267	326	350	676	8	80	0.44	13	7	23	82	3.89

Athletic SS is a top-notch defender. Runs well, with good range, and a plus arm. Defense is close to major league ready now. Makes good contact with solid plate discipline, but very little power and unlikely to be a base stealer. Will need to continue to hit to get MLB opportunity.

Adrianza,Ehire — 6 — San Francisco
EXP MLB DEBUT: 2013 | POTENTIAL: Backup SS | 6C

Bats B Age 24 | 2006 FA (Venezuela) | Pwr + | BAvg ++ | Spd +++ | Def ++++

Year	Lev	Team	AB	R	H	HR	RBI	Avg	OB	Slg	OPS	bb%	ct%	Eye	SB	CS	x/h%	Iso	RC/G
2011	A+	San Jose	230	34	69	3	27	300	364	470	833	9	80	0.50	5	1	43	170	6.02
2012	AA	Richmond	451	52	99	3	32	220	285	310	595	8	80	0.46	16	4	30	91	2.94
2013	AA	Richmond	250	31	60	2	23	240	324	312	636	11	82	0.69	11	6	23	72	3.59
2013	AAA	Fresno	145	23	45	0	12	310	405	441	846	14	79	0.74	6	2	29	131	6.54
2013	MLB	San Francisco	18	3	4	1	3	222	263	444	708	5	72	0.20	0	0	50	222	3.80

Athletic SS looked solid at two levels in 2013 before getting a cup of coffee. Makes quality contact and has good plate discipline, but whether he will hit enough in the majors is the biggest question. Has solid average speed on the bases and gives him good range at SS where he is a plus defender with a strong arm.

Aguilar,Jesus — 3 — Cleveland
EXP MLB DEBUT: 2014 | POTENTIAL: Starting 1B | 7D

Bats R Age 24 | 2007 FA (Venezuela) | Pwr ++++ | BAvg ++ | Spd + | Def ++

Year	Lev	Team	AB	R	H	HR	RBI	Avg	OB	Slg	OPS	bb%	ct%	Eye	SB	CS	x/h%	Iso	RC/G
2011	A	Lake County	349	58	102	19	69	292	357	544	901	9	72	0.36	1	0	47	252	6.91
2011	A+	Kinston	113	12	29	4	13	257	323	389	712	9	75	0.39	1	0	24	133	4.21
2012	A+	Carolina	368	63	102	12	58	277	356	454	810	11	75	0.49	0	1	38	177	5.72
2012	AA	Akron	72	12	21	3	13	292	400	500	900	15	67	0.54	0	0	43	208	7.53
2013	AA	Akron	499	66	137	16	105	275	348	427	775	10	79	0.52	0	1	32	152	5.14

Strong, consistent hitter who has solid offensive game. Lacks secondary skills as he doesn't have much speed and lacks athleticism and agility. Exhibits plus, raw power and makes contact with patient approach to draw walks. Crushes LHP, but can be beaten with good FB. Power is best chance at big league role.

Ahmed,Nick — 6 — Arizona
EXP MLB DEBUT: 2014 | POTENTIAL: Backup SS | 6B

Bats R Age 24 | 2011 (2) Connecticut | Pwr + | BAvg ++ | Spd ++++ | Def ++++

Year	Lev	Team	AB	R	H	HR	RBI	Avg	OB	Slg	OPS	bb%	ct%	Eye	SB	CS	x/h%	Iso	RC/G
2010	NCAA	Connecticut	267	57	80	4	43	300	368	375	743	10	88	0.94	34	8	15	75	4.86
2011	NCAA	Connecticut	183	51	61	2	35	333	416	448	864	12	90	1.44	23	6	25	115	6.54
2011	Rk	Danville	248	46	65	4	24	262	342	379	721	11	81	0.65	18	6	29	117	4.60
2012	A+	Lynchburg	506	84	136	6	49	269	333	391	725	9	80	0.48	40	10	34	123	4.58
2013	AA	Mobile	487	58	115	4	46	236	285	324	609	6	85	0.46	26	7	26	88	3.11

Came over in the Chris Johnson trade and struggled offensively. He is a plus runner with soft hands, good range, and a strong arm. Is patient at the plate and drives the ball into gaps, but has limited power and is not likely to be an asset on offense.

Alberto,Hanser — 6 — Texas
EXP MLB DEBUT: 2016 | POTENTIAL: Utility player | 7D

Bats R Age 21 | 2009 FA (DR) | Pwr ++ | BAvg +++ | Spd +++ | Def +++

Year	Lev	Team	AB	R	H	HR	RBI	Avg	OB	Slg	OPS	bb%	ct%	Eye	SB	CS	x/h%	Iso	RC/G
2011	A-	Spokane	187	21	50	0	16	267	301	321	622	5	92	0.60	7	1	18	53	3.37
2012	A	Hickory	246	37	83	4	38	337	383	463	846	7	91	0.82	15	4	27	126	5.89
2012	A+	Myrtle Beach	279	36	74	4	34	265	270	362	632	1	90	0.07	9	3	23	97	3.11
2013	A+	Myrtle Beach	97	6	25	0	7	258	287	309	596	4	92	0.50	3	1	20	52	3.04
2013	AA	Frisco	356	37	76	4	40	213	247	287	534	4	88	0.39	13	5	18	73	2.20

Short, quick INF who makes outstanding contact with fast bat and bat control. Not much power in frame or stroke, but can slash line drives to alleys. Very few swings and misses and should hit for BA. Could focus on hitting ball on ground to take advantage of solid-average speed. Strong arm accentuates quality defensive tools.

Alcantara,Arismendy — 46 — Chicago (N)
EXP MLB DEBUT: 2014 | POTENTIAL: Starting 2B | 8C

Bats B Age 22 | 2008 FA (DR) | Pwr +++ | BAvg ++ | Spd +++ | Def +++

Year	Lev	Team	AB	R	H	HR	RBI	Avg	OB	Slg	OPS	bb%	ct%	Eye	SB	CS	x/h%	Iso	RC/G
2010	A-	Boise	219	29	62	3	24	283	314	402	716	4	76	0.19	7	3	23	119	4.21
2011	A	Peoria	369	45	100	2	37	271	301	352	654	4	79	0.21	8	8	21	81	3.41
2012	A+	Daytona	331	47	100	7	51	302	340	447	787	5	82	0.31	25	4	27	145	5.09
2013	AA	Tennessee	494	69	134	15	69	271	353	451	804	11	75	0.50	31	6	41	180	5.70

Athletic player moved from SS to 2B to make room for J. Baez. Spike in power and new position gives him a clearer path to the majors. Needs to make more consistent contact, but walk total jumped to 62 in '13. Has a nice compact stroke with solid power.

Alcantara,Sergio — 6 — Arizona
EXP MLB DEBUT: 2017 | POTENTIAL: Starting SS | 7C

Bats B Age 17 | 2012 FA (DR) | Pwr + | BAvg +++ | Spd ++ | Def ++++

Year	Lev	Team	AB	R	H	HR	RBI	Avg	OB	Slg	OPS	bb%	ct%	Eye	SB	CS	x/h%	Iso	RC/G
2013	Rk	AZL D'backs	169	31	41	0	16	243	399	320	719	21	79	1.22	3	2	22	77	5.15

Skinny, athletic Dominican SS was signed for $700,000 and has developed into a plus defender. Quick, agile fielder with soft hands and a cannon for an arm. Doesn't project to have much power, but makes good contact and gets on base. Very little speed projection.

Alfaro,Jorge — 23 — Texas
EXP MLB DEBUT: 2016 | POTENTIAL: Starting C | 8C

Bats R Age 21 | 2010 FA (Colombia) | Pwr ++++ | BAvg ++ | Spd +++ | Def ++

Year	Lev	Team	AB	R	H	HR	RBI	Avg	OB	Slg	OPS	bb%	ct%	Eye	SB	CS	x/h%	Iso	RC/G
2011	A-	Spokane	160	18	48	6	23	300	317	481	798	2	66	0.07	1	0	33	181	5.48
2012	A	Hickory	272	40	71	5	34	261	302	430	732	6	69	0.19	7	3	44	169	4.71
2013	Rk	AZL Rangers	21	5	9	2	8	429	478	810	1288	9	71	0.33	2	0	44	381	12.11
2013	A	Hickory	372	63	96	16	53	258	310	452	762	7	70	0.25	16	3	41	194	4.94
2013	A+	Myrtle Beach	11	4	2	0	0	182	308	182	490	15	55	0.40	0	0	0	0	1.23

Strong, athletic backstop who set high in HR despite hand injury. Strong wrists and forearms produce ideal bat speed for brute power. Aggressive approach results in few walks and lots of Ks and needs better bat control to hit for BA. Receiving improving, but still raw. Has seen some action at 1B and bat works there, too.

Alford,Anthony — 8 — Toronto
EXP MLB DEBUT: 2018 | POTENTIAL: Starting OF | 8E

Bats R Age 19 | 2012 (3) HS (MS) | Pwr ++ | BAvg ++ | Spd ++++ | Def ++

Year	Lev	Team	AB	R	H	HR	RBI	Avg	OB	Slg	OPS	bb%	ct%	Eye	SB	CS	x/h%	Iso	RC/G
2012	Rk	GCL Blue Jays	18	1	3	1	1	167	250	333	583	10	78	0.50	4	0	33	167	2.48
2013	Rk	GCL Blue Jays	22	4	5	0	2	227	393	409	802	21	73	1.00	2	0	60	182	6.46

Very athletic outfielder who hasn't played much due to college football. Needs to focus on baseball to realize vast potential. Has elements of all five tools in repertoire, highlighted by plus-plus speed. Has quick, slashing stroke, but doesn't make contact as he lacks feel for bat control. Has potential to be above average CF.

Aliotti,Anthony — 3 — Oakland
EXP MLB DEBUT: 2014 | POTENTIAL: Reserve 1B | 6B

Bats L Age 26 | 2009 (15) St. Mary's | Pwr ++ | BAvg +++ | Spd + | Def +++

Year	Lev	Team	AB	R	H	HR	RBI	Avg	OB	Slg	OPS	bb%	ct%	Eye	SB	CS	x/h%	Iso	RC/G
2010	A	Kane County	478	75	133	5	77	278	395	379	773	16	72	0.70	14	4	27	100	5.63
2011	A+	Stockton	457	73	126	11	66	276	384	396	780	15	73	0.65	2	1	25	120	5.54
2012	AA	Midland	455	72	133	10	76	292	384	426	811	13	72	0.53	0	0	30	134	5.96
2013	AA	Midland	340	49	119	12	51	350	456	541	997	16	76	0.80	3	2	34	191	8.53
2013	AAA	Sacramento	154	17	41	2	20	266	331	344	676	9	71	0.34	0	0	17	78	3.87

Strong and patient hitter who led TL in BA and OBP. Set career high in HR, but doesn't have premium power requisite of corner INF. Pulling more and driving ball consistently has been key to numbers. Draws walks, but has struck out at least 123 times in each season. Inability to hit LHP and poor speed limit full-time role potential.

Allie,Stetson — 3 — Pittsburgh

EXP MLB DEBUT: 2015 | POTENTIAL: Starting 1B | 7D

Bats R Age 23 | 2010 (2) HS (OH)

Pwr ++++ | BAvg ++ | Spd +++ | Def +++

Year	Lev	Team	AB	R	H	HR	RBI	Avg	OB	Slg	OPS	bb%	ct%	Eye	SB	CS	x/h%	Iso	RC/G
2012	Rk	GCL Pirates	150	23	32	3	19	213	310	340	650	12	67	0.42	2	0	34	127	3.71
2013	A	West Virginia	244	42	79	17	61	324	411	607	1017	13	68	0.46	6	1	43	283	8.95
2013	A+	Bradenton	236	28	54	4	25	229	343	356	699	15	65	0.50	2	3	41	127	4.60

Strong hitter in Year Two of the move from SP to 1B. Shredded Low-A in the first half, but was not able to carry production forward upon promotion. On the year struck out 161 times, but did hit 21 HR. Has clear power, but MLB trajectory will depend on his ability to make contact.

Almanzar,Michael — 35 — Baltimore

EXP MLB DEBUT: 2015 | POTENTIAL: Backup 3B/1B | 7D

Bats R Age 23 | 2007 FA (DR)

Pwr +++ | BAvg ++ | Spd ++ | Def ++

Year	Lev	Team	AB	R	H	HR	RBI	Avg	OB	Slg	OPS	bb%	ct%	Eye	SB	CS	x/h%	Iso	RC/G
2010	A	Greenville	487	56	120	10	55	246	290	376	666	6	77	0.26	4	1	33	129	3.60
2011	A	Greenville	177	15	39	2	31	220	246	311	557	3	79	0.16	1	2	31	90	2.12
2011	A+	Salem	220	18	40	2	15	182	214	245	459	4	75	0.16	3	3	25	64	0.80
2012	A+	Salem	454	62	136	12	54	300	347	458	805	7	83	0.43	10	4	35	159	5.36
2013	AA	Portland	507	67	136	16	81	268	324	432	756	8	80	0.42	13	3	35	164	4.79

Tall, lanky INF who has put together consecutive productive seasons and chosen in Rule 5 by BAL. Set career highs in HR, SB, and BB while effective against LHP. Used cleaner swing to hit to all fields, though stroke can be inconsistent from AB to AB. Lacks athleticism and poor footwork and range may lead him to 1B.

Almonte,Abraham — 789 — Seattle

EXP MLB DEBUT: 2013 | POTENTIAL: Reserve OF | 6A

Bats B Age 25 | 2008 FA (DR)

Pwr ++ | BAvg +++ | Spd +++ | Def +++

Year	Lev	Team	AB	R	H	HR	RBI	Avg	OB	Slg	OPS	bb%	ct%	Eye	SB	CS	x/h%	Iso	RC/G
2012	Rk	GCL Yankees	18	2	4	0	0	222	300	333	633	10	78	0.50	2	0	50	111	3.56
2012	AA	Trenton	319	47	88	4	25	276	351	392	743	10	82	0.63	30	5	28	116	4.89
2013	AA	Jackson	102	18	26	4	18	255	367	451	818	15	73	0.64	6	1	42	196	6.05
2013	AAA	Tacoma	338	63	106	11	50	314	401	491	892	13	80	0.74	20	7	31	178	6.79
2013	MLB	SEA	72	10	19	2	9	264	321	403	723	8	71	0.29	1	0	32	139	4.46

Short and stocky outfielder who continues to improve in all facets of game. Posted career high in HR and consistently steals 25+ bases per year. Is better overall hitter from left side and makes good contact. Quick bats generates some power, though doesn't project well due to plane and size. Has usable range and arm in outfield.

Almonte,Zoilo — 79 — New York (A)

EXP MLB DEBUT: 2013 | POTENTIAL: Reserve OF | 6A

Bats B Age 25 | 2005 FA (DR)

Pwr +++ | BAvg ++ | Spd +++ | Def +++

Year	Lev	Team	AB	R	H	HR	RBI	Avg	OB	Slg	OPS	bb%	ct%	Eye	SB	CS	x/h%	Iso	RC/G
2011	A+	Tampa	259	38	76	12	54	293	369	514	882	11	77	0.52	14	4	39	220	6.57
2011	AA	Trenton	175	23	44	3	23	251	307	377	684	7	74	0.31	4	1	34	126	3.94
2012	AA	Trenton	419	64	116	21	70	277	318	487	804	6	75	0.24	15	4	39	210	5.26
2013	AAA	Scranton/W-B	259	30	77	6	36	297	370	421	791	10	82	0.64	4	1	25	124	5.39
2013	MLB	NYY	106	9	25	1	9	236	277	302	579	5	82	0.32	3	1	20	66	2.56

Switch-hitting outfielder who improved contact rate while showcasing average pop in solid season. Has good tools in repertoire, including solid defensive skills. Can still be free swinger, particularly by lunging at breaking balls. Has enough strength and bat speed to reach seats and learning to shorten stroke with two strikes.

Almora,Albert — 8 — Chicago (N)

EXP MLB DEBUT: 2016 | POTENTIAL: Starting CF | 9C

Bats R Age 20 | 2012 (1) HS (FL)

Pwr +++ | BAvg ++++ | Spd +++ | Def +++

Year	Lev	Team	AB	R	H	HR	RBI	Avg	OB	Slg	OPS	bb%	ct%	Eye	SB	CS	x/h%	Iso	RC/G
2012	Rk	AZL Cubs	75	18	26	1	13	347	364	480	844	3	89	0.25	5	1	27	133	5.57
2012	A-	Boise	65	9	19	1	6	292	292	446	738	0	92	0.00	0	1	42	154	4.32
2013	A	Kane County	249	39	82	3	23	329	372	466	838	6	88	0.57	4	4	29	137	5.81

Athletic OF is the best pure hitter in the system. Has quick hands and a smooth line-drive stroke. Needs to be more patient. Should develop above-avg power. Has good range, reads the ball well, and has a strong arm that will allow him to stay in CF.

Altherr,Aaron — 78 — Philadelphia

EXP MLB DEBUT: 2015 | POTENTIAL: Starting CF | 8C

Bats R Age 23 | 2009 (9) HS (AZ)

Pwr +++ | BAvg ++ | Spd ++++ | Def +++

Year	Lev	Team	AB	R	H	HR	RBI	Avg	OB	Slg	OPS	bb%	ct%	Eye	SB	CS	x/h%	Iso	RC/G
2010	A-	Williamsport	94	11	27	0	10	287	343	426	769	8	86	0.62	2	3	37	138	5.22
2011	A-	Williamsport	269	41	70	5	31	260	294	375	670	5	81	0.25	25	4	27	115	3.59
2011	A	Lakewood	147	20	31	1	15	211	266	272	538	7	68	0.23	12	0	23	61	1.89
2012	A	Lakewood	420	65	106	8	50	252	314	402	717	8	76	0.37	25	8	39	150	4.44
2013	A+	Clearwater	466	57	128	12	69	275	339	455	793	9	70	0.32	23	5	42	180	5.63

Raw athlete began to tap into his power (36 doubles, 12 HR) in a breakout season. Swing still needs work, as he can be beaten inside and strikes out frequently. But he's a plus base-stealer and has enough speed and arm to stick in CF. Double-A will be a good test.

Amaya,Gioskar — 4 — Chicago (N)

EXP MLB DEBUT: 2015 | POTENTIAL: Starting 3B/2B | 7C

Bats R Age 21 | 2009 FA (Venezuela)

Pwr ++ | BAvg ++++ | Spd ++ | Def ++

Year	Lev	Team	AB	R	H	HR	RBI	Avg	OB	Slg	OPS	bb%	ct%	Eye	SB	CS	x/h%	Iso	RC/G
2011	Rk	AZL Cubs	204	37	77	0	36	377	415	510	925	6	81	0.33	13	8	25	132	6.96
2012	A-	Boise	272	61	81	8	33	298	374	496	870	11	76	0.51	15	5	32	199	6.57
2012	AAA	Iowa	1	1	1	0	0	1000			3000	0	100		0	0	100	1000	27.71
2013	A	Kane County	453	65	114	5	28	252	315	369	684	8	76	0.39	13	6	32	117	4.03

Short, athletic 2B prospect took a step back in '13, hitting just .252. Has a quick bat and makes consistent contact, but doesn't have much power. Speed and range are average, but he does have soft hands and good instincts on defense.

Anderson,Tim — 6 — Chicago (A)

EXP MLB DEBUT: 2016 | POTENTIAL: Starting SS/2B | 8C

Bats R Age 21 | 2013 (1) East Central (MS) CC

Pwr ++ | BAvg +++ | Spd ++++ | Def ++

Year	Lev	Team	AB	R	H	HR	RBI	Avg	OB	Slg	OPS	bb%	ct%	Eye	SB	CS	x/h%	Iso	RC/G
2013	A	Kannapolis	267	45	74	1	21	277	334	363	698	8	71	0.29	24	4	22	86	4.26

Quick, very fast INF who is all about athleticism and projection. Packs punch with compact stroke and could reach double digit HR once he reads pitches better and adds loft. Has plus-plus speed for infield hits and SB. Profiles well with bat and can hit hard line drives. Footwork needs work and average arm may play better at 2B.

Andujar,Miguel — 5 — New York (A)

EXP MLB DEBUT: 2018 | POTENTIAL: Starting 3B | 8E

Bats R Age 19 | 2011 FA (DR)

Pwr +++ | BAvg +++ | Spd ++ | Def ++

Year	Lev	Team	AB	R	H	HR	RBI	Avg	OB	Slg	OPS	bb%	ct%	Eye	SB	CS	x/h%	Iso	RC/G
2012	Rk	GCL Yankees	177	21	41	1	19	232	284	299	584	7	79	0.35	1	3	24	68	2.66
2013	Rk	GCL Yankees 2	133	18	43	4	25	323	357	496	853	5	84	0.33	4	1	35	173	5.80

Young and projectable infielder who spent second season in Rookie ball. Has good pitch recognition for age and has ability to use entire field with line drive stroke. Bat speed and wiry strength should lead to more pop down the road, but could use better pitch selectivity. Good range and arm at 3B, but can be lazy with footwork.

Aplin,Andrew — 8 — Houston

EXP MLB DEBUT: 2015 | POTENTIAL: Fourth OF | 6B

Bats L Age 23 | 2012 (5) Arizona State

Pwr ++ | BAvg +++ | Spd +++ | Def +++

Year	Lev	Team	AB	R	H	HR	RBI	Avg	OB	Slg	OPS	bb%	ct%	Eye	SB	CS	x/h%	Iso	RC/G
2011	NCAA	Arizona St.	137	22	39	1	19	285	368	416	784	12	89	1.20	3	5	33	131	5.61
2012	NCAA	Arizona St.	219	48	66	5	27	301	376	470	846	11	95	2.17	6	2	35	169	6.25
2012	A-	Tri City	164	38	57	4	25	348	431	537	967	13	87	1.09	20	7	32	189	7.73
2012	A+	Lancaster	104	19	27	3	13	260	287	423	710	4	85	0.25	4	3	33	163	4.06
2013	A+	Lancaster	500	102	139	9	107	278	381	424	805	14	87	1.32	24	6	35	146	5.92

Instinctual prospect who maximizes average tools. Profiles as leadoff hitter with patient approach and contact ability. Controlled swing produces line drives to gaps and uses playable speed in CF. Can be solid defender due to routes and reads along with strong arm. Lack of power and impact speed may limit him to reserve role.

Aquino,Aristides — 9 — Cincinnati

EXP MLB DEBUT: 2017 | POTENTIAL: Starting RF | 8E

Bats R Age 20 | 2011 FA (DR)

Pwr ++++ | BAvg +++ | Spd +++ | Def ++

Year	Lev	Team	AB	R	H	HR	RBI	Avg	OB	Slg	OPS	bb%	ct%	Eye	SB	CS	x/h%	Iso	RC/G
2013	Rk	AZL Reds	194	37	54	4	38	278	314	479	793	5	79	0.25	4	3	46	201	5.27
2013	Rk	Billings	69	13	14	3	10	203	225	377	602	3	67	0.09	1	1	36	174	2.55

Wiry prospect with big-time tools and potential upside. Lack of plate patience and pitch recognition evidenced by inability to draw walks. Still very raw and should add muscle as he matures allowing him to tap into plus power potential. Showed nice pop and all-around skills during AZL season.

Arcia,Orlando | 6 | Milwaukee

EXP MLB DEBUT: 2016 | POTENTIAL: Starting SS | 7C

Bats R Age 19
2010 FA (Venezuela)
Pwr + +
BAvg + + +
Spd + + +
Def + + + +

Year	Lev	Team	AB	R	H	HR	RBI	Avg	OB	Slg	OPS	bb%	ct%	Eye	SB	CS	x/h%	Iso	RC/G
2013	A	Wisconsin	442	67	111	4	39	251	306	333	639	7	91	0.88	20	9	21	81	3.67

Small, athletic SS with contact oriented swing does not walk much, but he rarely strikes out, going gap-to-gap. Power is not a part of his game now, but has raw strength that should allow more as he matures. Plus SS, showing good range, footwork, and a strong arm. Not a burner but speed is a tick above average.

Arias,Junior | 8 | Cincinnati

EXP MLB DEBUT: 2016 | POTENTIAL: Backup OF | 6D

Bats R Age 22
2008 FA (DR)
Pwr + +
BAvg +
Spd + + + +
Def + +

Year	Lev	Team	AB	R	H	HR	RBI	Avg	OB	Slg	OPS	bb%	ct%	Eye	SB	CS	x/h%	Iso	RC/G
2010	Rk	AZL Reds	195	44	56	6	25	287	329	482	811	6	70	0.21	4	3	38	195	5.70
2011	Rk	Billings	219	47	55	8	30	251	311	452	763	8	66	0.26	7	5	45	201	5.25
2012	A	Dayton	361	52	75	7	35	208	249	313	562	5	73	0.21	28	7	28	105	2.16
2013	A	Dayton	271	45	77	10	33	284	317	469	786	5	73	0.18	40	10	34	185	5.08
2013	A+	Bakersfield	222	30	57	5	20	257	273	396	670	2	73	0.08	19	10	33	140	3.48

Athletic player has nice but undeveloped tools. Moved from 3B to OF, and is a work in progress, but has the arm, speed to play CF or RF. Hits the ball with hard contact to all fields, but poor pitch recognition leads to over-aggressiveness and untapped power potential. Needs to vastly improve ct%. Career high SB in '13.

Arroyo,Christian | 6 | San Francisco

EXP MLB DEBUT: 2016 | POTENTIAL: Starting SS | 8D

Bats R Age 19
2013 (1) HS (FL)
Pwr + +
BAvg + + + +
Spd + +
Def + +

Year	Lev	Team	AB	R	H	HR	RBI	Avg	OB	Slg	OPS	bb%	ct%	Eye	SB	CS	x/h%	Iso	RC/G
2013	Rk	AZL Giants	184	47	60	2	39	326	389	511	900	9	83	0.59	3	2	42	185	6.86

Instinctual, athletic SS impressed in debut, showing advanced feel for hitting, making consistent contact, and showing good plate discipline. Power will never be a big part of his game, though he sprays the ball to all fields. Below average speed limits range at SS, but his strong arm and reads would work from 2B/3B.

Arteaga,Humberto | 46 | Kansas City

EXP MLB DEBUT: 2017 | POTENTIAL: Utility INF | 6B

Bats R Age 20
2010 FA (Venezuela)
Pwr +
BAvg + +
Spd + +
Def + + + +

Year	Lev	Team	AB	R	H	HR	RBI	Avg	OB	Slg	OPS	bb%	ct%	Eye	SB	CS	x/h%	Iso	RC/G
2011	Rk	AZL Royals	213	30	54	0	28	254	284	324	608	4	82	0.23	8	2	24	70	2.91
2012	Rk	Burlington	234	40	64	2	29	274	300	380	681	4	87	0.29	7	3	28	107	3.82
2013	Rk	Idaho Falls	300	56	84	3	58	280	337	393	731	8	83	0.50	11	7	27	113	4.62
2013	A	Lexington	240	17	45	0	13	188	207	225	432	2	82	0.14	0	4	16	38	0.70

Lean, smooth INF who has value in defensive attributes. Struggled mightily in Low-A before demotion to short-season. Uses simple swing to make decent contact, though needs to get on base. Doesn't have enough strength for power and lacks ideal speed for SB. Plus defender with quick actions, plus range, and average arm.

Asencio,Yeison | 9 | San Diego

EXP MLB DEBUT: 2015 | POTENTIAL: Backup RF | 6D

Bats R Age 24
2009 FA (DR)
Pwr + +
BAvg + + +
Spd + +
Def + + +

Year	Lev	Team	AB	R	H	HR	RBI	Avg	OB	Slg	OPS	bb%	ct%	Eye	SB	CS	x/h%	Iso	RC/G
2011	Rk	AZL Padres	210	50	73	7	46	348	360	586	946	2	88	0.16	8	2	38	238	6.66
2012	A	Fort Wayne	350	47	113	8	61	323	352	474	827	4	89	0.42	7	6	29	151	5.47
2013	A+	Lake Elsinore	243	34	72	5	44	296	324	457	781	4	88	0.34	1	1	38	160	4.97
2013	AA	San Antonio	291	25	76	2	32	261	293	354	647	4	90	0.45	3	2	26	93	3.56

Big, strong OF who was healthy all season and continued to show BA potential. Makes easy, hard contact with repeatable stroke and has enough bat speed to lace line drives to gaps. Fringy pop limits upside. Free swinging approach leads to low OBP. Can play average RF with plus arm.

Aune,Austin | 96 | New York (A)

EXP MLB DEBUT: 2017 | POTENTIAL: Starting RF | 8E

Bats L Age 20
2012 (2) HS (TX)
Pwr + +
BAvg + +
Spd + +
Def + + +

Year	Lev	Team	AB	R	H	HR	RBI	Avg	OB	Slg	OPS	bb%	ct%	Eye	SB	CS	x/h%	Iso	RC/G
2012	Rk	GCL Yankees	139	19	38	1	20	273	361	410	771	12	68	0.42	6	4	37	137	5.65
2013	Rk	GCL Yankees	156	13	30	0	12	192	232	263	495	5	54	0.11	0	2	33	71	1.54

Raw, athletic prospect who moved from SS to RF in return to Rookie ball. Has significant issue with Ks and crude approach may be culprit. Swings at anything and needs to shorten stroke for more contact. Owns excellent raw power, but isn't game-ready. Strong arm and range in RF and will need time to develop instincts.

Austin,Tyler | 9 | New York (A)

EXP MLB DEBUT: 2014 | POTENTIAL: Starting OF | 8C

Bats R Age 22
2010 (13) HS (GA)
Pwr + + +
BAvg + + +
Spd + +
Def + + +

Year	Lev	Team	AB	R	H	HR	RBI	Avg	OB	Slg	OPS	bb%	ct%	Eye	SB	CS	x/h%	Iso	RC/G
2012	A	Charleston (Sc)	266	69	85	14	54	320	403	598	1000	12	74	0.54	17	2	48	278	8.36
2012	A+	Tampa	134	20	43	2	23	321	377	478	854	8	79	0.43	6	0	37	157	6.20
2012	AA	Trenton	7	2	2	0	1	286	375	286	661	13	86	1.00	0	0	0	0	4.04
2013	Rk	GCL Yankees 2	6	1	4	0	0	667	714	667	1381	14	100	1.00	0	0	0	0	12.11
2013	AA	Trenton	319	43	82	6	40	257	342	373	715	11	75	0.52	4	0	29	116	4.51

Advanced, athletic OF who missed time with wrist injury. Possesses short, fast stroke to hit hard line drives to gaps and has bat control for contact. Can be too patient at plate and get behind in counts. Power is average, but should hit for enough BA to warrant everyday corner OF. Runs OK and has excellent range in OF.

Avelino,Abiatal | 6 | New York (A)

EXP MLB DEBUT: 2018 | POTENTIAL: Starting SS | 7D

Bats R Age 19
2011 FA (DR)
Pwr +
BAvg + + +
Spd + + + +
Def + + +

Year	Lev	Team	AB	R	H	HR	RBI	Avg	OB	Slg	OPS	bb%	ct%	Eye	SB	CS	x/h%	Iso	RC/G
2013	Rk	GCL Yankees	58	14	15	0	4	259	338	328	666	11	88	1.00	9	3	20	69	4.16
2013	Rk	GCL Yankees 2	70	21	28	0	13	400	468	586	1054	11	94	2.25	17	1	32	186	8.73
2013	A-	Staten Island	70	10	17	0	6	243	284	271	555	5	91	0.67	2	0	12	29	2.65

Athletic, instinctual INF with advanced skills for his age. Made Rookie ball look easy by using plus speed and natural hitting skills. Uses whole field and has discerning eye for selectivity. Lacks punch in compact stroke, but has strength to line balls to gaps. Hands and feet work well at SS and exhibits above average arm.

Avery,Xavier | 78 | Seattle

EXP MLB DEBUT: 2012 | POTENTIAL: Starting OF | 8E

Bats L Age 24
2008 (2) HS (GA)
Pwr + +
BAvg + + +
Spd + + + +
Def + + +

Year	Lev	Team	AB	R	H	HR	RBI	Avg	OB	Slg	OPS	bb%	ct%	Eye	SB	CS	x/h%	Iso	RC/G
2012	AAA	Norfolk	390	57	92	8	34	236	324	356	681	12	73	0.48	22	7	28	121	4.05
2012	MLB	BAL	94	14	21	1	6	223	305	340	645	10	76	0.48	6	3	38	117	3.62
2013	AA	Bowie	160	34	48	1	12	300	388	406	794	13	73	0.52	12	3	27	106	5.80
2013	AAA	Norfolk	295	36	70	2	23	237	310	312	622	10	75	0.42	17	5	23	75	3.22
2013	AAA	Tacoma	12	5	6	1	3	500	538	833	1372	8	92	1.00	1	0	33	333	11.42

Very athletic outfielder who needs to get on base more in order to utilize plus speed. Exhibits clean, quick stroke mechanics, but doesn't read pitches well and chases out of zone. Struggles to hit LHP and doesn't own much power in lean frame. Steals lots of bases and has exemplary range in CF. Fringy arm may lead to move to LF.

Ayala,Sammy | 2 | Chicago (A)

EXP MLB DEBUT: 2018 | POTENTIAL: Starting C | 7E

Bats L Age 19
2012 (17) HS (CA)
Pwr + +
BAvg + +
Spd + +
Def + +

Year	Lev	Team	AB	R	H	HR	RBI	Avg	OB	Slg	OPS	bb%	ct%	Eye	SB	CS	x/h%	Iso	RC/G
2012	Rk	Bristol	84	12	17	1	5	202	247	274	521	6	73	0.22	0	1	24	71	1.62
2013	Rk	Bristol	105	9	22	1	7	210	272	267	539	8	69	0.27	0	0	18	57	1.89

Tall, athletic catcher who returned to Rookie ball and struggled with bat. Profiles well with raw, power potential. Swings with authority and has enough strength to reach seats, though mostly shows in BP. Can be very pull-conscious and isn't selective. Catch and throw skills improving, but needs to make strides with receiving.

Baez,Javier | 6 | Chicago (N)

EXP MLB DEBUT: 2014 | POTENTIAL: Starting SS/3B | 9B

Bats R Age 21
2011 (1) HS, PR
Pwr + + + + +
BAvg + + +
Spd + +
Def + +

Year	Lev	Team	AB	R	H	HR	RBI	Avg	OB	Slg	OPS	bb%	ct%	Eye	SB	CS	x/h%	Iso	RC/G
2011	A-	Boise	6	0	1	0	1	167	167	167	333	0	67	0.00	0	0	0	0	-1.38
2012	A	Peoria	213	41	71	12	33	333	360	596	957	4	77	0.19	20	3	38	263	7.08
2012	A+	Daytona	80	9	15	4	13	188	235	400	635	6	74	0.24	4	2	53	213	3.08
2013	A+	Daytona	299	59	82	17	57	274	322	535	857	7	74	0.27	12	2	49	261	6.08
2013	AA	Tennessee	218	39	64	20	54	294	350	638	988	8	68	0.28	8	2	55	344	8.11

Might have the best power of any prospect in the NL. Is physically strong and generates plenty of torque with aggressive swing. Has exciting bat speed, but can be overly aggressive. Decent tools at SS but rushed throws and poor footwork led to 44 errors.

Balaguert,Yasiel — 9 — Chicago (N)

EXP MLB DEBUT: 2018 | POTENTIAL: Starting LF | 7E

Bats R Age 21
2012 FA (Cuba)

- Pwr + + +
- BAvg + +
- Spd + +
- Def + +

Year	Lev	Team	AB	R	H	HR	RBI	Avg	OB	Slg	OPS	bb%	ct%	Eye	SB	CS	x/h%	Iso	RC/G
2012	Rk	AZL Cubs	115	16	27	2	15	235	296	357	653	8	77	0.37	1	1	30	122	3.55
2012	A	Peoria	149	10	31	1	18	208	234	262	496	3	67	0.10	0	1	19	54	1.13
2013	Rk	AZL Cubs	15	3	4	0	2	267	389	533	922	17	73	0.75	0	0	75	267	8.08
2013	A-	Boise	238	33	62	8	48	261	333	433	766	10	71	0.37	1	3	39	172	5.17

Strong, thick-bodied Cuban player was signed in '12 for $400,000 and looks to have modest potential. Has decent raw power, but makes below average contact due to uppercut swing and poor pitch recognition. Below avg runner and likely limited to LF.

Baldwin,James — 8 — Los Angeles (N)

EXP MLB DEBUT: 2016 | POTENTIAL: Starting CF | 7D

Bats L Age 22
2010 (4) HS (NC)

- Pwr + +
- BAvg + +
- Spd + + + +
- Def + + +

Year	Lev	Team	AB	R	H	HR	RBI	Avg	OB	Slg	OPS	bb%	ct%	Eye	SB	CS	x/h%	Iso	RC/G
2010	Rk	AZL Dodgers	179	25	49	2	22	274	309	363	672	5	66	0.15	17	3	20	89	3.79
2011	Rk	Ogden	196	47	49	10	39	250	313	480	793	8	62	0.24	22	5	45	230	5.87
2012	A	Great Lakes	440	62	92	7	40	209	282	334	617	9	60	0.25	53	8	36	125	3.36
2013	A	Great Lakes	369	49	88	7	49	238	315	388	702	10	58	0.27	42	11	40	149	4.92

Tall, athletic OF repeated Low-A and continued to struggle. Walk rate trending in the right direction, but struggles with breaking balls and making consistent contact, striking out 154 times. Has plus speed on the bases and shows good range and a strong arm in center.

Baltz,Jeremy — 7 — San Diego

EXP MLB DEBUT: 2016 | POTENTIAL: Starting OF | 7C

Bats R Age 23
2012 (2) St. John's

- Pwr + + +
- BAvg + + +
- Spd + +
- Def + +

Year	Lev	Team	AB	R	H	HR	RBI	Avg	OB	Slg	OPS	bb%	ct%	Eye	SB	CS	x/h%	Iso	RC/G
2011	NCAA	St. John's	209	42	65	6	60	311	426	483	910	17	78	0.89	7	2	32	172	7.35
2012	NCAA	St. John's	241	65	83	8	52	344	423	531	954	12	91	1.50	18	5	30	187	7.43
2012	A-	Eugene	263	44	74	5	43	281	361	414	776	11	84	0.77	12	2	31	133	5.32
2013	A	Fort Wayne	168	18	45	5	33	268	297	435	732	4	78	0.19	4	0	38	167	4.31
2013	A+	Lake Elsinore	262	42	81	10	54	309	363	511	874	8	78	0.38	2	1	38	202	6.31

Tall and strong OF who fared better in High-A than Low-A. Swings with authority and can put charge into ball with above average strength and raw power. Can steal a few bags despite limited speed, but is generally bat-only prospect. Relegated to LF with subpar range and below average arm strength.

Barnes,Austin — 2 — Miami

EXP MLB DEBUT: 2014 | POTENTIAL: Starting C | 7E

Bats R Age 24
2011 (9) Arizona State

- Pwr + +
- BAvg + + +
- Spd + +
- Def + + +

Year	Lev	Team	AB	R	H	HR	RBI	Avg	OB	Slg	OPS	bb%	ct%	Eye	SB	CS	x/h%	Iso	RC/G
2011	NCAA	Arizona St.	148	27	49	1	15	331	381	459	841	8	89	0.75	3	1	33	128	5.96
2011	A-	Jamestown	219	33	63	1	19	288	361	361	721	10	90	1.14	6	1	22	73	4.77
2012	A	Greensboro	478	76	152	12	65	318	393	481	874	11	87	0.97	9	2	34	163	6.47
2013	A+	Jupiter	350	42	91	4	38	260	356	343	699	13	83	0.88	5	2	22	83	4.47
2013	AA	Jacksonville	62	10	21	1	7	339	446	484	930	16	84	1.20	0	0	24	145	7.56

Small, athletic backstop with contact-oriented swing continued to impress in '13. Shows great patience at the plate, and makes hard contact going gap-to-gap. Power and speed will never be a big part of his game. Behind the plate his arm works but it is his good hands and receiving skills that will keep him there.

Barnes,Barrett — 8 — Pittsburgh

EXP MLB DEBUT: 2016 | POTENTIAL: Starting CF | 8D

Bats R Age 22
2012 (1) Texas Tech

- Pwr + + +
- BAvg + + +
- Spd + + +
- Def + + +

Year	Lev	Team	AB	R	H	HR	RBI	Avg	OB	Slg	OPS	bb%	ct%	Eye	SB	CS	x/h%	Iso	RC/G
2010	NCAA	Texas Tech	217	71	74	14	53	341	444	641	1084	16	77	0.80	12	3	47	300	9.46
2011	NCAA	Texas Tech	214	47	62	10	38	290	404	509	913	16	73	0.72	19	2	42	220	7.38
2012	NCAA	Texas Tech	206	53	67	9	49	325	416	597	1013	13	82	0.86	19	1	48	272	8.36
2012	A-	State College	125	16	36	5	24	288	373	456	829	12	83	0.81	10	6	31	168	5.87
2013	A	West Virginia	183	26	49	5	24	268	330	399	729	9	74	0.35	10	3	29	131	4.51

Injuries cost him season and logged just 308 AB in past two sesaons. When healthy, has good bat speed, solid plate discipline, and plus raw power. Has above-average speed, covers ground well, and should be able to stick in CF as he moves up.

Barnhart,Tucker — 2 — Cincinnati

EXP MLB DEBUT: 2015 | POTENTIAL: Starting C | 7C

Bats B Age 23
2009 (10) HS (IN)

- Pwr +
- BAvg + +
- Spd + +
- Def + + + +

Year	Lev	Team	AB	R	H	HR	RBI	Avg	OB	Slg	OPS	bb%	ct%	Eye	SB	CS	x/h%	Iso	RC/G
2010	Rk	Billings	111	17	34	0	12	306	403	387	790	14	77	0.72	4	1	26	81	5.76
2011	A	Dayton	326	47	89	3	43	273	347	387	734	10	82	0.63	2	1	33	113	4.79
2012	A+	Bakersfield	198	26	55	4	22	278	370	409	779	13	77	0.64	0	2	31	131	5.43
2012	AA	Pensacola	130	10	26	2	12	200	262	292	555	8	83	0.50	1	1	27	92	2.43
2013	AA	Pensacola	339	31	88	3	44	260	346	348	694	12	83	0.79	1	0	26	88	4.38

Athletic, defense-first catcher nailed 36% of baserunners in 2013 with just two passed balls. Defense will be his calling card to playing time, as power and speed are non-existent. Does possess nice plate discipline, posting solid bb%/ct% during repeat Double-A season. Respectable OBP could secure everyday role.

Barnum,Keon — 3 — Chicago (A)

EXP MLB DEBUT: 2017 | POTENTIAL: Starting 1B | 8E

Bats L Age 21
2012 (1-S) HS (FL)

- Pwr + + + +
- BAvg + +
- Spd +
- Def + +

Year	Lev	Team	AB	R	H	HR	RBI	Avg	OB	Slg	OPS	bb%	ct%	Eye	SB	CS	x/h%	Iso	RC/G
2012	Rk	Bristol	43	6	12	3	8	279	354	512	866	10	70	0.38	0	0	33	233	6.37
2013	A	Kannapolis	201	22	51	5	26	254	318	403	721	9	68	0.29	0	0	37	149	4.61

Big and powerful slugger who began season in June and missed time with knee and hand injuries. Showcases all-fields power with long arms and bat speed. Fails to recognize pitches and bails out against LHP (.186). Doesn't control strike zone. Possesses strong arm, but slow foot speed is issue in field and on base.

Barreto,Franklin — 6 — Toronto

EXP MLB DEBUT: 2018 | POTENTIAL: Starting INF | 8C

Bats R Age 18
2012 FA (Venezuela)

- Pwr + +
- BAvg + + +
- Spd + + +
- Def + +

Year	Lev	Team	AB	R	H	HR	RBI	Avg	OB	Slg	OPS	bb%	ct%	Eye	SB	CS	x/h%	Iso	RC/G
2013	Rk	Bluefield	54	4	11	0	7	204	232	333	565	4	74	0.14	0	2	55	130	2.39
2013	Rk	GCL Blue Jays	174	30	52	4	19	299	348	529	876	7	76	0.31	10	4	50	230	6.56

Short, quick INF who led GCL in SLG. Aggressive hitter who draws few walks, but makes hard contact with compact stroke. Should grow into solid-average power with experience. Recognizes pitches, but can't lay off pitches out of zone. Footwork and range may move him off SS, but has strong arm and good speed.

Bautista,Rafael — 8 — Washington

EXP MLB DEBUT: 2017 | POTENTIAL: Starting OF | 8D

Bats R Age 21
2012 FA (DR)

- Pwr +
- BAvg + + +
- Spd + + + +
- Def + + +

Year	Lev	Team	AB	R	H	HR	RBI	Avg	OB	Slg	OPS	bb%	ct%	Eye	SB	CS	x/h%	Iso	RC/G
2013	Rk	GCL Nationals	202	44	65	1	27	322	377	391	768	8	83	0.53	26	7	15	69	5.05

Great athlete with plus speed. Stole 26 bases in 202 AB. Has good defensive instincts and a strong arm; will be able to play CF for years to come. He won't ever hit many home runs, but nice gap power with solid bat speed and a contact-first approach.

Bean,Steve — 2 — St. Louis

EXP MLB DEBUT: 2017 | POTENTIAL: Starting C | 7D

Bats L Age 20
2012 (1-S) HS (TX)

- Pwr + +
- BAvg + + +
- Spd + +
- Def + + +

Year	Lev	Team	AB	R	H	HR	RBI	Avg	OB	Slg	OPS	bb%	ct%	Eye	SB	CS	x/h%	Iso	RC/G
2012	Rk	GCL Cardinals	50	8	16	0	7	320	414	400	814	14	78	0.73	0	0	25	80	6.05
2012	Rk	Johnson City	80	6	10	1	5	125	263	213	476	16	60	0.47	2	0	50	88	0.98
2013	Rk	Johnson City	118	15	27	2	14	229	295	314	608	9	63	0.25	0	0	22	85	2.99

Raw, athletic catcher has been slow to develop. Shows solid defensive tools with good agility and a strong arm. Has struggled offensively, hitting just ,229 while making poor contact. Isn't going to hit for much power, but still has time to develop.

Beckham,Tim — 46 — Tampa Bay

EXP MLB DEBUT: 2013 | POTENTIAL: Starting SS/2B | 7C

Bats R Age 24
2008 (1) HS (GA)

- Pwr + +
- BAvg + + +
- Spd + + +
- Def + + +

Year	Lev	Team	AB	R	H	HR	RBI	Avg	OB	Slg	OPS	bb%	ct%	Eye	SB	CS	x/h%	Iso	RC/G
2011	AA	Montgomery	418	82	115	7	57	275	337	395	732	9	78	0.43	15	4	30	120	4.60
2011	AAA	Durham	106	12	27	5	13	255	275	462	737	3	73	0.10	2	1	37	208	4.32
2012	AAA	Durham	285	40	73	6	28	256	325	361	686	9	75	0.41	6	0	23	105	3.98
2013	AAA	Durham	460	71	127	4	51	276	339	387	726	9	77	0.41	17	7	28	111	4.61
2013	MLB	TAM	7	1	3	0	1	429	429	429	857	0	100		0	0	0	0	5.47

Athletic infielder who tore ACL in offseason and will miss most of '14. Played mostly SS in '13 and may profile better as offensive 2B. Has sufficient bat speed to produce some power, though hasn't developed much. Long swing can result in Ks, but makes decent contact to gaps. Owns average speed, quickness, and range.

Bell,Josh — 9 — Pittsburgh

EXP MLB DEBUT: 2016 | POTENTIAL: Starting LF | 9D

Bats B Age 21
2011 (2) HS (TX)

- Pwr ++++
- BAvg +++
- Spd ++
- Def ++

Year	Lev	Team	AB	R	H	HR	RBI	Avg	OB	Slg	OPS	bb%	ct%	Eye	SB	CS	x/h%	Iso	RC/G
2012	A	West Virginia	62	6	17	1	11	274	297	403	700	3	66	0.10	1	0	35	129	4.19
2013	A	West Virginia	459	75	128	13	76	279	352	453	805	10	80	0.58	1	2	41	174	5.60

Athletic, switch-hitting OF was solid in his first full pro season. Has plus bat speed and plus raw power though swing is flat. Knee injury in '12 cut into his speed, which is average. Shows more power from the LH-side, but better contact from the right.

Belnome,Vince — 345 — Tampa Bay

EXP MLB DEBUT: 2014 | POTENTIAL: Utility player | 6B

Bats L Age 26
2009 (28) West Virginia

- Pwr ++
- BAvg +++
- Spd ++
- Def ++

Year	Lev	Team	AB	R	H	HR	RBI	Avg	OB	Slg	OPS	bb%	ct%	Eye	SB	CS	x/h%	Iso	RC/G
2011	AA	San Antonio	267	56	89	17	62	333	433	603	1036	15	78	0.80	0	5	42	270	8.71
2012	Rk	AZL Padres	10	1	4	1	5	400	500	1000	1500	17	100	1.00	0	0	75	600	13.47
2012	A+	Lake Elsinore	14	2	8	1	7	571	647	1000	1647	18	86	1.50	0	0	50	429	16.19
2012	AAA	Tucson	258	28	71	5	33	275	379	384	762	14	72	0.60	5	1	24	109	5.31
2013	AAA	Durham	444	77	133	8	67	300	411	446	857	16	75	0.77	0	2	35	146	6.71

Short and versatile infielder who continues to hit for BA with clean, level swing and disciplined approach. Lacks any semblance of frontline tools, but recognizes pitches and can use entire field. Power only to pull side and has below average speed. Has some arm strength, but isn't a polished defender at any position.

Beltre,Engel — 789 — Texas

EXP MLB DEBUT: 2013 | POTENTIAL: Starting OF | 7D

Bats L Age 24
2006 FA (DR)

- Pwr ++
- BAvg +++
- Spd ++++
- Def ++++

Year	Lev	Team	AB	R	H	HR	RBI	Avg	OB	Slg	OPS	bb%	ct%	Eye	SB	CS	x/h%	Iso	RC/G
2010	AA	Frisco	181	14	46	1	14	254	293	337	630	5	87	0.42	8	2	20	83	3.34
2011	AA	Frisco	437	64	101	1	28	231	277	300	577	6	76	0.27	16	6	22	69	2.52
2012	AA	Frisco	564	80	147	13	55	261	293	420	713	4	79	0.22	36	10	32	160	4.15
2013	AAA	Round Rock	394	58	115	7	34	292	339	398	737	7	79	0.33	15	12	23	107	4.52
2013	MLB	TEX	40	7	10	0	2	250	250	275	525	0	88	0.00	1	2	10	25	1.79

Athletic, rangy CF who can be free swinger at plate, but making better contact and having success against RHP. Mostly known for speed and defense. Patrols CF with above average range, speed, and routes. Raw power hasn't yet developed and LHP give him trouble. Solid all-around performer with good tools.

Beras,Jairo — 9 — Texas

EXP MLB DEBUT: 2018 | POTENTIAL: Starting OF | 9E

Bats R Age 18
2012 FA (DR)

- Pwr +++
- BAvg ++
- Spd ++
- Def ++

Year	Lev	Team	AB	R	H	HR	RBI	Avg	OB	Slg	OPS	bb%	ct%	Eye	SB	CS	x/h%	Iso	RC/G
2013	Rk	AZL Rangers	64	11	16	2	15	250	304	438	742	7	70	0.26	1	0	38	188	4.78

Very projectable OF who ended season after breaking hand. Showed glimpses of massive upside with all-around tools. Lean frame needs strength and needs to tone down aggressive, approach. Can hit breaking balls and should hit for moderate BA with plus-plus power. Has good feel for entire field, though lacks speed.

Betancourt,Javier — 456 — Detroit

EXP MLB DEBUT: 2018 | POTENTIAL: Starting 2B/SS | 7D

Bats R Age 19
2011 FA (Venezuela)

- Pwr ++
- BAvg ++++
- Spd ++
- Def +++

Year	Lev	Team	AB	R	H	HR	RBI	Avg	OB	Slg	OPS	bb%	ct%	Eye	SB	CS	x/h%	Iso	RC/G
2013	Rk	GCL Tigers	177	28	59	2	22	333	376	441	816	6	92	0.86	5	3	22	107	5.56

Fundamentally-sound INF who finished 2nd in GCL in BA. Spent most of time at SS. Takes contact approach to plate and possesses hand-eye coordination. Polished stroke helps to slash line drives to gaps. Below average power limits upside and won't rack up SB due to fringy speed. Steady defender with soft, quick hands.

Bethancourt,Christian — 2 — Atlanta

EXP MLB DEBUT: 2013 | POTENTIAL: Starting C | 8C

Bats R Age 22
2009 FA (Panama)

- Pwr ++
- BAvg ++
- Spd ++
- Def ++++

Year	Lev	Team	AB	R	H	HR	RBI	Avg	OB	Slg	OPS	bb%	ct%	Eye	SB	CS	x/h%	Iso	RC/G
2011	A	Rome	221	25	67	4	33	303	328	430	757	3	88	0.30	6	3	25	127	4.63
2011	A+	Lynchburg	166	11	45	1	20	271	284	325	609	2	79	0.09	3	2	16	54	2.66
2012	AA	Mississippi	268	30	65	2	26	243	272	291	563	4	83	0.24	8	6	12	49	2.31
2013	AA	Mississippi	358	42	99	12	45	277	307	436	743	4	84	0.28	11	7	33	159	4.42
2013	MLB	ATL	1	0	0	0	0	0	0	0	0	0	0	0.00	0	0	0	0	0.00

Plus defensive backstop with good actions, a quick release, and a strong arm. Nailed 33% of runners in 2013 and had a breakout season at the plate. Below avg plate discipline remains an issue, but good year at AA puts him in the frame for in 2014.

Betts,Mookie — 4 — Boston

EXP MLB DEBUT: 2015 | POTENTIAL: Starting 2B | 8C

Bats R Age 21
2011 (5) HS (TN)

- Pwr ++
- BAvg ++++
- Spd ++++
- Def +++

Year	Lev	Team	AB	R	H	HR	RBI	Avg	OB	Slg	OPS	bb%	ct%	Eye	SB	CS	x/h%	Iso	RC/G
2011	Rk	GCL Red Sox	4	0	2	0	2	500	500	500	1000	0	100	0.00	1	0	0	0	6.83
2012	A-	Lowell	251	34	67	0	31	267	350	307	657	11	88	1.07	20	4	13	40	4.04
2013	A	Greenville	277	63	82	8	26	296	418	477	894	17	86	1.45	18	2	40	181	7.12
2013	A+	Salem	185	30	63	7	39	341	413	551	965	11	91	1.35	20	2	35	211	7.47

Diminutive INF with breakout campaign. Swings bat with authority and combines contact ability with patient approach. Gets on base and steals bases with plus speed and quickness. Made tweaks to stroke and is compact and quicker. Hits for power, but frame lacks projection. Good defender with quick hands and ample range.

Bichette,Dante — 5 — New York (A)

EXP MLB DEBUT: 2016 | POTENTIAL: Starting 3B | 7E

Bats R Age 21
2011 (2) HS (FL)

- Pwr ++
- BAvg ++
- Spd ++
- Def ++

Year	Lev	Team	AB	R	H	HR	RBI	Avg	OB	Slg	OPS	bb%	ct%	Eye	SB	CS	x/h%	Iso	RC/G
2011	Rk	GCL Yankees	196	33	67	3	47	342	429	505	934	13	79	0.73	3	3	34	163	7.54
2011	A-	Staten Island	7	1	1	1	1	143	250	571	821	13	71	0.50	0	1	100	429	5.34
2012	A	Charleston (Sc)	471	67	117	3	46	248	313	331	644	9	80	0.47	3	4	26	83	3.54
2013	A	Charleston (Sc)	435	47	93	11	61	214	285	331	616	9	73	0.36	1	0	30	117	2.99

Streaky prospect who has seen stock drop after consecutive subar seasons in Low-A. Established career high in HR and has solid, usable power. Bat speed remains, but can be too passive at plate and struggles to recognize spin. K rate increased and may need to overhaul stroke. Has clean, quick hands, but fringy arm.

Bird,Gregory — 3 — New York (A)

EXP MLB DEBUT: 2016 | POTENTIAL: Starting 1B | 7B

Bats L Age 21
2011 (5) HS (CO)

- Pwr +++
- BAvg ++
- Spd +
- Def ++

Year	Lev	Team	AB	R	H	HR	RBI	Avg	OB	Slg	OPS	bb%	ct%	Eye	SB	CS	x/h%	Iso	RC/G
2011	Rk	GCL Yankees	12	0	1	0	0	83	154	83	237	8	67	0.25	0	0	0	0	-2.61
2012	Rk	GCL Yankees	49	9	14	0	5	286	417	367	784	18	73	0.85	0	0	21	82	5.95
2012	A-	Staten Island	40	4	16	2	8	400	478	650	1128	13	75	0.60	0	0	38	250	10.09
2013	A	Charleston (Sc)	458	84	132	20	84	288	423	511	934	19	71	0.81	1	1	45	223	7.94

Tall, instinctual hitter who led SAL in OBP. Drew over 100 walks and combined approach with bat speed and plus power to produce in pitchers park. Was consistent with bat all season, though has no other real value. Lacks athleticism and runs poorly. Long swing may eventually mute some of pop.

Blash,Jabari — 79 — Seattle

EXP MLB DEBUT: 2015 | POTENTIAL: Starting OF | 7D

Bats R Age 24
2010 (8) Miami Dade CC

- Pwr ++++
- BAvg ++
- Spd ++
- Def +++

Year	Lev	Team	AB	R	H	HR	RBI	Avg	OB	Slg	OPS	bb%	ct%	Eye	SB	CS	x/h%	Iso	RC/G
2011	A-	Everett	195	26	57	11	43	292	381	574	956	13	67	0.43	10	3	53	282	8.24
2011	A	Clinton	124	13	27	3	13	218	401	347	748	23	65	0.88	5	2	33	129	5.51
2012	A	Clinton	400	71	98	15	50	245	343	433	776	13	67	0.45	13	7	41	188	5.57
2013	A+	High Desert	283	42	73	16	53	258	350	505	855	12	70	0.47	14	8	48	247	6.47
2013	AA	Jackson	97	13	30	9	21	309	427	619	1046	17	71	0.71	1	1	40	309	9.09

Physically-gifted outfielder who remains raw, but is making incremental improvement in game. Posted career high in HR and has solid approach at plate. Works counts and can crush LHP with bat speed. Holes in swing have been exploited and will need to close in order to hit for BA. Natural RF with strong arm, but limited range.

Bogaerts,Xander — 56 — Boston

EXP MLB DEBUT: 2013 | POTENTIAL: Starting 3B | 9B

Bats R Age 21
2009 FA (Aruba)

- Pwr ++++
- BAvg +++
- Spd ++
- Def +++

Year	Lev	Team	AB	R	H	HR	RBI	Avg	OB	Slg	OPS	bb%	ct%	Eye	SB	CS	x/h%	Iso	RC/G
2012	A+	Salem	384	59	116	15	64	302	372	505	878	10	78	0.51	4	4	39	203	6.49
2012	AA	Portland	92	12	30	5	17	326	333	598	931	1	77	0.05	1	1	50	272	6.62
2013	AA	Portland	219	40	68	6	35	311	406	502	908	14	77	0.69	5	1	35	192	7.22
2013	AAA	Pawtucket	225	32	64	9	32	284	364	453	817	11	80	0.64	2	2	31	169	5.67
2013	MLB	BOS	44	7	11	1	5	250	327	364	690	10	70	0.38	1	0	27	114	4.11

Tall, athletic INF who reached BOS at 20. Impact bat potential thanks to plus bat speed and natural power to all fields. Became more selective in approach and uses smooth swing to put bat to ball. Can play either SS or 3B, though lacks ideal foot speed. Possesses quick actions and strong arm along with range.

Bonifacio,Jorge — 9 — Kansas City

EXP MLB DEBUT: 2015 | POTENTIAL: Starting OF | **8C**

Bats R Age 21
2009 FA (DR)

- Pwr + + +
- BAvg + + + +
- Spd + + +
- Def + + +

Year	Lev	Team	AB	R	H	HR	RBI	Avg	OB	Slg	OPS	bb%	ct%	Eye	SB	CS	x/h%	Iso	RC/G
2011	Rk	Burlington	236	26	67	7	30	284	329	492	821	6	75	0.28	5	6	46	208	5.71
2012	A	Kane County	412	54	116	10	61	282	330	432	762	7	80	0.36	6	3	31	150	4.86
2013	Rk	AZL Royals	30	4	9	0	6	300	382	533	916	12	80	0.67	1	0	56	233	7.45
2013	A+	Wilmington	206	32	61	2	29	296	367	408	775	10	81	0.58	0	2	26	112	5.27
2013	AA	NW Arkansas	93	15	28	2	19	301	375	441	816	11	75	0.48	2	1	32	140	5.83

Pure hitting OF who has been pushed despite raw skills. Hits for BA despite aggressive approach and subpar selectivity. Can put charge into ball with plus bat speed and strength. Has ability to go to opp field and use average speed. Should evolve into solid-average power or more in time. Owns strong arm and is solid defender.

Borenstein,Zach — 7 — Los Angeles (A)

EXP MLB DEBUT: 2016 | POTENTIAL: Reserve OF | **7D**

Bats L Age 23
2011 (23) Eastern Illinois

- Pwr + + +
- BAvg + + +
- Spd + +
- Def + +

Year	Lev	Team	AB	R	H	HR	RBI	Avg	OB	Slg	OPS	bb%	ct%	Eye	SB	CS	x/h%	Iso	RC/G
2010	NCAA	Eastern Illinois	207	50	73	11	47	353	425	575	1000	11	83	0.72	12	3	33	222	7.87
2011	NCAA	Eastern Illinois	195	38	68	7	29	349	412	554	966	10	85	0.72	9	5	34	205	7.44
2011	Rk	AZL Angels	113	21	31	2	21	274	369	451	821	13	81	0.81	12	1	39	177	6.05
2012	A	Cedar Rapids	293	42	78	11	50	266	328	485	813	8	80	0.45	13	5	50	218	5.59
2013	A+	Inland Empire	407	76	137	28	95	337	400	631	1031	10	78	0.49	5	5	42	295	8.28

Aggressive hitter who won CAL MVP by leading league in BA and HR. Breakout year predicated on improved plate discipline, and ability to hit LHP. Likes to attack FB, but has learned to lay off breaking pitches. Bat speed may not lead to same success at upper levels. Lacks plus tool and athleticism a little short for SB and defense.

Boss,Torsten — 45 — Baltimore

EXP MLB DEBUT: 2015 | POTENTIAL: Reserve INF | **7D**

Bats L Age 23
2012 (8) Michigan State

- Pwr + +
- BAvg + + +
- Spd + +
- Def + +

Year	Lev	Team	AB	R	H	HR	RBI	Avg	OB	Slg	OPS	bb%	ct%	Eye	SB	CS	x/h%	Iso	RC/G
2011	NCAA	Michigan St.	219	44	81	7	59	370	441	589	1030	11	83	0.74	7	2	36	219	8.44
2012	NCAA	Michigan St.	235	44	71	5	43	302	410	447	857	15	81	0.96	12	3	30	145	6.57
2012	A-	Aberdeen	237	33	61	5	27	257	341	414	754	11	78	0.57	9	3	38	156	5.06
2012	A+	Frederick	7	1	1	0	0	143	143	143	286	0	71	0.00	0	0	0	0	-1.83
2013	A	Delmarva	386	44	92	7	45	238	330	358	688	12	73	0.50	6	2	33	119	4.19

All-around INF who has more tools than performance suggests. Moved to 2B from 3B, though is below average defender at any spot. Owns excellent arm, but hands limit upside. Brings patient approach to plate and will work counts. Strikes out too often for limited power profile and can be beaten by good FB and LHP.

Bostick,Chris — 4 — Texas

EXP MLB DEBUT: 2016 | POTENTIAL: Starting 2B | **7C**

Bats R Age 21
2011 (44) HS (NY)

- Pwr + +
- BAvg + + +
- Spd + + +
- Def + +

Year	Lev	Team	AB	R	H	HR	RBI	Avg	OB	Slg	OPS	bb%	ct%	Eye	SB	CS	x/h%	Iso	RC/G
2011	Rk	AZL Athletics	52	13	23	1	5	442	473	654	1127	5	77	0.25	4	0	35	212	9.61
2012	A-	Vermont	279	41	70	3	29	251	317	369	686	9	76	0.41	12	5	33	118	4.09
2013	A	Beloit	489	75	138	14	89	282	350	452	802	9	75	0.42	25	8	34	170	5.57

Strong and athletic infielder who had impressive year in first assignment to full-season ball. Has excellent bat control and mature approach to get on base and has enough punch in stroke to hit HR. Uses entire field, but will need to make more consistent contact. Infield actions a little short, but can make routine plays.

Boyd,B.J. — 78 — Oakland

EXP MLB DEBUT: 2017 | POTENTIAL: Starting OF | **8E**

Bats L Age 20
2012 (4) HS (CA)

- Pwr + +
- BAvg + + +
- Spd + + +
- Def + +

Year	Lev	Team	AB	R	H	HR	RBI	Avg	OB	Slg	OPS	bb%	ct%	Eye	SB	CS	x/h%	Iso	RC/G
2012	Rk	AZL Athletics	143	37	43	1	20	301	398	434	831	14	75	0.64	16	4	30	133	6.36
2013	A-	Vermont	260	39	74	8	32	285	369	442	812	12	75	0.53	8	6	31	158	5.80
2013	A-	Vermont	260	39	74	8	32	285	369	442	812	12	75	0.53	8	6	31	158	5.80

Short and compact athlete who hasn't yet played full-season ball, but has talent to thrive. Possesses leadoff skills and knows how to get on base to use plus speed. Focusing on tapping into power by tweaking swing and adding more leverage. Still quite raw in LF with crude reads and arm strength is limited.

Boyd,Jayce — 3 — New York (N)

EXP MLB DEBUT: 2016 | POTENTIAL: Starting 1B | **7D**

Bats R Age 23
2012 (6) Florida State

- Pwr + +
- BAvg + + +
- Spd +
- Def + + + +

Year	Lev	Team	AB	R	H	HR	RBI	Avg	OB	Slg	OPS	bb%	ct%	Eye	SB	CS	x/h%	Iso	RC/G
2011	NCAA	Florida St.	233	38	78	6	56	335	419	515	934	13	86	1.06	9	2	33	180	7.32
2012	NCAA	Florida St.	255	47	96	4	61	376	455	506	961	13	90	1.42	8	1	26	129	7.62
2012	A-	Brooklyn	201	18	48	5	19	239	323	368	691	11	85	0.83	1	3	31	129	4.27
2013	A	Savannah	249	40	90	5	46	361	440	494	934	12	87	1.09	0	4	24	133	7.26
2013	A+	St. Lucie	209	28	61	4	37	292	370	421	791	11	86	0.90	2	0	30	129	5.51

Has demonstrated advanced plate approach both at collegiate level and Class-A. Makes very consistent, hard contact. Thus far has hit for better average and power against RHP. Going forward, high BA/OBP potential, but has below-average power potential for a 1B. Above-average defender with good range and hands.

Bradley,Jackie — 8 — Boston

EXP MLB DEBUT: 2013 | POTENTIAL: Starting CF | **8B**

Bats L Age 24
2011 (1-S) South Carolina

- Pwr + +
- BAvg + + +
- Spd + + +
- Def + + + +

Year	Lev	Team	AB	R	H	HR	RBI	Avg	OB	Slg	OPS	bb%	ct%	Eye	SB	CS	x/h%	Iso	RC/G
2011	A	Greenville	15	2	5	1	3	333	333	600	933	0	80	0.00	0	0	40	267	6.34
2012	A+	Salem	234	53	84	3	34	359	476	526	1001	18	83	1.30	16	6	37	167	8.65
2012	AA	Portland	229	37	62	6	29	271	367	437	804	13	79	0.71	8	3	39	166	5.77
2013	AAA	Pawtucket	320	57	88	10	35	275	357	469	826	11	77	0.55	7	7	44	194	5.98
2013	MLB	BOS	95	18	18	3	10	189	267	337	604	10	67	0.32	2	0	44	147	2.84

Small, instinctual OF who made BOS Opening Day roster, but struggled. Has leadoff potential due to ability to work counts and selectivity. Focuses on line drives and is terrific baserunner with average speed. Can play solid CF due to plus range and arm. Only weakness is power and even that could emerge.

Brentz,Bryce — 9 — Boston

EXP MLB DEBUT: 2014 | POTENTIAL: Starting OF | **7B**

Bats R Age 25
2010 (1-S) Middle TN State

- Pwr + + + +
- BAvg + +
- Spd + +
- Def + +

Year	Lev	Team	AB	R	H	HR	RBI	Avg	OB	Slg	OPS	bb%	ct%	Eye	SB	CS	x/h%	Iso	RC/G
2011	A+	Salem	288	48	79	19	58	274	334	531	866	8	72	0.33	1	1	44	257	6.25
2012	AA	Portland	456	62	135	17	76	296	353	478	831	8	71	0.31	7	5	36	182	5.94
2012	AAA	Pawtucket	17	0	2	0	0	118	167	118	284	6	65	0.17	0	0	0	0	-2.05
2013	Rk	GCL Red Sox	17	3	4	2	8	235	278	706	984	6	76	0.25	0	0	100	471	7.40
2013	AAA	Pawtucket	326	36	86	17	56	264	306	475	782	6	74	0.23	1	0	40	212	5.00

Powerful OF who missed time with knee injury. Possesses bat speed and strength and can pop balls out of park to all fields. Can sell out for power and become pull-conscious at times. Could be more patient and needs work with pitch recognition. Lacks speed, but range is OK in RF while he possesses very strong, accurate arm.

Brett,Ryan — 4 — Tampa Bay

EXP MLB DEBUT: 2015 | POTENTIAL: Starting 2B | **7B**

Bats R Age 22
2010 (3) HS (WA)

- Pwr + +
- BAvg + + + +
- Spd + + + +
- Def + +

Year	Lev	Team	AB	R	H	HR	RBI	Avg	OB	Slg	OPS	bb%	ct%	Eye	SB	CS	x/h%	Iso	RC/G
2011	Rk	Princeton	240	42	72	3	24	300	368	471	839	10	90	1.08	21	3	42	171	6.13
2012	A	Bowling Green	410	77	117	6	35	285	345	393	737	8	82	0.51	48	8	25	107	4.66
2013	Rk	GCL Rays	4	0	0	0	0	0	0	0	0	0	50	0.00	0	0		0	-7.85
2013	A+	Charlotte	206	38	70	4	22	340	385	490	875	7	87	0.56	22	7	27	150	6.21
2013	AA	Montgomery	105	19	25	3	16	238	292	400	692	7	87	0.57	4	0	40	162	4.10

Short, consistent INF who set career high in HR, but game is all about bat control and speed. Instinctual and natural hitter with hand-eye coordination. Began season in May after serving drug suspension and ended in Double-A. Runs very well and has quick first step at 2B. Hands and arm strength are only passable.

Briceno,Jose — 2 — Colorado

EXP MLB DEBUT: 2017 | POTENTIAL: Starting C | **8D**

Bats R Age 21
2010 FA (Venezuela)

- Pwr + + +
- BAvg + + +
- Spd + +
- Def + + +

Year	Lev	Team	AB	R	H	HR	RBI	Avg	OB	Slg	OPS	bb%	ct%	Eye	SB	CS	x/h%	Iso	RC/G
2012	Rk	Grand Junction	23	5	9	2	5	391	440	652	1092	8	91	1.00	0	0	22	261	8.29
2013	Rk	Grand Junction	153	32	51	9	30	333	354	614	969	3	80	0.17	8	2	49	281	7.07
2013	A	Asheville	91	12	24	1	8	264	302	363	665	5	78	0.25	1	0	29	99	3.58

Strong, agile backstop with good compact power stroke from the RH-side, but can be overly aggressive. Could be more patient at the plate. Defensively, has a strong arm and should be able to stick behind the plate.

Brinson,Lewis — 8 — Texas

EXP MLB DEBUT: 2017 | POTENTIAL: Starting OF | **9D**

Bats R Age 20
2012 (1) HS (FL)

- Pwr + + +
- BAvg + +
- Spd + + + +
- Def + + + +

Year	Lev	Team	AB	R	H	HR	RBI	Avg	OB	Slg	OPS	bb%	ct%	Eye	SB	CS	x/h%	Iso	RC/G
2012	Rk	AZL Rangers	237	54	67	7	42	283	341	523	864	8	69	0.28	14	2	54	241	6.76
2013	A	Hickory	447	64	106	21	52	237	311	427	738	10	57	0.25	24	7	39	190	5.36

Lean, long OF who led SAL in Ks, but has significant upside and potential to be multi-tooled CF. Lots of swing and miss in game and struggles to hit breaking balls. Plus bat speed leads to power to all fields and offers good speed on base and in field. Plays above average defense with excellent range and strong arm.

Brito,Socrates — 89 — Arizona

EXP MLB DEBUT: 2016 | POTENTIAL: Starting CF | **7D**

Bats L Age 21
2011 FA (DR)
Pwr ++
BAvg +++
Spd +++
Def +++

Year	Lev	Team	AB	R	H	HR	RBI	Avg	OB	Slg	OPS	bb%	ct%	Eye	SB	CS	x/h%	Iso	RC/G
2011	Rk	AZL D'backs	236	29	65	1	29	275	313	360	673	5	79	0.26	18	10	17	85	3.73
2012	Rk	Missoula	279	47	87	4	39	312	360	444	804	7	74	0.29	15	9	28	133	5.57
2013	A	South Bend	523	61	138	2	49	264	313	356	668	7	76	0.30	27	9	25	92	3.75

Physical player with good speed and raw power. Still raw in many phases, but has plus bat speed and should add power as he matures. Plays solid defense and can play all three OF positions. Needs to be more selective at the plate, but has tools.

Brown,Gary — 8 — San Francisco

EXP MLB DEBUT: 2014 | POTENTIAL: Starting OF | **7D**

Bats R Age 25
2010 (1) Cal State Fullerton
Pwr ++
BAvg ++
Spd ++++
Def +++

Year	Lev	Team	AB	R	H	HR	RBI	Avg	OB	Slg	OPS	bb%	ct%	Eye	SB	CS	x/h%	Iso	RC/G
2010	Rk	AZL Giants	22	6	4	0	0	182	308	227	535	15	77	0.80	2	0	25	45	2.40
2010	A-	Salem-Keizer	22	2	3	0	2	136	208	227	436	8	68	0.29	0	1	33	91	0.59
2011	A+	San Jose	559	115	188	14	80	336	387	519	906	8	86	0.60	53	19	32	182	6.63
2012	AA	Richmond	538	73	150	7	42	279	329	385	713	7	84	0.46	33	18	27	106	4.32
2013	AAA	Fresno	558	79	129	13	50	231	274	375	649	6	76	0.24	17	11	37	143	3.36

Another disappointing season as almost every offensive category trend in the wrong direction in the PCL. Still has an exciting mix of skills which include plus speed and good defense with plus range and a strong arm. Plate discipline is disappearing and ct% dwindling, as is his prospect upside.

Bruno,Stephen — 4 — Chicago (N)

EXP MLB DEBUT: 2015 | POTENTIAL: Starting 2B | **7D**

Bats R Age 23
2012 (7) Virginia
Pwr ++
BAvg +++
Spd ++
Def ++

Year	Lev	Team	AB	R	H	HR	RBI	Avg	OB	Slg	OPS	bb%	ct%	Eye	SB	CS	x/h%	Iso	RC/G
2010	NCAA	Virginia	98	30	38	3	30	388	455	592	1046	11	83	0.71	5	2	34	204	8.59
2011	NCAA	Virginia	25	4	6	0	2	240	240	320	560	0	72	0.00	0	1	33	80	2.03
2012	NCAA	Virginia	238	49	88	6	54	370	405	559	964	6	89	0.52	11	3	35	189	7.11
2012	A-	Boise	252	51	91	3	37	361	404	496	900	7	81	0.38	2	7	27	135	6.59
2013	A+	Daytona	69	16	25	0	7	362	405	478	884	7	77	0.31	2	1	32	116	6.61

Short 2B prospect continues to be a hitting machine, but a hamstring limited him to just 19 games. Has a short, compact stroke and a good understanding of the strike zone. Makes consistent contact with moderate power. Has decent speed with a good glove.

Bryant,Kris — 5 — Chicago (N)

EXP MLB DEBUT: 2015 | POTENTIAL: Starting RF/1B | **9C**

Bats R Age 22
2013 (1) San Diego
Pwr ++++
BAvg ++++
Spd ++
Def ++

Year	Lev	Team	AB	R	H	HR	RBI	Avg	OB	Slg	OPS	bb%	ct%	Eye	SB	CS	x/h%	Iso	RC/G
2012	NCAA	San Diego	213	59	78	14	57	366	464	671	1136	15	82	1.03	9	3	44	305	9.86
2013	NCAA	San Diego	228	80	75	31	62	329	480	820	1300	22	81	1.50	7	4	63	491	12.05
2013	Rk	AZL Cubs	6	0	1	0	2	167	167	333	500	0	83	0.00	0	0	100	167	1.68
2013	A-	Boise	65	13	23	4	16	354	425	692	1117	11	74	0.47	0	0	57	338	9.93
2013	A+	Daytona	57	9	19	5	14	333	367	719	1086	5	70	0.18	1	0	58	386	9.31

2nd pick from 2013 draft is one of the best hitters in the minors. Plus bat speed, pitch recognition, and ability to make consistent contact give him potential. Below avg defender with limited range and speed make a move to the OF or 1B likely, but his bat is big enough to survive it.

Buckley,Sean — 3 — Cincinnati

EXP MLB DEBUT: 2016 | POTENTIAL: Backup 3B | **6D**

Bats R Age 24
2011 (6) St. Petersburg JC
Pwr +++
BAvg ++
Spd ++
Def +++

Year	Lev	Team	AB	R	H	HR	RBI	Avg	OB	Slg	OPS	bb%	ct%	Eye	SB	CS	x/h%	Iso	RC/G
2010	NCAA	South Florida	60	11	15	1	8	250	318	383	702	9	57	0.23	2	1	40	133	5.02
2011	Rk	Billings	225	38	65	14	41	289	355	551	906	9	68	0.32	6	4	43	262	7.18
2012	A	Dayton	426	46	104	14	68	244	298	413	712	7	67	0.24	1	2	41	169	4.38
2013	A+	Bakersfield	19	1	1	0	2	53	100	53	153	5	53	0.11	0	0	0	0	-4.94

Above-average power potential, but struggles greatly in making contact. Injuries limited him to 19 AB, so will be old for level. Came up as 3B, but has played 1B and some OF; could bring some nice defensive versatility as a backup. Decent plate approach, but struggles with pitch recognition.

Burns,Andy — 56 — Toronto

EXP MLB DEBUT: 2015 | POTENTIAL: Starting 3B | **7B**

Bats R Age 23
2011 (11) Arizona
Pwr +++
BAvg +++
Spd +++
Def ++

Year	Lev	Team	AB	R	H	HR	RBI	Avg	OB	Slg	OPS	bb%	ct%	Eye	SB	CS	x/h%	Iso	RC/G
2011	Rk	GCL Blue Jays	16	5	10	1	7	625	667	813	1479	11	100		0	1	10	188	12.51
2011	A-	Vancouver	84	10	15	2	7	179	233	298	531	7	83	0.43	2	1	40	119	2.07
2012	A	Lansing	278	57	69	9	37	248	339	464	803	12	73	0.51	15	2	55	216	5.80
2013	A+	Dunedin	248	45	81	8	53	327	388	524	912	9	85	0.66	21	9	35	198	6.79
2013	AA	New Hampshire	265	40	67	7	32	253	313	419	731	8	79	0.42	12	5	42	166	4.56

Smooth, athletic INF who had career year with highs in HR and SB. Cooled off after promotion to AA, but has nice all-around game. Shows good pop to pull side and can hit RHP and LHP well. Makes contact, but could benefit from being more selective. Played mostly 3B and can play any infield spot thanks to hands, and strong arm.

Burns,Billy — 78 — Oakland

EXP MLB DEBUT: 2015 | POTENTIAL: Starting OF | **7E**

Bats B Age 24
2011 (32) Mercer
Pwr +
BAvg +++
Spd ++++
Def +++

Year	Lev	Team	AB	R	H	HR	RBI	Avg	OB	Slg	OPS	bb%	ct%	Eye	SB	CS	x/h%	Iso	RC/G
2011	NCAA	Mercer	224	72	80	6	33	357	452	509	961	15	87	1.34	29	3	25	152	7.73
2011	A-	Auburn	107	21	28	1	8	262	336	355	691	10	79	0.55	13	1	21	93	4.20
2012	A	Hagerstown	398	83	128	0	41	322	417	382	799	14	83	0.96	38	9	15	60	5.84
2013	A+	Potomac	330	70	103	0	29	312	406	391	797	14	89	1.41	54	5	17	79	5.87
2013	AA	Harrisburg	114	26	37	0	8	325	425	360	785	15	85	1.18	20	2	11	35	5.71

One of the fastest guys in the minors, and knows how to steal bases. Rarely strikes out and draws walks. Though lacking power, makes consistent contact and keeps ball on the ground to utilize speed. Can play CF or LF with above-average range and solid arm. Working on using lower half in swing more to drive ball into gaps.

Buss,Nick — 789 — Los Angeles (N)

EXP MLB DEBUT: 2013 | POTENTIAL: Backup OF | **6B**

Bats L Age 27
2008 (8) USC
Pwr ++
BAvg ++
Spd +++
Def ++

Year	Lev	Team	AB	R	H	HR	RBI	Avg	OB	Slg	OPS	bb%	ct%	Eye	SB	CS	x/h%	Iso	RC/G
2010	A	Great Lakes	242	42	69	1	23	285	350	351	701	9	88	0.80	20	5	17	66	4.39
2010	A+	Inland Empire	247	32	60	0	25	243	281	332	613	5	87	0.39	6	3	27	89	3.19
2011	A+	Rancho Cuca	479	86	157	14	55	328	364	511	875	5	87	0.43	28	10	33	184	6.08
2012	AA	Chattanooga	492	70	134	8	57	272	325	411	735	7	86	0.54	19	13	31	138	4.64
2013	AAA	Albuquerque	459	84	139	17	100	303	360	525	885	8	80	0.46	21	2	41	222	6.47

Strong, athletic OF had impressive season in AAA, hitting a career high 17 HR. Nothing stands out for Buss, but solid skills across the board make for a nice backup in the bigs. Medicore power-speed combo with solid contact rates are intriguing. Plays all three OF spots.

Buxton,Byron — 8 — Minnesota

EXP MLB DEBUT: 2015 | POTENTIAL: Starting OF | **9A**

Bats R Age 20
2012 (1) HS (GA)
Pwr +++
BAvg +++++
Spd ++++
Def ++++

Year	Lev	Team	AB	R	H	HR	RBI	Avg	OB	Slg	OPS	bb%	ct%	Eye	SB	CS	x/h%	Iso	RC/G
2012	Rk	Elizabethton	77	16	22	1	6	286	353	429	782	9	81	0.53	7	0	36	143	5.34
2012	Rk	GCL Twins	88	17	19	4	14	216	303	466	769	11	70	0.42	4	3	58	250	5.29
2013	A	Cedar Rapids	270	68	92	8	55	341	433	559	992	14	79	0.79	32	11	36	219	8.28
2013	A+	Fort Myers	218	41	71	4	22	326	412	472	884	13	78	0.65	23	8	23	147	6.85

Premier athlete who has extremely high ceiling with strong chance of reaching it. Owns all five tools that should continue to improve. Plus-plus speed is best weapon while power emerges. Recognizes pitches and uses clean swing path to make hard contact. CF defense with plus range and arm has shot for future Gold Glove.

Cabrera,Gustavo — 8 — San Francisco

EXP MLB DEBUT: 2017 | POTENTIAL: Starting OF | **8E**

Bats R Age 18
2012 FA (DR)
Pwr ++
BAvg ++
Spd ++++
Def ++++

Year	Lev	Team	AB	R	H	HR	RBI	Avg	OB	Slg	OPS	bb%	ct%	Eye	SB	CS	x/h%	Iso	RC/G
2013		Did not play in the US																	

Former top Int'l player oozes with potential showing plus-plus speed on the bases and in field where he has strong arm and good routes. Raw hitting mechanics hinder contact ability now, but with time he should develop better approach. He has great bat speed and the plus raw power that scouts dream on.

Cabrera,Ramon — 2 — Detroit

EXP MLB DEBUT: 2014 | POTENTIAL: Backup C | **6B**

Bats B Age 24
2008 FA (Venezuela)
Pwr ++
BAvg +++
Spd +
Def ++

Year	Lev	Team	AB	R	H	HR	RBI	Avg	OB	Slg	OPS	bb%	ct%	Eye	SB	CS	x/h%	Iso	RC/G
2011	A+	Bradenton	327	46	112	3	53	343	411	471	882	10	91	1.31	5	1	29	128	6.62
2012	AA	Altoona	384	47	106	3	50	276	343	367	710	9	89	0.89	0	3	25	91	4.54
2012	AAA	Indianapolis	5	1	2	0	0	400	400	600	1000	0	100		0	0	50	200	7.21
2013	AA	Erie	312	44	95	0	54	304	390	388	778	12	89	1.29	4	0	25	83	5.59
2013	AAA	Toledo	149	13	36	1	15	242	307	336	642	9	86	0.67	0	1	31	94	3.67

Short, stocky catcher who may not have much pop, but knows how to hit by putting ball in play. Hits well from both sides and focuses on hard line drives. Walk rate is sufficient, but can expand strike zone at times. Improved receiving and offers solid blocking technique. Needs to polish catch-and-throw skills as CS% too low.

Calixte,Orlando — 56 — Kansas City

EXP MLB DEBUT: 2015 | POTENTIAL: Starting SS | 7B

Bats R Age 22
2011 FA (DR)
Pwr ++
BAvg ++
Spd +++
Def +++

Year	Lev	Team	AB	R	H	HR	RBI	Avg	OB	Slg	OPS	bb%	ct%	Eye	SB	CS	x/h%	Iso	RC/G
2011	A	Kane County	289	19	60	3	31	208	259	263	522	6	76	0.29	11	4	15	55	1.71
2012	A	Kane County	228	31	55	10	34	241	305	465	770	8	81	0.48	2	5	49	224	5.00
2012	A+	Wilmington	256	38	72	4	28	281	321	426	747	6	75	0.23	8	3	35	145	4.73
2013	AA	NW Arkansas	484	59	121	8	36	250	310	368	678	8	73	0.32	14	11	31	118	3.89

Versatile INF who mostly played SS, but also saw time at 2B and 3B. Has talent in all facets, including some power in wiry frame. Works into hitters counts and gets on base to use speed. Has potential to hit for BA, but long swing needs to be tamed. Has makings of good defender, though can be erratic with routine plays.

Camargo,Johan — 6 — Atlanta

EXP MLB DEBUT: 2017 | POTENTIAL: Starting SS/2B | 7D

Bats B Age 20
2010 FA (Panama)
Pwr +
BAvg +++
Spd ++
Def +++

Year	Lev	Team	AB	R	H	HR	RBI	Avg	OB	Slg	OPS	bb%	ct%	Eye	SB	CS	x/h%	Iso	RC/G
2013	Rk	Danville	228	28	67	0	14	294	346	360	705	7	86	0.58	3	3	16	66	4.33

Impressive U.S. debut for switch-hitting SS from Panama. Solid approach at the plate with good strike zone judgment and consistent contact. Has limited power. Plus defender with soft hands and a strong arm, but only average range due to lack of speed.

Candelario,Jeimer — 5 — Chicago (N)

EXP MLB DEBUT: 2015 | POTENTIAL: Starting 3B | 7C

Bats B Age 20
2011 FA (DR)
Pwr ++
BAvg +++
Spd ++
Def ++

Year	Lev	Team	AB	R	H	HR	RBI	Avg	OB	Slg	OPS	bb%	ct%	Eye	SB	CS	x/h%	Iso	RC/G
2012	A-	Boise	278	34	78	6	47	281	342	396	738	9	80	0.47	2	1	26	115	4.62
2013	A	Kane County	500	71	128	11	57	256	345	396	741	12	82	0.77	1	0	37	140	4.92

Switch-hitting 3B had a solid season. 19-year-old has good power, a nice swing, and a good understanding of the strike zone. Makes consistent contact and could be in for a breakout in '14. He's an average defender at 3B with good hands, but limited speed.

Caratini,Victor — 52 — Atlanta

EXP MLB DEBUT: 2017 | POTENTIAL: Starting 3B | 8D

Bats B Age 20
2013 (2) Miami Dade JC
Pwr +++
BAvg +++
Spd +
Def ++

Year	Lev	Team	AB	R	H	HR	RBI	Avg	OB	Slg	OPS	bb%	ct%	Eye	SB	CS	x/h%	Iso	RC/G
2013	Rk	Danville	200	29	58	1	25	290	406	430	836	16	76	0.80	0	2	43	140	6.57

Switch-hitting 3B had an impressive debut. Uses a line-drive swing to shoot balls into the gaps and was disciplined at the plate. Could develop power as he matures. Swing can get long, but compensates with above-avg bat speed and makes decent contact.

Casali,Curt — 2 — Tampa Bay

EXP MLB DEBUT: 2014 | POTENTIAL: Backup C | 7D

Bats R Age 25
2011 (10) Vanderbilt
Pwr +++
BAvg +++
Spd +
Def ++

Year	Lev	Team	AB	R	H	HR	RBI	Avg	OB	Slg	OPS	bb%	ct%	Eye	SB	CS	x/h%	Iso	RC/G
2011	A	West Michigan	75	10	17	2	14	227	341	400	741	15	88	1.44	0	0	53	173	5.18
2012	A	West Michigan	170	25	49	8	25	288	386	500	886	14	89	1.50	2	1	41	212	6.69
2012	A+	Lakeland	160	18	40	1	18	250	298	350	648	6	83	0.39	0	0	35	100	3.55
2013	A+	Charlotte	165	15	44	5	22	267	339	406	745	10	81	0.58	1	0	27	139	4.75
2013	AA	Montgomery	120	25	46	5	31	383	475	600	1075	15	85	1.17	0	0	35	217	9.08

Tall, strong backstop who was standout performer in AA after promotion in July. Posted career high in HR with leveraged stroke and bat control. Power projects as average and can hit for BA as he knows strike zone and makes contact. Improving defender with average arm and needs to work on footwork and accuracy.

Casteel,Ryan — 2 — Colorado

EXP MLB DEBUT: 2016 | POTENTIAL: Starting C | 7D

Bats R Age 23
2010 (17) Cleveland St (TN) JC
Pwr +++
BAvg +++
Spd ++
Def ++

Year	Lev	Team	AB	R	H	HR	RBI	Avg	OB	Slg	OPS	bb%	ct%	Eye	SB	CS	x/h%	Iso	RC/G
2010	Rk	Casper	177	21	54	3	22	305	342	412	755	5	80	0.29	2	0	22	107	4.66
2011	A-	Tri-City	198	31	54	1	30	273	351	394	745	11	80	0.60	8	5	37	121	5.01
2012	A	Asheville	251	28	70	2	28	279	330	414	744	7	82	0.43	6	2	40	135	4.78
2013	A+	Modesto	411	67	111	22	76	270	349	523	872	11	71	0.42	1	0	50	253	6.63

Strong, agile catcher had a minor breakout in the hitter-friendly CAL, hitting 22 HR. Has a strong arm, but struggles blocking the ball and has work to do. Makes consistent contact, but will need to prove the power is legit outside of the CAL.

Castellanos,Nick — 57 — Detroit

EXP MLB DEBUT: 2013 | POTENTIAL: Starting LF/3B | 9C

Bats R Age 22
2010 (1-S) HS (FL)
Pwr ++++
BAvg ++++
Spd ++
Def ++

Year	Lev	Team	AB	R	H	HR	RBI	Avg	OB	Slg	OPS	bb%	ct%	Eye	SB	CS	x/h%	Iso	RC/G
2011	A	West Michigan	507	65	158	7	76	312	368	436	804	8	74	0.35	3	2	29	124	5.60
2012	A+	Lakeland	215	37	87	3	32	405	460	553	1013	9	80	0.52	3	2	26	149	8.21
2012	AA	Erie	322	35	85	7	25	264	295	382	677	4	76	0.18	5	4	27	118	3.61
2013	AAA	Toledo	533	81	147	18	76	276	342	450	793	9	81	0.54	4	1	38	174	5.33
2013	MLB	DET	18	1	5	0	0	278	278	278	556	0	94	0.00	0	0	0	0	2.35

Pure hitter who will move back to 3B. Established career highs in HR and BB while reducing K rate. Recognizes pitches and has plus bat speed for hard contact and above average pop. Uses entire field and can hit with two strikes. Lacks foot speed, but has strong arm and average range at 3B.

Castro,Harold — 4 — Detroit

EXP MLB DEBUT: 2017 | POTENTIAL: Starting 2B | 7D

Bats L Age 20
2011 FA (Venezuela)
Pwr ++
BAvg +++
Spd ++++
Def ++

Year	Lev	Team	AB	R	H	HR	RBI	Avg	OB	Slg	OPS	bb%	ct%	Eye	SB	CS	x/h%	Iso	RC/G
2012	Rk	GCL Tigers	193	24	60	1	21	311	345	420	765	5	87	0.40	15	3	28	109	4.88
2013	A	West Michigan	147	17	34	1	11	231	242	313	555	1	73	0.05	5	1	26	82	1.95
2013	A+	Lakeland	73	8	20	0	11	274	321	329	649	6	70	0.23	3	2	15	55	3.50

Lean, spry INF who was aggressively placed at High-A before moving back to Low-A. Speed is best tool, but doesn't get on base enough. Makes hard contact with good bat speed. Repeats swing mechanics, but lacks strength for any semblance of power. Lack of arm strength keeps him at 2B, but has quick, smooth actions.

Cecchini,Garin — 5 — Boston

EXP MLB DEBUT: 2015 | POTENTIAL: Starting 3B | 8B

Bats L Age 23
2010 (4) HS (LA)
Pwr +++
BAvg ++++
Spd +++
Def +++

Year	Lev	Team	AB	R	H	HR	RBI	Avg	OB	Slg	OPS	bb%	ct%	Eye	SB	CS	x/h%	Iso	RC/G
2011	A-	Lowell	114	21	34	3	23	298	389	500	889	13	83	0.89	12	2	47	202	6.84
2012	A	Greenville	455	84	139	4	62	305	388	433	821	12	80	0.68	51	6	33	127	5.99
2013	A+	Salem	214	44	75	5	33	350	459	547	1006	17	84	1.26	15	7	37	196	8.52
2013	AA	Portland	240	36	71	2	28	296	419	404	823	18	78	0.98	8	2	27	108	6.35

Advanced hitter who was consistently good all season. Posted career high in HR, though game is predicated on putting ball in play and using pro approach. Has ability to hit for BA with pitch recognition and knowledge of strike zone. Steals bases despite fringy speed and has clean feet and soft hands at 3B. Should hit lots of doubles.

Cecchini,Gavin — 6 — New York (N)

EXP MLB DEBUT: 2016 | POTENTIAL: Starting SS | 7D

Bats R Age 20
2012 (1) HS (LA)
Pwr ++
BAvg +++
Spd +++
Def +++

Year	Lev	Team	AB	R	H	HR	RBI	Avg	OB	Slg	OPS	bb%	ct%	Eye	SB	CS	x/h%	Iso	RC/G
2012	Rk	Kingsport	191	21	47	1	22	246	311	330	641	9	77	0.42	5	4	26	84	3.49
2012	A-	Brooklyn	5	2	0	0	0	0	0	0	0	0	80	0.00	0	0		0	-4.74
2013	A-	Brooklyn	194	18	53	0	14	273	322	314	637	7	85	0.47	2	3	15	41	3.42

Sprained ankle set back needed development season at plate. Though lacks a plus tool, does many things well with good instincts. Covers lots of ground at SS, with quick hands and strong arm. Goes opposite field quite a bit, but gaining pull-side power as gains strength. Pitch recognition needs to improve.

Centeno,Juan — 2 — New York (N)

EXP MLB DEBUT: 2013 | POTENTIAL: Backup C | 5D

Bats L Age 24
2007 (32) HS (PR)
Pwr +
BAvg ++
Spd +
Def +++

Year	Lev	Team	AB	R	H	HR	RBI	Avg	OB	Slg	OPS	bb%	ct%	Eye	SB	CS	x/h%	Iso	RC/G
2011	A+	St. Lucie	157	22	50	1	11	318	367	382	749	7	86	0.55	3	1	14	64	4.75
2012	AA	Binghamton	281	29	80	0	35	285	339	342	680	8	85	0.53	1	1	18	57	4.02
2013	AA	Binghamton	23	4	6	0	3	261	261	391	652	0	78	0.00	0	0	33	130	3.31
2013	AAA	Las Vegas	213	25	65	0	28	305	342	371	713	5	89	0.50	1	1	18	66	4.33
2013	MLB	New York (N)	10	0	3	0	1	300	300	300	600	0	90	0.00	0	0		0	3.30

Centeno's solid defensive efforts earned him a 10 AB September call-up. Offensively, he offers little besides decent BA potential. Defense and throwing arm his only plus skills. Power non-existent due to long, uppercut swing that doesn't utilize lower half and hands are slow to the ball. Will serve as backup catcher in the majors.

Chen, Pin-Chieh — 89 — Chicago (N)

			EXP MLB DEBUT: 2014	POTENTIAL: Starting CF	7D

Bats L Age 22
2010 FA (Taiwan)

	Pwr	++
	BAvg	++
	Spd	++++
	Def	+++

Year	Lev	Team	AB	R	H	HR	RBI	Avg	OB	Slg	OPS	bb%	ct%	Eye	SB	CS	x/h%	Iso	RC/G
2011	A-	Boise	229	34	69	2	30	301	370	424	794	10	81	0.57	20	6	29	122	5.52
2012	A	Peoria	464	75	120	2	51	259	346	347	693	12	83	0.79	36	14	23	88	4.41
2013	A	Kane County	161	25	39	0	15	242	344	298	642	13	86	1.09	9	6	18	56	3.95
2013	A+	Daytona	171	21	48	2	14	281	363	351	714	11	80	0.63	14	5	13	70	4.50
2013	AA	Tennessee	12	1	4	0	1	333	333	500	833	0	83	0.00	0	0	25	167	5.48

Athletic OF from Taiwan played at 3 different levels. Controls the bat well with good plate discipline and is willing to take a walk. Should be able to hit for average and has plus speed. Slashing stroke lets his speed play up, but limits power. Is still learning CF, but has good instincts and athleticism.

Choi, Ji-Man — 3 — Seattle

			EXP MLB DEBUT: 2015	POTENTIAL: Starting 1B	7C

Bats L Age 23
2009 FA (South Korea)

	Pwr	+++
	BAvg	+++
	Spd	+
	Def	++

Year	Lev	Team	AB	R	H	HR	RBI	Avg	OB	Slg	OPS	bb%	ct%	Eye	SB	CS	x/h%	Iso	RC/G
2010	A+	High Desert	43	7	13	1	7	302	388	442	830	12	79	0.67	0	0	23	140	6.02
2012	A	Clinton	242	43	72	8	43	298	395	463	858	14	77	0.71	0	2	32	165	6.46
2013	A+	High Desert	181	34	61	7	40	337	423	619	1042	13	82	0.82	0	1	56	282	8.76
2013	AA	Jackson	198	21	53	9	39	268	370	485	854	14	86	1.14	2	2	42	217	6.33
2013	AAA	Tacoma	45	9	11	2	6	244	306	422	728	8	84	0.57	0	0	36	178	4.43

Natural hitting prospect who produces offensively. Set career high in HR while using entire field in line drive approach. Possesses pretty swing and hangs in against LHP. May not have ideal pop for 1B, but draws walks to get on base. Secondary skills aren't as good as he is below average runner and defender.

Choice, Michael — 789 — Texas

			EXP MLB DEBUT: 2013	POTENTIAL: Starting OF	8C

Bats R Age 24
2010 (1) UT-Arlington

	Pwr	++++
	BAvg	+++
	Spd	++
	Def	+++

Year	Lev	Team	AB	R	H	HR	RBI	Avg	OB	Slg	OPS	bb%	ct%	Eye	SB	CS	x/h%	Iso	RC/G
2010	A-	Vancouver	102	20	29	7	26	284	376	627	1004	13	58	0.35	6	1	66	343	10.05
2011	A+	Stockton	467	79	133	30	82	285	367	542	909	12	71	0.46	9	5	44	257	7.07
2012	AA	Midland	359	59	103	10	58	287	347	423	770	8	75	0.38	5	1	26	136	5.04
2013	AAA	Sacramento	510	90	154	14	89	302	385	445	830	12	77	0.60	1	2	29	143	6.00
2013	MLB	OAK	18	2	5	0	0	278	316	333	649	5	67	0.17	0	0	20	56	3.52

Strong, consistent OF who parlayed productive campaign to big league callup. Brings patient approach along with exceptional bat speed. Produces power to all fields and should have more HR with polished swing. Makes good contact and offers decent speed despite few SB. Plays all OF positions and has nice instincts.

Ciuffo, Nick — 2 — Tampa Bay

			EXP MLB DEBUT: 2018	POTENTIAL: Starting C	8D

Bats L Age 19
2013 (1) HS (SC)

	Pwr	++
	BAvg	++
	Spd	++
	Def	+++

Year	Lev	Team	AB	R	H	HR	RBI	Avg	OB	Slg	OPS	bb%	ct%	Eye	SB	CS	x/h%	Iso	RC/G
2013	Rk	GCL Rays	159	11	41	0	25	258	298	308	606	5	75	0.23	0	0	17	50	2.83

Strong, all-around backstop with potential to be standout. Exhibits fundamental hitting skills with bat speed. Can be too aggressive, but hits hard line drives to all fields. Power projects as average unless he adds more loft and backspin. Strong arm is best attribute and he moves well with quick feet. Pitch recognition needs work.

Collier, Zach — 8 — Philadelphia

			EXP MLB DEBUT: 2015	POTENTIAL: Backup OF	6B

Bats L Age 23
2008 (1) HS (CA)

	Pwr	++
	BAvg	++
	Spd	+++
	Def	+++

Year	Lev	Team	AB	R	H	HR	RBI	Avg	OB	Slg	OPS	bb%	ct%	Eye	SB	CS	x/h%	Iso	RC/G
2009	A-	Williamsport	137	21	31	1	13	226	274	336	610	6	69	0.21	7	0	39	109	2.98
2009	A	Lakewood	298	40	65	0	32	218	274	319	593	7	73	0.29	13	7	35	101	2.84
2011	A	Lakewood	416	50	106	1	36	255	320	349	669	9	76	0.40	35	13	29	94	3.89
2012	A+	Clearwater	283	39	76	6	32	269	330	399	729	8	79	0.43	11	3	29	131	4.54
2013	AA	Reading	446	57	99	8	36	222	296	348	644	10	71	0.36	17	6	31	126	3.50

Toolsy athlete that has just not developed. Registered 129 Ks in 123 games in his first taste of Double-A, and has shown little game-usable power. Has some speed, but poor walk rate keeps him off the bases. Decent defender, but backup profile at best.

Collins, Tyler — 79 — Detroit

			EXP MLB DEBUT: 2015	POTENTIAL: Starting OF	7C

Bats L Age 24
2011 (6) Howard JC

	Pwr	+++
	BAvg	+++
	Spd	++
	Def	+++

Year	Lev	Team	AB	R	H	HR	RBI	Avg	OB	Slg	OPS	bb%	ct%	Eye	SB	CS	x/h%	Iso	RC/G
2010	NCAA	Baylor	89	19	36	0	10	404	459	506	965	9	91	1.13	3	2	22	101	7.47
2011	Rk	GCL Tigers	3	2	1	0	1	333	600	667	1267	40	100		0	0	100	333	13.39
2011	A-	Connecticut	163	28	51	8	31	313	353	534	886	6	90	0.59	6	1	37	221	6.14
2012	A+	Lakeland	473	68	137	7	66	290	367	429	796	11	86	0.91	20	3	34	140	5.62
2013	AA	Erie	466	67	112	21	79	240	315	438	753	10	74	0.42	4	5	45	197	4.85

Short, muscular hitter who is emerging in power department. Uses entire field and can hit LHP. Ks increased and will need to recognize breaking balls. Willing to draw walks by seeing lots of pitches, but doesn't have ideal speed. Can be an average defender in outfield corner with good instincts while arm strength is playable.

Colon, Christian — 46 — Kansas City

			EXP MLB DEBUT: 2014	POTENTIAL: Utility INF	6A

Bats R Age 25
2010 (1) Cal State Fullerton

	Pwr	++
	BAvg	++
	Spd	+++
	Def	+++

Year	Lev	Team	AB	R	H	HR	RBI	Avg	OB	Slg	OPS	bb%	ct%	Eye	SB	CS	x/h%	Iso	RC/G
2011	AA	NW Arkansas	491	69	126	8	61	257	320	342	662	9	90	0.90	17	7	19	86	3.91
2012	Rk	AZL Royals	22	6	8	0	4	364	462	500	962	15	100	1	1	38	136	8.07
2012	AA	NW Arkansas	273	33	79	5	27	289	362	392	754	10	90	1.15	12	6	20	103	5.06
2012	AAA	Omaha	17	4	7	1	5	412	474	647	1121	11	94	2.00	0	0	29	235	8.96
2013	AAA	Omaha	512	72	140	12	58	273	327	379	706	7	89	0.72	15	4	19	105	4.27

Instinctual INF who may never live up to first round billing, but is solid player. Set high in HR while maintaining extreme contact approach. Can be tough out and knows strike zone and value of walks. Not much power and is mostly singles hitter. Probable 2B with average defensive tools across board.

Cone, Zach — 78 — Texas

			EXP MLB DEBUT: 2016	POTENTIAL: Starting OF	7C

Bats R Age 24
2011 (1-S) Georgia

	Pwr	+++
	BAvg	++
	Spd	+++
	Def	++++

Year	Lev	Team	AB	R	H	HR	RBI	Avg	OB	Slg	OPS	bb%	ct%	Eye	SB	CS	x/h%	Iso	RC/G
2010	NCAA	Georgia	212	45	77	10	53	363	403	627	1030	6	84	0.42	13	0	38	264	7.94
2011	NCAA	Georgia	247	39	68	4	34	275	317	385	701	6	81	0.31	13	3	25	109	4.05
2011	A-	Spokane	224	37	45	4	29	201	254	339	593	7	75	0.28	11	2	47	138	2.73
2012	A	Hickory	432	66	113	17	64	262	323	461	783	8	75	0.35	10	0	42	199	5.22
2013	A+	Myrtle Beach	26	3	8	0	0	308	333	385	718	4	65	0.11	1	0	25	77	4.57

Athletic, strong OF who ended season in April after tearing achilles. May not hit for BA because of choppy swing mechanics and inability to hit breaking balls, but has solid power, particularly to pull side. Runs well and can steal bases with good instincts. Best skills are on defensive side with plus range and average arm.

Copeland, Kolby — 79 — Miami

			EXP MLB DEBUT: 2016	POTENTIAL: Backup OF	7D

Bats L Age 20
2012 (3) HS (LA)

	Pwr	+++
	BAvg	++
	Spd	++
	Def	+++

Year	Lev	Team	AB	R	H	HR	RBI	Avg	OB	Slg	OPS	bb%	ct%	Eye	SB	CS	x/h%	Iso	RC/G
2012	Rk	GCL Marlins	217	34	62	0	34	286	335	406	740	7	88	0.59	2	6	32	120	4.82
2012	A-	Jamestown	22	5	5	0	0	227	320	318	638	12	91	1.50	2	0	20	91	4.06

Athletic OF with a strong arm at the corners and good raw power. He has good bat speed that will allow him to make consistent contact but unusual swing mechanics may hinder his overall ability to hit for BA. He runs a tick below average but is smart on the bases.

Cordero, Franchy — 6 — San Diego

			EXP MLB DEBUT: 2017	POTENTIAL: Starting SS/3B	8D

Bats L Age 19
2012 FA (DR)

	Pwr	+++
	BAvg	+++
	Spd	+++
	Def	+++

Year	Lev	Team	AB	R	H	HR	RBI	Avg	OB	Slg	OPS	bb%	ct%	Eye	SB	CS	x/h%	Iso	RC/G
2013	Rk	AZL Padres	141	23	47	3	17	333	377	511	888	7	77	0.30	11	0	28	177	6.58

Toolsy and exciting young prospect with high ceiling and upside. Exhibits natural hitting skills with clean stroke and wiry strength. Led AZL in SLG and has chance to hit for both BA and power. Runs well and shows keen instincts on base. Range and above average arm are assets, but footwork needs work.

Correa, Carlos — 6 — Houston

			EXP MLB DEBUT: 2016	POTENTIAL: Starting SS	9B

Bats R Age 19
2012 (1) HS (PR)

	Pwr	+++
	BAvg	++++
	Spd	+++
	Def	++++

Year	Lev	Team	AB	R	H	HR	RBI	Avg	OB	Slg	OPS	bb%	ct%	Eye	SB	CS	x/h%	Iso	RC/G
2012	Rk	Greeneville	35	5	13	1	3	371	450	600	1050	13	77	0.63	1	0	38	229	9.05
2012	Rk	GCL Astros	155	23	36	2	9	232	265	355	620	4	77	0.19	5	1	39	123	3.00
2013	A	Quad Cities	450	73	144	9	86	320	398	467	864	11	82	0.70	10	10	31	147	6.43

Athletic, dynamic INF who finished 3rd in MWL in BA. Natural hitter with polished approach and contact ability. Makes hard contact with bat speed and offers above average power potential to all fields. Flashes slick glove at SS with clean hands and nimble feet. Doesn't project to many SB, but runs well underway.

Coulter,Clint | 2 | Milwaukee | EXP MLB DEBUT: 2016 | POTENTIAL: Starting C | 8E

Bats R Age 20
2012 (1) HS (WA)
Pwr + + +
BAvg + +
Spd + +
Def + + +

Year	Lev	Team	AB	R	H	HR	RBI	Avg	OB	Slg	OPS	bb%	ct%	Eye	SB	CS	x/h%	Iso	RC/G
2012	Rk	AZL Brewers	169	37	51	5	33	302	427	444	871	18	76	0.93	3	5	22	142	6.87
2013	Rk	AZL Brewers	60	12	21	3	15	350	400	617	1017	8	75	0.33	1	1	43	267	8.28
2013	Rk	Helena	74	8	16	1	8	216	256	311	567	5	81	0.29	1	0	31	95	2.40
2013	A	Wisconsin	116	18	24	3	13	207	276	345	620	9	73	0.35	1	0	38	138	3.08

Solid, athletic C with plus arm and above average power potential. Works counts well and finds pitches he can drive. Showed glimpses of his advanced approach at the plate, but his ct% was below average and poor pitch recognition led to inefficient adjustments. Solid behind the plate, but needs to work on receiving skills.

Cowart,Kaleb | 5 | Los Angeles (A) | EXP MLB DEBUT: 2015 | POTENTIAL: Starting 3B | 8B

Bats B Age 22
2010 (1) HS (GA)
Pwr + + + +
BAvg + + +
Spd + +
Def + + +

Year	Lev	Team	AB	R	H	HR	RBI	Avg	OB	Slg	OPS	bb%	ct%	Eye	SB	CS	x/h%	Iso	RC/G
2010	Rk	Orem	5	1	2	1	3	400	500	1000	1500	17	60	0.50	0	0	50	600	17.17
2011	Rk	Orem	283	49	80	7	40	283	341	420	761	8	71	0.31	11	4	28	138	5.02
2012	A	Cedar Rapids	263	42	77	9	54	293	347	479	826	8	83	0.50	9	4	36	186	5.66
2012	A+	Inland Empire	263	48	68	7	49	259	367	426	793	15	75	0.67	5	3	38	167	5.73
2013	AA	Arkansas	498	48	110	6	42	221	276	301	577	7	75	0.31	14	5	25	80	2.48

Instinctual, athletic INF who struggled with aggressive assignment in AA. Inconsistent swing resulted in few HR and approach not conducive for BA. Exhibits plus bat speed from both sides and can drive ball to all fields. Doesn't run well, but has good quickness at 3B with good range, clean hands, and plus arm.

Cox,Zack | 5 | Miami | EXP MLB DEBUT: 2014 | POTENTIAL: Backup 3B | 7D

Bats L Age 25
2010 (1) Arkansas
Pwr + +
BAvg + + +
Spd + +
Def + + +

Year	Lev	Team	AB	R	H	HR	RBI	Avg	OB	Slg	OPS	bb%	ct%	Eye	SB	CS	x/h%	Iso	RC/G
2011	A	Lake County	458	55	121	5	44	264	311	356	667	6	79	0.32	7	6	24	92	3.66
2012	AA	Jacksonville	95	14	24	1	13	253	324	368	692	10	72	0.37	0	0	33	116	4.23
2012	AAA	Memphis	299	27	76	9	30	254	283	421	704	4	79	0.19	1	0	42	167	3.96
2013	AA	Jacksonville	283	32	76	3	29	269	355	367	723	12	76	0.56	2	0	26	99	4.69
2013	AAA	New Orleans	5	0	0	0	0	0	167	0	167	17	100	1.00	0	0	0	0	-0.19

Short, big-bodied 3B had yet another disappointing season. Plate discipline still intact, but poor contact rates have started to erode offensive skill. Line-drive swing limits power. Solid defender with decent range and arm. At 25, there is hope but it is dwindling.

Coyle,Sean | 4 | Boston | EXP MLB DEBUT: 2015 | POTENTIAL: Starting 2B | 7C

Bats R Age 22
2010 (3) HS (PA)
Pwr + + +
BAvg + +
Spd + + +
Def + + +

Year	Lev	Team	AB	R	H	HR	RBI	Avg	OB	Slg	OPS	bb%	ct%	Eye	SB	CS	x/h%	Iso	RC/G
2011	A	Greenville	384	77	95	14	64	247	349	464	813	14	71	0.55	20	6	51	216	6.01
2012	A+	Salem	437	60	109	9	63	249	296	391	687	6	73	0.25	16	0	39	142	3.94
2013	Rk	GCL Red Sox	20	3	3	1	3	150	261	300	561	13	70	0.50	1	1	33	150	2.12
2013	A	Greenville	25	4	8	1	4	320	393	560	953	11	64	0.33	0	1	50	240	8.48
2013	A+	Salem	195	41	47	14	28	241	324	513	837	11	67	0.37	11	0	51	272	6.19

Short, instinctual INF who returned to High-A and set career high in HR despite missing June and most of July with knee injury. Struggles to hit for BA as he chases pitches and doesn't draw walks. Exhibits nice swing and hand-eye coordination, but can be easy out. Possesses decent range, arm strength, and speed.

Coyle,Tommy | 4 | Tampa Bay | EXP MLB DEBUT: 2015 | POTENTIAL: Reserve INF | 6B

Bats L Age 23
2012 (16) North Carolina
Pwr + +
BAvg + + +
Spd + + +
Def + +

Year	Lev	Team	AB	R	H	HR	RBI	Avg	OB	Slg	OPS	bb%	ct%	Eye	SB	CS	x/h%	Iso	RC/G
2010	NCAA	North Carolina	202	48	57	1	25	282	378	351	729	13	86	1.11	14	2	18	69	4.96
2011	NCAA	North Carolina	270	57	84	2	36	311	400	415	815	13	90	1.54	18	6	25	104	6.03
2012	NCAA	North Carolina	246	53	60	4	29	244	350	370	720	14	86	1.18	14	1	28	126	4.87
2012	A-	Hudson Valley	253	46	67	5	31	265	369	391	761	14	80	0.84	20	4	30	126	5.27
2013	A	Bowling Green	454	79	126	6	58	278	398	405	803	17	83	1.17	40	8	30	128	6.03

Small, hard-working infielder who maximizes minimal tools. Brings very disciplined approach to plate with discerning eye and barrel awareness. Makes easy contact with short, repeatable stroke and should hit for BA. Not much pop in game and lacks projection. Possesses passable speed, but is good baserunner.

Cozens,Dylan | 9 | Philadelphia | EXP MLB DEBUT: 2016 | POTENTIAL: Starting RF | 9D

Bats L Age 20
2012 (2) HS (AZ)
Pwr + + +
BAvg + +
Spd +
Def +

Year	Lev	Team	AB	R	H	HR	RBI	Avg	OB	Slg	OPS	bb%	ct%	Eye	SB	CS	x/h%	Iso	RC/G
2012	Rk	GCL Phillies	161	24	41	5	24	255	341	441	782	12	73	0.48	8	2	44	186	5.46
2013	A-	Williamsport	245	50	65	9	35	265	341	469	810	10	74	0.44	11	6	46	204	5.73

Former footballer with a classic corner-fielder power hitter's frame (6-6, 235), his swing can get long and breaking pitches tie him up. But he packs immense power when he connects, both in BP and in games. Struggles with routes in the outfield, but has athleticism to become above-average defender.

Crawford,J.P. | 6 | Philadelphia | EXP MLB DEBUT: 2017 | POTENTIAL: Starting SS | 9C

Bats L Age 19
2013 (1) HS (CA)
Pwr + + +
BAvg + + +
Spd + + +
Def + + + +

Year	Lev	Team	AB	R	H	HR	RBI	Avg	OB	Slg	OPS	bb%	ct%	Eye	SB	CS	x/h%	Iso	RC/G
2013	Rk	GCL Phillies	142	24	49	1	19	345	443	465	908	15	82	1.00	12	5	24	120	7.27
2013	A	Lakewood	53	10	11	0	2	208	300	226	526	12	81	0.70	2	1	9	19	2.23

Went from high school in June to the SAL in August and punished GCL pitching along the way. A natural SS with good range and a plus arm. Sprays balls to all fields and has excellent plate discipline and developing power. A dynamic, all-around shortstop prospect who is ready for full-season ball.

Crocker,Bobby | 78 | Oakland | EXP MLB DEBUT: 2015 | POTENTIAL: Starting OF | 7D

Bats R Age 24
2011 (4) Cal Poly
Pwr + + +
BAvg + +
Spd + + +
Def + +

Year	Lev	Team	AB	R	H	HR	RBI	Avg	OB	Slg	OPS	bb%	ct%	Eye	SB	CS	x/h%	Iso	RC/G
2011	NCAA	Cal Poly	189	37	64	5	20	339	396	497	893	9	79	0.46	9	2	30	159	6.61
2011	Rk	AZL Athletics	88	14	23	0	4	261	301	375	676	5	75	0.23	2	2	30	114	3.88
2011	A-	Vermont	118	19	38	3	15	322	365	441	806	6	81	0.36	6	1	21	119	5.28
2012	A	Burlington	406	56	109	6	53	268	333	369	702	9	73	0.36	17	10	25	101	4.24
2013	A+	Stockton	449	73	124	11	53	276	324	454	779	7	65	0.20	22	9	40	178	5.62

Instinctual, fast OF who is developing slowly, but posted career high in HR and SB. Hits doubles with strong, loose stroke. Chases pitches and gets himself out easily as breaking balls are problem. Has athletic build and runs well which allows him to play CF. Below avg arm relegates him to LF.

Cron,C.J. | 3 | Los Angeles (A) | EXP MLB DEBUT: 2014 | POTENTIAL: Starting 1B | 8C

Bats R Age 24
2011 (1) Utah
Pwr + + + +
BAvg + + +
Spd +
Def + +

Year	Lev	Team	AB	R	H	HR	RBI	Avg	OB	Slg	OPS	bb%	ct%	Eye	SB	CS	x/h%	Iso	RC/G
2010	NCAA	Utah	197	55	85	20	81	431	477	817	1294	8	88	0.74	0	0	42	386	10.68
2011	NCAA	Utah	198	51	86	15	59	434	511	803	1314	14	89	1.48	1	1	49	369	11.52
2011	Rk	Orem	143	30	44	13	41	308	353	629	982	7	76	0.29	0	0	43	322	7.40
2012	A+	Inland Empire	525	73	154	27	123	293	315	516	832	3	86	0.24	3	4	40	223	5.32
2013	AA	Arkansas	519	56	142	14	83	274	304	428	732	4	84	0.28	8	4	36	154	4.34

Powerful, free-swinging hitter who has plus power to all fields. Strong, quick swing and barrel control allow for consistent contact. Doesn't strike out much, though can chase breaking balls and doesn't walk much. Value tied to bat as he lacks foot speed and defense is only passable. Could become DH candidate.

Cuevas,Noel | 78 | Los Angeles (N) | EXP MLB DEBUT: 2015 | POTENTIAL: Starting CF | 7C

Bats R Age 22
2010 (21) PR
Pwr + +
BAvg + +
Spd + + + +
Def + + +

Year	Lev	Team	AB	R	H	HR	RBI	Avg	OB	Slg	OPS	bb%	ct%	Eye	SB	CS	x/h%	Iso	RC/G
2011	A+	Rancho Cuca	91	11	20	0	11	220	253	286	538	4	81	0.24	2	2	25	66	2.08
2012	Rk	AZL Dodgers	88	22	26	0	12	295	361	375	736	9	90	1.00	22	4	23	80	4.91
2012	Rk	Ogden	50	15	17	0	8	340	421	460	881	12	88	1.17	6	2	29	120	6.80
2012	A	Great Lakes	150	14	34	2	18	227	266	327	592	5	83	0.32	7	1	26	100	2.77
2013	A+	Rancho Cuca	476	80	135	12	66	284	335	454	789	7	78	0.35	38	15	35	170	5.27

Showed off the power/speed potential LA saw when they drafted him. Adjusted and tapped into his raw power, though his aggressive approach and poor plate discipline led to questions about his ability to make consistent contact going forward. Has plus speed and good range in CF where he will be an above average defender.

Culver,Cito | 6 | New York (A) | EXP MLB DEBUT: 2016 | POTENTIAL: Reserve INF | 7D

Bats B Age 21
2010 (1) HS (NY)
Pwr + +
BAvg + +
Spd + + +
Def + + + +

Year	Lev	Team	AB	R	H	HR	RBI	Avg	OB	Slg	OPS	bb%	ct%	Eye	SB	CS	x/h%	Iso	RC/G
2010	A-	Staten Island	43	2	8	0	0	186	314	209	523	16	77	0.80	1	1	13	23	2.20
2011	A-	Staten Island	276	40	69	2	33	250	324	337	660	10	79	0.53	10	0	26	87	3.81
2012	A	Charleston (Sc)	466	66	100	2	40	215	318	283	602	13	78	0.68	22	11	22	69	3.19
2013	A	Charleston (Sc)	410	57	95	8	29	232	312	344	656	10	70	0.39	13	5	29	112	3.68
2013	A+	Tampa	62	13	22	1	5	355	394	484	878	6	77	0.29	0	1	27	129	6.33

Smooth INF who repeated Low-A and showed glimpses of what made him first round pick, but not enough to raise stock. Glove is far ahead of bat due to quick feet and strong arm. Has hitch in swing which limits BA and pop, though he set easy high in HR and doubles. Knows balls from strikes, but has exploitable stroke.

Cunningham,Todd — 8 — Atlanta

EXP MLB DEBUT: 2013 | POTENTIAL: Starting CF | **6B**

Bats B | Age 25
2010 (2) Jacksonville State
Pwr ++
BAvg +++
Spd +++
Def ++

Year	Lev	Team	AB	R	H	HR	RBI	Avg	OB	Slg	OPS	bb%	ct%	Eye	SB	CS	x/h%	Iso	RC/G
2011	Rk	GCL Braves	11	2	2	0	4	182	250	364	614	8	55	0.20	1	0	50	182	3.98
2011	A+	Lynchburg	334	59	86	4	20	257	324	353	678	9	86	0.70	14	6	23	96	4.06
2012	AA	Mississippi	466	77	144	3	51	309	361	403	765	8	89	0.75	24	8	22	94	5.06
2013	AAA	Gwinnett	427	60	113	2	38	265	329	333	662	9	85	0.66	20	7	18	68	3.87
2013	MLB	ATL	8	2	2	0	0	250	250	250	500	0	63	0.00	0	0	0	0	1.04

Switch-hitter lacks a standout tool, but has a good approach at the plate. Makes consistent contact with a short stroke and good plate discipline. Strength and bat speed to hit for moderate power, but is more content with putting the ball in play. Runs well, but range is a little short for CF.

Curry,Matt — 3 — Pittsburgh

EXP MLB DEBUT: 2014 | POTENTIAL: Backup 1B | **6B**

Bats L | Age 25
2010 (16) TCU
Pwr ++
BAvg +++
Spd +
Def ++

Year	Lev	Team	AB	R	H	HR	RBI	Avg	OB	Slg	OPS	bb%	ct%	Eye	SB	CS	x/h%	Iso	RC/G
2011	AA	Altoona	302	38	73	6	39	242	316	374	691	10	70	0.37	1	1	34	132	4.17
2012	AA	Altoona	396	53	113	11	76	285	357	480	837	10	73	0.41	4	4	44	194	6.18
2012	AAA	Indianapolis	5	0	2	0	2	400	500	400	900	17	80	1.00	0	1	0	0	7.22
2013	Rk	GCL Pirates	9	0	1	0	0	111	200	111	311	10	78	0.50	0	0	0	0	-0.77
2013	AA	Altoona	105	11	26	4	16	248	282	400	682	5	67	0.14	2	0	31	152	3.77

Strong, stocky 1B missed most of 2013 following hamate surgery. When healthy, has a good understanding of the strike zone and a short, compact stroke. Drives the ball into the gaps, but doesn't make consistent contact and gets beat by good breaking balls. A below average runner but not a base clogger.

Cuthbert,Cheslor — 5 — Kansas City

EXP MLB DEBUT: 2015 | POTENTIAL: Starting 3B | **8D**

Bats R | Age 21
2009 FA (Nicaragua)
Pwr +++
BAvg ++
Spd ++
Def +++

Year	Lev	Team	AB	R	H	HR	RBI	Avg	OB	Slg	OPS	bb%	ct%	Eye	SB	CS	x/h%	Iso	RC/G
2010	Rk	Idaho Falls	60	10	14	2	10	233	270	433	703	5	73	0.19	1	0	50	200	4.08
2011	A	Kane County	300	33	80	8	51	267	345	397	742	11	78	0.55	2	0	28	130	4.77
2012	A+	Wilmington	475	47	114	7	59	240	295	322	617	7	83	0.46	6	3	22	82	3.13
2013	A+	Wilmington	225	32	63	2	31	280	357	418	775	11	84	0.73	1	2	40	138	5.38
2013	AA	NW Arkansas	237	25	51	6	28	215	276	359	635	8	78	0.39	5	2	43	143	3.30

Young, strong INF who is progressing at steady pace. Struggled in initial taste of AA, but still tied career high in HR. Smashes doubles by driving balls to gaps. Controls bat and has hand-eye coordination for contact. Still waiting for power, but has strength and bat speed to realize. Owns strong arm at 3B, but lacks quickness.

d'Arnaud,Travis — 2 — New York (N)

EXP MLB DEBUT: 2013 | POTENTIAL: Starting C | **8A**

Bats R | Age 25
2007 (1) HS (CA)
Pwr ++++
BAvg ++++
Spd ++
Def +++

Year	Lev	Team	AB	R	H	HR	RBI	Avg	OB	Slg	OPS	bb%	ct%	Eye	SB	CS	x/h%	Iso	RC/G
2012	AAA	Las Vegas	279	45	93	16	52	333	376	595	971	6	79	0.32	1	1	42	262	7.34
2013	Rk	GCL Mets	22	4	7	0	5	318	348	455	802	4	91	0.50	0	0	43	136	5.39
2013	AA	Binghamton	27	2	6	1	3	222	300	481	781	10	67	0.33	0	0	67	259	5.69
2013	AAA	Las Vegas	56	19	17	2	12	304	494	554	1047	27	79	1.75	0	0	59	250	9.77
2013	MLB	NYM	99	4	20	1	5	202	288	263	551	11	79	0.57	0	0	20	61	2.38

Broken foot in April delayed starting C job. Solid offensive and defensive skill set. Agile behind plate; blocks and throws well. Power is best offensive tool, and can hit to all fields. Good bat control, plate approach, and consistent contact with short swing. Improved pitch recognition and bb% in '13.

Dahl,David — 8 — Colorado

EXP MLB DEBUT: 2016 | POTENTIAL: Starting CF | **9D**

Bats L | Age 20
2012 (1) HS (AL)
Pwr ++++
BAvg ++++
Spd +++
Def +++

Year	Lev	Team	AB	R	H	HR	RBI	Avg	OB	Slg	OPS	bb%	ct%	Eye	SB	CS	x/h%	Iso	RC/G
2012	Rk	Grand Junction	280	62	106	9	57	379	422	625	1047	7	85	0.50	12	7	39	246	8.28
2013	A	Asheville	40	9	11	0	7	275	310	425	735	5	80	0.25	2	0	45	150	4.63

Natural, athletic hitter had a lost season in '13. Sent to extended ST for disciplinary reasons and then suffered a season-ending hamstring injury. Is a pure hitter who should hit for average due to a mature approach and short swing. Solid-average CF with plus speed and a good arm. Just needs to stay healthy.

Dantzler,L.B. — 3 — Toronto

EXP MLB DEBUT: 2016 | POTENTIAL: Reserve 1B | **7D**

Bats L | Age 23
2013 (14) South Carolina
Pwr +++
BAvg +++
Spd +
Def ++

Year	Lev	Team	AB	R	H	HR	RBI	Avg	OB	Slg	OPS	bb%	ct%	Eye	SB	CS	x/h%	Iso	RC/G
2012	NCAA	South Carolina	263	37	69	10	48	262	338	433	771	10	86	0.81	0	2	36	171	5.12
2013	NCAA	South Carolina	214	46	69	15	53	322	434	617	1050	16	77	0.84	2	1	46	294	9.01
2013	Rk	GCL Blue Jays	3	0	1	0	1	333	333	333	667	0	100	0.00	0	0	0	0	3.67
2013	A-	Vancouver	232	32	70	9	35	302	382	504	886	11	80	0.64	0	1	41	203	6.64

Short, stocky prospect who was NWL MVP after leading circuit in HR and SLG. Has advanced approach to draw walks and finds good pitches to drive. Makes consistent, hard contact, but swing may not result in success at higher levels as he sells out for power. Doesn't run well and lacks athleticism.

Darnell,James — 5 — Tampa Bay

EXP MLB DEBUT: 2012 | POTENTIAL: Starting LF | **7D**

Bats R | Age 27
2008 (2) USC
Pwr +++
BAvg +++
4.30 Spd ++
Def ++

Year	Lev	Team	AB	R	H	HR	RBI	Avg	OB	Slg	OPS	bb%	ct%	Eye	SB	CS	x/h%	Iso	RC/G
2011	AAA	Tucson	134	20	35	6	17	261	340	425	765	11	78	0.53	0	0	29	164	4.95
2011	MLB	SD	45	2	10	1	7	222	300	333	633	10	84	0.71	1	0	30	111	3.50
2012	AAA	Tucson	116	22	31	7	21	267	356	500	856	12	78	0.64	1	1	42	233	6.16
2012	MLB	SD	17	1	4	1	1	235	316	471	786	11	88	1.00	0	0	50	235	5.27
2013	AAA	Tucson	61	5	15	0	10	246	281	361	642	5	80	0.25	0	2	40	115	3.43

Tall and athletic prospect who has suffered thru multiple shoulder surgeries that have jeopardized his career. When healthy, has pure hitting talent with solid all-fields power and some BA. Uses nice approach to get on base and is lethal against LHP. Can play 3B and OF corners due to arm, but lacks range and speed.

Davidson,Matthew — 5 — Chicago (A)

EXP MLB DEBUT: 2013 | POTENTIAL: Starting 3B | **8C**

Bats R | Age 23
2009 (1) HS (CA)
Pwr ++++
BAvg ++
Spd ++
Def ++

Year	Lev	Team	AB	R	H	HR	RBI	Avg	OB	Slg	OPS	bb%	ct%	Eye	SB	CS	x/h%	Iso	RC/G
2010	A+	Visalia	71	6	12	2	11	169	289	268	557	14	65	0.48	0	0	25	99	2.18
2011	A+	Visalia	535	93	148	20	106	277	341	465	806	9	73	0.35	0	1	41	189	5.61
2012	AA	Mobile	486	81	127	23	76	261	353	469	822	12	74	0.55	3	4	42	208	5.90
2013	AAA	Reno	443	55	124	17	74	280	348	481	828	9	70	0.34	1	0	42	201	6.07
2013	MLB	ARI	76	8	18	3	12	237	326	434	760	12	68	0.42	0	1	50	197	5.20

Strong, powerful 3B continues to show solid power, but had mixed results once he got to the majors. BB rate held steady, but he doesn't make enough contact and his swing can get long. Does have good bat speed and 25+ HR potential. Made progress on defense, but lacks lateral quickness and remains somewhat stiff.

Davis,D.J. — 8 — Toronto

EXP MLB DEBUT: 2017 | POTENTIAL: Starting OF | **8C**

Bats L | Age 19
2012 (1) HS (MS)
Pwr ++
BAvg ++
Spd ++++
Def ++

Year	Lev	Team	AB	R	H	HR	RBI	Avg	OB	Slg	OPS	bb%	ct%	Eye	SB	CS	x/h%	Iso	RC/G
2012	Rk	Bluefield	47	9	16	1	6	340	392	511	903	8	79	0.40	6	2	31	170	6.76
2012	Rk	GCL Blue Jays	163	30	38	4	12	233	309	374	684	10	67	0.33	18	7	34	141	4.12
2012	A-	Vancouver	18	3	3	0	0	167	348	167	514	22	67	0.83	1	1	0	0	1.84
2013	Rk	Bluefield	225	35	54	6	25	240	319	418	737	10	66	0.34	13	8	39	178	5.00

Toolsy, athletic OF who is among most exciting prospects in baseball. Succeeds with quickness and plus-plus speed. Has exemplary range in CF which offsets arm. Exhibits bat speed and uses short swing for line drive pop. Power should evolve as he adds loft and strength. Swings and misses too often, but will work counts.

Davis,Kentrail — 9 — Milwaukee

EXP MLB DEBUT: 2014 | POTENTIAL: Backup OF | **7D**

Bats L | Age 26
2009 (1) Tennessee
Pwr ++
BAvg +++
Spd ++++
Def ++

Year	Lev	Team	AB	R	H	HR	RBI	Avg	OB	Slg	OPS	bb%	ct%	Eye	SB	CS	x/h%	Iso	RC/G
2010	A+	Brevard County	123	20	30	0	17	244	336	341	677	12	77	0.61	8	2	23	98	4.21
2011	A+	Brevard County	507	76	124	8	46	245	296	361	657	7	81	0.38	33	8	28	116	3.59
2012	AA	Huntsville	438	55	120	7	41	274	354	404	758	11	72	0.45	19	11	30	130	5.16
2013	AA	Huntsville	304	51	81	5	33	266	361	405	766	13	76	0.61	18	5	35	138	5.32
2013	AAA	Nashville	196	27	53	2	14	270	344	367	711	10	74	0.43	8	6	23	97	4.46

Short, athletic OF with plus speed had solid season across two levels in '13. Compact stroke with good patience will allow him to thrive, though aggressiveness leads to too many Ks and poor ct%. Defensive and arm are solid, though the move from CF to RF was neccessary.

De La Rosa,Bryan — 2 — Atlanta

EXP MLB DEBUT: 2016 | POTENTIAL: Backup C | **6C**

Bats R | Age 20
2012 (3) HS (FL)
Pwr ++
BAvg +
Spd +
Def ++++

Year	Lev	Team	AB	R	H	HR	RBI	Avg	OB	Slg	OPS	bb%	ct%	Eye	SB	CS	x/h%	Iso	RC/G
2012	Rk	GCL Braves	68	5	11	1	3	162	186	221	406	3	56	0.07	0	1	18	59	-0.32
2013	Rk	Danville	111	9	29	0	10	261	328	306	634	9	73	0.37	1	2	17	45	3.37

Short, compact backstop is a plus defender. Features a strong, accurate throwing arm and good receiving and blocking skills. Showed a better bat than anticipated, but almost no power. Does have good raw power and nice athleticism, but glove will be his ticket to the majors.

Dean, Austin — 7 — Miami
Bats R | Age 20 | 2012 (4) HS (TX)
EXP MLB DEBUT: 2017 | POTENTIAL: Starting OF | 7D
Pwr +++ | BAvg ++ | Spd ++ | Def ++

Year	Lev	Team	AB	R	H	HR	RBI	Avg	OB	Slg	OPS	bb%	ct%	Eye	SB	CS	x/h%	Iso	RC/G
2012	Rk	GCL Marlins	148	15	33	2	15	223	331	338	669	14	76	0.69	2	2	39	115	4.07
2013	A-	Batavia	213	28	57	2	19	268	322	418	740	7	78	0.36	0	2	37	150	4.77
2013	A	Greensboro	20	4	4	1	3	200	333	400	733	17	75	0.80	0	0	50	200	4.81

Athletic OF with plus bat speed and aggressive, pull-oriented approach. Stings the ball when he makes contact, but needs to be more selective and patient. With better swing mechanics he should tap into raw power. Solid defender in LF where arm and speed work well.

Dean, Matt — 35 — Toronto
Bats R | Age 21 | 2011 (13) HS (TX)
EXP MLB DEBUT: 2017 | POTENTIAL: Starting 1B | 8D
Pwr ++++ | BAvg +++ | Spd ++ | Def ++

Year	Lev	Team	AB	R	H	HR	RBI	Avg	OB	Slg	OPS	bb%	ct%	Eye	SB	CS	x/h%	Iso	RC/G
2012	Rk	Bluefield	167	22	37	2	24	222	274	353	627	7	64	0.20	3	2	38	132	3.37
2013	Rk	Bluefield	210	37	71	6	35	338	379	519	899	6	73	0.25	8	5	32	181	6.79

Tall, projectable INF who feasted on short-season pitching. Combines plus power to all fields with natural hitting ability. Approach can be inconsistent and has swing-and-miss in game, but recognizes spin well. Moved to 1B from 3B, but has bat to play at either position. Lacks speed and present defense.

DeCarlo, Joe — 5 — Seattle
Bats R | Age 20 | 2012 (2) HS (PA)
EXP MLB DEBUT: 2017 | POTENTIAL: Starting 3B | 7D
Pwr +++ | BAvg ++ | Spd ++ | Def +++

Year	Lev	Team	AB	R	H	HR	RBI	Avg	OB	Slg	OPS	bb%	ct%	Eye	SB	CS	x/h%	Iso	RC/G
2012	Rk	AZL Mariners	182	29	43	4	31	236	347	401	749	15	74	0.66	0	2	44	165	5.17
2013	Rk	Pulaski	96	18	24	4	15	250	363	417	779	15	56	0.40	0	1	33	167	6.27

Short and muscular infielder who needs time to develop all-around game. Possesses natural hitting talent with good pop and short stroke. Bat speed is impressive and could hit for BA with more game action. Hands and arm strength work well at 3B, though his range is a tad short due to lack of quickness.

Decker, Jaff — 9 — Pittsburgh
Bats R | Age 24 | 2008 (1) HS (AZ)
EXP MLB DEBUT: 2013 | POTENTIAL: Backup OF | 6B
Pwr +++ | BAvg ++ | Spd ++ | Def ++

Year	Lev	Team	AB	R	H	HR	RBI	Avg	OB	Slg	OPS	bb%	ct%	Eye	SB	CS	x/h%	Iso	RC/G
2011	AA	San Antonio	496	90	117	19	92	236	367	417	785	17	71	0.71	15	5	43	181	5.69
2012	Rk	AZL Padres	27	5	8	1	7	296	387	593	980	13	89	1.33	0	0	50	296	7.90
2012	AA	San Antonio	147	30	27	3	9	184	358	293	651	21	75	1.08	6	2	30	109	4.00
2013	AAA	Tucson	350	63	100	10	40	286	383	443	826	14	73	0.59	4	6	34	157	6.13
2013	MLB	SD	26	3	4	1	2	154	241	269	511	10	85	0.75	0	1	25	115	1.93

Short and strong outfielder who has extreme strike zone knowledge and discerning eye at plate. Exhibits good power to pull side, though vicious uppercut stroke limits contact and BA ability. Can be too patient as well. Strikes out too much and lacks foot speed for SB. Can play all OF spots, though best in corner.

Deglan, Kellin — 2 — Texas
Bats L | Age 22 | 2010 (1) HS (CAN)
EXP MLB DEBUT: 2015 | POTENTIAL: Reserve C | 7E
Pwr +++ | BAvg ++ | Spd ++ | Def +++

Year	Lev	Team	AB	R	H	HR	RBI	Avg	OB	Slg	OPS	bb%	ct%	Eye	SB	CS	x/h%	Iso	RC/G
2010	Rk	AZL Rangers	28	5	8	0	5	286	333	357	690	7	75	0.29	0	0	13	71	4.05
2010	A-	Spokane	82	7	13	1	4	159	225	220	444	8	74	0.33	0	0	23	61	0.70
2011	A	Hickory	291	39	66	6	39	227	308	347	655	10	69	0.37	2	0	33	120	3.67
2012	A	Hickory	320	46	75	12	41	234	304	438	741	9	70	0.33	4	4	52	203	4.83
2013	A+	Myrtle Beach	308	37	71	12	49	231	305	393	698	10	69	0.35	0	0	34	162	4.14

Instinctual backstop who made jump to High-A and posted almost identical numbers as Low-A. Carries a lot of promise on both sides of ball. Receiving isn't polished, but improving. Has feel for footwork and arm action. Tied career high in HR and has present pop. Not likely to hit for BA as he sells out for power and has long stroke.

DeJesus, Ivan — 4 — Baltimore
Bats R | Age 27 | 2005 (2) HS (PR)
EXP MLB DEBUT: 2011 | POTENTIAL: Utility INF | 6C
Pwr + | BAvg +++ | Spd ++ (4.35) | Def +++

Year	Lev	Team	AB	R	H	HR	RBI	Avg	OB	Slg	OPS	bb%	ct%	Eye	SB	CS	x/h%	Iso	RC/G
2011	MLB	LA	32	2	6	0	1	188	235	188	423	6	66	0.18	0	0	0	0	0.07
2012	AAA	Albuquerque	224	32	66	3	33	295	336	415	751	6	76	0.26	1	1	27	121	4.75
2012	AAA	Pawtucket	26	5	10	0	0	385	429	423	852	7	88	0.67	1	0	10	38	5.95
2012	MLB	LA/BOS	41	5	9	0	4	220	273	293	565	7	68	0.23	1	1	33	73	2.38
2013	AAA	Indianapolis	304	36	97	3	32	319	383	457	837	10	79	0.45	5	2	34	138	6.44

Athletic, sure-handed defender has bounced around. Quick bat allows to shoot line drives to all fields. Will not hit for power, but plays solid defense and uses short, compact stroke. Has a track record of hitting for average, but struggles to make contact and his speed has declined.

Delgado, Natanael — 789 — Los Angeles (A)
Bats L | Age 18 | 2012 FA (DR)
EXP MLB DEBUT: 2018 | POTENTIAL: Starting OF | 8D
Pwr ++ | BAvg +++ | Spd ++ | Def ++

Year	Lev	Team	AB	R	H	HR	RBI	Avg	OB	Slg	OPS	bb%	ct%	Eye	SB	CS	x/h%	Iso	RC/G
2013	Rk	AZL Angels	192	23	52	3	33	271	310	422	732	5	78	0.26	4	0	40	151	4.51

Young, lean OF who impressed with variety of skills. Sweet swing generated with good hands and wrist action. Offers average power potential, though needs strength. Focuses on contact more than working counts. Should hit for moderately high BA due to all-fields approach. Lacks speed and average arm limits him to LF.

Delmonico, Nick — 35 — Milwaukee
Bats L | Age 21 | 2011 (6) HS (TN)
EXP MLB DEBUT: 2015 | POTENTIAL: Starting 3B | 8D
Pwr ++++ | BAvg ++ | Spd ++ | Def ++

Year	Lev	Team	AB	R	H	HR	RBI	Avg	OB	Slg	OPS	bb%	ct%	Eye	SB	CS	x/h%	Iso	RC/G
2012	A	Delmarva	338	49	84	11	54	249	340	411	752	12	78	0.64	8	1	39	163	4.97
2013	A+	Brevard County	72	8	14	0	9	194	310	278	587	14	71	0.57	2	1	36	83	2.98
2013	A+	Frederick	226	33	55	13	30	243	347	469	816	14	74	0.61	5	1	45	226	5.80

Strong, LHH has struggled to make adjustments. MIL sees him as a power-hitting 3B. Understands strike zone and displays plus power, but making consistent contact has been issue. Has strong wrists and good bat speed. Needs to improve pitch recognition. Instinctual baserunner, but below average speed.

Demeritte, Travis — 56 — Texas
Bats R | Age 19 | 2013 (1) HS (GA)
EXP MLB DEBUT: 2017 | POTENTIAL: Starting SS/3B | 8D
Pwr +++ | BAvg +++ | Spd +++ | Def ++

Year	Lev	Team	AB	R	H	HR	RBI	Avg	OB	Slg	OPS	bb%	ct%	Eye	SB	CS	x/h%	Iso	RC/G
2013	Rk	AZL Rangers	144	31	41	4	20	285	405	444	849	17	66	0.59	5	1	29	160	6.92

Offensive, athletic INF who split time between SS and 3B. Defensive tools more suitable for 3B and has arm and hands to be asset. Swings and misses often, though bat speed offers above average power potential. Willing to work counts, though could benefit from swinging earlier in count. Runs well and can steal bases.

DeMichele, Joey — 46 — Chicago (A)
Bats L | Age 23 | 2012 Arizona State
EXP MLB DEBUT: 2015 | POTENTIAL: Starting 2B | 7C
Pwr ++ | BAvg +++ | Spd +++ | Def ++

Year	Lev	Team	AB	R	H	HR	RBI	Avg	OB	Slg	OPS	bb%	ct%	Eye	SB	CS	x/h%	Iso	RC/G
2011	NCAA	Arizona St.	182	37	67	9	48	368	413	665	1078	7	86	0.54	6	2	45	297	8.57
2012	NCAA	Arizona St.	209	47	70	6	44	335	390	550	941	8	85	0.61	10	4	37	215	7.12
2012	Rk	Bristol	46	7	16	2	9	348	388	696	1083	6	83	0.38	3	0	56	348	8.83
2012	A	Kannapolis	234	30	61	5	29	261	316	436	752	8	77	0.35	5	4	39	175	4.87
2013	A+	Winston-Salem	541	87	133	8	54	246	323	366	689	10	77	0.49	19	7	35	120	4.17

Short, compact INF who maximizes ability with limited tools. Used more patient approach to get on base, but also led to higher K rate. Hits LHP well and stays in against breaking balls. Power isn't part of game, though can steal bases with fringy speed. Limited range and arm limit him to right side of infield, though makes routine plays.

Denney, Jon — 2 — Boston
Bats R | Age 19 | 2013 (3) HS (OK)
EXP MLB DEBUT: 2017 | POTENTIAL: Starting C | 8D
Pwr +++ | BAvg ++ | Spd ++ | Def +++

Year	Lev	Team	AB	R	H	HR	RBI	Avg	OB	Slg	OPS	bb%	ct%	Eye	SB	CS	x/h%	Iso	RC/G
2013	Rk	GCL Red Sox	74	9	15	0	2	203	359	243	602	20	61	0.62	2	0	20	41	3.26

Agile, strong C who needs development, but has potential with bat and glove. Swings and misses often and needs to recognize pitches and control bat. Raw power potential is intriguing and can work counts and draw walks. Footwork is crude behind plate, but has shown improvement in receiving and blocking.

DeShields,Delino — 48 — Houston

EXP MLB DEBUT: 2015 | POTENTIAL: Starting 2B/OF | 7A

Bats R Age 21
2010 (1) HS (GA)
Pwr ++
BAvg +++
Spd ++++
Def ++

Year	Lev	Team	AB	R	H	HR	RBI	Avg	OB	Slg	OPS	bb%	ct%	Eye	SB	CS	x/h%	Iso	RC/G
2010	Rk	GCL Astros	9	3	1	0	0	111	200	111	311	10	78	0.50	0	0	0	0	-0.77
2011	A	Lexington	469	73	103	9	48	220	298	322	619	10	75	0.44	30	11	27	102	3.14
2012	A	Lexington	440	96	131	10	52	298	394	439	833	14	75	0.65	83	14	28	141	6.21
2012	A+	Lancaster	97	17	23	2	9	237	327	381	709	12	76	0.57	18	5	30	144	4.48
2013	A+	Lancaster	451	100	143	5	54	317	394	468	862	11	80	0.63	51	18	31	151	6.49

Short, speedy prospect who is moving to CF after manning position in AFL. Finished 3rd in CAL in BA and 2nd in SB. Gets on base, though can expand strike zone at times. Posted career high in BA and at best when using entire field. Has exemplary speed which should result in plus CF range. Arm strength may limit upside.

Dickerson,Alex — 79 — San Diego

EXP MLB DEBUT: 2015 | POTENTIAL: Starting 1B/OF | 8D

Bats L Age 24
2011 (3) Indiana
Pwr ++++
BAvg +++
Spd ++
Def ++

Year	Lev	Team	AB	R	H	HR	RBI	Avg	OB	Slg	OPS	bb%	ct%	Eye	SB	CS	x/h%	Iso	RC/G
2010	NCAA	Indiana	236	62	99	24	75	419	465	805	1270	8	85	0.57	3	2	43	386	10.56
2011	NCAA	Indiana	215	33	79	9	49	367	431	540	970	10	90	1.14	2	1	24	172	7.36
2011	A-	State College	150	25	47	3	19	313	380	493	873	10	81	0.57	0	0	43	180	6.48
2012	A+	Bradenton	488	65	144	13	90	295	347	451	798	7	81	0.42	12	7	33	156	5.32
2013	AA	Altoona	451	61	130	17	68	288	328	494	823	6	80	0.30	10	7	43	206	5.51

Tall, athletic player was moved back to the OF after playing 1B. Steady growth in power remains the most intriguing part of game. Has a smooth LH stroke, but needs to be more selective. Struggles with quality breaking balls and can be overly pull conscious.

Dickson,O'Koyea — 3 — Los Angeles (N)

EXP MLB DEBUT: 2015 | POTENTIAL: Backup 1B | 7C

Bats R Age 24
2011 (12) Sonoma State
Pwr +++
BAvg ++
Spd ++
Def ++

Year	Lev	Team	AB	R	H	HR	RBI	Avg	OB	Slg	OPS	bb%	ct%	Eye	SB	CS	x/h%	Iso	RC/G
2011	Rk	Ogden	189	33	63	13	38	333	394	603	997	9	77	0.43	1	1	38	270	7.85
2012	A	Great Lakes	386	63	105	17	48	272	350	479	829	11	83	0.71	11	6	43	207	5.81
2013	A+	Rancho Cuca	468	68	131	15	88	280	322	457	779	6	85	0.43	4	2	38	177	4.99

Short, strong-bodied 1B with average power and good plate coverage. Better plate discipline would help BA ceiling, but with good bat speed he puts the ball in play with ease. Slighlty below average runner and defender, limited to 1B. At 24, ceiling is not much higher.

Dixon,Brandon — 5 — Los Angeles (N)

EXP MLB DEBUT: 2016 | POTENTIAL: Starting 2B | 7D

Bats R Age 22
2013 (3) Arizona
Pwr +
BAvg ++
Spd ++++
Def ++

Year	Lev	Team	AB	R	H	HR	RBI	Avg	OB	Slg	OPS	bb%	ct%	Eye	SB	CS	x/h%	Iso	RC/G
2011	NCAA	Arizona	10	1	2	0	1	200	333	200	533	17	40	0.33	0	0	0	0	3.07
2012	NCAA	Arizona	155	30	38	1	14	245	299	323	622	7	78	0.35	8	4	26	77	3.15
2013	NCAA	Arizona	214	57	79	6	51	369	426	561	986	9	84	0.60	30	7	30	192	7.70
2013	A	Great Lakes	211	28	39	1	17	185	225	261	486	5	69	0.17	6	2	33	76	1.14

Athletic IF with plus speed drafted as a 3B, but lack of arm and fringe-average range will likely warrant a move to 2B in the future. Shows raw power in batting practice but flat stroke make him more of a gap-to-gap hitter. Lacks plate discipline and will rely on speed and contact to make impact.

Dozier,Hunter — 56 — Kansas City

EXP MLB DEBUT: 2015 | POTENTIAL: Starting 3B | 8B

Bats R Age 22
2013 (1) Stephen F. Austin
Pwr +++
BAvg +++
Spd ++
Def +++

Year	Lev	Team	AB	R	H	HR	RBI	Avg	OB	Slg	OPS	bb%	ct%	Eye	SB	CS	x/h%	Iso	RC/G
2011	NCAA	Stephen F. Austin	197	38	62	5	34	315	354	467	821	6	83	0.35	5	3	31	152	5.48
2012	NCAA	Stephen F. Austin	227	43	81	10	37	357	430	595	1024	11	81	0.69	8	6	41	238	8.32
2013	NCAA	Stephen F. Austin	212	47	84	17	52	396	480	755	1234	14	83	0.97	12	5	50	358	10.84
2013	Rk	Idaho Falls	218	43	66	7	43	303	399	509	908	14	85	1.09	3	1	47	206	7.07
2013	A	Lexington	55	6	18	0	9	327	362	436	798	5	91	0.60	0	0	33	109	5.36

Tall, strong INF who profiles as middle of order threat. Was surprise 1st round pick but justified spot with outstanding bat and defense. Makes plus contact and has advanced approach with bat control. Exhibits power to all fields, though bat speed is average. Played mostly 3B as pro and owns soft hands, plus arm and agility.

Drury,Brandon — 5 — Arizona

EXP MLB DEBUT: 2015 | POTENTIAL: Starting 3B | 7D

Bats R Age 21
2010 (13) HS (OR)
Pwr ++
BAvg ++
Spd ++
Def ++

Year	Lev	Team	AB	R	H	HR	RBI	Avg	OB	Slg	OPS	bb%	ct%	Eye	SB	CS	x/h%	Iso	RC/G
2010	Rk	GCL Braves	192	20	38	3	17	198	234	292	525	4	74	0.18	2	2	29	94	1.66
2011	Rk	Danville	265	40	92	8	54	347	362	525	886	2	87	0.17	3	0	34	177	5.95
2012	A	Rome	445	47	102	6	51	229	262	333	595	4	84	0.27	3	4	30	103	2.76
2013	A	South Bend	526	78	159	15	85	302	360	500	860	8	83	0.51	1	1	44	198	6.16

Bounce-back season. Nice compact stroke allows him to drive balls into gaps. Improved plate discipline fueled breakout. Improved defense now projects to be at least average with good hands and a strong arm. Speed is not a part of game, but there is potential for a power/average package.

Duenez,Samir — 37 — Kansas City

EXP MLB DEBUT: 2018 | POTENTIAL: Starting 1B/LF | 7C

Bats L Age 18
2012 FA (Venezuela)
Pwr ++
BAvg +++
Spd ++
Def +++

Year	Lev	Team	AB	R	H	HR	RBI	Avg	OB	Slg	OPS	bb%	ct%	Eye	SB	CS	x/h%	Iso	RC/G
2013	Rk	AZL Royals	187	26	55	0	19	294	337	380	716	6	86	0.44	6	4	25	86	4.40

Natural hitting prospect who owns simple approach and ability to use whole field. Has bat control and squares up balls for contact. Didn't hit HR, but has pull power potential. Has gap power at present and should grow into longball pop with added strength. Owns strong arm, but speed and defense are fringy.

Dugan,Kelly — 9 — Philadelphia

EXP MLB DEBUT: 2014 | POTENTIAL: Starting RF | 7C

Bats B Age 23
2009 (2) HS (CA)
Pwr +++
BAvg ++
Spd +
Def +++

Year	Lev	Team	AB	R	H	HR	RBI	Avg	OB	Slg	OPS	bb%	ct%	Eye	SB	CS	x/h%	Iso	RC/G
2010	A-	Williamsport	60	6	15	0	4	250	308	350	658	8	72	0.29	0	0	40	100	3.75
2011	A-	Williamsport	176	25	50	2	21	284	337	386	723	7	81	0.41	6	0	20	102	4.45
2012	A	Lakewood	430	83	129	12	60	300	370	470	840	10	72	0.39	5	1	36	170	6.23
2013	A+	Clearwater	217	37	69	10	36	318	386	539	925	10	72	0.40	1	3	36	221	7.28
2013	AA	Reading	212	25	56	10	23	264	281	472	753	2	75	0.09	0	1	41	208	4.46

Good athlete who has re-entered prospect sphere due to blossoming power. Noisy swing seems susceptible to timing issues, but so far has shown bat speed to make up for it. Patience took a big dive upon mid-season promotion to AA. Solid defender who shows quickness in outfield, but not likely to be SB threat.

Dunston,Shawon — 89 — Chicago (N)

EXP MLB DEBUT: 2017 | POTENTIAL: Backup OF | 6C

Bats L Age 21
2011 (11) HS (CA)
Pwr ++
BAvg +++
Spd +++
Def +++

Year	Lev	Team	AB	R	H	HR	RBI	Avg	OB	Slg	OPS	bb%	ct%	Eye	SB	CS	x/h%	Iso	RC/G
2012	Rk	AZL Cubs	161	30	46	2	24	286	358	410	767	10	80	0.55	4	2	26	124	5.18
2012	A-	Boise	65	10	12	1	2	185	232	323	555	6	78	0.29	1	2	50	138	2.29
2013	A-	Boise	193	27	56	1	19	290	380	358	738	13	87	1.12	12	2	18	67	5.03

Tall CF has yet to put it all together. Hit for BA in 2013, but still lacks power. Remains raw on both sides of the ball and should make his full-season debut in 2014. Has plus speed and decent plate discipline, but has a lot of work to do and is not young for this level.

Duvall,Adam — 5 — San Francisco

EXP MLB DEBUT: 2014 | POTENTIAL: Starting 3B | 7D

Bats R Age 25
2010 (11) Louisville
Pwr ++++
BAvg ++
Spd ++
Def ++

Year	Lev	Team	AB	R	H	HR	RBI	Avg	OB	Slg	OPS	bb%	ct%	Eye	SB	CS	x/h%	Iso	RC/G
2010	NCAA	Louisville	263	68	86	12	47	327	383	574	957	8	88	0.77	10	2	47	247	7.19
2010	A-	Salem-Keizer	192	30	47	4	18	245	296	370	666	7	77	0.31	2	3	32	125	3.63
2011	A	Augusta	431	69	123	22	87	285	371	527	898	12	77	0.60	4	4	46	241	6.83
2012	A+	San Jose	534	101	138	30	100	258	318	487	805	8	78	0.41	8	2	42	228	5.33
2013	AA	Richmond	385	61	97	17	58	252	314	465	779	8	81	0.49	2	1	45	213	5.09

Big, strong 3B continued to showcase power in AA and make a case for a starting role in the future. Aside from plus power, he is slightly below average across the board. Strikes out frequently and unlikely to hit for BA. Limited to a corner position and runs below average. Banking on the power.

Ehrlich,Adam — 2 — St. Louis

EXP MLB DEBUT: 2016 | POTENTIAL: Starting C | 7D

Bats L Age 21
2011 (6) HS (CA)
Pwr +++
BAvg +++
Spd +
Def +++

Year	Lev	Team	AB	R	H	HR	RBI	Avg	OB	Slg	OPS	bb%	ct%	Eye	SB	CS	x/h%	Iso	RC/G
2011	Rk	GCL Cardinals	59	3	14	1	6	237	318	339	657	11	73	0.44	1	0	29	102	3.69
2012	Rk	GCL Cardinals	74	12	21	0	6	284	384	365	749	14	77	0.71	0	0	24	81	5.21
2012	Rk	Johnson City	75	14	28	1	8	373	434	453	887	10	81	0.57	0	1	14	80	6.54
2013	A	Peoria	23	5	8	0	6	348	375	435	810	4	74	0.17	0	0	25	87	5.52
2013	A+	Palm Beach	20	1	3	0	3	150	292	150	442	17	80	1.00	0	0	0	0	1.29

Tall, strong-bodied backstop suffered a shoulder injury and was limited to just 43 AB. Has a smooth line-drive stroke at the plate and should hit for average with good contact, but limited power. Has a good arm, but is a bit stiff behind the plate and will need to work hard to stick.

Eibner, Brett — 89 — Kansas City
Bats R **Age** 25
2010 (2) Arkansas

Pwr	++++
BAvg	+
Spd	+++
Def	+++

EXP MLB DEBUT: 2015 **POTENTIAL:** Starting OF **8E**

Year	Lev	Team	AB	R	H	HR	RBI	Avg	OB	Slg	OPS	bb%	ct%	Eye	SB	CS	x/h%	Iso	RC/G
2009	NCAA	Arkansas	147	34	34	12	34	231	365	510	875	17	59	0.52	3	5	47	279	7.42
2010	NCAA	Arkansas	216	66	72	22	71	333	435	718	1153	15	75	0.71	3	0	54	384	10.28
2011	A	Kane County	272	46	58	12	31	213	331	408	739	15	67	0.53	2	3	47	195	4.99
2012	A+	Wilmington	423	60	83	15	53	196	292	388	679	12	61	0.35	5	2	55	191	4.29
2013	AA	NW Arkansas	441	74	107	19	41	243	324	451	775	11	66	0.36	7	3	42	209	5.47

Tall and powerful outfielder who has been mired in career-long slump, but shows signs of life. Established career high in HR and has modified swing to add more loft. Has trouble with good velocity and will always have swing and miss in game. Not likely to hit for BA, but plus power is asset. Plays solid CF with best arm in org.

Elander, Josh — 7 — Atlanta
Bats R **Age** 23
2012 (6) TCU

Pwr	+++
BAvg	+++
Spd	++
Def	++

EXP MLB DEBUT: 2016 **POTENTIAL:** Starting LF **7D**

Year	Lev	Team	AB	R	H	HR	RBI	Avg	OB	Slg	OPS	bb%	ct%	Eye	SB	CS	x/h%	Iso	RC/G
2011	NCAA	Texas Christian	171	38	57	5	38	333	427	509	936	14	79	0.78	9	0	32	175	7.50
2012	NCAA	Texas Christian	223	56	70	11	43	314	423	525	947	16	80	0.95	14	1	36	211	7.59
2012	Rk	Danville	123	19	32	4	19	260	345	439	784	12	85	0.84	3	1	38	179	5.40
2013	A	Rome	280	47	89	11	61	318	382	536	918	9	78	0.48	6	2	40	218	6.97
2013	A+	Lynchburg	221	28	58	4	32	262	340	371	711	11	78	0.54	3	1	28	109	4.41

Moved from behind the plate to LF where he was able to focus on hitting. Had impressive season offensively, hitting a combined .293 with 15 HR. Squares the ball up well and is willing to take a walk, but remains a below-average runner and defender. Has above-average power, but owns no other plus tools.

Encarnacion, Kevin — 78 — Chicago (N)
Bats B **Age** 22
2010 FA (DR)

Pwr	+++
BAvg	+++
Spd	+++
Def	+++

EXP MLB DEBUT: 2018 **POTENTIAL:** Starting OF **8D**

Year	Lev	Team	AB	R	H	HR	RBI	Avg	OB	Slg	OPS	bb%	ct%	Eye	SB	CS	x/h%	Iso	RC/G
2013	A-	Boise	166	34	59	8	30	355	428	566	994	11	80	0.64	10	5	31	211	7.90
2013	A	Kane County	60	9	13	1	3	217	309	333	642	12	77	0.57	1	3	31	117	3.59

Athletic OF had a nice breakout, hitting .355 at Boise, but struggling in the MWL. Showed solid plate discipline and contact ability. Struggled vs. LHP, but mashed vs. RHP. Shows good power and decent speed, but will need to prove he can hit at Low-A and beyond.

Encarnacion, Luis — 5 — Philadelphia
Bats R **Age** 16
2013 FA (DR)

Pwr	++++
BAvg	++
Spd	++
Def	++

EXP MLB DEBUT: 2019 **POTENTIAL:** Starting LF **9E**

Year	Lev	Team	AB	R	H	HR	RBI	Avg	OB	Slg	OPS	bb%	ct%	Eye	SB	CS	x/h%	Iso	RC/G
2013		Did not play in the US																	

One of the best hitters on the international market in 2013, he has a short, compact stroke that produces power from strong hands and wrists. Though young, already carries an athletic 6-2, 195 frame. Doesn't have defensive chops to stay at 3B, but bat could carry him in OF corner or at 1B. Long-term project.

Engel, Adam — 8 — Chicago (A)
Bats R **Age** 22
2013 (19) Louisville

Pwr	++
BAvg	+++
Spd	++++
Def	+++

EXP MLB DEBUT: 2016 **POTENTIAL:** Starting CF **8C**

Year	Lev	Team	AB	R	H	HR	RBI	Avg	OB	Slg	OPS	bb%	ct%	Eye	SB	CS	x/h%	Iso	RC/G
2011	NCAA	Louisville	144	27	36	0	9	250	321	264	585	9	85	0.68	16	7	6	14	2.94
2012	NCAA	Louisville	214	43	66	1	18	308	357	341	698	7	87	0.59	37	2	8	33	4.15
2013	NCAA	Louisville	246	51	58	1	18	236	324	301	625	12	86	0.91	41	13	21	65	3.61
2013	Rk	Great Falls	239	44	72	3	30	301	358	414	772	8	86	0.62	31	8	25	113	5.11

Strong, athletic OF who does everything well with no glaring weakness. Power a little short, but will still reach double digits due to moderate bat speed and strength. Runs very well on base and in CF. Can hit leadoff due to willingness to work counts and make consistent contact. Ranges well in outfield and has average, accurate arm.

Ervin, Phillip — 89 — Cincinnati
Bats R **Age** 21
2013 (1) HS (AL)

Pwr	+++
BAvg	++++
Spd	++++
Def	++++

EXP MLB DEBUT: 2016 **POTENTIAL:** Starting OF **9D**

Year	Lev	Team	AB	R	H	HR	RBI	Avg	OB	Slg	OPS	bb%	ct%	Eye	SB	CS	x/h%	Iso	RC/G
2011	NCAA	Samford	213	44	79	4	41	371	437	516	953	11	87	0.89	7	1	27	146	7.38
2012	NCAA	Samford	260	55	85	10	52	327	382	519	901	8	85	0.59	16	5	34	192	6.52
2013	NCAA	Samford	196	58	66	11	40	337	447	597	1044	17	87	1.56	21	2	41	260	8.71
2013	Rk	Billings	129	27	42	8	29	326	404	597	1001	12	81	0.71	12	0	43	271	7.94
2013	A	Dayton	43	7	15	1	6	349	451	465	916	16	77	0.80	2	1	20	116	7.37

Impressive pro debut despite nagging injuries. Above-average tools across the board and uses them well. Advanced plate approach and understanding of the strike zone. Despite small frame, brings nice power/speed combo with BA ability. Good baserunner (14 for 15 SB). Has arm and speed to play CF or RF.

Escobar, Elvis — 79 — Pittsburgh
Bats L **Age** 19
2011 FA (Venezuela)

Pwr	+
BAvg	+++
Spd	+++
Def	+++

EXP MLB DEBUT: 2017 **POTENTIAL:** Starting CF **7D**

Year	Lev	Team	AB	R	H	HR	RBI	Avg	OB	Slg	OPS	bb%	ct%	Eye	SB	CS	x/h%	Iso	RC/G
2012	Rk	GCL Pirates	190	29	52	2	18	274	337	374	710	9	76	0.39	6	5	21	100	4.36
2013	A-	Jamestown	183	25	49	1	23	268	302	350	652	5	74	0.19	9	4	22	82	3.41

Short, speedy OF was signed as an international FA for $570,000. At 5-9, is not likely to hit for much power, but has shown an ability to hit for average. Was 18 for most of the season and was one of the younger players in the NYPL. Needs to be more disciplined at the plate and make better contact, but has intriguing potential.

Estrada, Thairo — 46 — New York (A)
Bats R **Age** 18
2012 FA (Venezuela)

Pwr	++
BAvg	+++
Spd	+++
Def	+++

EXP MLB DEBUT: 2018 **POTENTIAL:** Starting 2B/SS **7D**

Year	Lev	Team	AB	R	H	HR	RBI	Avg	OB	Slg	OPS	bb%	ct%	Eye	SB	CS	x/h%	Iso	RC/G
2013	Rk	GCL Yankees 2	176	28	49	2	17	278	324	432	756	6	83	0.40	7	5	37	153	4.89

Quick, contact-oriented INF who packs surprising pop in lean frame. Can play both MIF positions with range to both sides and solid, accurate arm. Hands are beneficial at plate as he swings fast bat. Makes easy contact with repeatable stroke and uses entire field. Has potential to steal more bases.

Evans, Zane — 2 — Kansas City
Bats R **Age** 22
2013 (4) Georgia Tech

Pwr	+++
BAvg	+++
Spd	+
Def	++

EXP MLB DEBUT: 2016 **POTENTIAL:** Starting C **7C**

Year	Lev	Team	AB	R	H	HR	RBI	Avg	OB	Slg	OPS	bb%	ct%	Eye	SB	CS	x/h%	Iso	RC/G
2011	NCAA	Georgia Tech	226	34	61	5	46	270	329	398	727	8	77	0.38	2	0	31	128	4.49
2012	NCAA	Georgia Tech	224	34	66	4	51	295	363	433	796	10	80	0.53	1	0	33	138	5.49
2013	NCAA	Georgia Tech	244	47	88	14	66	361	437	590	1027	12	84	0.83	0	1	31	230	8.20
2013	Rk	Idaho Falls	162	26	57	4	31	352	393	537	930	6	85	0.44	1	0	39	185	6.85

Tall, durable C who exceeded expectations. Showed good power, particularly to pull side, and makes solid contact for slugging profile. Can be pull-conscious at times and will expand strike zone. Catching needs work in order to stay at position. Has improved as receiver, but footwork can be sloppy.

Fargas, Johneshwy — 8 — San Francisco
Bats R **Age** 19
2013 (11) HS (PR)

Pwr	+
BAvg	++
Spd	++++
Def	++++

EXP MLB DEBUT: 2017 **POTENTIAL:** Starting OF **8E**

Year	Lev	Team	AB	R	H	HR	RBI	Avg	OB	Slg	OPS	bb%	ct%	Eye	SB	CS	x/h%	Iso	RC/G
2013	Rk	AZL Giants	77	21	23	0	2	299	372	351	723	10	86	0.82	8	3	17	52	4.71

Lanky speedster impressed during limited look, showing solid contact and plus SB potential. Has good bat speed, but will need to shorten swing to maintain good ct% and utilize speed. Below average power could play average as he fully matures. SF sees his future in CF where his plus range and strong arm play well.

Featherston, Taylor — 4 — Colorado
Bats R **Age** 24
2011 (5) TCU

Pwr	+++
BAvg	++
Spd	+++
Def	++

EXP MLB DEBUT: 2017 **POTENTIAL:** Utility INF **6C**

Year	Lev	Team	AB	R	H	HR	RBI	Avg	OB	Slg	OPS	bb%	ct%	Eye	SB	CS	x/h%	Iso	RC/G
2010	NCAA	Texas Christian	231	59	78	8	52	338	398	571	969	9	82	0.55	6	4	40	234	7.56
2011	NCAA	Texas Christian	245	53	82	3	42	335	380	457	837	7	87	0.56	6	5	24	122	5.80
2011	A-	Tri-City	169	19	39	2	20	231	301	349	650	9	78	0.45	3	1	33	118	3.63
2012	A	Asheville	378	75	113	12	53	299	385	495	880	12	77	0.61	15	4	41	196	6.73
2013	A+	Modesto	469	87	137	13	81	292	335	484	819	6	77	0.27	17	4	39	192	5.62

5th rounder from TCU had a nice breakout, hitting .292 with 13 HR. Has offensive potential and above-avg speed. Makes consistent contact, but sells out plate discipline for power. Strong arm with good range and should be able to stick at 2B.

Fields, Daniel | 8 | Detroit

EXP MLB DEBUT: 2014 | POTENTIAL: Starting OF | 7C

Bats R Age 23
2009 (6) HS (MI)

	Pwr	+++
	BAvg	++
	Spd	+++
	Def	++++

Year	Lev	Team	AB	R	H	HR	RBI	Avg	OB	Slg	OPS	bb%	ct%	Eye	SB	CS	x/h%	Iso	RC/G
2010	A+	Lakeland	375	33	90	8	47	240	337	371	708	13	68	0.46	8	9	30	131	4.56
2011	A+	Lakeland	432	57	95	8	46	220	299	326	626	10	69	0.37	4	4	27	106	3.23
2012	A+	Lakeland	244	31	65	1	26	266	319	357	676	7	77	0.35	14	7	25	90	3.88
2012	AA	Erie	106	13	28	2	7	264	345	358	703	11	80	0.62	9	1	21	94	4.31
2013	AA	Erie	457	71	130	10	58	284	349	435	784	9	72	0.35	24	7	33	151	5.43

Athletic, fast OF who is quietly moving up ladder. Revamped approach resulted in harder contact. Tapping into raw power and should continue to grow, though he can expand strike zone. Swing-and-miss will always be part of game, but solid-average speed remains. Possesses above average range and shows better jumps in CF.

Fletcher, Brian | 37 | Kansas City

EXP MLB DEBUT: 2014 | POTENTIAL: Reserve 1B/LF | 6B

Bats R Age 25
2010 (18) Auburn

	Pwr	++++
	BAvg	+++
	Spd	+
	Def	++

Year	Lev	Team	AB	R	H	HR	RBI	Avg	OB	Slg	OPS	bb%	ct%	Eye	SB	CS	x/h%	Iso	RC/G
2011	A	Kane County	341	54	112	14	60	328	373	560	933	7	77	0.30	4	4	43	232	7.06
2012	A+	Wilmington	246	27	71	5	25	289	340	411	750	7	79	0.37	5	2	28	122	4.72
2012	AA	NW Arkansas	254	32	65	10	34	256	297	433	730	6	62	0.16	6	3	35	177	4.81
2013	AA	NW Arkansas	207	37	65	12	37	314	355	541	896	6	80	0.32	6	2	34	227	6.27
2013	AAA	Omaha	108	14	27	5	17	250	283	435	718	4	69	0.15	1	0	37	185	4.19

Slugging prospect who missed most of first two months of season, but rebounded to set high in HR. Produces steady and consistent pop with solid-average bat speed. Can hit for BA, but could benefit from being more patient. Secondary skills aren't up to snuff as he doesn't run well and is fringy defender at 1B or LF.

Flores, Ramon | 78 | New York (A)

EXP MLB DEBUT: 2015 | POTENTIAL: Starting OF | 7C

Bats L Age 22
2008 FA (Venezuela)

	Pwr	++
	BAvg	+++
	Spd	+++
	Def	++

Year	Lev	Team	AB	R	H	HR	RBI	Avg	OB	Slg	OPS	bb%	ct%	Eye	SB	CS	x/h%	Iso	RC/G
2010	A+	Tampa	28	0	7	0	2	250	250	250	500	0	82	0.00	0	0	0	0	1.26
2011	A	Charleston (Sc)	468	59	124	11	59	265	350	400	749	12	80	0.66	13	2	31	135	4.95
2012	A+	Tampa	517	83	156	6	39	302	368	420	788	9	84	0.64	24	9	27	118	5.39
2012	AA	Trenton	5	2	2	1	2	400	400		1400	0	100		0	0	50	600	10.25
2013	AA	Trenton	534	79	139	6	55	260	354	363	717	13	82	0.79	7	6	27	103	4.68

Small, pure-hitting OF who hasn't developed as much as hoped. Combines patient approach with sufficient bat speed to produce fringe-average pop. Knows strike zone and controls bat to put ball in play. Power projection is limited and may want to focus on line drives to gaps. Runs well, but lacks instincts in outfield with average arm.

Flores, Wilmer | 345 | New York (N)

EXP MLB DEBUT: 2013 | POTENTIAL: Starting 3B | 8C

Bats R Age 22
2007 FA (DR)

	Pwr	++++
	BAvg	++++
	Spd	++
	Def	++

Year	Lev	Team	AB	R	H	HR	RBI	Avg	OB	Slg	OPS	bb%	ct%	Eye	SB	CS	x/h%	Iso	RC/G
2011	A+	St. Lucie	516	52	139	9	81	269	306	380	686	5	87	0.40	2	2	27	110	3.89
2012	A+	St. Lucie	242	31	70	10	42	289	338	463	801	7	88	0.60	3	2	31	174	5.24
2012	AA	Binghamton	251	37	78	8	33	311	362	494	856	7	88	0.67	0	0	36	183	5.99
2013	AAA	Las Vegas	424	69	136	15	86	321	359	531	889	6	85	0.40	1	3	40	210	6.26
2013	MLB	NYM	95	8	20	1	13	211	250	295	545	5	76	0.22	0	0	30	84	2.00

Great hand-eye coordination and bat control. Natural strength provides plus power to all fields. Has made solid contact at every level. Won't draw a lot of walks or steal bases. Can get overly aggressive, but finds pitches to drive. Work in progress defensively but nice arm. Lots of offensive upside here.

Fontana, Nolan | 6 | Houston

EXP MLB DEBUT: 2015 | POTENTIAL: Reserve SS | 6B

Bats L Age 23
2012 (2) Florida

	Pwr	++
	BAvg	++
	Spd	+++
	Def	+++

Year	Lev	Team	AB	R	H	HR	RBI	Avg	OB	Slg	OPS	bb%	ct%	Eye	SB	CS	x/h%	Iso	RC/G
2010	NCAA	Florida	216	56	62	3	23	287	428	417	844	20	87	1.83	11	5	32	130	6.74
2011	NCAA	Florida	256	57	74	5	49	289	409	434	843	17	88	1.73	6	4	30	145	6.54
2012	NCAA	Florida	243	59	69	9	30	284	402	444	847	16	89	1.78	13	1	29	160	6.43
2012	A	Lexington	151	37	34	2	25	225	458	338	796	30	71	1.48	12	2	35	113	6.47
2013	A+	Lancaster	386	88	100	8	60	259	414	399	813	21	74	1.02	16	5	32	140	6.32

Patient, fundamentally-sound INF who started hot, but faded late. Walked over 100 times due to extensive knowledge of strike zone. Could stand to be more aggressive as he strikes out far too much for little pop. Swing can get choppy, but can hit hard line drives. Arm strength ideal for SS, but has fringy range.

Ford, Fred | 39 | Kansas City

EXP MLB DEBUT: 2017 | POTENTIAL: Starting OF | 7E

Bats R Age 22
2012 (7) Jefferson CC

	Pwr	++++
	BAvg	++
	Spd	++
	Def	++

Year	Lev	Team	AB	R	H	HR	RBI	Avg	OB	Slg	OPS	bb%	ct%	Eye	SB	CS	x/h%	Iso	RC/G
2012	Rk	Burlington	214	38	53	13	35	248	356	491	847	14	61	0.43	5	5	47	243	6.89
2013	A	Lexington	420	47	81	13	43	193	282	350	632	11	60	0.31	5	2	44	157	3.49

Long and lean outfielder who struggled to make contact and finished 2nd in SAL in K. Holes in long swing can be exploited and he sells out for power. Plus raw pop is best trait and he has surprising athleticism for size. Runs fairly well, though isn't a burner and offers some range in outfield corner. Needs to hit LHP better.

Franco, Carlos | 5 | Atlanta

EXP MLB DEBUT: 2017 | POTENTIAL: Starting 3B | 7D

Bats B Age 22
2009 FA (DR)

	Pwr	+++
	BAvg	++
	Spd	+++
	Def	+++

Year	Lev	Team	AB	R	H	HR	RBI	Avg	OB	Slg	OPS	bb%	ct%	Eye	SB	CS	x/h%	Iso	RC/G
2010	Rk	GCL Braves	65	9	8	2	5	123	219	231	450	11	63	0.33	1	0	38	108	0.41
2011	Rk	GCL Braves	155	22	37	1	21	239	306	329	635	9	75	0.39	10	0	30	90	3.40
2012	Rk	Danville	166	35	45	2	20	271	404	380	783	18	78	1.03	6	5	24	108	5.82
2013	A	Rome	454	54	104	1	48	229	307	284	591	10	73	0.41	15	9	21	55	2.82

Switch-hitting 3B took a step back in 2013. Should develop above-average power once he matures and fills out, but needs to make more consistent contact for it to be game usable. Good defender with a strong arm and average speed.

Franco, Maikel | 5 | Philadelphia

EXP MLB DEBUT: 2014 | POTENTIAL: Starting 3B | 9C

Bats R Age 21
2008 FA (DR)

	Pwr	++++
	BAvg	+++
	Spd	+
	Def	++

Year	Lev	Team	AB	R	H	HR	RBI	Avg	OB	Slg	OPS	bb%	ct%	Eye	SB	CS	x/h%	Iso	RC/G
2011	A-	Williamsport	202	19	58	2	38	287	366	411	777	11	85	0.83	0	0	34	124	5.40
2011	A	Lakewood	65	6	8	1	6	123	136	200	336	2	77	0.07	0	0	38	77	-0.81
2012	A	Lakewood	503	70	141	14	84	280	331	439	770	7	84	0.48	3	1	35	159	4.96
2013	A+	Clearwater	264	42	79	16	52	299	349	576	924	7	85	0.51	0	0	51	277	6.67
2013	AA	Reading	277	47	94	15	51	339	362	563	926	3	89	0.32	1	2	32	224	6.35

Breakout star from 2013, he showcased an explosive bat across two levels. Has uncanny bat-to-ball ability as well as the big power, but his long load leads many to wonder how he'll fare against upper-level pitching. Has hands and reflexes to play 3B, but could also be moved across the diamond if necessary.

Franklin, Kevin | 5 | Cincinnati

EXP MLB DEBUT: 2017 | POTENTIAL: Starting 3B | 8E

Bats R Age 19
2013 (2) HS (CA)

	Pwr	++++
	BAvg	++
	Spd	++
	Def	++

Year	Lev	Team	AB	R	H	HR	RBI	Avg	OB	Slg	OPS	bb%	ct%	Eye	SB	CS	x/h%	Iso	RC/G
2013	Rk	AZL Reds	173	17	45	1	25	260	312	364	676	7	69	0.25	1	1	36	104	3.96

Raw prospect with lots of tools and projection. Athletic with nice power potential. Needs to work on pitch recognition. Still developing at 3B, could move across diamond at some point due to his size. Strikes out a lot but possesses good hitting instincts, and can use the whole field. Has strong throwing arm.

Frazier, Adam | 6 | Pittsburgh

EXP MLB DEBUT: 2016 | POTENTIAL: Utility INF | 6C

Bats L Age 22
2013 (6) Mississippi State

	Pwr	+
	BAvg	++
	Spd	++
	Def	+++

Year	Lev	Team	AB	R	H	HR	RBI	Avg	OB	Slg	OPS	bb%	ct%	Eye	SB	CS	x/h%	Iso	RC/G
2011	NCAA	Mississippi St.	93	10	25	0	13	269	292	269	560	3	86	0.23	4	1	0	0	2.28
2012	NCAA	Mississippi St.	245	45	91	0	26	371	478	445	923	17	90	2.08	9	6	19	73	7.58
2013	NCAA	Mississippi St.	304	62	107	0	38	352	398	464	861	7	91	0.88	9	4	25	112	6.19
2013	A-	Jamestown	224	34	72	0	27	321	390	362	751	10	86	0.81	5	8	11	40	5.00

At 5-11 he is not likely to develop much power, but he showed solid plate discipline and has a good line-drive approach in impressive debut. He lacks the range to handle SS in the majors, but will stay there for now. Profiles as a good-hitting UT infielder with average speed.

Frazier, Clint | 8 | Cleveland

EXP MLB DEBUT: 2017 | POTENTIAL: Starting CF | 9C

Bats R Age 19
2013 (1) HS (GA)

	Pwr	++++
	BAvg	+++
	Spd	+++
	Def	+++

Year	Lev	Team	AB	R	H	HR	RBI	Avg	OB	Slg	OPS	bb%	ct%	Eye	SB	CS	x/h%	Iso	RC/G
2013	Rk	AZL Indians	172	32	51	5	28	297	360	506	866	9	65	0.28	3	2	41	209	7.06

Athletic, strong OF who possesses all requisite tools. High K rate from aggressive approach is alarming, but has bat speed and plus raw power. Could grow into middle-of-order threat, but will need to close holes in swing. Possesses range due to above average speed and patrols CF with passable instincts, routes, and jumps.

Freitas,David | 2 | Baltimore

EXP MLB DEBUT: 2014 | POTENTIAL: Reserve C | **6B**

Bats R Age 25	Year	Lev	Team	AB	R	H	HR	RBI	Avg	OB	Slg	OPS	bb%	ct%	Eye	SB	CS	x/h%	Iso	RC/G
2010 (15) Hawaii	2011	A	Hagerstown	427	67	123	13	73	288	403	450	852	16	80	0.94	2	1	35	162	6.50
Pwr +++	2012	A+	Potomac	273	37	74	5	46	271	362	407	769	13	81	0.75	0	0	36	136	5.30
BAvg ++	2012	AA	Midland	63	12	21	2	11	333	391	524	915	9	76	0.40	0	0	38	190	6.99
Spd +	2013	AA	Midland	224	34	48	9	21	214	279	362	640	8	83	0.51	0	0	31	147	3.33
Def +++	2013	AAA	Sacramento	97	13	26	1	9	268	343	381	724	10	86	0.79	0	0	35	113	4.71

Mobile and strong backstop with chance to become backup in big leagues. Receives well with good hands and has average arm strength. Not an accurate thrower and needs quicker release. Brings patient approach to plate and makes good contact. Power more to the pull side and hits hard line drives to gaps.

Fuentes,Reymond | 9 | San Diego

EXP MLB DEBUT: 2013 | POTENTIAL: Backup CF | **6B**

Bats L Age 23	Year	Lev	Team	AB	R	H	HR	RBI	Avg	OB	Slg	OPS	bb%	ct%	Eye	SB	CS	x/h%	Iso	RC/G
2009 (1) HS, (PR)	2011	A+	Lake Elsinore	510	84	140	5	45	275	332	369	701	8	77	0.38	41	14	21	94	4.19
Pwr ++	2012	AA	San Antonio	473	53	103	4	34	218	295	302	598	10	72	0.39	35	9	27	85	2.89
BAvg +++	2013	AA	San Antonio	345	56	109	6	35	316	389	441	829	11	79	0.58	29	10	27	125	5.95
Spd ++++	2013	AAA	Tucson	55	17	23	0	8	418	508	491	999	15	82	1.00	6	1	17	73	8.44
Def ++	2013	MLB	SD	33	4	5	0	1	152	222	152	374	8	52	0.19	3	0	0	0	-0.88

Lean and speedy outfielder who returned to AA and rebounded in major way. Made better contact and learned to keep ball on ground to utilize plus speed. Set high in HR, though power isn't game. Still strikes out too much and lacks juice for pop. Exemplary CF with solid-average range and OK arm strength.

Gallagher,Cameron | 2 | Kansas City

EXP MLB DEBUT: 2017 | POTENTIAL: Starting C | **7D**

Bats R Age 21	Year	Lev	Team	AB	R	H	HR	RBI	Avg	OB	Slg	OPS	bb%	ct%	Eye	SB	CS	x/h%	Iso	RC/G
2011 (2) HS (PA)																				
Pwr ++	2011	Rk	AZL Royals	78	6	11	1	7	141	212	179	391	8	81	0.47	0	0	9	38	0.30
BAvg ++	2011	Rk	Idaho Falls	30	2	6	1	2	200	273	300	573	9	87	0.75	0	0	17	100	2.70
Spd +	2012	Rk	Burlington	127	13	35	3	15	276	328	425	754	7	87	0.63	1	3	37	150	4.84
Def +++	2013	A	Lexington	222	19	47	2	18	212	289	306	595	10	87	0.86	0	0	36	95	3.23

Strong C who has yet to put together productive season, but still has desirable skills. Improving as a receiver and shows potential to control running game with strong arm and release. Controls strike zone and willing to draw walks. Long swing mutes above average raw power, but could realize with swing adjustments.

Gallo,Joey | 5 | Texas

EXP MLB DEBUT: 2016 | POTENTIAL: Starting 3B | **8D**

Bats L Age 20	Year	Lev	Team	AB	R	H	HR	RBI	Avg	OB	Slg	OPS	bb%	ct%	Eye	SB	CS	x/h%	Iso	RC/G
2012 (1-S) HS (NV)																				
Pwr +++++	2012	Rk	AZL Rangers	150	44	44	18	43	293	433	733	1166	20	65	0.71	6	0	66	440	11.47
BAvg ++	2012	A-	Spokane	56	9	12	4	9	214	343	464	808	16	54	0.42	0	0	50	250	6.85
Spd ++	2013	Rk	AZL Rangers	19	4	7	2	10	368	429	895	1323	10	63	0.29	1	0	86	526	14.22
Def ++	2013	A	Hickory	392	82	96	38	78	245	327	610	937	11	58	0.29	14	1	65	365	8.52

Big, powerful INF who finished 3rd in minors in HR despite missing month with groin strain. Quick hands and vicious swing produce well above average pop and can hit LHP with authority. Expands strike zone with long swing and lacks feel for contact. Runs well and should stick at 3B due to strong arm and sure hands.

Galvez,Jonathan | 4 | San Diego

EXP MLB DEBUT: 2015 | POTENTIAL: Starting 2B | **7C**

Bats R Age 23	Year	Lev	Team	AB	R	H	HR	RBI	Avg	OB	Slg	OPS	bb%	ct%	Eye	SB	CS	x/h%	Iso	RC/G
2008 FA (DR)	2010	A	Fort Wayne	398	64	103	10	49	259	353	397	750	13	70	0.48	18	7	31	138	5.11
Pwr ++	2011	A+	Lake Elsinore	488	84	142	13	86	291	346	465	811	8	75	0.33	37	9	38	174	5.64
BAvg +++	2012	AA	San Antonio	312	47	91	6	35	292	356	426	782	9	78	0.44	12	3	31	135	5.27
Spd +++	2013	Rk	AZL Padres	3	0	0	0	0	0	0	0	0	0	67	0.00	0	0	0	0	-6.12
Def ++	2013	AAA	Tucson	410	66	114	6	51	278	333	385	719	8	75	0.33	22	7	27	107	4.40

Tall and versatile infielder who hasn't lived up to power expectations, but has decent all-around game. Possesses clean, repeatable stroke and covers plate, but expands strike zone often and can be exploited. Runs well and is good baserunner. Can play variety of positions, including OF corner, though arm is short.

Gamel,Benjamin | 78 | New York (A)

EXP MLB DEBUT: 2015 | POTENTIAL: Reserve OF | **6B**

Bats L Age 22	Year	Lev	Team	AB	R	H	HR	RBI	Avg	OB	Slg	OPS	bb%	ct%	Eye	SB	CS	x/h%	Iso	RC/G
2010 (10) HS (FL)	2010	Rk	GCL Yankees	25	3	7	0	0	280	357	320	677	11	68	0.38	1	2	14	40	4.09
Pwr ++	2011	A-	Staten Island	190	20	55	2	30	289	369	432	801	11	74	0.48	7	2	40	142	5.81
BAvg +++	2012	A	Charleston (Sc)	444	56	136	2	61	306	340	394	735	5	84	0.32	19	10	22	88	4.48
Spd +++	2013	A+	Tampa	364	50	99	3	49	272	357	396	752	12	79	0.62	21	5	35	124	5.12
Def +++	2013	AA	Trenton	67	5	16	1	5	239	282	343	625	6	73	0.22	1	0	31	104	3.06

Versatile, athletic OF who doesn't have exciting upside, but does number of things well. Fluid stroke produces gap power and has speed to leg out extra base hits. Long ball pop not part of game and he understands that. Puts ball in play and uses wheels to steal bases. Outfield play is solid, though has fringy arm.

Garcia,Anthony | 7 | St. Louis

EXP MLB DEBUT: 2015 | POTENTIAL: Backup OF | **6C**

Bats R Age 22	Year	Lev	Team	AB	R	H	HR	RBI	Avg	OB	Slg	OPS	bb%	ct%	Eye	SB	CS	x/h%	Iso	RC/G
2009 (18) HS (PR)	2010	Rk	Johnson City	3	1	1	0	1	333	500	667	1167	25	67	1.00	0	0	100	333	12.77
Pwr +++	2011	Rk	Johnson City	182	38	56	6	31	308	379	527	907	10	80	0.58	4	1	43	220	6.91
BAvg ++	2012	A	Quad Cities	396	63	111	19	74	280	337	525	862	8	73	0.32	3	6	50	245	6.32
Spd ++	2013	Rk	GCL Cardinals	4	0	0	0	0	0	0	0	0	0	75	0.00	0	0	0	0	-5.26
Def ++	2013	A+	Palm Beach	345	37	75	13	45	217	272	383	655	7	72	0.27	6	2	40	165	3.42

Strong, power-hitting OF took a huge step back in '13, striking out 95 times in 345 AB and losing time to injury. Garcia has plus raw power and did hit 13 HR, but can be overly aggressive. Ball jumps off of his bat when he does make contact. Is a below-average runner and is questionable on defense.

Garcia,Leury | 4568 | Chicago (A)

EXP MLB DEBUT: 2013 | POTENTIAL: Starting 2B/SS | **7B**

Bats B Age 23	Year	Lev	Team	AB	R	H	HR	RBI	Avg	OB	Slg	OPS	bb%	ct%	Eye	SB	CS	x/h%	Iso	RC/G
2007 FA (DR)	2011	A+	Myrtle Beach	442	65	113	3	38	256	300	342	642	6	77	0.28	30	12	24	86	3.34
Pwr ++	2012	AA	Frisco	377	55	110	2	30	292	331	398	729	6	79	0.28	31	7	23	106	4.47
BAvg +++	2013	AAA	Charlotte	30	3	8	0	1	267	290	300	590	3	73	0.13	3	0	13	33	2.47
Spd ++++	2013	AAA	Round Rock	193	31	51	4	19	264	314	409	723	7	73	0.26	12	4	31	145	4.47
Def ++++	2013	MLB	CHW	101	10	20	0	2	198	250	228	478	6	66	0.21	7	2	10	30	0.98

Short, versatile INF who is best known for glove and plus speed. Has compact frame and offers some gap power, but focuses on line drives. Lacks OBP and BA potential as he owns long swing and will chase pitches. Speed bails him out of weak contact and helps him in field. Owns elite arm and has terrific range to both sides.

Garcia,Willy | 9 | Pittsburgh

EXP MLB DEBUT: 2015 | POTENTIAL: Starting OF | **7D**

Bats R Age 21	Year	Lev	Team	AB	R	H	HR	RBI	Avg	OB	Slg	OPS	bb%	ct%	Eye	SB	CS	x/h%	Iso	RC/G
2010 FA (DR)																				
Pwr +++	2011	Rk	GCL Pirates	177	26	47	5	35	266	309	446	755	6	72	0.22	7	5	38	181	4.85
BAvg ++	2011	A-	State College	7	1	2	0	0	286	286	286	571	0	100	1.00	0	0	0	0	2.76
Spd +++	2012	A	West Virginia	459	57	110	18	77	240	289	403	692	7	71	0.24	10	8	34	163	3.90
Def +++	2013	A+	Bradenton	449	51	115	16	60	256	292	437	729	5	66	0.15	13	6	37	180	4.62

Tall Dominican OF has good raw power, but has yet to hit for average. Also has above-average speed, but will not be a big part of his game. Can be overly aggressive and continues to struggle with breaking balls. Needs to tone down his approach and make more consistent contact.

Garfield,Cameron | 2 | Milwaukee

EXP MLB DEBUT: 2015 | POTENTIAL: Backup C | **6C**

Bats R Age 23	Year	Lev	Team	AB	R	H	HR	RBI	Avg	OB	Slg	OPS	bb%	ct%	Eye	SB	CS	x/h%	Iso	RC/G
2009 (2) HS (CA)	2010	A	Wisconsin	384	41	94	3	46	245	286	318	603	5	81	0.30	2	4	23	73	2.85
Pwr ++	2011	Rk	AZL Brewers	36	7	13	2	10	361	395	667	1061	5	75	0.22	0	0	46	306	8.74
BAvg ++	2011	A	Wisconsin	17	3	2	0	2	118	167	176	343	6	82	0.33	0	1	50	59	-0.14
Spd ++	2012	A	Wisconsin	225	33	67	11	33	298	373	524	897	11	81	0.64	3	1	43	227	6.66
Def +++	2013	A+	Brevard County	420	40	105	8	48	250	274	379	653	3	76	0.14	1	2	31	129	3.31

Strong, defensive-minded C stayed healthy and played in a career high 109 games in 2013. Shows some pop, but poor ct% and plate discipline will limit his ceiling offensively. Has a strong arm behind the plate with improved catch-and-throw skills. His speed is a non-factor.

Geiger,Dustin | 35 | Chicago (N)

EXP MLB DEBUT: 2017 | POTENTIAL: Starting 1B/3B | **7D**

Bats R Age 22	Year	Lev	Team	AB	R	H	HR	RBI	Avg	OB	Slg	OPS	bb%	ct%	Eye	SB	CS	x/h%	Iso	RC/G
2010 (24) HS (FL)	2010	Rk	AZL Cubs	123	17	30	1	15	244	311	358	669	9	80	0.48	3	1	37	114	3.91
Pwr +++	2011	Rk	AZL Cubs	79	14	27	2	20	342	366	582	948	4	81	0.20	1	3	48	241	7.06
BAvg ++	2011	A	Peoria	163	14	37	1	13	227	267	319	586	5	77	0.24	0	0	32	92	2.62
Spd ++	2012	A	Peoria	303	42	76	17	53	251	297	465	763	6	74	0.25	1	1	41	215	4.72
Def ++	2013	A+	Daytona	456	62	128	17	86	281	354	458	813	10	78	0.52	6	6	36	178	5.63

Tall and strong, improved plate discipline fueled the breakout, but is not young for this level. Solid defender can play 1B and 3B, but will likely stick at 1B as he moves up. Will need to prove that '13 was no fluke.

Gelalich,Jeff — 9 — Cincinnati

EXP MLB DEBUT: 2016 | POTENTIAL: Starting OF | **7C**

Bats L Age 23
2012 (1) UCLA
Pwr ++
BAvg +++
Spd +++
Def +++

Year	Lev	Team	AB	R	H	HR	RBI	Avg	OB	Slg	OPS	bb%	ct%	Eye	SB	CS	x/h%	Iso	RC/G
2010	NCAA	UCLA	78	17	25	2	13	321	430	474	904	16	71	0.65	7	0	28	154	7.50
2011	NCAA	UCLA	183	35	49	2	13	268	356	415	771	12	68	0.43	10	2	39	148	5.61
2012	NCAA	UCLA	245	56	86	11	48	351	430	535	965	12	82	0.76	16	5	26	184	7.54
2012	Rk	Billings	127	27	31	2	9	244	319	378	697	10	67	0.33	4	1	35	134	4.40
2013	A	Dayton	444	61	109	1	37	245	331	300	631	11	76	0.53	20	6	18	54	3.45

Has been hampered by injuries but really struggled in MWL, particularly for a college prospect. Played mostly RF, but hasn't shown power or arm to stick long-term. Has balanced tool set that's yet to develop. Runs well, has compact swing with good bat speed. Strikes out too much and needs to hit for power to advance.

Glaesmann,Todd — 79 — Arizona

EXP MLB DEBUT: 2015 | POTENTIAL: Starting OF | **8E**

Bats R Age 23
2009 (3) HS (TX)
Pwr +++
BAvg ++
Spd +++
Def +++

Year	Lev	Team	AB	R	H	HR	RBI	Avg	OB	Slg	OPS	bb%	ct%	Eye	SB	CS	x/h%	Iso	RC/G
2011	Rk	GCL Rays	37	7	8	0	0	216	310	243	553	12	73	0.50	6	1	13	27	2.34
2011	A	Bowling Green	210	28	48	4	21	229	277	343	620	6	60	0.16	6	0	29	114	3.30
2012	A	Bowling Green	352	57	99	13	53	281	324	469	792	6	75	0.25	8	3	35	188	5.21
2012	A+	Charlotte	139	20	41	8	22	295	333	554	887	5	75	0.23	0	0	44	259	6.37
2013	AA	Montgomery	487	53	117	11	54	240	279	378	657	5	77	0.24	6	2	36	138	3.44

Tall outfielder who had disappointing year in first season above High-A. Power potential is evident in long-armed stroke and plate coverage. Power not usable unless he makes better contact and becomes more selective. Offers nice speed and is excellent defender in either outfield corner. Strong arm is weapon and ranges well.

Goeddel,Tyler — 5 — Tampa Bay

EXP MLB DEBUT: 2016 | POTENTIAL: Starting 3B | **8D**

Bats R Age 21
2011 (1-S) HS (CA)
Pwr ++
BAvg +++
Spd +++
Def ++

Year	Lev	Team	AB	R	H	HR	RBI	Avg	OB	Slg	OPS	bb%	ct%	Eye	SB	CS	x/h%	Iso	RC/G
2012	A	Bowling Green	329	52	81	6	46	246	324	371	695	10	71	0.40	30	5	33	125	4.24
2013	A	Bowling Green	450	63	112	7	65	249	310	389	699	8	78	0.41	30	5	33	140	4.21

Athletic, projectable INF who repeated Low-A and had similar results. Possesses wiry strength in lean frame and has plus power potential. Focuses more on hard contact than long ball pop and has slightly above average speed. Exhibits strong arm and quick hands at 3B, but needs more reps.

Goodrum,Niko — 56 — Minnesota

EXP MLB DEBUT: 2016 | POTENTIAL: Starting 3B/SS | **8E**

Bats B Age 22
2010 (2) HS (GA)
Pwr ++
BAvg +++
Spd +++
Def +++

Year	Lev	Team	AB	R	H	HR	RBI	Avg	OB	Slg	OPS	bb%	ct%	Eye	SB	CS	x/h%	Iso	RC/G
2010	Rk	GCL Twins	118	10	19	0	5	161	220	195	415	7	71	0.26	4	2	21	34	0.23
2011	Rk	Elizabethton	204	39	56	2	20	275	342	382	725	9	73	0.38	8	1	27	108	4.64
2012	Rk	Elizabethton	227	38	55	4	38	242	351	419	769	14	75	0.68	6	3	44	176	5.49
2013	A	Cedar Rapids	385	62	100	4	45	260	360	369	728	13	73	0.57	20	4	30	109	4.88

Tall, quick INF who spent first year in Low-A after two years in short-season. Spent most of time at SS and can play any infield spot. Decent hitter from both sides and brings patient approach. Adding strength for additional gap power and has average profile. Possesses soft hands with strong arm, but remains unpolished.

Goodwin,Brian — 8 — Washington

EXP MLB DEBUT: 2015 | POTENTIAL: Starting CF | **9D**

Bats L Age 23
2011 (1) Miami Dade CC
Pwr ++++
BAvg +++
Spd +++
Def ++++

Year	Lev	Team	AB	R	H	HR	RBI	Avg	OB	Slg	OPS	bb%	ct%	Eye	SB	CS	x/h%	Iso	RC/G
2012	A	Hagerstown	216	47	70	9	38	324	436	542	978	17	82	1.10	15	4	40	218	8.07
2012	AA	Harrisburg	166	17	37	5	14	223	299	373	672	10	70	0.36	3	3	38	151	3.84
2013	AA	Harrisburg	457	82	115	10	40	252	346	407	753	13	74	0.55	19	11	35	155	5.14

A five-tool outfielder with 20/20 upside, but has struggled at Double-A level. Best tool is speed, but also has good raw power, plate patience, and short, compact swing. Defensively, covers lots of ground in OF with good reads off the bat. Needs to improve hitting against LHP and base-stealing instincts.

Green,Dean — 3 — Detroit

EXP MLB DEBUT: 2014 | POTENTIAL: Reserve 1B | **6B**

Bats L Age 25
2011 (11) Barry
Pwr +++
BAvg +++
Spd +
Def ++

Year	Lev	Team	AB	R	H	HR	RBI	Avg	OB	Slg	OPS	bb%	ct%	Eye	SB	CS	x/h%	Iso	RC/G
2012	A	West Michigan	219	34	67	9	38	306	372	502	874	10	82	0.59	0	3	37	196	6.30
2012	A+	Lakeland	141	16	49	3	36	348	378	518	896	5	82	0.28	2	0	33	170	6.38
2013	Rk	GCL Tigers	22	5	6	1	4	273	385	500	885	15	82	1.00	2	0	50	227	6.80
2013	A	West Michigan	107	15	30	5	23	280	347	495	843	9	82	0.58	3	0	40	215	5.89
2013	A+	Lakeland	118	18	37	2	13	314	362	458	820	7	81	0.41	0	0	30	144	5.63

Large-bodied prospect who has been injury-prone and has never gotten thru season unscathed. Uses powerful stroke and balanced approach to crush balls to pull side and has respectable feel for hitting. Reads spins well and can shorten stroke. Doesn't possess secondary skills as he has poor speed and fringy glove.

Green,Zach — 5 — Philadelphia

EXP MLB DEBUT: 2017 | POTENTIAL: Starting 3B | **8E**

Bats R Age 20
2012 (3) HS (CA)
Pwr ++++
BAvg ++
Spd ++
Def +++

Year	Lev	Team	AB	R	H	HR	RBI	Avg	OB	Slg	OPS	bb%	ct%	Eye	SB	CS	x/h%	Iso	RC/G
2012	Rk	GCL Phillies	169	20	48	3	21	284	316	426	742	5	75	0.19	2	2	35	142	4.59
2013	A-	Williamsport	270	52	68	13	41	252	329	478	807	10	66	0.34	8	5	50	226	5.91

First season at 3B, where he has prototypical size, strength and plus arm. But lots of work to do with the bat—set a team record with 91 Ks in 74 games. Led the team in homers and crushed fastballs, but fooled by breaking stuff. Improved defensively throughout season, and has the reputation of a coachable, cerebral player.

Greene,Larry — 7 — Philadelphia

EXP MLB DEBUT: 2016 | POTENTIAL: StartingLF | **7D**

Bats L Age 21
2011 (1) HS (GA)
Pwr +++
BAvg ++
Spd ++
Def ++

Year	Lev	Team	AB	R	H	HR	RBI	Avg	OB	Slg	OPS	bb%	ct%	Eye	SB	CS	x/h%	Iso	RC/G
2012	A-	Williamsport	257	36	70	2	26	272	372	381	754	14	70	0.53	1	2	34	109	5.35
2013	A	Lakewood	400	45	85	4	28	213	308	303	610	12	59	0.34	8	8	32	90	3.31

Former first rounder has taken a long time to adjust to pro ball; struggled mightily in his first full-season exposure. Contact is the most notable nemesis, and has shown very limited power so far. Off the field, conditioning and attitude could also use improvement. Still young, but definite bust potential.

Gregor,Conrad — 37 — Houston

EXP MLB DEBUT: 2016 | POTENTIAL: Starting 1B/LF | **7C**

Bats L Age 22
2013 (4) Vanderbilt
Pwr +++
BAvg +++
Spd +
Def +++

Year	Lev	Team	AB	R	H	HR	RBI	Avg	OB	Slg	OPS	bb%	ct%	Eye	SB	CS	x/h%	Iso	RC/G
2011	NCAA	Vanderbilt	170	33	60	3	32	353	455	471	926	16	82	1.07	2	2	23	118	7.45
2012	NCAA	Vanderbilt	229	37	75	3	35	328	430	463	893	15	82	1.00	10	0	32	135	7.06
2013	NCAA	Vanderbilt	227	47	70	3	48	308	441	410	851	19	87	1.86	21	3	24	101	6.78
2013	A-	Tri City	270	36	78	4	35	289	375	385	760	12	84	0.86	2	2	22	96	5.16

Big-framed prospect who hasn't developed much power despite strength and size. Has innate feel for strike zone and draws walks. Raw power still there and could tap into it with more loft and leverage in stroke. Not blessed with much speed, though is asset as 1B. Could see time in OF due to average arm strength.

Grichuk,Randal — 89 — St. Louis

EXP MLB DEBUT: 2015 | POTENTIAL: Starting OF | **7B**

Bats R Age 22
2009 (1) HS (TX)
Pwr ++++
BAvg ++
Spd +++
Def +++

Year	Lev	Team	AB	R	H	HR	RBI	Avg	OB	Slg	OPS	bb%	ct%	Eye	SB	CS	x/h%	Iso	RC/G
2011	Rk	AZL Angels	24	2	8	0	6	333	385	458	843	8	83	0.50	0	0	25	125	6.05
2011	A	Cedar Rapids	122	12	28	2	13	230	266	402	667	5	76	0.21	0	1	46	172	3.69
2011	A+	Inland Empire	53	13	15	1	6	283	283	491	774	0	75	0.00	0	0	47	208	4.85
2012	A+	Inland Empire	537	79	160	18	71	298	327	488	815	4	83	0.25	16	6	36	190	5.30
2013	AA	Arkansas	500	85	128	22	64	256	295	474	769	5	82	0.30	9	5	45	218	4.80

Athletic, strong OF who has stayed healthy and starting to realize vast power potential. Takes hard cut, but has ample bat control and plate coverage for good contact. Can go gap-to-gap, but long swing could result in more Ks in upper levels. Doesn't draw many walks to take advantage of average speed and instincts.

Grullon,Deivi — 2 — Philadelphia

EXP MLB DEBUT: 2018 | POTENTIAL: Starting C | **8C**

Bats R Age 18
2012 FA (DR)
Pwr +++
BAvg ++
Spd ++
Def ++++

Year	Lev	Team	AB	R	H	HR	RBI	Avg	OB	Slg	OPS	bb%	ct%	Eye	SB	CS	x/h%	Iso	RC/G
2013	Rk	GCL Phillies	121	13	33	1	14	273	328	364	692	8	85	0.56	0	0	27	91	4.15

Played in the GCL at 17 with modest success. Thickly built, his defense is a current strength, with excellent blocking skills and a strong throwing arm. Bat was better than expected: good plate discipline, bat speed with gap power, and the ability to make adjustments at the plate. On the low-minors watch list.

Guerrero,Alex

4 | **Los Angeles (N)** | EXP MLB DEBUT: 2014 | POTENTIAL: Starting 2B | **8D**

Bats R Age 27
2013 FA (Cuba)

- Pwr + + +
- BAvg + +
- Spd + + +
- Def + + +

Year	Lev	Team	AB	R	H	HR	RBI	Avg	OB	Slg	OPS	bb%	ct%	Eye	SB	CS	x/h%	Iso	RC/G
2012	FOR	Cuba	269	51	78	21	51	290	359	576	935	10	89	0.97	5	2	44	286	6.82

Strong MIF with power-speed combo. Defensive tools profile at 2B. Swing is stiff at times, but good bat speed and plus raw power should translate into 20+ HR potential. Needs to adjust to better velocity and refine his pitch recognition in order to reach his ceiling with the hit tool. Solid speed but not a SB threat.

Guerrero,Emilio

6 | **Toronto** | EXP MLB DEBUT: 2017 | POTENTIAL: Starting SS | **7C**

Bats R Age 21
2011 FA (DR)

- Pwr + +
- BAvg + + +
- Spd + + +
- Def + +

Year	Lev	Team	AB	R	H	HR	RBI	Avg	OB	Slg	OPS	bb%	ct%	Eye	SB	CS	x/h%	Iso	RC/G
2012	Rk	Bluefield	54	8	10	0	8	185	214	241	455	4	69	0.12	1	0	20	56	0.65
2012	Rk	GCL Blue Jays	82	14	20	2	9	244	340	427	767	13	76	0.60	3	3	50	183	5.33
2013	A	Lansing	343	48	95	8	52	277	351	402	753	10	83	0.67	17	6	26	125	4.93
2013	A+	Dunedin	7	1	1	0	0	143	143	286	429	0	71	0.00	0	0	100	143	0.45

Tall, lanky INF who is growing into power. Can turn on FB and drive ball to all fields. Puts bat on ball easily and has decent pitch recognition and bat control. Power could become average down line. Runs bases with good speed and defense has chance to be solid. Can be inconsistent with footwork, though has good lateral quickness.

Guerrero,Gabriel

9 | **Seattle** | EXP MLB DEBUT: 2017 | POTENTIAL: Starting OF | **8D**

Bats R Age 20
2011 FA (DR)

- Pwr + + +
- BAvg + + +
- Spd + +
- Def + +

Year	Lev	Team	AB	R	H	HR	RBI	Avg	OB	Slg	OPS	bb%	ct%	Eye	SB	CS	x/h%	Iso	RC/G
2012	Rk	AZL Mariners	75	17	25	4	18	333	359	560	919	4	83	0.23	0	0	36	227	6.40

Tall, projectable OF who got better as season progressed. Showed consistent swing path in second half and started to realize natural power. Free-swinging ways led to few walks, but covers plate and has hand-eye coordination. Raw defender in RF with crude routes and jumps, though arm is very strong.

Gumbs,Angelo

4 | **New York (A)** | EXP MLB DEBUT: 2016 | POTENTIAL: Starting 2B | **8D**

Bats R Age 21
2010 (2) HS (CA)

- Pwr + +
- BAvg + +
- Spd + + + +
- Def + + +

Year	Lev	Team	AB	R	H	HR	RBI	Avg	OB	Slg	OPS	bb%	ct%	Eye	SB	CS	x/h%	Iso	RC/G
2010	Rk	GCL Yankees	26	1	5	0	0	192	222	231	453	4	88	0.33	3	0	20	38	1.31
2011	A-	Staten Island	197	32	52	3	29	264	332	406	738	9	71	0.35	11	7	35	142	4.87
2012	A	Charleston (Sc)	257	40	70	7	36	272	320	432	752	7	77	0.30	26	3	34	160	4.73
2013	A	Charleston (Sc)	202	20	43	4	26	213	260	351	612	6	73	0.24	10	5	40	139	2.92
2013	A+	Tampa	159	16	34	0	11	214	251	302	553	5	81	0.26	6	1	35	88	2.31

Aggressive INF who struggled in High-A and demoted to Low-A in June. Never got going, but still has upside. Swings fast bat, but mechanics can be choppy and long. Breaking balls give him problems and he isn't very selective. Runs well and could steal more bags in time. Can be good defender with strong arm and range.

Guyer,Brandon

789 | **Tampa Bay** | EXP MLB DEBUT: 2011 | POTENTIAL: Starting OF | **7B**

Bats R Age 28
2007 (5) Virginia

- Pwr + + +
- BAvg + + +
- Spd + + +
- Def + + +

Year	Lev	Team	AB	R	H	HR	RBI	Avg	OB	Slg	OPS	bb%	ct%	Eye	SB	CS	x/h%	Iso	RC/G
2011	AAA	Durham	388	78	121	14	61	312	369	521	889	8	80	0.44	16	6	40	209	6.53
2011	MLB	TAM	41	7	8	2	3	195	214	366	580	2	78	0.11	0	0	38	171	2.18
2012	AAA	Durham	85	9	25	3	13	294	348	459	807	8	82	0.47	2	0	28	165	5.37
2012	MLB	TAM	7	2	1	1	1	143	143	571	714	0	86	0.00	0	0	100	429	3.45
2013	AAA	Durham	356	73	107	7	41	301	353	458	811	8	83	0.47	22	3	34	157	5.54

Athletic, solid OF who has missed a lot of time in past few seasons due to variety of injuries. Broken finger ended year in late July. Has good all-around skills with average tools. Can reach seats in strong swing while exhibiting good speed for SB. Can play all OF positions with nice range and sufficient arm strength.

Guzman,Ronald

3 | **Texas** | EXP MLB DEBUT: 2017 | POTENTIAL: Starting 1B | **8D**

Bats L Age 19
2011 FA (DR)

- Pwr + + +
- BAvg + + +
- Spd + +
- Def + +

Year	Lev	Team	AB	R	H	HR	RBI	Avg	OB	Slg	OPS	bb%	ct%	Eye	SB	CS	x/h%	Iso	RC/G
2012	Rk	AZL Rangers	212	29	68	1	33	321	377	434	811	8	80	0.45	7	1	28	113	5.66
2013	A	Hickory	173	17	47	4	26	272	315	387	703	6	84	0.41	0	0	26	116	4.07

Long, lean INF who had limited action due to torn meniscus. Uses controlled stroke to make easy contact and sprays line drives to gaps. Bat control is advanced for age, though will need strength and leverage for power. Bat is best tool and needs to improve defense. Arm strength is short and is poor runner with fringy instincts.

Ha,Jae-Hoon

789 | **Chicago (N)** | EXP MLB DEBUT: 2014 | POTENTIAL: Backup OF | **6B**

Bats R Age 23
2008 FA (South Korea)

- Pwr + +
- BAvg + +
- Spd + + +
- Def + + + +

Year	Lev	Team	AB	R	H	HR	RBI	Avg	OB	Slg	OPS	bb%	ct%	Eye	SB	CS	x/h%	Iso	RC/G
2011	A+	Daytona	294	35	81	8	47	276	304	422	726	4	87	0.31	7	8	31	146	4.25
2011	AA	Tennessee	226	32	64	3	25	283	316	403	719	5	88	0.39	6	9	31	119	4.31
2012	AA	Tennessee	465	63	127	6	47	273	344	385	729	10	79	0.52	11	5	29	112	4.65
2013	AA	Tennessee	95	21	27	1	14	284	370	368	739	12	75	0.54	8	1	22	84	4.89
2013	AAA	Iowa	228	22	55	5	21	241	288	364	652	6	82	0.36	7	2	33	123	3.46

22-year-od Korean OF has a good approach at the plate and makes consistent contact. Willing to work counts and grind out AB. Does have some OB ability, but very limited power. Runs well and can play all three OF spots. Likely a 4th OF at this point, but a steady producer.

Haase,Eric

2 | **Cleveland** | EXP MLB DEBUT: 2017 | POTENTIAL: Backup C | **6B**

Bats R Age 21
2011 (7) HS (MI)

- Pwr + + +
- BAvg + +
- Spd + +
- Def + +

Year	Lev	Team	AB	R	H	HR	RBI	Avg	OB	Slg	OPS	bb%	ct%	Eye	SB	CS	x/h%	Iso	RC/G
2011	Rk	AZL Indians	10	2	3	0	2	300	364	300	664	9	90	1.00	0	0	0	0	3.98
2012	Rk	AZL Indians	103	16	29	3	22	282	315	515	829	5	72	0.17	1	0	55	233	5.93
2012	A-	Mahoning Val	11	1	1	0	0	91	167	91	258	8	64	0.25	0	0	0	0	-2.49
2013	A	Lake County	376	49	94	14	47	250	322	439	761	10	69	0.34	2	2	43	189	5.13

Athletic C who is developing slowly. Offers strength in sound swing mechanics, though lacks bat speed. Knows strike zone and has average power to pull side. Could develop into platoon option as he hits LHP well and struggles with RHP. Footwork behind plate needs attention and has value in solid catch-and-throw skills.

Hager,Jake

6 | **Tampa Bay** | EXP MLB DEBUT: 2016 | POTENTIAL: Starting SS | **7C**

Bats R Age 21
2011 (1) HS (NV)

- Pwr + +
- BAvg + +
- Spd + + +
- Def + + +

Year	Lev	Team	AB	R	H	HR	RBI	Avg	OB	Slg	OPS	bb%	ct%	Eye	SB	CS	x/h%	Iso	RC/G
2011	Rk	Princeton	193	29	52	4	17	269	302	399	701	4	87	0.35	5	7	31	130	4.03
2012	A	Bowling Green	442	63	124	10	72	281	340	412	752	8	86	0.67	17	11	28	131	4.85
2013	Rk	GCL Rays	4	1	2	0	1	500	500	750	1250	0	100	0.00	0	0	50	250	9.68
2013	A+	Charlotte	449	56	116	0	33	258	316	305	621	8	82	0.47	12	8	16	47	3.26

Rangy INF who generally makes good contact with bat speed and pitch recognition skills. Contact rate fell in '13, but still has bat control and can use entire field. Power is very limited and can devolve into slap-hitting approach at times. Plays solid SS with sure hands and excellent range. Could return to High-A.

Hamilton,Billy

8 | **Cincinnati** | EXP MLB DEBUT: 2013 | POTENTIAL: Starting CF | **9C**

Bats B Age 23
2009 (2) HS (MS)

- Pwr +
- BAvg + + +
- Spd + + + + + (3.60)
- Def + + +

Year	Lev	Team	AB	R	H	HR	RBI	Avg	OB	Slg	OPS	bb%	ct%	Eye	SB	CS	x/h%	Iso	RC/G
2011	A	Dayton	550	99	153	3	50	278	341	360	701	9	76	0.39	103	20	20	82	4.25
2012	A+	Bakersfield	337	79	109	1	30	323	411	439	850	13	79	0.71	104	21	26	116	6.48
2012	AA	Pensacola	175	33	50	1	15	286	408	383	790	17	75	0.84	51	16	20	97	5.91
2013	AAA	Louisville	504	75	129	6	41	256	308	343	651	7	80	0.37	75	15	22	87	3.50
2013	MLB	CIN	19	9	7	0	1	368	429	474	902	10	79	0.50	13	1	29	105	6.94

Converted SS possesses the type of speed that rarely comes along. Struggled getting on-base at Triple-A, chasing pitches outside the zone and generating weak contact. Needs to refine plate approach and hit more line drives to become effective leadoff hitter. Elite range, improving reads, and adequate arm in OF.

Haniger,Mitch

89 | **Milwaukee** | EXP MLB DEBUT: 2015 | POTENTIAL: Starting OF | **7C**

Bats R Age 23
2012 (1) Cal Poly

- Pwr + + +
- BAvg + + +
- Spd + + +
- Def + + +

Year	Lev	Team	AB	R	H	HR	RBI	Avg	OB	Slg	OPS	bb%	ct%	Eye	SB	CS	x/h%	Iso	RC/G
2011	NCAA	Cal Poly	189	33	52	6	27	275	372	466	837	13	84	0.94	4	3	42	190	6.16
2012	NCAA	Cal Poly	211	48	73	13	64	346	441	626	1067	15	85	1.13	6	6	44	280	8.87
2012	A	Wisconsin	49	9	14	1	8	286	375	429	804	13	73	0.54	1	0	36	143	5.82
2013	A	Wisconsin	145	24	43	5	25	297	400	510	910	15	83	1.04	7	0	44	214	7.15
2013	A+	Brevard County	328	52	82	6	43	250	317	396	713	9	79	0.47	2	2	40	146	4.42

Athletic, toolsy OF whose above average plate discipline has allowed him to tap into raw power. With quick bat and good approach, he should move quickly. Played both CF and RF, but many see him in a corner where he has average arm and good reads. Average speed on the bases.

Hannemann,Jacob

8 | **Chicago (N)** | EXP MLB DEBUT: 2017 | POTENTIAL: Starting OF | **7D**

Bats L Age 23
2013 (3) Brigham Young

- Pwr +++
- BAvg ++
- Spd +++
- Def ++

Year	Lev	Team	AB	R	H	HR	RBI	Avg	OB	Slg	OPS	bb%	ct%	Eye	SB	CS	x/h%	Iso	RC/G
2013	NCAA	Brigham Young	215	53	74	5	29	344	410	553	964	10	83	0.65	14	1	38	209	7.60
2013	Rk	AZL Cubs	9	1	1	0	2	111	111	222	333	0	89	0.00	1	0	100	111	-0.02
2013	A-	Boise	62	8	18	1	5	290	313	468	780	3	82	0.18	3	1	39	177	4.97

Two-way player in college is somewhat raw on the diamond, but has good athleticism. Smooth LH stroke generates moderate power and consistent contact with good balance and bat speed. Runs well and should be able to stick in CF for now.

Hanson,Alen

6 | **Pittsburgh** | EXP MLB DEBUT: 2015 | POTENTIAL: Starting SS/2B | **8C**

Bats B Age 21
2009 FA (DR)

- Pwr +++
- BAvg +++
- Spd ++++
- Def ++

Year	Lev	Team	AB	R	H	HR	RBI	Avg	OB	Slg	OPS	bb%	ct%	Eye	SB	CS	x/h%	Iso	RC/G
2011	Rk	GCL Pirates	198	42	52	2	35	263	333	429	763	10	83	0.62	24	6	42	167	5.19
2011	A-	State College	10	1	2	0	0	200	273	200	473	9	80	0.50	0	0	0	0	1.36
2012	A	West Virginia	489	99	151	16	62	309	379	528	906	10	79	0.52	35	19	41	219	6.93
2013	A+	Bradenton	367	51	103	7	48	281	340	444	784	8	81	0.47	24	14	37	163	5.29
2013	AA	Altoona	137	13	35	1	10	255	297	380	676	6	81	0.31	6	2	29	124	3.85

Short, athletic SS came back to earth after a monster breakout. Has plus speed and a nice line-drive approach. Is aggressive at the plate and can put a charge into the ball, but makes enough contact that should be able to hit for avg. Is below-average defensively and could be moved from SS to 2B down the road.

Harrison,Travis

5 | **Minnesota** | EXP MLB DEBUT: 2016 | POTENTIAL: Starting 3B | **8D**

Bats R Age 21
2011 (1-S) HS (CA)

- Pwr ++++
- BAvg +++
- Spd +
- Def ++

Year	Lev	Team	AB	R	H	HR	RBI	Avg	OB	Slg	OPS	bb%	ct%	Eye	SB	CS	x/h%	Iso	RC/G
2012	Rk	Elizabethton	219	39	66	5	27	301	370	461	832	10	77	0.47	3	0	32	160	5.99
2013	A	Cedar Rapids	450	66	114	15	59	253	351	416	767	13	72	0.54	2	4	38	162	5.27

Strong INF who shows glimpses of pure hitting skills and tapping into raw power. Has improved approach that allows him to see pitches and make hard contact. Struggles with breaking balls, but can use entire field. Doesn't have much quickness at 3B, but has average, accurate arm and hands. Bat will have to carry him.

Hart,Josh

8 | **Baltimore** | EXP MLB DEBUT: 2017 | POTENTIAL: Starting CF | **8E**

Bats L Age 19
2013 (1-S) HS (GA)

- Pwr +
- BAvg ++
- Spd ++++
- Def ++++

Year	Lev	Team	AB	R	H	HR	RBI	Avg	OB	Slg	OPS	bb%	ct%	Eye	SB	CS	x/h%	Iso	RC/G
2013	Rk	GCL Orioles	123	14	28	0	9	228	301	301	602	10	81	0.57	11	3	25	73	3.15
2013	A-	Aberdeen	10	0	1	0	0	100	182	100	282	9	60	0.25	0	0	0	0	-2.30

Quick, athletic OF who projects as leadoff hitter. Focuses on contact and line drives by going gap to gap. Possesses good bat control, but will need to add strength and leverage to realize any semblance of power. Swing can get mechanical and choppy at times. Owns plus speed and patrols CF well with excellent range and jumps.

Hawkins,Courtney

789 | **Chicago (A)** | EXP MLB DEBUT: 2016 | POTENTIAL: Starting OF | **9D**

Bats R Age 20
2012 (1) HS (TX)

- Pwr ++++
- BAvg ++
- Spd +++
- Def +++

Year	Lev	Team	AB	R	H	HR	RBI	Avg	OB	Slg	OPS	bb%	ct%	Eye	SB	CS	x/h%	Iso	RC/G
2012	Rk	Bristol	147	25	40	3	16	272	305	401	707	5	75	0.19	8	2	30	129	4.06
2012	A	Kannapolis	65	11	20	4	15	308	348	631	979	6	74	0.24	3	2	55	323	7.74
2012	A+	Winston-Salem	17	3	5	1	2	294	294	588	882	0	88	0.00	0	1	60	294	5.74
2013	A+	Winston-Salem	383	48	68	19	62	178	235	384	619	7	58	0.18	10	5	56	206	3.22

Young, athletic OF who struggled, but was youngest player in league. Finished 3rd in HR, but led in strikeouts. Still owns huge upside predicated on bat speed, power, and secondary skills. Long swing and poor pitch recognition mute BA and will chase breaking balls. Runs well and can play solid CF with very strong arm.

Hazelbaker,Jeremy

79 | **Los Angeles (N)** | EXP MLB DEBUT: 2014 | POTENTIAL: Reserve OF | **6B**

Bats L Age 26
2009 (4) Ball State

- Pwr ++
- BAvg ++
- Spd ++++
- Def ++

Year	Lev	Team	AB	R	H	HR	RBI	Avg	OB	Slg	OPS	bb%	ct%	Eye	SB	CS	x/h%	Iso	RC/G
2011	A+	Salem	122	26	34	5	14	279	380	475	856	14	72	0.59	12	6	41	197	6.54
2011	AA	Portland	354	60	94	12	41	266	343	435	778	11	70	0.40	35	8	35	169	5.38
2012	AA	Portland	436	77	119	19	64	273	327	479	806	7	74	0.31	33	11	39	206	5.48
2012	AAA	Pawtucket	30	2	8	0	3	267	267	367	633	0	73	0.00	3	0	38	100	3.03
2013	AAA	Pawtucket	428	62	110	11	54	257	315	374	688	8	69	0.27	37	7	24	117	3.98

Tall, athletic OF who spent first full year in Triple-A. Runs very well and has been consistent 30+ SB guy in career. Won't hit many extra-base hits due to limited bat speed and lack of contact. Needs to get on base more to use speed more effectively. Fits profile of 4th OF, but can stand to improve range and fringy arm strength.

Head,Miles

35 | **Oakland** | EXP MLB DEBUT: 2015 | POTENTIAL: Starting 1B | **7D**

Bats R Age 23
2009 (26) HS (GA)

- Pwr ++++
- BAvg ++
- Spd +
- Def ++

Year	Lev	Team	AB	R	H	HR	RBI	Avg	OB	Slg	OPS	bb%	ct%	Eye	SB	CS	x/h%	Iso	RC/G
2011	A	Greenville	263	61	89	15	53	338	406	612	1018	10	80	0.57	4	2	46	274	8.17
2011	A+	Salem	232	27	59	7	29	254	313	405	719	8	76	0.36	0	2	34	151	4.34
2012	A+	Stockton	267	57	102	18	56	382	431	715	1146	8	79	0.42	3	0	46	333	9.64
2012	AA	Midland	213	25	58	5	28	272	323	404	727	7	65	0.21	0	1	28	131	4.73
2013	AA	Midland	148	13	29	2	8	196	256	264	520	8	72	0.29	0	1	21	68	1.63

Powerful, compact INF who couldn't repeat breakout campaign from 2012. Ended season in June due to shoulder injury. Has struggled in Double-A as quality stuff eats him up. Owns a quick stroke, but lacks bat speed to hit for BA. Exhibits plus power to entire field. Lacks range and quickness at 3B, but has strong arm.

Heathcott,Slade

8 | **New York (A)** | EXP MLB DEBUT: 2015 | POTENTIAL: Starting OF | **8D**

Bats L Age 23
2009 (1) HS (TX)

- Pwr +++
- BAvg ++
- Spd ++++
- Def +++

Year	Lev	Team	AB	R	H	HR	RBI	Avg	OB	Slg	OPS	bb%	ct%	Eye	SB	CS	x/h%	Iso	RC/G
2011	A	Charleston (Sc)	210	36	57	4	16	271	332	419	751	8	73	0.33	6	7	33	148	4.93
2011	A+	Tampa	5	2	3	1	1	600	600	1200	1800	0	80	0.00	0	0	33	600	16.14
2012	Rk	GCL Yankees	17	3	4	0	2	235	409	353	762	23	76	1.25	2	0	50	118	5.86
2012	A+	Tampa	215	38	66	5	27	307	366	470	836	9	69	0.30	17	4	35	163	6.24
2013	AA	Trenton	399	59	104	8	49	261	322	411	733	8	73	0.34	15	8	36	150	4.67

Athletic, aggressive OF who earned more AB than any other year in career. Set career high in HR in first year above High-A. Has knack for hitting LHP with hard line drives, though lack of plate discipline could mute upside. Swing can get long, resulting in minimal contact. Speed is best tool and is excellent defender with strong arm.

Hedges,Austin

2 | **San Diego** | EXP MLB DEBUT: 2015 | POTENTIAL: Starting C | **8B**

Bats R Age 21
2011 (1) HS (CA)

- Pwr ++
- BAvg +++
- Spd +++
- Def ++++

Year	Lev	Team	AB	R	H	HR	RBI	Avg	OB	Slg	OPS	bb%	ct%	Eye	SB	CS	x/h%	Iso	RC/G
2011	Rk	AZL Padres	16	3	5	1	4	313	476	500	976	24	94	5.00	1	0	20	188	8.32
2011	A-	Eugene	10	0	1	0	0	100	250	200	450	17	70	0.67	0	0	100	100	1.03
2012	A	Fort Wayne	337	44	94	10	56	279	325	451	776	6	82	0.37	14	9	40	172	4.99
2013	A+	Lake Elsinore	233	34	63	4	30	270	333	425	758	9	81	0.49	5	4	43	155	4.99
2013	AA	San Antonio	67	4	15	0	8	224	288	269	556	8	87	0.67	3	1	20	45	2.66

Strong and athletic backstop who is amazing defender and could catch in big leagues now. Owns very strong, accurate arm with polished blocking ability. Offers some BA potential along with average pop. Uses compact stroke to hit hard line drives to gaps, but can be fooled by breaking balls and offspeed stuff.

Hefflinger,Robby

7 | **Atlanta** | EXP MLB DEBUT: 2015 | POTENTIAL: Backup OF | **6C**

Bats R Age 24
2009 (11) Georgia Perimtr JC

- Pwr ++++
- BAvg ++
- Spd ++
- Def ++

Year	Lev	Team	AB	R	H	HR	RBI	Avg	OB	Slg	OPS	bb%	ct%	Eye	SB	CS	x/h%	Iso	RC/G
2011	A+	Lynchburg	44	2	5	0	2	114	170	159	329	6	57	0.16	0	0	40	45	-1.49
2012	A	Rome	296	44	84	12	58	284	365	483	848	11	73	0.47	7	1	40	199	6.30
2012	A+	Lynchburg	123	14	28	4	11	228	326	390	716	13	62	0.38	1	1	43	163	4.85
2013	A+	Lynchburg	280	44	80	21	52	286	338	579	916	7	75	0.31	1	1	49	293	6.76
2013	AA	Mississippi	188	19	32	6	25	170	232	319	551	7	66	0.23	2	1	47	149	2.00

Tall, athletic OF has some of the best power in the system, but struggles to make consistent contact. At 6-5, 235 has good size and plus raw strength and had a career best 27 HR. Needs a better approach against breaking balls if he is going to remain a prospect. Has some potential, but lots of work to do.

Heineman,Tyler

2 | **Houston** | EXP MLB DEBUT: 2016 | POTENTIAL: Backup C | **6B**

Bats B Age 23
2012 (8) UCLA

- Pwr ++
- BAvg +++
- Spd ++
- Def +++

Year	Lev	Team	AB	R	H	HR	RBI	Avg	OB	Slg	OPS	bb%	ct%	Eye	SB	CS	x/h%	Iso	RC/G
2010	NCAA	UCLA	8	2	1	0	0	125	222	125	347	11	63	0.33	0	0	0	0	-1.11
2011	NCAA	UCLA	46	8	12	0	7	261	346	304	651	12	89	1.20	0	1	17	43	4.03
2012	NCAA	UCLA	211	42	70	1	27	332	395	389	783	9	93	1.57	3	2	13	57	5.45
2012	A-	Tri City	193	33	69	0	26	358	434	430	864	12	94	2.17	6	2	20	73	6.57
2013	A+	Lancaster	370	67	106	13	71	286	343	476	819	8	87	0.68	2	3	38	189	5.59

Stocky, strong C who has shown ability to hit from both sides. Better hitter from left side, but makes good contact and has discerning eye. Adept at situational hitting and can hit for power to pull side. Pop is result of strength rather than bat speed. Catches and throws well with good mobility and agility. Has all-around game.

Hernandez, Cesar — 4 — Philadelphia

EXP MLB DEBUT: 2013 POTENTIAL: Starting 2B **7B**

Bats B Age 24
2006 FA (Venezuela)

Pwr	+
BAvg	+++
Spd	+++
Def	+++

Year	Lev	Team	AB	R	H	HR	RBI	Avg	OB	Slg	OPS	bb%	ct%	Eye	SB	CS	x/h%	Iso	RC/G
2012	AA	Reading	411	50	125	2	51	304	347	436	783	6	84	0.40	16	12	31	131	5.20
2012	AAA	Lehigh Valley	121	13	30	0	6	248	272	298	570	3	91	0.36	5	3	17	50	2.67
2013	AA	Reading	10	2	5	0	3	500	545	600	1145	9	90	1.00	1	0	20	100	9.46
2013	AAA	Lehigh Valley	391	59	121	2	34	309	375	402	777	9	79	0.51	32	8	19	92	5.28
2013	MLB	PHI	121	17	35	0	10	289	338	331	669	7	79	0.35	0	3	14	41	3.73

Diminutive but athletic infielder got a crash course in CF in August, and played both OF and some 2B for PHI in September. Despite 5-10, 175 frame, consistently stings the ball with a line-drive approach and has wheels to rack up SB. Excellent defender at 2B, continued to play OF in winter ball. Most likely a valuable utility piece.

Hernandez, Elier — 9 — Kansas City

EXP MLB DEBUT: 2017 POTENTIAL: Starting OF **9E**

Bats R Age 19
2011 FA (DR)

Pwr	++
BAvg	+++
Spd	+++
Def	+++

Year	Lev	Team	AB	R	H	HR	RBI	Avg	OB	Slg	OPS	bb%	ct%	Eye	SB	CS	x/h%	Iso	RC/G
2012	Rk	Idaho Falls	250	30	52	0	34	208	250	280	530	5	74	0.21	2	0	27	72	1.86
2013	Rk	Idaho Falls	289	44	87	3	44	301	342	439	781	6	79	0.29	9	2	30	138	5.16

Tall, projectable OF who repeated short-season ball and showed drastic improvement. Doesn't draw many walks and struggles to hit breaking balls, but starting to take advantage of bat speed and hard contact. Power is all about projection. Runs OK at present, though may slow down in future. Fits RF profile with strong arm and range.

Hernandez, Jan — 5 — Philadelphia

EXP MLB DEBUT: 2018 POTENTIAL: Starting 3B **7D**

Bats R Age 19
2013 (3) HS (PR)

Pwr	+++
BAvg	++
Spd	++
Def	++

Year	Lev	Team	AB	R	H	HR	RBI	Avg	OB	Slg	OPS	bb%	ct%	Eye	SB	CS	x/h%	Iso	RC/G
2013	Rk	GCL Phillies	124	16	26	3	14	210	279	347	626	9	60	0.24	7	2	38	137	3.44

Well-sized prospect with polished swing and good bat speed. Strikeouts an issue in first pro exposure in GCL, but exhibits good power with more likely to come as he matures. Pitch recognition needs work to fully realize potential. Good arm and hands on defense. Likely to be brought along slowly until hit tool improves.

Hernandez, Marco — 6 — Chicago (N)

EXP MLB DEBUT: 2016 POTENTIAL: Utility INF **6C**

Bats B Age 21
2010 FA (DR)

Pwr	+++
BAvg	++
Spd	+++
Def	+++

Year	Lev	Team	AB	R	H	HR	RBI	Avg	OB	Slg	OPS	bb%	ct%	Eye	SB	CS	x/h%	Iso	RC/G
2011	Rk	AZL Cubs	210	39	70	2	42	333	381	486	866	7	86	0.55	9	7	33	152	6.22
2012	A-	Boise	269	39	77	5	39	286	312	416	728	4	87	0.28	8	3	27	130	4.30
2012	A	Peoria	157	18	33	2	12	210	253	299	552	5	75	0.23	2	1	21	89	2.08
2013	A	Kane County	417	45	106	4	34	254	282	338	620	4	83	0.22	21	7	23	84	2.99

Lean, athletic SS from the Dominican Republic struggled in his 2nd stint in the MWL. Switch-hitter has gap power and the ability to make consistent contact. Needs to be more selective at the plate and drew only 16 BB in 417 AB. Is a capable defender with good range, soft hands, and a strong arm.

Hernandez, Oscar — 2 — Tampa Bay

EXP MLB DEBUT: 2016 POTENTIAL: Starting C **8D**

Bats R Age 20
2009 FA (Venezuela)

Pwr	+++
BAvg	++
Spd	++
Def	++++

Year	Lev	Team	AB	R	H	HR	RBI	Avg	OB	Slg	OPS	bb%	ct%	Eye	SB	CS	x/h%	Iso	RC/G
2012	Rk	Princeton	160	25	37	5	24	231	328	394	722	13	81	0.74	0	1	41	163	4.64
2013	A-	Hudson Valley	167	22	38	6	33	228	275	371	647	6	86	0.46	9	1	32	144	3.40
2013	A	Bowling Green	9	1	2	0	1	222	364	222	586	18	89	2.00	0	0	0	0	3.62

Defensive-oriented C with the potential to add more to bat. Has very strong arm and advanced receiving skills for age. Possesses footwork and catch-and-throw talent. Offers quick bat to make easy contact and pitch recognition should lead to average power. Runs well for catcher, but has limited BA upside and can be pull-conscious.

Hernandez, Teoscar — 89 — Houston

EXP MLB DEBUT: 2017 POTENTIAL: Starting OF **8E**

Bats R Age 21
2011 FA (DR)

Pwr	+++
BAvg	++
Spd	+++
Def	+++

Year	Lev	Team	AB	R	H	HR	RBI	Avg	OB	Slg	OPS	bb%	ct%	Eye	SB	CS	x/h%	Iso	RC/G
2012	Rk	GCL Astros	177	25	43	4	18	243	316	395	712	10	69	0.35	10	1	40	153	4.50
2012	A	Lexington	25	2	6	1	5	240	321	440	761	11	52	0.25	1	0	50	200	6.50
2013	A	Quad Cities	499	97	135	13	55	271	326	435	761	8	73	0.30	24	11	35	164	4.99

Physical, athletic OF who is deep sleeper in deep org. Can do many things well, especially hitting. Bat speed is above average and can hit for power to all fields. Exhibits feel for swing, but can get too aggressive and chase balls. Needs to recognize spin better. Plus arm ideal for corner and speed results in ample range.

Herrera, Carlos — 6 — Colorado

EXP MLB DEBUT: 2018 POTENTIAL: Starting SS **7D**

Bats L Age 17
2013 FA (Venezuela)

Pwr	+
BAvg	+++
Spd	+++
Def	+++

Year	Lev	Team	AB	R	H	HR	RBI	Avg	OB	Slg	OPS	bb%	ct%	Eye	SB	CS	x/h%	Iso	RC/G
2013		Did not play in the US																	

Short, slender SS from Venezuela was signed for $1.2 million in 2013. Good line-drive approach at the plate with above-average bat speed. Slight frame suggests limited power down the road. One of the better defenders on the international market, with good range, soft hands, and a strong arm.

Herrera, Dilson — 4 — New York (N)

EXP MLB DEBUT: 2016 POTENTIAL: Starting 2B **8D**

Bats R Age 20
2010 FA (Columbia)

Pwr	+++
BAvg	+++
Spd	++++
Def	++

Year	Lev	Team	AB	R	H	HR	RBI	Avg	OB	Slg	OPS	bb%	ct%	Eye	SB	CS	x/h%	Iso	RC/G
2012	Rk	GCL Pirates	199	41	56	7	27	281	341	482	823	8	79	0.44	11	4	39	201	5.70
2012	A-	State College	28	7	9	1	2	321	345	536	881	3	79	0.17	1	0	33	214	6.15
2013	A	Savannah	19	6	6	0	4	316	409	316	725	14	68	0.50	3	0	0	0	4.84
2013	A	West Virginia	423	69	112	11	56	265	324	421	745	8	74	0.34	11	6	37	156	4.76

Surprising power potential for small MI. Owns above-average bat control and hand-eye coordination. Troubling ct% and bb% trends in 2013 as he expanded strike zone, but still projects high BA. Works to hit everything back up the middle. Has the speed to do damage on the basepaths. Needs to shore up defense.

Herrera, Jose — 2 — Arizona

EXP MLB DEBUT: 2018 POTENTIAL: Starting C **7D**

Bats B Age 17
2013 FA (Venezuela)

Pwr	+++
BAvg	+++
Spd	++
Def	+++

Year	Lev	Team	AB	R	H	HR	RBI	Avg	OB	Slg	OPS	bb%	ct%	Eye	SB	CS	x/h%	Iso	RC/G
2013		Did not play in the US																	

The switch-hitter is the top catching prospect in this year's international class. The 17-year-old Venezuelan backstop moves well behind the plate, has a good feel for signal calling with a strong arm. At the plate, has good pop for size and makes consistent contact. Does have some swing-and-miss issues.

Herrera, Juan — 6 — St. Louis

EXP MLB DEBUT: 2017 POTENTIAL: Starting 2B/SS **7C**

Bats R Age 21
2011 FA (DR)

Pwr	+++
BAvg	++
Spd	++
Def	+++

Year	Lev	Team	AB	R	H	HR	RBI	Avg	OB	Slg	OPS	bb%	ct%	Eye	SB	CS	x/h%	Iso	RC/G
2012	Rk	AZL Indians	138	28	39	0	15	283	396	391	788	16	75	0.74	8	2	33	109	5.90
2013	A-	Mahoning Val	149	20	41	1	11	275	345	369	715	10	80	0.53	2	1	27	94	4.50
2013	A-	State College	15	1	1	0	0	67	176	67	243	12	93	2.00	0	0	0	0	-0.25
2013	A	Peoria	85	5	23	0	3	271	326	318	644	8	74	0.32	2	0	17	47	3.43

Short, skinny SS came over in the Rzepczynski trade in July. Solid approach at the plate with good plate discipline and contact ability and a career .370 OB%. Limited power cuts into his potential value. Above-average defender with good range and a strong arm. Should be able to stick at SS.

Herrera, Odubel — 4 — Texas

EXP MLB DEBUT: 2015 POTENTIAL: Utility player **6A**

Bats L Age 22
2008 FA (Venezuela)

Pwr	++
BAvg	+++
Spd	++++
Def	+++

Year	Lev	Team	AB	R	H	HR	RBI	Avg	OB	Slg	OPS	bb%	ct%	Eye	SB	CS	x/h%	Iso	RC/G
2010	A-	Spokane	9	0	2	0	0	222	222	333	556	0	89	0.00	0	0	50	111	2.36
2011	A	Hickory	464	72	142	3	56	306	340	394	735	5	83	0.31	34	11	23	88	4.46
2012	A+	Myrtle Beach	500	72	142	5	46	284	328	382	710	6	80	0.33	27	7	23	98	4.22
2013	A+	Myrtle Beach	95	13	28	1	5	295	396	368	765	14	80	0.84	2	2	14	74	5.34
2013	AA	Frisco	389	37	100	2	30	257	288	339	628	4	83	0.25	15	5	21	82	3.15

Quick and athletic infielder who plays small ball well. Doesn't own impact tools, but has excellent speed on basepaths. Makes surprisingly hard contact with simple swing, though will expand strike zone at times. Can be very good defender with sure, quick hands and strong arm. Range more suitable at 2B, but could play SS if needed.

Herrera,Rosell — 56 — Colorado

Bats B Age 21 | 2009 FA (DR) | EXP MLB DEBUT: 2015 | POTENTIAL: Starting SS | 9D

Pwr +++ | BAvg ++++ | Spd ++ | Def +++

Year	Lev	Team	AB	R	H	HR	RBI	Avg	OB	Slg	OPS	bb%	ct%	Eye	SB	CS	x/h%	Iso	RC/G
2011	Rk	Casper	243	38	69	6	34	284	356	449	804	10	74	0.44	5	4	29	165	5.67
2012	A-	Tri-City	194	30	55	1	30	284	332	351	682	7	82	0.41	7	3	16	67	3.92
2012	A	Asheville	213	22	43	1	26	202	274	272	546	9	77	0.43	6	3	26	70	2.25
2013	A	Asheville	472	83	162	16	76	343	418	515	933	11	80	0.64	21	8	30	172	7.23

Toolsy, athletic switch-hitting SS had a monster season. Has good size and is just starting to tap into power. Toned down aggressive approach and showed better pitch recognition. Despite notching 21 SB, is not a burner on the bases. Might be difficult to stick at SS, but he has the size and power for 3B.

Hicks,John — 2 — Seattle

Bats R Age 24 | 2011 (4) Virginia | EXP MLB DEBUT: 2015 | POTENTIAL: Starting C | 7E

Pwr ++ | BAvg +++ | Spd ++ | Def ++

Year	Lev	Team	AB	R	H	HR	RBI	Avg	OB	Slg	OPS	bb%	ct%	Eye	SB	CS	x/h%	Iso	RC/G
2010	NCAA	Virginia	244	59	75	8	48	307	350	488	838	6	88	0.55	9	1	37	180	5.69
2011	NCAA	Virginia	277	52	92	8	59	332	373	502	875	6	93	0.95	5	4	33	170	6.14
2011	A	Clinton	139	21	43	2	26	309	333	446	779	3	88	0.29	2	3	30	137	4.92
2012	A+	High Desert	506	87	158	15	79	312	348	472	821	5	86	0.38	22	8	31	160	5.41
2013	AA	Jackson	296	40	70	4	29	236	289	331	620	7	79	0.35	13	4	27	95	3.10

Tall, athletic C who has solid fundamentals across board. Power declined from 2012 season, but has improved defensively. Still fringy skills behind plate, though has average arm with quick release. Possesses bat control and doubles power from line drive stroke. Contact rate falling and doesn't draw many walks.

Holaday,Bryan — 2 — Detroit

Bats R Age 26 | 2010 (6) Texas Christian | EXP MLB DEBUT: 2012 | POTENTIAL: Backup C | 6A

Pwr ++ | BAvg ++ | Spd + | Def ++++

Year	Lev	Team	AB	R	H	HR	RBI	Avg	OB	Slg	OPS	bb%	ct%	Eye	SB	CS	x/h%	Iso	RC/G
2011	AA	Erie	330	35	80	7	42	242	300	361	660	8	77	0.36	6	1	31	118	3.59
2012	AAA	Toledo	250	18	60	2	25	240	301	320	621	8	83	0.51	2	0	25	80	3.28
2012	MLB	DET	12	3	3	0	0	250	250	333	583	0	83	0.00	0	0	33	83	2.44
2013	AAA	Toledo	288	28	75	4	24	260	304	372	675	6	80	0.32	0	1	31	111	3.77
2013	MLB	DET	27	8	8	1	2	296	345	444	789	7	89	0.67	0	0	25	148	5.12

Defensive-oriented backstop who has excellent shot at backup role. Has thick and durable frame and offers catch-and-throw skills. Moves well with clean footwork and has average arm and quick release to neutralize runners. Owns average, raw power, but not much else in way of bat. Lacks bat control and expands strike zone.

Houle,Dustin — 2 — Milwaukee

Bats R Age 20 | 2011 (8) HS (Canada) | EXP MLB DEBUT: 2016 | POTENTIAL: Backup C | 6C

Pwr ++ | BAvg ++ | Spd ++ | Def ++

Year	Lev	Team	AB	R	H	HR	RBI	Avg	OB	Slg	OPS	bb%	ct%	Eye	SB	CS	x/h%	Iso	RC/G
2012	Rk	AZL Brewers	175	19	36	1	19	206	261	280	541	7	81	0.39	0	1	31	74	2.21
2013	Rk	Helena	180	23	45	1	19	250	278	311	589	4	81	0.20	1	2	20	61	2.58
2013	A	Wisconsin	23	5	6	0	1	261	346	435	781	12	91	1.50	0	0	67	174	5.74

Raw, athletic C is slightly below average across the board, but has the attributes to be a decent backup. Solid bat speed allows for good ct%, but flat swing and poor pitch recognition will limit BA and power potential. Converted 3B should stick behind the plate with strong arm.

Jackson,Brett — 8 — Chicago (N)

Bats L Age 25 | 2009 (1) California | EXP MLB DEBUT: 2012 | POTENTIAL: Starting CF | 7D

Pwr ++ | BAvg ++ | 4.15 Spd ++++ | Def +++

Year	Lev	Team	AB	R	H	HR	RBI	Avg	OB	Slg	OPS	bb%	ct%	Eye	SB	CS	x/h%	Iso	RC/G
2012	AAA	Iowa	407	66	104	15	47	256	333	479	812	10	61	0.30	27	5	47	224	6.48
2012	MLB	CHC	120	14	21	4	9	175	303	342	644	15	51	0.37	0	3	52	167	4.30
2013	Rk	AZL Cubs	14	1	1	0	0	71	133	71	205	7	50	0.14	0	0	0	0	-4.15
2013	AA	Tennessee	95	10	19	0	4	200	296	284	581	12	61	0.35	2	2	32	84	2.87
2013	AAA	Iowa	215	24	48	6	23	223	292	367	660	9	64	0.27	7	5	33	144	3.77

Athletic OF continues to look overmatched at the plate, earning a demotion to AA. Overall, struck out 121 times in 324 AB. Still runs well and has decent power potential. Above-average defender with a strong arm and good instincts. At 25, Jackson might only have one more chance to carve out a role in the majors.

Jackson,Ryan — 6 — San Diego

Bats R Age 26 | 2009 (5) Miami | EXP MLB DEBUT: 2012 | POTENTIAL: Starting SS | 7C

Pwr ++ | BAvg ++ | Spd ++ | Def ++++

Year	Lev	Team	AB	R	H	HR	RBI	Avg	OB	Slg	OPS	bb%	ct%	Eye	SB	CS	x/h%	Iso	RC/G
2011	AA	Springfield	533	65	148	11	73	278	333	415	747	8	83	0.48	2	0	32	137	4.74
2012	AAA	Memphis	445	60	121	10	47	272	336	396	732	9	83	0.57	2	0	28	124	4.59
2012	MLB	STL	17	2	2	0	0	118	167	118	284	6	82	0.33	0	0	0	0	-0.96
2013	AAA	Memphis	442	49	123	3	34	278	354	346	700	11	79	0.57	9	0	19	68	4.32
2013	MLB	STL	7	0	0	0	0	0	0	0	0	0	71	0.00	0	0		0	-5.63

Tall and lean INF who was claimed off waivers by HOU before being traded to SD after season ended. Mostly known for plus glove and has added versatility to package. Has first-step quickness, plus instincts, and great hands. Possesses bat speed and gap power while showing enough patience to get on base.

Jacobs,Brandon — 7 — Arizona

Bats R Age 23 | 2009 (10) HS (GA) | EXP MLB DEBUT: 2014 | POTENTIAL: Starting OF | 8D

Pwr +++ | BAvg ++ | Spd +++ | Def +++

Year	Lev	Team	AB	R	H	HR	RBI	Avg	OB	Slg	OPS	bb%	ct%	Eye	SB	CS	x/h%	Iso	RC/G
2011	A	Greenville	442	75	134	17	80	303	365	505	869	9	72	0.35	30	7	39	201	6.51
2012	A+	Salem	437	62	110	13	61	252	313	410	723	8	71	0.30	17	9	39	158	4.49
2013	A+	Salem	291	44	71	11	44	244	321	440	761	10	70	0.38	10	4	49	196	5.13
2013	AA	Birmingham	156	13	37	2	22	237	287	327	614	7	68	0.22	2	3	27	90	2.97
2013	AA	Portland	8	2	3	0	0	375	375	750	1125	0	75	0.00	0	0	67	375	9.93

Athletic, muscular OF who hasn't recaptured success from 2011, but has impressive strength and bat speed. Muscles ball out of park with brute strength and has solid approach at bat. Will swing and miss often as breaking balls give him fits. BA upside limited without consistent swing, but he runs well and is average defender in LF.

Jagielo,Eric — 5 — New York (A)

Bats L Age 22 | 2013 (1) Notre Dame | EXP MLB DEBUT: 2016 | POTENTIAL: Starting 3B | 8C

Pwr +++ | BAvg ++++ | Spd + | Def ++

Year	Lev	Team	AB	R	H	HR	RBI	Avg	OB	Slg	OPS	bb%	ct%	Eye	SB	CS	x/h%	Iso	RC/G
2012	NCAA	Notre Dame	229	33	71	13	43	310	385	546	931	11	85	0.82	4	4	39	236	6.97
2013	NCAA	Notre Dame	196	47	76	9	53	388	481	633	1113	15	83	1.06	3	3	38	245	9.62
2013	Rk	GCL Yankees	2	1	0	0	0	0	0	0	0	0	100		0	0		0	-2.66
2013	Rk	GCL Yankees 2	7	2	2	0	0	286	375	571	946	13	71	0.50	0	0	100	286	8.37
2013	A-	Staten Island	184	19	49	6	27	266	357	451	808	12	71	0.48	0	0	43	185	5.91

Professional hitter who has BA and power potential. Secondary skills aren't polished, but has solid approach. Uses entire field with power and exhibits textbook lefty stroke. Has tendency to chase breaking balls and will strike out. Defense has potential with hands and arm, but lacks quickness and overall foot speed.

Jankowski,Travis — 8 — San Diego

Bats L Age 23 | 2012 (1) Stony Brook | EXP MLB DEBUT: 2016 | POTENTIAL: Backup OF | 7C

Pwr ++ | BAvg ++ | Spd ++++ | Def ++++

Year	Lev	Team	AB	R	H	HR	RBI	Avg	OB	Slg	OPS	bb%	ct%	Eye	SB	CS	x/h%	Iso	RC/G
2011	NCAA	Stony Brook	186	39	66	2	38	355	417	457	874	10	88	0.91	30	4	18	102	6.42
2012	NCAA	Stony Brook	266	79	110	5	46	414	462	620	1082	8	92	1.09	36	6	31	207	8.68
2012	Rk	AZL Padres	8	1	2	0	4	250	250	250	500	0	88	0.00	0	0	0	0	1.47
2012	A	Fort Wayne	238	32	67	1	23	282	319	370	688	5	82	0.30	17	7	22	88	3.94
2013	A+	Lake Elsinore	493	89	141	1	38	286	356	355	711	10	81	0.56	71	14	18	69	4.48

Tall and lean outfielder whose present game is all about speed and defense. Improved technique led to more SB and has instincts to be asset. Offers some pop potential if he fills out thin frame. Struggles with breaking stuff, though makes decent contact with line drive approach. Plays solid CF with plus range.

Jhang,Jin-De — 2 — Pittsburgh

Bats L Age 21 | 2010 FA (Taiwan) | EXP MLB DEBUT: 2016 | POTENTIAL: Starting C | 7C

Pwr ++ | BAvg +++ | 4.30 Spd ++ | Def ++++

Year	Lev	Team	AB	R	H	HR	RBI	Avg	OB	Slg	OPS	bb%	ct%	Eye	SB	CS	x/h%	Iso	RC/G
2012	Rk	GCL Pirates	128	12	39	1	23	305	373	398	772	10	88	0.88	1	1	21	94	5.26
2013	A-	Jamestown	184	22	51	5	34	277	338	413	751	8	87	0.71	0	1	27	136	4.83

Short, thick-bodied Taiwanese backstop has been solid since arrival to U.S. Moves well behind the plate, proving surprisingly agile. Has a strong, accurate arm and nailed 47% of baserunners.. Has good plate discipline, decent bat speed, and held his own vs. LHP. Scouts have reservations about hit tool.

Jimenez,A.J. — 2 — Toronto

Bats R Age 24 | 2008 (9) HS (PR) | EXP MLB DEBUT: 2014 | POTENTIAL: Starting C | 7C

Pwr ++ | BAvg +++ | Spd ++ | Def ++++

Year	Lev	Team	AB	R	H	HR	RBI	Avg	OB	Slg	OPS	bb%	ct%	Eye	SB	CS	x/h%	Iso	RC/G
2011	A+	Dunedin	379	49	115	4	52	303	351	417	768	7	84	0.47	11	2	30	113	5.00
2012	AA	New Hampshire	105	14	27	2	10	257	291	371	662	5	87	0.36	2	3	26	114	3.60
2013	A+	Dunedin	28	5	12	1	9	429	448	643	1091	3	89	0.33	0	0	33	214	8.28
2013	AA	New Hampshire	203	28	56	3	29	276	329	394	723	7	82	0.43	1	2	32	118	4.44
2013	AAA	Buffalo	30	0	7	0	0	233	258	267	525	3	93	0.50	0	1	14	33	2.28

Agile and strong backstop who returned in late May after TJ surgery in '12. Has valuable skills, especially behind plate where he stands out with his strong, accurate arm and quick transfer. Blocks and receives with excellence. Power is a little short, but recognizes pitches and not afraid to go to opposite field.

Jimenez,Eloy

8 | Chicago (N) | EXP MLB DEBUT: 2018 | POTENTIAL: Starting RF | 8D

Bats R Age 17
2013 FA (DR)
Pwr + + +
BAvg + +
Spd + + +
Def + + +

Year	Lev	Team	AB	R	H	HR	RBI	Avg	OB	Slg	OPS	bb%	ct%	Eye	SB	CS	x/h%	Iso	RC/G
2013		Did not play in the US																	

Top ranked international prospect is a lean, projectable OF with above-average raw power. Swing can get a bit long and scouts are mixed on whether he will hit for average or not. He has good speed, athleticism, and enough arm strength to play either corner in the OF.

Jimenez,Emerson

6 | Colorado | EXP MLB DEBUT: 2017 | POTENTIAL: Starting SS | 8D

Bats L Age 19
2012 FA (DR)
Pwr + +
BAvg + + +
Spd + + + +
Def + + + +

Year	Lev	Team	AB	R	H	HR	RBI	Avg	OB	Slg	OPS	bb%	ct%	Eye	SB	CS	x/h%	Iso	RC/G
2013	Rk	Grand Junction	181	32	56	3	20	309	342	414	756	5	77	0.21	6	3	21	105	4.67

Athletic SS from the DR has exciting potential and played well in his state-side debut. Has a good approach at the plate, but is more of a contact hitter. Needs to be more selective at the plate and improve pitch recognition. Defensively has good range, soft hands, a strong arm and should be able to stick at SS.

Jimenez,Luis

5 | Los Angeles (A) | EXP MLB DEBUT: 2013 | POTENTIAL: Starting 3B | 7D

Bats R Age 26
2006 FA (Venezuela)
Pwr + + +
BAvg + + +
Spd + +
Def + +

Year	Lev	Team	AB	R	H	HR	RBI	Avg	OB	Slg	OPS	bb%	ct%	Eye	SB	CS	x/h%	Iso	RC/G
2011	AA	Arkansas	490	62	142	18	94	290	327	486	813	5	85	0.38	15	6	42	196	5.32
2012	AAA	Salt Lake	485	78	150	16	85	309	335	495	830	4	86	0.27	17	7	37	186	5.44
2013	Rk	AZL Angels	13	3	6	1	4	462	462	692	1154	0	85	0.00	0	0	17	231	8.51
2013	AAA	Salt Lake	197	28	56	4	42	284	325	411	737	6	87	0.46	11	3	27	127	4.52
2013	MLB	LAA	104	15	27	0	5	260	274	317	591	2	73	0.07	0	2	22	58	2.47

Strong, aggressive INF who may lack upside, but has hitting utility. Reached big leagues due to offensive output and can steal bases thanks to instincts. Hits for BA and has pull power. Line drive focus limits HR upside, but can leg out doubles. Can be free swinger at plate. Plate discipline not a strength nor is speed or range.

Johnson,Micah

4 | Chicago (A) | EXP MLB DEBUT: 2015 | POTENTIAL: Starting 2B | 7C

Bats B Age 23
2012 (9) Indiana
Pwr + +
BAvg + + +
Spd + + + +
Def + +

Year	Lev	Team	AB	R	H	HR	RBI	Avg	OB	Slg	OPS	bb%	ct%	Eye	SB	CS	x/h%	Iso	RC/G
2012	Rk	Great Falls	271	49	74	4	25	273	373	391	764	14	73	0.58	19	6	26	118	5.36
2013	A	Kannapolis	304	76	104	6	42	342	419	530	948	12	78	0.60	61	19	33	188	7.65
2013	A+	Winston-Salem	211	28	58	1	15	275	308	360	668	5	87	0.37	22	7	21	85	3.74
2013	AA	Birmingham	21	2	5	0	1	238	238	238	476	0	81	0.00	1	0	0	0	0.95

Short, savvy INF who led minors in SB. Underwent elbow surgery after season, but will be ready for spring training. Gets on base and has plus speed and quickness. Offensive potential hindered by below average power, but puts bat to ball and goes to gaps. Despite quick first step, has poor hands and feet.

Jones,JaCoby

68 | Pittsburgh | EXP MLB DEBUT: 2016 | POTENTIAL: Starting OF | 7D

Bats R Age 22
2013 (3) LSU
Pwr + +
BAvg + +
Spd + + +
Def + + +

Year	Lev	Team	AB	R	H	HR	RBI	Avg	OB	Slg	OPS	bb%	ct%	Eye	SB	CS	x/h%	Iso	RC/G
2011	NCAA	Louisiana St.	195	36	66	4	32	338	377	467	843	6	81	0.32	13	8	24	128	5.77
2012	NCAA	Louisiana St.	245	42	62	4	29	253	296	363	659	6	81	0.32	11	5	29	110	3.55
2013	NCAA	Louisiana St.	201	42	59	6	31	294	385	448	833	13	78	0.68	12	3	31	154	6.08
2013	A-	Jamestown	61	14	19	1	10	311	344	459	803	5	77	0.21	3	2	26	148	5.34

3rd round pick after a standout career at LSU. Is a plus athlete who has good speed and plus raw power. Played SS and CF in his debut. Doesn't have the range or arm to stick on the infield over the long-term and a move to the OF seems likely. A knee injury limited him to just 15 games, but should be ready to go in '14.

Jones,James

789 | Seattle | EXP MLB DEBUT: 2014 | POTENTIAL: Starting OF | 7C

Bats R Age 25
2009 (4) Long Island
Pwr + +
BAvg + +
Spd + + +
Def + + +

Year	Lev	Team	AB	R	H	HR	RBI	Avg	OB	Slg	OPS	bb%	ct%	Eye	SB	CS	x/h%	Iso	RC/G
2010	A	Clinton	491	87	132	12	65	269	351	432	783	11	75	0.51	24	10	35	163	5.43
2011	A+	High Desert	296	42	73	5	29	247	340	378	719	12	69	0.46	16	3	34	132	4.74
2012	A+	High Desert	493	109	151	14	76	306	375	497	872	10	75	0.44	26	17	36	191	6.57
2013	AA	Jackson	363	44	100	6	45	275	347	419	766	10	80	0.56	28	9	30	143	5.15
2013	AAA	Tacoma	15	2	5	0	1	333	412	467	878	12	87	1.00	0	0	40	133	6.75

Strong-armed outfielder with outstanding athleticism in tall and lean package. Making better contact by taking more direct path to ball. Still needs work with pitch recognition, but has some wiry strength to reach seats. Set career high in SB, though speed is average at best. Plays solid RF with good range and incredible arm.

Jones,Ryder

5 | San Francisco | EXP MLB DEBUT: 2017 | POTENTIAL: Starting 3B | 8E

Bats L Age 20
2013 (2) HS (NC)
Pwr + + +
BAvg + +
Spd + +
Def + + +

Year	Lev	Team	AB	R	H	HR	RBI	Avg	OB	Slg	OPS	bb%	ct%	Eye	SB	CS	x/h%	Iso	RC/G
2013	Rk	AZL Giants	145	29	46	1	18	317	377	400	777	9	74	0.37	0	0	22	83	5.29

Strong, athletic 3B had good results in AZL. With good range and a strong arm, he should be an above average defender. Jones has a good approach in the box, with plus raw power and a good, smooth stroke from the left side. Still raw, many believe he could struggle against better pitching.

Joseph,Corban

4 | New York (A) | EXP MLB DEBUT: 2013 | POTENTIAL: Reserve 2B | 6C

Bats L Age 25
2008 (4) HS (TN)
Pwr + +
BAvg + + +
Spd +
Def + +

Year	Lev	Team	AB	R	H	HR	RBI	Avg	OB	Slg	OPS	bb%	ct%	Eye	SB	CS	x/h%	Iso	RC/G
2011	AA	Trenton	499	75	138	5	58	277	353	415	768	11	79	0.57	4	3	37	138	5.27
2012	AA	Trenton	86	9	27	2	6	314	416	430	846	15	85	1.15	0	0	22	116	6.34
2012	AAA	Scranton/W-B	327	50	87	13	56	266	368	474	842	14	83	0.93	0	1	46	208	6.21
2013	AAA	Scranton/W-B	188	30	45	6	19	239	316	383	699	10	79	0.54	2	0	33	144	4.16
2013	MLB	NYY	6	1	1	0	0	167	286	333	619	14	83	1.00	0	0	100	167	3.80

Athletic infielder whose season ended in May after shoulder surgery. Uses clean swing to make consistent, hard contact and has bat control for moderate BA potential. Has chance to hit for average pop but needs more leverage in stroke. Footwork isn't ideal for infield and lacks quickness and range to be average defender.

Joseph,Tommy

2 | Philadelphia | EXP MLB DEBUT: 2014 | POTENTIAL: Starting C | 7A

Bats R Age 22
2009 (2) HS (AZ)
Pwr + + + +
BAvg + +
Spd + +
Def + +

Year	Lev	Team	AB	R	H	HR	RBI	Avg	OB	Slg	OPS	bb%	ct%	Eye	SB	CS	x/h%	Iso	RC/G
2012	AA	Richmond	304	32	79	8	38	260	316	391	708	8	79	0.39	0	3	30	132	4.17
2013	Rk	GCL Phillies	3	0	1	0	0	333	600	333	933	40	67	2.00	0	0	0	0	9.29
2013	A+	Clearwater	42	0	4	0	1	95	95	143	238	0	69	0.00	0	0	50	48	-2.47
2013	AA	Reading	11	0	3	0	1	273	333	364	697	8	91	1.00	0	0	33	91	4.46
2013	AAA	Lehigh Valley	67	6	14	3	14	209	254	358	612	6	78	0.27	0	1	29	149	2.71

Played in only 36 games after a May concussion. Team eventually shut him down in August, though he caught during winter ball. Plus power his biggest draw, though defense has improved over past several seasons. Another concussion could move him out from behind the plate, where his value would plummet.

Judge,Aaron

9 | New York (A) | EXP MLB DEBUT: 2016 | POTENTIAL: Starting RF | 7C

Bats R Age 22
2013 (1) Fresno State
Pwr + + + +
BAvg + +
Spd + + +
Def + + +

Year	Lev	Team	AB	R	H	HR	RBI	Avg	OB	Slg	OPS	bb%	ct%	Eye	SB	CS	x/h%	Iso	RC/G
2011	NCAA	Fresno St.	187	38	67	2	30	358	434	465	899	12	78	0.60	11	1	22	107	6.99
2012	NCAA	Fresno St.	201	47	62	4	27	308	442	458	899	19	79	1.14	13	2	32	149	7.38
2013	NCAA	Fresno St.	206	45	76	12	36	369	461	655	1116	15	74	0.66	12	2	41	286	10.04
2013		Did not play/pros																	

Big, burly slugger who did not play after draft due to quad injury. Has significant power potential in long, strong arms and ability to put charge into ball. Power predicated more on strength than bat speed. Covers plate, but holes in swing may hinder BA and lead to K. Runs well for size and has arm strength ideal for RF.

Katoh,Gosuke

4 | New York (A) | EXP MLB DEBUT: 2018 | POTENTIAL: Starting 2B | 8D

Bats L Age 19
2013 (2) HS (CA)
Pwr + +
BAvg + + + +
Spd + + + +
Def + +

Year	Lev	Team	AB	R	H	HR	RBI	Avg	OB	Slg	OPS	bb%	ct%	Eye	SB	CS	x/h%	Iso	RC/G
2013	Rk	GCL Yankees	184	28	57	6	25	310	398	522	920	13	76	0.61	4	2	39	212	7.33

Lean, lanky INF who exceeded expectations with standout pro debut. Oozes athleticism and wiry strength to project as solid BA producer. Can be tough out due to disciplined eye and ability to make contact. Hits LHH well, though power potential is fringe-average at best. Has plus speed, but needs repetitions on defense.

Kelly,Carson — 25 — St. Louis

EXP MLB DEBUT: 2017 | POTENTIAL: Starting C/3B | 8D

Bats R | Age 19 | 2012 (2) HS (OR) | Pwr +++ | BAvg ++ | Spd ++ | Def ++

Year	Lev	Team	AB	R	H	HR	RBI	Avg	OB	Slg	OPS	bb%	ct%	Eye	SB	CS	x/h%	Iso	RC/G
2012	Rk	Johnson City	213	24	48	9	25	225	260	399	659	4	85	0.30	0	0	40	174	3.42
2013	A-	State College	271	35	75	4	32	277	326	387	714	7	89	0.65	1	0	28	111	4.40
2013	A	Peoria	146	18	32	2	13	219	283	301	584	8	83	0.52	0	0	25	82	2.80

Strong, agile player scuffled in full-season debut. Was a two-way player in high school and is still learning how to hit. Defensively has good hands and a strong arm. Could be more selective in his approach. The Cardinals have moved him behind the plate during instructional league and he is a work in progress.

Kelly,Ty — 457 — Seattle

EXP MLB DEBUT: 2014 | POTENTIAL: Utility player | 6B

Bats L | Age 25 | 2009 (13) UC-Davis | Pwr ++ | BAvg +++ | Spd ++ | Def ++

Year	Lev	Team	AB	R	H	HR	RBI	Avg	OB	Slg	OPS	bb%	ct%	Eye	SB	CS	x/h%	Iso	RC/G
2012	A+	Frederick	263	47	91	9	41	346	457	513	971	17	84	1.32	2	3	29	167	7.97
2012	AA	Bowie	172	24	53	1	27	308	383	413	796	11	84	0.75	1	0	26	105	5.62
2012	AAA	Norfolk	36	3	10	1	2	278	350	389	739	10	92	1.33	1	0	20	111	4.86
2013	AA	Bowie	283	51	80	1	47	283	392	382	774	15	83	1.04	4	2	30	99	5.62
2013	AAA	Tacoma	197	34	63	3	17	320	460	406	866	21	79	1.24	3	7	16	86	6.99

Instinctual prospect who draws tons of walks and has simple stroke with level swing path. Hits LHP well and slashes line drives to gaps. Power not part of game and lacks speed to steal bases. Can play variety of positions, though not a master of any. Range and arm are a bit short for infield and needs better routes in OF.

Kemp,Tony — 478 — Houston

EXP MLB DEBUT: 2016 | POTENTIAL: Utility player | 6B

Bats L | Age 22 | 2013 (5) Vanderbilt | Pwr + | BAvg +++ | Spd ++++ | Def ++

Year	Lev	Team	AB	R	H	HR	RBI	Avg	OB	Slg	OPS	bb%	ct%	Eye	SB	CS	x/h%	Iso	RC/G
2011	NCAA	Vanderbilt	252	58	83	0	34	329	415	417	832	13	87	1.16	17	5	18	87	6.22
2012	NCAA	Vanderbilt	241	55	63	1	31	261	364	386	750	14	83	0.93	21	4	32	124	5.28
2013	NCAA	Vanderbilt	266	64	104	0	33	391	462	485	947	12	88	1.09	34	14	18	94	7.47
2013	A	Quad Cities	98	21	25	1	9	255	376	316	692	16	82	1.06	4	2	12	61	4.53

Short-framed prospect who is tough out at top of lineup. Puts ball in play and draws walks, though may benefit from jumping on FB early in count. Hits LHP and has plus speed to steal bases. Has instincts on base and in field. Not a gifted defender, but getting better. Mostly played 2B in pro debut, but also saw action in OF.

Kepler,Max — 37 — Minnesota

EXP MLB DEBUT: 2016 | POTENTIAL: Starting 1B | 8E

Bats L | Age 21 | 2009 FA (Germany) | Pwr +++ | BAvg ++ | Spd +++ | Def ++

Year	Lev	Team	AB	R	H	HR	RBI	Avg	OB	Slg	OPS	bb%	ct%	Eye	SB	CS	x/h%	Iso	RC/G
2010	Rk	GCL Twins	140	15	40	0	11	286	346	343	689	8	81	0.48	6	1	18	57	4.12
2011	Rk	Elizabethton	191	29	50	1	24	262	341	366	708	11	72	0.43	1	1	30	105	4.53
2012	Rk	Elizabethton	232	40	69	10	49	297	371	539	909	10	86	0.82	7	0	45	241	6.81
2013	A	Cedar Rapids	236	35	56	9	40	237	308	424	731	9	82	0.56	2	0	41	186	4.57

Lanky, athletic prospect who is developing slowly and moving to 1B. Drives balls to all fields with balanced stroke and good contact. Struggles against LHP and still needs more strength to realize average power. Runs well underway and exhibits decent lateral movement, but lack of arm strength meant move to 1B.

Keys,Brent — 78 — Miami

EXP MLB DEBUT: 2015 | POTENTIAL: Starting CF | 7C

Bats L | Age 23 | 2009 (17) HS (CA) | Pwr + | BAvg +++ | Spd ++++ | Def +++

Year	Lev	Team	AB	R	H	HR	RBI	Avg	OB	Slg	OPS	bb%	ct%	Eye	SB	CS	x/h%	Iso	RC/G
2011	A-	Jamestown	106	13	36	1	12	340	352	387	739	2	92	0.22	6	2	8	47	4.29
2011	A	Greensboro	53	6	11	0	5	208	333	208	541	16	74	0.71	5	1	0	0	2.30
2012	A	Greensboro	370	72	124	5	51	335	391	449	840	8	92	1.13	18	5	23	114	5.96
2013	A+	Jupiter	381	57	132	2	33	346	417	399	816	11	93	1.77	13	9	12	52	5.88
2013	AA	Jacksonville	32	3	9	0	0	281	378	281	660	14	91	1.67	1	0	0	0	4.26

Quick, athletic OF with short, compact stroke and good approach at the plate. Keeps his strikeout totals low and draws walks. Power is not part of his game, but uses the whole field and keeps the ball on the ground to use his plus speed. With good range and solid reads, he has the athleticism to stick in CF as he progresses.

Kiermaier,Kevin — 8 — Tampa Bay

EXP MLB DEBUT: 2013 | POTENTIAL: Reserve OF | 6A

Bats L | Age 24 | 2010 (31) Parkland JC | Pwr ++ | BAvg +++ | Spd +++ | Def ++++

Year	Lev	Team	AB	R	H	HR	RBI	Avg	OB	Slg	OPS	bb%	ct%	Eye	SB	CS	x/h%	Iso	RC/G
2012	Rk	GCL Rays	6	0	1	0	0	167	167	167	333	0	67	0.00	0	0	0	0	-1.38
2012	A+	Charlotte	177	16	46	0	12	260	355	367	722	13	79	0.68	10	4	28	107	4.85
2012	AAA	Durham	9	2	3	0	1	333	500	333	833	25	89	3.00	0	0	0	0	7.01
2013	AA	Montgomery	371	65	114	5	28	307	361	434	795	8	84	0.51	14	11	25	127	5.36
2013	AAA	Durham	137	24	36	1	13	263	331	423	754	9	81	0.54	7	1	39	161	5.09

Instinctual, athletic OF who has made name as outstanding defender, but evolving into valued offensive contributor. Finished 2nd in SL in BA and uses quick, short stroke. Little punch in his bat, but has enough juice for gap power. Plays legit CF with great range, strong arm, and good speed.

Kivlehan,Patrick — 5 — Seattle

EXP MLB DEBUT: 2015 | POTENTIAL: Starting 3B | 7B

Bats R | Age 24 | 2012 (4) Rutgers | Pwr ++++ | BAvg +++ | Spd +++ | Def +++

Year	Lev	Team	AB	R	H	HR	RBI	Avg	OB	Slg	OPS	bb%	ct%	Eye	SB	CS	x/h%	Iso	RC/G
2012	NCAA	Rutgers	189	47	74	14	50	392	455	693	1148	10	79	0.55	24	4	36	302	9.76
2012	A-	Everett	282	46	85	12	52	301	346	511	856	6	67	0.20	14	1	38	209	6.46
2013	A	Clinton	223	26	63	3	31	283	333	386	719	7	81	0.40	5	3	25	103	4.36
2013	A+	High Desert	266	48	85	13	59	320	380	530	910	9	76	0.40	10	3	33	211	6.83

Natural-hitting infielder who is very athletic and has good strength in physical frame. Owns above average raw power and should grow as he learns to recognize pitches. Can focus on pulling ball too often and may benefit from using entire field. Has been average defender with good hands, though arm isn't strong.

Knapp,Andrew — 2 — Philadelphia

EXP MLB DEBUT: 2017 | POTENTIAL: Starting C | 7D

Bats B | Age 22 | 2013 (2) California | Pwr ++ | BAvg +++ | Spd + | Def +

Year	Lev	Team	AB	R	H	HR	RBI	Avg	OB	Slg	OPS	bb%	ct%	Eye	SB	CS	x/h%	Iso	RC/G
2011	NCAA	California	66	7	14	1	15	212	288	303	591	10	65	0.30	0	0	29	91	2.73
2012	NCAA	California	211	36	56	5	26	265	338	412	750	10	84	0.68	4	3	38	147	4.91
2013	NCAA	California	206	34	72	8	41	350	425	544	969	12	83	0.77	4	2	33	194	7.59
2013	A-	Williamsport	217	30	55	4	23	253	322	401	723	9	74	0.39	7	5	44	147	4.59

Advanced switch hitter with more of a gap-to-gap approach than raw power for now. Swing can get long, but health is priority #1: had off-season Tommy John surgery and will miss the beginning of 2014. Still work to do on defense, but could shift to OF, where there will be more emphasis on his bat to produce.

Kobernus,Jeff — 47 — Washington

EXP MLB DEBUT: 2013 | POTENTIAL: Backup OF | 7C

Bats R | Age 26 | 2009 (2) California | Pwr + | BAvg +++ | Spd ++++ | Def +++

Year	Lev	Team	AB	R	H	HR	RBI	Avg	OB	Slg	OPS	bb%	ct%	Eye	SB	CS	x/h%	Iso	RC/G
2010	A	Hagerstown	312	40	87	1	42	279	316	346	662	5	81	0.29	21	10	22	67	3.59
2011	A+	Potomac	489	67	138	7	52	282	312	387	698	4	82	0.24	53	8	24	104	3.93
2012	AA	Harrisburg	330	41	93	1	19	282	321	333	654	5	83	0.33	42	11	14	52	3.50
2013	AAA	Syracuse	371	59	118	1	36	318	366	388	754	7	84	0.47	42	9	19	70	4.83
2013	MLB	WAS	30	8	5	1	1	167	286	267	552	14	80	0.83	3	2	20	100	2.44

Doesn't have prototypical speedster frame, but continues to pile up 40+ SB. BA and bb% took a nice jump in '13. Has a quick bat and improving pitch recognition. Can contribute in every offensive category but power. Looks like he will spend most of his time as an OF going forward.

Kubitza,Kyle — 5 — Atlanta

EXP MLB DEBUT: 2015 | POTENTIAL: Backup 3B | 6C

Bats L | Age 23 | 2011 (3) Texas State | Pwr ++ | BAvg +++ | Spd +++ | Def ++

Year	Lev	Team	AB	R	H	HR	RBI	Avg	OB	Slg	OPS	bb%	ct%	Eye	SB	CS	x/h%	Iso	RC/G
2010	NCAA	Texas St.	229	59	82	11	58	358	447	607	1054	14	82	0.88	7	2	40	249	8.84
2011	NCAA	Texas St.	226	59	70	10	66	310	443	558	1000	19	79	1.13	16	3	41	248	8.61
2011	Rk	Danville	162	36	52	1	34	321	409	475	884	13	77	0.63	9	3	38	154	7.01
2012	A	Rome	448	68	107	9	59	239	345	393	738	14	72	0.57	18	11	39	154	5.03
2013	A+	Lynchburg	435	75	113	12	57	260	375	434	809	16	70	0.61	8	16	41	175	6.12

Solid utility type 3B had a better season in '13. Has above-average raw power and hit double-digit HR for the first time. Remains overly aggressive at the plate, striking out 132, but also drawing 80 walks. Has above-average speed for 3B and is solid defensively with soft hands, range, and a strong arm.

La Stella,Tommy — 4 — Atlanta

EXP MLB DEBUT: 2014 | POTENTIAL: Starting 2B | 7B

Bats L | Age 25 | 2011 (8) Coastal Carolina | Pwr ++ | BAvg +++ | Spd ++ | Def ++

Year	Lev	Team	AB	R	H	HR	RBI	Avg	OB	Slg	OPS	bb%	ct%	Eye	SB	CS	x/h%	Iso	RC/G
2011	A	Rome	232	46	76	9	40	328	395	543	938	10	88	0.93	2	2	36	216	7.11
2012	Rk	GCL Braves	13	4	3	1	3	231	412	615	1027	24	92	4.00	0	0	67	385	8.88
2012	A+	Lynchburg	298	43	90	5	56	302	377	460	837	11	92	1.50	13	2	36	158	6.15
2013	A+	Lynchburg	20	7	11	1	4	550	679	750	1429	29	95	8.00	1	1	18	200	14.04
2013	AA	Mississippi	283	32	97	4	41	343	419	473	892	12	88	1.09	7	1	28	131	6.77

Short, athletic 2B is one of the better pure hitters in the system. Has a polished approach at the plate and after three years has a .327 average. Has decent power for 2B and shoots balls into the gap with a short, quick stroke. Is below average defensively, but has enough offense to make him a big-league regular.

LaMarre,Ryan — 8 — Cincinnati
EXP MLB DEBUT: 2015 | POTENTIAL: Backup CF | 6C

Bats R Age 25 | 2010 (2) Michigan | Pwr ++ | BAvg ++ | Spd +++ | Def ++++

Year	Lev	Team	AB	R	H	HR	RBI	Avg	OB	Slg	OPS	bb%	ct%	Eye	SB	CS	x/h%	Iso	RC/G
2011	A+	Bakersfield	445	78	124	6	47	279	341	371	712	9	78	0.43	52	14	21	92	4.33
2011	AA	Carolina	15	3	4	0	0	267	389	333	722	17	80	1.00	3	0	25	67	5.01
2012	AA	Pensacola	482	68	127	5	32	263	345	353	698	11	75	0.50	30	10	24	89	4.30
2013	AA	Pensacola	451	55	111	10	39	246	313	373	686	9	79	0.47	22	13	30	126	4.00
2013	AAA	Louisville	11	4	2	0	0	182	250	182	432	8	91	1.00	1	0	0	0	1.43

Posted strong second half in '13, showing better plate discipline, cutting down Ks, and had nice power bump. Played hurt for much of '12 and showed better skills once healthy. Speed and defense are best tools. Utilizes line-drive stroke with gap power, draws walks, but needs to make better contact. Has the range to play CF.

Lamb,Jacob — 5 — Arizona
EXP MLB DEBUT: 2015 | POTENTIAL: Starting 3B | 8D

Bats L Age 23 | 2012 (6) Washington | Pwr +++ | BAvg +++ | Spd ++ | Def ++++

Year	Lev	Team	AB	R	H	HR	RBI	Avg	OB	Slg	OPS	bb%	ct%	Eye	SB	CS	x/h%	Iso	RC/G
2011	NCAA	Washington	212	20	66	3	26	311	351	434	785	6	85	0.41	2	0	27	123	5.11
2012	NCAA	Washington	190	32	61	3	30	321	414	442	856	14	86	1.15	4	4	26	121	6.46
2012	Rk	Missoula	280	47	92	9	57	329	382	539	921	8	82	0.47	8	2	39	211	6.88
2013	Rk	AZL D'backs	17	4	5	0	5	294	368	412	780	11	71	0.40	0	0	40	118	5.65
2013	A+	Visalia	231	44	70	13	47	303	423	558	981	17	70	0.69	0	0	47	255	8.55

Strong, athletic 3B had a breakout season. Has a good approach at the plate and showed solid power, though doesn't have premium bat speed and stroke can get long. Moves well for size and is a good defender. Missed action with a broken hamate bone, but fared well in the Arizona Fall League, where he hit .299 in 77 AB.

Lee,Hak-Ju — 6 — Tampa Bay
EXP MLB DEBUT: 2014 | POTENTIAL: Starting SS | 8B

Bats L Age 23 | 2008 FA (South Korea) | Pwr ++ | BAvg +++ | Spd ++++ | Def ++++

Year	Lev	Team	AB	R	H	HR	RBI	Avg	OB	Slg	OPS	bb%	ct%	Eye	SB	CS	x/h%	Iso	RC/G
2010	A	Peoria	485	85	137	1	40	282	348	351	699	9	82	0.57	32	7	20	68	4.30
2011	A+	Charlotte	400	82	127	4	23	318	382	443	825	10	82	0.58	28	14	24	125	5.87
2011	AA	Montgomery	100	16	19	1	7	190	270	310	580	10	78	0.50	5	2	32	120	2.80
2012	AA	Montgomery	475	68	124	4	37	261	333	360	693	10	79	0.50	37	9	23	99	4.21
2013	AAA	Durham	45	13	19	1	7	422	536	600	1136	20	80	1.22	6	2	26	178	10.51

Athletic, fast INF who tore knee ligaments in April and missed rest of season. Best tools revolve around speed and glove as he is consistent 30+ SB guy and plays plus SS defense. Owns soft hands and strong, accurate arm while ranging well. Can shoot gaps with line drive stroke, but likes to hit to opp field.

Lennerton,Jordan — 3 — Detroit
EXP MLB DEBUT: 2014 | POTENTIAL: Starting 1B | 7D

Bats L Age 28 | 2008 (33) Oregon State | Pwr +++ | BAvg +++ | Spd + | Def +++

Year	Lev	Team	AB	R	H	HR	RBI	Avg	OB	Slg	OPS	bb%	ct%	Eye	SB	CS	x/h%	Iso	RC/G
2010	A	West Michigan	214	21	62	3	23	290	380	402	781	13	70	0.48	0	0	29	112	5.64
2010	A+	Lakeland	206	25	62	9	33	301	390	505	895	13	74	0.56	1	0	39	204	6.94
2011	A+	Lakeland	484	75	138	14	75	285	399	444	844	16	74	0.74	0	0	35	159	6.47
2012	AA	Erie	495	73	133	21	82	269	369	469	838	14	72	0.56	2	4	42	200	6.29
2013	AAA	Toledo	514	68	143	17	57	278	380	430	810	14	74	0.63	0	3	30	152	5.85

Consistent hitter who is starting to emerge after 3 yrs in A ball. Season mirrored career stats and appeared in Futures Game. Draws walks with mature approach and offers strength and bat speed for average pop. Can be too patient at plate and will chase pitches with two strikes. Shows good glove at 1B, but offers little speed.

Leon,Sandy — 2 — Washington
EXP MLB DEBUT: 2012 | POTENTIAL: Backup C | 5B

Bats B Age 25 | 2007 FA (Venezuela) | Pwr + | BAvg ++ | Spd + | Def ++++

Year	Lev	Team	AB	R	H	HR	RBI	Avg	OB	Slg	OPS	bb%	ct%	Eye	SB	CS	x/h%	Iso	RC/G
2012	AAA	Syracuse	52	8	18	2	4	346	469	558	1026	19	77	1.00	0	0	39	212	9.01
2012	MLB	WAS	30	2	8	0	2	267	353	333	686	12	63	0.36	0	0	25	67	4.47
2013	A-	Auburn	13	0	1	0	0	77	77	77	154	0	77	0.00	0	0	0	0	-3.16
2013	AA	Harrisburg	310	35	55	3	26	177	286	252	537	13	82	0.82	0	0	29	74	2.45
2013	MLB	WAS	1	0	0	0	0	0	0	0	0	0	0	0.00	0	0	0	0	0.00

Took big step back in '13 after breakout '12. Plus defender with strong arm/quick release came nowhere near his previous offensive output. Seems doubtful he can ever hit enough to be a regular. Slow bat and poor pitch recognition; power non-existent, though can make decent contact.

Lin,Tzu-Wei — 6 — Boston
EXP MLB DEBUT: 2017 | POTENTIAL: Starting SS | 8E

Bats L Age 20 | 2012 FA (Taiwan) | Pwr + | BAvg +++ | Spd ++++ | Def +++

Year	Lev	Team	AB	R	H	HR	RBI	Avg	OB	Slg	OPS	bb%	ct%	Eye	SB	CS	x/h%	Iso	RC/G
2012	Rk	GCL Red Sox	110	21	28	0	16	255	349	318	667	13	75	0.57	4	2	21	64	4.03
2013	A-	Lowell	230	34	52	1	20	226	310	296	606	11	74	0.47	12	4	23	70	3.08

Diminutive, quick INF who could become leadoff hitter. Despite limited size, offers wiry strength and can punch balls to all fields with fast bat. Needs to make more contact and could stand to draw more walks and get on base. Can be terror once one; should stick at SS with great hands and range.

Lindor,Francisco — 6 — Cleveland
EXP MLB DEBUT: 2014 | POTENTIAL: Starting SS | 9B

Bats B Age 20 | 2011 (1) HS (PR) | Pwr ++ | BAvg ++++ | Spd ++++ | Def ++++

Year	Lev	Team	AB	R	H	HR	RBI	Avg	OB	Slg	OPS	bb%	ct%	Eye	SB	CS	x/h%	Iso	RC/G
2011	A-	Mahoning Val	19	4	6	0	2	316	350	316	666	5	74	0.20	1	0	0	0	3.48
2012	A	Lake County	490	83	126	6	42	257	339	355	694	11	84	0.78	27	12	26	98	4.35
2013	A+	Carolina	327	51	100	1	27	306	373	410	783	10	88	0.90	20	5	26	104	5.44
2013	AA	Akron	76	14	22	1	7	289	400	395	795	16	91	2.00	5	2	23	105	5.95

Pure, instinctual INF who found two levels to his liking. Game comes easy to him and he provides consistent and steady offensive production from both sides of plate. Has yet to tap into power, but has plus hand-eye coordination for easy BA. Owns plus glove with above average range and arm. Has great chance to realize vast potential.

Lindsey,Taylor — 4 — Los Angeles (A)
EXP MLB DEBUT: 2014 | POTENTIAL: Starting 2B | 7A

Bats L Age 22 | 2010 (1-S) HS (AZ) | Pwr +++ | BAvg +++ | Spd ++ | Def ++

Year	Lev	Team	AB	R	H	HR	RBI	Avg	OB	Slg	OPS	bb%	ct%	Eye	SB	CS	x/h%	Iso	RC/G
2010	Rk	AZL Angels	194	26	55	0	18	284	325	407	732	6	83	0.36	8	3	33	124	4.62
2011	Rk	Orem	290	64	105	9	46	362	389	593	983	4	84	0.28	10	4	41	231	7.34
2012	A+	Inland Empire	547	79	158	9	58	289	325	408	732	5	88	0.44	8	6	26	119	4.46
2013	AA	Arkansas	508	68	139	17	56	274	336	441	777	9	82	0.53	4	4	32	167	5.10

Fundamentally sound, steady INF who posted career high in HR, though focuses more on hard, line-drive contact. Uses entire field and has ideal hand-eye coordination and pitch recognition. Speed is below average and lack of range and quickness keep him at 2B. Could become offensive-oriented 2B in near-term.

Lipka,Matt — 8 — Atlanta
EXP MLB DEBUT: 2014 | POTENTIAL: Backup OF | 6C

Bats R Age 22 | 2010 (1) HS (TX) | Pwr ++ | BAvg ++ | Spd ++++ | Def ++

Year	Lev	Team	AB	R	H	HR	RBI	Avg	OB	Slg	OPS	bb%	ct%	Eye	SB	CS	x/h%	Iso	RC/G
2010	Rk	Danville	16	1	2	0	1	125	176	125	301	6	88	0.50	1	0	0	0	-0.37
2010	Rk	GCL Braves	192	33	58	1	24	302	350	401	751	7	89	0.64	20	3	22	99	4.86
2011	A	Rome	530	78	131	1	37	247	302	304	606	7	84	0.51	28	14	19	57	3.11
2012	A+	Lynchburg	199	32	54	2	13	271	338	337	675	9	84	0.63	12	6	15	65	3.96
2013	A+	Lynchburg	525	76	132	5	40	251	291	362	653	5	80	0.27	37	14	31	110	3.48

Speedy CF prospect took a step backwards as he struggled in repeat of High-A. Has plus speed and ability to create havoc on the bases, but has limited power and contact rate plummeted. Conversion from SS to CF has gone well defensively. Still has good athleticism and some potential, but clock is ticking.

Liriano,Rymer — 8 — San Diego
EXP MLB DEBUT: 2015 | POTENTIAL: Starting CF | 9D

Bats R Age 23 | 2007 FA (DR) | Pwr ++++ | BAvg +++ | Spd ++++ | Def +++

Year	Lev	Team	AB	R	H	HR	RBI	Avg	OB	Slg	OPS	bb%	ct%	Eye	SB	CS	x/h%	Iso	RC/G
2010	A+	Lake Elsinore	50	3	11	1	6	220	291	320	611	9	76	0.42	3	0	27	100	2.99
2011	A	Fort Wayne	455	81	145	12	62	319	382	499	881	9	79	0.49	65	20	34	180	6.54
2011	A+	Lake Elsinore	55	8	7	0	6	127	213	182	395	10	76	0.46	1	1	29	55	0.32
2012	A+	Lake Elsinore	282	41	84	5	41	298	347	443	790	7	76	0.30	22	7	35	145	5.33
2012	AA	San Antonio	183	24	46	3	20	251	325	377	702	10	73	0.40	10	1	33	126	4.33

Toolsy and strong outfielder who missed entire season after TJ surgery in February. Has potential to hit for power and steal bases due to eclectic mix of talents. Needs to make more contact and can expand strike zone due to lack of pitch recognition. Ranges very well in RF with plus arm and speed.

Lopes,Timmy — 4 — Seattle
EXP MLB DEBUT: 2016 | POTENTIAL: Utility player | 6B

Bats R Age 20 | 2012 (6) HS (CA) | Pwr ++ | BAvg +++ | Spd +++ | Def +++

Year	Lev	Team	AB	R	H	HR	RBI	Avg	OB	Slg	OPS	bb%	ct%	Eye	SB	CS	x/h%	Iso	RC/G
2012	Rk	AZL Mariners	215	42	68	0	32	316	385	479	864	10	87	0.83	7	3	34	163	6.51
2012	A+	High Desert	12	2	3	0	1	250	250	417	667	0	92	0.00	0	0	33	167	3.72
2013	A	Clinton	334	40	91	1	36	272	314	344	658	6	86	0.43	10	7	21	72	3.67

Smooth, balanced INF who is steady with glove and makes routine plays. Arm is best suited for 2B, but has range and actions for SS. Doesn't hit for much power, though puts ball in play with consistent approach and fluid swing. Owns average speed, but lacks impact tools to project as everyday player.

Lopez,Jack — 46 — Kansas City
EXP MLB DEBUT: 2016 | POTENTIAL: Starting SS | 7D

Bats R Age 21
2011 (16) HS (FL)
Pwr +
BAvg ++
Spd ++++
Def +++

Year	Lev	Team	AB	R	H	HR	RBI	Avg	OB	Slg	OPS	bb%	ct%	Eye	SB	CS	x/h%	Iso	RC/G
2012	Rk	Idaho Falls	13	6	5	0	3	385	467	538	1005	13	92	2.00	1	0	20	154	8.32
2012	A	Kane County	261	30	58	0	16	222	262	272	534	5	84	0.33	14	4	19	50	2.11
2013	A+	Wilmington	478	62	110	4	45	230	284	301	585	7	81	0.40	27	11	18	71	2.73

Short, quick INF who mostly plays SS, but can slide over and play 2B equally well. Most value comes on defensive side with smooth, quick actions and excellent range to both sides. Arm strength is sufficient for any spot. Steals bases with plus speed and instincts. Needs to be more patient as well as add strength for gap power.

Lugo,Dawel — 6 — Toronto
EXP MLB DEBUT: 2017 | POTENTIAL: Starting SS | 8E

Bats R Age 19
2011 FA (DR)
Pwr ++
BAvg +++
Spd ++
Def +++

Year	Lev	Team	AB	R	H	HR	RBI	Avg	OB	Slg	OPS	bb%	ct%	Eye	SB	CS	x/h%	Iso	RC/G
2012	Rk	GCL Blue Jays	170	20	38	2	20	224	254	329	584	4	85	0.28	5	1	24	106	2.68
2013	Rk	Bluefield	192	28	57	6	36	297	315	469	783	3	85	0.18	1	0	33	172	4.81
2013	A-	Vancouver	69	6	17	1	8	246	257	348	605	1	81	0.08	0	0	29	101	2.65

Pure-hitting INF with high upside thanks to impressive tools on both sides. Plays decent SS now, but may outgrow position and move to 3B. Has strong arm and quick actions. Has exceptional bat control, but swing-at-anything approach leads to contact issue. Has raw power with fast bat and can use entire field.

Mahtook,Mikie — 89 — Tampa Bay
EXP MLB DEBUT: 2014 | POTENTIAL: Starting OF | 7C

Bats R Age 24
2011 (1) LSU
Pwr ++
BAvg +++
Spd +++
Def +++

Year	Lev	Team	AB	R	H	HR	RBI	Avg	OB	Slg	OPS	bb%	ct%	Eye	SB	CS	x/h%	Iso	RC/G
2010	NCAA	Louisiana St.	239	68	80	14	50	335	426	623	1049	14	77	0.70	22	10	46	289	8.91
2011	NCAA	Louisiana St.	196	61	75	14	56	383	489	709	1199	17	84	1.28	29	9	41	327	10.68
2012	A+	Charlotte	341	44	99	5	37	290	346	419	765	8	79	0.41	19	6	27	129	5.01
2012	AA	Montgomery	153	17	38	4	25	248	299	405	704	7	80	0.35	4	3	39	157	4.13
2013	AA	Montgomery	511	71	130	7	68	254	312	386	698	8	80	0.42	25	8	35	131	4.19

All-around outfielder who brings several tools to the table, though none stand out. Puts charge into ball with clean, strong stroke. Has tendency to swing and miss while chasing breaking balls and could stand to be more selective. Runs very well on base and in outfield where routes and angles are ideal. Owns average, accurate arm.

Margot,Manuel — 8 — Boston
EXP MLB DEBUT: 2018 | POTENTIAL: Starting CF | 8D

Bats R Age 19
2011 FA (DR)
Pwr ++
BAvg +++
Spd ++++
Def +++

Year	Lev	Team	AB	R	H	HR	RBI	Avg	OB	Slg	OPS	bb%	ct%	Eye	SB	CS	x/h%	Iso	RC/G
2013	A-	Lowell	185	29	50	1	21	270	348	351	699	11	78	0.55	18	8	22	81	4.34

Raw, fast OF who impressed in first season in U.S. Knows strike zone and uses quick bat to make hard contact. Can expand the zone at times, but generally works counts. Has average power potential despite frame and should be menace on basepaths. Plays CF with fine routes and jumps while arm is good for corner.

Marin,Adrian — 6 — Baltimore
EXP MLB DEBUT: 2016 | POTENTIAL: Starting SS | 8D

Bats R Age 20
2012 (3) HS (FL)
Pwr ++
BAvg +++
Spd +++
Def +++

Year	Lev	Team	AB	R	H	HR	RBI	Avg	OB	Slg	OPS	bb%	ct%	Eye	SB	CS	x/h%	Iso	RC/G
2012	Rk	GCL Orioles	178	24	51	0	13	287	328	360	688	6	81	0.32	6	1	20	73	3.97
2012	A	Delmarva	21	5	6	0	2	286	318	286	604	5	90	0.50	2	0	0	0	3.02
2013	A	Delmarva	388	30	103	4	48	265	307	356	662	6	77	0.26	11	4	24	90	3.56

Pure SS with natural defensive instincts. Owns quickness and athleticism with ideal infield actions. Ranges well, but needs consistency and focus. Bat lags behind glove, though has projection with good bat speed and control. Strikes out a lot despite lack of power, but can beat out grounders with solid wheels.

Marisnick,Jake — 8 — Miami
EXP MLB DEBUT: 2013 | POTENTIAL: Starting CF | 9D

Bats R Age 23
2009 (3) HS (CA)
Pwr +++
BAvg ++
Spd ++++
Def +++++

Year	Lev	Team	AB	R	H	HR	RBI	Avg	OB	Slg	OPS	bb%	ct%	Eye	SB	CS	x/h%	Iso	RC/G
2012	A+	Dunedin	266	41	70	6	35	263	329	451	780	9	79	0.47	10	5	44	188	5.29
2012	AA	New Hampshire	223	25	52	2	15	233	269	336	606	5	80	0.24	14	4	31	103	2.87
2013	A+	Jupiter	15	2	3	0	0	200	200	267	467	0	93	0.00	0	0	33	67	1.53
2013	AA	Jacksonville	265	43	78	12	46	294	337	502	839	6	74	0.25	11	6	36	208	5.80
2013	MLB	MIA	109	6	20	1	5	183	226	248	474	5	75	0.22	3	1	20	64	1.05

Athletic OF with above average tools across board aside from hit tool. Has good bat speed, but has aggressive approach and chases pitches out of the zone. Has plus raw power that he is beginning to tap into, and plus speed, capable of 20+ SB. A plus-plus defender in CF, he has great range and super throwing arm.

Marlette,Tyler — 2 — Seattle
EXP MLB DEBUT: 2016 | POTENTIAL: Starting C | 7B

Bats R Age 21
2011 (5) HS (FL)
Pwr +++
BAvg +++
Spd ++
Def +++

Year	Lev	Team	AB	R	H	HR	RBI	Avg	OB	Slg	OPS	bb%	ct%	Eye	SB	CS	x/h%	Iso	RC/G
2011	Rk	Pulaski	45	4	7	0	2	156	156	200	356	0	71	0.00	0	0	29	44	-0.80
2012	Rk	Pulaski	208	23	59	5	23	284	304	423	727	3	78	0.13	3	1	32	139	4.18
2012	A-	Everett	5	0	2	0	0	400	400	600	1000	0	80	0.00	0	1	50	200	7.60
2013	A	Clinton	270	36	82	6	37	304	361	448	809	8	80	0.45	10	4	30	144	5.52

Short, strong C who fared well in first year in full-season ball. Combines bat speed and contact-oriented approach to produce BA while power starting to come along. Has punch to all fields, though has tendency to swing at pitches out of zone. Becoming good defender due to more accurate arm, though receiving still lags.

Marrero,Deven — 6 — Boston
EXP MLB DEBUT: 2015 | POTENTIAL: Starting SS | 7C

Bats R Age 23
2012 (1) Arizona State
Pwr ++
BAvg ++
Spd ++++
Def ++++

Year	Lev	Team	AB	R	H	HR	RBI	Avg	OB	Slg	OPS	bb%	ct%	Eye	SB	CS	x/h%	Iso	RC/G
2011	NCAA	Arizona St.	207	30	66	2	20	319	359	444	804	6	86	0.45	10	5	29	126	5.38
2012	NCAA	Arizona St.	208	36	58	4	32	279	333	438	771	8	92	1.06	10	3	34	159	5.19
2012	A-	Lowell	246	45	66	2	24	268	357	374	731	12	80	0.71	24	6	29	106	4.86
2013	A+	Salem	332	50	85	2	21	256	340	334	674	11	82	0.70	21	2	26	78	4.09
2013	AA	Portland	72	7	17	0	5	236	329	236	565	12	78	0.63	6	0	0	0	2.60

Natural, quick INF who has all attributes of above average defender. Gets to balls to both sides and has incredible arm. Swing and approach not conducive to much power, but recognizes spin and punches ball to gaps. Steals bases due to speed and honed instincts. If he can develop more with bat, he could be everyday shortstop.

Marte,Alfredo — 79 — Arizona
EXP MLB DEBUT: 2013 | POTENTIAL: Backup OF | 6B

Bats R Age 25
2005 FA (DR)
Pwr +++
BAvg ++
Spd ++
Def ++

Year	Lev	Team	AB	R	H	HR	RBI	Avg	OB	Slg	OPS	bb%	ct%	Eye	SB	CS	x/h%	Iso	RC/G
2011	A+	Visalia	234	35	70	7	33	299	339	479	817	6	82	0.33	5	0	36	179	5.45
2011	AA	Mobile	43	4	10	1	6	233	298	326	623	9	77	0.40	1	0	20	93	3.09
2012	AA	Mobile	398	68	117	20	75	294	350	523	872	8	82	0.47	6	6	41	229	6.15
2013	AAA	Reno	311	37	87	7	48	280	327	431	758	7	80	0.35	2	1	37	151	4.82
2013	MLB	ARI	43	4	8	0	4	186	255	256	511	9	72	0.33	0	0	38	70	1.70

Followed breakout with a decent campaign and made his MLB debut. Maintained gains in ct% at AAA, but power went AWOL. Solid defender with good range, but the raw power is going to be his calling card. Should see action in ARI in '14, but most likely as a 4th OF.

Marte,Ketel — 46 — Seattle
EXP MLB DEBUT: 2017 | POTENTIAL: Starting 2B/SS | 8E

Bats B Age 20
2010 FA (DR)
Pwr +
BAvg +++
Spd ++++
Def ++++

Year	Lev	Team	AB	R	H	HR	RBI	Avg	OB	Slg	OPS	bb%	ct%	Eye	SB	CS	x/h%	Iso	RC/G
2012	A-	Everett	251	36	62	0	22	247	281	279	560	5	86	0.34	14	4	10	32	2.44
2012	A	Clinton	14	3	4	0	2	286	375	286	661	13	79	0.67	1	0	0	0	3.87
2013	A	Clinton	378	61	115	0	29	304	331	370	701	4	90	0.38	16	8	17	66	4.11
2013	A+	High Desert	86	18	22	1	8	256	289	337	626	4	87	0.36	4	3	14	81	3.20

Flashy, quick INF whose glove far surpasses bat at present. Can easily play both MIF spots with plus range and first step quickness. Has instincts and speed to steal bases. Offensive production predicated on extreme amount of contact with short stroke. Doesn't swing hard and lacks strength for any power.

Martin,Brandon — 6 — Tampa Bay
EXP MLB DEBUT: 2016 | POTENTIAL: Starting SS | 8E

Bats R Age 20
2011 (1-S) HS (CA)
Pwr +++
BAvg ++
Spd +++
Def +++

Year	Lev	Team	AB	R	H	HR	RBI	Avg	OB	Slg	OPS	bb%	ct%	Eye	SB	CS	x/h%	Iso	RC/G
2011	Rk	GCL Rays	47	10	12	1	3	255	352	340	692	13	74	0.58	5	3	17	85	4.20
2012	Rk	Princeton	254	46	53	10	32	209	269	402	671	8	71	0.29	8	1	47	193	3.71
2013	A	Bowling Green	262	29	54	7	39	206	260	347	607	7	75	0.29	10	5	37	141	2.84

Quick, athletic INF who is excellent defender with solid instincts and feel for SS. Possesses strong, accurate arm and good range to both sides. Always in position to make routine plays. Offers good power with leveraged stroke and should grow into average pop. Long swing hinders BA and elevates K rate.

Martinez,Alberth — 789 — San Diego

EXP MLB DEBUT: 2016 | POTENTIAL: Starting CF | **7C**

Bats R Age 23
2010 FA (Venezuela)
Pwr +++
BAvg +++
Spd +++
Def ++++

Year	Lev	Team	AB	R	H	HR	RBI	Avg	OB	Slg	OPS	bb%	ct%	Eye	SB	CS	x/h%	Iso	RC/G
2011	A	Fort Wayne	13	0	0	0	0	0	71	0	71	7	54	0.17	0	1		0	-6.39
2011	AAA	Tucson	17	0	2	0	0	118	118	118	235	0	59	0.00	0	0	0	0	-3.14
2012	A-	Eugene	232	37	59	0	20	254	322	310	632	9	84	0.61	9	4	20	56	3.51
2012	A	Fort Wayne	62	8	8	0	3	129	182	194	375	6	77	0.29	3	0	50	65	0.01
2013	A	Fort Wayne	358	63	99	10	58	277	348	478	825	10	81	0.57	10	4	43	201	5.87

Long and lean outfielder who is taking awhile to develop, but has quality skills. Set career high in HR and has average power potential. Exhibits some feel for bat control and uses average speed well on base. Can be very good defender at all spots and has excellent range and instincts.

Martinez,Francisco — 5 — Detroit

EXP MLB DEBUT: 2015 | POTENTIAL: Starting 3B | **7D**

Bats R Age 23
2007 FA (Venezuela)
Pwr ++
BAvg +++
Spd ++++
Def +++

Year	Lev	Team	AB	R	H	HR	RBI	Avg	OB	Slg	OPS	bb%	ct%	Eye	SB	CS	x/h%	Iso	RC/G
2011	AA	Jackson	129	20	40	3	23	310	331	481	811	3	81	0.17	3	2	33	171	5.25
2012	Rk	AZL Mariners	28	7	8	0	7	286	310	500	810	3	79	0.17	1	0	50	214	5.63
2012	AA	Jackson	352	55	80	2	23	227	311	295	607	11	76	0.51	27	7	24	68	3.10
2013	A+	Lakeland	288	38	85	3	28	295	343	378	722	7	81	0.38	11	3	20	83	4.36
2013	AA	Jackson	126	8	26	0	5	206	242	254	496	5	66	0.14	7	0	23	48	1.24

Athletic prospect who has tools to succeed, but hasn't put everything together. Possesses very fast bat, but violent swing hinders shot at BA. Raw power hasn't yet translated to game action and won't reach potential without shortening stroke. Runs well for size and is good defender. Can play variety of positions.

Martinez,Wilton — 9 — Seattle

EXP MLB DEBUT: 2017 | POTENTIAL: Starting OF | **9E**

Bats R Age 20
2011 FA (DR)
Pwr ++++
BAvg ++
Spd ++
Def +++

Year	Lev	Team	AB	R	H	HR	RBI	Avg	OB	Slg	OPS	bb%	ct%	Eye	SB	CS	x/h%	Iso	RC/G
2013	Rk	Pulaski	201	29	42	12	33	209	254	443	696	6	68	0.18	3	2	52	234	3.94

Tall and projectable outfielder who led APPY in HR. Struggles to make consistent contact and can be easy out with long swing. Profiles very well in RF with excellent athleticism and power potential. Owns above average bat speed and runs fairly well for size. Plays solid defense due to strong arm and OK jumps.

Martinson,Jason — 6 — Washington

EXP MLB DEBUT: 2015 | POTENTIAL: Utility INF | **6C**

Bats R Age 25
2010 (5) Texas State
Pwr ++
BAvg ++
Spd +++
Def +++

Year	Lev	Team	AB	R	H	HR	RBI	Avg	OB	Slg	OPS	bb%	ct%	Eye	SB	CS	x/h%	Iso	RC/G
2011	A	Hagerstown	433	64	109	19	64	252	351	448	799	13	67	0.46	26	6	40	196	5.86
2012	A	Hagerstown	265	68	72	10	63	272	381	449	830	15	67	0.53	23	3	33	177	6.44
2012	A+	Potomac	237	36	51	12	43	215	279	409	688	8	67	0.27	7	2	35	194	3.95
2013	A+	Potomac	254	44	68	12	53	268	363	484	847	13	65	0.43	15	2	40	217	6.70
2013	AA	Harrisburg	173	19	32	4	19	185	269	306	576	10	68	0.36	2	0	31	121	2.49

Strong, athletic SS continues to show nice pop at the plate. Can be overly aggressive and strikes out too much, though he draws a good amount of walks. Needs to improve pitch recognition. Owns a plus arm defensively and possesses the speed and range to adequately cover 3B.

Mathisen,Wyatt — 2 — Pittsburgh

EXP MLB DEBUT: 2016 | POTENTIAL: Starting C | **8D**

Bats R Age 20
2012 (2) HS (TX)
Pwr ++
BAvg +++
Spd +++
Def ++

Year	Lev	Team	AB	R	H	HR	RBI	Avg	OB	Slg	OPS	bb%	ct%	Eye	SB	CS	x/h%	Iso	RC/G
2012	Rk	GCL Pirates	139	24	41	1	15	295	368	374	742	10	86	0.84	10	8	22	79	4.92
2013	Rk	GCL Pirates	22	5	9	0	3	409	552	455	1006	24	91	3.50	0	0	11	45	9.08
2013	A-	Jamestown	26	4	7	0	3	269	387	269	656	16	73	0.71	1	0	0	0	3.93
2013	A	West Virginia	119	13	22	0	9	185	242	210	452	7	82	0.41	1	0	14	25	1.12

Strong, athletic C struggled at Low-A. Shoulder injury may have been partially to blame and was shutdown in mid-May. Looked much better when returned to action. Good defensive catcher with a strong arm. At the plate, showed good plate discipline and should rebound nicely in '14, but has yet to show much power as a pro.

Mattair,Travis — 3 — Cincinnati

EXP MLB DEBUT: 2015 | POTENTIAL: Backup 3B/1B | **6D**

Bats R Age 25
2007 (2) HS (WA)
Pwr ++
BAvg +++
Spd ++
Def ++

Year	Lev	Team	AB	R	H	HR	RBI	Avg	OB	Slg	OPS	bb%	ct%	Eye	SB	CS	x/h%	Iso	RC/G
2009	A	Lakewood	450	55	106	3	39	236	317	333	651	11	71	0.41	12	2	32	98	3.71
2011	A	Lakewood	124	15	33	2	18	266	305	395	701	5	72	0.20	0	1	33	129	4.12
2011	A+	Clearwater	188	19	39	6	26	207	270	356	626	8	74	0.33	4	0	41	149	3.09
2012	A+	Bakersfield	492	73	135	19	82	274	341	465	807	9	76	0.42	3	6	39	191	5.55
2013	AA	Pensacola	475	52	115	13	57	242	302	364	667	8	78	0.39	2	2	26	122	3.64

Has split time between 3B and 1B the past two seasons. Followed breakout 2012 with a so-so 2013. Still strikes out way too much and batting average took a hit while plate approach took a step backwards. Shows decent power potential but not enough tools for more than backup corner IF ceiling.

Maxwell,Bruce — 2 — Oakland

EXP MLB DEBUT: 2015 | POTENTIAL: Starting C | **7C**

Bats L Age 23
2012 (2) Birmingham So.
Pwr ++
BAvg +++
Spd +
Def ++

Year	Lev	Team	AB	R	H	HR	RBI	Avg	OB	Slg	OPS	bb%	ct%	Eye	SB	CS	x/h%	Iso	RC/G
2012	Rk	AZL Athletics	21	8	11	0	4	524	615	714	1330	19	86	1.67	0	0	36	190	12.83
2012	A-	Vermont	228	22	58	0	22	254	331	316	646	10	85	0.74	1	0	24	61	3.79
2013	A	Beloit	199	25	57	2	28	286	363	387	750	11	85	0.83	0	0	28	101	5.04
2013	A+	Stockton	175	19	46	5	21	263	335	394	729	10	81	0.56	0	0	28	131	4.55

Tall, physical C who is sleeper, but could see prospect status rise with continued improvement behind plate. Exhibits arm strength with quick transfer, but receiving ability still raw. Lacks agility and athleticism. Owns mature eye at plate and exhibits line drive power at present. Has strength for power, but needs to pull ball more.

Mazara,Nomar — 9 — Texas

EXP MLB DEBUT: 2017 | POTENTIAL: Starting OF | **9E**

Bats L Age 19
2011 FA (DR)
Pwr +++
BAvg ++
Spd ++
Def +++

Year	Lev	Team	AB	R	H	HR	RBI	Avg	OB	Slg	OPS	bb%	ct%	Eye	SB	CS	x/h%	Iso	RC/G
2012	Rk	AZL Rangers	201	40	53	6	39	264	378	448	826	16	65	0.53	5	2	42	184	6.58
2013	A	Hickory	453	48	107	13	62	236	304	382	686	9	71	0.34	1	2	36	146	3.98

Young, exciting OF who started slow, but rebounded well in first full season. Showing improvement in all phases of game, especially with swing. Owns mature approach and can find pitches to drive. Produces easy power to all fields, though expands strike zone and struggles with LHP. Lacks speed, but has plus arm.

Mazzilli,L.J. — 4 — New York (N)

EXP MLB DEBUT: 2016 | POTENTIAL: Backup 2B | **6C**

Bats R Age 23
2013 (4) Connecticut
Pwr +++
BAvg ++
Spd ++
Def +++

Year	Lev	Team	AB	R	H	HR	RBI	Avg	OB	Slg	OPS	bb%	ct%	Eye	SB	CS	x/h%	Iso	RC/G
2010	NCAA	Connecticut	93	15	29	3	18	312	366	548	915	8	82	0.47	4	1	48	237	6.85
2011	NCAA	Connecticut	266	48	92	3	32	346	394	504	897	7	90	0.78	11	10	34	158	6.58
2012	NCAA	Connecticut	239	43	81	9	38	339	395	548	943	8	87	0.73	16	5	37	209	7.04
2013	NCAA	Connecticut	260	50	92	6	51	354	417	515	932	10	90	1.08	29	4	28	162	7.05
2013	A-	Brooklyn	273	24	76	4	34	278	332	381	713	7	81	0.42	3	0	24	103	4.30

The Mets 4th round pick lacks a standout tool or much more projection, but could bring decent BA value with a little pop, and makes consistent contact. He is a solid defender with good range. Knows how to steal a base despite just average speed.

McCann,James — 2 — Detroit

EXP MLB DEBUT: 2014 | POTENTIAL: Starting C | **7B**

Bats R Age 24
2011 (2) Arkansas
Pwr ++
BAvg +++
Spd ++
Def ++++

Year	Lev	Team	AB	R	H	HR	RBI	Avg	OB	Slg	OPS	bb%	ct%	Eye	SB	CS	x/h%	Iso	RC/G
2011	Rk	GCL Tigers	14	1	5	1	6	357	400	643	1043	7	93	1.00	0	0	40	286	7.81
2011	A	West Michigan	34	0	2	0	1	59	111	88	199	6	65	0.17	0	0	50	29	-3.26
2012	A+	Lakeland	160	24	46	0	20	288	329	350	679	6	82	0.34	3	0	22	63	3.86
2012	AA	Erie	220	15	44	2	19	200	228	282	510	4	80	0.18	3	2	32	82	1.61
2013	AA	Erie	441	50	122	8	54	277	323	404	726	6	81	0.35	3	3	32	127	4.41

Big, strong C who set career high in HR while tapping into average power potential. Hits well from both sides and shortened swing for more consistent contact. Exhibits little patience and doesn't get on base enough. Biggest value is with glove as he owns quick feet, very strong arm and good receiving ability.

McClure,D'Vone — 7 — Cleveland

EXP MLB DEBUT: 2018 | POTENTIAL: Starting OF | **8E**

Bats R Age 20
2012 (4) HS (AR)
Pwr +++
BAvg ++
Spd +++
Def ++

Year	Lev	Team	AB	R	H	HR	RBI	Avg	OB	Slg	OPS	bb%	ct%	Eye	SB	CS	x/h%	Iso	RC/G
2012	Rk	AZL Indians	90	15	19	1	12	211	297	289	586	11	79	0.58	2	1	26	78	2.86
2013	Rk	AZL Indians	101	16	22	0	5	218	255	297	552	5	60	0.13	1	0	32	79	2.27

Extremely athletic, toolsy OF who repeated Rookie ball and needs development time. Has live body and loose swing mechanics. Power has plenty of projection, but long, uppercut stroke and failure to recognize spin mute BA potential. Exhibits average speed, range, and arm strength, but gets poor jumps in OF.

McElroy, C.J. — 78 — St. Louis

EXP MLB DEBUT: 2016 **POTENTIAL:** Starting CF **7C**

Bats R Age 21
2011 (3) HS (TX)

Pwr	+
BAvg	++
Spd	++++
Def	+++

Year	Lev	Team	AB	R	H	HR	RBI	Avg	OB	Slg	OPS	bb%	ct%	Eye	SB	CS	x/h%	Iso	RC/G
2011	Rk	GCL Cardinals	79	10	18	0	7	228	291	278	569	8	81	0.47	8	2	17	51	2.62
2012	Rk	Johnson City	247	40	67	0	22	271	313	332	645	6	83	0.36	24	5	19	61	3.46
2013	Rk	GCL Cardinals	10	0	3	0	0	300	300	400	700	0	80	0.00	1	1	33	100	3.81
2013	A	Peoria	242	24	58	0	23	240	290	302	591	7	83	0.43	8	8	21	62	2.89

Fleet-footed CF has nice athleticism and a good line-drive stroke. Can occasionally drive the ball, but is not going to hit for power and has yet to hit a HR as a pro. Uses his plus speed well on the bases and in the field, but SB totals dropped from 24 to 8 and will need to rebound.

McGuiness, Chris — 3 — Pittsburgh

EXP MLB DEBUT: 2013 **POTENTIAL:** Backup 1B **6B**

Bats L Age 26
2009 (13) The Citadel

Pwr	+++
BAvg	++
Spd	+
Def	+++

Year	Lev	Team	AB	R	H	HR	RBI	Avg	OB	Slg	OPS	bb%	ct%	Eye	SB	CS	x/h%	Iso	RC/G
2010	A+	Bakersfield	120	19	30	7	22	250	375	450	825	17	73	0.75	1	1	33	200	6.01
2011	Rk	AZL Rangers	5	3	1	1	2	200	333	800	1133	17	80	1.00	0	0	100	600	9.12
2011	A+	Myrtle Beach	196	19	42	2	26	214	319	296	615	13	74	0.59	1	0	29	82	3.25
2012	AA	Frisco	456	65	122	23	77	268	364	474	837	13	77	0.64	0	1	39	206	6.05
2013	AAA	Round Rock	362	52	89	11	63	246	365	423	788	16	76	0.79	1	0	46	177	5.67

Big and strong prospect who could make impact with power off bench. Lacks skills of everyday 1B as he isn't very athletic and offers no speed. Hits with simple, patient approach and gets on base consistently. Makes decent contact despite long swing and projects to average pop. Can be good defender with some agility and sure hands.

McGuire, Reese — 2 — Pittsburgh

EXP MLB DEBUT: 2017 **POTENTIAL:** Starting C **8D**

Bats L Age 18
2013 (1) HS (WA)

Pwr	+++
BAvg	+++
Spd	++
Def	++++

Year	Lev	Team	AB	R	H	HR	RBI	Avg	OB	Slg	OPS	bb%	ct%	Eye	SB	CS	x/h%	Iso	RC/G
2013	Rk	GCL Pirates	176	30	58	0	21	330	382	392	774	8	90	0.83	5	1	19	63	5.20
2013	A-	Jamestown	16	3	4	0	0	250	294	250	544	6	94	1.00	1	0	0	0	2.62

13th pick was best backstop in the draft. Blocks and receives well and has a strong throwing arm. Has a good approach at the plate and solid plate discipline. Should develop moderate power and has good bat speed. Scouts are mixed on whether or not he will hit for average, but he showed well in his debut, hitting .330 in the GCL.

McKinney, Billy — 78 — Oakland

EXP MLB DEBUT: 2017 **POTENTIAL:** Starting OF **8D**

Bats L Age 19
2013 (1) HS (TX)

Pwr	+++
BAvg	+++
Spd	+++
Def	++

Year	Lev	Team	AB	R	H	HR	RBI	Avg	OB	Slg	OPS	bb%	ct%	Eye	SB	CS	x/h%	Iso	RC/G
2013	Rk	AZL Athletics	181	31	64	4	20	320	379	414	793	9	84	0.59	7	0	19	94	5.36
2013	A-	Vermont	34	5	12	1	6	353	405	559	964	8	88	0.75	1	1	33	206	7.32

Natural hitting OF who had terrific pro debut and should continue to evolve. Bat speed among best in org and brings polished eye to plate. Power potential only average, but offers other tools. Knows strike zone and reads spin. Average speed helps range, but relegated to LF due to subpar arm. Instincts make tools play up.

McMahon, Ryan — 5 — Colorado

EXP MLB DEBUT: 2017 **POTENTIAL:** Starting 3B **9D**

Bats R Age 18
2013 (2) HS (CA)

Pwr	++++
BAvg	+++
Spd	++
Def	+++

Year	Lev	Team	AB	R	H	HR	RBI	Avg	OB	Slg	OPS	bb%	ct%	Eye	SB	CS	x/h%	Iso	RC/G
2013	Rk	Grand Junction	218	42	70	11	52	321	398	583	981	11	73	0.47	4	6	46	261	8.13

Strong, athletic 3B was a two-sport star in HS. Rockies moved him to 3B and has a quick LH stroke and showed plus power in debut. He makes decent contact and has a solid approach at the plate. He's an average runner, but has soft hands, good lateral movement, and a strong arm.

Meadows, Austin — 8 — Pittsburgh

EXP MLB DEBUT: 2017 **POTENTIAL:** Starting LF **9D**

Bats L Age 19
2013 (1) HS (GA)

Pwr	+++
BAvg	++++
Spd	+++
Def	++

Year	Lev	Team	AB	R	H	HR	RBI	Avg	OB	Slg	OPS	bb%	ct%	Eye	SB	CS	x/h%	Iso	RC/G
2013	Rk	GCL Pirates	160	29	47	5	20	294	386	519	905	13	74	0.57	3	2	45	225	7.26
2013	A-	Jamestown	17	8	9	2	2	529	636	882	1519	23	76	1.25	0	0	22	353	15.49

9th overall pick had impressive debut. Showed better than expected power, and should be able to hit for BA. Has simple, compact stroke and ball jumps off bat. Above-average runner, but speed not likely to be part of game. Covers ground well in CF, but an average arm could result in a shift to LF where his power profiles well.

Medica, Tommy — 3 — San Diego

EXP MLB DEBUT: 2013 **POTENTIAL:** Starting 1B **6B**

Bats R Age 25
2010 (14) Santa Clara

Pwr	+++
BAvg	+++
Spd	++
Def	++

Year	Lev	Team	AB	R	H	HR	RBI	Avg	OB	Slg	OPS	bb%	ct%	Eye	SB	CS	x/h%	Iso	RC/G
2011	A+	Lake Elsinore	139	21	42	6	17	302	409	504	912	15	77	0.78	0	1	38	201	7.21
2012	A+	Lake Elsinore	355	65	117	19	87	330	399	623	1022	10	76	0.48	1	1	52	293	8.48
2013	Rk	AZL Padres	17	6	5	2	8	294	333	765	1098	6	59	0.14	0	0	80	471	10.97
2013	AA	San Antonio	280	48	83	18	57	296	360	582	943	9	76	0.42	4	2	49	286	7.23
2013	MLB	SD	69	9	20	3	10	290	380	449	829	13	67	0.43	0	0	25	159	6.23

Pure-hitting and aggressive prospect who parlayed success in minors to starting job with SD. Takes hard hacks at pitches, though has keen pitch recognition and plate coverage. Can be too impatient early in count, though has power to justify approach. Doesn't run well and is subpar defender at 1B with limited agility.

Mejia, Francisco — 2 — Cleveland

EXP MLB DEBUT: 2018 **POTENTIAL:** Starting C **8D**

Bats B Age 18
2012 FA (DR)

Pwr	++
BAvg	+++
Spd	++
Def	++

Year	Lev	Team	AB	R	H	HR	RBI	Avg	OB	Slg	OPS	bb%	ct%	Eye	SB	CS	x/h%	Iso	RC/G
2013	Rk	AZL Indians	105	16	32	4	24	305	336	524	860	5	83	0.28	3	1	44	219	5.88

Short, offensive-minded backstop who showed quality tools in first season in U.S. Puts ball in play with natural stroke from both sides and has bat speed to project to average power. Needs to add strength and become more selective to realize pop. Exhibits raw talent behind plate with suspect receiving, but arm is impressive.

Mejias-Brean, Seth — 35 — Cincinnati

EXP MLB DEBUT: 2016 **POTENTIAL:** Starting 1B/3B **7C**

Bats R Age 23
2012 (8) Arizona

Pwr	+++
BAvg	+++
Spd	+++
Def	++++

Year	Lev	Team	AB	R	H	HR	RBI	Avg	OB	Slg	OPS	bb%	ct%	Eye	SB	CS	x/h%	Iso	RC/G
2011	NCAA	Arizona	195	30	61	0	25	313	359	379	738	7	85	0.48	7	3	16	67	4.65
2012	NCAA	Arizona	265	57	94	1	61	355	404	479	883	8	91	0.96	10	4	29	125	6.47
2012	Rk	Billings	179	35	56	8	40	313	385	536	921	11	84	0.77	6	0	39	223	6.93
2013	A	Dayton	479	70	146	10	79	305	376	453	829	10	83	0.66	3	2	33	148	5.91
2013	A+	Bakersfield	13	3	4	1	3	308	308	615	923	0	100	1.00	1	0	50	308	6.10

Shows nice power, plate discipline, bat speed, contact rate and bb%. Plus defender at 3B with good range and strong arm. Won't steal a lot of bases but is decent baserunner. Hits the ball on the ground too much for his power profile. Older prospect for his level, needs to show he can duplicate numbers against advanced pitching.

Mercado, Oscar — 6 — St. Louis

EXP MLB DEBUT: 2018 **POTENTIAL:** Starting SS **7D**

Bats R Age 19
2013 (2) HS (FL)

Pwr	+
BAvg	+++
Spd	+++
Def	+++

Year	Lev	Team	AB	R	H	HR	RBI	Avg	OB	Slg	OPS	bb%	ct%	Eye	SB	CS	x/h%	Iso	RC/G
2013	Rk	GCL Cardinals	163	18	34	1	14	209	283	307	590	9	76	0.44	12	4	29	98	2.87

2nd round pick out of HS in FL struggled in his pro debut, hitting just .209 in the GCL. Has a line-drive approach that is geared more towards gap power and makes decent contact. Pitch recognition needs to improve for him to hit. Solid defender with good instincts and decent range.

Michael, Levi — 46 — Minnesota

EXP MLB DEBUT: 2015 **POTENTIAL:** Starting SS **7E**

Bats B Age 23
2011 (1) North Carolina

Pwr	++
BAvg	++
Spd	+++
Def	+++

Year	Lev	Team	AB	R	H	HR	RBI	Avg	OB	Slg	OPS	bb%	ct%	Eye	SB	CS	x/h%	Iso	RC/G
2009	NCAA	North Carolina	262	54	76	13	57	290	354	527	881	9	79	0.46	5	4	42	237	6.41
2010	NCAA	North Carolina	214	76	74	9	54	346	457	575	1032	17	88	1.69	20	2	36	229	8.68
2011	NCAA	North Carolina	242	53	70	5	48	289	409	434	843	17	81	1.04	15	1	31	145	6.48
2012	A+	Fort Myers	431	58	106	9	38	246	333	311	644	11	81	0.68	6	0	19	65	3.70
2013	A+	Fort Myers	315	40	72	4	28	229	332	340	672	13	79	0.73	21	2	32	111	4.12

Short, savvy INF who struggled in return to High-A. Drastically increased SB output and could provide more if he became better hitter. Has patient approach at plate, but doesn't have much pop and can expand zone with two strikes. Shows polish in infield with lateral quickness and average range. Has arm for 2B or SS.

Miller,Brandon — 9 — Washington
EXP MLB DEBUT: 2016 | POTENTIAL: Backup OF | 7C

Bats R Age 24
2012 (4) Samford
Pwr +++
BAvg ++
Spd ++
Def ++

Year	Lev	Team	AB	R	H	HR	RBI	Avg	OB	Slg	OPS	bb%	ct%	Eye	SB	CS	x/h%	Iso	RC/G
2011	NCAA	Samford	196	40	53	16	43	270	376	582	957	14	74	0.66	3	1	51	311	7.64
2012	A-	Auburn	113	20	33	4	21	292	350	549	898	8	68	0.28	0	0	55	257	7.27
2013	A	Hagerstown	395	62	96	18	72	243	303	456	759	8	66	0.25	3	1	48	213	5.13
2013	A+	Potomac	110	11	33	2	16	300	342	464	806	6	74	0.24	3	1	33	164	5.57

The catcher turned RF popped 20 HR in A ball, but was old for level. Obviously has good power tool, but still struggles to make contact and get on-base, posting weak bb% and Eye for second straight year. Strong arm and decent range in RF. Due to age, will need to move quickly.

Mitchell,Jared — 78 — Chicago (A)
EXP MLB DEBUT: 2014 | POTENTIAL: Starting OF | 7D

Bats L Age 25
2009 (1) LSU
Pwr +++
BAvg +
Spd +++
Def +++

Year	Lev	Team	AB	R	H	HR	RBI	Avg	OB	Slg	OPS	bb%	ct%	Eye	SB	CS	x/h%	Iso	RC/G
2011	A+	Winston-Salem	477	74	106	9	58	222	299	377	676	10	62	0.28	14	6	45	155	4.29
2012	AA	Birmingham	334	51	80	10	54	240	359	440	799	16	62	0.49	20	5	44	201	6.35
2012	AAA	Charlotte	121	18	28	1	13	231	321	364	685	12	56	0.30	1	1	46	132	4.91
2013	AA	Birmingham	247	23	43	5	20	174	292	275	567	14	61	0.43	13	5	30	101	2.45
2013	AAA	Charlotte	53	7	7	0	3	132	270	170	440	16	49	0.37	4	1	29	38	0.39

Very athletic OF who had horrendous campaign, but showed positive steps in AFL. Owns quick bat and average raw power, but inability to make contact mutes natural skills. Can be too patient at plate and has poor two-strike approach. Not as fast as he once was due to injuries, but still has speed. Solid defender with average arm.

Mondesi,Adalberto — 6 — Kansas City
EXP MLB DEBUT: 2017 | POTENTIAL: Starting SS | 9D

Bats B Age 18
2011 FA (DR)
Pwr +++
BAvg +++
Spd ++++
Def ++++

Year	Lev	Team	AB	R	H	HR	RBI	Avg	OB	Slg	OPS	bb%	ct%	Eye	SB	CS	x/h%	Iso	RC/G
2012	Rk	Idaho Falls	207	35	60	3	30	290	350	386	736	8	69	0.29	11	2	20	97	4.79
2013	A	Lexington	482	61	126	7	47	261	310	361	671	7	76	0.29	24	10	21	100	3.70

Quick, rangy INF who performed admirably for 17-year-old. Struggled with approach and putting bat to ball. Still has plenty of room to grow and add strength. Gap power at present, but should evolve into average long ball pop. Has exciting game with good speed and impact defense. Has clean, fast stroke from both sides.

Monsalve,Alex — 2 — Cleveland
EXP MLB DEBUT: 2015 | POTENTIAL: Starting C | 7C

Bats R Age 22
2008 FA (Venezuela)
Pwr +++
BAvg +++
Spd +
Def ++

Year	Lev	Team	AB	R	H	HR	RBI	Avg	OB	Slg	OPS	bb%	ct%	Eye	SB	CS	x/h%	Iso	RC/G
2011	A	Lake County	458	55	121	5	44	264	311	356	667	6	79	0.32	7	6	24	92	3.66
2012	A	Lake County	283	36	75	7	36	265	320	406	727	8	88	0.66	1	2	33	141	4.53
2012	A+	Carolina	116	10	27	1	6	233	276	293	570	6	85	0.41	1	0	19	60	2.57
2013	Rk	AZL Indians	13	1	3	0	2	231	286	231	516	7	92	1.00	0	0	0	0	2.34
2013	AA	Akron	78	9	23	2	8	295	304	449	753	1	81	0.07	0	0	30	154	4.39

Big, strong C who returned in July after elbow injury. Has quickness and athleticism which help defense. Still struggles with nuances of catching, though has good arm with quick release. Smoother and quicker swing help upside and exhibits some feel for bat control. Should hit for average power at his peak.

Moran,Colin — 5 — Miami
EXP MLB DEBUT: 2015 | POTENTIAL: Starting 3B | 9D

Bats L Age 21
2013 (1) North Carolina
Pwr ++
BAvg ++++
Spd ++
Def +++

Year	Lev	Team	AB	R	H	HR	RBI	Avg	OB	Slg	OPS	bb%	ct%	Eye	SB	CS	x/h%	Iso	RC/G
2011	NCAA	North Carolina	248	46	83	9	71	335	441	540	981	16	87	1.42	2	2	37	206	8.03
2012	NCAA	North Carolina	170	30	62	3	35	365	435	494	929	11	86	0.88	1	2	24	129	7.12
2013	NCAA	North Carolina	281	76	97	13	91	345	465	544	1010	18	91	2.52	1	0	28	199	8.43
2013	A	Greensboro	154	19	46	4	23	299	361	442	803	9	84	0.60	1	0	28	143	5.44

Big, strong 3B shows hand-eye coordination and good plate discipline which allow him to barrel ball to all fields. Bat projects to advance quickly but power will determine his MLB impact. Below average now, his power projects to be average. Has strong arm and average range which should allow him to stick at 3B.

Morban,Julio — 9 — Seattle
EXP MLB DEBUT: 2014 | POTENTIAL: Starting OF | 8D

Bats L Age 22
2008 FA (DR)
Pwr +++
BAvg +++
Spd ++
Def +++

Year	Lev	Team	AB	R	H	HR	RBI	Avg	OB	Slg	OPS	bb%	ct%	Eye	SB	CS	x/h%	Iso	RC/G
2011	A	Clinton	301	44	77	4	28	256	315	382	697	8	67	0.26	10	5	30	126	4.33
2012	Rk	AZL Mariners	21	2	5	0	3	238	238	238	476	0	86	0.00	0	0	0	0	1.13
2012	A+	High Desert	300	56	94	17	52	313	358	550	908	7	78	0.31	5	1	37	237	6.56
2013	AA	Jackson	295	46	87	7	44	295	356	468	824	9	68	0.29	7	2	37	173	6.18

Athletic, strong OF who broke leg in mid-August. Starting to realize potential with all-around tools and production. Owns good bat speed for average power and has balanced approach to hit to all fields. Needs to make more contact and has struggled with LHP. Staying healthy is key in order gain more at bats and polish selectivity.

Morris,Hunter — 3 — Milwaukee
EXP MLB DEBUT: 2014 | POTENTIAL: Starting 1B | 7C

Bats L Age 25
2010 (4) Auburn
Pwr ++++
BAvg +++
Spd ++
Def ++

Year	Lev	Team	AB	R	H	HR	RBI	Avg	OB	Slg	OPS	bb%	ct%	Eye	SB	CS	x/h%	Iso	RC/G
2010	A	Wisconsin	291	38	73	9	44	251	299	436	735	6	80	0.34	7	2	44	186	4.52
2011	A+	Brevard County	501	75	136	19	67	271	297	461	758	3	83	0.21	7	3	38	190	4.55
2011	AA	Huntsville	17	6	6	1	2	353	353	706	1059	0	94	0.00	0	0	50	353	7.64
2012	AA	Huntsville	522	77	158	28	113	303	352	563	916	7	78	0.34	2	1	47	261	6.77
2013	AAA	Nashville	497	61	123	24	73	247	307	457	764	8	75	0.35	3	1	43	209	4.87

Morris regressed, showing flaws in his swing. His power is a strength, but he makes below average contact, struggles against LHP, and Ks too often. This will limit his BA ceiling, though the strong-bodied 1B still has the potential to hit 20+ HR. He is a below average runner with limited range, making 1B his only option.

Moya,Steven — 9 — Detroit
EXP MLB DEBUT: 2016 | POTENTIAL: Starting OF | 8E

Bats L Age 22
2008 FA (PR)
Pwr ++++
BAvg ++
Spd ++
Def ++

Year	Lev	Team	AB	R	H	HR	RBI	Avg	OB	Slg	OPS	bb%	ct%	Eye	SB	CS	x/h%	Iso	RC/G
2010	Rk	GCL Tigers	137	12	26	2	11	190	224	299	523	4	53	0.09	0	0	35	109	2.00
2011	A	West Michigan	323	38	66	13	39	204	233	362	595	4	61	0.09	1	1	36	158	2.64
2012	A	West Michigan	243	28	70	9	47	288	319	481	800	4	76	0.19	5	3	37	193	5.22
2013	A+	Lakeland	365	52	93	12	55	255	290	433	723	5	71	0.17	6	0	39	178	4.34

Big, strong, athletic OF who missed time early after TJ surgery in '12. Has lots of leverage in swing and focused on shortening stroke. Doesn't draw many walks and long arms equate to exploitable swing. Has above average pop potential and is average runner with very strong arm. Good upside, but is still a project.

Muncy,Max — 3 — Oakland
EXP MLB DEBUT: 2015 | POTENTIAL: Starting 1B | 7C

Bats L Age 23
2012 (5) Baylor
Pwr +++
BAvg +++
Spd +
Def ++

Year	Lev	Team	AB	R	H	HR	RBI	Avg	OB	Slg	OPS	bb%	ct%	Eye	SB	CS	x/h%	Iso	RC/G
2011	NCAA	Baylor	227	40	73	9	44	322	417	511	928	14	84	1.03	6	3	30	189	7.23
2012	NCAA	Baylor	255	55	82	7	56	322	416	494	910	14	87	1.28	7	5	33	173	7.08
2012	A	Burlington	229	34	63	4	23	275	385	432	817	15	83	1.11	3	1	41	157	6.12
2013	A+	Stockton	351	67	100	21	76	285	395	507	902	15	81	0.94	1	1	35	222	6.90
2013	AA	Midland	172	22	43	4	24	250	342	413	755	12	80	0.71	0	1	42	163	5.11

Disciplined and natural hitter who had breakout year with power and patience, though hit tool may not last in upper minors. Recognizes pitches and shortens swing in situations. Makes hard contact, mostly to pull side, but bat speed merely average. Doesn't run well, but could be used in OF due to fine defensive acumen.

Munoz,Jose — 6 — Arizona
EXP MLB DEBUT: 2017 | POTENTIAL: Starting SS | 7D

Bats R Age 20
2012 (2) HS (CA)
Pwr ++
BAvg ++
Spd +
Def ++

Year	Lev	Team	AB	R	H	HR	RBI	Avg	OB	Slg	OPS	bb%	ct%	Eye	SB	CS	x/h%	Iso	RC/G
2012	Rk	AZL D'backs	173	25	45	2	20	260	323	341	664	8	69	0.30	4	4	18	81	3.73
2013	Rk	Missoula	194	32	51	6	30	263	332	448	780	9	69	0.33	5	0	41	186	5.48

Tall, athletic SS has yet to have a breakout. 2nd rounder has had extreme difficulty making contact and struck out 61 times in 194 AB. Has struggled defensively as well, but has solid tools. Could move to 3B, but will need to prove he can hit and hit for power.

Murphy,J.R. — 2 — New York (A)
EXP MLB DEBUT: 2013 | POTENTIAL: Starting C | 7C

Bats R Age 23
2009 (2) HS (FL)
Pwr +++
BAvg +++
Spd ++
Def ++

Year	Lev	Team	AB	R	H	HR	RBI	Avg	OB	Slg	OPS	bb%	ct%	Eye	SB	CS	x/h%	Iso	RC/G
2012	A+	Tampa	265	39	68	5	28	257	323	374	697	9	85	0.63	4	3	29	117	4.23
2012	AA	Trenton	147	23	34	4	16	231	307	408	715	10	78	0.50	0	0	50	177	4.46
2013	AA	Trenton	183	34	49	6	25	268	353	421	773	12	83	0.75	1	0	33	153	5.21
2013	AAA	Scranton/W-B	230	26	62	6	21	270	336	430	766	9	82	0.56	0	1	40	161	5.05
2013	MLB	NYY	27	3	4	0	1	148	179	185	364	4	67	0.11	0	0	25	37	-0.74

Solid all-around receiver who reached NYY for first time. Posted career high in HR, but focuses more on line drives. Makes nice contact with level swing and can work counts. Receiving has improved behind plate, but still needs polish. Best attributes as defender involve catch-and-throw skills with strong, accurate arm.

Murphy,Tanner — 2 — Atlanta

EXP MLB DEBUT: 2018 | POTENTIAL: Starting C | 7D

Bats R Age 19
2013 (4) HS (MO)

- Pwr ++
- BAvg ++
- Spd +
- Def +++

Year	Lev	Team	AB	R	H	HR	RBI	Avg	OB	Slg	OPS	bb%	ct%	Eye	SB	CS	x/h%	Iso	RC/G
2013	Rk	GCL Braves	97	7	22	0	8	227	312	258	570	11	65	0.35	5	0	14	31	2.50

Strong, athletic backstop who moves well behind the plate and has a plus arm. Swing can get a bit long and he struggled to make consistent contact in his pro debut. Has some good tools, but needs to refine his game on both sides of the ball.

Murphy,Tom — 2 — Colorado

EXP MLB DEBUT: 2016 | POTENTIAL: Starting C | 8D

Bats R Age 23
2012 (3) Buffalo

- Pwr +++
- BAvg +++
- Spd ++
- Def +++

Year	Lev	Team	AB	R	H	HR	RBI	Avg	OB	Slg	OPS	bb%	ct%	Eye	SB	CS	x/h%	Iso	RC/G
2011	NCAA	Buffalo	190	34	73	10	44	384	445	626	1072	10	87	0.84	7	4	36	242	8.56
2012	NCAA	Buffalo	219	46	68	13	51	311	398	616	1015	13	79	0.70	6	3	54	306	8.35
2012	A-	Tri-City	212	26	61	6	38	288	332	462	794	6	75	0.27	1	1	36	175	5.30
2013	A	Asheville	288	55	83	19	74	288	369	590	960	11	70	0.43	4	5	57	302	7.94
2013	AA	Tulsa	69	9	20	3	9	290	329	493	822	5	77	0.25	0	0	40	203	5.49

Strong catcher who continues to make progress. Has a good approach at the plate that generates power to all fields. Good bat speed, but struggles to make contact. Moves well behind the plate with a strong throwing arm, improved his blocking and receiving skills and should be able to stick.

Naquin,Tyler — 8 — Cleveland

EXP MLB DEBUT: 2015 | POTENTIAL: Starting CF | 7A

Bats L Age 23
2012 (1-S) Texas A&M

- Pwr ++
- BAvg +++
- Spd +++
- Def +++

Year	Lev	Team	AB	R	H	HR	RBI	Avg	OB	Slg	OPS	bb%	ct%	Eye	SB	CS	x/h%	Iso	RC/G
2011	NCAA	Texas A&M	273	68	104	2	44	381	440	538	979	10	87	0.83	6	7	31	158	7.72
2012	NCAA	Texas A&M	242	56	92	3	49	380	438	541	980	9	85	0.68	21	5	29	161	7.71
2012	A-	Mahoning Val	137	22	37	0	13	270	351	380	730	11	81	0.65	4	3	35	109	4.87
2013	A+	Carolina	448	69	124	9	42	277	337	424	762	8	75	0.37	14	7	34	147	5.02
2013	AA	Akron	80	9	18	1	6	225	271	300	571	6	73	0.23	1	3	22	75	2.29

Lean, athletic OF who does variety of things well. Lacks premium power projection and strikes out a lot for someone with profile, but has quick stroke and solid hand-eye coordination. Draws walks and offers value with speed. Defensive work is sound with strong arm, but may have to move to LF.

Navarro,Efren — 3 — Los Angeles (A)

EXP MLB DEBUT: 2011 | POTENTIAL: Reserve 1B | 6A

Bats L Age 28
2007 (50) Nevada-Las Vegas

- Pwr ++
- BAvg +++
- Spd ++
- Def +++

Year	Lev	Team	AB	R	H	HR	RBI	Avg	OB	Slg	OPS	bb%	ct%	Eye	SB	CS	x/h%	Iso	RC/G
2011	AAA	Salt Lake	492	76	156	12	73	317	371	488	859	8	84	0.54	5	5	35	171	6.10
2011	MLB	LAA	10	1	2	0	0	200	273	300	573	9	90	1.00	1	0	50	100	3.13
2012	AAA	Salt Lake	528	79	155	7	74	294	339	403	742	6	87	0.51	3	2	28	110	4.66
2013	AAA	Salt Lake	513	83	167	7	81	326	404	454	859	12	81	0.69	8	5	29	129	6.41
2013	MLB	LAA	4	0	1	0	1	250	500	250	750	33	75	2.00	1	0	0	0	6.01

Short, strong INF who has spent bulk of last three years in Triple-A. Has proven to be solid hitter with ability to get on base consistently. Knows strike zone and uses level swing to produce doubles power. Only hit 10+ HR once in career, though can hit LHP. Can be solid defender at 1B with soft hands and good range.

Nay,Mitch — 5 — Toronto

EXP MLB DEBUT: 2017 | POTENTIAL: Starting 3B | 8D

Bats R Age 20
2012 (1-S) HS (AZ)

- Pwr ++++
- BAvg +++
- Spd +
- Def ++

Year	Lev	Team	AB	R	H	HR	RBI	Avg	OB	Slg	OPS	bb%	ct%	Eye	SB	CS	x/h%	Iso	RC/G
2013	Rk	Bluefield	230	41	69	6	42	300	369	426	795	10	85	0.71	0	1	25	126	5.39

Projectable INF who made debut after missing 2012 with broken foot. Has mammoth projection with loose stroke and makes consistent contact for size. Bat speed and strength should lead to more pop once he enhances pitch recognition. Secondary skills are poor as he has well below average speed. Has OK range with strong arm.

Nessy,Santiago — 2 — Toronto

EXP MLB DEBUT: 2016 | POTENTIAL: Starting C | 7C

Bats R Age 21
2009 FA (Venezuela)

- Pwr +++
- BAvg ++
- Spd +
- Def +++

Year	Lev	Team	AB	R	H	HR	RBI	Avg	OB	Slg	OPS	bb%	ct%	Eye	SB	CS	x/h%	Iso	RC/G
2011	Rk	GCL Blue Jays	134	12	41	3	19	306	345	425	770	6	78	0.28	0	2	24	119	4.86
2012	Rk	Bluefield	160	26	41	8	23	256	312	456	768	8	71	0.28	0	0	39	200	4.98
2012	A-	Vancouver	22	4	2	1	3	91	200	273	473	12	68	0.43	0	0	100	182	0.88
2013	A	Lansing	224	23	54	5	23	241	283	375	658	5	74	0.22	0	0	37	134	3.47

Big and strong backstop who missed time with injuries. Possesses natural strength and good bat speed to produce above average raw power. Aggressive approach not conducive to OBP and will swing and miss quite a bit with exploitable stroke. Good catch-and-throw skills and agility make him solid receiver behind dish.

Neuhaus,Tucker — 56 — Milwaukee

EXP MLB DEBUT: 2017 | POTENTIAL: Starting 3B | 8E

Bats L Age 19
2013 (2) HS (FL)

- Pwr +++
- BAvg +++
- Spd +++
- Def +++

Year	Lev	Team	AB	R	H	HR	RBI	Avg	OB	Slg	OPS	bb%	ct%	Eye	SB	CS	x/h%	Iso	RC/G
2013	Rk	AZL Brewers	195	29	45	0	24	231	312	303	614	11	71	0.41	6	3	29	72	3.21

Strong INF with good approach and smooth stroke. Future will likely be at 3B where his strong arm and good hands work. Smooth swing should allow him to make plenty of contact and tap into raw power. He'll need to use the whole field for his swing to play up. Sound fundamentals on the bases with average speed.

Ngoepe,Gift — 6 — Pittsburgh

EXP MLB DEBUT: 2015 | POTENTIAL: Starting SS | 7D

Bats B Age 24
2008 FA (South Africa)

- Pwr +
- BAvg ++
- Spd +++
- Def ++++

Year	Lev	Team	AB	R	H	HR	RBI	Avg	OB	Slg	OPS	bb%	ct%	Eye	SB	CS	x/h%	Iso	RC/G
2011	Rk	GCL Pirates	6	0	1	0	0	167	167	167	333	0	83	0.00	0	0	0	0	-0.59
2011	A	West Virginia	85	14	26	2	5	306	359	459	818	8	84	0.50	3	3	31	153	5.58
2012	A+	Bradenton	456	66	106	9	36	232	326	338	663	12	71	0.48	22	14	24	105	3.82
2013	A+	Bradenton	96	17	28	0	6	292	419	427	846	18	64	0.60	7	1	36	135	7.35
2013	AA	Altoona	220	29	39	3	16	177	270	282	552	11	63	0.34	10	3	38	105	2.24

Switch-hitting SS had been pushed aggressively and it caught up to him at AA. He is a plus defender at SS with plus range and a strong arm. Struggles to make consistent contact raise questions about his ability to hit for average and he has shown little power.

Nieto,Adrian — 2 — Chicago (A)

EXP MLB DEBUT: 2014 | POTENTIAL: Backup C | 6C

Bats B Age 24
2008 (5) HS (FL)

- Pwr +++
- BAvg ++
- Spd +
- Def ++

Year	Lev	Team	AB	R	H	HR	RBI	Avg	OB	Slg	OPS	bb%	ct%	Eye	SB	CS	x/h%	Iso	RC/G
2011	A	Hagerstown	98	17	25	3	12	255	318	449	767	8	68	0.29	0	0	48	194	5.27
2011	A+	Potomac	5	1	1	0	0	200	333	200	533	17	60	0.50	0	0	0	0	1.98
2012	Rk	GCL Nationals	26	3	4	1	3	154	290	308	598	16	73	0.71	0	0	50	154	2.93
2012	A	Hagerstown	257	32	66	6	39	257	346	393	739	12	75	0.55	4	2	35	136	4.85
2013	A+	Potomac	390	68	111	11	53	285	370	449	819	12	79	0.65	4	2	37	164	5.86

Posted repeat offensive numbers with a bit more pop as he moved up a level to High-A in '13. As he matures, is showing a better feel for swing and plate approach. Defensively, has above-average arm but struggles blocking and receiving. Backup catcher ceiling. Selected in Rule 5 from WAS.

Nimmo,Brandon — 8 — New York (N)

EXP MLB DEBUT: 2017 | POTENTIAL: Starting LF/RF | 8D

Bats L Age 21
2011 (1) HS (WY)

- Pwr +++
- BAvg +++
- Spd +++
- Def +++

Year	Lev	Team	AB	R	H	HR	RBI	Avg	OB	Slg	OPS	bb%	ct%	Eye	SB	CS	x/h%	Iso	RC/G
2011	Rk	GCL Mets	29	5	7	2	4	241	313	448	761	9	69	0.33	0	0	29	207	4.81
2011	Rk	Kingsport	9	0	1	0	0	111	333	111	444	25	44	0.60	0	0	0	0	0.02
2012	A-	Brooklyn	266	41	66	6	40	248	359	406	765	15	71	0.59	1	5	42	158	5.44
2013	A	Savannah	395	62	108	2	40	273	384	359	744	15	67	0.54	10	7	22	86	5.33

Numbers play better than they appear; has played young at every level. Speed and athleticism haven't lived up to expectations. Does many things well but lacks standout tool. Should cut down on Ks with experience. Nice compact stroke, plus bat speed, and power potential. Decent range in OF but needs to improve reads.

Nunez,Renato — 5 — Oakland

EXP MLB DEBUT: 2016 | POTENTIAL: Starting 3B | 8D

Bats R Age 20
2010 FA (Venezuela)

- Pwr ++++
- BAvg ++
- Spd ++
- Def ++

Year	Lev	Team	AB	R	H	HR	RBI	Avg	OB	Slg	OPS	bb%	ct%	Eye	SB	CS	x/h%	Iso	RC/G
2012	Rk	AZL Athletics	160	31	52	4	42	325	390	550	940	10	80	0.53	4	0	48	225	7.36
2013	A	Beloit	508	69	131	19	85	258	297	423	720	5	73	0.21	2	2	35	165	4.20

Aggressive hitter who started strong, but faded late in first full season. Exhibits plate coverage and feel, but lacks requisite balance at plate to be BA producer. Above average bat speed and leverage to generate impact power. Doesn't draw walks and can be easy out. Defense improving, but still below average.

O'Brien,Peter — 25 — New York (A)

EXP MLB DEBUT: 2015 | **POTENTIAL:** Starting 3B | **8D**

Bats R Age 23
2012 (2) Miami (FL)
- Pwr ++++
- BAvg +++
- Spd +
- Def ++

Year	Lev	Team	AB	R	H	HR	RBI	Avg	OB	Slg	OPS	bb%	ct%	Eye	SB	CS	x/h%	Iso	RC/G
2012	NCAA	Miami	147	31	50	10	40	340	429	626	1055	14	84	1.00	1	2	44	286	8.62
2012	Rk	GCL Yankees	14	2	5	0	2	357	357	500	857	0	93	0.00	0	0	40	143	5.65
2012	A-	Staten Island	198	27	40	10	32	202	240	394	634	5	69	0.16	0	1	45	192	3.00
2013	A	Charleston (Sc)	194	47	63	11	41	325	394	619	1012	10	70	0.38	0	0	54	294	8.70
2013	A+	Tampa	253	31	67	11	55	265	316	486	802	7	70	0.25	0	1	46	221	5.57

Tall, strong C who is poor defender, but had offensive breakout. Has above average power to all fields with balanced approach and has bat speed to catch up to prime FB. Swing-and-miss will be part of game, but can hit for moderate BA. Lacks agility and profiles as subpar catcher. Arm is strong, but receiving needs attention.

O'Neill,Michael — 78 — New York (A)

EXP MLB DEBUT: 2016 | **POTENTIAL:** Starting OF | **7D**

Bats R Age 22
2013 (3) Michigan
- Pwr ++
- BAvg +++
- Spd ++++
- Def +++

Year	Lev	Team	AB	R	H	HR	RBI	Avg	OB	Slg	OPS	bb%	ct%	Eye	SB	CS	x/h%	Iso	RC/G
2011	NCAA	Michigan	218	30	67	2	29	307	346	390	736	6	79	0.28	29	8	18	83	4.48
2012	NCAA	Michigan	158	31	52	6	30	329	365	525	891	5	87	0.43	19	5	35	196	6.21
2013	NCAA	Michigan	239	46	85	5	37	356	384	498	882	4	83	0.28	23	4	27	142	6.12
2013	A-	Staten Island	256	26	56	0	14	219	259	293	552	5	64	0.15	9	7	32	74	2.19

Speedy OF with impressive all-around game. Started strong, but then had significant issues with plate discipline and pitch recognition that resulted in high number of strikeouts. Swing can get long, but has ample bat speed that projecst to average power. Strong arm and plus speed give him tools to play any OF position.

O'Neill,Mike — 7 — St. Louis

EXP MLB DEBUT: 2014 | **POTENTIAL:** Backup OF | **6A**

Bats L Age 26
2010 (31) USC
- Pwr +
- BAvg ++++
- Spd ++
- Def ++

Year	Lev	Team	AB	R	H	HR	RBI	Avg	OB	Slg	OPS	bb%	ct%	Eye	SB	CS	x/h%	Iso	RC/G
2011	A	Quad Cities	80	15	27	0	10	338	430	438	868	14	84	1.00	1	0	30	100	6.73
2012	A+	Palm Beach	386	56	132	0	35	342	443	417	860	15	94	2.92	12	10	18	75	6.80
2012	AA	Springfield	32	8	18	0	5	563	650	719	1369	20	94	4.00	3	0	28	156	12.94
2013	AA	Springfield	359	66	115	2	35	320	433	384	817	17	93	2.73	18	4	15	64	6.33
2013	AAA	Memphis	112	16	33	0	3	295	402	321	723	15	90	1.82	1	0	9	27	5.10

Short, sparkplug of a player is a pure hitter. Short, compact stroke and plus-plus strike zone judgment allow him to hit and get on base. Now has a career .435 OB%. Almost no power, but does have good speed and is a solid defender. Ideal 4th OF.

O'Neill,Tyler — 7 — Seattle

EXP MLB DEBUT: 2018 | **POTENTIAL:** Starting OF | **8D**

Bats R Age 19
2013 (3) HS (Canada)
- Pwr ++
- BAvg +++
- Spd ++
- Def ++

Year	Lev	Team	AB	R	H	HR	RBI	Avg	OB	Slg	OPS	bb%	ct%	Eye	SB	CS	x/h%	Iso	RC/G
2013	Rk	AZL Mariners	100	12	31	1	15	310	384	450	834	11	73	0.44	2	4	29	140	6.26

Stocky OF who has several intriguing tools, though not much projection. Should grow into above average power with more experience and compact stroke. Brings patience to plate and can hit with two strikes. Can be pull-conscious and too passive. Moved to OF from C and needs plenty of work with routes, though arm is strong.

Odor,Rougned — 4 — Texas

EXP MLB DEBUT: 2015 | **POTENTIAL:** Starting 2B | **8C**

Bats L Age 20
2011 FA (Venezuela)
- Pwr +++
- BAvg +++
- Spd +++
- Def ++++

Year	Lev	Team	AB	R	H	HR	RBI	Avg	OB	Slg	OPS	bb%	ct%	Eye	SB	CS	x/h%	Iso	RC/G
2011	A-	Spokane	233	33	61	2	29	262	301	352	653	5	84	0.35	10	4	23	90	3.52
2012	A	Hickory	432	60	112	10	47	259	300	400	700	5	85	0.38	19	10	33	141	4.07
2013	A+	Myrtle Beach	377	65	115	5	59	305	350	454	803	6	82	0.39	27	8	37	149	5.43
2013	AA	Frisco	134	20	41	6	19	306	350	530	880	6	82	0.38	5	2	39	224	6.18

Fundamentally-sound INF who had career year. Posted highs in BA, HR, BB, and SB and reached AA at 19. Finished 3rd in CAR in BA and is adept at hitting LHP and RHP. Increased strength resulted in more pop and uses compact, line-drive stroke to hit gaps. Strong arm and range ideal for MIF, but can get careless with feet.

Ohlman,Michael — 2 — Baltimore

EXP MLB DEBUT: 2015 | **POTENTIAL:** Backup C | **7C**

Bats R Age 23
2009 (11) HS (FL)
- Pwr ++++
- BAvg +++
- Spd ++
- Def +

Year	Lev	Team	AB	R	H	HR	RBI	Avg	OB	Slg	OPS	bb%	ct%	Eye	SB	CS	x/h%	Iso	RC/G
2010	A	Delmarva	109	14	19	2	17	174	280	284	564	13	69	0.47	1	0	42	110	2.43
2011	A	Delmarva	375	38	84	4	51	224	312	307	619	11	74	0.50	1	2	25	83	3.23
2012	Rk	GCL Orioles	29	5	8	1	3	276	323	483	805	6	66	0.20	1	0	50	207	5.90
2012	A	Delmarva	171	27	52	2	28	304	417	456	873	16	84	1.22	0	1	38	152	6.90
2013	A+	Frederick	361	61	113	13	53	313	405	524	929	13	74	0.60	5	0	41	211	7.52

Tall, strong C led CAR in BA while posting career high in HR. Consistent hitter has feel for bat and found success with shortened stroke and use of entire field. Has flown under radar due to rash of injuries and drug suspension, but can mash with above average pop. Poor defender behind dish and footwork needs attention.

Olson,Matt — 3 — Oakland

EXP MLB DEBUT: 2016 | **POTENTIAL:** Starting 1B | **8D**

Bats L Age 20
2012 (1-S) HS (GA)
- Pwr ++++
- BAvg ++
- Spd +
- Def +++

Year	Lev	Team	AB	R	H	HR	RBI	Avg	OB	Slg	OPS	bb%	ct%	Eye	SB	CS	x/h%	Iso	RC/G
2012	Rk	AZL Athletics	177	29	50	8	41	282	342	520	862	8	74	0.35	0	0	50	237	6.30
2012	A-	Vermont	11	3	3	1	4	273	429	545	974	21	64	0.75	0	0	33	273	8.67
2013	A	Beloit	481	69	108	23	93	225	325	435	760	13	69	0.49	4	3	51	210	5.16

Big and strong-swinging prospect who struggled with LHP and Ks, but has big-time power to all fields. Vicious, uppercut stroke and leads to high K totals. Stays patient at plate and works counts to advantage. Not much value outside bat, but has average defensive skills with instincts and quality hands.

Olt,Mike — 5 — Chicago (N)

EXP MLB DEBUT: 2012 | **POTENTIAL:** Starting 3B | **8D**

Bats R Age 25
2010 (1) Connecticut
- Pwr ++++
- BAvg ++
- Spd ++
- Def ++++

Year	Lev	Team	AB	R	H	HR	RBI	Avg	OB	Slg	OPS	bb%	ct%	Eye	SB	CS	x/h%	Iso	RC/G
2012	AA	Frisco	354	65	102	28	82	288	393	579	972	15	71	0.60	4	0	45	291	8.00
2012	MLB	TEX	33	2	5	0	5	152	263	182	445	13	61	0.38	1	1	20	30	0.51
2013	AA	Frisco	12	1	4	1	2	333	333	750	1083	0	50	0.00	0	0	75	417	13.03
2013	AAA	Iowa	131	11	22	3	8	168	278	275	553	13	72	0.54	0	0	32	107	2.27
2013	AAA	Round Rock	230	37	49	11	32	213	317	422	739	13	61	0.39	0	0	53	209	5.16

Big and strong 3B came over to the Cubs in the Garza trade. Suffered a concussion last winter and a related vision problem. Cubs hope that he can regain the form that saw him hit .288 with 28 HR but there are significant concerns. Prior to '13 Olt showed good power and solid plate discipline. He's a good defender at 3B.

Oropesa,Ricky — 3 — San Francisco

EXP MLB DEBUT: 2015 | **POTENTIAL:** Backup 1B | **6C**

Bats L Age 24
2011 (3) USC
- Pwr +++
- BAvg ++
- Spd +
- Def ++

Year	Lev	Team	AB	R	H	HR	RBI	Avg	OB	Slg	OPS	bb%	ct%	Eye	SB	CS	x/h%	Iso	RC/G
2010	NCAA	USC	235	53	83	20	67	353	433	711	1143	12	78	0.65	7	5	52	357	9.85
2011	NCAA	USC	208	35	67	7	44	322	405	481	886	12	78	0.63	4	2	27	159	6.70
2012	A+	San Jose	518	70	136	16	98	263	338	425	763	10	71	0.39	1	1	36	162	5.13
2013	A+	San Jose	220	30	65	8	38	295	365	477	842	10	75	0.44	0	0	37	182	6.07
2013	AA	Richmond	241	19	50	6	23	207	254	307	561	6	69	0.20	0	0	24	100	2.07

Strong 1B with average power hit 14 HR across two levels in '13. Struggles with off-speed pitches and while he shows some plate discipline he can be overly aggressive. Strikes out far too much to hit for BA. Runs well below average and below average D limits him to 1B.

Ortega,Rafael — 8 — St. Louis

EXP MLB DEBUT: 2012 | **POTENTIAL:** Starting CF | **8D**

Bats L Age 23
2008 FA (Venezuela)
- Pwr ++
- BAvg +++
- Spd ++++
- Def ++++

Year	Lev	Team	AB	R	H	HR	RBI	Avg	OB	Slg	OPS	bb%	ct%	Eye	SB	CS	x/h%	Iso	RC/G
2010	Rk	Casper	288	69	103	7	45	358	415	510	925	9	85	0.67	23	9	26	153	6.91
2011	A	Asheville	479	77	141	9	66	294	333	438	772	6	81	0.31	32	19	30	144	4.93
2012	A+	Modesto	495	81	140	8	60	283	344	410	754	9	81	0.49	36	18	28	127	4.89
2012	MLB	COL	4	0	2	0	0	500	600	500	1100	20	50	0.50	1	0	0	0	14.09
2013	AA	Tulsa	158	22	36	1	10	228	311	297	608	11	84	0.73	9	4	19	70	3.29

Leadoff-hitting OF who ended season in June due to leg injury. Exhibits plus defensive acumen with excellent range and strong, accurate arm. Runs very well and has 40+ SB potential. Learning to be more selective at plate should lead to higher OBP. Lacks strength and swing plane for much pop, but owns bat speed.

Ortiz,Jose — 2 — Cincinnati

EXP MLB DEBUT: 2017 | **POTENTIAL:** Starting C | **7D**

Bats R Age 20
2012 (17) HS (PR)
- Pwr +++
- BAvg ++
- Spd ++
- Def +++

Year	Lev	Team	AB	R	H	HR	RBI	Avg	OB	Slg	OPS	bb%	ct%	Eye	SB	CS	x/h%	Iso	RC/G
2012	Rk	AZL Reds	39	10	14	0	6	359	468	538	1007	17	74	0.80	3	0	43	179	9.11
2013	Rk	Billings	164	21	43	8	32	262	320	494	814	8	74	0.33	1	0	51	232	5.59

Plus power potential as seen by 8 HR in 164 AB in rookie ball. Allowed only three passed balls and threw out 23% of base stealers. Shows good plate patience and can draw a walk. Strong arm, but average blocking and receiving skills. Not as strong defensively as others in the system, will have to hit to play.

Osuna,Jose | 3 | Pittsburgh

Bats R Age 21 — 2010 FA (Venezuela) — EXP MLB DEBUT: 2015 — POTENTIAL: Backup 1B — **6C**

- Pwr ++++
- BAvg ++
- Spd +
- Def +

Year	Lev	Team	AB	R	H	HR	RBI	Avg	OB	Slg	OPS	bb%	ct%	Eye	SB	CS	x/h%	Iso	RC/G
2011	Rk	GCL Pirates	178	28	59	4	32	331	393	511	904	9	88	0.86	3	2	36	180	6.74
2011	A-	State College	8	2	2	0	1	250	333	375	708	11	100	0.00	0	0	50	125	5.15
2012	A	West Virginia	482	68	135	16	72	280	324	454	778	6	83	0.38	4	4	39	174	4.96
2013	A+	Bradenton	454	47	111	8	48	244	299	357	655	7	83	0.46	18	6	31	112	3.61

Strong RH hitter failed to follow-up on breakout of 2012. Does have good raw power and makes solid contact, but remains inconsistent. A below-average runner, he was moved to 1B, further undermining his value. Needs to regain power stroke in 2014.

Ovando,Ariel | 39 | Houston

Bats L Age 20 — 2010 FA (DR) — EXP MLB DEBUT: 2017 — POTENTIAL: Starting OF — **8E**

- Pwr +++
- BAvg ++
- Spd ++
- Def ++

Year	Lev	Team	AB	R	H	HR	RBI	Avg	OB	Slg	OPS	bb%	ct%	Eye	SB	CS	x/h%	Iso	RC/G
2011	Rk	Greeneville	170	16	40	2	30	235	286	365	650	7	70	0.24	0	0	38	129	3.56
2012	Rk	Greeneville	223	34	64	6	35	287	351	444	795	9	70	0.33	0	0	33	157	5.60
2013	Rk	Greeneville	171	25	37	4	21	216	310	333	643	13	73	0.50	0	1	32	117	3.27
2013	A	Quad Cities	169	12	29	1	13	172	251	219	470	10	66	0.32	3	0	21	47	0.92

Long, strong OF who was sent back to short-season ball for a third time. Has upside, but remains long-term project. Physical tools are evident with plus power potential, but low BA a result of long, exploitable swing and subpar hitting instincts. Speed is below average and may have to move to 1B due to weak arm.

Owings,Chris | 6 | Arizona

Bats R Age 22 — 2009 (1) HS (SC) — EXP MLB DEBUT: 2013 — POTENTIAL: Starting SS — **8C**

- Pwr ++++
- BAvg ++
- 4.15 Spd +++
- Def +++

Year	Lev	Team	AB	R	H	HR	RBI	Avg	OB	Slg	OPS	bb%	ct%	Eye	SB	CS	x/h%	Iso	RC/G
2011	A+	Visalia	521	67	128	11	50	246	267	388	655	3	75	0.12	10	4	36	142	3.32
2012	A+	Visalia	241	51	78	11	24	324	358	544	902	5	74	0.21	8	3	37	220	6.62
2012	AA	Mobile	297	35	78	6	28	263	289	377	666	4	77	0.16	4	3	24	114	3.45
2013	AAA	Reno	546	104	180	12	81	330	356	482	837	4	82	0.22	20	7	28	152	5.59
2013	MLB	Arizona	55	5	16	0	5	291	361	382	742	10	82	0.60	2	0	31	91	5.20

Followed up with an even bigger year and looked good in the majors. Short, compact strokes generates above-average power. Plate discipline and BB rate remain problematic and suggests a BA correction. Has the tools to make all of the plays defensively and has improved enough to remain at short over the long term.

Palka,Daniel | 3 | Arizona

Bats L Age 22 — 2013 (3) Georgia Tech — EXP MLB DEBUT: 2016 — POTENTIAL: Backup 1B — **6C**

- Pwr ++++
- BAvg ++
- Spd +
- Def +

Year	Lev	Team	AB	R	H	HR	RBI	Avg	OB	Slg	OPS	bb%	ct%	Eye	SB	CS	x/h%	Iso	RC/G
2011	NCAA	Georgia Tech	232	41	69	12	52	297	356	556	912	8	69	0.30	3	0	48	259	7.21
2012	NCAA	Georgia Tech	238	44	72	12	47	303	349	550	899	7	79	0.34	6	1	46	248	6.50
2013	NCAA	Georgia Tech	237	55	81	17	66	342	418	637	1055	12	75	0.52	6	0	41	295	8.89
2013	Rk	Missoula	205	36	62	7	38	302	389	502	891	12	78	0.64	2	2	44	200	6.84
2013	A-	Hillsboro	47	10	16	2	10	340	426	574	1000	13	66	0.44	1	0	31	234	9.07

3rd round pick out of Georgia Tech, had a solid pro debut, hitting .310 with 9 HR. Showed surprising discipline at the plate, drawing 36 BB. Below-avg defender and looks to be limited to 1B, though he does have a good arm. Could struggle as he moves up, but the power is legit.

Panik,Joe | 4 | San Francisco

Bats L Age 23 — 2011 (1) St. John's — EXP MLB DEBUT: 2014 — POTENTIAL: Starting 2B — **8D**

- Pwr ++
- BAvg +++
- Spd +++
- Def +++

Year	Lev	Team	AB	R	H	HR	RBI	Avg	OB	Slg	OPS	bb%	ct%	Eye	SB	CS	x/h%	Iso	RC/G
2010	NCAA	St. John's	227	66	85	10	53	374	464	621	1085	14	93	2.24	6	3	38	247	9.04
2011	NCAA	St. John's	226	60	90	10	57	398	496	642	1138	16	89	1.83	21	6	36	243	9.83
2011	A-	Salem-Keizer	270	49	92	6	54	341	403	467	869	9	91	1.12	13	5	21	126	6.29
2012	A+	San Jose	535	93	159	7	76	297	366	402	768	10	90	1.07	10	4	24	105	5.23
2013	AA	Richmond	522	64	134	4	57	257	331	347	678	10	87	0.85	10	5	26	90	4.18

Small MIF with good all-around game. He works deep into counts with plate discipline and the ability to make sound, consistent contact with gap power. Average speed with good instincts will lead to double-digit SB. Drafted as a SS, the move to 2B should improve his arm and overall defensive skill.

Parker,Kyle | 37 | Colorado

Bats R Age 24 — 2010 (1) Clemson — EXP MLB DEBUT: 2015 — POTENTIAL: Starting RF/1B — **8C**

- Pwr ++++
- BAvg ++
- Spd ++
- Def ++

Year	Lev	Team	AB	R	H	HR	RBI	Avg	OB	Slg	OPS	bb%	ct%	Eye	SB	CS	x/h%	Iso	RC/G
2009	NCAA	Clemson	231	48	59	12	52	255	338	442	780	11	77	0.56	6	0	32	186	5.14
2010	NCAA	Clemson	247	85	85	20	64	344	465	656	1121	18	76	0.93	4	2	42	312	10.06
2011	A	Asheville	445	75	127	21	95	285	355	483	838	10	70	0.36	2	0	35	198	6.11
2012	A+	Modesto	390	86	120	23	73	308	408	562	969	14	77	0.75	1	2	39	254	7.84
2013	AA	Tulsa	480	70	138	23	74	288	342	492	834	8	79	0.40	6	6	36	204	5.68

Good FB hitter has major league power, but struggles to hit quality breaking balls. Working to tweak his swing and played 1B in the AFL. Good bat speed, short, compact stroke, and raw strength should allow power to grow. Has hit 20+ home runs in all three seasons as a pro. Remains below average defensively.

Paroubeck,Jordan | 79 | San Diego

Bats B Age 19 — 2013 (2) HS (CA) — EXP MLB DEBUT: 2018 — POTENTIAL: Starting OF — **8E**

- Pwr ++
- BAvg +++
- Spd +++
- Def +++

Year	Lev	Team	AB	R	H	HR	RBI	Avg	OB	Slg	OPS	bb%	ct%	Eye	SB	CS	x/h%	Iso	RC/G
2013		Did not play in pros.																	

Long, athletic, and projectable outfielder who has potential to be contributor in a number of ways. Owns clean swing from both sides and covers plate with long arms. BA potential muted by long swing, but can be fixed. Power is best future tool while he runs OK at present and has strong arm for corner OF.

Paulino,Dorssys | 6 | Cleveland

Bats R Age 19 — 2011 FA (DR) — EXP MLB DEBUT: 2017 — POTENTIAL: Starting SS — **8C**

- Pwr ++
- BAvg +++
- Spd +++
- Def ++

Year	Lev	Team	AB	R	H	HR	RBI	Avg	OB	Slg	OPS	bb%	ct%	Eye	SB	CS	x/h%	Iso	RC/G
2012	Rk	AZL Indians	172	42	61	6	30	355	406	610	1017	8	82	0.48	9	1	43	256	8.10
2012	A-	Mahoning Val	59	5	16	1	8	271	306	407	713	5	76	0.21	2	1	38	136	4.20
2013	A	Lake County	476	56	117	5	46	246	291	349	639	6	81	0.33	12	7	31	103	3.35

Aggressive INF who started slowly in first full season. Uses short stroke and pitch recognition to hit hard line drives to gaps. Uses whole field in approach and covers plate. Power potential is average, but all-around offensive game is nice. Runs well and has range and arm. Can get lazy with feet and could move to 2B or 3B.

Pederson,Joc | 8 | Los Angeles (N)

Bats L Age 22 — 2010 (11) HS (CA) — EXP MLB DEBUT: 2014 — POTENTIAL: Starting CF — **9D**

- Pwr +++
- BAvg ++++
- Spd +++
- Def +++

Year	Lev	Team	AB	R	H	HR	RBI	Avg	OB	Slg	OPS	bb%	ct%	Eye	SB	CS	x/h%	Iso	RC/G
2010	Rk	AZL Dodgers	7	1	0	0	0	0	364	0	364	36	29	0.80	0	0	0	0	-4.69
2011	Rk	Ogden	266	54	94	11	64	353	430	568	998	12	80	0.67	24	5	35	214	8.08
2011	A	Great Lakes	50	4	8	0	1	160	263	160	423	12	82	0.78	2	0	0	0	0.99
2012	A+	Rancho Cuca	434	96	136	18	70	313	386	516	902	11	81	0.63	26	14	35	203	6.72
2013	AA	Chattanooga	439	81	122	22	58	278	377	497	874	14	74	0.61	31	8	40	219	6.66

Quick, athletic OF displays five-tool potential. Starting to translate raw power into HR output. Balanced approach at plate, with smooth stroke and good bat speed should allow him to hit for BA, though he needs to improve against LHP. Above average speed on the bases and in CF where he has a plus arm and the reads to stick.

Peguero,Francisco | 79 | Baltimore

Bats R Age 26 — 2006 FA (DR) — EXP MLB DEBUT: 2012 — POTENTIAL: Starting OF — **7D**

- Pwr ++
- BAvg +++
- Spd +++
- Def ++

Year	Lev	Team	AB	R	H	HR	RBI	Avg	OB	Slg	OPS	bb%	ct%	Eye	SB	CS	x/h%	Iso	RC/G
2012	AAA	Fresno	449	46	122	5	68	272	295	394	689	3	82	0.18	1	0	29	122	3.84
2012	MLB	SF	16	6	3	0	0	188	188	188	375	0	56	0.00	3	0	0	0	-0.87
2013	Rk	AZL Giants	26	5	8	1	7	308	308	500	808	0	92	0.00	0	0	25	192	4.92
2013	AAA	Fresno	272	38	86	3	30	316	347	408	755	5	81	0.25	3	0	20	92	4.64
2013	MLB	SF	29	4	6	1	1	207	233	345	578	3	93	0.50	2	0	33	138	2.74

Athletic OF got another shot at the bigs following impressive campaign in AAA. Makes consistent hard contact with no discipline, going gap-to-gap. Limited to a corner where his speed works and arm is above average. At 26, needs to be more selective to secure starting role.

Peoples-Walls,Kenneth | 64 | St. Louis

Bats R Age 20 — 2011 (4) HS (LA) — EXP MLB DEBUT: 2016 — POTENTIAL: Starting SS — **7D**

- Pwr ++
- BAvg +++
- Spd +++
- Def ++

Year	Lev	Team	AB	R	H	HR	RBI	Avg	OB	Slg	OPS	bb%	ct%	Eye	SB	CS	x/h%	Iso	RC/G
2012	Rk	GCL Cardinals	150	19	39	2	21	260	293	367	660	4	77	0.20	4	5	23	107	3.47
2013	Rk	Johnson City	237	41	71	7	35	300	341	468	810	6	69	0.21	9	3	31	169	5.69

4th round pick in '11 showed progress, hitting .300 in the APPY. Improved selectivity at the plate led to breakout, though poor ct% suggests caution. Average defender could be moved to a new position. Has moderate power and needs to draw more walks.

Peraza,Jose — 6 — Atlanta

Bats R Age 20 | 2010 FA (Venezuela) | EXP MLB DEBUT: 2016 | POTENTIAL: Starting SS | 7B

- Pwr +
- BAvg + + +
- Spd + + + +
- Def + + +

Year	Lev	Team	AB	R	H	HR	RBI	Avg	OB	Slg	OPS	bb%	ct%	Eye	SB	CS	x/h%	Iso	RC/G
2012	Rk	Danville	121	21	34	1	18	281	331	339	670	7	85	0.50	15	2	15	58	3.79
2012	Rk	GCL Braves	85	17	27	0	10	318	348	424	772	4	93	0.67	10	3	22	106	5.06
2013	A	Rome	448	72	129	1	47	288	338	371	709	7	86	0.53	64	15	21	83	4.36

Dynamic SS from Venezuela continues to make progress. Potential top-of-the-order hitter handles the bat well with a short compact stroke and consistent contact. Doesn't draw a ton of walks, but has plus speed and stole 64 bases. Not likely to hit for much power, but Is a plus defender with good range and soft hands.

Perez,Carlos — 2 — Houston

Bats R Age 23 | 2007 FA (DR) | EXP MLB DEBUT: 2014 | POTENTIAL: Starting C | 7D

- Pwr + +
- BAvg + + +
- Spd + +
- Def + + + +

Year	Lev	Team	AB	R	H	HR	RBI	Avg	OB	Slg	OPS	bb%	ct%	Eye	SB	CS	x/h%	Iso	RC/G
2011	A	Lansing	383	58	98	3	41	256	321	355	677	9	81	0.50	6	2	27	99	3.99
2012	A	Lansing	273	48	75	5	40	275	357	447	804	11	86	0.92	3	2	43	172	5.75
2012	A+	Lancaster	88	11	28	0	10	318	362	409	771	6	81	0.35	0	1	25	91	5.05
2013	AA	Corpus Christi	53	6	15	1	5	283	333	415	748	7	79	0.36	0	0	33	132	4.72
2013	AAA	Oklahoma City	264	29	71	2	32	269	332	345	677	9	85	0.64	1	1	23	76	4.02

Agile, fluid C who has solid all-around game, though no tool stands out. Can hit for BA with consistent, contact-oriented stroke and gap approach. Doesn't hit for much pop and lacks projection in flat swing. Can be terrific behind plate with mobility and receiving ability. Arm strength is sufficient and has quick release.

Perez,Eury — 8 — Washington

Bats R Age 24 | 2007 FA (DR) | EXP MLB DEBUT: 2012 | POTENTIAL: Backup OF | 7C

- Pwr +
- BAvg + + +
- Spd + + + +
- Def + + + +

Year	Lev	Team	AB	R	H	HR	RBI	Avg	OB	Slg	OPS	bb%	ct%	Eye	SB	CS	x/h%	Iso	RC/G
2012	AA	Harrisburg	351	34	105	0	30	299	313	342	655	2	85	0.13	26	10	12	43	3.32
2012	AAA	Syracuse	159	21	53	0	10	333	365	390	755	5	84	0.31	20	5	15	57	4.69
2012	MLB	WAS	5	3	1	0	0	200	200	200	400	0	100	1.00	3	0	0	0	1.14
2013	AAA	Syracuse	403	55	121	7	28	300	322	422	744	3	84	0.20	23	8	25	122	4.42
2013	MLB	WAS	8	1	1	0	0	125	125	125	250	0	63	0.00	1	0	0	0	-2.76

Prospect status took a hit in '13. Continues to struggle with plate patience and inability to draw walks. This is a problem for a speed guy lacking power. Still one of best bunters in the minors, he's also a plus OF defender with a strong arm, staying in CF will not be a problem.

Perez,Hernan — 46 — Detroit

Bats R Age 23 | 2007 FA (Venezuela) | EXP MLB DEBUT: 2012 | POTENTIAL: Reserve INF | 7D

- Pwr +
- BAvg + + +
- Spd + + + +
- Def + +

Year	Lev	Team	AB	R	H	HR	RBI	Avg	OB	Slg	OPS	bb%	ct%	Eye	SB	CS	x/h%	Iso	RC/G
2012	A+	Lakeland	441	50	115	5	44	261	299	338	637	5	84	0.34	27	4	17	77	3.28
2012	MLB	DET	2	1	1	0	0	500	500	500	1000	0	100	1.00	0	0	0	0	6.83
2013	AA	Erie	362	45	109	4	35	301	324	423	746	3	87	0.25	24	7	31	122	4.53
2013	AAA	Toledo	67	3	20	0	4	299	347	343	691	7	90	0.71	4	0	15	45	4.18
2013	MLB	DET	66	13	13	0	5	197	221	227	448	3	77	0.13	1	0	8	30	0.70

Slim, athletic INF who was on DET playoff roster. Can play either middle infield spot, though 2B is best position. Has instincts that benefit on both sides of ball. Starting to hit for BA as he puts ball in play and can hit with two strikes. Power is mostly to gaps and can leg out doubles with plus speed. Defense hindered by careless actions.

Perez,Michael — 2 — Arizona

Bats L Age 21 | 2011 (5) HS (PR) | EXP MLB DEBUT: 2016 | POTENTIAL: Starting C | 7D

- Pwr + + +
- BAvg + +
- Spd +
- Def + + + +

Year	Lev	Team	AB	R	H	HR	RBI	Avg	OB	Slg	OPS	bb%	ct%	Eye	SB	CS	x/h%	Iso	RC/G
2011	Rk	AZL D'backs	23	5	5	2	3	217	280	565	845	8	57	0.20	1	0	80	348	7.15
2012	Rk	Missoula	225	43	66	10	60	293	351	542	893	8	68	0.28	0	1	47	249	7.09
2013	A	South Bend	162	20	40	2	14	247	307	383	690	8	66	0.25	0	0	40	136	4.29
2013	A+	Visalia	179	21	31	5	24	173	221	307	528	6	56	0.14	1	1	45	134	1.83

Strong, offensive-minded catcher struggled in full-season debut. Needs to be more selective at the plate and make more consistent contact. Was raw behind the plate when drafted and is still a work in progress, but has a very strong arm and most observers now believe in him as major league catcher.

Perio,Noah — 4 — Miami

Bats L Age 22 | 2009 (3) HS (CA) | EXP MLB DEBUT: 2015 | POTENTIAL: Backup 2B | 6C

- Pwr + +
- BAvg + + +
- Spd + + +
- Def + +

Year	Lev	Team	AB	R	H	HR	RBI	Avg	OB	Slg	OPS	bb%	ct%	Eye	SB	CS	x/h%	Iso	RC/G
2010	A-	Jamestown	225	30	58	0	31	258	310	302	612	7	89	0.68	7	0	17	44	3.30
2011	A	Greensboro	488	76	144	6	52	295	321	406	727	4	87	0.30	15	6	27	111	4.32
2012	A+	Jupiter	463	50	115	1	40	248	290	311	601	6	85	0.40	6	4	22	63	2.97
2013	A+	Jupiter	162	17	39	0	16	241	285	265	550	6	93	0.83	6	2	10	25	2.67
2013	AA	Jacksonville	177	20	41	1	14	232	295	288	583	8	85	0.59	2	0	20	56	2.88

Small, wiry 2B took another step back in '13. Makes good contact, but poor pitch recognition and plate discipline hinder his overall ability. Has some loft for a little guy, but his power is gap-to-gap. Runs average, though SB has dwindled. Below average defender moved from SS to 2B.

Perkins,Cameron — 9 — Philadelphia

Bats R Age 23 | 2012 (6) Purdue | EXP MLB DEBUT: 2105 | POTENTIAL: Backup OF | 7D

- Pwr + + +
- BAvg + + +
- Spd + +
- Def + +

Year	Lev	Team	AB	R	H	HR	RBI	Avg	OB	Slg	OPS	bb%	ct%	Eye	SB	CS	x/h%	Iso	RC/G
2012	NCAA	Purdue	242	53	86	9	61	355	388	529	917	5	92	0.65	8	3	28	174	6.44
2012	Rk	GCL Phillies	19	0	3	0	3	158	158	158	316	0	89	0.00	0	0	0	0	-0.40
2012	A-	Williamsport	270	31	82	1	38	304	338	407	745	5	85	0.34	5	2	30	104	4.65
2013	Rk	GCL Phillies	7	1	4	1	1	571	625	1143	1768	13	100	1.00	0	0	50	571	15.46
2013	A+	Clearwater	387	54	114	6	53	295	337	444	782	6	85	0.44	4	5	36	150	5.13

Polished college hitter had a solid full-season debut. Though can be overly aggressive at the plate, has shown he can hit for average. Some feel that with his 6-5, 195 frame, more power is on the way; for now, it's been mainly of the doubles variety. Relegated to OF corner, he'll need to add some pop to make an impact.

Peterson,D.J. — 5 — Seattle

Bats R Age 22 | 2013 (1) New Mexico | EXP MLB DEBUT: 2015 | POTENTIAL: Starting 3B/1B | 8C

- Pwr + + + +
- BAvg + + + +
- Spd + +
- Def + +

Year	Lev	Team	AB	R	H	HR	RBI	Avg	OB	Slg	OPS	bb%	ct%	Eye	SB	CS	x/h%	Iso	RC/G
2011	NCAA	New Mexico	246	39	78	6	48	317	356	545	901	6	79	0.29	0	0	53	228	6.68
2012	NCAA	New Mexico	248	57	104	17	78	419	488	734	1221	12	88	1.14	1	1	39	315	10.35
2013	NCAA	New Mexico	218	68	89	18	72	408	511	807	1319	17	84	1.31	5	1	53	399	12.15
2013	A-	Everett	109	20	34	6	27	312	385	532	917	11	83	0.72	0	1	35	220	6.80
2013	A	Clinton	99	16	29	7	20	293	340	576	915	7	76	0.29	1	0	45	283	6.68

Outstanding hitting prospect who leveraged bat speed and natural strength to high draft slot. Makes easy, hard contact with simple swing and has potential to hit in middle of order. Recognizes spin and works counts. Should hit for BA and pop. Secondary skills not as honed as speed and range limit him on base and in field.

Peterson,Dustin — 5 — San Diego

Bats R Age 19 | 2013 (2) HS, (AZ) | EXP MLB DEBUT: 2018 | POTENTIAL: Starting 3B | 7C

- Pwr + + +
- BAvg + + +
- Spd + +
- Def + +

Year	Lev	Team	AB	R	H	HR	RBI	Avg	OB	Slg	OPS	bb%	ct%	Eye	SB	CS	x/h%	Iso	RC/G
2013	Rk	AZL Padres	157	20	46	0	18	293	331	344	675	5	79	0.27	3	0	17	51	3.74

Pure-hitting infielder who moved to 3B from SS immediately upon signing. Profiles as offensive player with ability to hit for both BA and power. Has leverage in stroke to reach seats and uses entire field. Can be overzealous at plate and swing at bad pitches. Lacks speed and may not have enough arm for 3B.

Peterson,Jace — 6 — San Diego

Bats L Age 24 | 2011 (1) McNeese State | EXP MLB DEBUT: 2015 | POTENTIAL: Starting SS | 8C

- Pwr + +
- BAvg + + +
- Spd + + + +
- Def + + + +

Year	Lev	Team	AB	R	H	HR	RBI	Avg	OB	Slg	OPS	bb%	ct%	Eye	SB	CS	x/h%	Iso	RC/G
2010	NCAA	McNeese St.	232	68	82	4	49	353	451	491	942	15	85	1.17	35	5	26	138	7.59
2011	NCAA	McNeese St.	224	67	75	2	34	335	442	473	915	16	88	1.54	30	10	25	138	7.41
2011	A-	Eugene	276	48	67	2	27	243	359	333	692	15	81	0.94	39	10	24	91	4.53
2012	A	Fort Wayne	444	78	127	2	48	286	374	392	765	12	86	0.98	51	13	27	106	5.37
2013	A+	Lake Elsinore	423	78	128	7	66	303	382	454	835	11	86	0.93	42	10	29	151	6.10

Very athletic infielder who has good tools and well above average savvy. Can be flashy defender with ideal quickness and SS range. Arm isn't strong, but makes routine plays. Hits LHP in simple approach and has line drive pop. Steals loads of bases which is enhanced by on-base skills.

Phillips,Dane — 2 — San Diego

Bats L Age 23 | 2012 (2) HS (TX) | EXP MLB DEBUT: 2016 | POTENTIAL: Starting C | 7D

- Pwr + +
- BAvg + + +
- Spd + +
- Def + +

Year	Lev	Team	AB	R	H	HR	RBI	Avg	OB	Slg	OPS	bb%	ct%	Eye	SB	CS	x/h%	Iso	RC/G
2010	NCAA	Oklahoma St.	193	33	65	3	34	337	410	477	887	11	79	0.59	1	2	29	140	6.76
2011	NCAA	Oklahoma St.	245	44	83	4	32	339	389	518	907	8	79	0.38	2	0	34	180	6.86
2012	A-	Eugene	234	33	53	4	30	226	335	350	685	14	77	0.72	4	2	40	124	4.27
2013	A	Fort Wayne	224	34	63	5	23	281	337	433	770	8	76	0.36	1	0	35	152	5.08
2013	A+	Lake Elsinore	52	7	9	0	6	173	204	308	511	4	85	0.25	0	0	56	135	1.99

Big and strong catcher who needs refinement behind dish, but could evolve into offensive-minded backstop. Uses entire field in approach and has potential to hit for moderately high BA. Makes contact, but needs to pull more for pop. Quickness and receiving below average at present, but has nice arm.

Pierre,Nicolas — 8 — Milwaukee

EXP MLB DEBUT: 2017 | POTENTIAL: Starting OF | 7C

Bats R Age 18 | 2013 FA (DR)
Pwr +++ | BAvg +++ | Spd +++ | Def +++

Year	Lev	Team	AB	R	H	HR	RBI	Avg	OB	Slg	OPS	bb%	ct%	Eye	SB	CS	x/h%	Iso	RC/G
2013		Did not play in the US																	

Toolsy, athletic OF with good bat speed and line-drive oriented swing. Room to fill out will allow him to tap into more power. An above-average runner, Pierre will be a threat on the bases and in the outfield where he has a strong arm and good range.

Pillar,Kevin — 789 — Toronto

EXP MLB DEBUT: 2013 | POTENTIAL: Reserve OF | 6A

Bats R Age 25 | 2011 (32) Cal St/DomngzHills
Pwr ++ | BAvg ++++ | Spd +++ | Def +++

Year	Lev	Team	AB	R	H	HR	RBI	Avg	OB	Slg	OPS	bb%	ct%	Eye	SB	CS	x/h%	Iso	RC/G
2012	A	Lansing	335	49	108	5	57	322	386	451	837	9	84	0.66	35	6	27	128	5.97
2012	A+	Dunedin	164	16	53	1	34	323	343	415	758	3	90	0.29	16	3	21	91	4.66
2013	AA	New Hampshire	304	44	95	5	30	313	353	441	794	6	90	0.61	15	8	28	128	5.25
2013	AAA	Buffalo	201	30	60	4	27	299	338	493	831	6	81	0.31	8	5	45	194	5.74
2013	MLB	TOR	102	11	21	3	13	206	236	333	569	4	72	0.14	0	1	33	127	2.12

Consistent hitter who leveraged easy contact ability and speed into big league role. Posted high in HR while maintaining high BA. Puts ball in play with bat control and short, simple swing. Power is more of gap variety, though can showcase pull pop at times. Walk rate is low and iffy arm is neutralized by range and instincts in OF.

Pimentel,Guillermo — 7 — Seattle

EXP MLB DEBUT: 2016 | POTENTIAL: Starting OF | 8E

Bats L Age 21 | 2009 FA (DR)
Pwr ++++ | BAvg ++ | Spd ++ | Def ++

Year	Lev	Team	AB	R	H	HR	RBI	Avg	OB	Slg	OPS	bb%	ct%	Eye	SB	CS	x/h%	Iso	RC/G
2011	Rk	Pulaski	245	33	65	11	46	265	308	441	749	6	70	0.21	4	1	32	176	4.64
2012	A	Clinton	372	37	91	9	51	245	281	366	647	5	69	0.17	5	2	30	121	3.30
2013	Rk	AZL Mariners	20	1	6	0	2	300	300	400	700	0	70	0.00	0	0	33	100	3.99
2013	A	Clinton	202	24	52	6	30	257	324	416	740	9	66	0.29	4	3	35	158	4.92
2013	A+	High Desert	63	10	21	4	14	333	354	603	957	3	71	0.11	0	0	38	270	7.31

Strong and athletic slugger who repeated Low-A and showed little progress. Ceiling remains very high, but won't reach it without cutting down on Ks and recognizing spin. Still owns plus, raw power, but hasn't yet translated to games. Can be pull-conscious as well. Fringy speed, range, and arm keep him in LF.

Pinder,Chad — 56 — Oakland

EXP MLB DEBUT: 2017 | POTENTIAL: Starting SS | 7D

Bats R Age 22 | 2013 (2-S) Virginia Tech
Pwr ++ | BAvg ++ | Spd +++ | Def +++

Year	Lev	Team	AB	R	H	HR	RBI	Avg	OB	Slg	OPS	bb%	ct%	Eye	SB	CS	x/h%	Iso	RC/G
2011	NCAA	Virginia Tech	104	21	33	3	14	317	360	510	870	6	82	0.37	4	1	30	192	6.16
2012	NCAA	Virginia Tech	212	36	69	7	37	325	367	538	905	6	80	0.33	6	5	43	212	6.61
2013	NCAA	Virginia Tech	240	49	77	8	50	321	375	483	859	8	84	0.55	5	4	29	163	6.02
2013	A-	Vermont	140	14	28	3	8	200	263	293	556	8	71	0.29	1	0	25	93	2.10

Tall, rangy INF who mostly played SS in debut. Steady performer with good quickness, agility and arm. Offense development will dictate future as he has sufficient bat speed, but lacks projection in level swing path. Has tendency to expand strike zone and needs to get on base more. Likely to move to 2B or 3B long-term.

Pinto,Josmil — 2 — Minnesota

EXP MLB DEBUT: 2013 | POTENTIAL: Starting C | 7B

Bats R Age 25 | 2006 FA (Venezuela)
Pwr +++ | BAvg +++ | Spd + | Def ++

Year	Lev	Team	AB	R	H	HR	RBI	Avg	OB	Slg	OPS	bb%	ct%	Eye	SB	CS	x/h%	Iso	RC/G
2012	A+	Fort Myers	349	45	103	12	51	295	366	473	839	10	82	0.62	0	0	35	178	5.94
2012	AA	New Britain	47	8	14	2	9	298	353	553	906	8	79	0.40	0	0	50	255	6.76
2013	AA	New Britain	386	59	119	14	68	308	407	482	889	14	82	0.90	0	2	32	174	6.79
2013	AAA	Rochester	70	6	22	1	6	314	333	486	819	3	83	0.17	0	0	45	171	5.40
2013	MLB	MIN	76	10	26	4	12	342	390	566	956	7	71	0.27	0	0	35	224	7.58

Short, stout C who burst onto scene and fared well in MIN. Has drastically improved in last two seasons and posted high in HR. Has mature approach and is consistent producer. Draws walks and make easy contact. Power projects as average, mostly to pull side. Becoming better receiver, but poor footwork negates strong arm.

Piscotty,Stephen — 9 — St. Louis

EXP MLB DEBUT: 2014 | POTENTIAL: Starting RF | 8C

Bats R Age 23 | 2012 (1) Stanford
Pwr +++ | BAvg +++ | Spd +++ | Def +++

Year	Lev	Team	AB	R	H	HR	RBI	Avg	OB	Slg	OPS	bb%	ct%	Eye	SB	CS	x/h%	Iso	RC/G
2011	NCAA	Stanford	216	34	80	3	39	370	416	477	893	7	88	0.63	2	3	20	106	6.42
2012	NCAA	Stanford	246	44	81	5	56	329	402	467	870	11	91	1.30	4	0	26	138	6.44
2012	A	Quad Cities	210	29	62	4	27	295	351	448	798	8	88	0.72	3	0	37	152	5.44
2013	A+	Palm Beach	243	30	71	9	35	292	341	477	818	7	89	0.67	4	5	35	185	5.50
2013	AA	Springfield	184	17	55	6	24	299	365	446	810	9	90	1.00	7	3	27	147	5.57

Does everything above-average, but doesn't have a plus tool besides the ability to hit. Makes consistent contact and uses the whole field. Moved to RF where he runs well and has a plus arm and range. Does have good bat speed and a discerning eye so power spike looks legit.

Plawecki,Kevin — 2 — New York (N)

EXP MLB DEBUT: 2015 | POTENTIAL: Starting C | 7B

Bats R Age 23 | 2012 (1) Purdue
Pwr ++ | BAvg +++ | Spd + | Def +++

Year	Lev	Team	AB	R	H	HR	RBI	Avg	OB	Slg	OPS	bb%	ct%	Eye	SB	CS	x/h%	Iso	RC/G
2011	NCAA	Purdue	211	46	72	2	39	341	393	436	829	8	95	1.80	3	2	22	95	5.87
2012	NCAA	Purdue	223	54	80	7	47	359	426	578	1004	10	96	3.25	3	3	39	220	7.92
2012	A-	Brooklyn	216	26	54	7	27	250	328	384	712	10	89	1.04	0	0	28	134	4.50
2013	A	Savannah	245	35	77	6	43	314	373	494	867	9	87	0.72	1	0	40	180	6.26
2013	A+	St. Lucie	204	25	60	2	37	294	354	392	746	9	90	0.90	0	0	27	98	4.92

Doesn't have the upside of a d'Arnaud but prospect status took nice bump up in '13. Exhibits advanced plate approach, solid Eye, and utilizes whole field for base hits. Still some untapped power potential despite contact-first approach. Solid blocker behind plate, decent arm, and good mobility for his size.

Polanco,Gregory — 8 — Pittsburgh

EXP MLB DEBUT: 2014 | POTENTIAL: Starting CF | 9C

Bats L Age 22 | 2009 FA (DR)
Pwr ++++ | BAvg +++ | Spd ++++ | Def ++++

Year	Lev	Team	AB	R	H	HR	RBI	Avg	OB	Slg	OPS	bb%	ct%	Eye	SB	CS	x/h%	Iso	RC/G
2011	A-	State College	10	0	1	0	1	100	100	100	200	0	80	0.00	0	0	0	0	-2.36
2012	A	West Virginia	437	84	142	16	85	325	387	522	908	9	85	0.69	40	15	34	197	6.70
2013	A+	Bradenton	218	29	68	6	30	312	359	472	831	7	83	0.43	24	4	34	161	5.67
2013	AA	Altoona	243	36	64	6	41	263	358	407	766	13	85	1.00	13	7	33	144	5.29
2013	AAA	Indianapolis	9	1	2	0	0	222	222	222	444	0	100	####	1	0	0	0	1.56

Tall, lanky CF is a legitimate 5-tool prospect. Just starting to tap into power. Continues to make strides as a hitter, becoming more selective. Swing can get long, but he makes up for it with a lightning-quick bat. Has plus speed on the bases and in CF, where he covers tons of ground and has a strong throwing arm.

Polanco,Jorge — 46 — Minnesota

EXP MLB DEBUT: 2016 | POTENTIAL: Starting SS | 7B

Bats B Age 20 | 2009 FA (DR)
Pwr ++ | BAvg +++ | Spd +++ | Def +++

Year	Lev	Team	AB	R	H	HR	RBI	Avg	OB	Slg	OPS	bb%	ct%	Eye	SB	CS	x/h%	Iso	RC/G
2010	Rk	GCL Twins	103	12	23	1	12	223	304	301	605	10	91	1.33	2	4	26	78	3.51
2011	Rk	GCL Twins	172	21	43	1	16	250	310	349	659	8	86	0.63	6	4	28	99	3.85
2012	Rk	Elizabethton	173	35	55	5	27	318	389	514	903	10	85	0.77	6	3	40	197	6.79
2013	A	Cedar Rapids	465	76	143	5	78	308	365	452	817	8	87	0.71	4	4	33	144	5.72

Consistent, steady INF who had successful first full season. Split time between 2B and SS and has ample range at both. Has reliable glove with quick actions and soft hands. Controls plate with discerning eye and makes contact from both sides. Could grow into power as he adds strength, but generally has gap approach.

Pompey,Dalton — 78 — Toronto

EXP MLB DEBUT: 2016 | POTENTIAL: Reserve OF | 7D

Bats B Age 21 | 2010 (16) HS (CAN)
Pwr ++ | BAvg ++ | Spd ++++ | Def +++

Year	Lev	Team	AB	R	H	HR	RBI	Avg	OB	Slg	OPS	bb%	ct%	Eye	SB	CS	x/h%	Iso	RC/G
2011	Rk	GCL Blue Jays	158	34	41	4	12	259	357	405	762	13	78	0.69	19	0	32	146	5.20
2012	Rk	Bluefield	14	2	5	0	1	357	357	571	929	0	86	0.00	1	0	40	214	6.61
2012	A-	Vancouver	34	11	10	0	4	294	442	441	883	21	79	1.29	3	0	40	147	7.44
2012	A	Lansing	22	1	5	0	3	227	261	364	625	4	77	0.20	1	1	40	136	3.22
2013	A	Lansing	437	68	114	6	40	261	354	394	748	13	76	0.59	38	10	32	133	5.08

Quick and athletic outfielder who is significant sleeper after breakthrough campaign. Spent most of time in CF where he has ample range and good arm strength. Speed is best present attribute, but could grow into good hitter with emerging power. Has quick hands and short stroke and can be too patient for own good.

Puello,Cesar — 9 — New York (N)

EXP MLB DEBUT: 2015 | POTENTIAL: Starting RF | 8C

Bats R Age 23 | 2007 FA (DR)
Pwr ++++ | BAvg ++ | Spd ++++ | Def +++

Year	Lev	Team	AB	R	H	HR	RBI	Avg	OB	Slg	OPS	bb%	ct%	Eye	SB	CS	x/h%	Iso	RC/G
2009	Rk	Kingsport	196	37	58	5	23	296	330	423	754	5	74	0.20	15	5	26	128	4.65
2010	A	Savannah	404	80	118	1	34	292	344	359	703	7	80	0.39	45	10	20	67	4.21
2011	A+	St. Lucie	441	67	114	10	50	259	288	397	684	4	77	0.17	19	9	32	138	3.73
2012	A+	St. Lucie	227	36	59	4	21	260	282	423	705	3	74	0.12	19	2	42	163	4.07
2013	AA	Binghamton	331	63	108	16	73	326	379	547	926	8	75	0.34	24	7	36	221	7.01

Biogenesis suspension clouds 2013 breakout. Mid-season swing adjustment boosted HRs and BA. Has above average speed, impressive power, and plus arm. Uppercut swing with good bat speed. Knows how to steal bases. Good opposite field power. Needs to improve reads but adequate range for either corner OF spot.

Pullin,Andrew — 4 — Philadelphia

EXP MLB DEBUT: 2016 | POTENTIAL: Starting 2B | **8D**

Bats L Age 20 | 2012 (5) HS (WA)

- Pwr +++
- BAvg ++++
- Spd ++
- Def ++

Year	Lev	Team	AB	R	H	HR	RBI	Avg	OB	Slg	OPS	bb%	ct%	Eye	SB	CS	x/h%	Iso	RC/G
2012	Rk	GCL Phillies	140	16	45	2	13	321	375	436	811	8	77	0.38	3	5	27	114	5.59
2013	A-	Williamsport	211	20	55	3	23	261	284	412	697	3	82	0.19	1	3	38	152	3.96

Made transition from OF to 2B and improved defensively as season wore on, convincing most that he can stick in the IF. Bat will play up there, as he has great hitting instincts, a smooth, quiet stroke and opposite-field power. Upside here if he can improve his patience and maintain his defense.

Quinn,Roman — 6 — Philadelphia

EXP MLB DEBUT: 2016 | POTENTIAL: Starting SS | **8D**

Bats B Age 21 | 2011 (2) HS (FL)

- Pwr ++
- BAvg +++
- 4.00 Spd ++++
- Def ++

Year	Lev	Team	AB	R	H	HR	RBI	Avg	OB	Slg	OPS	bb%	ct%	Eye	SB	CS	x/h%	Iso	RC/G
2012	A-	Williamsport	267	56	75	1	23	281	349	408	757	9	77	0.46	30	6	28	127	5.13
2013	A	Lakewood	260	37	62	5	21	238	310	346	656	9	75	0.42	32	9	24	108	3.62

Quick-twitch INF with a bit of pop and blazing speed despite slight frame. Can get on base, and the SB have followed. Broken hand stalled 2013 and a ruptured Achilles tendon will wipe out half of 2014. With shaky defense, there has been talk of returning him to CF, a position he played in high school, or perhaps to 2B.

Quintana,Gabriel — 5 — San Diego

EXP MLB DEBUT: 2016 | POTENTIAL: Starting 3B | **7D**

Bats R Age 21 | 2009 FA (DR)

- Pwr +++
- BAvg +++
- Spd ++
- Def ++

Year	Lev	Team	AB	R	H	HR	RBI	Avg	OB	Slg	OPS	bb%	ct%	Eye	SB	CS	x/h%	Iso	RC/G
2011	Rk	AZL Padres	30	3	8	1	3	267	333	400	733	9	80	0.50	0	1	25	133	4.52
2012	Rk	AZL Padres	151	25	44	5	36	291	318	483	802	4	75	0.16	2	1	39	192	5.25
2012	A-	Eugene	61	2	14	1	8	230	242	311	553	2	70	0.06	0	0	21	82	1.84
2013	Rk	AZL Padres	21	4	7	0	3	333	364	429	792	5	81	0.25	0	0	29	95	5.19
2013	A	Fort Wayne	347	50	106	9	44	305	327	447	774	3	74	0.12	6	2	28	141	4.84

Tall and athletic infielder who is big-time sleeper. Possesses natural hitting skills with average power potential. Free swinging approach may not play well at higher levels, but can hit with two strikes. Focuses on hard contact to gaps and should increase HR with more loft. OK defender with quick hands and feet.

Ragira,Brian — 39 — San Francisco

EXP MLB DEBUT: 2016 | POTENTIAL: Starting 1B/OF | **7D**

Bats R Age 22 | 2013 (4) Stanford

- Pwr ++
- BAvg +++
- Spd ++
- Def +++

Year	Lev	Team	AB	R	H	HR	RBI	Avg	OB	Slg	OPS	bb%	ct%	Eye	SB	CS	x/h%	Iso	RC/G
2011	NCAA	Stanford	206	30	66	4	43	320	364	461	825	6	78	0.30	2	2	24	141	5.67
2012	NCAA	Stanford	252	41	83	5	50	329	374	448	822	7	81	0.38	3	2	24	119	5.56
2013	NCAA	Stanford	222	34	71	8	42	320	360	482	842	6	89	0.58	4	1	27	162	5.67
2013	Rk	AZL Giants	28	4	10	0	6	357	379	464	844	3	79	0.17	0	0	20	107	5.81
2013	A-	Salem-Keizer	179	29	47	3	36	263	356	391	747	13	70	0.48	1	1	34	128	5.14

Strong, athletic 1B split time in the OF where he has a strong arm and runs well enough to cover ground. Good bat speed and smooth stroke from the right side will make him an average hitter, but lack of power potential hinders positional value. Lacks plate discipline, but should develop ability to make consistent contact.

Rahier,Tanner — 5 — Cincinnati

EXP MLB DEBUT: 2016 | POTENTIAL: Starting 3B | **7D**

Bats R Age 20 | 2012 (2) HS (CA)

- Pwr ++
- BAvg ++
- Spd ++
- Def +++

Year	Lev	Team	AB	R	H	HR	RBI	Avg	OB	Slg	OPS	bb%	ct%	Eye	SB	CS	x/h%	Iso	RC/G
2012	Rk	AZL Reds	193	21	37	4	30	192	271	311	582	10	78	0.49	5	2	38	119	2.71
2013	A	Dayton	410	31	91	7	61	222	244	320	564	3	80	0.15	0	5	26	98	2.18

Second straight disappointing season, but still a lot of potential and tools. Athletic, plays hard, plus defender with plus arm, and plus power potential. Over-aggressiveness at plate hinders bb% and power numbers. Still has time to develop plate patience and become solid all-around 3B.

Ramirez,Harold — 789 — Pittsburgh

EXP MLB DEBUT: 2016 | POTENTIAL: Starting CF | **8D**

Bats R Age 19 | 2011 FA (Colombia)

- Pwr +++
- BAvg +++
- Spd +++
- Def +++

Year	Lev	Team	AB	R	H	HR	RBI	Avg	OB	Slg	OPS	bb%	ct%	Eye	SB	CS	x/h%	Iso	RC/G
2012	Rk	GCL Pirates	135	18	35	1	12	259	291	333	624	4	85	0.30	9	5	20	74	3.13
2013	A-	Jamestown	274	42	78	5	40	285	340	409	749	8	81	0.44	23	11	26	124	4.76

Spark-plug type put up impressive numbers. Has an aggressive approach with good pop for his size and plus speed. Is raw as a base-stealer and got nabbed 11 times, but should improve. Struggled somewhat vs. LHP and split time between all three OF spots, but will likely stick in CF for now.

Ramirez,Jose — 456 — Cleveland

EXP MLB DEBUT: 2013 | POTENTIAL: Utility player | **6A**

Bats B Age 21 | 2009 FA (DR)

- Pwr +
- BAvg +++
- Spd +++
- Def +++

Year	Lev	Team	AB	R	H	HR	RBI	Avg	OB	Slg	OPS	bb%	ct%	Eye	SB	CS	x/h%	Iso	RC/G
2011	Rk	AZL Indians	194	30	63	1	20	325	348	448	797	3	91	0.41	12	6	29	124	5.20
2012	A-	Mahoning Val	11	2	4	0	0	364	417	545	962	8	100	1.00	2	1	50	182	7.55
2012	A	Lake County	277	54	98	3	27	354	405	462	867	8	91	0.92	15	6	20	108	6.23
2013	AA	Akron	482	78	131	3	38	272	326	349	675	7	91	0.95	38	16	19	77	4.11
2013	MLB	CLE	12	5	4	0	0	333	429	500	929	14	83	1.00	0	1	25	167	7.60

Short, diminutive INF who has been promoted aggressively. Led EL in SB and focuses on small ball. Makes extreme contact with simple stroke, yet can slash line drives to gaps. Controls bat from both sides and could hit leadoff with more patience. Has low ceiling due to below average pop, but has defensive versatility.

Ramsey,James — 8 — St. Louis

EXP MLB DEBUT: 2014 | POTENTIAL: Starting CF | **7C**

Bats L Age 24 | 2012 (1) Florida State

- Pwr ++
- BAvg +++
- Spd +++
- Def +++

Year	Lev	Team	AB	R	H	HR	RBI	Avg	OB	Slg	OPS	bb%	ct%	Eye	SB	CS	x/h%	Iso	RC/G
2012	NCAA	Florida St.	233	78	88	13	58	378	510	652	1162	21	82	1.50	11	5	36	275	10.66
2012	A+	Palm Beach	210	36	48	1	14	229	333	314	648	14	72	0.56	10	2	27	86	3.78
2013	A+	Palm Beach	61	17	22	1	7	361	466	557	1023	16	80	1.00	1	0	36	197	8.89
2013	AA	Springfield	347	61	87	15	44	251	350	424	774	13	69	0.49	8	4	32	173	5.36
2013	AAA	Memphis	3	0	0	0	0	0	0	0	0	0	67	0.00	0	0	0	0	-6.12

Solid season for this former 1st rounder. Is a good athlete, but none of his tools are plus. Has enough speed to stick in CF and showed improved power at AA. Contact rate dropped when he moved up and raises concerns about his ability to hit for both average and power. Has a simple swing and still has potential.

Ratterree,Michael — 9 — Milwaukee

EXP MLB DEBUT: 2016 | POTENTIAL: Backup OF | **6C**

Bats R Age 23 | 2013 (10) Rice

- Pwr +++
- BAvg +++
- Spd ++
- Def ++

Year	Lev	Team	AB	R	H	HR	RBI	Avg	OB	Slg	OPS	bb%	ct%	Eye	SB	CS	x/h%	Iso	RC/G
2010	NCAA	Rice	224	60	63	10	64	281	404	464	868	17	80	1.05	3	2	32	183	6.64
2011	NCAA	Rice	260	46	85	6	53	327	379	481	860	8	83	0.50	6	2	32	154	6.11
2012	NCAA	Rice	189	39	44	6	32	233	372	407	780	18	79	1.08	6	2	45	175	5.66
2013	NCAA	Rice	226	48	59	9	41	261	381	425	806	16	81	1.00	13	3	32	164	5.83
2013	Rk	Helena	258	63	81	12	58	314	377	585	962	9	72	0.36	7	3	49	271	7.86

Small, athletic OF continued to hit well in Rookie ball. Known for his plus makeup and ability to hit for BA in college, the Brewers hope he carries it over to pro ranks. Has some patience and power in the box, though his aggressive approach was seen in his ct%. Coverted from 2B, athleticsm works in a corner OF spot.

Realmuto, Jacob — 2 — Miami

EXP MLB DEBUT: 2014 | POTENTIAL: Starting C | **7C**

Bats R Age 23 | 2010 (3) HS (OK)

- Pwr ++
- BAvg ++
- Spd +++
- Def +++

Year	Lev	Team	AB	R	H	HR	RBI	Avg	OB	Slg	OPS	bb%	ct%	Eye	SB	CS	x/h%	Iso	RC/G
2010	Rk	GCL Marlins	40	2	7	0	4	175	298	175	473	15	73	0.64	0	1	0	0	1.27
2011	A	Greensboro	348	46	100	12	49	287	337	454	791	7	78	0.33	13	6	31	167	5.18
2012	A+	Jupiter	446	63	114	8	46	256	313	345	658	8	86	0.58	13	5	21	90	3.68
2013	AA	Jacksonville	368	41	88	5	39	239	307	353	660	9	82	0.53	9	1	33	114	3.78

Another disappointing year raises questions about hit tool. Has raw power and good bat speed, but results have been minimal. Defense is MLB ready now. Continues to impress with his receiving skills and strong arm, nailing 34% of attempted base-stealers. On the bases, he is not a burner but runs better than most catchers.

Reed,Michael — 79 — Milwaukee

EXP MLB DEBUT: 2016 | POTENTIAL: Backup OF | **7D**

Bats R Age 21 | 2011 (5) HS (TX)

- Pwr +
- BAvg +++
- Spd ++++
- Def +++

Year	Lev	Team	AB	R	H	HR	RBI	Avg	OB	Slg	OPS	bb%	ct%	Eye	SB	CS	x/h%	Iso	RC/G
2011	Rk	AZL Brewers	56	11	13	0	5	232	295	375	670	8	70	0.29	1	0	46	143	4.07
2012	Rk	Helena	179	29	44	1	20	246	335	302	637	12	68	0.41	11	1	16	56	3.51
2012	A+	Brevard County	32	5	9	0	5	281	425	281	706	20	75	1.00	3	0	0	0	4.82
2012	AA	Huntsville	7	0	0	0	0	0	0	0	0	0	57	0.00	0	0	0	0	-7.11
2013	A	Wisconsin	455	68	130	1	40	286	382	400	782	13	76	0.66	26	10	28	114	5.67

Small, strong corner OF had great season in '13. Flat, line-drive oriented swing limits his power potential, and poor pitch recognition and ct% reflect in his BA. Relies on his speed and patience to make an impact offensively. Good defender in either corner, though may not hit enough to stick full-time.

Reinheimer, Jack — 46 — Seattle
EXP MLB DEBUT: 2016 — POTENTIAL: Starting 2B/SS — 7C
Bats R — Age 21 — 2013 (5) East Carolina
Pwr ++ / BAvg +++ / Spd +++ / Def +++

Year	Lev	Team	AB	R	H	HR	RBI	Avg	OB	Slg	OPS	bb%	ct%	Eye	SB	CS	x/h%	Iso	RC/G
2011	NCAA	East Carolina	212	33	66	0	23	311	381	330	712	10	86	0.80	3	1	6	19	4.51
2012	NCAA	East Carolina	238	36	70	2	22	294	333	374	707	6	88	0.48	9	1	20	80	4.22
2013	NCAA	East Carolina	221	32	60	2	21	271	356	339	695	12	81	0.67	10	3	18	68	4.31
2013	A-	Everett	249	39	67	2	30	269	352	325	678	11	80	0.63	18	5	13	56	4.05

Athletic and quick infielder whose average tools play up because of his knowledge of game and instincts. Plays game with mature approach and possesses solid defensive skills, including range and arm strength. Waits for pitches to hit, though lacks strength to hit for much gap power, much less HR. Has good speed, but not a burner.

Renda, Tony — 4 — Washington
EXP MLB DEBUT: 2016 — POTENTIAL: Backup 2B — 7D
Bats R — Age 23 — 2012 (2) California
Pwr + / BAvg +++ / Spd +++ / Def ++

Year	Lev	Team	AB	R	H	HR	RBI	Avg	OB	Slg	OPS	bb%	ct%	Eye	SB	CS	x/h%	Iso	RC/G
2010	NCAA	California	217	55	81	3	37	373	421	548	970	8	84	0.53	13	2	35	175	7.49
2011	NCAA	California	265	38	88	3	44	332	363	434	797	5	89	0.46	9	2	22	102	5.18
2012	NCAA	California	219	41	75	5	27	342	419	484	903	12	92	1.61	16	3	28	142	6.87
2012	A-	Auburn	295	47	78	0	32	264	334	295	629	10	89	0.94	15	3	12	31	3.63
2013	A	Hagerstown	521	99	153	3	51	294	375	405	780	12	88	1.05	30	6	32	111	5.52

Put together nice first full season though he lacks a standout tool. Can hit for average to all fields, draw walks, run the bases, and defend 2B well with a strong arm. Utilizes short, compact swing. Excellent at pitch recognition and situational hitting.

Renfroe, Hunter — 9 — San Diego
EXP MLB DEBUT: 2016 — POTENTIAL: Starting RF — 9C
Bats R — Age 20 — 2013 (1) Mississippi State
Pwr ++++ / BAvg +++ / Spd +++ / Def +++

Year	Lev	Team	AB	R	H	HR	RBI	Avg	OB	Slg	OPS	bb%	ct%	Eye	SB	CS	x/h%	Iso	RC/G
2011	NCAA	Mississippi St.	26	4	4	0	2	154	241	192	434	10	69	0.38	0	0	25	38	0.53
2012	NCAA	Mississippi St.	230	24	58	4	25	252	315	374	689	8	78	0.41	7	1	34	122	4.04
2013	NCAA	Mississippi St.	255	56	88	16	65	345	424	620	1044	12	83	0.81	9	4	40	275	8.44
2013	A-	Eugene	104	20	32	4	18	308	339	510	849	5	75	0.19	2	0	41	202	5.89
2013	A	Fort Wayne	66	6	14	2	7	212	257	379	636	6	65	0.17	0	0	50	167	3.31

Big and strong outfielder who fits classic RF profile with plus power and arm strength. Has tendency to expand strike zone with unrefined approach, but has decent hitting instincts. Generates plus bat speed, but can be fooled by breaking balls. Runs well for size and has enough range and savvy in the OF.

Reyes, Victor — 79 — Atlanta
EXP MLB DEBUT: 2018 — POTENTIAL: Starting OF — 8D
Bats L — Age 19 — 2011 FA (Venezuela)
Pwr +++ / BAvg +++ / Spd ++ / Def +++

Year	Lev	Team	AB	R	H	HR	RBI	Avg	OB	Slg	OPS	bb%	ct%	Eye	SB	CS	x/h%	Iso	RC/G
2013	Rk	Danville	81	12	26	0	4	321	345	358	703	4	89	0.33	0	0	12	37	4.04
2013	Rk	GCL Braves	112	22	40	0	21	357	419	446	866	10	82	0.60	5	1	23	89	6.41

Tall, athletic OF was impressive in his state-side debut. Has a polished approach at the plate and a good understanding of the strike zone. Didn't show much power in debut, but it should develop into at least an average tool down the road. Should have enough range and arm strength to play either corner in the majors.

Reynoso, Jonathan — 8 — Cincinnati
EXP MLB DEBUT: 2017 — POTENTIAL: Starting CF — 8E
Bats R — Age 21 — 2010 FA (DR)
Pwr +++ / BAvg ++ / Spd ++++ / Def +++

Year	Lev	Team	AB	R	H	HR	RBI	Avg	OB	Slg	OPS	bb%	ct%	Eye	SB	CS	x/h%	Iso	RC/G
2012	Rk	AZL Reds	190	37	59	2	16	311	332	411	742	3	88	0.26	30	9	20	100	4.45
2013	Rk	Billings	160	16	38	2	12	238	261	306	567	3	82	0.17	9	5	18	69	2.25

Tough year battling knee injury, and numbers dipped. Still very toolsy, high upside prospect. Rarely walks but makes consistent contact. Swing gets long and could make better contact by shortening swing path. Has plus speed and runs bases well. Shows above-average power potential. Strong arm and range to stick in CF.

Rijo, Wendell — 4 — Boston
EXP MLB DEBUT: 2018 — POTENTIAL: Starting 2B — 8E
Bats R — Age 18 — 2012 FA (DR)
Pwr ++ / BAvg +++ / Spd +++ / Def ++

Year	Lev	Team	AB	R	H	HR	RBI	Avg	OB	Slg	OPS	bb%	ct%	Eye	SB	CS	x/h%	Iso	RC/G
2013	Rk	GCL Red Sox	170	28	46	0	20	271	354	359	713	11	83	0.76	15	5	33	88	4.67
2013	A-	Lowell	14	1	5	0	0	357	357	571	929	0	79	0.00	0	1	40	214	6.85

Smart, instinctual INF who is advanced for age. Focuses on making hard contact with line drive stroke and legs out doubles with average speed. Controls bat with repeatable stroke and has enough juice for average power potential. Owns soft, quick hands at 2B and can turn double play well. Arm strength limits him to that position.

Rivera, Alexis — 79 — Kansas City
EXP MLB DEBUT: 2017 — POTENTIAL: Starting OF — 7D
Bats L — Age 20 — 2012 (10) HS (FL)
Pwr +++ / BAvg +++ / Spd +++ / Def ++

Year	Lev	Team	AB	R	H	HR	RBI	Avg	OB	Slg	OPS	bb%	ct%	Eye	SB	CS	x/h%	Iso	RC/G
2012	Rk	AZL Royals	176	35	60	3	34	341	417	477	894	12	84	0.79	9	3	23	136	6.79
2013	Rk	Idaho Falls	212	44	57	4	26	269	340	363	704	10	83	0.62	9	5	21	94	4.29

Strong, compact OF who hasn't played full-season ball. Uses mature approach to get on base and has above average raw power. Bat speed is a little short, but can muscle balls out. Loose swing helps BA, but struggles against LHP. Runs well and is slightly below average defender with average arm in OF corner.

Rivera, Yadiel — 6 — Milwaukee
EXP MLB DEBUT: 2015 — POTENTIAL: Backup SS — 6C
Bats R — Age 22 — 2010 (9) HS (PR)
Pwr ++ / BAvg ++ / Spd +++ / Def ++++

Year	Lev	Team	AB	R	H	HR	RBI	Avg	OB	Slg	OPS	bb%	ct%	Eye	SB	CS	x/h%	Iso	RC/G
2010	Rk	AZL Brewers	206	22	43	0	23	209	242	257	499	4	65	0.13	6	2	21	49	1.27
2011	Rk	Helena	330	47	82	8	38	248	279	406	685	4	72	0.15	7	3	35	158	3.82
2011	A	Wisconsin	103	6	20	1	5	194	224	262	486	4	67	0.12	0	0	20	68	1.01
2012	A	Wisconsin	465	60	115	12	49	247	287	402	689	5	74	0.22	7	3	37	155	3.88
2013	A+	Brevard County	478	51	115	5	37	241	288	314	602	6	83	0.40	13	8	20	73	2.92

Tall, skinny SS turned himself into a plus defender with good actions and strong arm. Offensive contributions are minimal. Contact rate trending in right direction, but poor plate discipline and aggressive approach rack up the strikeout totals. Some pop in his bat, but will be a challenge to translate into results.

Roache, Victor — 7 — Milwaukee
EXP MLB DEBUT: 2016 — POTENTIAL: Starting OF — 8D
Bats R — Age 22 — 2012 (1) Georgia Southern
Pwr ++++ / BAvg ++ / Spd ++ / Def ++

Year	Lev	Team	AB	R	H	HR	RBI	Avg	OB	Slg	OPS	bb%	ct%	Eye	SB	CS	x/h%	Iso	RC/G
2010	NCAA	Georgia Southern	151	38	38	8	38	252	379	464	843	17	72	0.74	7	2	39	212	6.38
2011	NCAA	Georgia Southern	230	58	75	30	84	326	419	778	1198	14	82	0.88	3	4	56	452	10.16
2012	NCAA	Georgia Southern	17	6	7	2	5	412	583	765	1348	29	94	7.00	0	0	29	353	12.67
2013	A	Wisconsin	459	62	114	22	74	248	317	440	757	9	70	0.34	6	2	35	192	4.90

Big, strong OF with plus raw power. Struggles with the breaking stuff, making his BA ceiling low, but with good plate discipline and bat speed his approach should fare well. Limited to LF, has an average arm and good reads, given his below average speed. His power is a weapon and will carry him through the minors.

Robertson, Daniel — 56 — Oakland
EXP MLB DEBUT: 2016 — POTENTIAL: Starting 3B — 8D
Bats R — Age 20 — 2012 (1-S) HS (CA)
Pwr +++ / BAvg +++ / Spd ++ / Def +++

Year	Lev	Team	AB	R	H	HR	RBI	Avg	OB	Slg	OPS	bb%	ct%	Eye	SB	CS	x/h%	Iso	RC/G
2012	Rk	AZL Athletics	101	25	30	4	22	297	393	554	948	14	85	1.07	2	0	53	257	7.53
2012	A-	Vermont	94	9	17	1	8	181	238	234	472	7	67	0.23	1	1	18	53	0.85
2013	A	Beloit	401	59	111	9	46	277	344	401	745	9	80	0.52	1	7	28	125	4.77

Advanced INF with excellent fundamentals and approach to game. Makes consistent, hard contact and shoots balls to gaps. Blisters LHP and has fluid swing and pitch recognition to post BA. Potential for slightly above average pop, but may take time to develop. Lacks ideal speed, but flashes quick hands and strong arm at SS.

Robinson, Drew — 5 — Texas
EXP MLB DEBUT: 2016 — POTENTIAL: Starting 3B — 7C
Bats L — Age 22 — 2010 (4) HS (NV)
Pwr ++ / BAvg +++ / Spd ++ / Def ++

Year	Lev	Team	AB	R	H	HR	RBI	Avg	OB	Slg	OPS	bb%	ct%	Eye	SB	CS	x/h%	Iso	RC/G
2012	A	Hickory	410	72	112	13	67	273	399	444	843	17	70	0.70	10	7	36	171	6.63
2013	A+	Myrtle Beach	436	62	112	8	70	257	362	404	766	14	72	0.58	10	2	37	147	5.44

Smooth and patient prospect who is sleeper in deep org. Gets on base consistently with mature approach and knows how to put bat to ball and goes gap to gap. Offers line drive stroke at present, but could get to average pop with more leverage and loft. May not have enough pop for 3B, but is passable defender with average arm.

Rodriguez,Jonathan

3 | **St. Louis** | EXP MLB DEBUT: 2017 | POTENTIAL: Utility INF | **6C**

Bats R Age 24
2009 (17) Manatee CC
Pwr ++
BAvg ++
Spd +++
Def ++

Year	Lev	Team	AB	R	H	HR	RBI	Avg	OB	Slg	OPS	bb%	ct%	Eye	SB	CS	x/h%	Iso	RC/G
2009	Rk	Johnson City	68	9	17	2	7	250	354	412	766	14	74	0.61	1	1	41	162	5.31
2010	A-	Batavia	244	46	63	12	40	258	335	500	835	10	77	0.50	3	2	48	242	5.93
2011	A	Quad Cities	394	67	99	20	70	251	374	472	846	16	72	0.71	4	5	47	221	6.43
2012	A+	Palm Beach	222	24	56	6	28	252	320	405	725	9	69	0.32	2	2	39	153	4.62
2013	A+	Palm Beach	455	71	129	18	72	284	367	481	848	12	78	0.59	21	4	41	198	6.19

Strong, physically mature 1B prospect had his best offensive season, hitting .284 with 18 HR in repeat of High-A. Makes decent contact, is patient at the plate, and cut down his K rate. Also has good speed and almost went 20/20 in '13. Solid defender at 1B, but power might be a bit short.

Rodriguez,Luigi

78 | **Cleveland** | EXP MLB DEBUT: 2015 | POTENTIAL: Starting OF | **7C**

Bats B Age 21
2009 FA (DR)
Pwr ++
BAvg +++
Spd ++++
Def +++

Year	Lev	Team	AB	R	H	HR	RBI	Avg	OB	Slg	OPS	bb%	ct%	Eye	SB	CS	x/h%	Iso	RC/G
2011	Rk	AZL Indians	95	18	36	3	14	379	410	579	989	5	80	0.26	12	5	31	200	7.54
2011	A	Lake County	132	10	33	0	5	250	322	311	633	10	73	0.39	6	5	18	61	3.40
2012	A	Lake County	463	75	124	11	48	268	339	406	745	10	71	0.38	24	9	30	138	4.89
2013	A	Lake County	76	14	20	1	9	263	349	329	678	12	67	0.40	5	3	15	66	4.06
2013	A+	Carolina	113	16	32	0	11	283	382	398	780	14	68	0.50	3	4	38	115	5.88

Lean, projectable OF who ended season in June due to shoulder injury. Power dissipated, but generates bat speed from both sides and has wiry strength. Draws walks with approach, but long swing can be exploited. Runs extremely well and should steal more bases. Crude routes and instincts in outfield, but has plus range.

Rodriguez,Ronny

46 | **Cleveland** | EXP MLB DEBUT: 2015 | POTENTIAL: Starting 2B/SS | **8D**

Bats R Age 22
2010 FA (DR)
Pwr +++
BAvg ++
Spd +++
Def +++

Year	Lev	Team	AB	R	H	HR	RBI	Avg	OB	Slg	OPS	bb%	ct%	Eye	SB	CS	x/h%	Iso	RC/G
2011	A	Lake County	370	41	91	11	42	246	272	449	720	3	78	0.16	10	7	51	203	4.22
2012	A+	Carolina	454	67	120	19	66	264	294	452	745	4	81	0.22	7	7	36	187	4.40
2013	AA	Akron	468	62	124	5	52	265	289	376	665	3	84	0.21	12	3	29	111	3.56

Lean, quick INF who is advancing one level per year. Power output decreased, but still possesses bat speed and strength. Makes good contact with simple stroke, but doesn't work counts. Pitch recognition needs to be honed. Runs very well and has quick hands. Played mostly SS, but some 2B with strong arm.

Rodriguez,Wilfredo

2 | **Colorado** | EXP MLB DEBUT: 2018 | POTENTIAL: Starting C | **7D**

Bats R Age 20
2012 (7) HS (PR)
Pwr ++
BAvg +++
Spd ++
Def ++

Year	Lev	Team	AB	R	H	HR	RBI	Avg	OB	Slg	OPS	bb%	ct%	Eye	SB	CS	x/h%	Iso	RC/G
2012	Rk	Grand Junction	166	26	53	2	27	319	369	452	821	7	86	0.57	1	1	32	133	5.66
2013	A-	Tri-City	141	15	38	1	19	270	352	326	678	11	82	0.72	2	4	16	57	4.11

Athletic catcher moves well behind the plate with an average arm. Improved defensively, but still has work to do. Does have a good approach at the plate with a short, balanced stroke. He shoots balls into the gap and could develop average power with decent plate discipline. Bat gives him value if he can stick at C..

Rodriguez,Yorman

8 | **Cincinnati** | EXP MLB DEBUT: 2015 | POTENTIAL: Starting CF | **8D**

Bats R Age 21
2009 FA (Venezuela)
Pwr ++
BAvg ++
Spd ++++
Def ++++

Year	Lev	Team	AB	R	H	HR	RBI	Avg	OB	Slg	OPS	bb%	ct%	Eye	SB	CS	x/h%	Iso	RC/G
2011	A	Dayton	280	38	71	7	40	254	315	393	708	8	70	0.30	20	8	30	139	4.31
2012	A	Dayton	258	35	70	6	44	271	304	430	734	4	76	0.20	7	5	37	159	4.43
2012	A+	Bakersfield	90	7	14	0	7	156	183	200	383	3	57	0.08	4	0	29	44	-0.58
2013	A+	Bakersfield	251	41	63	9	35	251	311	470	781	8	69	0.29	6	3	52	219	5.43
2013	AA	Pensacola	262	30	70	4	31	267	331	385	717	9	71	0.33	4	0	30	118	4.50

Lots of raw tools, though he continues to struggle making consistent contact. Plus power began to materialize in '13. Can go to the opposite field with authority. Owns plus speed and arm in OF, and can cover a lot of ground. Future hinges on correcting contact issues; other tools major-league ready.

Rogers,Jason

3 | **Milwaukee** | EXP MLB DEBUT: 2014 | POTENTIAL: Starting 1B | **7D**

Bats R Age 26
2010 (32) Columbus State
Pwr +++
BAvg +++
Spd ++
Def ++

Year	Lev	Team	AB	R	H	HR	RBI	Avg	OB	Slg	OPS	bb%	ct%	Eye	SB	CS	x/h%	Iso	RC/G
2011	Rk	Helena	27	3	8	1	3	296	345	444	789	7	81	0.40	0	1	25	148	5.07
2011	A	Wisconsin	240	29	66	6	37	275	336	429	765	8	80	0.46	6	1	35	154	4.99
2012	A	Wisconsin	239	39	72	6	43	301	395	485	880	13	81	0.80	5	0	43	184	6.77
2012	A+	Brevard County	233	33	70	5	23	300	407	412	819	15	82	1.00	7	1	23	112	6.04
2013	AA	Huntsville	481	69	130	22	87	270	350	468	818	11	82	0.69	7	2	38	198	5.66

Strong, big-bodied 1B came into his own in '13, tapping into his raw power, hitting 22 HR. Continues to show decent ct% and bb% that should allow him to utilize his power and hit for a respectable BA. At his size, speed will not be a part of his game and he is limited to 1B where he plays well.

Romero,Avery

4 | **Miami** | EXP MLB DEBUT: 2016 | POTENTIAL: Starting 2B | **8D**

Bats R Age 21
2012 (3) HS (FL)
Pwr ++
BAvg +++
Spd ++
Def +++

Year	Lev	Team	AB	R	H	HR	RBI	Avg	OB	Slg	OPS	bb%	ct%	Eye	SB	CS	x/h%	Iso	RC/G
2012	Rk	GCL Marlins	121	8	27	3	15	223	282	347	630	8	83	0.48	0	1	33	124	3.27
2012	A-	Jamestown	21	3	8	0	4	381	458	381	839	13	100	1.00	1	0	0	0	6.42
2013	A-	Batavia	209	27	62	2	30	297	344	411	755	7	84	0.44	3	4	32	115	4.84
2013	A	Greensboro	34	5	5	1	5	147	237	265	502	11	85	0.80	0	0	40	118	1.95

Officially moved to 2B in '13, where he continued to hit. Strong hands and quick wrists generate above average bat speed that allows him to go gap-to-gap now. Below average speed, but a good base runner. Transition to 2B has been smooth where his strong arm and good reads work, though 3B could be an option.

Romero,Stefen

7 | **Seattle** | EXP MLB DEBUT: 2014 | POTENTIAL: Starting OF | **7B**

Bats R Age 25
2010 (12) Oregon State
Pwr +++
BAvg +++
Spd ++
Def ++

Year	Lev	Team	AB	R	H	HR	RBI	Avg	OB	Slg	OPS	bb%	ct%	Eye	SB	CS	x/h%	Iso	RC/G
2011	A	Clinton	429	62	120	16	65	280	330	462	791	7	84	0.46	16	9	35	182	5.16
2012	A+	High Desert	258	47	92	11	51	357	387	581	969	5	86	0.37	6	2	36	225	7.06
2012	AA	Jackson	216	38	75	12	50	347	387	620	1007	6	83	0.38	6	3	41	273	7.66
2013	A+	High Desert	18	1	5	0	2	278	350	333	683	10	94	2.00	0	0	20	56	4.50
2013	AAA	Tacoma	375	51	104	11	74	277	328	448	776	7	77	0.32	8	4	37	171	5.06

Balanced, consistent hitter who moved to OF full-time. Has high BA potential along with average power. Possesses barrel awareness and clean swing to make contact and could add more pop if he becomes more selective. Speed and range are below average, though he's showing marked improvement in LF.

Rondon,Cleuluis

46 | **Chicago (A)** | EXP MLB DEBUT: 2017 | POTENTIAL: Starting 2B/SS | **7D**

Bats R Age 20
2010 FA (Venezuela)
Pwr +
BAvg ++
Spd ++++
Def +++

Year	Lev	Team	AB	R	H	HR	RBI	Avg	OB	Slg	OPS	bb%	ct%	Eye	SB	CS	x/h%	Iso	RC/G
2012	Rk	GCL Red Sox	182	19	42	0	16	231	267	352	619	5	77	0.21	2	2	38	121	3.13
2012	A-	Lowell	4	0	0	0	0	0	0	0	0	0	75	0.00	0	0	###	0	-5.26
2013	A-	Lowell	123	13	34	1	10	276	315	350	665	5	79	0.27	6	1	18	73	3.57
2013	A	Kannapolis	94	11	19	1	6	202	257	234	491	7	74	0.29	1	0	5	32	1.25

Lean, savvy INF who played mostly 2B, but also saw action at SS. Best tools revolve around wheels and defense as he owns quick hands and clean actions. Needs to get on base more in order to use speed. Not much pop in slender frame, but has quick bat. Pitch recognition needs work in order for bat to catch up to glove.

Rondon,Jose

6 | **Los Angeles (A)** | EXP MLB DEBUT: 2017 | POTENTIAL: Starting SS | **7C**

Bats R Age 20
2011 FA (Venezuela)
Pwr ++
BAvg +++
Spd +++
Def +++

Year	Lev	Team	AB	R	H	HR	RBI	Avg	OB	Slg	OPS	bb%	ct%	Eye	SB	CS	x/h%	Iso	RC/G
2012	Rk	AZL Angels	192	26	50	1	20	260	311	365	675	7	88	0.58	5	5	32	104	4.01
2012	Rk	Orem	20	4	6	0	1	300	364	450	814	9	85	0.67	1	0	33	150	5.84
2013	Rk	Orem	276	45	81	1	50	293	363	399	761	10	89	0.97	13	8	31	105	5.22

Aggressive, dynamic INF who spent second year in Rookie ball. Knows how to play game and understands that contact and getting on base are keys. Rarely strikes out and exhibits terrific bat control. Doesn't own a power profile, but should hit for BA. Possesses all requisite tools to become solid defender.

Rosa,Gabriel

789 | **Cincinnati** | EXP MLB DEBUT: 2017 | POTENTIAL: Starting 3B/OF | **8E**

Bats R Age 21
2011 (2) HS (PR)
Pwr +++
BAvg ++
Spd +++
Def +++

Year	Lev	Team	AB	R	H	HR	RBI	Avg	OB	Slg	OPS	bb%	ct%	Eye	SB	CS	x/h%	Iso	RC/G
2011	Rk	AZL Reds	106	17	26	2	10	245	298	406	704	7	74	0.29	6	3	38	160	4.25
2012	Rk	Billings	78	8	14	0	5	179	190	256	446	1	68	0.04	2	0	43	77	0.50
2013	Rk	Billings	180	29	38	6	23	211	307	339	646	12	74	0.54	13	2	29	128	3.49

High risk/high upside prospect who could become either 3B or OF. Exciting power/speed combo, who's a breakout candidate if he can ever stay healthy. Contact rate and bb% took nice steps forward in '13. Nice speed, arm, and range defensively. Needs to barrel more pitches to turn contact into base hits.

Rosario,Amed — 6 — New York (N)

EXP MLB DEBUT: 2018 | POTENTIAL: Starting SS | 8D

Bats R Age 18 — 2013 FA (DR)

Pwr ++ | BAvg +++ | Spd ++++ | Def ++++

Year	Lev	Team	AB	R	H	HR	RBI	Avg	OB	Slg	OPS	bb%	ct%	Eye	SB	CS	x/h%	Iso	RC/G
2013	Rk	Kingsport	212	22	51	3	23	241	278	358	637	5	80	0.26	2	6	29	118	3.24

Jumped GCL to APPY as 17 y/o and considered top prospect in the league. Plus speed, strong arm, and quick feet bode well for sticking at SS. Runs bases well, possesses good bat speed, and makes solid contact. Power should land at slightly above-average as he matures. Needs to shorten swing and improve plate discipline.

Rosario,Eddie — 4 — Minnesota

EXP MLB DEBUT: 2015 | POTENTIAL: Starting 2B | 8C

Bats L Age 22 — 2010 (4) HS (PR)

Pwr +++ | BAvg ++++ | Spd +++ | Def ++

Year	Lev	Team	AB	R	H	HR	RBI	Avg	OB	Slg	OPS	bb%	ct%	Eye	SB	CS	x/h%	Iso	RC/G
2011	Rk	Elizabethton	270	71	91	21	60	337	397	670	1068	9	78	0.45	17	6	43	333	8.73
2012	Rk	GCL Twins	19	2	7	1	4	368	400	684	1084	5	89	0.50	0	0	57	316	8.38
2012	A	Beloit	392	60	116	12	70	296	348	490	837	7	82	0.45	11	11	41	194	5.81
2013	A+	Fort Myers	207	40	68	6	35	329	379	527	906	8	86	0.59	3	6	35	198	6.63
2013	AA	New Britain	289	40	82	4	38	284	332	412	744	7	77	0.31	7	4	32	128	4.71

Natural hitting INF who will miss first 50 games due to drug suspension. Posts high BA with bat control and hand-eye coordination. Uses quick bat to lace line drives to gaps. Has strength for more power, but focuses on contact. Biggest question mark is defense where hands are below average. Has moderate SB potential.

Rua,Ryan — 45 — Texas

EXP MLB DEBUT: 2015 | POTENTIAL: Starting 2B/3B | 7D

Bats R Age 24 — 2011 (17) Lake Erie

Pwr +++ | BAvg ++ | Spd ++ | Def ++

Year	Lev	Team	AB	R	H	HR	RBI	Avg	OB	Slg	OPS	bb%	ct%	Eye	SB	CS	x/h%	Iso	RC/G
2011	Rk	AZL Rangers	162	41	52	3	34	321	396	512	908	11	79	0.59	10	0	38	191	7.08
2011	A-	Spokane	26	2	5	1	3	192	222	308	530	4	77	0.17	0	0	20	115	1.57
2012	A-	Spokane	280	40	82	7	43	293	359	432	791	9	77	0.45	4	1	29	139	5.37
2013	A	Hickory	367	70	92	29	82	251	339	559	898	12	75	0.54	13	2	59	308	6.70
2013	AA	Frisco	86	19	20	3	9	233	290	384	674	8	72	0.29	1	0	30	151	3.70

Tall, power-hitting infielder who had breakout year at plate with surprising production. Added leverage and strength to swing for more power and crushed LHP. Can sell out for power and may not hit for BA as he struggles with pitch recognition and spin. Played 2B at Low-A before getting big jump to Double-A and moved to 3B.

Ruiz,Rio — 5 — Houston

EXP MLB DEBUT: 2016 | POTENTIAL: Starting 3B | 8C

Bats L Age 20 — 2012 (4) HS (CA)

Pwr +++ | BAvg +++ | Spd ++ | Def ++

Year	Lev	Team	AB	R	H	HR	RBI	Avg	OB	Slg	OPS	bb%	ct%	Eye	SB	CS	x/h%	Iso	RC/G
2012	Rk	Greeneville	50	8	11	1	7	220	278	380	658	7	80	0.40	0	0	45	160	3.67
2012	Rk	GCL Astros	85	13	23	0	11	271	361	412	773	12	74	0.55	2	0	43	141	5.58
2013	A	Quad Cities	416	46	108	12	63	260	339	430	769	11	78	0.54	12	3	43	171	5.17

Very athletic INF who is better than numbers suggest. Increased BA and HR each month. Puts bat to ball easily and has strength and bat speed to produce BA and power. Can also hit LHP and use entire field when his swing is on. Lack of speed limits range at 3B, but makes plays with soft hands and plus arm strength.

Rupp,Cameron — 2 — Philadelphia

EXP MLB DEBUT: 2013 | POTENTIAL: Backup C | 6A

Bats R Age 25 — 2010 (3) Texas

Pwr +++ | BAvg + | Spd + | Def +++

Year	Lev	Team	AB	R	H	HR	RBI	Avg	OB	Slg	OPS	bb%	ct%	Eye	SB	CS	x/h%	Iso	RC/G
2011	A	Lakewood	324	33	88	4	44	272	335	373	709	9	70	0.32	0	0	27	102	4.40
2012	A+	Clearwater	344	32	92	10	49	267	344	424	768	10	78	0.52	0	0	36	157	5.12
2013	AA	Reading	143	18	35	8	21	245	312	455	767	9	75	0.39	0	0	40	210	4.88
2013	AAA	Lehigh Valley	182	18	49	6	24	269	307	423	730	5	70	0.18	1	1	33	154	4.45
2013	MLB	Philadelphia	13	1	4	0	2	308	357	385	742	7	69	0.25	0	0	25	77	5.10

Continued improvement in the high minors led to a cup of coffee in September. Doesn't have great hitting mechanics, but does have some pop in his swing, though probably not enough to be a long-term starter. Also made strides defensively, where he's now slightly above average.

Russell,Addison — 6 — Oakland

EXP MLB DEBUT: 2015 | POTENTIAL: Starting SS | 9C

Bats R Age 20 — 2012 (1) HS (FL)

Pwr +++ | BAvg ++++ | Spd ++++ | Def +++

Year	Lev	Team	AB	R	H	HR	RBI	Avg	OB	Slg	OPS	bb%	ct%	Eye	SB	CS	x/h%	Iso	RC/G
2012	Rk	AZL Athletics	106	29	44	6	29	415	483	717	1200	12	78	0.61	9	1	34	302	10.72
2012	A-	Vermont	53	9	18	1	7	340	386	509	895	7	75	0.31	2	0	28	170	6.75
2012	A	Burlington	58	8	18	0	9	310	365	448	813	8	79	0.42	5	1	33	138	5.78
2013	A+	Stockton	429	85	118	17	60	275	365	508	873	12	73	0.53	21	3	47	233	6.76
2013	AAA	Sacramento	13	1	1	0	0	77	77	77	154	0	31	0.00	0	0	0	0	-5.10

Advanced INF who owns average to plus tools across board and has strong, athletic frame. Average power exceeds expectations while BA potential remains high due to quick hands and ability to make contact. Hits hard line drives with simple swing. Footwork can get sloppy, but arm and range sufficient.

Saladino,Tyler — 46 — Chicago (A)

EXP MLB DEBUT: 2014 | POTENTIAL: Reserve INF | 6B

Bats R Age 24 — 2010 (7) Oral Roberts

Pwr ++ | BAvg ++ | Spd +++ | Def +++

Year	Lev	Team	AB	R	H	HR	RBI	Avg	OB	Slg	OPS	bb%	ct%	Eye	SB	CS	x/h%	Iso	RC/G
2010	A	Kannapolis	165	40	51	2	18	309	390	442	833	12	73	0.50	4	2	33	133	6.26
2011	A+	Winston-Salem	397	75	107	16	55	270	353	501	854	11	77	0.57	7	7	48	232	6.31
2012	AA	Birmingham	418	71	99	4	39	237	353	321	674	15	78	0.82	38	8	23	84	4.21
2012	AAA	Charlotte	49	9	11	0	6	224	283	265	548	8	67	0.25	1	0	18	41	2.09
2013	AA	Birmingham	424	49	97	5	55	229	312	314	625	11	80	0.59	28	8	25	85	3.37

Patient, smart INF who repeated AA, but hasn't yet mastered level. Knows strike zone and draws walks, but fringy bat speed and choppy stroke limit BA. Power has regressed and he has focused more on line drives to gaps. Runs well and is good baserunner. Possesses quick hands and strong arm and can play either MIF spot.

Salcedo,Edward — 5 — Atlanta

EXP MLB DEBUT: 2014 | POTENTIAL: Starting 3B | 7D

Bats R Age 22 — 2010 FA (DR)

Pwr ++++ | BAvg ++ | Spd ++ | Def +

Year	Lev	Team	AB	R	H	HR	RBI	Avg	OB	Slg	OPS	bb%	ct%	Eye	SB	CS	x/h%	Iso	RC/G
2010	A	Rome	193	23	38	2	16	197	240	295	536	5	71	0.20	6	5	29	98	1.86
2011	A	Rome	508	83	126	12	68	248	304	396	700	7	79	0.39	23	10	36	148	4.13
2012	A+	Lynchburg	471	65	113	17	61	240	290	412	702	7	72	0.25	23	14	40	172	4.06
2013	AA	Mississippi	468	52	112	12	55	239	305	372	676	9	76	0.40	20	10	32	132	3.83

Strong 3B has some of the best raw power in the system, but has yet to prove he can hit for average. Has good bat speed and can drive the ball out of the park, but struck out 111 times. Does have decent speed and a strong arm, but his glove and footwork are well below average (29 errors in '13).

Sanchez,Alexander — 2 — New York (N)

EXP MLB DEBUT: 2019 | POTENTIAL: Starting C | 8D

Bats R Age 17 — 2013 FA (Venezuela)

Pwr ++ | BAvg +++ | Spd ++ | Def ++++

Year	Lev	Team	AB	R	H	HR	RBI	Avg	OB	Slg	OPS	bb%	ct%	Eye	SB	CS	x/h%	Iso	RC/G
2011	Rk	Kingsport	59	7	15	2	10	254	267	407	673	2	93	0.25	1	0	33	153	3.65
2012	A-	Brooklyn	184	11	48	2	15	261	303	342	645	6	85	0.41	0	0	23	82	3.45

Exhibits solid blocking and receiving skills with a strong arm. Though still very young, his contact approach and swing path may not leave much power projection going forward. However, he does appear to have advanced plate discipline for his age.

Sanchez,Carlos — 46 — Chicago (A)

EXP MLB DEBUT: 2014 | POTENTIAL: Starting 2B/SS | 7A

Bats R Age 22 — 2009 FA (Venezuela)

Pwr + | BAvg +++ | Spd +++ | Def ++++

Year	Lev	Team	AB	R	H	HR	RBI	Avg	OB	Slg	OPS	bb%	ct%	Eye	SB	CS	x/h%	Iso	RC/G
2011	A	Kannapolis	264	44	76	1	27	288	326	345	671	5	81	0.31	7	8	16	57	3.68
2012	A+	Winston-Salem	365	58	115	1	42	315	369	395	763	8	82	0.48	19	10	18	79	5.00
2012	AA	Birmingham	119	17	44	0	13	370	419	462	881	8	82	0.45	7	5	23	92	6.47
2012	AAA	Charlotte	39	4	10	0	1	256	256	308	564	0	85	0.00	0	0	20	51	2.18
2013	AAA	Charlotte	432	50	104	0	28	241	289	296	585	6	82	0.38	16	7	21	56	2.76

Steady INF who hasn't hit HR since early '12, but has excellent defensive skills and good speed. Exhibits clean, soft hands at both SS and 2B while range enhanced by quick first step. Arm strength more than enough. Sprays line drives to gaps, but lacks bat path for HR. Aggressive approach not conducive for high OBP.

Sanchez,Gary — 2 — New York (A)

EXP MLB DEBUT: 2015 | POTENTIAL: Starting C | 9C

Bats R Age 21 — 2009 FA (DR)

Pwr ++++ | BAvg +++ | Spd ++ | Def ++

Year	Lev	Team	AB	R	H	HR	RBI	Avg	OB	Slg	OPS	bb%	ct%	Eye	SB	CS	x/h%	Iso	RC/G
2011	A	Charleston (Sc)	301	49	77	17	52	256	335	485	820	11	69	0.39	2	1	44	229	5.90
2012	A	Charleston (Sc)	263	44	78	13	56	297	351	517	868	8	75	0.34	11	4	41	221	6.23
2012	A+	Tampa	172	21	48	5	29	279	319	436	755	5	76	0.24	4	0	33	157	4.69
2013	A+	Tampa	362	38	92	13	61	254	308	420	728	7	80	0.39	3	1	37	166	4.38
2013	AA	Trenton	92	12	23	2	10	250	343	380	723	12	83	0.81	0	0	35	130	4.71

Big, strong C who has posted nice numbers despite age for level and has more power to come. Well above average pop is best tool, but also owns clean, smooth swing for easy contact. BA doesn't project as well as he can expand K zone. No speed, but defense showing vast improvement, especially receiving.

Sanchez,Tony — 2 — Pittsburgh

EXP MLB DEBUT: 2013 | POTENTIAL: Starting C | **7C**

Bats R Age 26
2009 (1) Boston College
- Pwr ++
- BAvg ++
- Spd ++
- Def +++

Year	Lev	Team	AB	R	H	HR	RBI	Avg	OB	Slg	OPS	bb%	ct%	Eye	SB	CS	x/h%	Iso	RC/G
2012	AA	Altoona	141	22	39	0	17	277	358	390	749	11	77	0.55	1	1	38	113	5.13
2012	AAA	Indianapolis	206	21	48	8	26	233	310	408	718	10	78	0.50	0	0	42	175	4.39
2013	AA	Altoona	17	2	3	0	0	176	176	235	412	0	82	0.00	0	0	33	59	0.39
2013	AAA	Indianapolis	260	35	75	10	42	288	358	504	861	10	77	0.47	0	0	48	215	6.31
2013	MLB	PIT	60	9	14	2	5	233	270	400	670	5	77	0.21	0	0	43	167	3.55

Short, stocky backstop finally made his MLB debut, but saw limited action. 4th pick in '09 draft has been slow to develop. Remains inconsistent behind the plate with a strong arm, but poor footwork. At the plate, Sanchez has decent power, but his swing can get long and he struggles to make consistent contact.

Sandberg,Cord — 78 — Philadelphia

EXP MLB DEBUT: 2018 | POTENTIAL: Starting LF | **8D**

Bats L Age 19
2013 (3) HS (FL)
- Pwr +++
- BAvg ++
- Spd ++
- Def ++

Year	Lev	Team	AB	R	H	HR	RBI	Avg	OB	Slg	OPS	bb%	ct%	Eye	SB	CS	x/h%	Iso	RC/G
2013	Rk	GCL Phillies	169	23	35	2	14	207	306	272	578	12	79	0.67	4	3	17	65	2.79

Two-sport athlete in HS chose baseball over QB at Mississippi St. Good size at 6-3, 215, and athleticism to match. Fluid swing with good bat speed and raw power as well as decent foot speed. Likely ends up as a corner outfielder, though 5 tools are there. Unrefined player who needs baseball reps.

Sano,Miguel — 5 — Minnesota

EXP MLB DEBUT: 2014 | POTENTIAL: Starting 3B | **9B**

Bats R Age 21
2009 FA (DR)
- Pwr +++++
- BAvg ++++
- Spd ++
- Def ++

Year	Lev	Team	AB	R	H	HR	RBI	Avg	OB	Slg	OPS	bb%	ct%	Eye	SB	CS	x/h%	Iso	RC/G
2010	Rk	GCL Twins	148	23	43	4	19	291	335	466	802	6	71	0.23	2	2	42	176	5.56
2011	Rk	Elizabethton	267	58	78	20	59	292	348	637	985	8	71	0.30	5	4	58	345	8.03
2012	A	Beloit	457	75	118	28	100	258	369	521	890	15	68	0.56	8	3	51	263	7.12
2013	A+	Fort Myers	206	51	68	16	48	330	413	655	1068	12	70	0.48	9	2	49	325	9.42
2013	AA	New Britain	233	35	55	19	55	236	338	571	909	13	65	0.44	2	1	67	335	7.48

Big, strong INF who has among best power in minors. Posted career high in HR and has patient approach to draw walks. Destroys LHP and has improved pitch recognition to hit for BA. Will expand strike zone at times. Doesn't run well and footwork needs work at 3B. Owns very strong arm and should stick at position.

Santana,Alex — 5 — Los Angeles (N)

EXP MLB DEBUT: 2016 | POTENTIAL: Starting 3B | **8D**

Bats R Age 20
2011 (2) HS (FL)
- Pwr +++
- BAvg +++
- Spd +++
- Def +++

Year	Lev	Team	AB	R	H	HR	RBI	Avg	OB	Slg	OPS	bb%	ct%	Eye	SB	CS	x/h%	Iso	RC/G
2011	Rk	AZL Dodgers	189	30	45	1	19	238	276	339	615	5	66	0.16	8	1	31	101	3.07
2012	Rk	AZL Dodgers	96	12	23	1	12	240	318	323	641	10	57	0.27	4	1	22	83	3.88
2012	Rk	Ogden	93	14	25	1	19	269	299	409	708	4	69	0.14	1	2	40	140	4.32
2013	Rk	Ogden	205	39	67	2	27	327	387	444	831	9	81	0.51	7	3	24	117	5.90

Tall, strong 3B who has plus bat speed and good leverage in his swing that should translate gap-to-gap power to HR production. Plate discipline is taking forward strides, but longer swing and below average pitch recognition make him aggressive at times. At 3B, he has good hands, a strong arm, and decent range.

Santana,Daniel — 46 — Minnesota

EXP MLB DEBUT: 2014 | POTENTIAL: Utility player | **7C**

Bats B Age 23
2007 FA (DR)
- Pwr +
- BAvg +++
- Spd ++++
- Def ++++

Year	Lev	Team	AB	R	H	HR	RBI	Avg	OB	Slg	OPS	bb%	ct%	Eye	SB	CS	x/h%	Iso	RC/G
2010	Rk	Elizabethton	140	23	37	4	16	264	280	421	701	2	79	0.10	5	4	35	157	3.81
2010	A	Beloit	130	14	31	0	11	238	277	315	593	5	69	0.18	10	4	23	77	2.71
2011	A	Beloit	365	55	90	7	41	247	295	373	667	6	73	0.26	24	15	30	126	3.66
2012	A+	Fort Myers	507	70	145	8	60	286	325	410	735	5	85	0.38	17	11	26	124	4.49
2013	AA	New Britain	539	66	160	2	45	297	327	386	713	4	83	0.26	30	13	21	89	4.18

Short, quick INF who finished 3rd in EL in SB. Spent majority of time at SS and has range, smooth actions, and arm to thrive at position. Has above average wheels, but isn't a polished baserunner. Doesn't walk much for someone with well below average power and needs to make more contact to take advantage of speed.

Santana,Domingo — 9 — Houston

EXP MLB DEBUT: 2015 | POTENTIAL: Starting RF | **9D**

Bats R Age 21
2009 FA (DR)
- Pwr ++++
- BAvg +++
- Spd +++
- Def +++

Year	Lev	Team	AB	R	H	HR	RBI	Avg	OB	Slg	OPS	bb%	ct%	Eye	SB	CS	x/h%	Iso	RC/G
2010	A	Lakewood	165	27	30	3	16	182	304	297	601	15	54	0.38	5	6	43	115	3.35
2011	A	Lakewood	350	45	94	7	32	269	319	434	753	7	66	0.22	4	1	43	166	5.20
2011	A	Lexington	68	13	26	5	21	382	432	662	1094	8	78	0.40	1	0	35	279	8.93
2012	A+	Lancaster	457	87	138	23	97	302	377	536	913	11	68	0.37	7	1	40	234	7.42
2013	AA	Corpus Christi	416	72	105	25	64	252	327	498	824	10	67	0.33	12	5	48	245	6.05

Tall, strong OF who finished 3rd in TL in HR. Set highs in HR and SB and has ideal RF skills. Long arms result in plate coverage, but subject to Ks due to long swing. Makes hard contact with leveraged stroke and has plus, raw power. Not blessed with great speed, but runs bases well. Strong arm is best defensive attribute.

Santander,Anthony — 9 — Cleveland

EXP MLB DEBUT: 2017 | POTENTIAL: Starting OF | **8D**

Bats B Age 19
2011 FA (Venezuela)
- Pwr +++
- BAvg ++
- Spd +++
- Def ++

Year	Lev	Team	AB	R	H	HR	RBI	Avg	OB	Slg	OPS	bb%	ct%	Eye	SB	CS	x/h%	Iso	RC/G
2012	Rk	AZL Indians	154	27	47	4	32	305	359	494	853	8	76	0.35	6	3	43	188	6.19
2013	A	Lake County	219	27	53	5	31	242	284	370	654	6	80	0.30	6	3	34	128	3.44

Athletic OF who was young for level and ended year in July due to injury. Better hitter from left side and average power could grow into more with added loft. Needs to read pitches better and has tendency to swing at pitches out of zone. Has average speed at present for some SB and good range, but outfield play needs work.

Sardinas,Luis — 46 — Texas

EXP MLB DEBUT: 2015 | POTENTIAL: Starting SS | **8C**

Bats B Age 21
2009 FA (Venezuela)
- Pwr ++
- BAvg +++
- Spd ++++
- Def ++++

Year	Lev	Team	AB	R	H	HR	RBI	Avg	OB	Slg	OPS	bb%	ct%	Eye	SB	CS	x/h%	Iso	RC/G
2010	Rk	AZL Rangers	103	22	32	0	8	311	355	350	704	6	85	0.47	8	2	13	39	4.19
2011	Rk	AZL Rangers	52	11	16	0	7	308	357	385	742	7	81	0.40	2	1	19	77	4.72
2012	A	Hickory	374	65	109	2	30	291	342	356	698	7	86	0.56	32	9	17	64	4.19
2013	A+	Myrtle Beach	383	69	114	1	31	298	352	360	712	8	86	0.59	27	8	17	63	4.40
2013	AA	Frisco	135	12	35	1	15	259	281	311	592	3	84	0.19	5	2	14	52	2.61

Steady IF who is consistent performer at any level. Lacks power projection, but has feel for bat control with loose, balanced stroke. Speed and arm are best attributes and has quick first step at SS. Can be lazy at times with throwing, but has all tools to be standout defender. Understands role and knows limitations.

Scavuzzo,Jacob — 78 — Los Angeles (N)

EXP MLB DEBUT: 2017 | POTENTIAL: Starting CF | **8E**

Bats R Age 20
2012 (21) HS (CA)
- Pwr +++
- BAvg +++
- Spd ++
- Def ++

Year	Lev	Team	AB	R	H	HR	RBI	Avg	OB	Slg	OPS	bb%	ct%	Eye	SB	CS	x/h%	Iso	RC/G
2012	Rk	AZL Dodgers	82	11	18	1	5	220	264	317	581	6	67	0.19	7	2	28	98	2.50
2013	Rk	Ogden	244	49	75	14	42	307	352	578	930	7	81	0.36	3	5	47	270	6.81

Athleitc, raw OF had an impressive season in 2013, showing the skills that got him drafted. Makes solid contact with good bat speed. Plus raw power should continue to develop into HR production. Plays LF and CF but slightly below average speed will likely make his future in the corner.

Schebler,Scott — 79 — Los Angeles (N)

EXP MLB DEBUT: 2015 | POTENTIAL: Starting OF | **7D**

Bats L Age 23
2010 (28) Des Moines CC
- Pwr +++
- BAvg ++
- Spd ++
- Def ++

Year	Lev	Team	AB	R	H	HR	RBI	Avg	OB	Slg	OPS	bb%	ct%	Eye	SB	CS	x/h%	Iso	RC/G
2010	Rk	AZL Dodgers	17	3	5	0	1	294	333	529	863	6	71	0.20	1	0	40	235	6.81
2011	Rk	Ogden	295	44	84	13	58	285	315	529	844	4	67	0.13	1	1	45	244	6.25
2012	A	Great Lakes	515	67	134	6	67	260	301	388	689	6	81	0.30	17	11	34	128	3.97
2013	A+	Rancho Cuca	477	95	141	27	91	296	344	581	924	7	71	0.25	16	5	49	285	7.23

Strong OF raked in High-A, showing a power/speed combo that is quite intriguing. His biggest asset is his power, though his below average ct% and poor discipline drive down the value. Holes in swing will limit BA and while smart on bases, he is a below average runner, limited to a corner where arm works.

Schoop,Jonathan — 456 — Baltimore

EXP MLB DEBUT: 2013 | POTENTIAL: Starting 3B/2B | **8C**

Bats R Age 22
2008 FA (Curacao)
- Pwr +++
- BAvg +++
- Spd ++
- Def +++

Year	Lev	Team	AB	R	H	HR	RBI	Avg	OB	Slg	OPS	bb%	ct%	Eye	SB	CS	x/h%	Iso	RC/G
2012	AA	Bowie	485	68	119	14	56	245	316	386	701	9	79	0.49	5	3	33	140	4.18
2013	Rk	GCL Orioles	25	9	9	3	9	360	484	800	1284	19	76	1.00	0	0	56	440	12.10
2013	A-	Aberdeen	14	3	8	2	9	571	600	1071	1671	7	93	1.00	0	1	38	500	14.23
2013	AAA	Norfolk	270	30	69	9	34	256	290	396	686	5	80	0.24	1	2	29	141	3.69
2013	MLB	BAL	14	5	4	1	1	286	333	500	833	7	86	0.50	0	0	25	214	5.39

Aggressive hitter who posted high in HR despite missing time due to stress fracture in back. Split time between 2B and SS, though most at 2B. Has hands and arm for any infield spot, though range is short at SS. Focuses on hard contact with above average raw pop. Pitch recognition needs work, but can catch up to good FB.

Schotts,Austin — 8 — Detroit

EXP MLB DEBUT: 2017 | POTENTIAL: Starting OF | 8D

Bats R Age 20
2012 (3) HS (TX)
Pwr ++
BAvg ++
Spd ++++
Def +++

Year	Lev	Team	AB	R	H	HR	RBI	Avg	OB	Slg	OPS	bb%	ct%	Eye	SB	CS	x/h%	Iso	RC/G
2012	Rk	GCL Tigers	155	31	48	3	21	310	359	452	811	7	74	0.29	15	4	31	142	5.65
2012	A+	Lakeland	3	1	1	0	0	333	333	333	667	0	67	0.00	1	0	0	0	3.37
2013	A-	Connecticut	218	25	50	1	13	229	294	303	597	8	67	0.28	22	3	22	73	2.85
2013	A	West Michigan	193	22	37	1	17	192	246	249	495	7	61	0.19	9	5	22	57	1.26

Athletic OF who was demoted to SS ball after nightmare in Low-A. Plus-plus speed is highlight, but rarely hits ball with authority. At his best, exhibits bat speed and punch to gaps while wreaking havoc. At worst, flails at pitches and has trouble making contact. Should become plus defender with range, but arm is a little short.

Seager,Corey — 56 — Los Angeles (N)

EXP MLB DEBUT: 2015 | POTENTIAL: Starting 3B | 9D

Bats L Age 20
2012 (1) HS (NC)
Pwr ++++
BAvg +++
Spd ++
Def +++

Year	Lev	Team	AB	R	H	HR	RBI	Avg	OB	Slg	OPS	bb%	ct%	Eye	SB	CS	x/h%	Iso	RC/G
2012	Rk	Ogden	175	34	54	8	33	309	383	520	903	11	81	0.64	8	2	35	211	6.73
2013	A	Great Lakes	272	45	84	12	57	309	386	529	915	11	79	0.59	9	4	39	221	6.99
2013	A+	Rancho Cuca	100	10	16	4	15	160	250	320	570	11	69	0.39	1	0	44	160	2.31

Big, strong IF impressed in first full season, hitting for power and showing mature approach. Makes hard contact with plus bat speed and leverage in swing. Struggles with off-speed, seen in his ct%, though given his age, adjustments will come. May switch to 3B where his strong arm and good hands will play plus.

Semien,Marcus — 456 — Chicago (A)

EXP MLB DEBUT: 2013 | POTENTIAL: Starting 2B/3B | 8C

Bats R Age 23
2011 (6) California
Pwr +++
BAvg +++
Spd +++
Def +++

Year	Lev	Team	AB	R	H	HR	RBI	Avg	OB	Slg	OPS	bb%	ct%	Eye	SB	CS	x/h%	Iso	RC/G
2011	A	Kannapolis	229	35	58	3	26	253	319	376	694	9	77	0.42	3	4	34	122	4.17
2012	A+	Winston-Salem	418	80	114	14	59	273	357	471	829	12	77	0.57	11	5	44	199	6.01
2013	AA	Birmingham	393	90	114	15	49	290	415	483	899	18	83	1.27	20	5	36	193	7.12
2013	AAA	Charlotte	125	20	33	4	17	264	338	464	802	10	81	0.58	4	0	48	200	5.56
2013	MLB	Chicago (A)	69	7	18	2	7	261	268	406	673	1	68	0.05	2	2	33	145	3.40

Breakout performer who led SL in OBP. Exhibits strong eye at plate with nice bat control while showcasing some power. Flat swing path may not translate to much more pop, but makes hard, line drive contact and gets on base consistently. Possesses average speed and sufficient arm, but range may not be enough for SS.

Severino,Pedro — 2 — Washington

EXP MLB DEBUT: 2017 | POTENTIAL: Starting C | 7D

Bats R Age 20
2010 FA (DR)
Pwr +
BAvg ++
Spd ++
Def ++++

Year	Lev	Team	AB	R	H	HR	RBI	Avg	OB	Slg	OPS	bb%	ct%	Eye	SB	CS	x/h%	Iso	RC/G
2011	Rk	GCL Nationals	115	16	21	2	9	183	248	287	535	8	77	0.37	0	0	33	104	2.00
2012	Rk	GCL Nationals	109	9	24	0	8	220	280	266	546	8	92	1.00	0	0	17	46	2.74
2013	A	Hagerstown	282	28	68	1	45	241	275	333	608	4	81	0.24	1	0	32	92	2.93

Athletic, top-flight defensive catching prospect made nice strides offensively during his first full season. Being best defensive catcher in WAS system will give him time to develop offensive skills, and he's shown the ability to make consistent contact, though he could benefit from taking more pitches.

Shaffer,Richie — 5 — Tampa Bay

EXP MLB DEBUT: 2015 | POTENTIAL: Starting 3B/1B | 8D

Bats R Age 23
2012 (1) Clemson
Pwr +++
BAvg +++
Spd ++
Def ++

Year	Lev	Team	AB	R	H	HR	RBI	Avg	OB	Slg	OPS	bb%	ct%	Eye	SB	CS	x/h%	Iso	RC/G
2010	NCAA	Clemson	158	45	51	7	36	323	392	525	917	10	77	0.50	2	0	35	203	6.98
2011	NCAA	Clemson	222	62	70	13	55	315	429	577	1005	17	76	0.83	8	1	43	261	8.50
2012	NCAA	Clemson	232	49	78	10	46	336	478	573	1051	21	77	1.19	8	2	42	237	9.48
2012	A-	Hudson Valley	117	25	36	4	26	308	391	487	878	12	74	0.52	0	0	31	179	6.74
2013	A+	Charlotte	469	55	119	11	73	254	306	399	704	7	77	0.33	6	0	38	145	4.15

Tall INF who showed glimpses of solid tools in mediocre season. Struggled with swing and chased pitches out of zone. Has natural hitting skills and owns power potential to all fields. Recognizes pitches and has bat speed for plus power down road. Lacks foot speed and defense is iffy, though exhibits arm strength.

Shaw,Travis — 35 — Boston

EXP MLB DEBUT: 2015 | POTENTIAL: Starting 1B | 7D

Bats L Age 24
2011 (9) Kent State
Pwr +++
BAvg ++
Spd ++
Def +++

Year	Lev	Team	AB	R	H	HR	RBI	Avg	OB	Slg	OPS	bb%	ct%	Eye	SB	CS	x/h%	Iso	RC/G
2011	A-	Lowell	202	33	53	8	36	262	369	446	814	14	77	0.72	3	0	40	183	5.88
2011	A	Greenville	9	1	3	0	1	333	400	444	844	10	100	1.00	0	0	33	111	6.41
2012	A+	Salem	354	69	108	16	73	305	404	545	950	14	77	0.73	11	2	46	240	7.69
2012	AA	Portland	110	13	25	3	12	227	351	427	778	16	69	0.62	1	1	64	200	5.75
2013	AA	Portland	444	57	98	16	50	221	337	394	731	15	74	0.67	7	3	42	173	4.82

Big, strong INF who has struggled above High-A. Started strong, but faded late. Draws walks with patient approach and combines clean stroke with bat speed. Can be overly passive at plate and swing timidly. Ks will always be an issue and doesn't project to high BA. Limited agility impacts defense, though owns strong arm.

Shipman,Aaron — 789 — Oakland

EXP MLB DEBUT: 2016 | POTENTIAL: Starting OF | 7E

Bats L Age 22
2010 (3) HS (GA)
Pwr ++
BAvg ++
Spd ++++
Def ++++

Year	Lev	Team	AB	R	H	HR	RBI	Avg	OB	Slg	OPS	bb%	ct%	Eye	SB	CS	x/h%	Iso	RC/G
2010	Rk	AZL Athletics	17	2	2	0	2	118	118	118	235	0	65	0.00	3	0	0	0	-2.87
2011	A-	Vermont	201	34	51	0	19	254	383	303	686	17	81	1.08	17	3	18	50	4.56
2012	A	Burlington	360	40	74	0	32	206	319	261	580	14	76	0.70	11	11	22	56	2.93
2013	Rk	AZL Athletics	19	7	8	0	3	421	522	579	1101	17	100	1.00	2	0	25	158	9.71
2013	A	Beloit	244	44	68	0	16	279	395	324	719	16	80	0.94	17	8	13	45	4.90

Very athletic and lean outfielder who repeated Low-A and showed some improvement. Has yet to hit HR in career and could be more aggressive at plate. Possesses slashing stroke that isn't conducive to XBH, but controls bat to make good contact. Exhibits well above average speed and terrific defensive skills, especially strong arm.

Silva,Juan — 789 — Cincinnati

EXP MLB DEBUT: 2015 | POTENTIAL: Starting LF | 7C

Bats L Age 23
2009 (8) HS (PR)
Pwr ++
BAvg ++
Spd +++
Def +++

Year	Lev	Team	AB	R	H	HR	RBI	Avg	OB	Slg	OPS	bb%	ct%	Eye	SB	CS	x/h%	Iso	RC/G
2009	Rk	GCL Reds	143	26	40	1	16	280	372	462	833	13	69	0.47	7	4	43	182	6.66
2010	Rk	AZL Reds	178	26	41	3	24	230	318	371	689	11	73	0.48	4	1	34	140	4.24
2011	Rk	Billings	150	30	44	4	21	293	404	413	818	16	71	0.65	4	6	18	120	6.13
2012	A	Dayton	380	58	103	8	42	271	383	413	796	15	71	0.63	25	12	34	142	5.90
2013	A+	Bakersfield	336	51	91	8	44	271	383	414	797	15	77	0.80	31	13	31	143	5.78

Duplicated 2012 numbers in 2013 except for drop in strikeouts which is huge for the speedy OF. Career high 31 SB, but also caught 13 times. Shows advanced plate approach, can hit the ball to all fields with power. Split time at all three OF positions, but LF is most likely where he ends up. Continues to post excellent bb%.

Singleton,Jonathan — 3 — Houston

EXP MLB DEBUT: 2014 | POTENTIAL: Starting 1B | 9D

Bats L Age 22
2009 (8) HS (CA)
Pwr ++++
BAvg +++
Spd ++
Def ++

Year	Lev	Team	AB	R	H	HR	RBI	Avg	OB	Slg	OPS	bb%	ct%	Eye	SB	CS	x/h%	Iso	RC/G
2011	A+	Lancaster	129	20	43	4	16	333	399	512	910	10	69	0.35	0	0	33	178	7.34
2012	AA	Corpus Christi	461	94	131	21	79	284	399	497	896	16	72	0.67	7	2	40	213	7.20
2013	A	Quad Cities	21	6	6	3	5	286	400	810	1210	16	76	0.80	0	0	83	524	10.76
2013	AA	Corpus Christi	38	5	10	2	8	263	404	526	931	19	58	0.56	0	0	50	263	8.92
2013	AAA	Oklahoma City	245	31	54	6	31	220	344	347	691	16	64	0.52	1	0	35	127	4.45

Patient slugger who returned in May after drug suspension. Struggled upon return, but has hitting skills. Possesses smooth stroke and has knowledge of strike zone. Gets on base and can hit for BA despite Ks. Pitch recognition needs work, but can put charge into ball. Offers little speed and suspect defense with fringy hands.

Sisco,Chance — 2 — Baltimore

EXP MLB DEBUT: 2017 | POTENTIAL: Starting C | 8D

Bats L Age 19
2013 (2) HS (CA)
Pwr ++
BAvg +++
Spd ++
Def ++

Year	Lev	Team	AB	R	H	HR	RBI	Avg	OB	Slg	OPS	bb%	ct%	Eye	SB	CS	x/h%	Iso	RC/G
2013	Rk	GCL Orioles	97	15	36	1	11	371	465	464	929	15	78	0.81	1	1	17	93	7.54
2013	A-	Aberdeen	5	1	1	0	0	200	333	200	533	17	60	0.50	0	0	0	0	1.98

Athletic, improving C who combines pro approach and bat control to give offensive upside. Focuses on line drives and lacks present power. Has tendency to lengthen swing, but can hit LHP. Relatively new to catching and has good arm with surprising receiving skills. Has high ceiling, but could take time to develop.

Skole,Matt — 35 — Washington

EXP MLB DEBUT: 2015 | POTENTIAL: Starting 1B | 8D

Bats L Age 24
2011 (5) Georgia Tech
Pwr ++++
BAvg +++
Spd ++
Def +

Year	Lev	Team	AB	R	H	HR	RBI	Avg	OB	Slg	OPS	bb%	ct%	Eye	SB	CS	x/h%	Iso	RC/G
2011	NCAA	Georgia Tech	233	56	81	10	58	348	451	545	996	16	86	1.33	1	3	32	197	8.15
2011	A-	Auburn	272	43	79	5	48	290	385	438	823	13	81	0.81	2	1	37	147	6.05
2012	A	Hagerstown	343	73	98	27	92	286	439	574	1014	22	66	0.81	10	0	46	289	9.27
2012	A+	Potomac	70	11	22	0	12	314	360	486	846	7	76	0.29	1	0	50	171	6.26
2013	AA	Harrisburg	5	1	1	0	2	200	429	400	829	29	60	1.00	0	0	100	200	7.54

Elbow injury cost him most of 2013. Power stroke appeared to be back during AFL. Led SAL in HR/BB in 2012 and has big-time power potential. Strong build coupled with bat speed and plate discipline gives ability to hit for average and power. Would benefit from shortening swing. Below-average defender with limited range.

Smith,Dominic — 3 — New York (N)

Bats L Age 19 | 2013 (1) HS (CA) | EXP MLB DEBUT: 2017 | POTENTIAL: Starting 1B | **9D**

Pwr ++++ | BAvg ++++ | Spd + | Def ++++

Year	Lev	Team	AB	R	H	HR	RBI	Avg	OB	Slg	OPS	bb%	ct%	Eye	SB	CS	x/h%	Iso	RC/G
2013	Rk	GCL Mets	167	23	48	3	22	287	377	407	784	13	78	0.65	2	4	27	120	5.49
2013	Rk	Kingsport	6	2	4	0	4	667	750	1333	2083	25	100	1.00	0	0	100	667	21.29

The 11th overall pick of 2013 draft has plus hit tool, smooth swing, great plate approach, and pitch recognition. Can square up any pitch and flashes raw power that will continue to develop. Hand-eye coordination allows for fewer Ks than prototypical power hitter. Plus defender with strong arm, good footwork, and hands.

Smith,Dwight — 78 — Toronto

Bats L Age 21 | 2011 (1-S) HS (GA) | EXP MLB DEBUT: 2016 | POTENTIAL: Starting OF | **7C**

Pwr +++ | BAvg +++ | Spd +++ | Def +++

Year	Lev	Team	AB	R	H	HR	RBI	Avg	OB	Slg	OPS	bb%	ct%	Eye	SB	CS	x/h%	Iso	RC/G
2012	Rk	Bluefield	159	20	36	4	21	226	276	340	616	6	86	0.50	1	1	28	113	3.12
2012	A-	Vancouver	63	5	11	0	8	175	246	254	500	9	83	0.55	0	0	36	79	1.93
2013	A	Lansing	423	57	120	7	46	284	362	388	750	11	81	0.63	25	5	23	104	4.94

Short, strong OF who has average tools across board. Has enough patience to draw walks and uses good speed to steal bases. Makes hard contact with simple swing mechanics and offers at least average power potential. May be platoon option as he struggles with LHP. Below average arm relegates him to LF.

Smith,Jordan — 89 — Cleveland

Bats L Age 23 | 2011 (9) St. Cloud State | EXP MLB DEBUT: 2015 | POTENTIAL: Fourth OF | **6B**

Pwr ++ | BAvg +++ | Spd ++ | Def +++

Year	Lev	Team	AB	R	H	HR	RBI	Avg	OB	Slg	OPS	bb%	ct%	Eye	SB	CS	x/h%	Iso	RC/G
2011	A-	Mahoning Val	243	36	73	0	47	300	388	391	779	13	88	1.17	3	1	29	91	5.60
2012	A	Lake County	468	70	148	9	74	316	364	453	817	7	89	0.67	9	3	26	137	5.56
2013	A+	Carolina	518	71	151	5	54	292	367	400	767	11	86	0.86	18	9	26	108	5.25

Tall and natural hitting outfielder who increased walk rate while sustaining contact-making ability. Uses simple swing and has bat control to spray balls to entire field. Has raw power, but doesn't pull ball much and can slap at times. Can dig in against LHP and is tough to fan. Lacks foot speed, but runs bases with quality instincts.

Smith,Kevan — 2 — Chicago (A)

Bats R Age 26 | 2011 (7) Pittsburgh | EXP MLB DEBUT: 2015 | POTENTIAL: Backup C | **6B**

Pwr +++ | BAvg +++ | Spd ++ | Def ++

Year	Lev	Team	AB	R	H	HR	RBI	Avg	OB	Slg	OPS	bb%	ct%	Eye	SB	CS	x/h%	Iso	RC/G
2011	Rk	Bristol	96	24	38	7	32	396	473	740	1212	13	85	1.00	1	2	47	344	10.44
2011	Rk	Great Falls	107	22	34	2	16	318	397	523	920	12	85	0.88	1	0	47	206	7.18
2012	A	Kannapolis	340	48	96	7	60	282	332	421	752	7	82	0.40	0	1	34	138	4.75
2012	A+	Winston-Salem	77	8	21	3	23	273	317	494	811	6	78	0.29	0	0	43	221	5.44
2013	A+	Winston-Salem	384	66	110	12	73	286	351	464	814	9	83	0.58	4	1	37	177	5.60

Big, athletic C who has surprising agility and quickness for size. Still raw with glove and needs to become better receiver to catch in big leagues. Posted high in HR while crushing LHP and driving ball to all fields. Power is best attribute, but isn't very selective with aggressive approach. Has profile of backup catcher.

Smith,Mallex — 8 — San Diego

Bats L Age 21 | 2012 (5) HS (FL) | EXP MLB DEBUT: 2017 | POTENTIAL: Starting CF | **7D**

Pwr ++ | BAvg ++ | Spd ++++ | Def ++++

Year	Lev	Team	AB	R	H	HR	RBI	Avg	OB	Slg	OPS	bb%	ct%	Eye	SB	CS	x/h%	Iso	RC/G
2012	Rk	AZL Padres	96	23	33	1	10	344	376	417	793	5	80	0.26	13	3	12	73	5.09
2012	A-	Eugene	32	6	6	1	5	188	316	281	597	16	75	0.75	4	1	17	94	2.94
2013	A	Fort Wayne	424	81	111	4	29	262	352	340	692	12	80	0.70	64	16	21	78	4.31

Short and quick outfielder who has potential as leadoff hitter. Has plus-plus speed and instincts on base for SB and extra base hits. Knows value of getting on base and keeping ball on ground. Makes easy contact and can hit LHP. Raw defender in CF, but getting better. Arm isn't asset, but covers lots of ground.

Soler,Jorge — 9 — Chicago (N)

Bats R Age 22 | 2012 FA (Cuba) | EXP MLB DEBUT: 2015 | POTENTIAL: Starting RF | **8C**

Pwr +++ | BAvg +++ | Spd ++ | Def +++

Year	Lev	Team	AB	R	H	HR	RBI	Avg	OB	Slg	OPS	bb%	ct%	Eye	SB	CS	x/h%	Iso	RC/G
2012	Rk	AZL Cubs	54	14	13	2	10	241	317	389	706	10	76	0.46	8	0	31	148	4.19
2012	A	Peoria	80	14	27	3	15	338	384	513	896	7	93	1.00	4	1	30	175	6.37
2013	A+	Daytona	210	38	59	8	35	281	346	467	813	9	82	0.55	5	1	37	186	5.55

Missed 3 months with a stress fracture in his leg. Has some of best raw power in system, but is far from one-dimensional player. Has plus bat speed and continues to show solid plate discipline and contact ability, but can be overly aggressive. Has above-average speed with a strong arm and profiles well in RF.

Solorzano,Jesus — 8 — Miami

Bats R Age 23 | 2009 FA (Venezuela) | EXP MLB DEBUT: 2016 | POTENTIAL: Starting CF | **8D**

Pwr ++ | BAvg +++ | Spd ++++ | Def ++++

Year	Lev	Team	AB	R	H	HR	RBI	Avg	OB	Slg	OPS	bb%	ct%	Eye	SB	CS	x/h%	Iso	RC/G
2011	Rk	GCL Marlins	194	34	58	3	31	299	343	454	797	6	85	0.43	18	7	34	155	5.32
2012	A-	Jamestown	210	36	66	8	27	314	366	519	885	7	77	0.35	7	6	36	205	6.47
2013	A	Greensboro	484	72	138	15	66	285	319	450	769	5	77	0.22	33	4	34	165	4.82

Small, athletic OF showed off potential five-tool ability in first full season. Aggressive approach allows him to make quality hard contact, and while it hurts bb%, stays clear of the strikeout. With adjustments he could tap into raw power. Plus runner and defender where his strong arm and good range can stick in CF.

Sosa,Francisco — 78 — Colorado

Bats R Age 24 | 2007 FA (DR) | EXP MLB DEBUT: 2017 | POTENTIAL: Starting OF | **7D**

Pwr +++ | BAvg ++ | Spd +++ | Def +++

Year	Lev	Team	AB	R	H	HR	RBI	Avg	OB	Slg	OPS	bb%	ct%	Eye	SB	CS	x/h%	Iso	RC/G
2010	Rk	Casper	17	3	3	0	1	176	222	176	399	6	71	0.20	0	1	0	0	-0.15
2011	Rk	Casper	185	21	47	6	28	254	303	438	741	7	69	0.23	7	4	40	184	4.75
2012	A-	Tri-City	251	35	69	4	36	275	338	394	733	9	77	0.42	21	2	29	120	4.63
2013	A	Asheville	461	85	145	20	89	315	390	529	919	11	73	0.46	30	10	39	215	7.25

Tall, strong Dominican OF had a huge breakout season in '13. Turns 24 in March '14 so was definitely not young for the SAL, but the power/speed package is legit. Has an aggressive approach at the plate, but makes decent contact. He has good range in the OF and above-average speed.

Soto,Neftali — 35 — Cincinnati

Bats R Age 26 | 2007 (3) HS (PR) | EXP MLB DEBUT: 2013 | POTENTIAL: Starting 1B/3B | **7D**

Pwr ++++ | BAvg ++ | Spd +++ (4.30) | Def ++

Year	Lev	Team	AB	R	H	HR	RBI	Avg	OB	Slg	OPS	bb%	ct%	Eye	SB	CS	x/h%	Iso	RC/G
2011	AA	Carolina	379	70	103	30	76	272	317	575	892	6	75	0.26	0	1	50	303	6.36
2011	AAA	Louisville	17	1	7	1	4	412	444	588	1033	6	88	0.50	0	0	14	176	7.57
2012	AAA	Louisville	465	55	114	14	59	245	306	400	706	8	75	0.35	2	1	39	155	4.20
2013	AAA	Louisville	461	54	125	15	61	271	310	414	724	5	78	0.25	3	1	29	143	4.22
2013	MLB	CIN	12	0	0	0	0	0	0	0	0	0	50	0.00	0	0		0	-7.85

Shifted back to 3B, as he's blocked at 1B by Votto. Big-time plus power potential, though has yet to again get near the 31 HR posted in 2011. Showed nice defensive improvement at 3B. Has lightning quick bat speed and can hit with power to all fields. Lack of plate discipline and pitch recognition has kept BA < .300 at higher levels.

Souza,Steven — 9 — Washington

Bats R Age 25 | 2007 (3) HS (WA) | EXP MLB DEBUT: 2014 | POTENTIAL: Starting RF | **7D**

Pwr ++++ | BAvg ++ | Spd +++ | Def +++

Year	Lev	Team	AB	R	H	HR	RBI	Avg	OB	Slg	OPS	bb%	ct%	Eye	SB	CS	x/h%	Iso	RC/G
2011	A+	Potomac	390	58	89	11	56	228	353	367	719	16	66	0.57	25	9	34	138	4.82
2012	A	Hagerstown	262	48	76	17	72	290	345	576	921	8	81	0.45	7	7	51	286	6.72
2012	A+	Potomac	91	16	29	6	13	319	404	560	964	13	73	0.52	7	1	31	242	7.79
2013	Rk	GCL Nationals	10	3	2	0	2	200	385	300	685	23	60	0.75	2	0	50	100	4.83
2013	AA	Harrisburg	273	54	82	15	44	300	392	557	948	13	72	0.54	20	6	48	256	7.75

Has plus power and can hit HR to both fields. Excellent bat speed allows him to power up on high velocity pitches, and has shortened swing to be less susceptible to offspeed pitches. Average speed and good baserunning instincts. Can cover either OF corner and has enough arm strength to play RF.

Spangenberg,Cory — 4 — San Diego

Bats L Age 23 | 2011 (1) Indian River JC | EXP MLB DEBUT: 2014 | POTENTIAL: Starting 2B | **7B**

Pwr + | BAvg +++ | Spd +++ | Def +++

Year	Lev	Team	AB	R	H	HR	RBI	Avg	OB	Slg	OPS	bb%	ct%	Eye	SB	CS	x/h%	Iso	RC/G
2011	A-	Eugene	86	20	33	1	20	384	547	535	1082	26	83	2.07	10	4	33	151	10.25
2011	A	Fort Wayne	189	35	54	2	24	286	335	365	700	7	78	0.33	15	4	19	79	4.09
2012	A+	Lake Elsinore	384	53	104	1	40	271	317	352	669	6	81	0.36	27	9	20	81	3.77
2013	A+	Lake Elsinore	226	33	67	4	31	296	361	460	822	9	77	0.45	17	3	34	164	5.87
2013	AA	San Antonio	287	35	83	2	20	289	329	366	695	6	79	0.28	19	11	18	77	3.97

Lean and athletic infielder who tweaked swing and focused on more consistent, hard contact. Lacks present power as strength and bat speed a little short, but reads pitches well and uses entire field. Has excellent speed and good quickness for 2B, though still needs work on nuances of infield play. Could be utility player.

Springer,George
89 | **Houston** | EXP MLB DEBUT: 2014 | POTENTIAL: Starting OF | **8A**

Bats R Age 24
2011 (1) Connecticut
Pwr ++++
BAvg +++
Spd ++++
Def ++++

Year	Lev	Team	AB	R	H	HR	RBI	Avg	OB	Slg	OPS	bb%	ct%	Eye	SB	CS	x/h%	Iso	RC/G
2011	A-	Tri City	28	8	5	1	3	179	233	393	626	7	93	1.00	4	0	80	214	3.57
2012	A+	Lancaster	433	101	137	22	82	316	395	557	951	11	70	0.43	28	6	36	240	7.87
2012	AA	Corpus Christi	73	8	16	2	5	219	278	342	621	8	66	0.24	4	2	31	123	3.06
2013	AA	Corpus Christi	273	56	81	19	55	297	390	579	969	13	65	0.44	23	5	48	282	8.49
2013	AAA	Oklahoma City	219	50	68	18	53	311	419	626	1045	16	70	0.63	22	3	43	315	9.19

Consistent, strong OF who was equally good on two levels. Set easy highs in HR and SB while showing patient approach. Can hit LHP and RHP with plus bat speed and leveraged stroke. Can be too patient and will swing and miss. Struggles to read spin and may post below average BA. Offers above average speed and solid CF play.

Stamets,Eric
6 | **Los Angeles (A)** | EXP MLB DEBUT: 2015 | POTENTIAL: Reserve INF | **6B**

Bats R Age 22
2012 (6) Evansville
Pwr ++
BAvg ++
Spd ++++
Def ++++

Year	Lev	Team	AB	R	H	HR	RBI	Avg	OB	Slg	OPS	bb%	ct%	Eye	SB	CS	x/h%	Iso	RC/G
2010	NCAA	Evansville	234	57	75	4	27	321	402	436	838	12	86	0.97	43	8	25	115	6.12
2011	NCAA	Evansville	212	51	62	2	21	292	364	382	746	10	84	0.71	27	10	24	90	4.92
2012	NCAA	Evansville	225	41	71	1	27	316	396	422	818	12	92	1.76	30	7	30	107	6.05
2012	A	Cedar Rapids	248	34	68	1	20	274	316	347	662	6	86	0.43	7	2	22	73	3.71
2013	A+	Inland Empire	506	80	142	4	53	281	326	375	701	6	87	0.52	16	4	25	95	4.22

Athletic, rangy INF who is tough out with extreme ability to put bat to ball. Sprays balls to all fields and has plus speed to leg out doubles and steal bases. Lacks selectivity at plate and won't draw walks. Keeps ball on ground which is good for speed, but bad for HR. Has plus range at SS with quick hands and strong arm.

Starling,Bubba
8 | **Kansas City** | EXP MLB DEBUT: 2016 | POTENTIAL: Starting OF | **9E**

Bats R Age 21
2011 (1) HS (KS)
Pwr ++++
BAvg ++
Spd ++++
Def ++++

Year	Lev	Team	AB	R	H	HR	RBI	Avg	OB	Slg	OPS	bb%	ct%	Eye	SB	CS	x/h%	Iso	RC/G
2012	Rk	Burlington	200	35	55	10	33	275	364	485	849	12	65	0.40	10	1	36	210	6.65
2013	A	Lexington	435	51	105	13	63	241	324	398	721	11	71	0.41	22	3	36	156	4.59

Tall, athletic OF who started slowly, but ended year well. Possesses exceptional tools across board and has upside. Lacks intellect and gets himself out with poor pitch recognition. Tendency to chase hinders BA, but has plus, raw power and well above average speed. Owns range and very strong arm in CF.

Stassi,Max
2 | **Houston** | EXP MLB DEBUT: 2013 | POTENTIAL: Starting C | **8D**

Bats R Age 23
2009 (4) HS (CA)
Pwr +++
BAvg +++
Spd ++
Def +++

Year	Lev	Team	AB	R	H	HR	RBI	Avg	OB	Slg	OPS	bb%	ct%	Eye	SB	CS	x/h%	Iso	RC/G
2010	A	Kane County	411	54	94	13	51	229	305	380	684	10	66	0.32	3	3	37	151	4.10
2011	A+	Stockton	121	22	28	2	19	231	321	331	652	12	82	0.73	1	1	29	99	3.78
2012	A+	Stockton	314	48	84	15	45	268	326	468	794	8	74	0.33	3	1	39	201	5.28
2013	AA	Corpus Christi	289	40	80	17	60	277	321	529	851	6	76	0.28	1	1	48	253	5.86
2013	MLB	HOU	7	0	2	0	1	286	286	286	571	0	71	0.00	0	0	0	0	1.97

Short, compact C who reached HOU despite starting season late due to sports hernia. Has all-around skill set worthy of future starting spot. Realizing power potential and learning to lay off pitches. Can be too aggressive at plate and Ks will likely be part of game. Receiving getting better while strong, accurate arm is asset.

Story,Trevor
6 | **Colorado** | EXP MLB DEBUT: 2015 | POTENTIAL: Starting SS | **8D**

Bats R Age 21
2011 (2) HS (TX)
Pwr +++
BAvg +++
Spd +++
Def +++

Year	Lev	Team	AB	R	H	HR	RBI	Avg	OB	Slg	OPS	bb%	ct%	Eye	SB	CS	x/h%	Iso	RC/G
2011	Rk	Casper	179	37	48	6	28	268	361	436	797	13	77	0.63	13	1	33	168	5.59
2012	A	Asheville	477	96	132	18	63	277	358	505	863	11	75	0.50	15	3	51	229	6.50
2013	A+	Modesto	497	71	116	12	65	233	297	394	691	8	63	0.25	23	1	44	161	4.37

Had a disastrous season and struggled with pitch recognition. Can be overly aggressive and pull-conscious, but does have good raw power. Has good bat speed and is stronger than he looks. Runs well and is a smart base runner. Can make all of the plays on defense and shows good range and a plus arm.

Suarez,Eugenio
6 | **Detroit** | EXP MLB DEBUT: 2015 | POTENTIAL: Starting SS/2B | **7B**

Bats B Age 22
2008 FA (Venezuela)
Pwr ++
BAvg +++
Spd +++
Def +++

Year	Lev	Team	AB	R	H	HR	RBI	Avg	OB	Slg	OPS	bb%	ct%	Eye	SB	CS	x/h%	Iso	RC/G
2011	Rk	GCL Tigers	44	11	15	2	9	341	383	636	1019	6	91	0.75	2	0	60	295	7.78
2011	A-	Connecticut	204	37	51	5	24	250	311	426	737	8	79	0.42	9	5	41	176	4.68
2012	A	West Michigan	511	82	147	6	67	288	368	409	777	11	77	0.56	21	9	31	121	5.39
2013	A+	Lakeland	103	17	32	1	12	311	393	437	830	12	76	0.56	2	3	28	126	6.18
2013	AA	Erie	442	53	112	9	45	253	324	387	711	9	78	0.47	9	11	33	133	4.37

Smooth INF who is developing quickly. Owns gap power, but set high in HR while hitting loads of doubles. Works counts to get on base, but can be beaten with good velocity. Pull conscious at times and prone to Ks. Doesn't run particularly well, but is solid-average defender with quick hands and above average arm strength.

Susac,Andrew
2 | **San Francisco** | EXP MLB DEBUT: 2014 | POTENTIAL: Starting C | **7C**

Bats R Age 24
2011 (2) Oregon State
Pwr ++
BAvg ++
Spd ++
Def ++++

Year	Lev	Team	AB	R	H	HR	RBI	Avg	OB	Slg	OPS	bb%	ct%	Eye	SB	CS	x/h%	Iso	RC/G
2010	NCAA	Oregon St.	96	15	25	2	13	260	360	365	725	14	76	0.65	0	1	24	104	4.71
2011	NCAA	Oregon St.	134	31	42	5	32	313	429	552	981	17	76	0.84	0	1	43	239	8.36
2012	A+	San Jose	361	58	88	9	52	244	344	380	723	13	72	0.55	1	1	32	136	4.70
2013	AA	Richmond	262	32	67	12	46	256	359	458	817	14	74	0.62	1	0	43	202	5.89

Athletic C with plus arm and good receiving skills put together impressive season in AA. Moderate power and good plate discipline make offensive upside promising, though improved ct% would increase chances of hitting for BA. Regardless of his BA, glove will keep him in the lineup.

Swanner,Will
2 | **Colorado** | EXP MLB DEBUT: 2015 | POTENTIAL: Starting C | **7D**

Bats R Age 22
2010 (15) HS (CA)
Pwr +++
BAvg +++
Spd ++
Def ++

Year	Lev	Team	AB	R	H	HR	RBI	Avg	OB	Slg	OPS	bb%	ct%	Eye	SB	CS	x/h%	Iso	RC/G
2010	Rk	Casper	76	14	23	7	13	303	303	632	934	0	57	0.00	0	1	48	329	8.37
2011	Rk	Casper	159	33	42	10	24	264	346	553	900	11	62	0.33	1	2	60	289	7.65
2012	A	Asheville	325	60	98	16	61	302	375	529	904	10	69	0.38	3	2	42	228	7.19
2013	A+	Modesto	355	52	85	13	51	239	323	425	749	11	64	0.34	7	4	46	186	5.23

Strong, stocky C took a step back in '13. Has good bat speed and legit power, but swing can be long and contact rate and pitch recognition are problematic. Can be overly aggressive in his approach. Still raw behind the plate, so there is work to do. Needs to improve on signal calling and blocking and receiving skills.

Swihart,Blake
2 | **Boston** | EXP MLB DEBUT: 2015 | POTENTIAL: Starting C | **8B**

Bats B Age 22
2011 (1) HS (NM)
Pwr ++
BAvg +++
Spd ++
Def +++

Year	Lev	Team	AB	R	H	HR	RBI	Avg	OB	Slg	OPS	bb%	ct%	Eye	SB	CS	x/h%	Iso	RC/G
2011	Rk	GCL Red Sox	6	0	0	0	0	0	0	0	0	0	67	0.00	0	0		0	-6.12
2012	A	Greenville	344	44	90	7	53	262	314	395	709	7	80	0.38	6	2	31	134	4.22
2013	A+	Salem	376	45	112	2	42	298	367	428	795	10	83	0.65	7	8	34	130	5.58

Athletic, smooth-swinging hitter with potential to become all-around catcher. Power not developing as much as hoped, but makes hard line drive contact. Controls bat and recognizes pitches while maintaining aggressive nature. Has shown improvement behind plate, especially with footwork and catch-and-throw skills.

Szczur,Matt
789 | **Chicago (N)** | EXP MLB DEBUT: 2014 | POTENTIAL: Starting CF | **7C**

Bats R Age 24
2010 (5) Villanova
Pwr ++
BAvg +++
Spd ++++
Def +++

Year	Lev	Team	AB	R	H	HR	RBI	Avg	OB	Slg	OPS	bb%	ct%	Eye	SB	CS	x/h%	Iso	RC/G
2011	A	Peoria	274	55	86	5	27	314	363	431	793	7	90	0.75	17	5	24	117	5.30
2011	A+	Daytona	173	20	45	5	19	260	281	410	691	3	88	0.25	7	0	31	150	3.83
2012	A+	Daytona	295	68	87	2	34	295	392	407	799	14	83	0.94	38	12	29	112	5.83
2012	AA	Tennessee	143	24	30	2	6	210	280	357	637	9	80	0.48	4	2	43	147	3.51
2013	AA	Tennessee	512	78	144	3	44	281	345	367	712	9	85	0.67	22	12	24	86	4.49

Another solid season and held his own at AA. Has plus speed and continues to draw walks and demonstrate solid strike zone judgment. Isn't likely to develop power due to a slashing swing, but should hit for average. Continues to improve defensively and should stick in CF. Has the tools to develop into a top-of-the-order hitter.

Tapia,Raimel
789 | **Colorado** | EXP MLB DEBUT: 2016 | POTENTIAL: Starting OF | **8D**

Bats L Age 20
2011 FA (DR)
Pwr ++
BAvg +++
Spd +++
Def +++

Year	Lev	Team	AB	R	H	HR	RBI	Avg	OB	Slg	OPS	bb%	ct%	Eye	SB	CS	x/h%	Iso	RC/G
2013	Rk	Grand Junction	258	53	92	7	47	357	392	562	954	5	88	0.48	10	9	36	205	7.02

Tall, skinny Dominican OF has a good approach at the plate and posted very good contact rate. Also has good strike zone judgment and a quick LH stroke. Has above-average power and it should continue to develop as he matures. Also has enough speed to stick in CF, though he did play all three OF slots in 2013.

Taveras,Oscar | 8 | St. Louis | EXP MLB DEBUT: 2014 | POTENTIAL: Starting CF | 9B

Bats L Age 22
2008 FA (DR)
- Pwr ++++
- BAvg ++++
- Spd +++
- Def ++++

Year	Lev	Team	AB	R	H	HR	RBI	Avg	OB	Slg	OPS	bb%	ct%	Eye	SB	CS	x/h%	Iso	RC/G
2010	Rk	Johnson City	211	39	68	8	43	322	359	526	885	5	81	0.29	8	5	35	204	6.24
2011	A	Quad Cities	308	52	119	8	62	386	444	584	1029	9	83	0.62	1	4	34	198	8.28
2012	AA	Springfield	477	83	153	23	94	321	376	572	948	8	88	0.75	10	1	44	252	7.05
2013	Rk	GCL Cardinals	1	0	1	0	0	1000	0	2000	3000	50	100	1.00	0	0	100	1000	35.11
2013	AAA	Memphis	173	25	53	5	32	306	341	462	803	5	87	0.41	5	1	32	156	5.20

Continues to be one of the most dynamic prospects in baseball, but a high-ankle sprain cost him most 2013. Takes a vicious hack at the plate, but makes consistent contact and has good balance. Plus bat speed, excellent hand-eye coordination, and good strike zone judgment enable him to hit for power and average.

Taylor,Chris | 46 | Seattle | EXP MLB DEBUT: 2015 | POTENTIAL: Starting 2B/SS | 7B

Bats R Age 23
2012 (5) Virginia
- Pwr ++
- BAvg ++++
- Spd ++++
- Def +++

Year	Lev	Team	AB	R	H	HR	RBI	Avg	OB	Slg	OPS	bb%	ct%	Eye	SB	CS	x/h%	Iso	RC/G
2012	NCAA	Virginia	236	57	67	5	47	284	376	445	821	13	84	0.92	12	2	34	161	6.00
2012	A-	Everett	137	26	45	2	18	328	418	474	892	13	87	1.17	13	5	33	146	6.91
2012	A	Clinton	46	5	14	0	4	304	333	304	638	4	91	0.50	4	1	0	0	3.38
2013	A+	High Desert	269	62	90	7	44	335	428	524	952	14	77	0.71	20	2	33	190	7.83
2013	AA	Jackson	256	46	75	1	16	293	389	383	771	14	79	0.73	18	3	23	90	5.46

Polished INF who ended first full season in AA. Split time between 2B and SS and has quickness and fundamentals to play both. Draws walks with consistent approach and shoots gaps with quick, line-drive stroke. May not reach seats too often, but uses above average wheels and baserunning ability to get fair share of doubles.

Taylor,Michael A. | 8 | Washington | EXP MLB DEBUT: 2015 | POTENTIAL: Starting CF | 8D

Bats R Age 23
2009 (6) HS (FL)
- Pwr +++
- BAvg ++
- Spd ++++
- Def +++

Year	Lev	Team	AB	R	H	HR	RBI	Avg	OB	Slg	OPS	bb%	ct%	Eye	SB	CS	x/h%	Iso	RC/G
2010	Rk	GCL Nationals	128	14	25	1	12	195	275	297	572	10	76	0.45	1	2	32	102	2.63
2010	A	Hagerstown	13	0	3	0	1	231	286	308	593	7	85	0.50	0	0	33	77	3.01
2011	A	Hagerstown	442	64	112	13	68	253	304	432	736	7	73	0.27	23	12	41	179	4.61
2012	A+	Potomac	384	51	93	3	37	242	314	362	676	9	71	0.35	19	9	41	120	4.05
2013	A+	Potomac	509	79	134	10	87	263	335	426	761	10	74	0.42	51	7	43	163	5.14

Athletic, toolsy SS turned CF made strides in repeat High-A season. Improved base running skills and saw a nice bump in power. Also made progress toning down overly-aggressive plate approach, allowing him to hit the ball with more authority. Best defensive OF in system, but needs to improve ct% to utilize speed.

Taylor,Michael D. | 79 | Oakland | EXP MLB DEBUT: 2011 | POTENTIAL: Starting OF | 7C

Bats R Age 28
2007 (5) Stanford
- Pwr +++
- BAvg +++
- Spd +++
- Def +++

Year	Lev	Team	AB	R	H	HR	RBI	Avg	OB	Slg	OPS	bb%	ct%	Eye	SB	CS	x/h%	Iso	RC/G
2011	MLB	OAK	30	4	6	1	1	200	314	300	614	14	63	0.45	0	0	17	100	3.04
2012	AAA	Sacramento	449	81	129	12	67	287	402	441	843	16	77	0.82	18	3	34	154	6.43
2012	MLB	OAK	21	2	3	0	0	143	143	190	333	0	52	0.00	0	0	33	48	-1.39
2013	AAA	Sacramento	420	54	118	18	85	281	357	474	831	11	79	0.57	5	2	37	193	5.85
2013	MLB	OAK	23	0	1	0	0	43	120	43	163	8	78	0.40	0	0	0	0	-2.68

Tall, athletic OF who has been on prospect charts for years, but can't break through for big league role. Spent 3½ years in AAA and has solid tools across board. Swings with authority and uses entire field in line drive approach. Natural strength results in average power. Doesn't run as well as he once did.

Taylor,Tyrone | 8 | Milwaukee | EXP MLB DEBUT: 2016 | POTENTIAL: Starting OF | 7B

Bats R Age 20
2012 (2) HS (CA)
- Pwr +++
- BAvg +++
- Spd +++
- Def +++

Year	Lev	Team	AB	R	H	HR	RBI	Avg	OB	Slg	OPS	bb%	ct%	Eye	SB	CS	x/h%	Iso	RC/G
2012	Rk	AZL Brewers	36	11	14	0	6	389	405	694	1100	3	92	0.33	3	1	57	306	8.72
2012	Rk	Helena	39	11	15	2	5	385	455	641	1096	11	79	0.63	3	2	40	256	9.26
2013	A	Wisconsin	485	69	133	8	57	274	323	400	723	7	87	0.56	19	8	32	126	4.47

Athletic two-sport star excelled in first full season. True five-tool player tinkered with mechanics, allowing quick bat speed to tap into raw power. Makes good contact for aggressive hitter. Needs to be more selective to realize power. Has legitimate CF talent with above average speed, reads and instincts.

Tellez,Rowdy | 3 | Toronto | EXP MLB DEBUT: 2018 | POTENTIAL: Starting 1B | 8E

Bats L Age 19
2013 (30) HS (CA)
- Pwr ++++
- BAvg ++
- Spd ++
- Def ++

Year	Lev	Team	AB	R	H	HR	RBI	Avg	OB	Slg	OPS	bb%	ct%	Eye	SB	CS	x/h%	Iso	RC/G
2013	Rk	GCL Blue Jays	124	10	29	2	20	234	317	371	688	11	79	0.58	1	0	34	137	4.20

Big and strong hitter who fell in draft due to bonus demands. Has as much raw power as any in org and can crush balls to all fields. Not much value outside of present strength. Exhibits good bat control, but not likely to hit for BA without cleaner stroke. Can bail out against breaking balls. Has OK hands and arm at 1B.

Thompson,Trayce | 89 | Chicago (A) | EXP MLB DEBUT: 2014 | POTENTIAL: Starting OF | 8D

Bats R Age 23
2009 (2) HS (CA)
- Pwr ++++
- BAvg ++
- Spd ++++
- Def +++

Year	Lev	Team	AB	R	H	HR	RBI	Avg	OB	Slg	OPS	bb%	ct%	Eye	SB	CS	x/h%	Iso	RC/G
2011	A	Kannapolis	519	95	125	24	87	241	320	457	776	10	67	0.35	8	4	50	216	5.42
2012	A+	Winston-Salem	449	77	114	22	90	254	322	486	807	9	68	0.31	18	3	48	232	5.79
2012	AA	Birmingham	50	10	14	3	6	280	379	520	899	14	68	0.50	2	0	36	240	7.23
2012	AAA	Charlotte	18	1	3	0	0	167	250	278	528	10	67	0.33	1	0	67	111	2.00
2013	AA	Birmingham	507	78	116	15	73	229	310	383	693	11	73	0.43	25	8	37	154	4.15

Tall, athletic OF who suffers from inconsistency on both sides of ball. Focused on shortening swing, but still finished 3rd in league in strikeouts. Stroke and strength lead to above average pop, but breaking balls still give him fits. Posted high in SB and has plentiful tools. Split time between CF and RF with improved reads and jumps.

Tilson,Charlie | 8 | St. Louis | EXP MLB DEBUT: 2015 | POTENTIAL: Starting CF | 7C

Bats L Age 21
2011 (2) HS (IL)
- Pwr ++
- BAvg +++
- Spd +++
- Def +++

Year	Lev	Team	AB	R	H	HR	RBI	Avg	OB	Slg	OPS	bb%	ct%	Eye	SB	CS	x/h%	Iso	RC/G
2011	Rk	GCL Cardinals	12	2	2	0	1	167	286	167	452	14	75	0.67	1	0	0	0	1.08
2011	Rk	Johnson City	15	2	7	0	4	467	500	600	1100	6	93	1.00	0	0	29	133	8.69
2013	A	Peoria	376	49	114	4	30	303	347	388	735	6	85	0.43	15	6	16	85	4.52
2013	A+	Palm Beach	34	1	9	0	0	265	359	353	712	13	82	0.83	0	0	22	88	4.73

Fully recovered from shoulder surgery that caused him to miss all of 2012. Had a solid year in his full-season debut. High-energy CF with a smooth compact LH stroke and is willing to drive the ball the other way. Is more of a contact hitter and is not likely to hit for much power, but has good speed.

Tocci,Carlos | 8 | Philadelphia | EXP MLB DEBUT: 2017 | POTENTIAL: Starting CF | 8D

Bats R Age 18
2011 FA (DR)
- Pwr ++
- BAvg +++
- Spd +++
- Def ++++

Year	Lev	Team	AB	R	H	HR	RBI	Avg	OB	Slg	OPS	bb%	ct%	Eye	SB	CS	x/h%	Iso	RC/G
2012	Rk	GCL Phillies	97	13	27	0	9	278	320	299	619	6	81	0.33	9	2	7	21	3.05
2013	A	Lakewood	421	40	88	0	26	209	248	249	498	5	82	0.29	6	7	19	40	1.60

Rail-thin at 160 pounds, but is all about projection. Was overmatched in the SAL, but has the fluid actions of a plus athlete. Made good contact, hit to the opposite field, and showed promising instincts on the bases. But a lack of strength is an issue until he fills out. Covers a lot of ground in CF and has a strong arm.

Toles,Andrew | 78 | Tampa Bay | EXP MLB DEBUT: 2016 | POTENTIAL: Starting OF | 8C

Bats L Age 22
2012 (3) Chipola JC
- Pwr ++
- BAvg +++
- Spd ++++
- Def +++

Year	Lev	Team	AB	R	H	HR	RBI	Avg	OB	Slg	OPS	bb%	ct%	Eye	SB	CS	x/h%	Iso	RC/G
2011	NCAA	Tennessee	204	30	55	1	25	270	284	368	651	2	89	0.17	21	7	27	98	3.44
2012	NCAA	Chipola College	166	41	61	5	33	367	429	554	984				29	7	31	187	7.66
2012	Rk	Princeton	199	31	56	7	33	281	322	482	805	6	82	0.33	14	5	41	201	5.29
2013	A	Bowling Green	519	79	169	2	57	326	353	466	819	4	80	0.21	62	17	31	141	5.56

Athletic OF who led MWL in BA and finished 2nd in SB. Owns incredible speed which enhances CF range and has sufficient arm. Exhibits bat speed and offers some power potential, but needs to focus on more contact. Rarely draws walks and long swing results in strikeouts. Has knack for hard contact, but next step is plate discipline.

Torrens,Luis | 2 | New York (A) | EXP MLB DEBUT: 2018 | POTENTIAL: Starting C | 8E

Bats R Age 18
2012 FA (Venezuela)
- Pwr ++
- BAvg ++
- Spd ++
- Def ++

Year	Lev	Team	AB	R	H	HR	RBI	Avg	OB	Slg	OPS	bb%	ct%	Eye	SB	CS	x/h%	Iso	RC/G
2013	Rk	GCL Yankees 2	174	17	42	1	14	241	343	299	642	13	77	0.68	2	0	19	57	3.69

Strong-armed backstop who has plenty of work to do behind plate, but has high ceiling. Very raw blocker and receiver, but shuts down running game with quick release. Offense is advanced for age as he owns mature approach and clean swing mechanics. Bat speed and loft should lead to at least average power in future.

Torres, Gleyber — 6 — Chicago (N)

EXP MLB DEBUT: 2018 | POTENTIAL: Starting SS | 8D

Bats R Age 17
2013 FA (Venezuela)

Pwr	+++
BAvg	+++
Spd	++
Def	++++

Year	Lev	Team	AB	R	H	HR	RBI	Avg	OB	Slg	OPS	bb%	ct%	Eye	SB	CS	x/h%	Iso	RC/G
2013		Did not play in the US																	

Polished SS prospect has five above-average tools. Has a good approach at the plate with bat speed, nice pop for his size, and makes consistent contact. Has decent range, soft hands, and a strong arm, though some scouts question whether he will stick at SS.

Towey, Cal — 5 — Los Angeles (A)

EXP MLB DEBUT: 2016 | POTENTIAL: Reserve 3B | 7E

Bats L Age 24
2013 (17) Baylor

Pwr	++
BAvg	+++
Spd	++
Def	++

Year	Lev	Team	AB	R	H	HR	RBI	Avg	OB	Slg	OPS	bb%	ct%	Eye	SB	CS	x/h%	Iso	RC/G
2010	NCAA	Baylor	105	21	33	3	20	314	424	514	938	16	69	0.61	3	2	36	200	8.15
2011	NCAA	Baylor	131	22	32	4	15	244	377	397	774	18	63	0.57	6	5	31	153	5.88
2012	NCAA	Baylor	224	43	66	6	51	295	399	469	868	15	72	0.62	9	7	35	174	6.87
2013	NCAA	Baylor	199	34	58	4	45	291	400	457	857	15	78	0.84	10	2	34	166	6.64
2013	Rk	Orem	230	69	73	8	53	317	471	543	1015	23	74	1.14	13	3	41	226	9.23

Extremely patient hitter who surprised after 17th round selection. Walk rate was exceptionally high, but can be too passive at plate. Upon contact, can drive ball to all fields with average power. Doesn't possess plus tool and power doesn't project. Strong arm is best attribute and has fringy range and hands.

Trahan, Stryker — 2 — Arizona

EXP MLB DEBUT: 2016 | POTENTIAL: Starting C | 8D

Bats L Age 20
2012 (1) HS (LA)

Pwr	+++
BAvg	+++
Spd	++
Def	++

Year	Lev	Team	AB	R	H	HR	RBI	Avg	OB	Slg	OPS	bb%	ct%	Eye	SB	CS	x/h%	Iso	RC/G
2012	Rk	AZL D'backs	167	29	47	5	25	281	420	473	893	19	71	0.83	8	1	40	192	7.46
2013	Rk	Missoula	236	44	60	10	33	254	323	462	785	9	76	0.42	1	0	45	208	5.26

Strong, offensive-minded backstop continues his steady development. Has good bat speed, raw power, and a good walk rate. Struggled to make consistent contact and will need to improve to hit for average. Made strides defensively, throwing out 40% of runners and improving his receiving skills. Should be able to stick at C.

Travis, Devon — 4 — Detroit

EXP MLB DEBUT: 2014 | POTENTIAL: Starting 2B/3B | 8C

Bats R Age 23
2012 (13) Florida State

Pwr	++
BAvg	++++
Spd	+++
Def	+++

Year	Lev	Team	AB	R	H	HR	RBI	Avg	OB	Slg	OPS	bb%	ct%	Eye	SB	CS	x/h%	Iso	RC/G
2011	NCAA	Florida St.	220	54	72	6	33	327	431	514	944	15	86	1.33	4	4	40	186	7.61
2012	NCAA	Florida St.	268	63	87	8	44	325	393	504	896	10	85	0.75	7	2	37	179	6.66
2012	A-	Connecticut	93	17	26	3	11	280	337	441	777	8	89	0.80	3	1	27	161	5.13
2013	A	West Michigan	290	55	102	6	42	352	402	486	908	11	89	1.09	14	3	25	134	6.84
2013	A+	Lakeland	214	38	75	10	34	350	401	561	962	8	85	0.56	8	1	31	210	7.16

Breakout prospect in system and finished 2nd in minors in BA. Makes easy contact with short stroke and has strength to reach seats when turning on pitches. Doesn't project to much power, but can reach seats when turning on pitches. Willing to work counts and use speed. Possesses average range and hands.

Triunfel, Carlos — 46 — Seattle

EXP MLB DEBUT: 2012 | POTENTIAL: Reserve INF | 6B

Bats R Age 24
2006 FA (DR)

Pwr	++
BAvg	++
Spd	++
Def	++++

Year	Lev	Team	AB	R	H	HR	RBI	Avg	OB	Slg	OPS	bb%	ct%	Eye	SB	CS	x/h%	Iso	RC/G
2011	AAA	Tacoma	111	7	31	0	10	279	292	351	643	2	85	0.12	1	0	23	72	3.24
2012	AAA	Tacoma	496	74	129	10	62	260	293	391	684	4	82	0.26	3	2	33	131	3.78
2012	MLB	SEA	22	2	5	0	3	227	261	318	579	4	82	0.25	0	0	40	91	2.63
2013	AAA	Tacoma	383	55	108	5	31	282	313	394	707	4	80	0.22	6	4	28	112	4.06
2013	MLB	SEA	44	1	6	0	2	136	136	159	295	0	75	0.00	0	0	17	23	-1.46

Strong and versatile defender who hasn't developed as much as hoped with bat, but continues to stand out with glove. Has cannon for arm that is asset at any position. Hands and quick actions work well in MIF. Had power potential, but focuses more on contact with free-swinging nature and rarely draws walks.

Tucker, Preston — 79 — Houston

EXP MLB DEBUT: 2015 | POTENTIAL: Reserve OF | 6B

Bats L Age 23
2012 (7) Florida

Pwr	++++
BAvg	++
Spd	+
Def	++

Year	Lev	Team	AB	R	H	HR	RBI	Avg	OB	Slg	OPS	bb%	ct%	Eye	SB	CS	x/h%	Iso	RC/G
2011	NCAA	Florida	286	55	88	15	74	308	369	545	915	9	90	0.97	5	3	43	238	6.68
2012	NCAA	Florida	262	57	84	16	50	321	401	584	985	12	90	1.30	6	3	42	263	7.63
2012	A-	Tri City	165	32	53	8	38	321	388	509	897	10	90	1.13	1	2	28	188	6.50
2013	A+	Lancaster	298	61	97	15	74	326	385	544	929	9	85	0.64	3	0	35	218	6.84
2013	AA	Corpus Christi	237	36	62	10	29	262	337	456	793	10	81	0.59	0	1	40	194	5.35

Thick-bodied OF who stands out for offensive production. Struggled in AA, but makes good contact and offers all-fields power. Can be pitched to and has to start swing early to catch up to good FB. Uses entire field, though doesn't have speed and has limited value beyond bat. Doesn't have much mobility or range in outfield.

Turner, Stuart — 2 — Minnesota

EXP MLB DEBUT: 2015 | POTENTIAL: Starting C | 7C

Bats R Age 22
2013 (3) Mississippi

Pwr	++
BAvg	++
Spd	++
Def	++++

Year	Lev	Team	AB	R	H	HR	RBI	Avg	OB	Slg	OPS	bb%	ct%	Eye	SB	CS	x/h%	Iso	RC/G
2013	NCAA	Mississippi	222	44	83	5	51	374	444	518	962	11	83	0.76	2	4	25	144	7.55
2013	Rk	Elizabethton	121	15	32	3	19	264	331	380	711	9	82	0.55	0	1	25	116	4.30
2013	AA	New Britain	4	1	2	0	0	500	500	500	1000	0	75	0.00	0	0	0	0	7.40

Big and agile backstop who is known for defensive acumen. Catch and throw skills unmatched in org and moves well behind plate. Footwork is sound and arm neutralizes runners. Can be passable hitter, but is pull-conscious. Controls bat and knows strike zone. Has some power potential, but focuses more on line drives.

Unroe, Riley — 6 — Tampa Bay

EXP MLB DEBUT: 2018 | POTENTIAL: Starting SS | 8E

Bats B Age 18
2013 (2) HS (AZ)

Pwr	++
BAvg	+++
Spd	+++
Def	+++

Year	Lev	Team	AB	R	H	HR	RBI	Avg	OB	Slg	OPS	bb%	ct%	Eye	SB	CS	x/h%	Iso	RC/G
2013	Rk	GCL Rays	167	34	41	1	15	246	370	341	711	17	74	0.77	7	2	27	96	4.79

Short, versatile INF who has plus bat speed from both sides of plate. Has good offensive skills, highlighted by plate patience and average power potential. Likely not going to be middle of order run producer, but is good situational hitter. Provides solid-average speed and quickness at SS. Also has sure hands and strong arm.

Urena, Jhoan — 5 — New York (N)

EXP MLB DEBUT: 2018 | POTENTIAL: Starting 3B | 7D

Bats B Age 19
2013 FA (DR)

Pwr	+++
BAvg	+++
Spd	++
Def	+++

Year	Lev	Team	AB	R	H	HR	RBI	Avg	OB	Slg	OPS	bb%	ct%	Eye	SB	CS	x/h%	Iso	RC/G
2013	Rk	GCL Mets	157	19	47	0	20	299	353	376	729	8	78	0.38	4	1	19	76	4.59

Shows nice agility for his size at 3B. Has good hands and strong arm with adequate range defensively. Gap power could translate to home runs as he gains strength; good raw power potential and bat speed. Switch hits though he appears to be a stronger batter from the left side.

Urena, Jose — 79 — San Diego

EXP MLB DEBUT: 2018 | POTENTIAL: Starting OF | 7E

Bats R Age 19
2011 FA (Mexico)

Pwr	++++
BAvg	++
Spd	++
Def	++

Year	Lev	Team	AB	R	H	HR	RBI	Avg	OB	Slg	OPS	bb%	ct%	Eye	SB	CS	x/h%	Iso	RC/G
2013	Rk	AZL Padres	191	32	49	9	34	257	333	508	841	10	72	0.41	1	2	51	251	6.21

Raw and projectable outfielder who led AZL in HR in pro debut. Hitting instincts aren't as evident as approach is inconsistent and swing can get long. Uses entire field and has ample strength and bat speed. Best defensive attribute is arm, though isn't very quick and doesn't take good routes to balls in corner.

Urena, Richard — 6 — Toronto

EXP MLB DEBUT: 2018 | POTENTIAL: Starting SS | 8D

Bats L Age 18
2012 FA (DR)

Pwr	++
BAvg	+++
Spd	++
Def	+++

Year	Lev	Team	AB	R	H	HR	RBI	Avg	OB	Slg	OPS	bb%	ct%	Eye	SB	CS	x/h%	Iso	RC/G
2013	Rk	GCL Blue Jays	27	3	9	0	3	333	400	407	807	10	78	0.50	0	0	22	74	5.73

Young, projectable INF who has solid potential, especially on defense. Makes routine plays with quick feet and soft, sure hands. Arm strength is sufficient for any infield spot. Average tools enhanced by instincts and should be able to provide gap power with wiry strength. Simply needs time and experience to realize potential.

Urrutia,Henry — 9 — Baltimore
EXP MLB DEBUT: 2013 | POTENTIAL: Starting OF | 7C

Bats B Age 27
2012 FA (Cuba)
Pwr ++
BAvg +++
Spd ++
Def +++

Year	Lev	Team	AB	R	H	HR	RBI	Avg	OB	Slg	OPS	bb%	ct%	Eye	SB	CS	x/h%	Iso	RC/G
2013	AA	Bowie	200	33	73	7	37	365	433	550	983	11	82	0.67	1	1	32	185	7.75
2013	AAA	Norfolk	114	16	36	2	13	316	361	430	790	7	87	0.53	0	0	22	114	5.19
2013	MLB	BAL	58	5	16	0	2	276	276	310	586	0	81	0.00	0	0	6	34	2.32

Long, lean OF who reached BAL after easy success in minors on two levels. Makes line drive contact with clean stroke and can shoot gaps. Power mostly of pull variety and tough on RHP. Lacks ideal athleticism and quickness, but can play solid defense in RF with strong arm. Not much upside, but safe bet for playing time.

Urshela,Giovanny — 5 — Cleveland
EXP MLB DEBUT: 2015 | POTENTIAL: Starting 3B | 7C

Bats R Age 22
2008 FA (Colombia)
Pwr +++
BAvg ++
Spd ++
Def ++++

Year	Lev	Team	AB	R	H	HR	RBI	Avg	OB	Slg	OPS	bb%	ct%	Eye	SB	CS	x/h%	Iso	RC/G
2009	Rk	AZL Indians	105	10	27	0	11	257	322	276	598	9	89	0.83	3	0	7	19	3.20
2010	A-	Mahoning Val	221	22	64	3	35	290	326	367	693	5	86	0.38	5	3	17	77	3.93
2011	A	Lake County	505	57	120	9	46	238	258	347	605	3	86	0.20	3	0	29	109	2.82
2012	A+	Carolina	439	50	122	14	59	278	303	446	750	4	86	0.27	1	1	37	169	4.49
2013	AA	Akron	445	42	120	8	43	270	292	384	676	3	89	0.29	1	1	28	115	3.72

Smooth, natural hitting INF who brings extreme contact-oriented approach to plate. Rarely fans, but quick AB result in few walks. Has good strength with level stroke, but power projects as only average. Struggled against LHP (.189, 0 HR) and may need to be more patient. Well above average 3B with plus arm, hands, and range.

Valentin,Jesmuel — 6 — Los Angeles (N)
EXP MLB DEBUT: 2017 | POTENTIAL: Starting SS | 7D

Bats B Age 20
2012 (S-1) HS (PR)
Pwr ++
BAvg ++
Spd +++
Def +++

Year	Lev	Team	AB	R	H	HR	RBI	Avg	OB	Slg	OPS	bb%	ct%	Eye	SB	CS	x/h%	Iso	RC/G
2012	Rk	AZL Dodgers	152	34	32	2	18	211	358	316	674	19	84	1.46	5	2	31	105	4.52
2013	Rk	Ogden	250	53	71	4	24	284	367	396	763	12	86	0.97	11	7	24	112	5.23
2013	A	Great Lakes	99	12	21	0	5	212	322	293	615	14	72	0.57	4	3	33	81	3.36

Quick, athletic glove-first SS has above-average range and a strong arm with good hands. Switch-hitter makes hard contact and has good plate discipline, but needs to improve pitch recognition. Speed plays well and should bring double-digit stolen bases.

Valera,Breyvic — 47 — St. Louis
EXP MLB DEBUT: 2016 | POTENTIAL: Starting 2B | 7D

Bats B Age 21
2010 FA (Venezuela)
Pwr +
BAvg +++
Spd +++
Def +++

Year	Lev	Team	AB	R	H	HR	RBI	Avg	OB	Slg	OPS	bb%	ct%	Eye	SB	CS	x/h%	Iso	RC/G
2011	Rk	GCL Cardinals	110	23	28	1	13	255	317	364	680	8	85	0.59	7	1	29	109	4.07
2011	Rk	Johnson City	73	16	29	0	8	397	436	479	915	6	88	0.56	7	5	17	82	6.68
2012	A-	Batavia	282	39	89	1	33	316	357	418	775	6	90	0.67	10	6	26	103	5.12
2012	AA	Springfield	5	2	1	0	1	200	200	200	400	0	100	1.00	0	0	0	0	1.14
2013	A	Peoria	515	71	159	0	48	309	359	367	726	7	94	1.33	13	7	15	58	4.73

Short, switch-hitting 2B prospect put up another impressive season, hitting .309 with 40 BB/30 K in the MWL. Hits well from both sides of the plate and uses the whole field. Doesn't have much power, but has good speed. Solid range and actions at 2B and also saw action in LF.

Vargas,Kennys — 3 — Minnesota
EXP MLB DEBUT: 2015 | POTENTIAL: Reserve 1B | 6B

Bats B Age 23
2009 FA (PR)
Pwr ++++
BAvg +++
Spd +
Def +

Year	Lev	Team	AB	R	H	HR	RBI	Avg	OB	Slg	OPS	bb%	ct%	Eye	SB	CS	x/h%	Iso	RC/G
2009	Rk	GCL Twins	109	12	28	3	18	257	357	404	761	13	69	0.50	2	0	36	147	5.31
2010	Rk	GCL Twins	142	24	46	3	26	324	381	507	888	8	72	0.33	1	0	41	183	6.90
2011	Rk	Elizabethton	174	27	56	6	33	322	376	489	864	8	71	0.30	0	0	30	167	6.40
2012	A	Beloit	154	22	49	11	36	318	423	610	1033	15	73	0.68	0	0	45	292	8.88
2013	A+	Fort Myers	457	68	122	19	93	267	339	468	808	10	77	0.48	0	0	43	201	5.56

Large-bodied slugger who started season hot, but faded last two months. Works counts to find balls to drive, but has too much swing and miss in game. Doesn't recognize spin and can be beaten with good FB. Has some feel for hitting and makes OK contact for profile. All-fields power is best tool whereas speed is worst.

Vasquez,Danry — 7 — Houston
EXP MLB DEBUT: 2016 | POTENTIAL: Starting OF | 8D

Bats L Age 20
2010 FA (Venezuela)
Pwr +++
BAvg +++
Spd ++
Def ++

Year	Lev	Team	AB	R	H	HR	RBI	Avg	OB	Slg	OPS	bb%	ct%	Eye	SB	CS	x/h%	Iso	RC/G
2011	Rk	GCL Tigers	206	25	56	2	30	272	296	350	645	3	83	0.21	3	2	20	78	3.26
2012	A-	Connecticut	289	36	90	2	35	311	341	401	742	4	84	0.29	6	4	22	90	4.51
2012	A	West Michigan	99	5	16	1	7	162	217	222	439	7	80	0.35	0	0	25	61	0.83
2013	A	Quad Cities	118	12	34	3	20	288	323	398	721	5	87	0.40	2	0	18	110	4.22
2013	A	West Michigan	375	47	106	6	40	283	337	400	737	8	85	0.55	9	8	25	117	4.66

Tall, lanky OF who is all about projection, but showcases natural hitting skills. Makes easy contact due to balanced stroke and not afraid to go to opp field. Can hit LHP and improving pitch recognition could lead to average pop. Lacks foot speed for SB and defense is subpar. Currently a bat-only prospect.

Vaughn,Cory — 7 — New York (N)
EXP MLB DEBUT: 2014 | POTENTIAL: Starting RF/LF | 7D

Bats R Age 25
2010 (4) San Diego State
Pwr ++++
BAvg ++
Spd +++
Def +++

Year	Lev	Team	AB	R	H	HR	RBI	Avg	OB	Slg	OPS	bb%	ct%	Eye	SB	CS	x/h%	Iso	RC/G
2011	A+	St. Lucie	210	29	46	9	29	219	296	395	691	10	75	0.43	2	3	39	176	3.99
2012	A+	St. Lucie	456	73	111	23	69	243	338	463	801	12	75	0.57	21	4	46	219	5.57
2013	Rk	GCL Mets	29	4	5	0	1	172	368	345	713	24	69	1.00	2	0	60	172	5.22
2013	A+	St. Lucie	39	5	8	0	3	205	340	282	622	17	77	0.89	5	0	25	77	3.67
2013	AA	Binghamton	262	40	70	10	50	267	329	424	752	8	70	0.31	9	1	29	156	4.84

Nagged by injuries, he didn't make progress hoped for in improving ct%. In AFL, struck out 25 times in 88 AB. Could become a nice power/speed combo OF if he can ever put it all together; has huge power potential. Covers lots of ground in OF with strong arm. Swing gets long and struggles against offspeed pitches.

Vazquez,Christian — 2 — Boston
EXP MLB DEBUT: 2014 | POTENTIAL: Starting C | 7C

Bats R Age 23
2008 (9) HS (PR)
Pwr ++
BAvg +++
Spd ++
Def +++

Year	Lev	Team	AB	R	H	HR	RBI	Avg	OB	Slg	OPS	bb%	ct%	Eye	SB	CS	x/h%	Iso	RC/G
2011	A	Greenville	392	71	111	18	84	283	354	505	859	10	79	0.51	1	1	43	222	6.19
2012	A+	Salem	293	43	78	7	41	266	354	396	750	12	76	0.57	2	2	31	130	4.98
2012	AA	Portland	73	11	15	0	5	205	284	260	544	10	88	0.89	0	0	27	55	2.68
2013	AA	Portland	342	48	99	5	48	289	375	395	770	12	87	1.07	7	5	25	105	5.35
2013	AAA	Pawtucket	3	0	0	0	0	0	250	0	250	25	100	1.00	0	0	0	0	1.04

Short backstop who walked more than he fanned, though power regression is troubling. Showed ability to hit for BA by shortening swing and being more selective. Swing path not conducive to much power, but uses entire field. Becoming excellent defender who can receive while average arm plays up due to release.

Vettleson,Drew — 9 — Tampa Bay
EXP MLB DEBUT: 2016 | POTENTIAL: Starting OF | 8D

Bats L Age 22
2010 (1-S) HS (WA)
Pwr +++
BAvg +++
Spd +++
Def +++

Year	Lev	Team	AB	R	H	HR	RBI	Avg	OB	Slg	OPS	bb%	ct%	Eye	SB	CS	x/h%	Iso	RC/G
2011	Rk	Princeton	234	33	66	7	40	282	356	462	818	10	77	0.51	20	6	36	179	5.79
2012	A	Bowling Green	505	80	139	15	69	275	342	432	773	9	77	0.44	20	11	32	156	5.12
2013	A+	Charlotte	467	50	128	4	62	274	331	388	719	8	83	0.51	5	7	30	113	4.49

Strong, athletic OF who had year of ups and downs. Drastically cut down on Ks, but HR and SB production dropped. Possesses short stroke and has strength and bat speed to drive ball to all fields. Controlled stroke enhances BA and still offers average pop. Not a big SB guy to begin with, but runs well and has strong arm for RF.

Villalona,Angel — 3 — San Francisco
EXP MLB DEBUT: 2014 | POTENTIAL: Backup 1B | 6C

Bats R Age 23
2006 FA (DR)
Pwr +++
BAvg ++
Spd ++
Def ++

Year	Lev	Team	AB	R	H	HR	RBI	Avg	OB	Slg	OPS	bb%	ct%	Eye	SB	CS	x/h%	Iso	RC/G
2009	A+	San Jose	292	47	78	9	42	267	289	397	686	3	75	0.12	0	1	26	130	3.61
2013	A+	San Jose	284	37	65	14	42	229	268	433	701	5	73	0.20	0	0	46	204	3.90
2013	AA	Richmond	196	23	46	8	28	235	265	413	678	4	69	0.13	0	0	41	179	3.65

First season back since being charged with murder in the DR, Villalona was once regarded as a top prospect in the Giants org. Power is still intact, hitting 22 HR across two levels. Struggles to draw walks and making consistent contact hinder BA ceiling. Below average defender and runner limited to 1B.

Villanueva,Christian — 5 — Chicago (N)
EXP MLB DEBUT: 2014 | POTENTIAL: Starting 3B | 7C

Bats R Age 23
2008 FA (Mexico)
Pwr +++
BAvg ++
Spd ++
Def ++++

Year	Lev	Team	AB	R	H	HR	RBI	Avg	OB	Slg	OPS	bb%	ct%	Eye	SB	CS	x/h%	Iso	RC/G
2010	Rk	AZL Rangers	188	30	59	2	35	314	358	431	789	6	78	0.31	6	2	29	117	5.26
2011	A	Hickory	467	78	130	17	84	278	331	465	796	7	82	0.43	32	6	38	186	5.25
2012	A+	Daytona	84	14	21	4	9	250	330	452	782	11	71	0.42	5	2	43	202	5.31
2012	A+	Myrtle Beach	375	45	107	10	59	285	328	421	750	6	78	0.29	9	9	28	136	4.62
2013	AA	Tennessee	490	60	128	19	72	261	309	469	779	6	76	0.29	5	7	48	208	5.06

Short, strong-bodied 3B took a step back, though he did have 62 XBH. Short, compact stroke and good bat speed result in above-average power, but aggressive approach could cut into batting average and scouts are not convinced he will hit for average. Is a plus defender with good hands, range, and strong, accurate arm.

Vitters,Josh — 7 — Chicago (N) — EXP MLB DEBUT: 2012 — POTENTIAL: Starting LF — 7D

Bats R Age 24
2007 (1) HS (CA)
Pwr +++
BAvg ++
Spd ++
Def ++

Year	Lev	Team	AB	R	H	HR	RBI	Avg	OB	Slg	OPS	bb%	ct%	Eye	SB	CS	x/h%	Iso	RC/G
2011	AA	Tennessee	449	56	127	14	81	283	316	448	764	5	88	0.41	4	10	35	165	4.75
2012	AAA	Iowa	415	54	126	17	68	304	351	513	864	7	81	0.39	6	3	40	210	6.04
2012	MLB	CHC	99	7	12	2	5	121	179	202	381	7	67	0.21	2	0	33	81	-0.54
2013	Rk	AZL Cubs	13	1	1	0	0	77	294	154	448	24	62	0.80	0	0	100	77	0.63
2013	AAA	Iowa	88	14	26	5	12	295	374	511	885	11	78	0.58	1	0	35	216	6.48

Showed some signs of progress in 2013 . Posted a career best BB%, but hamstring injury limited him to 101 AB. Hit well when he returned to action. The Cubs will move him to LF in the spring after trading for Mike Olt and drafting K. Bryant. Third overall pick still has potential.

Vogelbach,Dan — 3 — Chicago (N) — EXP MLB DEBUT: 2016 — POTENTIAL: Starting 1B — 8D

Bats L Age 21
2011 (2) HS (FL)
Pwr ++++
BAvg +++
Spd +
Def +

Year	Lev	Team	AB	R	H	HR	RBI	Avg	OB	Slg	OPS	bb%	ct%	Eye	SB	CS	x/h%	Iso	RC/G
2011	Rk	AZL Cubs	24	4	7	1	6	292	346	542	888	8	92	1.00	1	0	57	250	6.41
2012	Rk	AZL Cubs	102	16	33	7	31	324	395	686	1081	11	86	0.86	1	0	64	363	8.78
2012	A-	Boise	143	23	46	10	31	322	416	608	1024	14	76	0.68	0	1	43	287	8.52
2013	A	Kane County	433	55	123	17	71	284	367	450	818	12	82	0.75	4	4	31	166	5.72
2013	A+	Daytona	50	13	14	2	5	280	455	440	895	24	74	1.23	1	0	29	160	7.47

Strong, thick-bodied 1B has plus raw power, good plate discipline, and a short, compact stroke. Held his own in the MWL, earning a late bump to High-A. Makes consistent contact for a power hitter, giving him the potential to hit for power and average. Is below-average defensively with limited range and stiff hands.

Vollmuth,B.A. — 5 — Oakland — EXP MLB DEBUT: 2015 — POTENTIAL: Starting 3B — 7E

Bats R Age 24
2011 (3) Southern Miss
Pwr ++++
BAvg ++
Spd +
Def ++

Year	Lev	Team	AB	R	H	HR	RBI	Avg	OB	Slg	OPS	bb%	ct%	Eye	SB	CS	x/h%	Iso	RC/G
2011	Rk	AZL Athletics	27	3	4	1	2	148	233	259	493	10	78	0.50	0	0	25	111	1.39
2011	A-	Vermont	14	8	7	0	6	500	563	929	1491	13	79	0.67	0	1	71	429	15.26
2012	A	Burlington	265	37	69	7	44	260	333	411	745	10	72	0.39	7	1	36	151	4.87
2012	A+	Stockton	264	45	69	7	29	261	330	398	728	9	73	0.39	0	2	32	136	4.55
2013	A+	Stockton	471	66	100	21	70	212	296	408	704	11	66	0.35	0	0	48	195	4.35

Tall and strong infielder who set easy career-high in HR, but BA plummeted. Expands strike zone and misses pitches often. Struggles to read pitches and has noted problems with spin. Hands work well in powerful stroke, but pulls off ball often. Can be sufficient defender, but makes careless errors with sloppy footwork.

Walding,Mitch — 5 — Philadelphia — EXP MLB DEBUT: 2016 — POTENTIAL: Backup 3B — 7D

Bats L Age 21
2011 (5) HS (CA)
Pwr ++
BAvg ++
Spd ++
Def ++

Year	Lev	Team	AB	R	H	HR	RBI	Avg	OB	Slg	OPS	bb%	ct%	Eye	SB	CS	x/h%	Iso	RC/G
2012	A-	Williamsport	253	33	59	1	31	233	317	308	625	11	74	0.47	5	2	24	75	3.35
2013	A	Lakewood	402	50	90	1	42	224	320	286	606	12	70	0.47	6	7	23	62	3.12

Suffered through tough first full season, though it was hampered by a rib injury. Owns a discerning eye at the plate, but way too much present swing and miss, and his balance is easily disrupted. Improved defensively, flashed athleticism and a strong arm. May not hit enough to be a starter.

Walker,Adam Brett — 9 — Minnesota — EXP MLB DEBUT: 2015 — POTENTIAL: Starting OF — 8D

Bats R Age 22
2012 (3) Jacksonville
Pwr ++++
BAvg ++
Spd +++
Def ++

Year	Lev	Team	AB	R	H	HR	RBI	Avg	OB	Slg	OPS	bb%	ct%	Eye	SB	CS	x/h%	Iso	RC/G
2010	NCAA	Jacksonville	192	44	60	16	58	313	389	635	1024	11	61	0.32	7	0	50	323	9.59
2011	NCAA	Jacksonville	242	65	99	13	74	409	484	682	1166	13	74	0.56	14	0	38	273	10.65
2012	NCAA	Jacksonville	210	44	72	12	42	343	423	581	1004	12	78	0.62	19	1	36	238	8.13
2012	Rk	Elizabethton	232	44	58	14	45	250	307	496	802	8	67	0.25	4	0	43	246	5.60
2013	A	Cedar Rapids	508	83	141	27	109	278	319	526	845	6	77	0.27	10	0	46	248	5.78

Tall, athletic OF who led MWL in HR. Produces plus, consistent pop from strong, uppercut stroke. Long swing can be exploited and will chase breaking balls. Has BA potential, but may be trade-off for power. Runs well for size, though will likely slow down with age. Defense needs work, particularly with jumps and routes.

Walker,Christian — 3 — Baltimore — EXP MLB DEBUT: 2014 — POTENTIAL: Starting 1B — 7B

Bats R Age 23
2012 (4) South Carolina
Pwr ++
BAvg ++++
Spd +
Def ++

Year	Lev	Team	AB	R	H	HR	RBI	Avg	OB	Slg	OPS	bb%	ct%	Eye	SB	CS	x/h%	Iso	RC/G
2012	NCAA	South Carolina	240	48	77	11	55	321	440	525	965	18	90	2.13	3	2	32	204	7.86
2012	A-	Aberdeen	81	12	23	2	9	284	363	420	782	11	83	0.71	2	1	30	136	5.33
2013	A	Delmarva	116	19	41	3	20	353	409	474	884	9	86	0.69	0	3	20	121	6.34
2013	A+	Frederick	215	25	62	8	35	288	341	479	820	7	81	0.41	2	0	40	191	5.54
2013	AA	Bowie	62	7	15	0	1	242	309	323	631	9	84	0.60	0	0	33	81	3.54

Instinctual hitter who played on three levels and selected for Futures Game. Uses patient approach and keen pitch recognition to make easy contact. Has short swing that produces avg pop, but may not be enough for full-time 1B. BA shouldn't be issue. Doesn't run well and footwork and arm limit him to 1B.

Walker,Keenyn — 89 — Chicago (A) — EXP MLB DEBUT: 2015 — POTENTIAL: Starting OF — 7C

Bats B Age 23
2011 (1-S) Central AZ JC
Pwr ++
BAvg ++
Spd ++++
Def ++++

Year	Lev	Team	AB	R	H	HR	RBI	Avg	OB	Slg	OPS	bb%	ct%	Eye	SB	CS	x/h%	Iso	RC/G
2011	Rk	Great Falls	60	16	20	0	9	333	403	483	886	10	72	0.41	11	5	40	150	7.16
2011	A	Kannapolis	162	25	37	0	15	228	290	259	549	8	60	0.22	10	4	8	31	2.16
2012	A	Kannapolis	266	53	75	1	39	282	396	387	783	16	65	0.54	39	11	28	105	6.08
2012	A+	Winston-Salem	143	31	34	3	16	238	347	364	711	14	65	0.48	17	4	32	126	4.74
2013	AA	Birmingham	462	77	93	3	32	201	305	277	582	13	67	0.45	38	15	26	76	2.76

Athletic, quick OF who led SL in strikeouts and finished 2nd in SB. Has discerning eye to work counts and get on base despite limited hit tool. Swing can get long and loopy which results in strikeouts. Doesn't have much pop and many hits are of infield variety. Has plus-plus speed which enhances OF play. Also has solid arm strength.

Wallach,Chad — 2 — Miami — EXP MLB DEBUT: 2016 — POTENTIAL: Backup C — 6C

Bats R Age 22
2013 (5) Cal State Fullerton
Pwr ++
BAvg ++
Spd ++
Def +++

Year	Lev	Team	AB	R	H	HR	RBI	Avg	OB	Slg	OPS	bb%	ct%	Eye	SB	CS	x/h%	Iso	RC/G
2011	NCAA	Cal St. Fullerton	27	2	6	0	3	222	323	222	545	13	81	0.80	0	1	0	0	2.51
2012	NCAA	Cal St. Fullerton	68	7	14	0	7	206	270	265	535	8	82	0.50	1	0	29	59	2.27
2013	NCAA	Cal St. Fullerton	162	24	50	2	32	309	367	444	812	8	90	0.88	2	2	34	136	5.67
2013	A-	Batavia	146	19	33	0	13	226	280	267	547	7	82	0.41	0	0	18	41	2.30

Big, strong backstop with average receiving and throwing skills. Bat is below average. Poor plate discipline and plate coverage hinder his BA ceiling. Shows decent raw power, but approach in the box will prevent him from using it. Runs below average, but instinctual on the bases.

Walsh,Colin — 4 — St. Louis — EXP MLB DEBUT: 2015 — POTENTIAL: Utility player — 6C

Bats B Age 23
2010 (13) Stanford
Pwr +++
BAvg +++
Spd ++
Def ++

Year	Lev	Team	AB	R	H	HR	RBI	Avg	OB	Slg	OPS	bb%	ct%	Eye	SB	CS	x/h%	Iso	RC/G
2012	Rk	GCL Cardinals	8	1	1	0	1	125	125	125	250	0	88	0.00	0	0	0	0	-1.25
2012	A	Quad Cities	353	69	111	16	68	314	414	530	944	15	82	0.92	4	3	35	215	7.48
2013	A+	Palm Beach	351	59	92	4	34	262	367	387	754	14	81	0.85	11	1	33	125	5.26
2013	AA	Springfield	118	15	26	2	6	220	313	314	627	12	80	0.67	3	0	27	93	3.42

Switch hitter failed to follow-up on his 2012 breakout and his production was down across the board, though he did reach AA. Has good bat speed and controls the strike zone well. Has below-average speed and defense, but has shown the ability to hit. Will need a rebound in 2014.

Walters,Zach — 6 — Washington — EXP MLB DEBUT: 2013 — POTENTIAL: Backup INF — 7D

Bats B Age 24
2010 (9) San Diego
Pwr ++++
BAvg ++
Spd ++
Def +++

Year	Lev	Team	AB	R	H	HR	RBI	Avg	OB	Slg	OPS	bb%	ct%	Eye	SB	CS	x/h%	Iso	RC/G
2011	A+	Potomac	116	15	34	0	11	293	339	371	709	6	72	0.24	7	1	24	78	4.35
2012	A+	Potomac	193	24	52	5	24	269	305	399	704	5	78	0.23	6	3	27	130	3.98
2012	AA	Harrisburg	164	23	48	6	19	293	326	518	844	5	77	0.21	1	0	44	226	5.84
2012	AAA	Syracuse	98	9	21	1	6	214	260	286	545	6	71	0.21	0	0	24	71	1.95
2013	AAA	Syracuse	487	69	123	29	77	253	282	517	800	4	72	0.15	4	3	54	265	5.22

Not your prototypical SS prospect: 6-2 switch hitter with compact power stroke. Finally tapped into plus power, hitting 29 HR in 487 AB. Power spike due to aggressive approach, causing drop in OBP. Other plus tool is throwing arm, allowing him to play SS despite below-average range. Can play three INF positions and some OF.

Ward,Drew — 5 — Washington — EXP MLB DEBUT: 2018 — POTENTIAL: Starting 3B/1B — 7D

Bats L Age 19
2013 (3) HS (OK)
Pwr ++++
BAvg +++
Spd ++
Def +++

Year	Lev	Team	AB	R	H	HR	RBI	Avg	OB	Slg	OPS	bb%	ct%	Eye	SB	CS	x/h%	Iso	RC/G
2013	Rk	GCL Nationals	168	24	49	1	28	292	383	387	770	13	74	0.57	2	4	29	95	5.45

Solid debut for corner infielder with good bat speed and plate approach. Selective hitter who knows how to draw walks. Exhibits power to all fields with solid pitch recognition and leveraged swing. Offense will be his path to playing time, as he has below-average speed and is just an average defender with decent arm.

Washington,LeVon

78 | **Cleveland** | EXP MLB DEBUT: 2015 | POTENTIAL: Starting CF | **7C**

Bats L Age 22
2010 (2) Chipola JC
- Pwr + +
- BAvg + + +
- Spd + + + +
- Def + + +

Year	Lev	Team	AB	R	H	HR	RBI	Avg	OB	Slg	OPS	bb%	ct%	Eye	SB	CS	x/h%	Iso	RC/G
2012	Rk	AZL Indians	9	3	4	0	2	444	500	444	944	10	78	0.50	1	0	0	0	7.36
2012	A	Lake County	25	8	11	0	1	440	548	480	1028	19	68	0.75	0	3	9	40	9.84
2012	A+	Carolina	14	2	1	0	1	71	133	71	205	7	79	0.33	0	0	0	0	-2.17
2013	Rk	AZL Indians	37	9	18	4	13	486	548	946	1494	12	78	0.63	2	0	39	459	14.27
2013	A	Lake County	193	33	62	1	19	321	418	477	894	14	76	0.70	14	4	39	155	7.25

Extremely athletic OF who has rarely seen field last two years due to variety of ailments. Plays heady CF with plus range and jumps, though arm is below average. Still possesses great bat speed, but swing not tailored for pop. Can be too pull-conscious and bails out against LHP. Can thrive by playing small ball with plus speed.

Wates,Austin

79 | **Houston** | EXP MLB DEBUT: 2014 | POTENTIAL: Backup OF | **6B**

Bats R Age 25
2010 (3) Virginia Tech
- Pwr + +
- BAvg + + +
- Spd + + + +
- Def + + +

Year	Lev	Team	AB	R	H	HR	RBI	Avg	OB	Slg	OPS	bb%	ct%	Eye	SB	CS	x/h%	Iso	RC/G
2011	A+	Lancaster	526	85	158	6	75	300	358	413	770	8	84	0.55	26	7	24	112	5.10
2012	Rk	GCL Astros	9	2	5	1	2	556	556	889	1444	0	78	0.00	0	0	20	333	12.39
2012	AA	Corpus Christi	359	58	109	7	48	304	359	429	788	8	80	0.44	17	11	25	125	5.24
2013	AA	Corpus Christi	87	14	27	1	5	310	406	448	854	14	79	0.78	11	1	26	138	6.54
2013	AAA	Oklahoma City	49	5	15	0	5	306	333	347	680	4	94	0.67	4	0	13	41	3.97

Natural-hitting OF who ended season in late May due to fractured forearm. Has hit at least .300 each season due to balanced swing and ideal bat control. Likes to go to opp field with inside-out stroke and rarely pulls ball. Has 4th OF profile as he lacks power and isn't great defender. Possesses OK arm and instincts.

Wendle,Joseph

4 | **Cleveland** | EXP MLB DEBUT: 2015 | POTENTIAL: Starting 2B | **7D**

Bats L Age 24
2012 (6) West Chester
- Pwr + +
- BAvg + + +
- Spd + + +
- Def + +

Year	Lev	Team	AB	R	H	HR	RBI	Avg	OB	Slg	OPS	bb%	ct%	Eye	SB	CS	x/h%	Iso	RC/G
2012	A-	Mahoning Val	245	32	80	4	37	327	365	469	835	6	90	0.60	4	1	29	143	5.71
2013	A+	Carolina	413	73	122	16	64	295	363	513	877	10	81	0.56	10	2	43	218	6.42

Offensive INF who plays above limited tools. Bypassed Low-A and impressed with whole field approach and surprising power. Uses level stroke and may not have bat speed or loft for pop at upper levels. Can hit for BA due to hand-eye coordination. Runs well, but defense is suspect. Lacks smooth actions and hands.

Westbrook,Jamie

46 | **Arizona** | EXP MLB DEBUT: 2017 | POTENTIAL: Starting 2B/SS | **7D**

Bats R Age 19
2013 (5) HS (AZ)
- Pwr + + +
- BAvg +
- Spd + + +
- Def + + +

Year	Lev	Team	AB	R	H	HR	RBI	Avg	OB	Slg	OPS	bb%	ct%	Eye	SB	CS	x/h%	Iso	RC/G
2013	Rk	AZL D'backs	154	31	45	1	20	292	363	468	830	10	86	0.81	3	3	38	175	6.07
2013	Rk	Missoula	67	12	17	1	13	254	315	343	658	8	70	0.30	1	0	24	90	3.62

Has a nice compact RH stroke, but tends to try to pull everything and plate discipline eroded when moved up. Despite being just 5-9 he does have some good pop in his bat and has average speed. Played SS in HS, but saw action mainly at 2B in his debut. Defensively he moves well and has good hands.

Wheeler,Tim

9 | **Colorado** | EXP MLB DEBUT: 2014 | POTENTIAL: Starting OF | **7C**

Bats R Age 26
2009 (1) Sacramento State
- Pwr + + +
- BAvg + + +
- Spd + + +
- Def + + +

Year	Lev	Team	AB	R	H	HR	RBI	Avg	OB	Slg	OPS	bb%	ct%	Eye	SB	CS	x/h%	Iso	RC/G
2009	A-	Tri-City	273	44	70	5	35	256	328	381	709	10	78	0.48	10	4	30	125	4.36
2010	A+	Modesto	510	88	127	12	63	249	328	384	712	11	78	0.53	22	8	31	135	4.42
2011	AA	Tulsa	561	105	161	33	86	287	355	535	890	10	75	0.42	21	12	42	248	6.59
2012	AAA	Colorado Springs	379	67	115	2	37	303	353	412	765	7	82	0.42	7	7	29	108	5.00
2013	AAA	Colorado Springs	397	59	104	5	42	262	319	355	674	8	78	0.38	12	7	23	93	3.81

Has been in a tailspin since his breakout season in 2011. A hand injury limited his production in 2012, but was healthy this year and still hit just 5 HR. Continues to hit for average, but is likely limited to LF in the majors. In the offseason, was removed from the 40-man roster.

White,Max

8 | **Colorado** | EXP MLB DEBUT: 2017 | POTENTIAL: Backup OF | **6C**

Bats L Age 20
2012 (2) HS (FL)
- Pwr + +
- BAvg + +
- Spd + + +
- Def + + +

Year	Lev	Team	AB	R	H	HR	RBI	Avg	OB	Slg	OPS	bb%	ct%	Eye	SB	CS	x/h%	Iso	RC/G
2012	Rk	Grand Junction	170	30	34	4	18	200	317	335	652	15	58	0.40	6	5	35	135	4.05
2013	A	Asheville	243	25	55	3	21	226	285	337	623	8	67	0.25	11	8	36	111	3.19

Fleet-footed OF has a projectable body, but has yet to hit as a professional. Swing can get long and his contact rate was atrocious. If he can figure things out, he has good speed and raw power. Covers ground well in CF, but needs to work on taking proper routes.

Wilkins,Andy

3 | **Chicago (A)** | EXP MLB DEBUT: 2014 | POTENTIAL: Backup 1B | **6B**

Bats L Age 25
2010 (5) Arkansas
- Pwr + + + +
- BAvg + +
- Spd +
- Def + +

Year	Lev	Team	AB	R	H	HR	RBI	Avg	OB	Slg	OPS	bb%	ct%	Eye	SB	CS	x/h%	Iso	RC/G
2010	Rk	Great Falls	218	37	67	6	40	307	398	463	862	13	86	1.06	7	2	31	156	6.44
2011	A+	Winston-Salem	493	72	137	23	89	278	352	485	836	10	82	0.62	2	2	41	207	5.86
2012	AA	Birmingham	435	68	104	17	69	239	335	425	761	13	78	0.67	6	4	44	186	5.09
2013	AA	Birmingham	243	37	70	10	49	288	384	477	862	14	76	0.66	3	0	37	189	6.47
2013	AAA	Charlotte	215	25	57	7	30	265	310	423	733	6	76	0.27	2	1	35	158	4.42

Consistent and powerful hitter who is on verge of earning time in big leagues. Has big and strong frame that produces lots of leverage in stroke. Can overswing and focus on pulling too often. May be platoon option as he struggles with LHP. Can be passable defensively with strong arm, but bat is ticket to playing time.

Williams,Everett

7 | **San Diego** | EXP MLB DEBUT: 2014 | POTENTIAL: Starting CF | **7D**

Bats L Age 23
2009 (2) HS (TX)
- Pwr + +
- BAvg + +
- Spd + + + +
- Def + + + +

Year	Lev	Team	AB	R	H	HR	RBI	Avg	OB	Slg	OPS	bb%	ct%	Eye	SB	CS	x/h%	Iso	RC/G
2010	A	Fort Wayne	390	53	95	5	59	244	331	372	703	12	66	0.39	10	5	37	128	4.58
2011	A	Fort Wayne	20	5	6	0	1	300	364	300	664	9	85	0.67	3	0	0	0	3.83
2012	A+	Lake Elsinore	397	38	96	5	50	242	292	363	654	7	72	0.25	9	4	35	121	3.57
2013	AA	San Antonio	331	37	85	2	31	257	315	314	629	8	76	0.35	10	4	16	57	3.21

Strong and very athletic outfielder whose time is running out as prospect. Still exhibits all five tools in spurts, but is inconsistent at plate and in field. Struggles against LHP and makes minimal contact. Owns bat speed with line drive stroke, though power hasn't developed. Plays mostly LF with average range and speed.

Williams,Justin

7 | **Arizona** | EXP MLB DEBUT: 2018 | POTENTIAL: Starting LF | **7D**

Bats L Age 18
2013 (2) HS (LA)
- Pwr + + + +
- BAvg + +
- Spd + +
- Def + +

Year	Lev	Team	AB	R	H	HR	RBI	Avg	OB	Slg	OPS	bb%	ct%	Eye	SB	CS	x/h%	Iso	RC/G
2013	Rk	AZL D'backs	148	17	51	1	32	345	378	446	824	5	76	0.23	0	1	25	101	5.66
2013	Rk	Missoula	51	12	21	0	5	412	423	529	952	2	86	0.14	0	0	29	118	6.81
2013	A	South Bend	9	3	1	0	0	111	273	111	384	18	78	1.00	0	0	0	0	0.44

2nd round pick had an impressive debut. Physically mature and has some of the better raw power in the 2013 draft class. Has good athleticism and played SS in high school, but was moved to LF. Has good speed, but is raw in the OF. Can crush even the best fastballs, but needs to be more selective at the plate.

Williams,Mason

8 | **New York (A)** | EXP MLB DEBUT: 2015 | POTENTIAL: Starting OF | **8C**

Bats L Age 22
2010 (4) HS (FL)
- Pwr + +
- BAvg + + +
- Spd + + + +
- Def + + + +

Year	Lev	Team	AB	R	H	HR	RBI	Avg	OB	Slg	OPS	bb%	ct%	Eye	SB	CS	x/h%	Iso	RC/G
2011	A-	Staten Island	269	42	94	3	31	349	394	468	863	7	85	0.49	28	12	21	119	6.11
2012	A	Charleston (Sc)	276	55	84	8	28	304	354	489	843	7	88	0.64	19	9	37	185	5.85
2012	A+	Tampa	83	13	23	3	7	277	302	422	724	3	83	0.21	1	4	26	145	4.08
2013	A+	Tampa	406	56	106	3	24	261	326	350	676	9	85	0.64	15	9	25	89	4.03
2013	AA	Trenton	72	7	11	1	4	153	164	264	428	1	75	0.06	0	0	45	111	0.36

Very athletic, thin OF who struggled thru poor season. Still owns plus speed and above average bat speed for high ceiling. Drives ball with authority with quick stroke, but drop off in power output was alarming. Can settle for slap approach when behind in count. Excellent CF with plus range and average arm.

Williams,Nick

7 | **Texas** | EXP MLB DEBUT: 2017 | POTENTIAL: Starting OF | **8D**

Bats L Age 20
2012 (2) HS (TX)
- Pwr + + +
- BAvg + + +
- Spd + + +
- Def + + +

Year	Lev	Team	AB	R	H	HR	RBI	Avg	OB	Slg	OPS	bb%	ct%	Eye	SB	CS	x/h%	Iso	RC/G
2012	Rk	AZL Rangers	201	34	63	2	27	313	364	448	812	7	75	0.32	15	2	27	134	5.70
2013	A	Hickory	376	70	110	17	60	293	320	543	862	4	71	0.14	8	5	44	250	6.26

Tall, lean OF who posted outstanding numbers despite raw, aggressive approach. Uses controlled swing to make hard contact. Plus bat speed should lead to more power. Draws very few walks and swings at everything. Poor arm limits him to LF, but runs well with solid range.

Williamson,Mac — 9 — San Francisco

EXP MLB DEBUT: 2015 | POTENTIAL: Starting OF | 8D

Bats R Age 23 — 2012 (3) Wake Forest — Pwr ++++ / BAvg +++ / Spd +++ / Def ++

Year	Lev	Team	AB	R	H	HR	RBI	Avg	OB	Slg	OPS	bb%	ct%	Eye	SB	CS	x/h%	Iso	RC/G
2011	NCAA	Wake Forest	205	33	56	12	49	273	352	493	845	11	72	0.43	11	3	38	220	6.11
2012	NCAA	Wake Forest	192	42	55	17	52	286	363	589	951	11	79	0.56	12	3	44	302	7.14
2012	Rk	AZL Giants	17	4	3	2	7	176	263	529	793	11	71	0.40	0	0	67	353	5.02
2012	A-	Salem-Keizer	114	22	39	7	25	342	375	596	971	5	83	0.32	0	0	38	254	7.06
2013	A+	San Jose	520	94	152	25	89	292	356	504	859	9	75	0.39	10	1	38	212	6.20

Big, physical OF had impressive first full season, showing plus power, leading all Giants in the minors with HR. Power is biggest asset, going to all fields, though breaking balls are weakness and have led to lots of swings and misses, driving down his ct% and Eye. Good athlete who runs well and has good range with strong arm.

Wilson,Austin — 9 — Seattle

EXP MLB DEBUT: 2016 | POTENTIAL: Starting OF | 8D

Bats R Age 22 — 2013 (2) Stanford — Pwr ++++ / BAvg ++ / Spd +++ / Def ++++

Year	Lev	Team	AB	R	H	HR	RBI	Avg	OB	Slg	OPS	bb%	ct%	Eye	SB	CS	x/h%	Iso	RC/G
2011	NCAA	Stanford	188	25	58	5	27	309	333	420	754	4	70	0.13	1	0	19	112	4.64
2012	NCAA	Stanford	221	56	63	10	54	285	355	493	848	10	80	0.55	7	0	38	208	6.01
2013	NCAA	Stanford	118	26	34	5	26	288	359	475	833	10	85	0.72	5	2	35	186	5.81
2013	A-	Everett	203	22	49	6	27	241	300	414	714	8	79	0.40	2	4	41	172	4.31

Tall, strong OF who fell in draft because of elbow injury, but has big bat potential. Long swing and choppy mechanics mute BA, but top-notch strength and bat speed give him plus pop. Runs well and features plus range, arm, and instincts in outfield. Has classic RF profile, but needs to focus on more consistent contact.

Wilson,Jacob — 4 — St. Louis

EXP MLB DEBUT: 2016 | POTENTIAL: Utility INF | 6C

Bats R Age 23 — 2012 (10) Memphis — Pwr ++ / BAvg +++ / Spd ++ / Def +++

Year	Lev	Team	AB	R	H	HR	RBI	Avg	OB	Slg	OPS	bb%	ct%	Eye	SB	CS	x/h%	Iso	RC/G
2011	NCAA	Memphis	217	51	62	6	51	286	382	433	816	14	85	1.03	11	3	32	147	5.90
2012	NCAA	Memphis	231	47	74	17	64	320	391	615	1006	10	87	0.87	7	9	46	294	7.75
2012	A-	Batavia	160	28	44	6	25	275	329	444	773	8	79	0.39	2	1	32	169	4.95
2013	A	Peoria	348	63	92	15	72	264	340	468	809	10	84	0.74	6	5	43	204	5.56
2013	A+	Palm Beach	117	12	21	3	10	179	284	291	574	13	83	0.85	0	1	33	111	2.85

Older 2B prospect was a 10th round pick. Has shown an ability to hit; hat solid plate discipline and makes good contact with surprising pop. Struggled when moved up, but hit well in the AFL. Solid defender at 2B, but is likely destined to a UTL role down the road.

Winker,Jesse — 7 — Cincinnati

EXP MLB DEBUT: 2016 | POTENTIAL: Starting LF | 8C

Bats L Age 20 — 2012 (1) HS (FL) — Pwr ++++ / BAvg ++++ / Spd ++ / Def ++

Year	Lev	Team	AB	R	H	HR	RBI	Avg	OB	Slg	OPS	bb%	ct%	Eye	SB	CS	x/h%	Iso	RC/G
2012	Rk	Billings	228	42	77	5	35	338	437	500	937	15	78	0.80	1	3	31	162	7.64
2013	A	Dayton	417	73	117	16	76	281	375	463	838	13	82	0.84	6	1	33	182	6.09

Advanced LH hitting approach with plus power. A disciplined hitter that will make pitchers work. Makes consistent, hard contact against both LHP and RHP. Plus bat speed and pitch recognition; not afraid to use opposite field. Has enough offensive skills to advance despite below-average speed and arm.

Wisdom,Patrick — 35 — St. Louis

EXP MLB DEBUT: 2015 | POTENTIAL: Starting 3B | 8D

Bats R Age 22 — 2012 (1) St. Marys — Pwr +++ / BAvg ++ / Spd ++ / Def +++

Year	Lev	Team	AB	R	H	HR	RBI	Avg	OB	Slg	OPS	bb%	ct%	Eye	SB	CS	x/h%	Iso	RC/G
2011	NCAA	St. Mary's CA	208	33	73	8	46	351	416	553	968	10	80	0.56	5	2	34	202	7.57
2012	NCAA	St. Mary's CA	191	39	50	9	24	262	382	476	858	16	77	0.86	4	2	44	215	6.51
2012	A-	Batavia	241	40	68	6	32	282	364	465	829	11	76	0.53	2	1	40	183	6.07
2013	A	Peoria	372	54	86	13	62	231	309	411	720	10	69	0.37	4	1	43	180	4.56
2013	A+	Palm Beach	92	8	23	2	11	250	317	359	676	9	75	0.39	1	0	26	109	3.82

Works hard to get the most of his tools and looked just fine in full season debut. Has a good all-around game with average bat speed, moderate power, and decent plate discipline. He has good athleticism, but is a below-average runner and is limited to a corner INF slot.

Witherspoon,Travis — 789 — Seattle

EXP MLB DEBUT: 2014 | POTENTIAL: Reserve OF | 6B

Bats R Age 25 — 2009 (12) Spartanburg — Pwr ++ / BAvg ++ / Spd ++++ / Def ++++

Year	Lev	Team	AB	R	H	HR	RBI	Avg	OB	Slg	OPS	bb%	ct%	Eye	SB	CS	x/h%	Iso	RC/G
2011	A	Cedar Rapids	404	60	99	12	42	245	307	394	700	8	75	0.35	44	9	32	149	4.12
2011	A+	Inland Empire	68	15	19	1	10	279	329	382	711	7	79	0.36	2	2	26	103	4.23
2012	A+	Inland Empire	270	52	86	7	27	319	393	470	863	11	81	0.63	25	7	26	152	6.34
2012	AA	Arkansas	208	28	42	6	21	202	284	351	635	10	74	0.44	9	4	40	149	3.35
2013	AA	Arkansas	448	58	96	11	38	214	300	342	642	11	74	0.47	30	10	33	127	3.46

Long and athletic outfielder who has experienced tough time in Double-A for past two years. Finished 2nd in TL in SB and speed is best attribute. Gets good jumps in outfield and has plus range and average arm. Inconsistent approach can be exploited and lacks strength for power. Needs to cultivate natural bat speed.

Wolters,Tony — 2 — Cleveland

EXP MLB DEBUT: 2015 | POTENTIAL: Utility player | 7D

Bats L Age 22 — 2010 (3) HS (CA) — Pwr ++ / BAvg +++ / Spd ++ / Def ++

Year	Lev	Team	AB	R	H	HR	RBI	Avg	OB	Slg	OPS	bb%	ct%	Eye	SB	CS	x/h%	Iso	RC/G
2010	Rk	AZL Indians	19	2	4	0	3	211	286	211	496	10	74	0.40	2	0	0	0	1.44
2011	A-	Mahoning Val	267	50	78	1	20	292	364	363	727	10	82	0.61	19	4	18	71	4.68
2012	A+	Carolina	485	66	126	8	58	260	311	404	715	7	79	0.35	5	9	37	144	4.35
2013	A+	Carolina	289	36	80	3	33	277	367	353	720	12	80	0.71	3	6	20	76	4.66

Raw, athletic C who moved to position in '12 and returned to High-A to polish skills. Started slowly, but hit over .300 last 3 months. Has strong, accurate arm along with agility. Still needs to work on footwork and receiving. Shows natural hitting skills and gap power could lead to moderate pop down line.

Wong,Kolten — 4 — St. Louis

EXP MLB DEBUT: 2013 | POTENTIAL: Starting 2B | 8B

Bats L Age 23 — 2011 (1) Hawaii — Pwr ++ / BAvg +++ / Spd +++ / Def +++

Year	Lev	Team	AB	R	H	HR	RBI	Avg	OB	Slg	OPS	bb%	ct%	Eye	SB	CS	x/h%	Iso	RC/G
2011	NCAA	Hawaii	209	48	79	7	53	378	482	560	1042	17	90	2.10	23	7	27	182	8.77
2011	A	Quad Cities	194	39	65	5	25	335	400	510	910	10	88	0.88	9	5	34	175	6.81
2012	AA	Springfield	523	79	150	9	52	287	342	405	748	8	86	0.59	21	11	25	119	4.78
2013	AAA	Memphis	412	68	125	10	45	303	366	466	832	9	85	0.68	20	1	31	163	5.86
2013	MLB	STL	59	6	9	0	0	153	194	169	363	5	80	0.25	3	0	11	17	-0.18

Has quickly developed into one of the best 2B prospects, but he looked overmatched in his MLB debut. Uses a short, compact LH stroke and gets surprising pop. Has a disciplined eye and is a good situational hitter. Has improved as a defender with a good arm, good range, and soft hands.

Wren,Kyle — 8 — Atlanta

EXP MLB DEBUT: 2016 | POTENTIAL: Starting CF | 8D

Bats L Age 23 — 2013 (8) Georgia Tech — Pwr ++ / BAvg +++ / Spd ++++ / Def +++

Year	Lev	Team	AB	R	H	HR	RBI	Avg	OB	Slg	OPS	bb%	ct%	Eye	SB	CS	x/h%	Iso	RC/G
2012	NCAA	Georgia Tech	258	56	66	2	22	256	340	364	705	11	88	1.10	16	6	27	109	4.64
2013	NCAA	Georgia Tech	272	50	98	2	28	360	422	467	889	10	87	0.81	28	13	19	107	6.61
2013	Rk	Danville	22	6	9	0	4	409	458	636	1095	8	86	0.67	3	0	44	227	9.15
2013	A	Rome	195	36	64	2	20	328	379	456	836	8	89	0.76	32	6	27	128	5.88
2013	A+	Lynchburg	1	0	0	0	0	0	500	0	500	50	100	1.00	0	1	0	0	4.75

Son of ATL GM had a nice pro debut, hitting .335 at three different levels. Wren has plus speed and stole 35 bases in 42 attempts. Above-average defender in CF, but with a below-average arm. Solid approach at the plate with a good understanding of the strike zone and a good line-drive swing.

Wright,Ryan — 4 — Cincinnati

EXP MLB DEBUT: 2016 | POTENTIAL: Starting 2B | 7C

Bats R Age 24 — 2011 (5) Louisville — Pwr ++ / BAvg ++ / Spd +++ / Def +++

Year	Lev	Team	AB	R	H	HR	RBI	Avg	OB	Slg	OPS	bb%	ct%	Eye	SB	CS	x/h%	Iso	RC/G
2011	Rk	AZL Reds	22	4	7	1	5	318	318	636	955	0	77	0.00	1	2	57	318	7.04
2011	Rk	Billings	161	28	48	7	32	298	335	522	857	5	83	0.33	6	1	42	224	5.84
2012	A	Dayton	389	53	111	5	50	285	340	424	764	8	87	0.63	14	1	34	139	5.04
2012	A+	Bakersfield	96	17	26	5	16	271	286	521	807	2	82	0.12	3	1	46	250	5.03
2013	A+	Bakersfield	411	53	109	8	52	265	309	384	693	6	84	0.39	5	3	29	119	3.99

Offensive-minded 2B continues to post solid numbers. Instincts and work ethic allow tools to play up, including HR totals despite below-average power. Good strike zone judgment, compact stroke, and contact rates. Smart baserunner and solid defender. Not much projection left.

Yarbrough,Alex — 4 — Los Angeles (A)

EXP MLB DEBUT: 2015 | POTENTIAL: Starting 2B | 7B

Bats B Age 22 — 2012 (4) Mississippi — Pwr ++ / BAvg +++ / Spd ++ / Def +++

Year	Lev	Team	AB	R	H	HR	RBI	Avg	OB	Slg	OPS	bb%	ct%	Eye	SB	CS	x/h%	Iso	RC/G
2011	NCAA	Mississippi	214	49	75	7	38	350	409	542	951	9	87	0.78	4	1	32	192	7.18
2012	NCAA	Mississippi	250	43	95	3	43	380	430	508	938	8	90	0.92	4	0	24	128	7.03
2012	A	Cedar Rapids	244	35	70	0	27	287	315	410	725	4	92	0.50	9	2	30	123	4.53
2012	AA	Arkansas	18	1	2	0	0	111	111	167	278	0	83	0.00	0	0	50	56	-1.10
2013	A+	Inland Empire	582	77	182	11	80	313	343	459	802	4	82	0.25	14	4	29	146	5.22

Steady INF who had breakout campaign. Shows natural hitting skills and can hit for BA despite lack of plate patience. Knows value of going to opp field and has strength for some pop. Bat speed is fringy, but knows how to hit with gap approach. Doesn't commit many errors, but isn't a standout defender as range and arm are short.

Pitchers are classified as Starters (SP) or Relievers (RP).

THROWS: Handedness — right (RH) or left (LH).

AGE: Pitcher's age, as of April 1, 2014.

DRAFTED: The year, round, and school that the pitcher performed at as an amateur if drafted, or the year and country where the player was signed from, if a free agent.

EXP MLB DEBUT: The year a player is expected to debut in the major leagues.

PROJ ROLE: The role that the pitcher is expected to have for the majority of his major league career, not necessarily his greatest upside.

PITCHES: Each pitch that a pitcher throws is graded and designated with a "+", indicating the quality of the pitch, taking into context the pitcher's age and level pitched. Pitches are graded for their velocity, movement, and command. An average pitch will receive three "+" marks. If known, a pitcher's velocity for each pitch is indicated.

FB	fastball
CB	curveball
SP	split-fingered fastball
SL	slider
CU	change-up
CT	cut-fastball
KC	knuckle-curve
KB	knuckle-ball
SC	screwball
SU	slurve

PLAYER STAT LINES: Pitchers receive statistics for the last five teams that they played for (if applicable), including college and the major leagues.

TEAM DESIGNATIONS: Each team that the pitcher performed for during a given year is included.

LEVEL DESIGNATIONS: The level for each team a player performed is included. "AAA" means Triple-A, "AA" means Double-A, "A+" means high Class-A, "A-" means low Class-A and "Rk" means rookie level.

SABERMETRIC CATEGORIES: Descriptions of all the sabermetric categories appear in the glossary.

CAPSULE COMMENTARIES: For each pitcher, a brief analysis of their skills/statistics, and their future potential is provided.

ELIGIBILITY: Eligibility for inclusion is the standard for which Major League Baseball adheres to; 50 innings pitched or 45 days on the 25-man roster, not including the month of September.

POTENTIAL RATINGS: The Potential Ratings are a two-part system in which a player is assigned a number rating based on his upside potential (1-10) and a letter rating based on the probability of reaching that potential (A-E).

Potential

10:	Hall of Famer	5:	MLB reserve
9:	Elite player	4:	Top minor leaguer
8:	Solid regular	3:	Average minor leaguer
7:	Average regular	2:	Minor league reserve
6:	Platoon player	1:	Minor league roster filler

Probability Rating

A:	90% probability of reaching potential
B:	70% probability of reaching potential
C:	50% probability of reaching potential
D:	30% probability of reaching potential
E:	10% probability of reaching potential

FASTBALL: Scouts grade a fastball in terms of both velocity and movement. Movement of a pitch is purely subjective, but one can always watch the hitter to see how he reacts to a pitch or if he swings and misses. Pitchers throw four types of fastballs with varying movement. A two-seam fastball is often referred to as a sinker. A four-seam fastball appears to maintain its plane at high velocities. A cutter can move in different directions and is caused by the pitcher both cutting-off his extension out front and by varying the grip. A split-fingered fastball (forkball) is thrown with the fingers spread apart against the seams and demonstrates violent downward movement. Velocity is often graded on the 20-80 scale and is indicated by the chart below.

Scout Grade	Velocity (mph)
80	96+
70	94-95
60	92-93
50 (avg)	89-91
40	87-88
30	85-86
20	82-84

PITCHER RELEASE TIMES: The speed (in seconds) that a pitcher releases a pitch from the stretch is extremely important in terms of halting the running game and establishing good pitching mechanics. Pitchers are timed from the movement of the front leg until the baseball reaches the catcher's mitt. The phrases "slow to the plate" or "quick to the plate" may often appear in the capsule commentary box.

1.0-1.2	+
1.3-1.4	MLB average
1.5+	−

Adam,Jason — SP — Kansas City

EXP MLB DEBUT: 2015 | POTENTIAL: #3 starter | **8D**

Thrws R Age 22
2010 (5) HS (KS)

- 88-95 FB +++
- 76-81 CB +++
- 80-84 CU ++

Year	Lev	Team	W	L	Sv	IP	K	ERA	WHIP	BF/G	OBA	H%	S%	xERA	Ctl	Dom	Cmd	hr/9	BPV
2011	A	Kane County	6	9	0	104	76	4.24	1.14	19.6	243	28	64	3.18	2.2	6.6	3.0	0.8	78
2012	A+	Wilmington	7	12	0	158	123	3.53	1.16	23.3	249	29	73	3.55	2.1	7.0	3.4	1.0	89
2013	AA	NW Arkansas	8	11	0	144	126	5.19	1.44	23.6	274	33	64	4.30	3.4	7.9	2.3	0.8	69

Tall, powerful, and durable SP who finished 3rd in TL in Ks. Advancing one level per year and has pitch mix to be better than stats indicate. Throws all pitches for strikes and gets ahead in count with stellar FB. Clean arm action produces pitch movement, but hittable when around middle of plate. Keeps ball on ground.

Adams,Austin — RP — Cleveland

EXP MLB DEBUT: 2014 | POTENTIAL: Setup reliever | **7C**

Thrws R Age 27
2009 (5) Faulkner

- 93-98 FB ++++
- 81-83 SL +++
- 80-82 CB ++
- CU ++

Year	Lev	Team	W	L	Sv	IP	K	ERA	WHIP	BF/G	OBA	H%	S%	xERA	Ctl	Dom	Cmd	hr/9	BPV
2009	A-	Mahoning Val	3	1	1	37	29	4.86	1.46	9.3	272	32	68	4.55	3.6	7.1	1.9	1.0	46
2010	A	Lake County	2	4	1	53	61	3.57	1.15	16.2	211	27	74	3.15	3.6	10.4	2.9	1.2	108
2010	A+	Kinston	6	1	0	58	51	1.55	1.12	17.6	234	29	92	2.99	2.3	7.9	3.4	0.8	98
2011	AA	Akron	11	10	0	136	131	3.77	1.54	22.8	277	36	75	4.28	4.2	8.7	2.1	0.4	61
2013	AA	Akron	3	2	4	55	76	2.62	1.33	5.1	221	34	81	3.04	4.7	12.4	2.6	0.5	114

Short and stocky RP who moved to bullpen after missing entire '12 season due to shoulder surgery. Continued to post high K rate due to plus FB and fine breaking balls. Will likely stick in role as he lacks stamina in long stints and throws across body. FB command is still below par, but can reach mid-90s when healthy.

Agosta,Martin — SP — San Francisco

EXP MLB DEBUT: 2016 | POTENTIAL: #4 Starter/Reliever | **8E**

Thrws R Age 23
2012 (2) St. Mary's

- 90-94 FB ++++
- SL +++
- CT +++
- CU ++

Year	Lev	Team	W	L	Sv	IP	K	ERA	WHIP	BF/G	OBA	H%	S%	xERA	Ctl	Dom	Cmd	hr/9	BPV
2010	NCAA	St. Mary's CA	3	6	1	70	52	5.40	1.54	18.0	283				3.9	6.7	1.7		34
2011	NCAA	St. Mary's CA	7	6	0	89	76	2.83	1.12	23.4	244				1.9	7.7	4.0		104
2012	NCAA	St. Mary's CA	9	2	0	103	95	2.18	1.11	28.9	230	30	81	2.51	2.4	8.3	3.5	0.3	104
2012	Rk	AZL Giants	0	0	0	10	19	4.50	1.70	9.0	221	47	71	3.47	8.1	17.1	2.1	0.0	107
2013	A	Augusta	9	3	0	91	109	2.08	1.10	19.8	182	26	82	1.93	4.3	10.8	2.5	0.4	97

Small, undersized SP with good pitch sequencing excelled in his first full season. Uses his low-90s FB up to 96, with good run and sink. He complements it with an average SL and a below average CU. He has clean arm action and deceptive delivery, but his lack of the CU could push him to a relief role if he cannot refine it.

Alcantara,Raul — SP — Oakland

EXP MLB DEBUT: 2015 | POTENTIAL: #3 starter | **8D**

Thrws R Age 21
2009 FA (DR)

- 90-95 FB +++
- 80-84 SL +++
- 77-80 CB ++
- 80-83 CU +++

Year	Lev	Team	W	L	Sv	IP	K	ERA	WHIP	BF/G	OBA	H%	S%	xERA	Ctl	Dom	Cmd	hr/9	BPV
2011	Rk	GCL Red Sox	1	1	0	48	36	0.75	0.60	18.3	145	19	86		1.1	6.8	6.0	0.0	109
2011	A-	Lowell	0	3	0	17	14	6.35	1.82	19.7	343	42	61	5.66	3.2	7.4	2.3	0.0	66
2012	A	Burlington	6	11	0	102	57	5.12	1.54	16.5	293	32	68	5.15	3.4	5.0	1.5	1.1	18
2013	A	Beloit	7	1	0	77	58	2.45	1.18	23.7	279	34	80	3.37	0.8	6.8	8.3	0.4	118
2013	A+	Stockton	5	5	0	79	66	3.76	1.14	22.3	247	29	70	3.34	1.9	7.5	3.9	0.9	101

Tall, lean righty with clean, quick arm that produces quality FB and nifty CU. Pitches to all quadrants of zone and rarely beats himself. Can be hittable without dependable breaking ball and FB often lacks movement. Projectable frame could add velocity and K rate could increase with more polished SL.

Almonte,Miguel — SP — Kansas City

EXP MLB DEBUT: 2016 | POTENTIAL: #3 starter | **8C**

Thrws R Age 21
2010 FA (DR)

- 90-95 FB +++
- 77-79 CB +++
- 80-83 CU +++

Year	Lev	Team	W	L	Sv	IP	K	ERA	WHIP	BF/G	OBA	H%	S%	xERA	Ctl	Dom	Cmd	hr/9	BPV
2012	Rk	AZL Royals	2	1	0	27	28	2.33	1.00	17.2	224	31	74	1.82	1.7	9.3	5.6	0.0	141
2013	A	Lexington	6	9	0	130	132	3.12	1.16	20.7	239	32	73	2.80	2.5	9.1	3.7	0.4	115

Tall, lean SP who was selected for Futures Game in first year above Rookie ball. Repeats athletic delivery and shows polish. Generates solid velocity with smooth arm action and throws strikes with all pitches. Induces GB with heavy FB and can get hitters to chase better CB. Nifty CU may be best pitch at present.

Alvarez,R.J. — RP — Los Angeles (A)

EXP MLB DEBUT: 2014 | POTENTIAL: Closer | **8D**

Thrws R Age 23
2012 (3) Florida Atlantic

- 93-99 FB ++++
- 83-86 SL +++
- 80-82 CU +

Year	Lev	Team	W	L	Sv	IP	K	ERA	WHIP	BF/G	OBA	H%	S%	xERA	Ctl	Dom	Cmd	hr/9	BPV
2010	NCAA	Florida Atlantic	3	1	0	60	49	5.10	1.50	16.2	284	34	67	4.75	3.5	7.4	2.1	0.9	57
2011	NCAA	Florida Atlantic	6	6	0	74	72	5.23	1.64	20.6	292	37	67	4.92	4.3	8.8	2.1	0.6	61
2012	NCAA	Florida Atlantic	5	0	8	37	47	0.73	0.81	6.1	161	25	93	0.82	2.4	11.4	4.7	0.2	158
2012	A	Cedar Rapids	3	2	0	27	38	3.33	1.22	4.7	224	34	74	2.97	3.7	12.7	3.5	0.7	147
2013	A+	Inland Empire	4	2	4	48	79	3.00	1.27	5.3	201	36	76	2.52	5.1	14.8	2.9	0.4	148

Quick-armed RP who can dominate in short stints with heavy FB and knockout SL. Admirable arm strength generates quality velocity and counters with hard SL that misses bats. Pitch movement results in Ks, but tough to command. Needs pitch to battle LHH and max effort, violent delivery keeps him in bullpen.

Ames,Jeff — SP — Tampa Bay

EXP MLB DEBUT: 2015 | POTENTIAL: #4 starter | **7C**

Thrws R Age 23
2011 (1-S) Lower Columbia JC

- 87-94 FB +++
- 82-85 SL +++
- 80-83 CU ++

Year	Lev	Team	W	L	Sv	IP	K	ERA	WHIP	BF/G	OBA	H%	S%	xERA	Ctl	Dom	Cmd	hr/9	BPV
2011	Rk	Princeton	4	2	1	30	39	7.20	1.57	12.0	321	44	53	5.73	2.1	11.7	5.6	1.2	172
2012	A-	Hudson Valley	6	1	0	64	70	1.97	1.00	17.5	196	28	79	1.61	2.8	9.8	3.5	0.1	119
2013	A	Bowling Green	9	4	0	114	83	3.00	1.10	19.4	213	24	76	2.70	3.0	6.6	2.2	0.8	55

Tall, strong RHP with good command due to consistent release point and delivery. Velocity can be inconsistent from outing to outing, but changes speeds well and uses height to throw downhill. Can be flyball pitcher and K rate not indicative of natural stuff. Hard SL misses bats and CU could improve to be third pitch.

Ames,Steven — RP — Miami

EXP MLB DEBUT: 2013 | POTENTIAL: Setup reliever | **7D**

Thrws R Age 26
2009 (17) Gonzaga

- 90-93 FB +++
- 81-83 SL +++

Year	Lev	Team	W	L	Sv	IP	K	ERA	WHIP	BF/G	OBA	H%	S%	xERA	Ctl	Dom	Cmd	hr/9	BPV
2011	AA	Chattanooga	2	2	5	32	41	2.53	1.34	4.8	262	37	85	3.95	3.1	11.5	3.7	0.8	142
2012	AA	Chattanooga	3	3	18	63	72	1.57	1.03	4.5	226	32	86	2.19	1.9	10.3	5.5	0.3	153
2013	AAA	Albuquerque	2	2	8	34	29	3.71	1.71	5.1	319	38	81	5.96	3.4	7.7	2.2	1.1	63
2013	AAA	New Orleans	1	0	0	12	5	3.75	1.50	5.8	293	29	81	5.48	3.0	3.8	1.3	1.5	5
2013	MLB	MIA	0	1	0	4	4	4.50	2.00	4.8	347	45	75	6.16	4.5	9.0	2.0	0.0	59

Short, strong-armed RP was traded over to MIA from LA as part of the Nolasco deal. Has shown the ability to dominate hitters with his FB/SL mix. FB sits in the low-90s and pairs with his low-80s SL to generate swings and misses. Upside is not huge, but shows good enough Cmd for a late-inning RP.

Anderson,Chase — SP — Arizona

EXP MLB DEBUT: 2014 | POTENTIAL: #4 starter/reliever | **6B**

Thrws R Age 26
2009 (9) Oklahoma

- 88-92 FB ++
- SL ++
- CB ++
- CU ++++

Year	Lev	Team	W	L	Sv	IP	K	ERA	WHIP	BF/G	OBA	H%	S%	xERA	Ctl	Dom	Cmd	hr/9	BPV
2010	A	South Bend	2	4	0	38	31	2.84	1.18	21.7	251	31	75	2.88	2.1	7.3	3.4	0.2	93
2010	A+	Visalia	5	3	3	70	83	3.60	1.06	14.3	227	31	69	2.83	2.1	10.7	5.2	0.9	155
2011	A+	Visalia	1	1	0	13	20	5.54	1.15	17.2	276	44	50	3.51	0.7	13.8	20.0	0.7	249
2012	AA	Mobile	5	4	0	104	97	2.86	1.12	19.5	237	29	78	3.01	2.2	8.4	3.9	0.8	111
2013	AAA	Reno	4	7	0	88	80	5.73	1.59	14.9	301	36	65	5.44	3.4	8.2	2.4	1.1	74

Small RH scuffled in a full season at AAA. Attacks hitters with an 88-92 mph FB, a plus CU, and a breaking ball. Anderson isn't overpowering, but has some of the best control in the system. Worked both as a starter and in relief.

Anderson,Chris — SP — Los Angeles (N)

EXP MLB DEBUT: 2016 | POTENTIAL: #3 starter | **8D**

Thrws R Age 21
2013 (1) Jacksonville

- 90-94 FB ++++
- 83-85 SL ++++
- CB ++
- CU +++

Year	Lev	Team	W	L	Sv	IP	K	ERA	WHIP	BF/G	OBA	H%	S%	xERA	Ctl	Dom	Cmd	hr/9	BPV
2011	NCAA	Jacksonville	4	2	11	50	39	3.96	1.48	6.0	221	26	75	3.86	6.1	7.0	1.1	0.9	-21
2012	NCAA	Jacksonville	5	4	1	88	69	4.50	1.52	23.9	275	33	70	4.41	4.1	7.1	1.7	0.6	35
2013	NCAA	Jacksonville	7	5	0	104	101	2.51	1.13	29.3	235	31	79	2.68	2.3	8.7	3.7	0.4	112
2013	A	Great Lakes	3	0	0	46	50	1.96	1.22	15.5	198	29	82	2.05	4.7	9.8	2.1	0.0	67

Pitches with good downhill plane, pounding the K-zone with four pitches. Features a low-to-mid-90s FB up to 98, a tight, wipeout SL, a CU that flashes potential and a show-me CB. He holds his velocity deep into games and while he pitches with deception, he has clean arm action and repeatable mechanics.

Anderson,Cody — SP — Cleveland

EXP MLB DEBUT: 2014 | POTENTIAL: #4 starter | **7B**

Thrws R Age 23
2011 (14) Feather River JC

- 89-94 FB +++
- 77-80 CB +++
- 82-83 CU ++

Year	Lev	Team	W	L	Sv	IP	K	ERA	WHIP	BF/G	OBA	H%	S%	xERA	Ctl	Dom	Cmd	hr/9	BPV
2011	A-	Mahoning Val	0	0	0	5	3	1.80	1.60	7.4	221	26	88	3.33	7.2	5.4	0.8	0.0	-79
2012	A	Lake County	4	7	0	98	72	3.21	1.23	16.6	250	29	76	3.46	2.7	6.6	2.5	0.7	65
2013	A+	Carolina	9	4	0	123	112	2.34	1.11	21.0	232	30	80	2.61	2.3	8.2	3.6	0.4	104
2013	AA	Akron	0	0	0	12	10	6.00	2.08	19.6	321	37	74	7.36	6.8	7.5	1.1	1.5	-29

Consistent SP who led CAR in ERA and was named pitcher of year. Increased K rate by being more aggressive and improving CB. Throws quality strikes by spotting FB to both sides of plate. Velocity is average at best, and must improve CU by repeating delivery and arm speed. Upside muted by lack of true out pitch.

Anderson,Tyler — SP — Colorado

EXP MLB DEBUT: 2014 | POTENTIAL: #3 starter | **7C**

Thrws L Age 24
2011 (1) Oregon

Velo	Pitch	Grade
88-93	FB	+++
77-80	SL	+++
74-77	CB	++
81-83	CU	+++

Year	Lev	Team	W	L	Sv	IP	K	ERA	WHIP	BF/G	OBA	H%	S%	xERA	Ctl	Dom	Cmd	hr/9	BPV
2010	NCAA	Oregon	7	5	0	102	105	3.00	1.15	23.8	226	29	78	3.13	2.9	9.3	3.2	1.0	106
2011	NCAA	Oregon	8	3	0	107	114	2.36	1.03	27.4	199	28	76	1.74	2.9	9.6	3.3	0.2	111
2012	A	Asheville	12	3	0	120	81	2.48	1.08	23.4	232	27	78	2.51	2.1	6.1	2.9	0.4	71
2013	A-	Tri-City	1	1	0	15	13	0.60	0.80	18.1	175	23	92	0.76	1.8	7.8	4.3	0.0	110
2013	A+	Modesto	3	2	0	74	63	3.28	1.16	22.7	229	26	78	3.45	2.9	7.7	2.6	1.2	77

Solid season of growth for finesse lefty. Has a decent 89-93 mph FB and complements it with a SL, CB, and avg CU. Has good command of all offerings and deception from funky delivery. Thrived due to FB/CU combination, but lack of dominance is a concern.

Andriese,Matt — SP — San Diego

EXP MLB DEBUT: 2014 | POTENTIAL: #3 starter | **8C**

Thrws R Age 24
2011 (3) UC-Riverside

Velo	Pitch	Grade
88-94	FB	+++
85-86	SP	++++
77-79	CB	++

Year	Lev	Team	W	L	Sv	IP	K	ERA	WHIP	BF/G	OBA	H%	S%	xERA	Ctl	Dom	Cmd	hr/9	BPV
2011	NCAA	Cal-Riverside	4	5	0	95	74	2.65	1.23	27.5	256	32	76	2.83	2.4	7.0	3.0	0.0	80
2011	A-	Eugene	5	1	0	41	42	1.54	0.95	12.9	201	28	82	1.41	2.2	9.2	4.2	0.0	125
2012	A+	Lake Elsinore	10	8	0	146	131	3.58	1.22	21.8	254	32	71	3.29	2.3	8.1	3.4	0.6	100
2013	AA	San Antonio	8	2	0	76	63	2.37	1.16	20.2	249	31	80	2.89	2.0	7.5	3.7	0.4	98
2013	AAA	Tucson	3	5	0	58	42	4.50	1.31	20.0	281	34	64	3.69	1.9	6.5	3.5	0.3	85

Durable and strong SP who was promoted to AAA midseason. Pitches off sinker and rarely allows hitters to put ball in air. Throws consistent strikes and has good enough breaking stuff to miss some bats. CB could become plus, though needs better offspeed pitch to counter LHH.

Appel,Mark — SP — Houston

EXP MLB DEBUT: 2015 | POTENTIAL: #1 starter | **9C**

Thrws R Age 22
2013 (1) Stanford

Velo	Pitch	Grade
93-98	FB	++++
83-87	SL	++++
80-83	CU	++

Year	Lev	Team	W	L	Sv	IP	K	ERA	WHIP	BF/G	OBA	H%	S%	xERA	Ctl	Dom	Cmd	hr/9	BPV
2011	NCAA	Stanford	6	6	0	104	83	3.03	1.28	26.6	267	34	74	3.19	2.3	7.2	3.2	0.1	87
2012	NCAA	Stanford	10	2	0	123	130	2.56	1.03	29.6	219	30	74	2.04	2.2	9.5	4.3	0.2	130
2013	NCAA	Stanford	10	4	0	106	130	2.12	0.97	28.7	211	32	77	1.73	2.0	11.0	5.7	0.2	164
2013	A-	Tri City	0	0	0	5	6	3.60	1.20	10.1	299	43	67	3.33	0.0	10.8		0.0	212
2013	A	Quad Cities	3	1	0	33	27	3.82	1.18	16.5	244	30	68	3.06	2.5	7.4	3.0	0.5	84

Tall, athletic SP who has all ingredients to become ace. Generates arm speed with clean delivery and can pepper zone with plus FB. Downhill plane enhances pitch mix and hard SL is swing-and-miss offering. Learning to mix in CU, but throws strikes with all pitches. Has tendency to nibble which impacts command.

Aquino,Jayson — SP — Colorado

EXP MLB DEBUT: 2016 | POTENTIAL: #3 starter | **7C**

Thrws L Age 21
2009 FA (DR)

Velo	Pitch	Grade
88-92	FB	+++
	CB	+
	CU	+++

Year	Lev	Team	W	L	Sv	IP	K	ERA	WHIP	BF/G	OBA	H%	S%	xERA	Ctl	Dom	Cmd	hr/9	BPV
2012	Rk	Grand Junction	4	0	0	43	36	1.88	1.00	23.5	209	26	83	2.04	2.3	7.5	3.3	0.4	91
2013	A-	Tri-City	0	1	0	23	16	3.13	1.13	22.7	245	29	72	2.81	2.0	6.3	3.2	0.4	78
2013	A	Asheville	0	9	0	64	57	4.78	1.36	24.3	268	33	64	3.84	3.0	8.0	2.7	0.6	83

Lefty had mixed results, getting off to a strong start, but struggling in the SAL. Has a good 87-91 mph FB and avg CU that allows him to keep hitters off-balance. Mixes in an inconsistent CB. Works his FB well to both corners and keeps the ball down.

Armstrong,Mark — RP — Cincinnati

EXP MLB DEBUT: 2017 | POTENTIAL: #4 starter | **7D**

Thrws R Age 19
2013 (3) HS (NY)

Velo	Pitch	Grade
88-92	FB	+++
	CB	+++
	CU	+++

Year	Lev	Team	W	L	Sv	IP	K	ERA	WHIP	BF/G	OBA	H%	S%	xERA	Ctl	Dom	Cmd	hr/9	BPV
2013	Rk	AZL Reds	0	0	0	3	2	0.00	0.33	4.7	106	13	100	0.00	0.0	6.0		0.0	126

Strong, stocky RHP was CIN 3rd round pick in 2013. Advanced skills for a high school pitcher. CIN took precautions with IP due to heavy prep work load. FB sits at 88-92 with some projection left. Complements FB with solid-average CB and CU. Command pitcher with a lot of potential.

Armstrong,Shawn — RP — Cleveland

EXP MLB DEBUT: 2014 | POTENTIAL: Middle reliever | **7D**

Thrws R Age 23
2011 (18) East Carolina

Velo	Pitch	Grade
89-96	FB	++++
83-87	SL	+++
81-83	CU	+

Year	Lev	Team	W	L	Sv	IP	K	ERA	WHIP	BF/G	OBA	H%	S%	xERA	Ctl	Dom	Cmd	hr/9	BPV
2012	A	Lake County	0	0	0	3	4	0.00	1.00	5.7	106	18	100	0.52	6.0	12.0	2.0	0.0	72
2012	A+	Carolina	1	3	1	43	52	2.09	1.26	6.7	204	31	81	2.20	4.8	10.9	2.3	0.0	84
2012	AA	Akron	1	0	3	20	22	0.90	1.20	4.7	175	26	92	1.75	5.4	9.9	1.8	0.0	50
2013	Rk	AZL Indians	0	0	0	4	5	4.50	0.75	4.8	210	24	50	3.11	0.0	11.3		2.3	221
2013	AA	Akron	2	3	0	33	43	4.09	1.61	4.9	256	37	75	4.25	5.7	11.7	2.0	0.5	74

Tall and strong RP who missed 3 months, but still owns sneaky stuff with deceptive delivery. FB remains plus pitch and has explosive, late action. Keeps ball in park by living in lower half of zone. Secondary pitches need work. Tight SL can be good, but patient hitters lay off it. Needs better pitch to battle LHH as CU is poor.

Asher,Alec — SP — Texas

EXP MLB DEBUT: 2015 | POTENTIAL: #4 starter | **7C**

Thrws R Age 22
2012 (4) Polk County JC

Velo	Pitch	Grade
90-95	FB	++++
84-87	SL	+++
78-81	CB	++
83-85	CU	++

Year	Lev	Team	W	L	Sv	IP	K	ERA	WHIP	BF/G	OBA	H%	S%	xERA	Ctl	Dom	Cmd	hr/9	BPV
2012	A-	Spokane	2	3	5	35	50	3.09	1.14	6.9	227	34	78	3.15	2.8	12.9	4.5	1.0	173
2013	A+	Myrtle Beach	9	7	0	133	139	2.91	1.20	20.6	242	32	78	3.20	2.7	9.4	3.5	0.7	114

Big-framed starter who led CAR in Ks. Aggressive placement in High-A to begin season and made transition look easy. Tough to hit with plus FB that he locates to both sides. Holds velocity and has two decent secondary pitches. Throws from high ¾ slot with good arm speed, but not much pitch movement.

Astin,Barrett — SP — Milwaukee

EXP MLB DEBUT: 2016 | POTENTIAL: Setup reliever | **7C**

Thrws R Age 22
2013 (3) Arkansas

Velo	Pitch	Grade
89-92	FB	+++
	SL	+++
	CU	++

Year	Lev	Team	W	L	Sv	IP	K	ERA	WHIP	BF/G	OBA	H%	S%	xERA	Ctl	Dom	Cmd	hr/9	BPV
2011	NCAA	Arkansas	5	2	3	59	57	2.75	1.31	9.0	255	33	81	3.57	3.1	8.7	2.9	0.6	92
2012	NCAA	Arkansas	3	5	11	58	61	2.02	1.22	7.3	220	31	82	2.33	3.9	9.5	2.4	0.0	84
2013	NCAA	Arkansas	4	4	1	90	74	1.80	1.17	19.9	251	32	84	2.70	2.0	7.4	3.7	0.1	97
2013	Rk	Helena	1	1	0	37	31	4.38	1.41	13.0	282	32	74	5.01	2.7	7.5	2.8	1.5	81

Small, athletic RHP saw time in the rotation and pen. A closer in college, future role will likely be in the late innings as he has never shown durability. His FB sits in the low 90s and has a solid SL and show-me CU. Could move fast if transitioned to the pen full-time.

Baez,Angel — SP — Kansas City

EXP MLB DEBUT: 2016 | POTENTIAL: #4 starter / Setup reliever | **7D**

Thrws R Age 23
2008 FA (DR)

Velo	Pitch	Grade
90-96	FB	+++
81-83	SL	+++
77-79	CB	++
83-86	CU	++

Year	Lev	Team	W	L	Sv	IP	K	ERA	WHIP	BF/G	OBA	H%	S%	xERA	Ctl	Dom	Cmd	hr/9	BPV
2010	Rk	AZL Royals	0	2	0	15	14	5.40	1.27	8.8	175	22	56	2.50	6.0	8.4	1.4	0.6	7
2011	Rk	Burlington	0	6	0	47	41	7.09	2.06	16.4	336	41	64	6.68	5.7	7.9	1.4	0.6	4
2012	A	Kane County	6	5	0	76	83	3.20	1.26	19.4	233	31	76	3.14	3.7	9.8	2.7	0.6	96
2013	Rk	AZL Royals	1	0	0	14	17	2.57	1.43	9.9	301	43	80	3.94	1.9	10.9	5.7	0.0	163
2013	A+	Wilmington	3	1	0	37	35	4.38	1.68	20.8	246	31	75	4.49	6.8	8.5	1.3	0.7	-13

Tall and thick SP who missed all of May and June with broken hand. Pitches from low arm slot and keeps ball down with heavy FB. Has trouble repeating delivery that has effort and struggles to command plate. SL has moments, but gets on side of CB too often. Likely to convert to reliever to take advantage of arm.

Baker,Dylan — SP — Cleveland

EXP MLB DEBUT: 2016 | POTENTIAL: #4 starter / Setup reliever | **7B**

Thrws R Age 22
2012 (5) Western Nevada JC

Velo	Pitch	Grade
90-95	FB	+++
83-86	SL	+++
78-82	CB	++
80-84	CU	++

Year	Lev	Team	W	L	Sv	IP	K	ERA	WHIP	BF/G	OBA	H%	S%	xERA	Ctl	Dom	Cmd	hr/9	BPV
2012	Rk	AZL Indians	0	1	0	24	30	4.13	1.63	13.3	262	38	74	4.22	5.6	11.3	2.0	0.4	69
2013	A	Lake County	7	6	0	143	117	3.65	1.30	21.8	235	30	70	2.91	3.9	7.4	1.9	0.2	45

Athletic SP who has seen prospect status rise with excellent FB/SL combo. Keeps ball in yard by inducing high number of GB with sinking FB. Can battle hitters from both sides of plate with solid-average stuff, but effort in delivery may eventually lead to bullpen role. CU and CB have moments, but aren't yet dependable.

Ball,Trey — SP — Boston

EXP MLB DEBUT: 2017 | POTENTIAL: #2 starter | **9D**

Thrws L Age 20
2013 (1) HS (IN)

Velo	Pitch	Grade
88-94	FB	+++
74-78	CB	+++
78-82	CU	++

Year	Lev	Team	W	L	Sv	IP	K	ERA	WHIP	BF/G	OBA	H%	S%	xERA	Ctl	Dom	Cmd	hr/9	BPV
2013	Rk	GCL Red Sox	0	1	0	7	5	6.43	2.29	7.1	336	38	73	7.93	7.7	6.4	0.8	1.3	-75

Tall, angular LHP with significant upside. Oozes projection and has solid present stuff. Delivery is smooth and functional and will need to continue to repeat to enhance CU. Very thin frame needs strength in order to maintain velocity. CB is average at present and can get hitters to chase.

Balog,Alex | SP | Colorado

EXP MLB DEBUT: 2017 | POTENTIAL: #4 starter | 7D

Thrws R Age 21
2013 (2) San Francisco

Velo	Pitch	Grade
91-94	FB	+++
78-81	CB	++
81-83	SL	+++
78-80	CU	+

Year	Lev	Team	W	L	Sv	IP	K	ERA	WHIP	BF/G	OBA	H%	S%	xERA	Ctl	Dom	Cmd	hr/9	BPV
2011	NCAA	San Francisco	2	2	0	17	5	6.35	1.82	4.9	315	34	61	5.23	4.8	2.6	0.6	0.0	-63
2012	NCAA	San Francisco	4	4	0	78	57	3.46	1.19	20.9	220	26	71	2.71	3.6	6.6	1.8	0.5	40
2013	NCAA	San Francisco	3	4	0	91	67	3.66	1.40	27.4	268	31	75	4.07	3.3	6.6	2.0	0.7	49
2013	Rk	Grand Junction	1	4	0	30	17	9.30	1.97	20.5	376	39	54	8.62	2.4	5.1	2.1	2.1	45

70th overall pick struggled in debut, going 1-4 with a 9.30 ERA. At 6-5, 210 has ideal size and a good power arm. FB sits at 91-94 and mixes in a power CB and a good SL Gave up 7 HR in 30 IP in debut. Good potential, but needs to pitch down in the zone.

Bandilla,Bryce | RP | San Francisco

EXP MLB DEBUT: 2015 | POTENTIAL: Reliever | 7D

Thrws L Age 24
2011 (4) Arizona

Velo	Pitch	Grade
92-95	FB	++++
	SL	+++
	CU	++

Year	Lev	Team	W	L	Sv	IP	K	ERA	WHIP	BF/G	OBA	H%	S%	xERA	Ctl	Dom	Cmd	hr/9	BPV
2010	NCAA	Arizona	6	4	1	77	70	4.09	1.61	11.8	293	37	74	4.75	4.0	8.2	2.1	0.5	58
2011	NCAA	Arizona	5	3	1	46	48	3.72	1.52	6.2	208	29	74	3.12	7.0	9.4	1.3	0.2	-3
2012	Rk	AZL Giants	0	0	0	14	20	1.93	0.64	12.1	151	24	75	0.65	1.3	12.9	10.0	0.6	215
2012	A	Augusta	2	4	0	44	48	3.07	1.64	17.8	262	36	80	4.10	5.7	9.8	1.7	0.2	40
2013	A+	San Jose	1	4	5	44	72	3.68	1.16	4.6	173	29	72	2.53	5.1	14.7	2.9	1.0	145

Drafted as a SP, made the move to the pen in '13 and had great results. Comes at hitters with a low-to-mid-90s FB. Complements with a solid average SL and developing CU. FB/SL combo used to put away hitters and led to 14.7 Dom. Struggles with command of pitches and needs to execute better to have bigger role in relief.

Banuelos,Manny | SP | New York (A)

EXP MLB DEBUT: 2015 | POTENTIAL: #2 starter | 8C

Thrws L Age 23
2008 FA (Mexico)

Velo	Pitch	Grade
89-94	FB	++++
79-82	CB	+++
80-83	CU	+++

Year	Lev	Team	W	L	Sv	IP	K	ERA	WHIP	BF/G	OBA	H%	S%	xERA	Ctl	Dom	Cmd	hr/9	BPV
2010	A+	Tampa	0	3	0	44	62	2.25	1.18	17.6	234	37	80	2.57	2.9	12.7	4.4	0.2	169
2010	AA	Trenton	0	1	0	15	17	3.60	1.53	21.8	262	34	81	4.78	4.8	10.2	2.1	1.2	72
2011	AA	Trenton	4	5	0	95	94	3.60	1.54	20.7	260	33	78	4.26	4.9	8.9	1.8	0.7	45
2011	AAA	Scranton/W-B	2	2	0	34	31	4.24	1.62	21.6	273	34	74	4.53	5.0	8.2	1.6	0.5	30
2012	AAA	Scranton/W-B	0	2	0	24	22	4.50	1.63	17.8	300	37	73	5.16	3.8	8.3	2.2	0.8	65

Quick-armed SP who hasn't pitched since May '12 due to TJ surgery. When healthy, has plenty of weapons in toolbox. FB has lots of life and can get hitters to chase CB and excellent CU. Delivery has some deception due to arm action, though has been hit harder than stuff would suggest. Still has youth on his side.

Barbato,John | RP | San Diego

EXP MLB DEBUT: 2015 | POTENTIAL: #4 starter/reliever | 7D

Thrws R Age 21
2010 (6) HS (FL)

Velo	Pitch	Grade
90-96	FB	+++
	CB	++
	CU	+

Year	Lev	Team	W	L	Sv	IP	K	ERA	WHIP	BF/G	OBA	H%	S%	xERA	Ctl	Dom	Cmd	hr/9	BPV
2011	A-	Eugene	1	4	0	57	50	4.89	1.46	16.2	244	30	66	3.84	4.9	7.9	1.6	0.6	28
2012	A	Fort Wayne	6	1	3	73	84	1.85	1.14	6.0	202	28	86	2.35	3.8	10.4	2.7	0.5	101
2013	A+	Lake Elsinore	3	6	14	88	89	5.01	1.40	7.6	266	34	64	4.15	3.4	9.1	2.7	0.8	91

Big and strong RP who started handful of games late in season. Should stay in pen as he struggles to repeat delivery. Regressed from '12 campaign, but misses bats with explosive, hard FB. Mixes in fringy overhand CB, but FB is go-to offering. Lacks touch and feel for CU and needs to be more aggressive.

Bard,Luke | RP | Minnesota

EXP MLB DEBUT: 2016 | POTENTIAL: Setup reliever | 7C

Thrws R Age 23
2012 (1-S) Georgia Tech

Velo	Pitch	Grade
89-95	FB	++++
80-84	SL	+++
80-83	CU	++

Year	Lev	Team	W	L	Sv	IP	K	ERA	WHIP	BF/G	OBA	H%	S%	xERA	Ctl	Dom	Cmd	hr/9	BPV
2012	Rk	Elizabethton	0	0	1	3	4	0.00	1.33	3.1	191	31	100	2.24	6.0	12.0	2.0	0.0	72
2012	Rk	GCL Twins	0	0	0	4	3	6.75	2.00	6.4	210	27	63	4.19	11.3	6.8	0.6	0.0	-164
2013	Rk	Elizabethton	1	0	0	8	6	1.13	1.00	4.4	81	11	88	0.35	6.8	6.8	1.0	0.0	-43
2013	Rk	GCL Twins	0	0	0	3	1	12.00	2.67	4.1	371	40	50	8.35	9.0	3.0	0.3	0.0	-171
2013	A+	Fort Myers	0	0	0	1	2	0.00	0.00	2.8	0	0	0	0.00	0.0	18.0		0.0	342

Strong-armed RP who hasn't pitched much since '12 draft. Had sore elbow to start '13 and only pitched 12 innings. Future role still to be determined, but has plus FB thrown with clean arm action and fluid delivery. Lacks consistent secondary pitch, but both SL and CU show promise. Pitch sequencing needs work.

Barlow,Scott | SP | Los Angeles (N)

EXP MLB DEBUT: 2017 | POTENTIAL: #5 starter | 6B

Thrws R Age 21
2011 (6) HS (CA)

Velo	Pitch	Grade
89-93	FB	+++
	CB	++
	SL	+++
83-85	CU	++

Year	Lev	Team	W	L	Sv	IP	K	ERA	WHIP	BF/G	OBA	H%	S%	xERA	Ctl	Dom	Cmd	hr/9	BPV
2011	Rk	AZL Dodgers	0	1	0	1	1	45.00	7.00	4.9	639	69	33	36.52	18.0	9.0	0.5	9.0	-306
2013	Rk	Ogden	4	3	0	69	51	6.26	1.65	20.6	296	32	65	6.08	4.2	6.7	1.6	1.7	25

Tall, lanky SP had a disappointing season in his return from TJ surgery. Sits in the low-90s with the FB, but projectable frame could lead to more. SL is his best secondary, used to get swing-and-misses, though CB and CU have chance to play average. Cmd was erratic for most of season and needs further refinement.

Barnes,Matt | SP | Boston

EXP MLB DEBUT: 2014 | POTENTIAL: #3 starter | 8C

Thrws R Age 24
2011 (1) Connecticut

Velo	Pitch	Grade
90-96	FB	++++
75-80	CB	+++
84-88	CU	++

Year	Lev	Team	W	L	Sv	IP	K	ERA	WHIP	BF/G	OBA	H%	S%	xERA	Ctl	Dom	Cmd	hr/9	BPV
2011	NCAA	Connecticut	11	4	0	116	111	1.71	0.88	26.8	178	24	82	1.28	2.4	8.6	3.6	0.3	108
2012	A	Greenville	2	0	0	26	42	0.35	0.62	17.9	141	28	94	0.00	1.4	14.5	10.5	0.0	242
2012	A+	Salem	5	5	0	93	91	3.58	1.18	18.6	245	32	70	3.10	2.4	8.8	3.6	0.6	111
2013	AA	Portland	5	10	0	108	135	4.33	1.46	19.3	269	37	72	4.42	3.8	11.3	2.9	0.9	117
2013	AAA	Pawtucket	1	0	0	5	7	0.00	1.00	19.1	175	30	100	1.22	3.6	12.6	3.5	0.0	148

Tall, aggressive SP who had solid, yet up-and-down season. Induces GB and can register Ks with lively FB. Pitches effectively to all areas of strike zone. Can be inefficient with pitch counts and needs to find consistency in CB. Repeats arm speed on CU, but not yet an average offering. Has been hittable despite stuff.

Barrett,Aaron | RP | Washington

EXP MLB DEBUT: 2014 | POTENTIAL: Reliever | 7B

Thrws R Age 26
2010 (9) Mississippi

Velo	Pitch	Grade
93-95	FB	+++
83-85	SL	++++

Year	Lev	Team	W	L	Sv	IP	K	ERA	WHIP	BF/G	OBA	H%	S%	xERA	Ctl	Dom	Cmd	hr/9	BPV
2010	A-	Vermont	0	5	0	21	25	9.43	2.29	10.7	305	40	58	7.38	9.4	10.7	1.1	1.3	-44
2011	A-	Auburn	1	2	9	26	32	4.15	1.38	5.8	179	25	71	2.89	6.9	11.1	1.6	0.7	30
2012	A	Hagerstown	3	2	16	34	52	2.65	1.06	4.3	207	34	76	2.21	2.9	13.8	4.7	0.5	187
2012	A+	Potomac	0	0	1	17	21	1.06	0.71	5.4	158	25	83	0.30	1.6	11.1	7.0	0.0	175
2013	AA	Harrisburg	1	1	26	50	69	2.16	1.10	3.8	221	35	81	2.34	2.7	12.4	4.6	0.4	169

Move from starter to closer has been very successful, racking up 52 saves since 2011. Best pitch is plus SL used as an out pitch and thrown for strikes. Follows SL with average velocity FB with good downward movement. Has yet to post Dom under 10 and reigned in control issues that plauged him early in career.

Barrett,Jake | RP | Arizona

EXP MLB DEBUT: 2014 | POTENTIAL: Setup reliever | 8C

Thrws R Age 22
2012 (3) Arizona State

Velo	Pitch	Grade
94-98	FB	++++
85-87	SL	++++
78-80	CU	++

Year	Lev	Team	W	L	Sv	IP	K	ERA	WHIP	BF/G	OBA	H%	S%	xERA	Ctl	Dom	Cmd	hr/9	BPV
2011	NCAA	Arizona St.	7	4	0	76	72	4.14	1.26	22.2	259	34	66	3.28	2.5	8.5	3.4	0.4	104
2012	NCAA	Arizona St.	2	4	11	32	35	1.41	0.81	3.9	174	25	84	1.02	2.0	9.8	5.0	0.3	142
2012	A	South Bend	0	3	6	24	25	6.00	1.71	4.3	293	38	64	5.24	4.9	9.4	1.9	0.8	55
2013	A+	Visalia	2	1	15	27	37	2.00	1.11	3.8	216	33	86	2.60	3.0	12.3	4.1	0.7	159
2013	AA	Mobile	1	1	14	24	22	0.38	0.88	3.7	210	26	105	2.05	1.1	8.3	7.3	0.8	136

Relief prospect posted a 1.21 ERA with a 10.2 Dome. Has a plus 94-98 mph FB that can hit 99. Adds a plus 85-87 SL and an inconsistent CU. Has a solid frame and is durable. Notched 29 SV and is one of the better relief prospects in the NL.

Barrios,Yhonathan | SP | Pittsburgh

EXP MLB DEBUT: 2017 | POTENTIAL: #3 starter | 7E

Thrws R Age 22
2008 FA (Colombia)

Velo	Pitch	Grade
91-95	FB	++++
	SL	++
	CU	+

Year	Lev	Team	W	L	Sv	IP	K	ERA	WHIP	BF/G	OBA	H%	S%	xERA	Ctl	Dom	Cmd	hr/9	BPV
2013	Rk	GCL Pirates	2	1	1	11	10	0.82	0.91	4.1	162	22	90	0.89	3.3	8.2	2.5	0.0	77

Strong-armed Colombian hurler converted from INF to SP. Generates easy velocity and already has a FB that sits at 91-95 mph, a SL, and a CU. He is very raw on the mound and has poor front-side mechanics, but does have a lively arm.

Bassitt,Chris | SP | Chicago (A)

EXP MLB DEBUT: 2015 | POTENTIAL: #4 starter | 7C

Thrws R Age 25
2011 (16) Akron

Velo	Pitch	Grade
90-95	FB	+++
82-84	SL	+++
81-85	CU	++

Year	Lev	Team	W	L	Sv	IP	K	ERA	WHIP	BF/G	OBA	H%	S%	xERA	Ctl	Dom	Cmd	hr/9	BPV
2011	A	Kannapolis	3	1	1	25	30	1.80	1.04	5.4	212	31	84	2.10	2.5	10.8	4.3	0.4	144
2011	A+	Winston-Salem	0	0	0	1	1	9.00	2.00	4.8	415	52	50	7.49	0.0	9.0		0.0	180
2012	A+	Winston-Salem	5	4	4	91	75	3.66	1.41	10.1	224	27	75	3.42	5.3	7.4	1.4	0.6	7
2013	A+	Winston-Salem	7	2	0	101	101	3.48	1.31	23.2	240	31	76	3.55	3.7	9.0	2.4	0.8	79
2013	AA	Birmingham	4	2	0	47	37	2.30	1.11	23.1	209	26	80	2.28	3.3	7.1	2.2	0.4	58

Tall pitcher who has been unheralded as starter for last two seasons, though may likely move back to pen long-term. Thrives with excellent sinking FB that induces lots of groundballs and mixes in decent, sweeping SL from low ¾ slot. Doesn't have good enough CU to retire LHH and will have bouts of wildness.

Bauer,Trevor — SP — Cleveland

EXP MLB DEBUT: 2012 | POTENTIAL: #3 starter | 8C

Thrws R Age 23
2011 (1) UCLA

Velo	Pitch	Grade
90-96	FB	+++
81-83	SL	+++
74-78	CB	++++
	CU	+++

Year	Lev	Team	W	L	Sv	IP	K	ERA	WHIP	BF/G	OBA	H%	S%	xERA	Ctl	Dom	Cmd	hr/9	BPV
2012	AA	Mobile	7	1	0	48	60	1.69	1.23	24.3	196	30	86	2.22	4.9	11.3	2.3	0.2	89
2012	AAA	Reno	5	1	0	82	97	2.85	1.33	24.3	242	33	82	3.69	3.8	10.6	2.8	0.9	106
2012	MLB	ARI	1	2	0	16	17	6.19	1.69	18.0	237	30	64	4.77	7.3	9.6	1.3	1.1	-7
2013	AAA	Columbus	6	7	0	121	106	4.17	1.59	24.2	259	31	76	4.74	5.4	7.9	1.5	1.0	13
2013	MLB	CLE	1	2	0	17	11	5.29	1.82	19.7	238	25	75	5.60	8.5	5.8	0.7	1.6	-106

Athletic SP who seemed to regress with velocity and inefficiency. FB command was issue, but hope remains with impressive arsenal and deceptive delivery. Can sequence pitches, but walks too many and loses steam as game goes on. FB and CB are plus pitches when on while SL and CU are average at best.

Beck,Christopher — SP — Chicago (A)

EXP MLB DEBUT: 2015 | POTENTIAL: #4 starter | 7C

Thrws R Age 23
2012 (2) Georgia Southern

Velo	Pitch	Grade
89-95	FB	+++
83-86	SL	++
80-82	CU	+++

Year	Lev	Team	W	L	Sv	IP	K	ERA	WHIP	BF/G	OBA	H%	S%	xERA	Ctl	Dom	Cmd	hr/9	BPV
2011	NCAA	Georgia Southern	9	5	0	103	109	3.23	1.15	20.4	214	30	70	2.30	3.4	9.5	2.8	0.3	97
2012	NCAA	Georgia Southern	6	7	1	103	115	3.93	1.42	25.7	287	38	75	4.62	2.5	10.0	4.0	1.0	130
2012	Rk	Great Falls	4	3	0	40	36	4.73	1.58	11.7	311	38	70	5.14	2.7	8.1	3.0	0.7	91
2013	A+	Winston-Salem	11	8	0	118	57	3.13	1.35	23.4	260	28	80	4.00	3.2	4.3	1.4	0.8	10
2013	AA	Birmingham	2	2	0	28	22	2.89	1.04	21.6	248	31	69	2.23	1.0	7.1	7.3	0.0	119

Tall starter who possesses good frame and arm action that could result in more velocity. Improved mechanics led to better control, but decline in K rate is disturbing. Owns decent repertoire, including FB that he spots to both sides of plate and induces groundballs. CU may be best pitch, but SL continues to be hittable.

Bedrosian,Cam — RP — Los Angeles (A)

EXP MLB DEBUT: 2015 | POTENTIAL: Setup reliever | 7C

Thrws R Age 22
2010 (1) HS (GA)

Velo	Pitch	Grade
89-95	FB	+++
77-80	SL	+++
78-80	CU	++

Year	Lev	Team	W	L	Sv	IP	K	ERA	WHIP	BF/G	OBA	H%	S%	xERA	Ctl	Dom	Cmd	hr/9	BPV
2010	Rk	AZL Angels	0	2	0	12	10	4.50	1.67	10.8	278	35	70	4.23	5.3	7.5	1.4	0.0	11
2012	A	Cedar Rapids	3	11	0	82	48	6.37	1.74	17.8	282	32	62	5.03	5.7	5.3	0.9	0.5	-41
2013	A	Burlington	1	5	7	54	69	5.33	1.43	6.2	265	38	62	4.04	3.7	11.5	3.1	0.7	126
2013	A+	Inland Empire	0	0	0	8	9	0.00	1.38	4.8	151	23	100	1.92	7.9	10.1	1.3	0.0	-12

Short, strong pitcher who was moved to RP and doubled K rate. Missed all '11 due to TJ surgery, but velocity returned to normal. FB looks quicker due to arm action and starting to throw more strikes. Keeps ball low in zone and aggressively goes after hitters. Lacks feel for CU and will need more velocity on SL.

Belfiore,Mike — RP — Baltimore

EXP MLB DEBUT: 2013 | POTENTIAL: Setup reliever | 6A

Thrws L Age 25
2009 (1-S) Boston College

Velo	Pitch	Grade
89-92	FB	+++
80-83	SL	++
79-82	CU	+++

Year	Lev	Team	W	L	Sv	IP	K	ERA	WHIP	BF/G	OBA	H%	S%	xERA	Ctl	Dom	Cmd	hr/9	BPV
2010	A	South Bend	3	10	0	126	105	4.00	1.44	21.5	281	35	71	4.11	3.0	7.5	2.5	0.4	72
2011	A+	Visalia	4	4	0	79	79	5.92	1.81	10.5	279	32	72	6.41	6.5	9.0	1.4	1.9	5
2012	A+	Visalia	0	0	1	19	28	2.37	0.95	6.0	195	30	81	2.19	2.4	13.3	5.6	0.9	193
2012	AA	Bowie	5	1	2	47	50	2.87	1.36	7.0	245	33	79	3.35	4.0	9.6	2.4	0.4	82
2013	AAA	Norfolk	2	1	1	76	82	3.20	1.45	8.8	274	36	81	4.50	3.4	9.7	2.8	0.9	100

Tall, angular pitcher who has found success since turning into RP in '11. Posts nice K rate with combo of avg stuff and deception. Lively FB is best pitch and allows him to get ahead of hitters. Effectively mixes in fringy SL and solid CU. Pitches up often and lacks out pitch while command is short for prominent role.

Benincasa,Robert — RP — Washington

EXP MLB DEBUT: 2015 | POTENTIAL: Reliever | 7B

Thrws R Age 23
2012 (7) Florida State

Velo	Pitch	Grade
93-96	FB	+++
	SL	++++

Year	Lev	Team	W	L	Sv	IP	K	ERA	WHIP	BF/G	OBA	H%	S%	xERA	Ctl	Dom	Cmd	hr/9	BPV
2011	NCAA	Florida St.	2	2	0	32	24	3.38	1.28	6.9	250	27	81	4.20	3.1	6.8	2.2	1.4	56
2012	NCAA	Florida St.	4	2	16	41	58	1.32	0.76	4.6	172	28	86	0.97	1.5	12.7	8.3	0.4	206
2012	A-	Auburn	2	0	3	23	32	3.13	1.30	5.9	294	45	73	3.51	1.2	12.5	10.7	0.0	212
2013	A	Hagerstown	0	1	10	21	30	2.57	1.05	4.1	223	34	80	2.70	2.1	12.9	6.0	0.9	192
2013	A+	Potomac	0	4	17	30	34	3.30	1.23	4.9	249	34	74	3.28	2.7	10.2	3.8	0.6	129

Another closer with plus SL in WAS system. FB works off slider, and he can dial it up to 98 but struggles to command it at times. Because of FB inconsistency, goes to SL often, which will get exposed at higher levels. Needs to add strength as he tired late in the season.

Bergman,Christian — SP — Colorado

EXP MLB DEBUT: 2015 | POTENTIAL: #5 starter/reliever | 6C

Thrws R Age 26
2010 (24) UC-Irvine

Velo	Pitch	Grade
89-92	FB	+++
	CB	++
	CU	+++

Year	Lev	Team	W	L	Sv	IP	K	ERA	WHIP	BF/G	OBA	H%	S%	xERA	Ctl	Dom	Cmd	hr/9	BPV
2010	NCAA	Cal-Irvine	9	3	1	101	78	3.74	1.24	20.5	277	33	70	3.65	1.4	7.0	4.9	0.5	105
2010	Rk	Casper	1	4	0	48	37	6.00	1.52	14.9	314	37	60	5.30	2.1	6.9	3.4	0.9	87
2011	A-	Tri-City	7	5	0	97	68	2.60	0.97	24.5	233	28	73	2.23	1.0	6.3	6.2	0.4	104
2012	A+	Modesto	16	5	0	162	121	3.67	1.22	24.3	261	30	73	3.72	2.1	6.7	3.3	0.9	84
2013	AA	Tulsa	8	7	0	171	111	3.37	1.08	24.7	251	27	76	3.65	1.2	5.8	4.8	1.3	90

Finesse RH continues to put up impressive numbers despite avg stuff. Rarely breaks 90 with FB, but complements it with a CU that keeps hitters off-balance. Is an extreme strike-thrower, but lacks dominance. Remains a starter, but could move to relief.

Berrios,Jose — SP — Minnesota

EXP MLB DEBUT: 2016 | POTENTIAL: #2 starter | 8B

Thrws R Age 20
2012 (1-S) HS (PR)

Velo	Pitch	Grade
90-96	FB	++++
78-81	SL	+++
80-82	CU	+++

Year	Lev	Team	W	L	Sv	IP	K	ERA	WHIP	BF/G	OBA	H%	S%	xERA	Ctl	Dom	Cmd	hr/9	BPV
2012	Rk	Elizabethton	2	0	0	14	22	1.29	0.64	16.2	168	29	88	0.83	0.6	14.1	22.0	0.6	255
2012	Rk	GCL Twins	1	0	4	16	27	1.13	0.63	6.9	134	28	80	0.00	1.7	15.2	9.0	0.0	246
2013	A	Cedar Rapids	7	7	0	103	100	4.02	1.41	22.9	266	34	71	3.89	3.5	8.7	2.5	0.5	81

Short, strong RHP who has pure arm strength and pitch mix that leads to high Dom and low oppBA. Was hittable as SL can be flat at times, but plus FB is go-to offering. Maintains velocity and sequences well. At his best, FB and SL are K pitches while CU effective against LHH. Generates good movement with fast arm.

Berry,Timothy — SP — Baltimore

EXP MLB DEBUT: 2014 | POTENTIAL: #3 starter | 7B

Thrws L Age 23
2009 (50) HS (CA)

Velo	Pitch	Grade
88-94	FB	+++
79-82	CB	+++
80-82	CU	+++

Year	Lev	Team	W	L	Sv	IP	K	ERA	WHIP	BF/G	OBA	H%	S%	xERA	Ctl	Dom	Cmd	hr/9	BPV
2011	A	Delmarva	3	7	0	116	96	5.20	1.45	19.0	246	29	64	4.06	4.7	7.4	1.6	0.9	24
2012	A	Delmarva	2	7	0	52	44	5.02	1.48	22.4	290	36	65	4.44	2.9	7.6	2.6	0.5	76
2012	A+	Frederick	5	5	0	75	61	4.32	1.37	21.0	282	34	69	4.23	2.4	7.3	3.1	0.7	85
2012	AA	Bowie	0	1	0	1	4	63.00	9.00	11.8	713	120	22	38.14	18.0	36.0	2.0	0.0	180
2013	A+	Frederick	11	7	0	152	119	3.85	1.29	23.1	267	32	72	3.86	2.4	7.0	3.0	0.8	81

Athletic, projectable lefty who returned to High-A and cleaned up delivery for much better command and control. Gets consistent groundballs by living in lower half of strike zone and can retire hitters with effective CB. Needs to add strength and maintain velocity. Shows solid CU with good arm speed.

Betances,Dellin — RP — New York (A)

EXP MLB DEBUT: 2011 | POTENTIAL: Setup reliever | 7C

Thrws R Age 26
2006 (8) HS (NJ)

Velo	Pitch	Grade
92-97	FB	++++
80-82	CB	+++
84-88	CU	++

Year	Lev	Team	W	L	Sv	IP	K	ERA	WHIP	BF/G	OBA	H%	S%	xERA	Ctl	Dom	Cmd	hr/9	BPV
2011	MLB	New York (A)	0	0	0	3	2	6.75	2.63	8.0	125	15	71	14.90	20.3	6.8	0.3	0.0	-433
2012	AA	Trenton	3	4	0	56	53	6.59	1.84	23.7	316	40	63	5.85	4.8	8.5	1.8	0.6	41
2012	AAA	Scranton/W-B	3	5	0	74	71	6.45	1.89	21.8	254	31	66	5.49	8.4	8.6	1.0	1.1	-53
2013	AAA	Scranton/W-B	6	4	5	84	108	2.68	1.12	8.7	180	28	75	1.78	4.5	11.6	2.6	0.2	105
2013	MLB	NYY	0	0	0	5	10	10.80	2.20	4.2	390	66	50	9.07	3.6	18.0	5.0	1.8	245

Tall, large RHP who moved to bullpen and was dominant after April. K rate increased and induced more gb in short stints. Dominated RHH (.153 oppBA) with plus, heavy FB and power CB can also miss bats. Has difficulty repeating release point and has stiff delivery. If command improves, he could earn integral role.

Bettis,Chad — SP — Colorado

EXP MLB DEBUT: 2013 | POTENTIAL: #2 starter/reliever | 9D

Thrws R Age 25
2010 (2) Texas Tech

Velo	Pitch	Grade
88-94	FB	++++
81-84	SL	+++
	CU	++

Year	Lev	Team	W	L	Sv	IP	K	ERA	WHIP	BF/G	OBA	H%	S%	xERA	Ctl	Dom	Cmd	hr/9	BPV
2010	A-	Tri-City	4	1	0	48	39	1.13	1.13	18.9	245	31	89	2.43	1.9	7.3	3.9	0.0	99
2010	A	Asheville	2	0	0	18	17	1.00	0.94	22.6	216	28	94	2.06	1.5	8.5	5.7	0.5	131
2011	A+	Modesto	12	5	0	169	184	3.36	1.11	24.6	230	31	70	2.65	2.4	9.8	4.1	0.5	130
2013	AA	Tulsa	3	4	0	63	68	3.71	1.16	20.9	252	32	73	3.79	1.9	9.7	5.2	1.3	143
2013	MLB	COL	1	3	0	45	30	5.60	1.67	12.6	302	34	68	5.74	4.0	6.0	1.5	1.2	18

Short, strong-armed fRHP who was back in action after missing '12. FB velocity was 92-94, topping out at 96 mph. Showed improved CU and a knee-buckling SL. Dominated at times, but struggled with ctl when called up. Good long-term potential, but work to do.

Biddle,Jesse — SP — Philadelphia

EXP MLB DEBUT: 2014 | POTENTIAL: #3 starter | 8C

Thrws L Age 22
2010 (1) HS (PA)

Velo	Pitch	Grade
90-92	FB	++++
70-74	CB	++++
80-82	SL	++
75-80	CU	+++

Year	Lev	Team	W	L	Sv	IP	K	ERA	WHIP	BF/G	OBA	H%	S%	xERA	Ctl	Dom	Cmd	hr/9	BPV
2010	Rk	GCL Phillies	3	1	0	33	41	4.36	1.33	15.2	273	39	67	3.81	2.5	11.2	4.6	0.5	153
2010	A-	Williamsport	1	0	0	10	9	2.70	1.60	14.7	151	21	81	2.51	9.9	8.1	0.8	0.0	-104
2011	A	Lakewood	7	8	0	133	124	2.98	1.28	21.8	217	28	76	2.76	4.5	8.4	1.9	0.3	48
2012	A+	Clearwater	10	6	0	142	151	3.23	1.29	22.4	244	32	76	3.39	3.4	9.6	2.8	0.6	98
2013	AA	Reading	5	14	0	138	154	3.65	1.35	21.3	211	29	74	3.14	5.3	10.0	1.9	0.7	54

Strikeout machine battled through whooping cough and ankle injury and surrendered too many walks in 2013. Best pitch is tight, 12-to-6 CB; CU has shown flashes. Without big FB, needs to spot pitches to succeed. Excellent size and repeatable delivery points to durability, but command still inconsistent.

Binford,Christian — SP — Kansas City

EXP MLB DEBUT: 2016 | POTENTIAL: #4 starter | 7C

Thrws R Age 21
2011 (30) HS (PA)

Velo	Pitch	Grade
88-93	FB	++++
77-80	CB	++
83-85	CU	++

Year	Lev	Team	W	L	Sv	IP	K	ERA	WHIP	BF/G	OBA	H%	S%	xERA	Ctl	Dom	Cmd	hr/9	BPV
2012	Rk	Burlington	2	3	0	40	31	2.03	1.10	19.6	262	32	81	2.80	0.9	7.0	7.8	0.2	119
2013	A	Lexington	8	7	0	135	130	2.67	1.14	23.2	253	33	78	2.99	1.7	8.7	5.2	0.5	129

Tall, advanced pitcher who finished 3rd in SAL in ERA. Doesn't have a true knockout pitch, but pitches with good angle and locates FB. Pitch movement has been key in lower levels and will need to enhance CB. Lacks projection despite height and needs pitch to retire LHH. Keeps ball down and throws strikes.

Bird,Zach — SP — Los Angeles (N)

EXP MLB DEBUT: 2016 | POTENTIAL: #3 starter | 8D

Thrws R Age 19
2012 (9) HS (MS)

Velo	Pitch	Grade
88-92	FB	+++
70-73	CB	++
	SL	++
	CU	++

Year	Lev	Team	W	L	Sv	IP	K	ERA	WHIP	BF/G	OBA	H%	S%	xERA	Ctl	Dom	Cmd	hr/9	BPV
2012	Rk	AZL Dodgers	1	2	0	39	46	4.59	1.35	16.4	246	35	65	3.40	3.9	10.6	2.7	0.5	103
2013	Rk	Ogden	2	4	0	43	44	5.83	1.44	20.4	261	34	58	3.99	4.0	9.2	2.3	0.6	76
2013	A	Great Lakes	2	5	0	60	50	5.10	1.68	14.2	249	30	70	4.58	6.8	7.5	1.1	0.8	-29

Tall, lean RHP with projection continues to show signs of his raw ability, but fails to find consistency in his mechanics. He now sits in the low-90s, seen up to 96 with a tight CB that flashes plus. His delivery is a mess with no repeatability or command of his pitch selection, but added strength will allow refinement.

Blach,Ty — SP — San Francisco

EXP MLB DEBUT: 2015 | POTENTIAL: #3 starter | 7B

Thrws L Age 23
2012 (5) Creighton

Velo	Pitch	Grade
90-94	FB	+++
	CB	++
	CU	+++

Year	Lev	Team	W	L	Sv	IP	K	ERA	WHIP	BF/G	OBA	H%	S%	xERA	Ctl	Dom	Cmd	hr/9	BPV
2010	NCAA	Creighton	3	3	0	75	58	3.12	1.08	20.9	229	27	74	2.89	2.2	7.0	3.2	0.8	85
2011	NCAA	Creighton	10	3	0	102	100	2.65	1.21	21.6	246	33	78	2.88	2.6	8.8	3.4	0.3	108
2012	NCAA	Creighton	6	6	0	120	83	2.70	1.02	21.9	217	26	74	2.16	2.1	6.2	3.0	0.4	73
2013	A+	San Jose	12	4	0	130	117	2.91	1.09	23.1	253	32	75	2.95	1.2	8.1	6.5	0.6	130

Advanced LHP dominated in '13, showing plus feel and ability to miss bats. Sits in the low-90s with FB, complemented by a solid average SL and CB that flashes potential. Works down in the zone with his clean arm and delivery, generating ground balls, and sequences pitches to generate swings and misses.

Black,Victor — RP — New York (N)

EXP MLB DEBUT: 2013 | POTENTIAL: Reliever | 7C

Thrws R Age 26
2009 (1) Dallas Baptist

Velo	Pitch	Grade
92-94	FB	+++
82-84	SL	++
	CU	++

Year	Lev	Team	W	L	Sv	IP	K	ERA	WHIP	BF/G	OBA	H%	S%	xERA	Ctl	Dom	Cmd	hr/9	BPV
2011	A	West Virginia	2	1	1	29	23	5.28	1.59	5.8	268	34	63	3.90	5.0	7.1	1.4	0.0	12
2011	A+	Bradenton	1	0	0	6	5	4.35	1.94	5.9	314	36	82	6.83	5.8	7.3	1.3	1.5	-8
2012	AA	Altoona	2	3	13	60	85	1.65	1.15	4.7	191	31	87	2.05	4.4	12.8	2.9	0.3	130
2013	AAA	Indianapolis	5	3	17	46	63	2.53	1.06	4.7	177	28	77	1.76	4.1	12.3	3.0	0.4	128
2013	MLB	NYM/PIT	3	0	1	17	15	3.71	1.35	3.9	262	33	73	3.71	3.2	7.9	2.5	0.5	75

Move to reliever has been successful. Throws from 3/4 arm slot using primarily two pitches: FB that can hit 97 and average SL. Rarely uses CU. Arm action creates deception and good movement on pitches. Has struggled with mechanics, but Dom/Cmd/Ctl all trending the right direction the past three years.

Blackburn,Clayton — SP — San Francisco

EXP MLB DEBUT: 2015 | POTENTIAL: #2 starter | 8D

Thrws R Age 21
2011 (16) HS (OK)

Velo	Pitch	Grade
87-93	FB	+++
74-77	CB	++++
	SL	++
	CU	++

Year	Lev	Team	W	L	Sv	IP	K	ERA	WHIP	BF/G	OBA	H%	S%	xERA	Ctl	Dom	Cmd	hr/9	BPV
2011	Rk	AZL Giants	3	1	0	33	30	1.09	0.57	9.4	146	18	88	0.39	0.8	8.2	10.0	0.5	143
2012	A	Augusta	8	4	0	131	143	2.54	1.02	22.9	239	33	74	2.25	1.2	9.8	7.9	0.2	161
2013	A+	San Jose	7	5	0	133	138	3.65	1.10	22.7	228	29	69	2.88	2.4	9.3	3.9	0.8	122

Big, durable SP dealt with some nagging injuries but continued to show durability and dominance. Low 90s with his FB, complemented by a plus power CB, and an average SL and CU. Has good feel for all his pitches, throwing them in any count for strikes. Durable frame and clean arm action; frontline starter potential.

Blackburn,Paul — SP — Chicago (N)

EXP MLB DEBUT: 2016 | POTENTIAL: #3 starter | 7D

Thrws R Age 20
2012 (1) HS (CA)

Velo	Pitch	Grade
91-93	FB	+++
	CB	++
	CU	++

Year	Lev	Team	W	L	Sv	IP	K	ERA	WHIP	BF/G	OBA	H%	S%	xERA	Ctl	Dom	Cmd	hr/9	BPV
2012	Rk	AZL Cubs	2	0	0	20	13	3.56	1.49	9.7	288	32	79	4.78	3.1	5.8	1.9	0.9	38
2013	A-	Boise	2	3	0	46	38	3.33	1.52	15.4	240	29	79	3.91	5.7	7.4	1.3	0.6	-1

1st rounder has potential, but struggled with control, walking 5.7/9. FB sits at 91-93. Secondary offerings include a CB and CU that have potential, but remain inconsistent. Cubs limited him to just 46 IP as he works on consistency and arm strength.

Blair,Aaron — SP — Arizona

EXP MLB DEBUT: 2016 | POTENTIAL: #3 starter | 8D

Thrws R Age 22
2013 (1-S) Marshall

Velo	Pitch	Grade
92-94	FB	+++
75-79	CB	++
82-85	CU	++++

Year	Lev	Team	W	L	Sv	IP	K	ERA	WHIP	BF/G	OBA	H%	S%	xERA	Ctl	Dom	Cmd	hr/9	BPV
2011	NCAA	Marshall	2	3	0	36	34	2.74	1.33	12.5	256	33	80	3.54	3.2	8.5	2.6	0.5	83
2012	NCAA	Marshall	2	8	0	83	82	4.00	1.25	24.2	245	32	66	3.02	3.0	8.9	2.9	0.3	96
2013	NCAA	Marshall	5	5	0	82	84	2.85	1.16	25.1	203	28	73	2.07	4.0	9.2	2.3	0.1	77
2013	A-	Hillsboro	1	1	0	31	28	2.90	1.23	15.7	222	28	78	2.92	3.8	8.1	2.2	0.6	62
2013	A	South Bend	0	2	0	17	13	3.66	1.34	23.8	281	35	70	3.46	2.1	6.8	3.3	0.0	84

Physical RH was the 41st pick. FB sits at 92-94 mph with good late life. FB and straight CU are his best offerings and breaking ball is just average. Sometimes has difficulty harnessing the movement on his lively FB, but can be overpowering.

Blair,Seth — SP — St. Louis

EXP MLB DEBUT: 2014 | POTENTIAL: #5 starter | 6D

Thrws R Age 25
2010 (S-1) Arizona State

Velo	Pitch	Grade
88-94	FB	+++
78-81	CB	+++
80-82	CU	+

Year	Lev	Team	W	L	Sv	IP	K	ERA	WHIP	BF/G	OBA	H%	S%	xERA	Ctl	Dom	Cmd	hr/9	BPV
2010	NCAA	Arizona St.	12	1	0	106	108	3.65	1.33	24.5	272	35	75	4.17	2.5	9.2	3.7	0.9	116
2011	A	Quad Cities	6	3	0	81	70	5.32	1.74	17.6	257	31	70	5.05	6.9	7.8	1.1	1.0	-28
2012	Rk	GCL Cardinals	0	0	0	3	1	0.00	1.00	5.7	106	12	100	0.61	6.0	3.0	0.5	0.0	-90
2012	A+	Palm Beach	1	3	0	16	12	5.56	1.98	15.5	283	34	71	5.61	7.8	6.7	0.9	0.6	-72
2013	AA	Springfield	3	9	0	129	117	5.09	1.52	23.4	290	35	69	5.23	3.3	8.2	2.4	1.3	74

2010 1st rounder was healthy, but results were not stellar. Has a nice four-pitch mix featuring a 92-94 mph FB, CB, SL, and a CU. Breaking balls need work but have potential. Does have some recoil on his low 3/4 delivery and an inconsistent arm slot.

Bochy,Brett — RP — San Francisco

EXP MLB DEBUT: 2014 | POTENTIAL: Reliever | 6B

Thrws R Age 26
2010 (20) Kansas

Velo	Pitch	Grade
88-90	FB	+++
	SL	+++

Year	Lev	Team	W	L	Sv	IP	K	ERA	WHIP	BF/G	OBA	H%	S%	xERA	Ctl	Dom	Cmd	hr/9	BPV
2009	NCAA	Kansas	5	0	0	37	54	4.37	1.35	5.2	245	37	70	3.84	3.9	13.1	3.4	1.0	149
2010	NCAA	Kansas	2	0	5	23	34	0.78	0.70	6.7	122	23	88	0.00	2.7	13.3	4.9	0.0	184
2011	A	Augusta	1	0	10	39	53	1.38	0.77	4.0	167	27	83	0.76	1.8	12.2	6.6	0.2	188
2012	AA	Richmond	7	3	14	53	69	2.54	0.89	4.8	162	24	73	1.27	3.1	11.7	3.8	0.5	146
2013	AAA	Fresno	1	1	2	56	57	4.01	1.19	5.0	244	33	65	2.86	2.6	9.1	3.6	0.3	113

The son of Giants manager Bruce Bochy continues to succeed in high leverage relief roles despite subpar FB/SL combo. FB sits in the upper 80s with good movement; average SL has late break. Misses bats with regularity and limits the walks. Nothing overpowering, but good command and deception warrant look during ST.

Boer,Madison — RP — Minnesota

EXP MLB DEBUT: 2015 | POTENTIAL: Setup reliever | 7D

Thrws R Age 24
2011 (2) Oregon

Velo	Pitch	Grade
88-93	FB	+++
82-86	SL	+++
79-84	CU	++

Year	Lev	Team	W	L	Sv	IP	K	ERA	WHIP	BF/G	OBA	H%	S%	xERA	Ctl	Dom	Cmd	hr/9	BPV
2012	A	Beloit	2	2	0	27	20	3.64	1.32	22.5	253	31	71	3.35	3.3	6.6	2.0	0.3	48
2012	A+	Fort Myers	7	10	0	111	66	6.41	1.61	22.4	320	35	61	5.90	2.6	5.4	2.1	1.2	44
2013	Rk	GCL Twins	0	0	1	3	5	0.00	1.67	6.7	371	59	100	5.71	0.0	15.0		0.0	288
2013	A	Cedar Rapids	1	1	7	26	23	3.09	1.30	6.0	260	34	74	3.06	2.7	7.9	2.9	0.0	86
2013	A+	Fort Myers	1	0	0	10	5	12.35	2.65	18.6	410	43	52	10.72	6.2	4.4	0.7	1.8	-69

Tall, projectable pitcher who worked out of pen after starting in '12. Hasn't found success past Low-A and needs to produce to advance. Throws with clean arm action, but lacks movement and is hittable. Can rush delivery, limiting command. FB has potential to be plus offering in short stints, but needs polish to SL.

Bonilla,Lisalberto — RP — Texas

EXP MLB DEBUT: 2014 | POTENTIAL: Setup reliever | 7B

Thrws R Age 24
2008 FA (DR)

Velo	Pitch	Grade
91-96	FB	++++
78-81	SL	++
82-84	CU	+++

Year	Lev	Team	W	L	Sv	IP	K	ERA	WHIP	BF/G	OBA	H%	S%	xERA	Ctl	Dom	Cmd	hr/9	BPV
2011	A	Lakewood	4	5	4	106	95	2.80	1.13	16.1	233	29	78	2.92	2.5	8.1	3.3	0.7	97
2012	A+	Clearwater	1	1	1	13	18	1.37	0.99	5.0	196	32	85	1.43	2.7	12.4	4.5	0.0	166
2012	AA	Reading	2	1	3	33	46	1.64	1.18	6.3	191	31	87	2.11	4.6	12.5	2.7	0.3	119
2013	AA	Frisco	2	0	6	30	50	0.30	0.83	5.2	159	31	96	0.58	2.7	15.0	5.6	0.0	214
2013	AAA	Round Rock	5	5	0	43	56	7.95	1.77	7.6	300	40	56	6.35	5.0	11.7	2.3	1.7	93

Lean and athletic reliever who was demoted to Double-A in June and only allowed 1 ER in 30 innings. Establishes plate with plus FB with potential for more velocity. Has tendency to overthrow and FB can lack life. SL flashes above average, but CU is most polished secondary pitch with good arm speed.

Borden, Buddy — SP — Pittsburgh

Thrws R | Age 22
2013 (7) Nevada-Las Vegas

90-93	FB	+++
	CB	+
	CU	+++

EXP MLB DEBUT: 2017 | POTENTIAL: #4 starter | 7D

Year	Lev	Team	W	L	Sv	IP	K	ERA	WHIP	BF/G	OBA	H%	S%	xERA	Ctl	Dom	Cmd	hr/9	BPV
2011	NCAA	UNLV	1	2	0	22	10	10.59	2.26	11.2	391	42	50	8.46	4.1	4.1	1.0	0.8	-19
2012	NCAA	UNLV	2	5	1	54	63	4.98	1.66	15.2	268	36	71	4.83	5.6	10.5	1.9	0.8	54
2013	NCAA	UNLV	8	2	0	100	77	2.60	1.23	27.0	237	29	79	2.92	3.1	6.9	2.2	0.4	58
2013	A-	Jamestown	0	0	0	16	23	1.11	0.93	10.1	180	31	87	1.07	2.8	12.8	4.6	0.0	173

Athletic RH could be a steal in the 7th round. Has a lively 90-93 mph FB that can hit 95. Also has a decent CU and a CB that needs refinement. Solid debut; he profiles as a back-end starter, but could be more.

Bostick, Akeem — SP — Texas

Thrws R | Age 19
2013 (2) HS (SC)

90-96	FB	++++
78-82	CB	+++
80-83	CU	+++

EXP MLB DEBUT: 2018 | POTENTIAL: #3 starter | 8D

Year	Lev	Team	W	L	Sv	IP	K	ERA	WHIP	BF/G	OBA	H%	S%	xERA	Ctl	Dom	Cmd	hr/9	BPV
2013	Rk	AZL Rangers	4	1	1	41	33	2.85	1.31	12.1	266	34	76	3.18	2.6	7.2	2.8	0.0	77

Lean, athletic RHP who has raw ability, but potential to become standout. Loose, fast arm is very projectable and could add more ticks to existing FB. Velocity can be inconsistent and needs to reduce effort in delivery. Secondary pitches are average and can get hitters to chase CB out of zone. Needs better CU.

Boyd, Hudson — SP — Minnesota

Thrws R | Age 21
2011 (1-S) HS (FL)

86-92	FB	+++
77-80	CB	+++
81-83	CU	++

EXP MLB DEBUT: 2016 | POTENTIAL: #4 starter | 7D

Year	Lev	Team	W	L	Sv	IP	K	ERA	WHIP	BF/G	OBA	H%	S%	xERA	Ctl	Dom	Cmd	hr/9	BPV
2012	Rk	Elizabethton	2	5	0	58	36	2.95	1.48	19.2	278	31	85	4.82	3.6	5.6	1.6	1.1	22
2013	A	Cedar Rapids	4	5	0	103	72	4.98	1.52	15.4	258	29	68	4.43	4.9	6.3	1.3	0.9	-1

Large-framed RHP who lost weight prior to '13 and moved to bullpen. Fared much better as RP (1.48 ERA) than SP (6.06), but Dom remains low. CB was once top-notch offering, but has regressed with minimal break. Pitches up too often with fringy FB. Became more aggressive as reliever and could see velocity increase.

Bradley, Archie — SP — Arizona

Thrws R | Age 21
2011 (1) HS (OK)

93-96	FB	+++++
80-83	CB	++++
83-85	CU	++

EXP MLB DEBUT: 2014 | POTENTIAL: #1 starter | 9B

Year	Lev	Team	W	L	Sv	IP	K	ERA	WHIP	BF/G	OBA	H%	S%	xERA	Ctl	Dom	Cmd	hr/9	BPV
2011	Rk	Missoula	0	0	0	2	4	0.00	0.50	3.3	151	38	100	0.00	0.0	18.0		0.0	342
2012	A	South Bend	12	6	0	136	152	3.84	1.26	20.5	185	26	68	2.37	5.6	10.1	1.8	0.4	49
2013	A+	Visalia	2	0	0	28	43	1.28	1.13	22.3	217	37	90	2.32	3.2	13.7	4.3	0.3	179
2013	AA	Mobile	12	5	0	123	119	1.97	1.23	23.8	211	28	85	2.60	4.3	8.7	2.0	0.4	58

Top pitching prospect in NL and generates easy velocity. Has a plus 93-96 mph FB that hits 98. CB continues to improve and is a second plus offering, CU remains a work in progress, but with potential. 9.6 Dom and limited opposing batters to a .215 BA.

Bradley, Jed — SP — Milwaukee

Thrws L | Age 24
2011 (1) Georgia Tech

90-94	FB	+++
80-83	SL	++
	CU	+++

EXP MLB DEBUT: 2015 | POTENTIAL: #3 starter | 8E

Year	Lev	Team	W	L	Sv	IP	K	ERA	WHIP	BF/G	OBA	H%	S%	xERA	Ctl	Dom	Cmd	hr/9	BPV
2009	NCAA	Georgia Tech	2	3	0	44	49	6.72	1.61	16.3	302	37	61	6.14	3.5	10.0	2.9	1.8	104
2010	NCAA	Georgia Tech	9	5	0	91	99	4.84	1.45	24.3	294	39	66	4.46	2.5	9.8	4.0	0.6	127
2011	NCAA	Georgia Tech	7	3	0	98	106	3.49	1.22	24.8	244	34	69	2.72	2.8	9.7	3.4	0.1	116
2012	A+	Brevard County	5	10	0	107	60	5.55	1.67	24.1	310	34	66	5.47	3.6	5.0	1.4	0.8	11
2013	A+	Brevard County	4	4	0	78	58	4.15	1.54	21.3	269	32	74	4.44	4.5	6.7	1.5	0.7	17

Returned to High-A and continued to struggle with consistency. Missed more bats, but inability to repeat his mechanics led to an increased Ctl. He features a low-90s FB, an inconsistent SL, and an average CU. Has the making of a middle-of-the-rotation starter but inconsistencies are holding him back.

Brady, Sean — SP — Cleveland

Thrws L | Age 20
2013 (5) HS (FL)

86-91	FB	++
77-80	CB	+++
80-82	CU	+++

EXP MLB DEBUT: 2017 | POTENTIAL: #4 starter | 7C

Year	Lev	Team	W	L	Sv	IP	K	ERA	WHIP	BF/G	OBA	H%	S%	xERA	Ctl	Dom	Cmd	hr/9	BPV
2013	Rk	AZL Indians	0	1	0	32	30	1.97	0.94	12.0	210	27	82	2.03	1.7	8.4	5.0	0.6	124

Short LHP who posted solid numbers in debut. Lacks size, arm strength, and projection for high ceiling, but knows how to pitch. Used sharp CB to hold LHH to .071 BA and induces GB by burying ball low. Repeats delivery and has enough stuff to succeed. Fastball velocity may not be good enough.

Brasier, Ryan — RP — Los Angeles (A)

Thrws R | Age 26
2007 (6) Weatherford JC

90-96	FB	+++
79-84	SL	+++
81-82	CU	+

EXP MLB DEBUT: 2013 | POTENTIAL: Middle reliever | 7D

Year	Lev	Team	W	L	Sv	IP	K	ERA	WHIP	BF/G	OBA	H%	S%	xERA	Ctl	Dom	Cmd	hr/9	BPV
2011	AA	Arkansas	0	1	16	25	26	0.72	1.27	4.1	203	28	97	2.59	5.0	9.3	1.9	0.4	50
2011	AAA	Salt Lake	2	1	3	27	26	5.00	1.30	4.4	255	32	61	3.59	3.0	8.7	2.9	0.7	93
2012	AAA	Salt Lake	7	3	13	59	54	4.41	1.52	4.7	283	37	69	4.08	3.6	8.2	2.3	0.2	67
2013	AAA	Salt Lake	5	2	10	56	57	4.16	1.51	6.4	303	38	75	5.11	2.6	9.1	3.6	1.0	113
2013	MLB	LAA	0	0	0	9	7	2.00	1.22	5.2	216	25	90	3.25	4.0	7.0	1.8	1.0	36

Short, aggressive RP who has spent last 2½ years in AAA. Uses short, quick arm action to generate velocity and movement of solid-average FB. Improved control, but is hittable as breaking ball lacks depth and bite. Has effort in delivery, but generally repeats arm speed and slot. Has tendency to leave ball up in zone.

Brault, Steven — SP — Baltimore

Thrws L | Age 22
2013 (11) Regis

87-93	FB	+++
80-82	SL	+++
	CU	++

EXP MLB DEBUT: 2015 | POTENTIAL: #4 starter | 7C

Year	Lev	Team	W	L	Sv	IP	K	ERA	WHIP	BF/G	OBA	H%	S%	xERA	Ctl	Dom	Cmd	hr/9	BPV
2013	A-	Aberdeen	1	2	0	43	38	2.09	1.09	14.0	224	29	80	2.26	2.5	8.0	3.2	0.2	93

Athletic, deceptive LHP who relies on FB to succeed. Velocity is merely average but he locates it with precision and keeps ball down. Throws with clean arm and offers ideal, late pitch movement. Secondary offerings aren't overwhelming and lacks CU to keep RHH at bay. He needs to polish delivery.

Brennan, Brandon — SP — Chicago (A)

Thrws R | Age 22
2012 (4) Orange Coast CC

89-93	FB	+++
81-83	SL	++
82-84	CU	++

EXP MLB DEBUT: 2016 | POTENTIAL: #4 starter | 7D

Year	Lev	Team	W	L	Sv	IP	K	ERA	WHIP	BF/G	OBA	H%	S%	xERA	Ctl	Dom	Cmd	hr/9	BPV
2012	Rk	Great Falls	3	2	0	37	31	4.37	1.62	11.8	296	36	72	4.84	3.9	7.5	1.9	0.5	49
2013	A	Kannapolis	4	9	0	81	54	5.55	1.55	23.6	302	34	64	5.06	3.0	6.0	2.0	0.8	45

Powerful RHP whose season ended in June. Throws from high ¾ slot and keeps ball low in zone. FB is best pitch and gets ahead of hitters. Lacks dependable breaking ball or CU, though SL has shown flashes of becoming go-to pitch. Could end up in bullpen as he may be too hittable to start.

Brice, Austin — SP — Miami

Thrws R | Age 22
2010 (9) HS (NC)

92-95	FB	++++
80-82	CB	++++
	CU	+++

EXP MLB DEBUT: 2016 | POTENTIAL: #3 starter | 7D

Year	Lev	Team	W	L	Sv	IP	K	ERA	WHIP	BF/G	OBA	H%	S%	xERA	Ctl	Dom	Cmd	hr/9	BPV
2010	Rk	GCL Marlins	0	1	0	8	8	4.44	1.73	6.1	235	32	71	3.79	7.8	8.9	1.1	0.0	-32
2011	Rk	GCL Marlins	6	0	0	48	55	2.99	1.35	18.3	191	27	78	2.64	6.2	10.3	1.7	0.4	36
2012	A	Greensboro	8	6	3	109	122	4.37	1.50	18.9	238	31	74	4.26	5.6	10.1	1.8	1.1	48
2013	A	Greensboro	8	11	0	113	111	5.73	1.77	19.9	270	34	68	5.20	6.5	8.8	1.4	0.9	1

Tall, projectable SP continues to make hitters look foolish, finishing '13 with an 8.8 Dom. Works with a 92-94 FB, CB that flashes plus, and a show-me CU that flashes average. Pure stuff allows him to dominate at times, but after repeated control issues, his mechanics will need work in order to succeed.

Briceno, Endrys — SP — Detroit

Thrws R | Age 22
2009 FA (VZ)

90-97	FB	+++
81-84	SL	++
80-83	CU	+++

EXP MLB DEBUT: 2016 | POTENTIAL: #4 starter | 7E

Year	Lev	Team	W	L	Sv	IP	K	ERA	WHIP	BF/G	OBA	H%	S%	xERA	Ctl	Dom	Cmd	hr/9	BPV
2011	Rk	GCL Tigers	2	5	0	59	49	5.34	1.54	21.4	302	37	63	4.57	2.9	7.5	2.6	0.3	74
2012	A-	Connecticut	4	3	0	57	30	5.19	1.43	20.3	271	30	62	4.02	3.5	4.7	1.4	0.5	10
2013	A	West Michigan	7	9	0	116	65	4.49	1.51	20.1	275	31	69	4.17	4.0	5.0	1.3	0.4	2

Tall SP who is all about projection with long, lean frame. Has high ceiling predicated on size and stuff. Needs to repeat delivery. Solid velocity at present and should tick higher. Throws with good arm speed which adds to pitch movement. SL is below average and lacks break and has impressive CU.

Brickhouse,Bryan — SP — Kansas City

EXP MLB DEBUT: 2017 | POTENTIAL: #4 starter | 7C

Thrws R Age 22
2011 (3) HS (TX)

Velo	Pitch	Grade
90-96	FB	+++
75-79	CB	+++
82-83	CU	++

Year	Lev	Team	W	L	Sv	IP	K	ERA	WHIP	BF/G	OBA	H%	S%	xERA	Ctl	Dom	Cmd	hr/9	BPV
2012	Rk	Idaho Falls	0	0	0	1	1	52.50	6.67	11.4	596	63	14	32.07	22.5	7.5	0.3	7.5	-455
2012	A	Kane County	3	3	0	51	40	5.64	1.43	21.7	258	31	59	3.85	4.1	7.0	1.7	0.5	35
2013	A	Lexington	4	4	0	60	49	2.25	1.25	22.2	242	30	83	3.12	3.2	7.4	2.3	0.5	65

Short, strong SP who will be on sidelines after undergoing TJ surgery in June. When healthy, features FB with wicked movement. Sinker sets up secondary offerings, led by good CB. Uses drop and drive delivery to deliver heat, though has effort and may move to pen. Command is erratic and CU can lack movement.

Bridwell,Parker — SP — Baltimore

EXP MLB DEBUT: 2015 | POTENTIAL: #3 starter | 8D

Thrws R Age 22
2010 (9) HS (TX)

Velo	Pitch	Grade
87-94	FB	++++
80-82	CB	+++
81-83	SL	++
80-83	CU	++

Year	Lev	Team	W	L	Sv	IP	K	ERA	WHIP	BF/G	OBA	H%	S%	xERA	Ctl	Dom	Cmd	hr/9	BPV
2010	A-	Aberdeen	0	0	0	4	2	0.00	1.00	7.6	210	24	100	1.70	2.3	4.5	2.0	0.0	38
2011	A-	Aberdeen	2	5	0	53	57	4.57	1.47	19.0	272	37	67	3.94	3.7	9.6	2.6	0.3	91
2011	A	Delmarva	0	3	0	21	13	7.22	1.70	19.2	278	33	53	4.33	5.5	5.5	1.0	0.0	-32
2012	A	Delmarva	5	9	0	114	71	5.99	1.62	22.0	275	30	64	5.21	5.0	5.6	1.1	1.2	-15
2013	A	Delmarva	8	9	0	142	144	4.75	1.41	23.1	260	34	65	3.85	3.7	9.1	2.4	0.6	81

Athletic starter who finished 2nd in SAL in Ks upon return to level. Still has room for improvement, especially with command and repeating delivery. Posted much higher K rate while reducing BB. Features heavy FB and loose arm action should lead to more velocity down road. CB is best secondary pitch.

Britton,Drake — SP — Boston

EXP MLB DEBUT: 2013 | POTENTIAL: #3 starter / Reliever | 8D

Thrws L Age 25
2007 (23) HS (TX)

Velo	Pitch	Grade
88-96	FB	+++
74-78	CB	+++
81-84	SL	++
82-85	CU	+++

Year	Lev	Team	W	L	Sv	IP	K	ERA	WHIP	BF/G	OBA	H%	S%	xERA	Ctl	Dom	Cmd	hr/9	BPV
2012	A+	Salem	3	5	0	45	42	5.80	1.36	18.8	249	30	57	3.98	3.8	8.4	2.2	1.0	67
2012	AA	Portland	4	7	0	84	76	3.74	1.47	22.6	266	34	74	3.87	4.1	8.1	2.0	0.3	55
2013	AA	Portland	7	6	0	97	80	3.52	1.34	23.8	256	31	74	3.54	3.3	7.4	2.2	0.5	61
2013	AAA	Pawtucket	0	1	0	5	5	8.82	2.16	25.4	410	52	55	7.78	1.8	8.8	5.0	0.0	129
2013	MLB	BOS	1	1	0	21	17	3.86	1.33	4.8	262	32	70	3.58	3.0	7.3	2.4	0.4	68

Big, strong pitcher who reached BOS and pitched out of pen. Has starter profile due to deep repertoire. Has been potent against LHH and lives in lower half of zone. FB shows plus and uses two breaking balls. CU has deceptive action and sink. Struggles to repeat delivery which detracts from overall command.

Brown,Mitch — SP — Cleveland

EXP MLB DEBUT: 2017 | POTENTIAL: #3 starter | 8E

Thrws R Age 20
2012 (2) HS (MN)

Velo	Pitch	Grade
90-94	FB	+++
84-86	SL	+++
77-79	CB	++
81-84	CU	++

Year	Lev	Team	W	L	Sv	IP	K	ERA	WHIP	BF/G	OBA	H%	S%	xERA	Ctl	Dom	Cmd	hr/9	BPV
2012	Rk	AZL Indians	2	0	0	27	26	3.64	1.10	13.3	207	25	70	2.81	3.3	8.6	2.6	1.0	84
2013	Rk	AZL Indians	2	4	0	52	48	5.37	1.65	19.4	280	36	65	4.55	5.0	8.3	1.7	0.3	32
2013	A	Lake County	1	1	0	15	18	11.84	2.11	15.0	329	41	43	8.32	6.5	10.7	1.6	2.4	34

Strong, durable SP who began in Low-A, but got demoted. Has plenty to work on, but has desirable tools. Exhibits inconsistent velocity, but hard CB can be used as chase pitch or dropped in zone. Throws across body which limits command and has tendency to slow arm speed on CU.

Buchanan,Jake — SP — Houston

EXP MLB DEBUT: 2014 | POTENTIAL: #5 starter | 6B

Thrws R Age 24
2010 (8) North Carolina State

Velo	Pitch	Grade
88-91	FB	+++
85-88	CT	+++
75-78	CB	+
81-82	CU	++

Year	Lev	Team	W	L	Sv	IP	K	ERA	WHIP	BF/G	OBA	H%	S%	xERA	Ctl	Dom	Cmd	hr/9	BPV
2011	AA	Corpus Christi	0	0	0	7	2	1.29	1.00	26.7	233	25	86	2.00	1.3	2.6	2.0	0.0	30
2012	AA	Corpus Christi	5	9	0	134	83	4.97	1.52	21.6	311	35	67	5.09	2.2	5.6	2.5	0.7	58
2012	AAA	Oklahoma City	0	1	0	8	5	10.13	2.75	14.9	430	48	62	10.80	5.6	5.6	1.0	1.1	-33
2013	AA	Corpus Christi	7	2	1	82	44	2.09	0.93	17.1	225	25	79	2.10	1.0	4.8	4.9	0.4	78
2013	AAA	Oklahoma City	5	5	0	76	55	3.90	1.29	26.1	284	33	71	4.04	1.5	6.5	4.2	0.7	94

Efficient and command-oriented starter who lacks premium velocity, but throws strikes with clean delivery. Proved tougher to hit than in past and learning to cut and sink FB with precision. CB is well below average pitch, but can hit corners effectively. Keeps ball in lower half of strike zone and doesn't beat himself.

Buckel,Cody — SP — Texas

EXP MLB DEBUT: 2015 | POTENTIAL: #3 starter | 8E

Thrws R Age 22
2010 (2) HS (CA)

Velo	Pitch	Grade
88-94	FB	+++
77-80	CB	+++
83-86	SL	++
81-84	CU	+++

Year	Lev	Team	W	L	Sv	IP	K	ERA	WHIP	BF/G	OBA	H%	S%	xERA	Ctl	Dom	Cmd	hr/9	BPV
2011	A	Hickory	8	3	0	96	120	2.62	1.14	16.6	234	33	80	2.91	2.5	11.2	4.4	0.7	152
2012	A+	Myrtle Beach	5	3	0	75	91	1.32	0.98	22.0	188	28	88	1.56	3.0	10.9	3.6	0.2	133
2012	AA	Frisco	5	5	0	69	68	3.78	1.14	21.0	223	28	69	3.04	3.0	8.9	3.0	0.9	97
2013	Rk	AZL Rangers	0	1	0	1	4	32.73	6.36	5.1	0	0	43	12.94	57.3	32.7	0.6	0.0	-939
2013	AA	Frisco	0	5	0	9	9	20.77	4.18	10.6	280	32	47	12.44	27.7	8.9	0.3	2.0	-569

Durable RHP who had severe control problems. No health concerns, but couldn't throw strikes. Has deep repertoire of solid offerings including tailing FB and solid-average SL with late break. FB plane can be flat due to limited height and can leave balls up. At best when mixing well with deceptive arm speed.

Bundy,Dylan — SP — Baltimore

EXP MLB DEBUT: 2012 | POTENTIAL: #1 starter | 9A

Thrws R Age 21
2011 (1) HS (OK)

Velo	Pitch	Grade
93-99	FB	+++++
77-82	CB	++++
79-84	CU	+++

Year	Lev	Team	W	L	Sv	IP	K	ERA	WHIP	BF/G	OBA	H%	S%	xERA	Ctl	Dom	Cmd	hr/9	BPV
2012	A	Delmarva	1	0	0	30	40	0.00	0.23	11.5	56	10	100	0.00	0.6	12.0	20.0	0.0	218
2012	A+	Frederick	6	3	0	57	66	2.84	1.16	18.9	230	31	79	3.02	2.8	10.4	3.7	0.8	129
2012	AA	Bowie	2	0	0	16	13	3.33	1.36	22.6	235	28	76	3.40	4.4	7.2	1.6	0.6	28
2012	MLB	BAL	0	0	0	2	0	0.00	1.18	3.4	173	17	100	1.76	5.3	0.0	0.0	0.0	-125

Advanced, strong RHP who missed entire season and underwent TJ surgery in June. Reached BAL at age 19 and has high upside despite injury. Owns powerful repertoire highlighted by plus-plus FB when healthy. Can tantalize with CB and CU and can cut and sink FB. Body control and feel unmatched for age.

Burgos,Hiram — RP — Milwaukee

EXP MLB DEBUT: 2013 | POTENTIAL: #5 starter | 6C

Thrws R Age 26
2009 (6) Bethune-Cookman

Velo	Pitch	Grade
87-91	FB	++
70-72	CB	+++
	SL	++
79-81	CU	++

Year	Lev	Team	W	L	Sv	IP	K	ERA	WHIP	BF/G	OBA	H%	S%	xERA	Ctl	Dom	Cmd	hr/9	BPV
2012	AAA	Nashville	2	2	0	46	35	2.93	1.17	23.0	231	27	78	3.09	2.9	6.8	2.3	0.8	62
2013	A	Wisconsin	0	1	0	2	3	4.50	1.50	8.6	262	43	67	3.53	4.5	13.5	3.0	0.0	140
2013	A+	Brevard County	0	0	0	4	4	4.50	1.25	16.3	307	41	60	3.61	0.0	9.0		0.0	180
2013	AAA	Nashville	1	4	0	30	24	3.87	1.23	17.5	227	24	77	4.12	3.6	7.2	2.0	1.8	50
2013	MLB	MIL	1	2	0	29	18	6.45	1.67	21.9	315	34	64	6.28	3.4	5.5	1.6	1.5	26

Short, durable SP made his ML debut in '13 with little success. Lacks dominant stuff, but simple mechanics and solid control have allowed him to succeed. FB sits in upper-80s, and mixes in the occasional CT. CB is best pitch; also throws a SL and CU. Nothing is dominant, but throws strikes and competes.

Butler,Eddie — SP — Colorado

EXP MLB DEBUT: 2015 | POTENTIAL: #2 starter | 9C

Thrws R Age 23
2012 (1-S) Radford

Velo	Pitch	Grade
92-95	FB	++++
85-88	SL	+++
71-74	CB	+
87-88	CU	+++

Year	Lev	Team	W	L	Sv	IP	K	ERA	WHIP	BF/G	OBA	H%	S%	xERA	Ctl	Dom	Cmd	hr/9	BPV
2012	NCAA	Radford	7	4	0	98	95	2.20	1.03	27.0	220	29	80	2.28	2.1	8.7	4.1	0.5	118
2012	Rk	Grand Junction	7	1	0	67	55	2.14	1.07	20.1	237	30	79	2.31	1.7	7.4	4.2	0.1	104
2013	A	Asheville	5	1	0	54	51	1.66	0.92	22.5	141	18	83	1.01	4.2	8.5	2.0	0.3	58
2013	A+	Modesto	3	4	0	67	67	2.41	1.18	20.7	234	29	85	3.28	2.8	9.0	3.2	0.9	104
2013	AA	Tulsa	1	0	0	27	25	0.66	0.70	16.0	145	20	89	0.18	2.0	8.3	4.2	0.0	113

22-year-old RH comes after hitters with a heavy 92-95 mph sinking FB that hits 98. Also has a hard SL and an improved CU, giving him three plus offerings. Clean, repeatable mechanics with a low 3/4 arm slot and good command of all three pitches.

Buttrey,Ty — SP — Boston

EXP MLB DEBUT: 2016 | POTENTIAL: #3 starter | 8E

Thrws R Age 21
2012 (4) HS (NC)

Velo	Pitch	Grade
86-93	FB	++
77-80	CB	+++
83-86	CU	+++

Year	Lev	Team	W	L	Sv	IP	K	ERA	WHIP	BF/G	OBA	H%	S%	xERA	Ctl	Dom	Cmd	hr/9	BPV
2012	Rk	GCL Red Sox	0	0	0	5	5	1.80	1.20	5.0	262	35	83	2.82	1.8	9.0	5.0	0.0	131
2013	A-	Lowell	4	3	0	61	35	2.21	1.23	19.0	239	28	80	2.63	3.1	5.2	1.7	0.0	27

Lean, angular RHP who has potential, but struggles to repeat delivery that features moving parts. Doesn't have much velocity, though has projection remaining. Hasn't allowed HR as a pro and keeps ball down in zone. Hard CB can be out pitch, but hasn't been ahead of hitters to use as knockout.

Cabrera,Alberto — RP — Chicago (N)

EXP MLB DEBUT: 2012 | POTENTIAL: Reliever | 7C

Thrws R Age 25
2005 FA (DR)

Velo	Pitch	Grade
93-98	FB	++++
80-83	SL	+++
	CU	++

Year	Lev	Team	W	L	Sv	IP	K	ERA	WHIP	BF/G	OBA	H%	S%	xERA	Ctl	Dom	Cmd	hr/9	BPV
2012	AAA	Iowa	2	0	0	19	29	4.24	1.73	6.7	350	50	83	7.25	1.9	13.7	7.3	1.9	213
2012	MLB	CHC	1	1	0	22	27	5.39	1.57	3.8	207	30	64	3.41	7.5	11.2	1.5	0.4	18
2013	AA	Tennessee	9	3	0	112	107	3.21	1.26	25.4	244	31	77	3.48	3.1	8.6	2.7	0.8	88
2013	AAA	Iowa	1	3	0	20	19	7.16	1.89	6.3	314	37	65	7.03	5.4	8.5	1.6	1.8	26
2013	MLB	CHC	0	0	0	6	4	4.50	2.00	4.1	293	35	75	5.31	7.5	6.0	0.8	0.0	-77

Tall RH worked as a starter at AA, but in relief for the Cubs. FB sits at 94-98 mph. CU and SL can be plus at times, but remain inconsistent. Can struggle with control, but work at AA hints at the potential. Most likely that will be in relief.

Cabrera, Edwar — SP — Texas
Thrws L | Age 26 | 2008 FA (DR)
88-92 FB +++ | CU ++++ | SL ++
EXP MLB DEBUT: 2012 | POTENTIAL: #4 starter | 7C

Year	Lev	Team	W	L	Sv	IP	K	ERA	WHIP	BF/G	OBA	H%	S%	xERA	Ctl	Dom	Cmd	hr/9	BPV
2011	A	Asheville	4	2	0	86	110	3.14	1.10	26.0	241	34	76	3.26	1.9	11.5	6.1	1.0	174
2011	A+	Modesto	4	1	0	81	107	3.56	1.25	25.3	255	37	74	3.65	2.6	11.9	4.7	0.9	163
2012	AA	Tulsa	8	4	0	98	82	2.94	0.90	24.3	190	20	77	2.47	2.1	7.5	3.6	1.4	97
2012	AAA	Colorado Springs	3	1	0	31	39	3.46	1.22	21.0	228	29	81	4.03	3.5	11.3	3.3	1.7	127
2012	MLB	COL	0	2	0	6	5	11.05	2.81	16.0	359	35	69	12.87	11.1	7.9	0.7	4.7	-138

Short, smooth SP who missed entire season with shoulder injury. Mostly a two-pitch guy with average FB and above average CU. K rate has been high at all levels despite mediocre velocity, but has deceptive CU thrown with same arm speed. CB remains below average, but rarely walks hitters or allows HR.

Cabrera, Mauricio — SP — Atlanta
Thrws R | Age 20 | 2010 FA (DR)
93-97 FB ++++ | 80-82 SL ++ | CU +++
EXP MLB DEBUT: 2016 | POTENTIAL: #3 starter | 8D

Year	Lev	Team	W	L	Sv	IP	K	ERA	WHIP	BF/G	OBA	H%	S%	xERA	Ctl	Dom	Cmd	hr/9	BPV
2012	Rk	Danville	2	2	0	57	48	2.99	1.19	19.1	218	28	74	2.53	3.6	7.6	2.1	0.3	56
2013	A	Rome	3	8	0	131	107	4.19	1.44	23.3	242	30	69	3.37	4.9	7.3	1.5	0.2	19

Short Dominican hurler has an electric FB and an improved CU. FB sits at 93-97 mph and hits 100 mph with good sink. SL remains inconsistent and can struggle with command to develop. Elite power arm gives him time to develop. At worst, he has the stuff to be a power RP.

Callahan, Jamie — SP — Boston
Thrws R | Age 19 | 2012 (2) HS (SC)
86-94 FB +++ | 77-80 CB +++ | 80-83 SL ++ | 80-83 CU +
EXP MLB DEBUT: 2016 | POTENTIAL: #3 starter | 8E

Year	Lev	Team	W	L	Sv	IP	K	ERA	WHIP	BF/G	OBA	H%	S%	xERA	Ctl	Dom	Cmd	hr/9	BPV
2012	Rk	GCL Red Sox	1	0	0	8	7	5.49	1.34	6.8	257	33	55	3.12	3.3	7.7	2.3	0.0	67
2013	A-	Lowell	5	1	0	59	54	3.95	1.10	17.8	223	28	64	2.64	2.6	8.2	3.2	0.6	96

Tall, strong RHP who has youth on his side. Can be tough to hit with variety of pitches. Gets ahead of hitters with solid-average FB and uses two breaking balls with varying velocities. FB can be straight and has been flyball pitcher. Poor CU needs to get better as he lacks feel for repeating arm speed and slot.

Caminero, Arquimedes — RP — Miami
Thrws R | Age 27 | 2005 FA (DR)
89-98 FB ++++ | 80-82 SL +++
EXP MLB DEBUT: 2013 | POTENTIAL: Reliever | 7D

Year	Lev	Team	W	L	Sv	IP	K	ERA	WHIP	BF/G	OBA	H%	S%	xERA	Ctl	Dom	Cmd	hr/9	BPV
2012	A+	Jupiter	1	0	1	20	27	0.45	1.04	4.1	174	29	95	1.31	4.0	12.0	3.0	0.0	126
2012	AA	Jacksonville	0	0	2	17	17	3.14	1.51	6.2	248	34	77	3.42	5.2	8.9	1.7	0.0	37
2013	AA	Jacksonville	5	2	5	52	68	3.63	1.06	4.8	188	28	67	2.15	3.6	11.7	3.2	0.7	131
2013	AAA	New Orleans	1	0	0	2	1	0.00	1.00	5.6	0	0	100	0.00	0.0	4.5		0.0	99
2013	MLB	MIA	0	0	0	13	12	2.77	1.00	3.8	214	24	82	3.01	2.1	8.3	4.0	1.4	111

Strong, big-bodied RP dominated two levels of the minors before getting 13 IP with MIA. FB sits in the mid-90s up to 100 and he also cuts it in the low-90s. Pairs the FB with his average, low-80s SL that shows good bite. It has taken a few years for him to develop and stay healthy, but his power FB is ready for a relief role.

Campos, Jose — SP — New York (A)
Thrws R | Age 21 | 2009 FA (Venezuela)
90-95 FB +++ | 77-80 CB +++ | 80-83 CU +++
EXP MLB DEBUT: 2016 | POTENTIAL: #2 starter | 9E

Year	Lev	Team	W	L	Sv	IP	K	ERA	WHIP	BF/G	OBA	H%	S%	xERA	Ctl	Dom	Cmd	hr/9	BPV
2011	A-	Everett	5	5	0	81	85	2.33	0.97	22.0	224	30	77	2.17	1.4	9.4	6.5	0.4	149
2012	A	Charleston (Sc)	3	0	0	24	26	4.09	1.16	19.2	227	30	65	2.94	3.0	9.7	3.3	0.7	112
2013	A	Charleston (Sc)	4	2	2	87	77	3.41	1.13	13.2	251	31	70	2.98	1.7	8.0	4.8	0.5	117

Tall SP who is still getting back to speed after elbow inflammation in '12. Velocity not all the way back, but FB shows plus at times. Keeps ball down and uses pinpoint location to stay ahead. Can wipe out hitters with power CB and CU can be good as well. Pitch movement has been key and simply needs innings.

Cardona, Adonys — SP — Toronto
Thrws R | Age 20 | 2010 FA (VZ)
89-96 FB ++++ | 81-85 SL ++ | 81-84 CU +++
EXP MLB DEBUT: 2017 | POTENTIAL: #2 starter | 9E

Year	Lev	Team	W	L	Sv	IP	K	ERA	WHIP	BF/G	OBA	H%	S%	xERA	Ctl	Dom	Cmd	hr/9	BPV
2011	Rk	GCL Blue Jays	1	3	0	31	35	4.62	1.38	13.1	261	35	66	3.78	3.5	10.1	2.9	0.6	106
2012	Rk	GCL Blue Jays	0	1	0	15	20	6.51	1.64	8.5	259	38	58	4.43	5.9	11.8	2.0	0.6	71
2013	Rk	Bluefield	0	2	1	25	27	6.81	1.91	14.8	331	44	62	5.99	4.7	9.7	2.1	0.4	66

Strong, athletic SP whose season ended early due to elbow issue, but exhibits fast arm speed which produces quality FB. Can change speeds with both FB and excellent CU while SL lags behind. Can be dominant with multiple out pitches and keeps ball down. Could move to RP due to effort in delivery.

Carroll, Damion — SP — Tampa Bay
Thrws R | Age 20 | 2012 (6) HS (VA)
87-95 FB +++ | 80-81 CB ++ | 82-84 SL ++ | CU ++
EXP MLB DEBUT: 2017 | POTENTIAL: #3 starter | 8E

Year	Lev	Team	W	L	Sv	IP	K	ERA	WHIP	BF/G	OBA	H%	S%	xERA	Ctl	Dom	Cmd	hr/9	BPV
2012	Rk	GCL Rays	1	0	0	19	20	2.36	1.68	8.6	194	28	84	3.16	9.0	9.4	1.1	0.0	-54
2013	Rk	GCL Rays	0	0	0	2	3	4.29	0.95	4.0	0	0	50	0.00	8.6	12.9	1.5	0.0	18

Tall and very projectable pitcher with limited pro experience, but has high ceiling. Needs to iron out crude mechanics and find consistency in release point. Throws hard now with natural strength and has potential to reach high 90s with adjustments. Uses two breaking balls and CU, though none are average yet.

Cash, Ralston — RP — Los Angeles (N)
Thrws R | Age 22 | 2010 (2) HS (GA)
88-92 FB ++ | 75-77 CB ++ | CU ++
EXP MLB DEBUT: 2016 | POTENTIAL: #4 starter | 7D

Year	Lev	Team	W	L	Sv	IP	K	ERA	WHIP	BF/G	OBA	H%	S%	xERA	Ctl	Dom	Cmd	hr/9	BPV
2010	Rk	AZL Dodgers	2	2	0	30	25	3.60	1.33	13.8	255	33	70	3.08	3.3	7.5	2.3	0.0	64
2010	Rk	Ogden	0	0	0	6	5	12.00	2.33	15.5	394	43	56	10.72	4.5	7.5	1.7	3.0	32
2012	A	Great Lakes	1	6	0	40	29	6.49	1.72	20.3	284	33	62	5.30	5.4	6.5	1.2	0.9	-10
2013	Rk	AZL Dodgers	0	0	0	2	5	0.00	0.50	6.6	151	61	100	0.00	0.0	22.5		0.0	423
2013	A	Great Lakes	4	3	0	53	56	3.21	1.37	13.9	210	28	78	3.23	5.6	9.5	1.7	0.7	38

Tall RHP put together his best season since he was drafted in '10. FB control still an issue as his 5.6 Ctl was a career worst, but 9.5 Dom was his best. Arm action is clean, though he needs to learn to repeat his mechanics better. CB is showing better depth and bite while CU is becoming a more usable third offering.

Castillo, Jose — SP — Tampa Bay
Thrws L | Age 18 | 2012 FA (Venezuela)
88-95 FB +++ | 75-78 CB ++ | 82-84 CU ++
EXP MLB DEBUT: 2018 | POTENTIAL: #3 starter | 8D

Year	Lev	Team	W	L	Sv	IP	K	ERA	WHIP	BF/G	OBA	H%	S%	xERA	Ctl	Dom	Cmd	hr/9	BPV
2013	Rk	GCL Rays	2	2	0	30	25	5.96	1.39	10.6	285	35	54	3.93	2.4	7.5	3.1	0.3	88

Tall and projectable lefty who needs time to develop. Has raw ingredients to be special, though may pitch in short-season for a few years. Very tough on LHH due to height and angle. Uses solid-average FB that can add ticks. CU shows improvement and will need polish to battle RHH. CB is distant third offering.

Chaffee, Ryan — RP — Los Angeles (A)
Thrws R | Age 26 | 2008 (3) Chipola JC
90-95 FB ++++ | 78-82 CB +++ | 81-84 CU ++
EXP MLB DEBUT: 2014 | POTENTIAL: Setup reliever | 7C

Year	Lev	Team	W	L	Sv	IP	K	ERA	WHIP	BF/G	OBA	H%	S%	xERA	Ctl	Dom	Cmd	hr/9	BPV
2011	A+	Inland Empire	2	10	0	96	87	7.30	1.68	14.4	296	36	56	5.51	4.5	8.1	1.8	1.0	43
2011	AAA	Salt Lake	1	1	0	9	8	6.85	1.85	10.7	334	36	71	8.32	3.9	7.8	2.0	2.9	53
2012	A+	Inland Empire	2	0	7	22	28	2.43	1.17	4.9	214	30	83	2.86	3.6	11.4	3.1	0.8	124
2012	AA	Arkansas	5	1	0	43	56	2.72	1.19	4.7	165	24	79	2.17	5.7	11.7	2.1	0.6	76
2013	AA	Arkansas	3	2	0	61	73	2.94	1.24	5.3	192	28	77	2.45	5.1	10.7	2.1	0.4	72

Tall pitcher who saved career by moving to pen in '11. Can be tough to hit due to arm speed and FB thrown on downhill plane. Has been menace to RHH with solid-average FB that can register Ks. Has bouts of wildness and needs better FB location to stay ahead in count. Has lots of effort in deceptive delivery.

Chafin, Andrew — SP — Arizona
Thrws L | Age 24 | 2011 (1) Kent State
90-93 FB +++ | 81-83 SL ++++ | CU ++
EXP MLB DEBUT: 2014 | POTENTIAL: #4 starter | 7C

Year	Lev	Team	W	L	Sv	IP	K	ERA	WHIP	BF/G	OBA	H%	S%	xERA	Ctl	Dom	Cmd	hr/9	BPV
2011	NCAA	Kent St.	8	1	0	89	105	2.02	0.92	23.8	190	28	78	1.40	2.3	10.6	4.6	0.2	146
2011	Rk	AZL D'backs	0	0	0	1	2	0.00	1.00	3.8	262	55	100	2.23	0.0	18.0		0.0	342
2012	A+	Visalia	6	6	0	122	150	4.94	1.48	17.5	245	34	67	4.12	5.1	11.1	2.2	0.9	80
2013	A+	Visalia	3	1	0	31	32	4.65	1.48	22.2	268	36	67	3.89	4.1	9.3	2.3	0.3	75
2013	AA	Mobile	10	7	0	126	87	2.85	1.26	24.5	249	30	77	3.17	2.9	6.2	2.1	0.4	51

Another solid season, going 13-8 with a 3.20 ERA, but drop in Dom is a concern. Good 90-93 mph FB, a plus SL, CB, and a decent CU. Competes on the mound and has the stuff to dominate. Future could be in relief where he shows better velocity.

Chapman,Kevin — RP — Houston

EXP MLB DEBUT: 2013 | POTENTIAL: Setup reliever | 6A

Thrws L Age 26
2010 (4) Florida

Velo	Pitch	Grade
89-94	FB	+++
79-83	SL	+++
	CU	+

Year	Lev	Team	W	L	Sv	IP	K	ERA	WHIP	BF/G	OBA	H%	S%	xERA	Ctl	Dom	Cmd	hr/9	BPV
2011	A+	Wilmington	0	2	7	22	40	4.89	1.40	6.2	278	51	63	3.87	2.9	16.3	5.7	0.4	234
2011	AA	NW Arkansas	1	2	3	39	50	5.05	1.48	6.7	251	35	68	4.43	4.8	11.5	2.4	1.1	94
2012	AA	Corpus Christi	6	3	2	58	59	2.64	1.40	5.0	231	31	81	3.19	5.0	9.2	1.8	0.3	49
2013	AAA	Oklahoma City	1	2	2	50	61	3.23	1.55	4.9	229	33	79	3.59	6.5	10.9	1.7	0.4	41
2013	MLB	HOU	1	1	1	20	15	1.77	1.28	3.3	185	22	88	2.51	5.8	6.7	1.2	0.4	-18

Strong, durable RP who reached HOU and was reliable out of pen. Upside is limited due to crude arm action and lack of offspeed pitch. Dominates LHH with excellent FB/SL combo. FB features average life. SL has late break and can be legitimate out pitch, but doesn't throw for strikes. Could become setup guy.

Chargois,J.T. — RP — Minnesota

EXP MLB DEBUT: 2016 | POTENTIAL: Closer | 7C

Thrws R Age 23
2012 (2) Rice

Velo	Pitch	Grade
90-97	FB	++++
80-82	SL	+++
81-83	CU	+

Year	Lev	Team	W	L	Sv	IP	K	ERA	WHIP	BF/G	OBA	H%	S%	xERA	Ctl	Dom	Cmd	hr/9	BPV
2010	NCAA	Rice	3	2	0	27	14	3.32	1.37	7.6	302	32	79	4.79	1.3	4.6	3.5	1.0	66
2011	NCAA	Rice	0	2	2	6	7	14.52	2.74	4.9	314	36	47	10.19	13.1	10.2	0.8	2.9	-152
2012	NCAA	Rice	4	1	8	37	38	2.18	1.08	5.8	211	29	79	2.07	2.9	9.2	3.2	0.2	105
2012	Rk	Elizabethton	0	0	5	16	22	1.69	0.94	5.0	181	30	80	1.13	2.8	12.4	4.4	0.0	165

Big, strong RP who didn't pitch in '13 due to strained elbow and underwent TJ surgery in September. Will likely miss all of '14. When healthy, can dominate with explosive FB that features late life. Complements heater with excellent, power SL. Keeps ball low in ground and has deception to keep hitters off guard.

Church,Andrew — SP — New York (N)

EXP MLB DEBUT: 2018 | POTENTIAL: #4 starter | 7E

Thrws R Age 19
2013 (2) HS (NV)

Velo	Pitch	Grade
91-93	FB	+++
73-76	CB	+++
	CU	++

Year	Lev	Team	W	L	Sv	IP	K	ERA	WHIP	BF/G	OBA	H%	S%	xERA	Ctl	Dom	Cmd	hr/9	BPV
2013	Rk	GCL Mets	3	3	0	35	19	5.91	1.63	17.3	332	37	62	5.49	2.1	4.9	2.4	0.5	50

Very inexperienced prep pitcher with a lot of projection left in his arsenal. Follows 91-93 mph FB with a curve that could become plus. Good arm action but inconsistent mechanics; doesn't yet get a lot of movement on his FB and it finds bats. High ceiling due to his raw stuff, but needs to learn the art of pitching.

Cisco,Drew — SP — Cincinnati

EXP MLB DEBUT: 2015 | POTENTIAL: #4 starter | 7D

Thrws R Age 22
2010 (6) HS (SC)

Velo	Pitch	Grade
88-92	FB	+++
74-76	CB	++
75-78	CU	++

Year	Lev	Team	W	L	Sv	IP	K	ERA	WHIP	BF/G	OBA	H%	S%	xERA	Ctl	Dom	Cmd	hr/9	BPV
2012	Rk	Billings	4	1	0	58	45	3.41	1.15	15.4	268	32	71	3.39	1.1	7.0	6.4	0.6	114
2013	A	Dayton	5	7	0	130	99	3.87	1.26	22.1	287	34	71	4.07	1.1	6.8	6.2	0.8	111

Has advanced feel for pitching and excellent command of all three pitches though not overpowering stuff. Was brought back slowly following TJ surgery, but innings will ramp up and could move quickly. FB has nice late action that he complements with above-average CB and decent CU.

Clark,Tyler — RP — Detroit

EXP MLB DEBUT: 2014 | POTENTIAL: Middle reliever | 6B

Thrws R Age 25
2010 (24) Missouri

Velo	Pitch	Grade
90-96	FB	++++
75-78	CB	++
82-84	CU	++

Year	Lev	Team	W	L	Sv	IP	K	ERA	WHIP	BF/G	OBA	H%	S%	xERA	Ctl	Dom	Cmd	hr/9	BPV
2011	Rk	GCL Tigers	0	0	0	17	25	3.71	1.65	5.8	238	38	78	4.09	6.9	13.2	1.9	0.5	70
2011	A	West Michigan	0	0	0	9	6	2.97	1.43	6.4	260	29	83	4.33	4.0	5.9	1.5	1.0	18
2012	A+	Lakeland	6	1	9	42	59	0.64	0.85	5.0	138	23	94	0.65	3.6	12.6	3.5	0.2	147
2012	AA	Erie	0	0	0	7	7	7.61	1.97	4.9	285	35	62	6.29	7.6	8.9	1.2	1.3	-28
2013	AA	Erie	1	0	0	32	33	3.63	1.80	6.8	290	38	79	4.99	5.9	9.2	1.6	0.3	26

Hard-throwing RP who may not throw consistent strikes, but has excellent cutting action to plus FB. Throws with deceptive delivery to keep hitters off-guard. Mostly works with FB and cutter while mixing in fringy CB and decent CU. Has been tough on LHH and keeps ball in park despite flyball tendencies.

Clarkin,Ian — SP — New York (A)

EXP MLB DEBUT: 2018 | POTENTIAL: #3 starter | 8D

Thrws L Age 19
2013 (1) HS (CA)

Velo	Pitch	Grade
87-94	FB	+++
75-78	CB	+++
80-83	CU	++

Year	Lev	Team	W	L	Sv	IP	K	ERA	WHIP	BF/G	OBA	H%	S%	xERA	Ctl	Dom	Cmd	hr/9	BPV
2013	Rk	GCL Yankees	0	2	0	5	4	10.80	1.80	7.7	262	23	43	7.73	7.2	7.2	1.0	3.6	-47

High upside arm whose focus will be on polishing delivery and improving FB command and location. Showcases quality offerings consisting of FB and CB that can be tough, though erratic. Has feel for CU, but can be inconsistent. Frame and arm speed suggests projection and should be high Dom pitcher.

Claudio,Alexander — RP — Texas

EXP MLB DEBUT: 2015 | POTENTIAL: Setup reliever | 6B

Thrws L Age 22
2010 (27) HS (PR)

Velo	Pitch	Grade
84-89	FB	++
74-78	CB	++
64-70	CU	++++

Year	Lev	Team	W	L	Sv	IP	K	ERA	WHIP	BF/G	OBA	H%	S%	xERA	Ctl	Dom	Cmd	hr/9	BPV
2011	Rk	AZL Rangers	4	0	1	25	29	2.15	1.16	6.7	220	31	82	2.49	3.2	10.4	3.2	0.4	118
2011	A-	Spokane	1	0	0	3	2	0.00	1.00	11.5	191	24	100	1.46	3.0	6.0	2.0	0.0	45
2012	Rk	AZL Rangers	4	0	1	45	54	1.80	0.91	12.0	221	32	80	1.72	1.0	10.8	10.8	0.2	185
2013	A	Hickory	3	1	11	47	62	1.15	0.62	6.7	142	22	85	0.27	1.3	11.9	8.9	0.4	196
2013	AA	Frisco	1	5	0	31	29	2.88	1.25	6.0	241	31	78	3.22	3.2	8.4	2.6	0.6	83

Tall, very thin RP who thrives with sidearm delivery. Bypassed High-A upon promotion in June in first full season as pro. Lacks velocity and big-breaking CB, but has great success with unusual CU. Thrown at very low velocity, but features screwball action. Hitters can't square it up and make weak contact.

Cleto,Maikel — RP — Kansas City

EXP MLB DEBUT: 2011 | POTENTIAL: Setup reliever | 7C

Thrws R Age 25
2006 FA (DR)

Velo	Pitch	Grade
94-98	FB	++++
84-87	SL	+++
81-83	CU	+

Year	Lev	Team	W	L	Sv	IP	K	ERA	WHIP	BF/G	OBA	H%	S%	xERA	Ctl	Dom	Cmd	hr/9	BPV
2012	AAA	Memphis	3	2	2	53	66	5.41	1.37	5.0	254	36	59	3.76	3.7	11.2	3.0	0.7	118
2012	MLB	STL	0	0	0	9	15	7.00	1.67	4.5	339	46	73	8.88	2.0	15.0	7.5	4.0	234
2013	AAA	Memphis	2	3	0	53	53	6.95	1.92	15.7	247	32	62	5.07	9.0	9.0	1.0	0.7	-63
2013	AAA	Omaha	1	2	1	38	36	3.55	1.47	8.6	246	32	75	3.53	5.0	8.5	1.7	0.2	37
2013	MLB	KC	0	0	0	2	5	19.57	2.61	12.5	435	73	20	13.06	3.9	19.6	5.0	3.9	265

Big, durable RP who has seen majors in each of past 3 seasons. Converted to RP in '12 to take advantage of arm strength. Owns explosive, plus FB, though can be straight at upper velocity. Hasn't found consistent secondary offering, though hard SL can wipe out hitters. Max effort delivery tough to repeat.

Clevinger,Michael — SP — Los Angeles (A)

EXP MLB DEBUT: 2016 | POTENTIAL: #3 starter | 8E

Thrws R Age 23
2011 (4) Seminole State JC

Velo	Pitch	Grade
89-94	FB	+++
81-83	SL	+++
77-80	CB	++
81-84	CU	++

Year	Lev	Team	W	L	Sv	IP	K	ERA	WHIP	BF/G	OBA	H%	S%	xERA	Ctl	Dom	Cmd	hr/9	BPV
2010	NCAA	The Citadel	5	3	0	92	77	5.17	1.63	25.6	307	37	68	5.21	3.4	7.5	2.2	0.7	61
2011	Rk	Orem	0	0	0	4	5	2.25	1.25	5.4	210	32	80	2.26	4.5	11.3	2.5	0.0	99
2012	A	Cedar Rapids	1	1	0	41	34	3.73	1.22	20.7	242	29	70	3.24	2.9	7.5	2.6	0.7	75
2013	Rk	AZL Angels	0	0	0	3	3	3.00	1.33	6.2	191	27	75	2.27	6.0	9.0	1.5	0.0	18
2013	Rk	Orem	0	1	0	2	2	20.45	3.64	14.2	492	59	38	13.55	8.2	8.2	1.0	0.0	-56

Tall, quick-armed SP who returned in August after TJ surgery in '12. Has potential to own four average or better offerings. Above average SL is best pitch and can miss bats. Solid FB used to set up secondary pitches and CU has potential. Tendency to overthrow and can be inefficient when going for Ks.

Clinard,Will — RP — Detroit

EXP MLB DEBUT: 2015 | POTENTIAL: Middle reliever | 6B

Thrws R Age 24
2012 (19) Vanderbilt

Velo	Pitch	Grade
88-92	FB	+++
87-89	CT	+++
80-83	SL	++

Year	Lev	Team	W	L	Sv	IP	K	ERA	WHIP	BF/G	OBA	H%	S%	xERA	Ctl	Dom	Cmd	hr/9	BPV
2012	NCAA	Vanderbilt	7	3	5	54	47	4.83	1.50	7.8	265	32	68	4.42	4.3	7.8	1.8	0.8	42
2012	A-	Connecticut	2	1	2	13	19	1.38	0.77	6.7	179	31	80	0.67	1.4	13.2	9.5	0.0	217
2012	A	West Michigan	1	1	2	24	20	2.99	1.41	7.3	284	35	79	4.04	2.6	7.5	2.9	0.4	82
2013	A+	Lakeland	1	2	2	28	23	1.60	0.93	7.0	209	26	84	1.77	1.6	7.4	4.6	0.3	107
2013	AA	Erie	2	3	1	34	26	5.54	1.67	7.0	278	31	71	5.74	5.3	6.9	1.3	1.6	-1

Polished, tall RP who is advancing quickly. Uses height and arm slot to throw on downhill plane which makes it tough for hitters to elevate. Repeats delivery, though has erratic control and command. Not much upside or projection in average FB, but has hard cutter that serves as K pitch. Improving SL is key.

Cole,A.J. — SP — Washington

EXP MLB DEBUT: 2015 | POTENTIAL: #2 starter | 9D

Thrws R Age 22
2010 (4) HS (FL)

Velo	Pitch	Grade
90-97	FB	++++
77-79	CB	+++
	CU	+++

Year	Lev	Team	W	L	Sv	IP	K	ERA	WHIP	BF/G	OBA	H%	S%	xERA	Ctl	Dom	Cmd	hr/9	BPV
2011	A	Hagerstown	4	7	0	89	108	4.04	1.25	18.1	257	36	68	3.43	2.4	10.9	4.5	0.6	149
2012	A	Burlington	6	3	0	95	102	2.08	1.02	19.2	225	30	83	2.50	1.8	9.6	5.4	0.7	143
2012	A+	Stockton	0	7	0	38	31	7.82	1.84	22.1	359	41	59	7.55	2.4	7.3	3.1	1.7	86
2013	A+	Potomac	6	3	0	97	102	4.26	1.23	21.8	260	33	68	3.89	2.1	9.5	4.4	1.1	131
2013	AA	Harrisburg	4	2	0	45	49	2.20	0.91	24.0	196	26	79	1.81	2.0	9.8	4.9	0.6	140

Tall, athletic pitcher posted lights-out second half at Double-A. Throws consistent strikes from 3/4 arm slot, with ideal mix of power and control. Even without a lot of deception, pitches good enough to get hitters out. FB shows good late action, CU and CB on verge of becoming plus.

Colome,Alex — SP — Tampa Bay

Thrws R Age 25 | 2007 FA (DR)

EXP MLB DEBUT: 2013 | POTENTIAL: #3 starter | 8C

Velo	Pitch	Grade
88-95	FB	++++
77-79	CB	+++
81-86	SL	++
80-84	CU	++

Year	Lev	Team	W	L	Sv	IP	K	ERA	WHIP	BF/G	OBA	H%	S%	xERA	Ctl	Dom	Cmd	hr/9	BPV
2011	AA	Montgomery	3	4	0	52	31	4.15	1.33	24.0	219	24	70	3.43	4.8	5.4	1.1	0.9	-16
2012	AA	Montgomery	8	3	0	75	75	3.48	1.37	22.5	246	33	73	3.27	4.1	9.0	2.2	0.2	70
2012	AAA	Durham	0	1	0	16	15	3.33	1.30	22.2	208	26	75	2.90	5.0	8.3	1.7	0.6	33
2013	AAA	Durham	4	6	0	70	72	3.08	1.31	20.7	242	32	78	3.43	3.7	9.2	2.5	0.6	84
2013	MLB	TAM	1	1	0	16	12	2.25	1.44	22.7	237	27	90	4.17	5.1	6.8	1.3	1.1	3

Injury-prone, high-upside SP who has potential to make impact. Season ended in June due to elbow strain, but healthy now. Exhibits pitch movement which results in high K totals. Plus FB is best pitch and CB and hard SL are complements. CB is best secondary, but needs better CU and overall command/control.

Colvin,Brody — SP — Philadelphia

Thrws R Age 23 | 2009 (7) HS (LA)

EXP MLB DEBUT: 2015 | POTENTIAL: Middle reliever | 7D

Velo	Pitch	Grade
90-94	FB	+++
75-77	CB	+++
	CU	++

Year	Lev	Team	W	L	Sv	IP	K	ERA	WHIP	BF/G	OBA	H%	S%	xERA	Ctl	Dom	Cmd	hr/9	BPV
2010	A	Lakewood	6	8	0	138	120	3.39	1.30	21.1	262	33	74	3.52	2.7	7.8	2.9	0.5	85
2011	A+	Clearwater	3	8	0	116	78	4.72	1.49	22.8	286	33	69	4.64	3.3	6.0	1.9	0.8	39
2012	A+	Clearwater	5	6	0	105	93	4.28	1.56	20.0	276	35	72	4.34	4.4	8.0	1.8	0.4	43
2012	AA	Reading	1	4	0	32	16	11.18	2.05	22.4	321	33	43	7.47	6.4	4.5	0.7	1.7	-75
2013	AA	Reading	3	2	0	77	36	6.42	1.73	16.7	267	28	63	5.24	6.3	4.2	0.7	1.1	-77

Highly regarded when signed away from an LSU scholarship, his progression has stalled above Low-A. PHI still sees him as SP, but much better in short bullpen stints at AA. Inconsistent release point has led to a ton of walks in the past two seasons, and strikeouts in decline. Future looks like a two-pitch reliever.

Comer,Kevin — SP — Houston

Thrws R Age 21 | 2011 (1-S) HS (NJ)

EXP MLB DEBUT: 2017 | POTENTIAL: #3 starter | 8E

Velo	Pitch	Grade
88-95	FB	+++
74-78	CB	+++
	CU	++

Year	Lev	Team	W	L	Sv	IP	K	ERA	WHIP	BF/G	OBA	H%	S%	xERA	Ctl	Dom	Cmd	hr/9	BPV
2012	Rk	Bluefield	3	3	0	43	29	3.97	1.18	17.3	261	30	68	3.59	1.7	6.1	3.6	0.8	82
2012	Rk	Greeneville	0	1	0	6	5	9.00	2.00	14.5	371	40	60	9.44	3.0	7.5	2.5	3.0	72
2013	A-	Tri City	2	5	1	45	44	4.98	1.50	13.0	282	37	65	4.24	3.6	8.8	2.4	0.4	79

Tall and projectable starter who hasn't pitched in full-season ball. Future role still in question as he possesses inconsistent velocity and below average CU. Uses athletic delivery that he repeats well, but has tendency to slow arm when aiming. Induces groundballs with quality sinker and CB could evolve into plus pitch.

Conley,Adam — SP — Miami

Thrws L Age 24 | 2011 (2) Washington State

EXP MLB DEBUT: 2014 | POTENTIAL: #3 starter | 8D

Velo	Pitch	Grade
88-95	FB	++++
	SL	+++
	CU	++++

Year	Lev	Team	W	L	Sv	IP	K	ERA	WHIP	BF/G	OBA	H%	S%	xERA	Ctl	Dom	Cmd	hr/9	BPV
2011	NCAA	Washington St.	6	7	0	108	83	3.50	1.30	27.8	271	33	72	3.44	2.3	6.9	3.1	0.3	82
2011	Rk	GCL Marlins	0	0	0	2	2	0.00	0.50	3.3	151	22	100	0.00	0.0	9.0		0.0	180
2012	A	Greensboro	7	3	0	74	84	2.79	1.11	20.8	217	30	76	2.45	2.9	10.2	3.5	0.5	123
2012	A+	Jupiter	4	2	0	52	51	4.48	1.49	18.8	286	38	67	3.91	3.3	8.8	2.7	0.0	88
2013	AA	Jacksonville	11	7	0	138	129	3.26	1.17	21.2	243	31	72	2.93	2.4	8.4	3.5	0.5	104

Continues to be successful in the rotation, improving his Ctl and Cmd from '12. Comes at hitters with a upper-80s, low-90s FB that tops out at 97, a solid average CU with good fade, and an inconsistent, sweeping SL that flashes above average. Durability concerns, and funk in his delivery affect control.

Constante,Jacob — SP — Cincinnati

Thrws L Age 20 | 2012 FA (DR)

EXP MLB DEBUT: 2018 | POTENTIAL: #4 starter | 8E

Velo	Pitch	Grade
89-92	FB	+++
80-83	SL	+++
83-84	CU	++

Year	Lev	Team	W	L	Sv	IP	K	ERA	WHIP	BF/G	OBA	H%	S%	xERA	Ctl	Dom	Cmd	hr/9	BPV
2013		Did not pitch in the US																	

Big, durable power lefty posted great numbers in the DSL in 2013 (12.8 Dom, 1.86 ERA), though struggled with control at times. Throws with easy arm action and works down in the zone. Plus FB has good life. As with most young pitchers, needs to gain consistency with secondary pitches.

Contreras,Carlos — SP — Cincinnati

Thrws R Age 23 | 2008 FA (DR)

EXP MLB DEBUT: 2016 | POTENTIAL: #4 starter/reliever | 8E

Velo	Pitch	Grade
91-93	FB	++++
80-83	CU	++++
75-78	CB	+++

Year	Lev	Team	W	L	Sv	IP	K	ERA	WHIP	BF/G	OBA	H%	S%	xERA	Ctl	Dom	Cmd	hr/9	BPV
2011	Rk	Billings	2	1	0	36	38	5.00	1.61	8.9	256	32	72	4.95	5.8	9.5	1.7	1.3	34
2012	A	Dayton	0	1	16	50	51	3.23	0.96	4.7	170	20	71	2.09	3.4	9.1	2.7	1.1	91
2012	A+	Bakersfield	1	0	4	10	12	2.70	1.40	4.7	242	33	85	3.89	4.5	10.8	2.4	0.9	91
2013	A+	Bakersfield	5	7	0	90	96	3.80	1.23	20.3	216	28	72	3.15	4.1	9.6	2.3	0.9	80
2013	AA	Pensacola	3	2	0	42	26	2.78	1.35	22.0	233	27	80	3.26	4.5	5.6	1.2	0.4	-3

Short, RHP moved back to starting rotation for first time since '09 as CB developed enough to give viable third pitch. Posted 2.20 ERA final month at Double-A. Two plus pitches are FB and CU with exceptional movement. Consistency with mechanics and release point would help limit walks.

Cooney,Tim — SP — St. Louis

Thrws L Age 23 | 2012 (3) Wake Forest

EXP MLB DEBUT: 2015 | POTENTIAL: #4 starter | 7B

Velo	Pitch	Grade
88-92	FB	++
75-77	CB	++
82-85	SL	+++

Year	Lev	Team	W	L	Sv	IP	K	ERA	WHIP	BF/G	OBA	H%	S%	xERA	Ctl	Dom	Cmd	hr/9	BPV
2011	NCAA	Wake Forest	7	3	0	98	91	3.02	1.23	28.4	271	33	79	3.90	1.6	8.3	5.1	0.9	124
2012	NCAA	Wake Forest	6	7	0	99	90	3.82	1.38	27.7	262	33	72	3.72	3.5	8.2	2.4	0.5	72
2012	A-	Batavia	3	3	0	55	43	3.42	1.16	16.9	265	32	72	3.39	1.3	7.0	5.4	0.7	109
2013	A+	Palm Beach	3	3	0	36	23	2.75	1.17	23.9	272	32	76	3.15	1.0	5.8	5.8	0.3	95
2013	AA	Springfield	7	10	0	118	125	3.81	1.27	24.2	284	37	70	3.88	1.4	9.5	6.9	0.6	152

Finesse LHP has a good feel for pitching. Keeps hitters off-balance with four quality offerings. FB sits at 89-93 with good movement. Mixes in a mid-70s CB, CT, and CU. Locates all pitches well and changes speed. Dom spike raises profile with good Ctl.

Corcino,Daniel — SP — Cincinnati

Thrws R Age 23 | 2008 FA (DR)

EXP MLB DEBUT: 2015 | POTENTIAL: #3 starter | 8D

Velo	Pitch	Grade
91-95	FB	++++
75-78	SL	++++
84-85	CU	+++

Year	Lev	Team	W	L	Sv	IP	K	ERA	WHIP	BF/G	OBA	H%	S%	xERA	Ctl	Dom	Cmd	hr/9	BPV
2010	Rk	Billings	1	3	0	39	31	3.44	1.40	18.4	256	31	75	3.70	3.9	7.1	1.8	0.5	41
2010	A	Dayton	1	1	0	31	29	4.34	1.48	22.3	261	34	69	3.79	4.3	8.4	1.9	0.3	52
2011	A	Dayton	11	7	0	139	156	3.43	1.16	21.3	246	33	72	3.12	2.2	10.1	4.6	0.6	140
2012	AA	Pensacola	8	8	0	143	126	3.02	1.23	22.3	216	27	77	2.84	4.1	7.9	1.9	0.6	50
2013	AAA	Louisville	7	14	0	129	90	5.86	1.66	20.6	279	31	66	5.36	5.1	6.3	1.2	1.2	-6

Command and mechanics poor in '13, but stuff good as ever. Short RH attacks hitters with plus 90-94 FB, good SL, and CU with nice sink. Overthrows to make up for lack of downward action on pitches; adding deception to delivery would help him miss more bats. Cmd issues limited IP so needs to prove durability.

Cote,Jordan — SP — New York (A)

Thrws R Age 21 | 2011 (3) HS (NH)

EXP MLB DEBUT: 2017 | POTENTIAL: #3 starter | 8E

Velo	Pitch	Grade
88-92	FB	+++
77-80	CB	++
80-82	SL	++
	CU	+++

Year	Lev	Team	W	L	Sv	IP	K	ERA	WHIP	BF/G	OBA	H%	S%	xERA	Ctl	Dom	Cmd	hr/9	BPV
2012	Rk	GCL Yankees	3	0	0	27	25	0.99	0.92	17.0	215	29	88	1.51	1.3	8.3	6.3	0.0	131
2013	Rk	GCL Yankees 2	0	1	0	28	20	0.96	0.82	11.3	186	22	91	1.24	1.6	6.4	4.0	0.3	90

Tall, projectable SP who returned to Rookie ball and showed progress with cleaner and more efficient delivery. Hasn't yet realized power potential, but spots FB in lower half to induce GB. Inconsistent secondary pitches need time to develop, particularly CB which can be good. CU may be best present pitch.

Cotton,Jharel — RP — Los Angeles (N)

Thrws R Age 22 | 2012 (20) East Carolina

EXP MLB DEBUT: 2015 | POTENTIAL: Reliever | 7D

Velo	Pitch	Grade
91-95	FB	++++
	CB	++

Year	Lev	Team	W	L	Sv	IP	K	ERA	WHIP	BF/G	OBA	H%	S%	xERA	Ctl	Dom	Cmd	hr/9	BPV
2012	NCAA	East Carolina	8	3	0	74	62	3.65	1.35	20.6	267	34	71	3.52	2.9	7.5	2.6	0.2	75
2012	Rk	Ogden	1	0	0	15	20	1.20	0.80	10.9	175	29	83	0.72	1.8	12.0	6.7	0.0	185
2013	A	Great Lakes	2	5	0	58	58	3.56	1.02	20.3	204	26	65	2.20	2.6	9.0	3.4	0.6	109
2013	A+	Rancho Cuca	0	0	0	5	3	1.73	1.35	10.8	214	26	86	2.61	5.2	5.2	1.0	0.0	-29
2013	AA	Chattanooga	0	2	0	10	11	8.10	1.80	5.8	347	47	50	5.65	2.7	9.9	3.7	0.0	123

Hard-throwing RP had an impressive first full season of pro ball in '13, reaching AA. Sits in the low-to-mid 90s with his FB, seen up to 98. The CB a tick below average, though it flashes the potential to play average. Saw time as a starter, but mechanics point to a bullpen role in the future.

Crabbe,Timothy — RP — Cincinnati

Thrws R Age 26 | 2009 (14) Westmont College

EXP MLB DEBUT: 2015 | POTENTIAL: #4 starter/reliever | 7D

Velo	Pitch	Grade
90-95	FB	+++
	SL	++++
	CB	+
	CU	+

Year	Lev	Team	W	L	Sv	IP	K	ERA	WHIP	BF/G	OBA	H%	S%	xERA	Ctl	Dom	Cmd	hr/9	BPV
2011	A+	Bakersfield	5	5	0	111	123	3.41	1.29	21.7	237	32	75	3.38	3.7	10.0	2.7	0.7	97
2012	A+	Bakersfield	5	2	0	57	60	3.30	1.07	22.2	222	29	71	2.70	2.4	9.4	4.0	0.8	124
2012	AA	Pensacola	3	6	0	86	93	4.91	1.71	21.7	250	32	72	4.82	6.9	9.7	1.4	0.9	7
2013	AA	Pensacola	7	8	0	140	101	3.28	1.27	22.9	264	31	77	3.78	2.3	6.5	2.8	0.8	72
2013	AAA	Louisville	0	1	0	12	8	0.74	1.31	25.2	207	25	94	2.43	5.2	5.9	1.1	0.0	-15

Has risen further than most expected. Throws nice mid 90s FB with a plus SL. Dom dropped in '13 but better overall results. Has shown the ability to dominate hitters at times, though stuff is not overpowering. Could move to pen if he doesn't develop his CB or CU to average in near future.

Crawford, Jonathon — SP — Detroit

EXP MLB DEBUT: 2015 | POTENTIAL: #3 starter / Closer | 8C

Thrws R Age 22
2013 (1) Florida

90-96	FB	++++
82-87	SL	+++
83-86	CU	+

Year	Lev	Team	W	L	Sv	IP	K	ERA	WHIP	BF/G	OBA	H%	S%	xERA	Ctl	Dom	Cmd	hr/9	BPV
2011	NCAA	Florida	0	0	0	3	4	5.63	2.19	3.2	399	50	83	10.25	2.8	11.3	4.0	2.8	145
2012	NCAA	Florida	6	2	0	77	73	3.15	1.28	16.7	256	34	74	3.18	2.8	8.5	3.0	0.2	96
2013	NCAA	Florida	3	6	0	86	69	3.86	1.36	24.0	248	30	71	3.43	3.9	7.2	1.9	0.4	43
2013	A-	Connecticut	0	2	0	19	21	1.89	1.26	9.7	219	32	83	2.41	4.3	9.9	2.3	0.0	82

Durable, strong SP with an extreme GB tendency. FB can be explosive and tough for hitters to pick up, especially low in zone. Maintains velocity and counters with hard SL that can be plus. Development of CU will dictate future role, but has some feel for it. Command hindered by inconsistent release point.

Crick, Kyle — SP — San Francisco

EXP MLB DEBUT: 2015 | POTENTIAL: #2 starter | 9D

Thrws R Age 21
2011 (1) HS (TX)

94-98	FB	++++
72-74	CB	++
81-83	SL	+++
78-82	CU	+++

Year	Lev	Team	W	L	Sv	IP	K	ERA	WHIP	BF/G	OBA	H%	S%	xERA	Ctl	Dom	Cmd	hr/9	BPV
2011	Rk	AZL Giants	1	0	0	7	8	6.43	2.43	5.2	313	43	71	6.66	10.3	10.3	1.0	0.0	-75
2012	A	Augusta	7	6	0	111	128	2.51	1.28	19.8	193	29	79	2.22	5.4	10.4	1.9	0.1	58
2013	A+	San Jose	3	1	0	68	95	1.58	1.28	20.0	200	33	87	2.31	5.1	12.5	2.4	0.1	105

Big, strong RH dominated hitters in High-A, getting Ks using his mid-90s FB and plus SL. He also throws an average CU and CB that has some potential. Plus arm speed makes the ball explode out of his hand, making all his offerings lively and difficult to pick up. Like most raw SP, just needs time to further develop his arsenal.

Crockett, Kyle — RP — Cleveland

EXP MLB DEBUT: 2014 | POTENTIAL: Situational reliever | 6A

Thrws L Age 22
2013 (4) Virginia

89-92	FB	+++
79-82	SL	+++
	CU	+

Year	Lev	Team	W	L	Sv	IP	K	ERA	WHIP	BF/G	OBA	H%	S%	xERA	Ctl	Dom	Cmd	hr/9	BPV
2012	NCAA	Virginia	5	2	0	60	57	2.25	0.93	7.0	206	28	73	1.44	1.8	8.6	4.8	0.0	123
2013	NCAA	Virginia	4	1	12	58	71	1.70	0.84	7.3	204	31	78	1.16	1.1	11.0	10.1	0.0	187
2013	A-	Mahoning Val	0	0	0	9	16	0.00	0.77	4.1	163	34	100	0.47	2.0	15.8	8.0	0.0	249
2013	A	Lake County	0	0	0	5	7	1.80	1.00	4.8	221	30	100	3.44	1.8	12.6	7.0	1.8	196
2013	AA	Akron	1	0	0	10	9	0.00	0.89	4.2	197	26	100	1.24	1.8	8.0	4.5	0.0	114

Sinkerball RP who was used as closer in college and could reach majors quickly. Exhibits plus command despite long arm action. Rarely walks hitters and induces weak contact due to arm slot and movement on FB. Doesn't own true out pitch, but keeps hitters on toes by spotting FB and SL well.

Crosby, Casey — SP — Detroit

EXP MLB DEBUT: 2012 | POTENTIAL: #4 starter | 7C

Thrws L Age 25
2007 (5) HS (IL)

90-95	FB	++++
80-84	CB	+++
82-84	CU	++

Year	Lev	Team	W	L	Sv	IP	K	ERA	WHIP	BF/G	OBA	H%	S%	xERA	Ctl	Dom	Cmd	hr/9	BPV
2010	Rk	GCL Tigers	0	1	0	12	10	8.93	2.07	19.7	381	45	54	7.67	3.0	7.4	2.5	0.7	72
2011	AA	Erie	9	7	0	131	121	4.12	1.52	22.8	248	31	74	4.15	5.3	8.3	1.6	0.8	25
2012	AAA	Toledo	7	9	0	125	112	4.03	1.41	24.1	241	29	73	3.90	4.7	8.1	1.7	0.9	37
2012	MLB	DET	1	1	0	12	9	9.51	2.11	20.2	302	34	54	7.10	8.0	6.6	0.8	1.5	-81
2013	AAA	Toledo	2	5	0	57	61	4.88	1.66	19.7	254	34	70	4.32	6.3	9.6	1.5	0.5	21

Tall, angular LHP who has yet to breakout at AAA or majors. Season ended in June due to shoulder and knee ailments. Injury history gives pause to durability, but showcases plus arm when healthy. Has been lethal against LHH (.154 oppBA) with plus FB and power CB. Varies velocity with breaking ball.

Cruz, Luis — SP — Houston

EXP MLB DEBUT: 2015 | POTENTIAL: #4 starter | 7D

Thrws L Age 23
2008 (9) HS (PR)

87-91	FB	+++
78-80	CB	++
81-83	CU	+++

Year	Lev	Team	W	L	Sv	IP	K	ERA	WHIP	BF/G	OBA	H%	S%	xERA	Ctl	Dom	Cmd	hr/9	BPV
2011	A	Lexington	5	4	0	91	92	4.45	1.34	21.0	278	34	72	4.80	2.3	9.1	4.0	1.5	120
2011	A+	Lancaster	0	1	0	13	10	14.54	2.31	16.7	396	39	39	12.43	4.2	6.9	1.7	4.8	30
2012	A	Lexington	9	8	0	146	135	4.06	1.36	21.8	269	34	71	4.03	2.9	8.3	2.9	0.7	89
2013	A+	Lancaster	8	6	2	113	129	5.17	1.34	17.4	258	35	61	3.85	3.2	10.3	3.2	0.8	117
2013	AA	Corpus Christi	2	0	0	17	21	0.53	0.53	14.2	94	16	89	0.00	2.1	11.1	5.3	0.0	161

Very short, deceptive SP who had big spike in K rate while maintaining GB tendency. Crossfire delivery tough on RHH, but wasn't as solid against LHH. FB features good life and bottom falls out of CU on occasion. CU can be K pitch. Velocity might play up in shorter stints and could eventually move to pen.

Cumpton, Brandon — RP — Pittsburgh

EXP MLB DEBUT: 2013 | POTENTIAL: #5 SP / Setup RP | 6B

Thrws R Age 25
2010 (9) Georgia Tech

89-93	FB	+++
	SL	++
	CU	+

Year	Lev	Team	W	L	Sv	IP	K	ERA	WHIP	BF/G	OBA	H%	S%	xERA	Ctl	Dom	Cmd	hr/9	BPV
2011	A+	Bradenton	3	3	0	66	42	3.68	1.29	20.9	281	32	73	4.11	1.6	5.7	3.5	0.8	77
2012	AA	Altoona	12	11	0	152	88	3.85	1.28	23.1	258	29	70	3.51	2.7	5.2	1.9	0.5	38
2013	AA	Altoona	0	1	0	9	7	7.83	1.74	21.0	298	37	50	4.72	4.9	6.8	1.4	0.0	9
2013	AAA	Indianapolis	6	7	0	122	90	3.32	1.30	24.0	251	30	75	3.37	3.2	6.6	2.0	0.4	50
2013	MLB	PIT	2	1	0	31	22	2.05	1.01	19.6	231	28	80	2.23	1.5	6.4	4.4	0.3	95

Strong, stocky RHP succeeds without dominating. FB sits at 89-93, but can hit 96 in relief. Mixes in a decent SL and a below-average CU. Has excellent control and looked good in five starts for the Pirates. Lack of dominance makes him a likely swing-man.

Danish, Tyler — SP — Chicago (A)

EXP MLB DEBUT: 2017 | POTENTIAL: #3 starter | 8D

Thrws R Age 19
2013 (2) HS (FL)

90-94	FB	++++
82-86	SL	+++
79-82	CU	++

Year	Lev	Team	W	L	Sv	IP	K	ERA	WHIP	BF/G	OBA	H%	S%	xERA	Ctl	Dom	Cmd	hr/9	BPV
2013	Rk	Bristol	1	0	0	26	22	1.38	0.77	7.2	170	21	84	0.95	1.7	7.6	4.4	0.3	108
2013	A	Kannapolis	0	0	0	4	6	0.00	0.50	6.6	151	27	100	0.00	0.0	13.5		0.0	261

Athletic, aggressive RHP who combines pitchability with stuff. FB exhibits wicked late action to produce high GB rate. Quick arm generates pitch movement, but he has effort in unusual delivery. Hard SL is solid #2 pitch, though CU lags behind. Commands plate with FB and has feel for secondaries.

Davies, Zach — SP — Baltimore

EXP MLB DEBUT: 2015 | POTENTIAL: #4 starter | 7C

Thrws R Age 21
2011 (26) HS (AZ)

87-92	FB	+++
73-75	CB	+++
81-83	SL	++
	CU	+++

Year	Lev	Team	W	L	Sv	IP	K	ERA	WHIP	BF/G	OBA	H%	S%	xERA	Ctl	Dom	Cmd	hr/9	BPV
2012	A	Delmarva	5	7	1	114	91	3.87	1.36	19.1	253	30	74	3.93	3.6	7.2	2.0	0.9	49
2013	A+	Frederick	7	9	0	148	132	3.70	1.23	23.1	258	32	71	3.43	2.3	8.0	3.5	0.6	100

Polished, advanced starter who finished 2nd in CAR in Ks despite age for league. Has small, thin frame and lacks overpowering stuff, but mixes pitches and commands with repeatable delivery and slot. Throws with quick arm and keeps ball down. Upside is a tad short, but can throw four pitches for strikes.

Davis, Rookie — SP — New York (A)

EXP MLB DEBUT: 2017 | POTENTIAL: #4 starter | 7C

Thrws R Age 21
2011 (14) HS (NC)

89-93	FB	+++
77-80	CB	+++
82-84	CU	+++

Year	Lev	Team	W	L	Sv	IP	K	ERA	WHIP	BF/G	OBA	H%	S%	xERA	Ctl	Dom	Cmd	hr/9	BPV
2012	Rk	GCL Yankees	2	1	0	17	17	2.65	1.24	9.8	262	34	80	3.41	2.1	9.0	4.3	0.5	123
2013	A-	Staten Island	2	4	0	42	39	2.36	1.40	16.1	280	36	83	3.80	2.8	8.4	3.0	0.2	93
2013	A	Charleston (Sc)	0	0	0	10	8	0.00	0.90	18.6	242	31	100	1.82	0.0	7.2		0.0	148

Imposing, big-bodied pitcher who is emerging as prospect. Lack of FB command limits effectiveness, but has decent velocity and pitch movement. Throws on downward angle and has average CB that flashes plus. Likes to challenge hitters and register Ks, but could be more efficient with use of impressive CU.

Dayton, Grant — RP — Miami

EXP MLB DEBUT: 2014 | POTENTIAL: Reliever | 7D

Thrws L Age 26
2010 (11) Auburn

91-94	FB	+++
81-84	SL	+++
	CU	++

Year	Lev	Team	W	L	Sv	IP	K	ERA	WHIP	BF/G	OBA	H%	S%	xERA	Ctl	Dom	Cmd	hr/9	BPV
2010	A-	Jamestown	1	1	1	28	23	1.28	1.17	6.6	185	24	88	1.80	4.8	7.3	1.5	0.0	21
2011	A	Greensboro	7	1	5	71	99	2.91	1.17	5.8	227	35	77	2.84	3.0	12.5	4.1	0.6	161
2012	A+	Jupiter	2	5	2	60	71	2.10	1.10	7.6	221	32	80	2.16	2.7	10.7	3.9	0.2	137
2012	AA	Jacksonville	2	1	0	13	19	4.15	1.23	7.5	247	36	71	3.95	2.8	13.2	4.8	1.4	180
2013	AA	Jacksonville	4	4	1	38	56	2.37	1.18	5.1	235	36	85	3.28	2.8	13.3	4.7	0.9	180

Strong, durable lefty finally found his home in the pen where his FB sits 92-94 with late life. Hitters struggle picking up on it and can complement it with a low-80s SL. CU is a tick below average, though it has decent fade and keeps RHH at ease. Continues to show good command of all his pitches.

De Horta, Adrian — SP — San Diego

EXP MLB DEBUT: 2018 | POTENTIAL: #3 starter | 7E

Thrws R Age 19
2013 (8) HS (CA)

88-93	FB	+++
	CU	++++
	CB	++

Year	Lev	Team	W	L	Sv	IP	K	ERA	WHIP	BF/G	OBA	H%	S%	xERA	Ctl	Dom	Cmd	hr/9	BPV
2013	Rk	AZL Padres	0	2	0	31	40	4.06	1.32	10.7	243	36	68	3.12	3.8	11.6	3.1	0.3	125

Athletic, projectable SP who needs time to fill out frame, but has tools to build on. FB thrown from high arm slot and features nice movement. CU is best pitch and thrown with impressive arm speed. CB lags behind as distant third pitch and will need to find consistency with pitch sequencing and efficiency.

De Leon,Victor

RP | St. Louis | EXP MLB DEBUT: 2015 | POTENTIAL: Reliever | 7D

Thrws R Age 22
2009 FA (DR)

Velo	Pitch	Grade
95-97	FB	++++
80-82	SL	+++
	CU	++

Year	Lev	Team	W	L	Sv	IP	K	ERA	WHIP	BF/G	OBA	H%	S%	xERA	Ctl	Dom	Cmd	hr/9	BPV
2011	Rk	GCL Cardinals	0	6	0	50	30	4.49	1.60	22.1	284	33	71	4.51	4.3	5.4	1.3	0.4	-1
2012	Rk	Johnson City	3	0	0	44	42	3.27	1.34	18.3	239	32	74	3.06	4.1	8.6	2.1	0.2	62
2013	A-	State College	5	2	0	37	37	2.90	1.29	9.0	228	30	78	3.06	4.1	9.0	2.2	0.5	68

Strong-armed Dominican has a live 95-97 mph FB. Also has a SL and a workable CU. Move to relief allows him to focus on FB/SL. Continues to struggle with control and FB can flatten out when over-thrown, but gives the Cardinals a good bullpen arm.

De Paula,Rafael

SP | New York (A) | EXP MLB DEBUT: 2016 | POTENTIAL: #3 starter | 8C

Thrws R Age 23
2010 FA (DR)

Velo	Pitch	Grade
92-97	FB	++++
81-83	CB	++
83-84	CU	++

Year	Lev	Team	W	L	Sv	IP	K	ERA	WHIP	BF/G	OBA	H%	S%	xERA	Ctl	Dom	Cmd	hr/9	BPV
2013	A	Charleston (Sc)	6	2	0	64	96	2.95	1.03	19.0	192	32	71	1.87	3.2	13.5	4.2	0.4	173
2013	A+	Tampa	1	3	0	49	50	6.06	1.71	20.2	281	36	65	5.25	5.5	9.2	1.7	0.9	35

Big, strong righty who dominated Low-A, but struggled in High-A in first year. Registers Ks with plus FB and hard CB. Athletic for large frame and pitches aggressively to both sides. Can overthrow and could use upgrade in control. CU shows promise due to repeating of arm speed. Needs better overall command.

deGrom,Jacob

SP | New York (N) | EXP MLB DEBUT: 2014 | POTENTIAL: #3 starter | 7D

Thrws R Age 26
2010 (9) Stetson

Velo	Pitch	Grade
92-95	FB	++++
	SL	++++
	CU	++

Year	Lev	Team	W	L	Sv	IP	K	ERA	WHIP	BF/G	OBA	H%	S%	xERA	Ctl	Dom	Cmd	hr/9	BPV
2012	A	Savannah	6	3	0	89	78	2.52	1.02	22.8	234	30	75	2.30	1.4	7.9	5.6	0.3	122
2012	A+	St. Lucie	3	0	0	21	18	2.12	0.94	19.9	190	24	79	1.68	2.5	7.6	3.0	0.4	87
2013	A+	St. Lucie	1	0	0	12	13	3.00	1.17	23.9	262	35	77	3.43	1.5	9.8	6.5	0.8	153
2013	AA	Binghamton	2	5	0	60	44	4.80	1.48	25.8	290	34	67	4.52	3.0	6.6	2.2	0.6	56
2013	AAA	Las Vegas	4	2	0	75	63	4.55	1.48	23.1	291	35	70	4.62	2.9	7.5	2.6	0.7	76

Didn't start pitching until junior year of college and missed '11 for TJS, which is why an older prospect. Athletic frame with plus FB/SL combo. CU coming along nicely - needs it as third viable pitch. Throws strikes and goes to SL when needs a K. Could benefit from pitching off plate more.

DeJong,Chase

SP | Toronto | EXP MLB DEBUT: 2017 | POTENTIAL: #3 starter | 8D

Thrws R Age 20
2012 (2) HS (CA)

Velo	Pitch	Grade
87-94	FB	+++
74-78	CB	+++
80-81	CU	+++

Year	Lev	Team	W	L	Sv	IP	K	ERA	WHIP	BF/G	OBA	H%	S%	xERA	Ctl	Dom	Cmd	hr/9	BPV
2012	Rk	GCL Blue Jays	1	0	0	12	15	1.50	0.67	7.0	171	27	75	0.35	0.8	11.3	15.0	0.0	200
2013	Rk	Bluefield	2	3	0	56	66	3.05	1.21	17.4	269	38	74	3.24	1.6	10.6	6.6	0.3	166

Tall, loose-armed starter who revamped delivery and became more consistent with arm slot and release point. Uses height to throw on downhill plane and has overhand CB with sharp, late-breaking action. Could add a few ticks to FB, but can spot at will within zone. CB is out pitch while CU keeps LHH at bay.

Del Rosario,Yeyfry

RP | Toronto | EXP MLB DEBUT: 2017 | POTENTIAL: Setup reliever | 7D

Thrws R Age 20
2011 FA (DR)

Velo	Pitch	Grade
88-95	FB	++++
77-80	CB	++
82-85	CU	++

Year	Lev	Team	W	L	Sv	IP	K	ERA	WHIP	BF/G	OBA	H%	S%	xERA	Ctl	Dom	Cmd	hr/9	BPV
2012	Rk	GCL Blue Jays	1	5	0	44	52	3.67	1.11	13.4	229	33	65	2.33	2.4	10.6	4.3	0.2	143
2013	Rk	Bluefield	4	2	2	28	33	2.56	1.39	7.4	232	31	86	3.79	4.8	10.6	2.2	1.0	79

Lean and projectable pitcher who spent season working out of pen. Can pump strike zone with outstanding, sinking FB that he uses to induce groundballs. Secondary pitches aren't nearly as polished and will take a while to develop. Adding strength to throw CB with more conviction. Lacks command at present.

DeSclafani,Anthony

SP | Miami | EXP MLB DEBUT: 2014 | POTENTIAL: #3 starter | 8D

Thrws R Age 24
2011 (6) Florida

Velo	Pitch	Grade
90-96	FB	++++
	SL	++++
	CU	++++
	CB	+++

Year	Lev	Team	W	L	Sv	IP	K	ERA	WHIP	BF/G	OBA	H%	S%	xERA	Ctl	Dom	Cmd	hr/9	BPV
2010	NCAA	Florida	2	3	0	40	29	7.16	1.69	9.5	346	40	55	6.02	1.8	6.5	3.6	0.7	87
2011	NCAA	Florida	5	3	3	43	39	4.38	1.25	6.3	283	34	67	4.23	1.3	8.1	6.5	1.0	131
2012	A	Lansing	11	3	0	123	92	3.37	1.38	18.5	295	36	74	3.98	1.8	6.7	3.7	0.2	90
2013	A+	Jupiter	4	2	0	54	53	1.67	1.06	17.4	240	31	87	2.63	1.5	8.8	5.9	0.5	137
2013	AA	Jacksonville	5	4	0	75	62	3.36	1.17	23.0	259	31	74	3.52	1.7	7.4	4.4	0.8	107

Took another huge leap forward in '13, improving Ctl, Dom, and Cmd. Comes at hitters with a low-90s FB, a power SL, straight CU, and a CB. His SL generates most swing-and-miss, but he is aggressive and pounds the zone with all his pitches, especially the FB.

Diaz,Edwin

SP | Seattle | EXP MLB DEBUT: 2017 | POTENTIAL: #2 starter | 9D

Thrws R Age 20
2012 (3) HS (PR)

Velo	Pitch	Grade
91-96	FB	++++
74-77	CB	+++
81-84	SL	+++
82-85	CU	++

Year	Lev	Team	W	L	Sv	IP	K	ERA	WHIP	BF/G	OBA	H%	S%	xERA	Ctl	Dom	Cmd	hr/9	BPV
2012	Rk	AZL Mariners	2	1	0	19	20	5.21	1.53	9.2	183	23	67	3.55	8.1	9.5	1.2	0.9	-29
2013	Rk	Pulaski	5	2	0	69	79	1.43	0.91	19.8	188	26	90	1.77	2.3	10.3	4.4	0.7	140

Lean and loose starter who led APPY in ERA. Has proven difficult to hit due to plus FB and two breaking balls. Quick arm produces pitch movement and tight SL serves as out pitch. Should add velocity down the road, but needs to add strength to maintain velocity. CU still in infancy stage, but has excellent arm speed.

Diaz,Miller

SP | New York (N) | EXP MLB DEBUT: 2017 | POTENTIAL: Reliever | 6D

Thrws R Age 22
2009 FA (Venezuela)

Velo	Pitch	Grade
92-94	FB	+++
80-82	SL	++
	CU	++

Year	Lev	Team	W	L	Sv	IP	K	ERA	WHIP	BF/G	OBA	H%	S%	xERA	Ctl	Dom	Cmd	hr/9	BPV
2011	Rk	GCL Mets	0	0	0	8	5	0.00	0.63	13.8	117	15	100	0.00	2.3	5.6	2.5	0.0	59
2011	Rk	Kingsport	1	1	1	33	22	5.42	1.81	17.1	294	35	68	5.10	5.7	6.0	1.0	0.3	-28
2012	Rk	Kingsport	2	1	0	43	45	3.56	1.26	15.9	229	31	71	2.92	3.8	9.4	2.5	0.4	86
2012	A	Savannah	0	1	0	4	8	6.43	1.90	19.8	371	65	63	6.28	2.1	17.1	8.0	0.0	269
2013	A-	Brooklyn	7	3	0	66	87	2.04	1.16	20.3	191	30	82	1.94	4.5	11.8	2.6	0.1	110

Stocky pitcher throws from a 3/4 arm slot with some effort. Led NYPL in Ks. Good mid 90s FB that has overpowered hitters in low minors. Needs to develop secondary pitches and has really struggled at times with command. Profiles long-term as a reliever where he could be very effective if SL develops.

Dickson,Cody

SP | Pittsburgh | EXP MLB DEBUT: 2016 | POTENTIAL: #4 starter | 7D

Thrws L Age 22
2013 (4) Sam Houston State

Velo	Pitch	Grade
90-95	FB	+++
	CB	++
	CU	++

Year	Lev	Team	W	L	Sv	IP	K	ERA	WHIP	BF/G	OBA	H%	S%	xERA	Ctl	Dom	Cmd	hr/9	BPV
2011	NCAA	Sam Houston St.	4	1	0	45	52	4.38	1.59	14.2	230	33	70	3.56	6.8	10.4	1.5	0.2	22
2012	NCAA	Sam Houston St.	4	5	0	72	46	3.25	1.47	17.2	251	29	78	3.86	4.8	5.8	1.2	0.5	-7
2013	NCAA	Sam Houston St.	9	5	0	95	91	4.26	1.18	21.1	185	24	62	2.18	4.8	8.6	1.8	0.4	43
2013	A-	Jamestown	2	0	0	57	59	2.37	1.16	16.2	207	28	81	2.46	3.8	9.3	2.5	0.5	83

Tall, lean LHP was impressive in debut, going 2-0 with a 2.37 ERA. Has a good 90-95 mph FB, but CB and CU both need refinement. Can rush delivery resulting in inconsistent command, but was tough on RHB, limiting them to a .171 BA.

Dominguez,Jose

RP | Los Angeles (N) | EXP MLB DEBUT: 2013 | POTENTIAL: Setup reliever | 7C

Thrws R Age 23
2007 FA (DR)

Velo	Pitch	Grade
96-100	FB	+++++
	SL	+++
	CU	+++

Year	Lev	Team	W	L	Sv	IP	K	ERA	WHIP	BF/G	OBA	H%	S%	xERA	Ctl	Dom	Cmd	hr/9	BPV
2012	A	Great Lakes	4	3	4	72	78	5.25	1.72	9.9	275	37	68	4.78	5.9	9.8	1.7	0.5	35
2012	AA	Chattanooga	0	1	1	7	9	1.29	0.29	4.3	92	16	50	0.00	0.0	11.6		0.0	226
2013	AA	Chattanooga	1	0	5	17	28	2.63	0.94	4.6	142	28	69	0.68	4.2	14.7	3.5	0.0	170
2013	AAA	Albuquerque	1	0	0	8	12	0.00	0.75	3.6	42	9	100	0.00	5.6	13.5	2.4	0.0	109
2013	MLB	LA	0	0	0	8	4	2.17	1.69	4.2	320	36	86	4.96	3.3	4.3	1.3	0.0	8

Petite, undersized RP overpowers hitters with a plus-plus FB that sits in the upper 90s, showing 100 mph consistently. His all-out delivery has led to control issues in the past, but he seems to have learned to harness it and repeat his mechanics. He also offers a solid average SL in the mid-80s that complements the FB well.

Drake,Oliver

RP | Baltimore | EXP MLB DEBUT: 2014 | POTENTIAL: Setup reliever | 7D

Thrws R Age 27
2008 (43) Navy

Velo	Pitch	Grade
89-94	FB	+++
82-85	SL	+++
78-80	CB	++
80-83	CU	++

Year	Lev	Team	W	L	Sv	IP	K	ERA	WHIP	BF/G	OBA	H%	S%	xERA	Ctl	Dom	Cmd	hr/9	BPV
2011	A+	Frederick	8	3	0	96	80	2.15	1.00	26.2	223	29	77	1.91	1.7	7.5	4.4	0.1	107
2011	AA	Bowie	3	5	0	64	47	5.20	1.58	23.5	299	34	69	5.39	3.4	6.6	2.0	1.1	46
2011	AAA	Norfolk	0	0	0	2	2	0.00	1.00	7.6	151	22	100	0.99	4.5	9.0	2.0	0.0	59
2012	AA	Bowie	1	1	0	18	15	1.50	0.67	20.9	136	16	82	0.48	2.0	7.5	3.8	0.5	99
2013	AA	Bowie	3	0	8	31	38	1.74	1.03	6.3	179	27	84	1.62	3.8	11.0	2.9	0.3	115

Tall, strong RP who returned in June from shoulder surgery. Has been brought along slowly and may stick in pen. Has four pitches in toolbox, though secondary offerings are inconsistent. Uses SL as K pitch and mixes in slower CB for different look. FB has good sinking action and may eventually get bigger.

Duffey,Tyler — SP — Minnesota

EXP MLB DEBUT: 2016 | POTENTIAL: #5 starter | 6B

Thrws R Age 23
2012 (5) Rice

- 88-94 FB +++
- 80-83 SL +++
- 82-83 CU ++

Year	Lev	Team	W	L	Sv	IP	K	ERA	WHIP	BF/G	OBA	H%	S%	xERA	Ctl	Dom	Cmd	hr/9	BPV
2011	NCAA	Rice	8	2	2	60	76	2.54	1.20	8.1	241	35	81	3.07	2.7	11.4	4.2	0.6	150
2012	NCAA	Rice	1	1	7	51	68	1.94	1.06	5.5	186	29	83	1.82	3.7	12.0	3.2	0.4	134
2012	Rk	Elizabethton	2	0	2	19	27	1.42	0.63	5.5	157	25	82	0.54	0.9	12.8	13.5	0.5	223
2013	A	Cedar Rapids	3	2	0	58	47	2.79	0.95	24.3	230	27	74	2.51	0.9	7.3	7.8	0.8	124
2013	A+	Fort Myers	4	5	0	62	44	4.49	1.35	17.3	276	33	65	3.84	2.5	6.4	2.6	0.4	66

Aggressive, durable pitcher who was college reliever, but tried hand as starter in '13. Has limited upside as he lacks premium velocity or knockout breaking ball. Throws three pitches for strikes with quality location. FB has some late run while hard SL can be effective against RHH. Likely has more value as reliever.

Dwyer,Chris — SP — Kansas City

EXP MLB DEBUT: 2013 | POTENTIAL: #3 SP / Setup RP | 8E

Thrws L Age 26
2009 (4) Clemson

- 88-94 FB +++
- 80-82 CB ++++
- 80-82 CU ++

Year	Lev	Team	W	L	Sv	IP	K	ERA	WHIP	BF/G	OBA	H%	S%	xERA	Ctl	Dom	Cmd	hr/9	BPV
2011	AA	NW Arkansas	8	10	0	141	126	5.61	1.43	22.2	238	29	61	3.93	5.0	8.0	1.6	0.9	28
2012	AA	NW Arkansas	5	8	0	85	71	5.28	1.44	21.4	247	28	66	4.55	4.6	7.5	1.6	1.4	28
2012	AAA	Omaha	3	4	0	50	33	7.01	1.94	26.5	341	37	67	7.61	4.3	5.9	1.4	1.8	8
2013	AAA	Omaha	10	11	0	159	112	3.56	1.33	22.8	238	27	76	3.65	4.1	6.3	1.6	0.8	22
2013	MLB	KC	0	0	0	3	2	0.00	1.00	5.7	191	24	100	1.46	3.0	6.0	2.0	0.0	45

Quick-armed, durable LHP who hasn't matched success from '10. Has solid arsenal, but inconsistent command and inability to repeat arm slot have hindered development. Shows flashes of promise thanks to solid FB and CB that can exhibit fantastic breaking action. CU is improving, though still below average.

Eades,Ryan — SP — Minnesota

EXP MLB DEBUT: 2016 | POTENTIAL: #3 starter | 8D

Thrws R Age 22
2013 (2) Louisiana State

- 88-95 FB +++
- 79-83 CB +++
- 80-82 CU ++

Year	Lev	Team	W	L	Sv	IP	K	ERA	WHIP	BF/G	OBA	H%	S%	xERA	Ctl	Dom	Cmd	hr/9	BPV
2011	NCAA	Louisiana St.	4	1	0	43	31	4.81	1.56	10.5	288	33	70	4.90	3.8	6.5	1.7	0.8	33
2012	NCAA	Louisiana St.	5	3	0	94	63	3.83	1.44	23.5	288	33	75	4.53	2.7	6.0	2.3	0.8	54
2013	NCAA	Louisiana St.	8	1	0	100	78	2.79	1.33	24.4	264	32	78	3.45	2.9	7.0	2.4	0.3	67
2013	Rk	Elizabethton	0	0	0	15	13	4.74	1.64	6.8	233	30	68	3.57	7.1	7.7	1.1	0.0	-35

Thin, athletic SP who has a lot of talent, but will need time to develop pitch mix. Has makings of three solid-average offerings. FB is best current pitch and can effectively take a few ticks off for cut and sink. Keeps ball in lower half for weak contact. Can register Ks with CB, but needs to repeat arm speed on improving CU.

Edwards,C.J. — SP — Chicago (N)

EXP MLB DEBUT: 2014 | POTENTIAL: #2 starter | 9C

Thrws R Age 22
2011 (48) HS (SC)

- 92-95 FB ++++
- 75-78 CB ++++
- 80-83 SL ++
- 82-85 CU ++

Year	Lev	Team	W	L	Sv	IP	K	ERA	WHIP	BF/G	OBA	H%	S%	xERA	Ctl	Dom	Cmd	hr/9	BPV
2012	Rk	AZL Rangers	3	0	0	20	25	0.00	0.60	17.1	96	16	100	0.00	2.7	11.3	4.2	0.0	148
2012	A-	Spokane	2	3	0	47	60	2.11	0.96	17.8	164	26	76	1.00	3.6	11.5	3.2	0.0	127
2013	A	Hickory	8	2	0	93	122	1.84	1.03	19.9	191	31	80	1.48	3.3	11.8	3.6	0.0	142
2013	A+	Daytona	0	0	0	23	33	1.96	0.91	14.3	178	29	80	1.39	2.7	12.9	4.7	0.4	176

Athletic RH came over in the Garza trade and has a high-upside arm. FB sits at 92-95 with cutting action. Complements it with a 12-6 CB, a SL and CU. Dominated going 8-2 with 155 K and a 1.86 ERA, but size raises some concerns about durability.

Eflin,Zach — SP — San Diego

EXP MLB DEBUT: 2016 | POTENTIAL: #3 starter | 8D

Thrws R Age 20
2012 (1) HS (FL)

- 88-94 FB ++++
- CB ++
- 81-83 CU +++

Year	Lev	Team	W	L	Sv	IP	K	ERA	WHIP	BF/G	OBA	H%	S%	xERA	Ctl	Dom	Cmd	hr/9	BPV
2012	Rk	AZL Padres	0	1	0	7	4	7.71	1.71	7.9	313	36	50	4.91	3.9	5.1	1.3	0.0	6
2013	A	Fort Wayne	7	6	0	118	86	2.74	1.19	21.6	248	29	78	3.14	2.4	6.5	2.8	0.5	72

Athletic and durable SP who was consistently good all season. Likes to change speeds by cutting and sinking plus FB and mixing in excellent CU with similar arm speed. Has feel for pitching and can throw strikes, but fails to adequately drop CB in zone. Dom a bit low, and he is more of flyball pitcher.

Emanuel,Kent — SP — Houston

EXP MLB DEBUT: 2015 | POTENTIAL: #4 starter | 7C

Thrws L Age 22
2013 (3) North Carolina

- 86-91 FB +++
- 76-79 CB +++
- 82-84 SL +++
- 80-83 CU +++

Year	Lev	Team	W	L	Sv	IP	K	ERA	WHIP	BF/G	OBA	H%	S%	xERA	Ctl	Dom	Cmd	hr/9	BPV
2011	NCAA	North Carolina	9	1	0	104	89	2.33	1.14	20.6	246	31	79	2.73	2.0	7.7	3.9	0.3	103
2012	NCAA	North Carolina	8	4	0	110	100	1.96	1.04	25.0	227	30	81	2.19	1.9	8.2	4.3	0.2	114
2013	NCAA	North Carolina	11	5	1	131	98	3.16	1.17	24.9	246	30	73	3.00	2.2	6.7	3.1	0.5	80
2013	Rk	GCL Astros	0	0	0	9	8	0.00	0.89	8.3	191	26	100	1.16	2.0	8.0	4.0	0.0	108

Long and athletic pitcher with power frame, but lacks frontline velocity and projection. Has feel for throwing strikes and pitching to all quadrants of zone. Pitches with good angle to plate, though has little margin for error. Uses four average pitches and knows how to mix. Repeats delivery which converts to low walk rate.

Encinas,Gabe — SP — New York (A)

EXP MLB DEBUT: 2017 | POTENTIAL: #4 starter | 7D

Thrws R Age 22
2010 (6) HS (CA)

- 90-96 FB ++++
- 75-79 CB ++
- 80-82 CU ++

Year	Lev	Team	W	L	Sv	IP	K	ERA	WHIP	BF/G	OBA	H%	S%	xERA	Ctl	Dom	Cmd	hr/9	BPV
2011	Rk	GCL Yankees	3	0	0	51	46	5.11	1.47	18.3	283	36	64	4.31	3.2	8.1	2.6	0.5	78
2012	A-	Staten Island	3	7	0	70	48	5.00	1.60	19.4	269	30	70	4.91	5.0	6.2	1.2	1.0	-6
2013	A	Charleston (Sc)	3	0	0	35	31	0.77	1.09	19.5	182	25	92	1.56	4.1	8.0	1.9	0.0	50

Tall starter who underwent TJ surgery in May and will likely be back at midseason. Has flown under radar despite plus FB that continues to increase in velocity. Will take time to return to mid-90s heat. CB was evolving into swing-and-miss offering while CU lagged behind. Ingredients are there, but patience is needed.

Escobar,Edwin — SP — San Francisco

EXP MLB DEBUT: 2014 | POTENTIAL: #2 starter | 8D

Thrws L Age 22
2009 FA (Venezuela)

- 91-94 FB ++++
- SL +++
- CU +++

Year	Lev	Team	W	L	Sv	IP	K	ERA	WHIP	BF/G	OBA	H%	S%	xERA	Ctl	Dom	Cmd	hr/9	BPV
2011	Rk	AZL Giants	2	4	0	46	42	5.09	1.48	13.2	282	36	64	4.18	3.3	8.2	2.5	0.4	76
2011	A	Augusta	1	3	0	6	5	18.00	3.33	9.2	470	56	40	12.19	7.5	7.5	1.0	0.0	-50
2012	A	Augusta	7	8	0	130	122	2.97	1.18	23.6	248	32	75	3.03	2.2	8.4	3.8	0.5	110
2013	A+	San Jose	3	4	0	74	92	2.91	1.15	18.4	245	36	74	2.78	2.1	11.2	5.4	0.4	163
2013	AA	Richmond	5	4	0	54	54	2.67	1.06	20.9	224	30	75	2.28	2.2	9.0	4.2	0.3	122

Strong, stocky LHP turned heads with three pitches that play average or better. FB sits in the low 90s up to 94 with good sink and cutting action, complemented by a SL that flashes plus, and a CU with good fade. Cross-body delivery has some deception, but he repeats it well with clean arm action and plus control.

Familia,Jeurys — RP — New York (N)

EXP MLB DEBUT: 2012 | POTENTIAL: Setup reliever | 7D

Thrws R Age 24
2007 FA (DR)

- 94-96 FB ++++
- 83-85 SL +++
- CU ++

Year	Lev	Team	W	L	Sv	IP	K	ERA	WHIP	BF/G	OBA	H%	S%	xERA	Ctl	Dom	Cmd	hr/9	BPV
2012	MLB	NYM	0	0	0	12	10	5.85	1.54	6.7	224	29	58	3.21	6.6	7.3	1.1	0.0	-28
2013	A-	Brooklyn	0	0	0	1	0	0.00	1.00	3.8	262	26	100	2.41	0.0	0.0		0.0	18
2013	A+	St. Lucie	0	1	0	3	3	3.00	1.33	4.2	191	27	75	2.27	6.0	9.0	1.5	0.0	18
2013	AAA	Las Vegas	0	0	1	5	4	0.00	1.20	5.0	262	33	100	2.84	1.8	7.2	4.0	0.0	99
2013	MLB	NYM	0	0	1	11	8	4.21	1.96	5.7	285	31	84	6.67	7.6	6.7	0.9	1.7	-65

Elbow surgery in June limited him to 19.2 IP. Appears headed to bullpen. FB that can reach triple digits and SL a lethal 1-2 punch when he commands them. Lack of consistent mechanics plays into Cmd issues, and needs to tighten up delivery. Will shelf below-average CU out of pen. Works slow allowing too many SB.

Feliz,Michael — SP — Houston

EXP MLB DEBUT: 2017 | POTENTIAL: #3 starter | 8D

Thrws R Age 20
2010 FA (DR)

- 91-97 FB ++++
- 84-87 SL +++
- 79-83 CU ++

Year	Lev	Team	W	L	Sv	IP	K	ERA	WHIP	BF/G	OBA	H%	S%	xERA	Ctl	Dom	Cmd	hr/9	BPV
2011	Rk	GCL Astros	0	3	0	50	44	4.32	1.48	17.9	273	34	69	4.03	3.8	7.9	2.1	0.4	59
2012	Rk	Greeneville	1	1	0	26	28	5.17	1.61	19.3	276	37	66	4.36	4.8	9.7	2.0	0.3	61
2012	Rk	GCL Astros	5	0	0	38	35	1.65	0.89	20.2	189	24	84	1.58	2.1	8.3	3.9	0.5	109
2013	A-	Tri City	4	2	1	69	78	1.96	0.96	18.6	214	30	80	1.82	1.7	10.2	6.0	0.3	155

Tall, athletic RHP who has spent 3 years in Rookie/SS ball, but has upside. Possesses 2 average-to-plus pitches in FB and power SL. Doesn't change speeds well and could use better CU to battle LHH. Dom continues to rise while he minimizes walks with good FB location. Could be intriguing in late-innings role.

Figueroa,Pedro — RP — Tampa Bay

EXP MLB DEBUT: 2012 | POTENTIAL: Setup reliever | 7D

Thrws L Age 28
2003 FA (DR)

- 93-98 FB +++
- 82-84 SL ++
- 80-82 CU ++

Year	Lev	Team	W	L	Sv	IP	K	ERA	WHIP	BF/G	OBA	H%	S%	xERA	Ctl	Dom	Cmd	hr/9	BPV
2011	Rk	AZL Athletics	0	0	0	2	6	4.50	1.50	4.3	347	114	67	4.72	0.0	27.0		0.0	504
2012	AAA	Sacramento	0	2	1	44	40	2.65	1.20	5.6	219	29	77	2.46	3.7	8.1	2.2	0.2	66
2012	MLB	OAK	0	0	0	22	14	3.32	1.43	4.9	207	23	79	3.51	6.2	5.8	0.9	0.8	-45
2013	AAA	Sacramento	3	4	2	59	49	4.11	1.52	5.6	255	29	78	4.84	5.0	7.5	1.5	1.4	17
2013	MLB	OAK	0	0	0	3	3	12.00	3.00	3.5	415	42	71	15.65	9.0	9.0	1.0	6.0	-63

Short, stocky RP who converted from SP in '12. Uses whippy arm to generate excellent movement and velocity to FB. Has tendency to rush delivery and leave ball up, though is GB pitcher. Hard SL serves as out pitch, though struggles to command it. Arm injuries in past bring stamina and durability into question.

Flexen,Chris — SP — New York (N)

EXP MLB DEBUT: 2017 | POTENTIAL: #2/#3 starter | 7C

Thrws R Age 20
2012 (14) HS (CA)

Velo	Pitch	Grade
90-92	FB	+++
	SL	+++
	CB	++
	CU	+++

Year	Lev	Team	W	L	Sv	IP	K	ERA	WHIP	BF/G	OBA	H%	S%	xERA	Ctl	Dom	Cmd	hr/9	BPV
2012	Rk	Kingsport	1	3	0	32	26	5.63	1.63	20.3	296	36	64	4.93	3.9	7.3	1.9	0.6	43
2013	Rk	Kingsport	8	1	0	69	62	2.09	0.94	23.6	214	26	83	2.30	1.6	8.1	5.2	0.8	121

Repeated APPY league at 19 and won Player of the Year award. Commands pitches well, SL flashes plus with hard, late bite. Mature body for his age but needs to shore up mechanics. Projectable with good stuff now. Throws strikes and knows how to use his arsenal. Worked deep into games, including 2 CG.

Floro,Dylan — SP — Tampa Bay

EXP MLB DEBUT: 2015 | POTENTIAL: #5 starter | 7E

Thrws R Age 23
2012 (13) Cal State Fullerton

Velo	Pitch	Grade
87-92	FB	+++
76-79	SL	+++
79-82	CU	++

Year	Lev	Team	W	L	Sv	IP	K	ERA	WHIP	BF/G	OBA	H%	S%	xERA	Ctl	Dom	Cmd	hr/9	BPV
2011	NCAA	Cal St. Fullerton	4	2	1	55	39	4.25	1.58	9.7	323	39	70	4.71	2.1	6.4	3.0	0.0	75
2012	NCAA	Cal St. Fullerton	10	4	0	114	70	2.84	1.09	26.2	256	30	73	2.72	1.0	5.5	5.4	0.2	90
2012	A-	Hudson Valley	4	1	2	30	21	2.40	1.00	6.4	235	29	73	1.99	1.2	6.3	5.3	0.0	99
2013	A	Bowling Green	9	2	0	109	85	1.81	1.12	22.6	251	31	85	2.79	1.6	7.0	4.5	0.3	102
2013	A+	Charlotte	2	0	0	28	14	1.61	0.75	25.0	194	23	76	0.88	0.6	4.5	7.0	0.0	82

Deceptive and athletic pitcher who dominated Low-A despite lack of true out pitch. Succeeds with ability to induce weak contact thanks to pitch movement. Lively FB is rarely straight and can spot it well to both sides. Keeps ball on ground and doesn't allow many HR. SL gives him reliable breaking ball, but CU is inconsistent.

Flynn,Brian — SP — Miami

EXP MLB DEBUT: 2013 | POTENTIAL: #3 starter | 7C

Thrws L Age 24
2011 (7) Wichita State

Velo	Pitch	Grade
88-95	FB	++++
	SL	++++
	CU	+++
	CB	+++

Year	Lev	Team	W	L	Sv	IP	K	ERA	WHIP	BF/G	OBA	H%	S%	xERA	Ctl	Dom	Cmd	hr/9	BPV
2012	AA	Erie	0	1	0	5	3	9.00	2.00	24.1	362	39	56	8.16	3.6	5.4	1.5	1.8	18
2012	AA	Jacksonville	3	0	0	45	32	3.80	1.36	23.5	274	32	72	3.98	2.6	6.4	2.5	0.6	63
2013	AA	Jacksonville	1	1	0	23	25	1.57	0.91	21.5	217	29	89	2.25	1.2	9.8	8.3	0.8	162
2013	AAA	New Orleans	6	11	0	138	122	2.80	1.21	24.2	246	31	78	3.07	2.6	8.0	3.1	0.5	91
2013	MLB	MIA	0	2	0	18	15	8.50	2.22	22.7	347	39	64	8.62	6.5	7.5	1.2	2.0	-23

Athletic, big-bodied LHP struggled in pro debut, but with solid four pitch arsenal he has the making of a workhorse starter. He works mostly with his low-90s FB and hard SL, mixing in a CU and CB on occassion. Uses size well to work downhill, repeating mechanics and getting solid ground ball rates.

Foltynewicz,Mike — SP — Houston

EXP MLB DEBUT: 2015 | POTENTIAL: #3 starter | 8B

Thrws R Age 22
2010 (1) HS (SC)

Velo	Pitch	Grade
93-99	FB	++++
77-80	CB	+++
80-83	CU	++

Year	Lev	Team	W	L	Sv	IP	K	ERA	WHIP	BF/G	OBA	H%	S%	xERA	Ctl	Dom	Cmd	hr/9	BPV
2010	Rk	Greeneville	0	3	0	44	39	4.07	1.38	15.5	270	33	71	3.97	3.1	7.9	2.6	0.6	78
2011	A	Lexington	5	11	0	134	88	4.97	1.49	22.2	283	32	66	4.52	3.4	5.9	1.7	0.7	32
2012	A	Lexington	14	4	0	152	125	3.14	1.36	23.5	253	31	79	3.73	3.7	7.4	2.0	0.7	52
2013	A+	Lancaster	1	0	0	26	29	3.81	1.73	16.9	297	38	83	5.96	4.8	10.0	2.1	1.4	68
2013	AA	Corpus Christi	5	3	3	103	95	2.88	1.23	18.2	205	26	79	2.84	4.5	8.3	1.8	0.7	45

Consistent RHP who owns ideal frame to be impact power pitcher. Can be tough to make hard contact against and uses height to keep ball down. FB command comes and goes, but generates Ks with velocity and pitch movement. Key to success is throwing CB for strikes. Tough on LHH with CU.

Font,Wilmer — RP — Texas

EXP MLB DEBUT: 2012 | POTENTIAL: Setup reliever / Closer | 7A

Thrws R Age 24
2006 FA (DR)

Velo	Pitch	Grade
92-99	FB	++++
79-84	SL	++
80-82	CU	+++

Year	Lev	Team	W	L	Sv	IP	K	ERA	WHIP	BF/G	OBA	H%	S%	xERA	Ctl	Dom	Cmd	hr/9	BPV
2012	AA	Frisco	2	0	1	15	29	3.00	1.07	5.8	175	38	73	1.90	4.2	17.4	4.1	0.6	218
2012	MLB	TEX	0	0	0	2	1	9.00	2.00	3.2	0	0	50	2.23	18.0	4.5	0.3	0.0	-387
2013	AA	Frisco	1	2	10	32	45	1.41	1.19	4.9	134	21	92	1.79	6.8	12.7	1.9	0.6	64
2013	AAA	Round Rock	1	0	4	20	26	0.45	0.90	4.7	124	21	94	0.44	4.5	11.7	2.6	0.0	107
2013	MLB	TEX	0	0	0	1	0	0.00	2.31	3.3	214	21	100	5.09	13.8	0.0	0.0	0.0	-356

Big-bodied RP with intimidating presence and big FB to match. Hits high 90s, but can take a little off to give hitters different looks. Lacks feel for SL, but fluid arm action makes CU solid-average offering. Command comes and goes, but tough to hit when on. Uses height well and keeps ball in park.

Fornataro,Eric — RP — St. Louis

EXP MLB DEBUT: 2014 | POTENTIAL: Reliever | 6C

Thrws R Age 26
2008 (6) Miami Dade CC

Velo	Pitch	Grade
96-98	FB	++++
80-83	CB	+++
	SP	++

Year	Lev	Team	W	L	Sv	IP	K	ERA	WHIP	BF/G	OBA	H%	S%	xERA	Ctl	Dom	Cmd	hr/9	BPV
2010	A	Quad Cities	7	15	0	140	100	5.27	1.57	22.0	290	33	67	4.96	3.8	6.4	1.7	0.8	31
2011	A+	Palm Beach	7	13	0	144	116	3.68	1.39	25.3	269	33	73	3.83	3.1	7.2	2.3	0.4	64
2012	AA	Springfield	3	3	5	67	41	2.41	1.07	4.6	225	27	76	2.17	2.3	5.5	2.4	0.1	55
2013	Rk	GCL Cardinals	0	0	0	3	3	3.00	1.33	4.2	262	35	75	3.16	3.0	9.0	3.0	0.0	99
2013	AAA	Memphis	1	4	1	55	39	6.04	1.60	6.6	295	34	61	5.09	3.8	6.4	1.7	0.8	31

Strong-armed reliever struggled at Triple-A Memphis. Has some of the best velocity in the system, with a FB that sits at 95-98, but lacks movement and the PCL hit .300 against him. Power CB is a second plus offering, but needs to miss more bats.

Freeman,Sam — RP — St. Louis

EXP MLB DEBUT: 2012 | POTENTIAL: Lefty reliever | 7B

Thrws L Age 27
2008 (32) Kansas

Velo	Pitch	Grade
94-97	FB	++++
79-81	SL	+++
84-86	CU	++

Year	Lev	Team	W	L	Sv	IP	K	ERA	WHIP	BF/G	OBA	H%	S%	xERA	Ctl	Dom	Cmd	hr/9	BPV
2012	AA	Springfield	1	3	1	17	12	1.58	0.94	4.3	199	23	87	1.88	2.1	6.3	3.0	0.5	75
2012	AAA	Memphis	2	2	0	30	27	2.09	1.23	4.5	228	28	88	3.30	3.6	8.1	2.3	0.9	66
2012	MLB	STL	0	2	0	20	18	5.40	1.35	3.5	232	28	60	3.65	4.5	8.1	1.8	0.9	42
2013	AAA	Memphis	7	2	2	69	66	2.99	1.21	5.7	226	29	76	2.88	3.5	8.6	2.4	0.5	78
2013	MLB	STL	1	0	0	12	8	2.20	1.06	3.7	187	23	77	1.56	3.7	5.9	1.6	0.0	25

Short LH reliever has good stuff and knows how to pitch. FB sits at 94-96, topping out at 97 mph. Mixes in a sinker and a nice slurve to keep hitters off-balance. Inconsistent command remains a red-flag, but 1.62 GB/FB gives him nice upside in the pen.

Fried,Max — SP — San Diego

EXP MLB DEBUT: 2016 | POTENTIAL: #2 starter | 9C

Thrws L Age 20
2012 (1) HS (CA)

Velo	Pitch	Grade
90-95	FB	++++
74-78	CB	++++
80-83	CU	++

Year	Lev	Team	W	L	Sv	IP	K	ERA	WHIP	BF/G	OBA	H%	S%	xERA	Ctl	Dom	Cmd	hr/9	BPV
2012	Rk	AZL Padres	0	1	0	17	17	3.66	1.16	6.9	224	29	68	2.72	3.1	8.9	2.8	0.5	93
2013	A	Fort Wayne	6	7	0	118	100	3.50	1.38	21.6	243	30	75	3.53	4.3	7.6	1.8	0.5	40

Very projectable lefty who has huge upside. Needs to add strength, but has quick, clean arm action to generate velocity and movement. Best pitch is hard CB that he can throw for strikes or get hitters to chase. Dominates LHH (.174 oppBA), but has a few things to improve. Needs to reduce walk rate and polish CU.

Fulmer,Michael — RP — New York (N)

EXP MLB DEBUT: 2016 | POTENTIAL: #3 starter | 8D

Thrws R Age 21
2011 (1) HS (OK)

Velo	Pitch	Grade
92-95	FB	++++
83-85	SL	++++
	CU	+

Year	Lev	Team	W	L	Sv	IP	K	ERA	WHIP	BF/G	OBA	H%	S%	xERA	Ctl	Dom	Cmd	hr/9	BPV
2011	Rk	GCL Mets	0	1	0	5	10	10.59	2.55	6.8	385	67	54	8.16	7.1	17.6	2.5	0.0	145
2012	A	Savannah	7	6	0	108	101	2.75	1.20	20.7	232	30	78	2.91	3.2	8.4	2.7	0.5	84
2013	Rk	GCL Mets	1	1	0	12	13	3.00	0.83	21.9	210	30	60	1.22	0.8	9.8	13.0	0.0	173
2013	A+	St. Lucie	2	2	0	34	29	3.44	1.24	19.7	200	26	71	2.39	4.8	7.7	1.6	0.3	28

Had meniscus surgery in spring training, then made nine starts before knee issues shut him down. In limited exposure, stuff looked as good as ever. Plus FB/SL combo misses lots of bats. CU a work in progress, but improving to solid-average. Needs to gain consistency with mechanics and build stamina.

Gagnon,Drew — SP — Milwaukee

EXP MLB DEBUT: 2014 | POTENTIAL: #4 starter | 7D

Thrws R Age 24
2011 (3) Long Beach State

Velo	Pitch	Grade
90-92	FB	+++
	CB	++
	CU	+++

Year	Lev	Team	W	L	Sv	IP	K	ERA	WHIP	BF/G	OBA	H%	S%	xERA	Ctl	Dom	Cmd	hr/9	BPV
2011	Rk	Helena	0	3	1	19	27	8.05	1.84	11.1	318	47	53	5.68	4.7	12.8	2.7	0.5	120
2012	A	Wisconsin	6	1	0	82	65	2.85	1.05	22.7	224	27	75	2.58	2.1	7.1	3.4	0.7	90
2012	A+	Brevard County	1	2	0	67	49	2.82	1.10	23.9	229	27	75	2.55	2.4	6.6	2.7	0.4	71
2013	A+	Brevard County	3	4	0	45	50	5.19	1.35	18.8	266	36	59	3.62	3.0	10.0	3.3	0.4	117
2013	AA	Huntsville	4	9	0	84	58	5.57	1.62	23.3	284	31	68	5.43	4.5	6.2	1.4	1.3	8

Tall, strong SP had a disappointing season following a breakout year in '12. Not overpowering with a low 90s FB, complements it with an average CU and a developing CB. Attacks the zone with decent control. Mechanics are solid, but overall command needs refinement as strikeouts won't be a big part of his game.

Garcia,Christian — RP — Washington

EXP MLB DEBUT: 2012 | POTENTIAL: Reliever | 7B

Thrws R Age 28
2004 (4) HS (FL)

Velo	Pitch	Grade
95-98	FB	+++
	SL	++++
	CB	+++
	CU	+++

Year	Lev	Team	W	L	Sv	IP	K	ERA	WHIP	BF/G	OBA	H%	S%	xERA	Ctl	Dom	Cmd	hr/9	BPV
2012	AAA	Syracuse	1	1	14	32	38	0.56	0.90	4.4	166	26	93	0.89	3.1	10.7	3.5	0.0	127
2012	MLB	WAS	0	0	0	13	15	2.13	0.79	3.5	183	22	88	2.11	1.4	10.6	7.5	1.4	171
2013	A-	Auburn	0	0	0	1	2	0.00	0.00	2.8	0	0	100	0.00	0.0	18.0		0.0	342
2013	AA	Harrisburg	0	1	0	4	4	2.25	1.75	6.1	307	41	86	4.87	4.5	9.0	2.0	0.0	59
2013	AAA	Syracuse	1	0	0	8	10	3.33	1.36	4.8	180	28	73	2.18	6.7	11.1	1.7	0.0	38

2013 brought another injury setback after an outstanding '12 had him figuring heavily into WAS plans. Can pump his FB up to 98 with plus movement. Also has a plus SL that misses bats. Height, arm angle, and pitch movement creates many groundball outs. Should provide late-inning value if he stays healthy.

Garcia,Onelki — RP — Los Angeles (N)

EXP MLB DEBUT: 2013 | POTENTIAL: Setup reliever | 7C

Thrws L Age 24
2012 (3) Cuba

- 90-95 FB ++++
- CB +++
- SL ++
- CU +

Year	Lev	Team	W	L	Sv	IP	K	ERA	WHIP	BF/G	OBA	H%	S%	xERA	Ctl	Dom	Cmd	hr/9	BPV
2012	A+	Rancho Cuca	0	0	0	2	4	0.00	0.00	5.6	0	0	100	0.00	0.0	18.0		0.0	342
2013	AA	Chattanooga	2	3	1	52	53	2.76	1.40	8.8	218	29	81	3.25	5.5	9.2	1.7	0.5	34
2013	AAA	Albuquerque	0	1	0	9	14	3.91	0.98	3.5	188	33	56	1.29	2.9	13.7	4.7	0.0	185

Big LH made the transition to the pen and jumped on the fast track to LA. He shows four pitches: a FB in low-to-mid 90s, a good 12-6 CB, SL, and a well below average CU, though now in relief his FB/CB combo will do the most damage. Has good arm action, but struggles to repeat, hindering his overall Ctl.

Garcia,Yimi — RP — Los Angeles (N)

EXP MLB DEBUT: 2014 | POTENTIAL: Setup reliever | 7C

Thrws R Age 23
2009 FA (DR)

- 92-96 FB +++
- SL +++
- CU ++

Year	Lev	Team	W	L	Sv	IP	K	ERA	WHIP	BF/G	OBA	H%	S%	xERA	Ctl	Dom	Cmd	hr/9	BPV
2010	Rk	AZL Dodgers	1	2	1	30	22	7.15	1.82	10.8	356	42	57	6.17	2.4	6.6	2.8	0.3	72
2011	Rk	Ogden	4	2	4	52	71	3.11	1.25	10.6	238	36	77	3.24	3.3	12.3	3.7	0.7	150
2012	A	Great Lakes	4	4	14	41	60	3.06	1.43	4.4	266	43	76	3.41	3.7	13.1	3.5	0.0	154
2012	A+	Rancho Cuca	2	1	2	10	22	2.65	1.18	4.5	196	51	75	1.82	4.4	19.4	4.4	0.0	248
2013	AA	Chattanooga	4	6	19	60	85	2.55	0.82	4.5	171	24	80	1.97	2.1	12.7	6.1	1.3	191

Lean, undersized RP continues to make a case for a late-inning reliever. FB sits in the mid-90s and he pairs it with an average SL that gets strikeouts and mixes in the occassional CU. Delivery has some effort. Mixes FB-SL combo well and continues to rack of the Ks and improve his Cmd.

Gardner,Joe — RP — Colorado

EXP MLB DEBUT: 2014 | POTENTIAL: #4 starter/reliever | 7C

Thrws R Age 26
2009 (3) UC Santa Barbara

- 87-92 FB +++
- 74-78 SL ++
- 78-82 CU ++

Year	Lev	Team	W	L	Sv	IP	K	ERA	WHIP	BF/G	OBA	H%	S%	xERA	Ctl	Dom	Cmd	hr/9	BPV
2010	A+	Kinston	12	6	0	122	104	2.65	1.11	21.8	198	25	76	2.09	3.8	7.7	2.0	0.3	54
2011	AA	Akron	7	8	0	97	60	5.01	1.60	22.6	283	32	68	4.67	4.4	5.6	1.3	0.6	0
2011	AA	Tulsa	3	3	0	36	22	2.49	1.08	23.5	233	27	76	2.41	2.0	5.5	2.8	0.2	63
2012	AA	Tulsa	8	8	1	138	99	3.98	1.22	19.9	249	29	69	3.51	2.5	6.5	2.5	0.8	66
2013	AA	Tulsa	6	4	2	55	60	5.55	1.27	6.4	251	33	56	3.76	2.9	9.8	3.3	1.0	115

Tall, strong hurler was limited to 55 IP due to illness and was not effective when in action. When healthy has a good 89-93 mph sinking FB. CU and SL remain below avg, making a move to relief likely. Does have good Dom, striking out more than a batter per inning in 2013.

Garrett,Amir — SP — Cincinnati

EXP MLB DEBUT: 2016 | POTENTIAL: #3 starter | 8D

Thrws L Age 22
2011 (22) HS (NV)

- 90-94 FB +++
- CB +
- CU +

Year	Lev	Team	W	L	Sv	IP	K	ERA	WHIP	BF/G	OBA	H%	S%	xERA	Ctl	Dom	Cmd	hr/9	BPV
2012	Rk	AZL Reds	0	2	0	14	13	5.79	1.86	9.4	262	33	68	5.09	7.7	8.4	1.1	0.6	-40
2012	Rk	Billings	0	0	0	6	5	0.00	0.83	11.0	191	25	100	1.03	1.5	7.5	5.0	0.0	113
2013	Rk	Billings	1	1	0	23	17	2.72	1.38	19.5	252	31	78	3.16	3.9	6.6	1.7	0.0	32
2013	A	Dayton	1	3	0	34	15	6.88	1.65	19.0	294	31	58	5.46	4.2	4.0	0.9	1.1	-25

Tall, athletic pitcher with considerable upside and potential. Needs polish and reps. All three pitches could become plus if he puts the work in. Has starting pitcher frame. Arm speed will change pitch-to-pitch and doesn't repeat mechanics well. FB needs less arm-side run to get more of plate.

Garvin,Grayson — SP — Tampa Bay

EXP MLB DEBUT: 2015 | POTENTIAL: #4 starter | 7C

Thrws L Age 24
2011 (1-S) Vanderbilt

- 88-94 FB +++
- 82-85 SL ++
- 79-81 CU +++

Year	Lev	Team	W	L	Sv	IP	K	ERA	WHIP	BF/G	OBA	H%	S%	xERA	Ctl	Dom	Cmd	hr/9	BPV
2010	NCAA	Vanderbilt	1	1	1	36	38	1.25	1.17	11.0	240	32	93	2.91	2.5	9.5	3.8	0.5	122
2011	NCAA	Vanderbilt	13	2	0	112	101	2.49	1.10	24.4	236	29	81	2.98	2.0	8.1	4.0	0.8	110
2012	A+	Charlotte	2	4	0	46	37	5.08	1.39	17.6	257	33	59	3.25	3.7	7.2	1.9	0.0	48
2013	Rk	GCL Rays	0	1	0	11	12	2.41	1.34	7.8	258	34	86	3.87	3.2	9.6	3.0	0.8	105
2013	A+	Charlotte	0	1	0	16	12	1.11	0.74	11.5	149	19	83	0.34	2.2	6.7	3.0	0.0	78

Tall, angular LHP who returned in July after elbow surgery. Shows promise of returning to full strength and getting FB back to solid-average status. Pitches inside and uses FB to set up quality secondary offerings. SL can be too slurvy and needs more power, but CU can be good. Upside and K rate are limited.

Gast,John — RP — St. Louis

EXP MLB DEBUT: 2013 | POTENTIAL: Reliever | 7C

Thrws L Age 25
2010 (6) Florida State

- 88-92 FB +++
- 76-78 CB ++
- CU ++

Year	Lev	Team	W	L	Sv	IP	K	ERA	WHIP	BF/G	OBA	H%	S%	xERA	Ctl	Dom	Cmd	hr/9	BPV
2011	AA	Springfield	4	4	0	79	54	4.10	1.43	25.9	264	30	74	4.42	3.8	6.1	1.6	1.0	27
2012	AA	Springfield	4	2	0	51	41	1.94	1.00	24.4	209	24	87	2.48	2.3	7.2	3.2	0.9	86
2012	AAA	Memphis	9	5	0	109	86	5.11	1.52	23.7	287	34	67	4.79	3.5	7.1	2.0	0.8	52
2013	AAA	Memphis	3	1	0	38	35	1.18	1.07	21.2	206	28	88	1.80	3.1	8.2	2.7	0.0	84
2013	MLB	STL	2	0	0	12	8	5.12	1.30	16.9	241	27	60	3.51	3.7	5.9	1.6	0.7	25

Move to relief was effective, but struggled once called up. Short lefty works off a 90-93 FB. Also features a solid CB and a CU. Delivery is max-effort and concerns about durabillity prompted the move to relief. Held opposing hitters to a .214 BA.

Gausman,Kevin — SP — Baltimore

EXP MLB DEBUT: 2013 | POTENTIAL: #2 starter | 9C

Thrws R Age 23
2012 (1) Louisiana State

- 92-98 FB ++++
- 77-79 CB ++
- 83-86 SL +++
- 82-86 CU ++++

Year	Lev	Team	W	L	Sv	IP	K	ERA	WHIP	BF/G	OBA	H%	S%	xERA	Ctl	Dom	Cmd	hr/9	BPV
2012	A-	Aberdeen	0	0	0	6	5	0.00	0.17	9.0	56	8	100	0.00	0.0	7.5			153
2012	A+	Frederick	0	1	0	9	8	6.00	1.22	12.1	283	29	63	6.00	1.0	8.0	8.0	3.0	135
2013	AA	Bowie	2	4	0	46	49	3.12	1.06	22.4	253	34	72	2.90	1.0	9.6	9.8	0.6	164
2013	AAA	Norfolk	1	2	0	35	33	4.09	1.28	18.0	266	35	66	3.32	2.3	8.4	3.7	0.3	108
2013	MLB	BAL	3	5	0	48	49	5.66	1.34	9.9	275	33	61	4.78	2.5	9.2	3.8	1.5	118

Athletic pitcher who earned time with BAL, mostly as RP. Has pitch mix to front rotation and only needs consistent secondary pitches to take jump. FB and well above average CU are best pitches. SL and CB can register Ks when on. Can throw too many strikes and could benefit from getting hitters to chase.

Geltz,Steve — RP — Tampa Bay

EXP MLB DEBUT: 2012 | POTENTIAL: Setup reliever | 6B

Thrws R Age 26
2008 FA (Buffalo)

- 89-95 FB ++++
- 77-80 SL ++
- 82-85 CU +

Year	Lev	Team	W	L	Sv	IP	K	ERA	WHIP	BF/G	OBA	H%	S%	xERA	Ctl	Dom	Cmd	hr/9	BPV
2011	AAA	Salt Lake	0	0	0	1	1	30.00	5.00	4.7	542	63	33	18.61	15.0	7.5	0.5	0.0	-252
2012	AA	Arkansas	3	0	6	25	37	0.36	0.76	4.3	155	28	95	0.38	2.2	13.3	6.2	0.0	199
2012	AAA	Salt Lake	0	1	5	33	33	5.15	1.30	5.5	236	29	62	3.74	3.8	8.9	2.4	1.1	77
2012	MLB	LAA	0	0	0	2	1	4.50	2.50	5.3	262	30	80	6.14	13.5	4.5	0.3	0.0	-266
2013	AAA	Durham	5	3	3	67	80	2.82	0.88	6.0	156	20	75	1.74	3.2	10.7	3.3	1.1	124

Short, durable RP who has spent entire career in pen. Size will keep him in role, but thrives with deceptive, high ¾ slot and sneaky, late-moving FB. Works quickly and aggressively on inner half of plate. Spots FB well and throws strikes with all pitches. Has been tough to hit, but needs to be careful with leaving balls up.

Gibson,Daniel — RP — Arizona

EXP MLB DEBUT: 2015 | POTENTIAL: Setup reliever | 7C

Thrws L Age 22
2013 (7) Florida

- 92-95 FB ++++
- SL +++
- CB +
- CU +

Year	Lev	Team	W	L	Sv	IP	K	ERA	WHIP	BF/G	OBA	H%	S%	xERA	Ctl	Dom	Cmd	hr/9	BPV
2011	NCAA	Florida	1	0	0	10	10	13.37	2.57	3.9	447	55	42	9.67	2.7	8.9	3.3	0.0	106
2012	NCAA	Florida	1	1	1	24	17	2.99	1.45	4.5	261	31	79	3.82	4.1	6.3	1.5	0.4	21
2013	NCAA	Florida	2	1	0	38	31	4.48	1.47	5.1	250	30	70	4.02	4.7	7.3	1.6	0.7	22
2013	A-	Hillsboro	1	0	3	20	22	0.45	1.25	5.8	232	33	96	2.54	3.6	9.9	2.8	0.0	99
2013	A	South Bend	0	1	0	8	5	1.11	0.99	5.1	208	25	88	1.63	2.2	5.6	2.5	0.0	58

Strong lefty reliever from Florida had an impressive debut. Comes after hitters with a plus 92-95 mph FB and a quality SL. Also features a CB and CU when starting, but both are below-average. Smooth easy delivery with good control. Could move up quickly.

Giles,Kenneth — RP — Philadelphia

EXP MLB DEBUT: 2015 | POTENTIAL: Setup reliever | 8E

Thrws R Age 23
2011 (7) Yavapai JC

- 95-98 FB +++++
- 87-90 SL +++

Year	Lev	Team	W	L	Sv	IP	K	ERA	WHIP	BF/G	OBA	H%	S%	xERA	Ctl	Dom	Cmd	hr/9	BPV
2011	Rk	GCL Phillies	1	1	0	4	7	6.43	2.14	6.9	336	51	75	8.29	6.4	15.0	2.3	2.1	114
2012	A	Lakewood	3	3	5	67	86	3.62	1.46	9.9	222	32	76	3.56	5.9	11.5	2.0	0.7	66
2012	A+	Clearwater	1	0	3	14	25	3.17	1.13	5.6	200	37	73	2.38	3.8	15.8	4.2	0.6	201
2013	A+	Clearwater	2	2	6	25	34	6.43	1.67	4.7	245	34	63	5.07	6.8	12.1	1.8	1.4	53

Gained notice in 2013 AFL with repeated triple-digit radar run readings. In reality, he's a lottery ticket: always had the blazing FB with a high Dom, but as his numbers show, has little idea where it's going. Slider is improving, but throwing strikes needs to the focus. Rib injury limited his IP in 2013; was again old for his level.

Gilmartin,Sean — SP — Minnesota

EXP MLB DEBUT: 2014 | POTENTIAL: #4 starter | 7C

Thrws L Age 24
2011 (1) Florida State

- 88-91 FB +++
- 75-77 CU +++
- 78-80 SL +++
- 70-72 CB ++

Year	Lev	Team	W	L	Sv	IP	K	ERA	WHIP	BF/G	OBA	H%	S%	xERA	Ctl	Dom	Cmd	hr/9	BPV
2012	AA	Mississippi	5	8	0	119	86	3.55	1.15	23.6	248	29	70	3.18	2.0	6.5	3.3	0.7	82
2012	AAA	Gwinnett	1	2	0	37	25	4.84	1.45	22.7	281	30	71	5.12	3.1	6.0	1.9	1.5	42
2013	Rk	GCL Braves	0	0	0	9	11	0.00	0.11	8.8	38	7	100	0.00	0.0	11.0		0.0	216
2013	A	Rome	1	0	0	5	5	1.80	0.80	18.1	221	31	75	1.28	0.0	9.0		0.0	180
2013	AAA	Gwinnett	3	8	0	91	65	5.74	1.59	23.6	304	34	65	5.56	3.3	6.4	2.0	1.2	46

Polished lefty struggled in his 2nd stint at Triple-A before being shut-down with tendinitis. Was then traded to the Twins. Knows how to pitch, but lack of FB velocity makes him hittable. Does have good control and a 4-pitch mix. Look for a rebound in 2014.

Giolito,Lucas — SP — Washington

EXP MLB DEBUT: 2016 | POTENTIAL: #1 starter | **9C**

Thrws R Age 19
2012 (1) HS (CA)

Velo	Pitch	Grade
95-97	FB	+++++
84-86	CB	++++
82-84	CU	++

Year	Lev	Team	W	L	Sv	IP	K	ERA	WHIP	BF/G	OBA	H%	S%	xERA	Ctl	Dom	Cmd	hr/9	BPV
2012	Rk	GCL Nationals	0	0	0	2	1	4.50	1.00	7.6	262	30	50	2.36	0.0	4.5		0.0	99
2013	Rk	GCL Nationals	1	1	0	22	25	2.84	1.31	11.5	233	34	76	2.69	4.1	10.1	2.5	0.0	91
2013	A-	Auburn	1	0	0	14	14	0.64	0.93	17.5	186	24	100	1.79	2.6	9.0	3.5	0.6	111

Missed most of '12'-13 to TJ surgery, but encouraging results in 11 starts. Plus-plus fastball with good downward angle that can hit triple digits. Complements with power curve and CU with late sinking action. Commands all his pitches with smooth, easy delivery. Mature pitching approach for this future ace.

Glasnow,Tyler — SP — Pittsburgh

EXP MLB DEBUT: 2016 | POTENTIAL: #1 starter | **9D**

Thrws R Age 20
2011 (5) HS (CA)

Velo	Pitch	Grade
93-96	FB	++++
75-78	CB	+++
	CU	+++

Year	Lev	Team	W	L	Sv	IP	K	ERA	WHIP	BF/G	OBA	H%	S%	xERA	Ctl	Dom	Cmd	hr/9	BPV
2012	Rk	GCL Pirates	0	3	0	34	40	2.11	1.03	11.9	165	22	84	1.93	4.2	10.6	2.5	0.8	94
2012	A-	State College	0	0	0	4	4	0.00	1.25	16.3	262	35	100	2.95	2.3	9.0	4.0	0.0	119
2013	A	West Virginia	9	3	0	111	164	2.19	1.04	17.8	147	23	83	1.68	4.9	13.3	2.7	0.7	124

RH had a huge breakout striking out 164 in 111.1 IP. FB jumped to 93-96 mph and tops at 99 mph. Improved CB is a swing-and-miss offering. CU shows potential. Struggled with control, but was difficult to hit, posting a minor league-leading .142 oppBA.

Goforth,David — SP — Milwaukee

EXP MLB DEBUT: 2014 | POTENTIAL: Closer | **8D**

Thrws R Age 25
2011 (7) Mississippi

Velo	Pitch	Grade
93-98	FB	++++
	CB	+++
90-93	CT	+++
	CU	++

Year	Lev	Team	W	L	Sv	IP	K	ERA	WHIP	BF/G	OBA	H%	S%	xERA	Ctl	Dom	Cmd	hr/9	BPV
2011	NCAA	Mississippi	4	8	0	83	63	4.88	1.37	24.9	271	32	63	3.92	2.9	6.8	2.3	0.5	62
2011	Rk	Helena	0	4	2	40	42	4.48	1.34	8.8	280	35	69	4.48	2.2	9.4	4.2	1.1	127
2012	A	Wisconsin	10	8	0	150	93	4.67	1.44	22.9	267	29	69	4.44	3.8	5.6	1.5	1.0	16
2013	A+	Brevard County	7	5	0	78	58	3.11	1.22	22.5	233	28	75	2.94	3.2	6.7	2.1	0.5	51
2013	AA	Huntsville	4	3	5	46	36	3.31	1.08	9.0	197	25	67	1.91	3.5	7.0	2.0	0.2	50

Returned to the pen in '13 and had promising results. Works with upper-90s FB and above average CT, showing an occasional CB and CU. Limits walks, but overall command needs refinement. He has a plus FB but he does not generate the amount of Ks one would expect.

Gohara,Luiz — SP — Seattle

EXP MLB DEBUT: 2018 | POTENTIAL: #1 starter | **9E**

Thrws L Age 17
2012 FA (Brazil)

Velo	Pitch	Grade
90-96	FB	++++
77-79	CB	++
81-84	CU	++

Year	Lev	Team	W	L	Sv	IP	K	ERA	WHIP	BF/G	OBA	H%	S%	xERA	Ctl	Dom	Cmd	hr/9	BPV
2013	Rk	Pulaski	1	2	0	21	27	4.25	1.46	15.1	269	39	70	3.95	3.8	11.5	3.0	0.4	121

Big, young SP with huge upside predicated on frame and arm strength. Needs to keep body under control, but generates velocity and power with effortless delivery. Has tendency to rush and overthrow, but plus FB very effective when on. Mixes in CB that has plus potential, but doesn't have much feel for CU.

Gonsalves,Stephen — SP — Minnesota

EXP MLB DEBUT: 2017 | POTENTIAL: #3 starter | **8E**

Thrws L Age 19
2013 (4) HS (CA)

Velo	Pitch	Grade
86-92	FB	+++
77-80	CB	++
81-83	CU	+++

Year	Lev	Team	W	L	Sv	IP	K	ERA	WHIP	BF/G	OBA	H%	S%	xERA	Ctl	Dom	Cmd	hr/9	BPV
2013	Rk	Elizabethton	1	1	0	14	21	1.29	1.00	17.8	202	35	86	1.51	2.6	13.5	5.3	0.0	192
2013	Rk	GCL Twins	1	0	0	14	18	0.64	1.06	11.0	167	27	93	1.30	4.5	11.5	2.6	0.0	104

Thin and projectable lefty who had terrific pro debut after falling in draft. Lean frame oozes projection and should add ticks to average FB. Shows advanced feel for solid-average CU, but needs to enhance below average CB. Slows arm speed at times and needs to clean up delivery to realize velocity potential.

Gonzales,Marco — RP — St. Louis

EXP MLB DEBUT: 2015 | POTENTIAL: #3 starter | **7B**

Thrws L Age 22
2013 (1) Gonzaga

Velo	Pitch	Grade
88-92	FB	+++
75-77	CB	++
	SL	++
77-79	CU	++++

Year	Lev	Team	W	L	Sv	IP	K	ERA	WHIP	BF/G	OBA	H%	S%	xERA	Ctl	Dom	Cmd	hr/9	BPV
2011	NCAA	Gonzaga	11	2	0	105	90	2.57	0.99	26.7	219	27	75	2.15	1.8	7.7	4.3	0.4	108
2012	NCAA	Gonzaga	8	2	0	92	92	1.56	0.93	28.8	195	26	84	1.58	2.2	9.0	4.0	0.3	119
2013	NCAA	Gonzaga	7	3	1	106	96	2.80	1.20	25.1	254	33	74	2.72	2.1	8.2	3.8	0.0	107
2013	Rk	GCL Cardinals	0	0	0	6	10	5.81	1.77	7.1	314	52	64	4.98	4.4	14.5	3.3	0.0	162
2013	A+	Palm Beach	0	0	0	16	13	1.67	0.93	15.2	180	22	86	1.65	2.8	7.2	2.6	0.6	73

Solid pro debut, posting a 2.70 ERA in 23.1 IP. Has a fluid, clean arm action that leads to plus command of a four-pitch mix. FB sits at 88-92 and has best change-up in the system. Improved CB and an inconsistent SL. Locates well and changes speeds.

Gonzales,Tyler — SP — Toronto

EXP MLB DEBUT: 2017 | POTENTIAL: #3 starter | **8E**

Thrws R Age 21
2012 (1-S) HS (TX)

Velo	Pitch	Grade
90-95	FB	++
84-87	SL	+++
82-84	CU	++

Year	Lev	Team	W	L	Sv	IP	K	ERA	WHIP	BF/G	OBA	H%	S%	xERA	Ctl	Dom	Cmd	hr/9	BPV
2012	Rk	GCL Blue Jays	1	1	0	15	7	8.40	1.60	7.4	321	35	43	5.32	2.4	4.2	1.8	0.6	29
2013	Rk	GCL Blue Jays	1	1	0	10	9	10.69	2.38	5.8	296	38	50	6.29	10.7	8.0	0.8	0.0	-126

Long and lean starter who has significant problem with command. Struggles to maintain arm slot and velocity while FB lacks movement. Hard SL is best present pitch and can miss bats. Needs greater separation between FB and CU. Pure stuff is impressive, but is still very raw. Effort in delivery could lead to pen.

Gonzalez,Alex — SP — Texas

EXP MLB DEBUT: 2015 | POTENTIAL: #2 starter | **8C**

Thrws R Age 22
2013 (1) Oral Roberts

Velo	Pitch	Grade
89-95	FB	++++
83-87	SL	++++
84-86	CU	++

Year	Lev	Team	W	L	Sv	IP	K	ERA	WHIP	BF/G	OBA	H%	S%	xERA	Ctl	Dom	Cmd	hr/9	BPV
2011	NCAA	Oral Roberts	8	7	0	105	100	3.51	1.32	22.9	244	32	73	3.22	3.7	8.6	2.3	0.3	73
2012	NCAA	Oral Roberts	6	3	0	86	66	2.30	1.01	19.4	206	26	76	1.85	2.5	6.9	2.8	0.2	75
2013	NCAA	Oral Roberts	9	5	0	113	126	1.83	0.97	28.6	206	29	83	1.90	2.1	10.0	4.7	0.4	140
2013	A-	Spokane	0	4	0	23	20	4.66	1.59	11.4	314	39	69	4.97	2.7	7.8	2.9	0.4	84
2013	A+	Myrtle Beach	0	0	0	19	15	2.84	1.26	15.5	219	27	78	2.88	4.3	7.1	1.7	0.5	31

Sinkerballer who keeps hitters off-balance with solid-average to plus offerings. FB features exceptional movement with sink and cut. Hard SL serves as out pitch while CU shows potential to be dependable. Delivery can be too mechanical at times, but limits walks. Could use better command of SL and can be reliant on FB.

Gonzalez,Miguel — SP — Philadelphia

EXP MLB DEBUT: 2014 | POTENTIAL: #3 starter | **8B**

Thrws R Age 27
2013 FA (Cuba)

Velo	Pitch	Grade
91-94	FB	+++
78-82	SP	++
78-82	CU	++
75-79	CB	+

Year	Lev	Team	W	L	Sv	IP	K	ERA	WHIP	BF/G	OBA	H%	S%	xERA	Ctl	Dom	Cmd	hr/9	BPV
2009	FOR	Cuba	8	4	0	126	101	2.14								7.2		2.9	
2010	FOR	Cuba	6	6	0	100	77	1.44	0.08	3.2	21	30	26	0.82	0.2	6.9	38.5	3.5	138
2011	FOR	Cuba	8	5	0	113	74	2.31	0.10	3.0	27	30	50	1.15	0.2	5.9	37.0	3.7	120

Cuban defector with athletic body, but missed time during last two seasons in his trek to U.S. Threw well in Fall Instructional League, and will have shot at earning a rotation spot. Decent FB, uses splitter and change-up as primarly off-speed pitches. Some concern about lack of MLB-ready breaking pitch.

Gonzalez,Severino — SP — Philadelphia

EXP MLB DEBUT: 2015 | POTENTIAL: #4/#5 starter | **7D**

Thrws R Age 21
2011 FA (Panama)

Velo	Pitch	Grade
90-92	FB	+++
	CB	++
	SL	++

Year	Lev	Team	W	L	Sv	IP	K	ERA	WHIP	BF/G	OBA	H%	S%	xERA	Ctl	Dom	Cmd	hr/9	BPV
2013	A	Lakewood	3	0	0	21	31	1.71	0.62	18.1	144	24	75	0.31	1.3	13.2	10.3	0.4	221
2013	A+	Clearwater	3	5	0	75	82	2.03	1.13	14.9	237	32	84	2.76	2.3	9.8	4.3	0.5	133
2013	AA	Reading	1	0	0	6	6	2.90	1.29	25.5	314	41	75	3.82	0.0	8.7		0.0	175

Unheralded, skinny hurler had a breakout season in High-A. Gets by on exquisite control for now, but question is will it hold up in the future. Sports only an average arsenal, which points to probability that Ks will go down as he rises through the system. Working on a CU to combat lefty hitters.

Graham,J.R. — SP — Atlanta

EXP MLB DEBUT: 2014 | POTENTIAL: #2 starter | **9D**

Thrws R Age 24
2011 (4) Santa Clara

Velo	Pitch	Grade
92-95	FB	++++
82-85	SL	+++
	CU	++

Year	Lev	Team	W	L	Sv	IP	K	ERA	WHIP	BF/G	OBA	H%	S%	xERA	Ctl	Dom	Cmd	hr/9	BPV
2011	NCAA	Santa Clara	3	5	3	62	45	3.34	1.00	10.3	233	29	64	2.09	1.3	6.5	5.0	0.1	100
2011	Rk	Danville	5	2	0	57	52	1.73	1.14	17.4	244	32	83	2.43	2.0	8.2	4.0	0.0	110
2012	A+	Lynchburg	9	1	0	102	68	2.64	1.03	23.1	234	27	76	2.54	1.5	6.0	4.0	0.5	85
2012	AA	Mississippi	3	1	0	45	42	3.19	1.15	19.9	216	28	72	2.49	3.4	8.4	2.5	0.4	77
2013	AA	Mississippi	1	3	0	35	28	4.09	1.39	18.5	282	35	67	3.61	2.6	7.2	2.8	0.0	78

Short, strong-armed RHP made just 8 starts before being shut down. Did not require surgery and he should be 100% in 2014. When healthy has a plus 92-95 FB and SL. CU is average and attacks hitters low in the strike zone, inducing plenty of ground balls.

Granier,Drew — SP — Oakland — EXP MLB DEBUT: 2014 — POTENTIAL: Middle reliever — 6B

Thrws R Age 25
2011 (32) Louisiana-Monroe

Velo	Pitch	Grade
87-92	FB	+++
75-79	CB	+++
79-81	CU	+++

Year	Lev	Team	W	L	Sv	IP	K	ERA	WHIP	BF/G	OBA	H%	S%	xERA	Ctl	Dom	Cmd	hr/9	BPV
2011	Rk	AZL Athletics	5	1	0	23	35	1.57	0.83	14.0	156	27	83	0.93	2.7	13.7	5.0	0.4	191
2011	A-	Vermont	1	1	0	28	34	1.92	1.53	17.5	209	32	86	2.96	7.0	10.9	1.5	0.0	24
2012	A	Burlington	11	10	0	162	167	3.22	1.25	23.6	246	32	76	3.34	2.9	9.3	3.2	0.7	105
2013	A+	Stockton	6	3	0	83	97	3.25	1.34	24.6	233	33	76	3.28	4.3	10.5	2.4	0.5	90
2013	AA	Midland	3	6	0	72	56	5.24	1.72	23.4	287	33	71	5.57	5.2	7.0	1.3	1.1	2

Short, strong SP who lacks premium velocity, but gets plus pitch movement due to arm action. FB misses bats and pitch sequencing is strong suit. Doesn't throw with much angle to plate which can leave ball up in zone. Doesn't throw enough strikes and lacks ideal breaking ball to register Ks at upper levels.

Gray,Jonathan — SP — Colorado — EXP MLB DEBUT: 2015 — POTENTIAL: #1 starter — 9C

Thrws R Age 22
2013 (1) Oklahoma

Velo	Pitch	Grade
95-97	FB	++++
85-88	SL	++++
81-84	CU	++

Year	Lev	Team	W	L	Sv	IP	K	ERA	WHIP	BF/G	OBA	H%	S%	xERA	Ctl	Dom	Cmd	hr/9	BPV
2012	NCAA	Oklahoma	8	4	0	102	104	3.17	1.39	23.9	258	34	76	3.49	3.7	9.2	2.5	0.3	83
2013	NCAA	Oklahoma	10	3	0	126	147	1.64	0.85	27.2	189	28	79	1.08	1.7	10.5	6.1	0.1	161
2013	Rk	Grand Junction	0	0	0	13	15	4.12	1.30	13.5	289	41	65	3.44	1.4	10.3	7.5	0.0	166
2013	A+	Modesto	4	0	0	24	36	0.75	0.67	16.7	129	24	88	0.00	2.3	13.5	6.0	0.0	200

3rd pick in the draft has an ideal power frame. Attacks hitters with a plus 95-97 mph FB. Holds velocity deep into games and commands FB to both sides of the plate. SL is a true swing-and-miss pitch. CU is undeveloped but has potential. Impressive debut.

Green,Hunter — SP — Los Angeles (A) — EXP MLB DEBUT: 2018 — POTENTIAL: #3 starter — 8D

Thrws L Age 18
2013 (2) HS (KY)

Velo	Pitch	Grade
85-93	FB	+++
76-79	CB	+++
78-80	CU	++

Year	Lev	Team	W	L	Sv	IP	K	ERA	WHIP	BF/G	OBA	H%	S%	xERA	Ctl	Dom	Cmd	hr/9	BPV
2013	Rk	AZL Angels	0	1	0	16	11	4.44	1.98	9.7	259	32	75	4.77	8.9	6.1	0.7	0.0	-112

Raw LHP who may take a while to develop, but owns upside. Has athletic delivery and uses clean, quick arm to generate FB. Needs to find consistency in secondary pitches, especially CB. Has trouble repeating delivery which negatively impacts CU. Could stand to add strength in order to increase velocity.

Gregorio,Joan — SP — San Francisco — EXP MLB DEBUT: 2016 — POTENTIAL: #4 starter — 7D

Thrws R Age 22
2010 FA (DR)

Velo	Pitch	Grade
88-93	FB	+++
	SL	++
	CU	+

Year	Lev	Team	W	L	Sv	IP	K	ERA	WHIP	BF/G	OBA	H%	S%	xERA	Ctl	Dom	Cmd	hr/9	BPV
2011	Rk	AZL Giants	3	0	0	50	43	2.34	1.18	16.7	233	30	79	2.57	2.9	7.7	2.7	0.2	79
2012	A-	Salem-Keizer	7	7	0	76	69	5.56	1.42	20.2	284	34	62	4.69	2.7	8.2	3.0	1.1	91
2013	A	Augusta	6	3	0	69	84	4.03	1.18	19.8	250	36	65	2.97	2.2	10.9	4.9	0.4	155

Tall, lean SP with good low-90s FB had nice rebound season in 2013. Dom, Ctl, and Cmd all trending in the right direction and secondary pitches are developing. Complements FB with SL that flashes average and a below average CU. Arm works well and he repeats his delivery. Someone to keep an eye on in 2014.

Gsellman,Robert — SP — New York (N) — EXP MLB DEBUT: 2017 — POTENTIAL: #4 starter — 7C

Thrws R Age 21
2011 (13) HS (CA)

Velo	Pitch	Grade
89-92	FB	+++
79-82	CB	+++
81-84	CU	+++

Year	Lev	Team	W	L	Sv	IP	K	ERA	WHIP	BF/G	OBA	H%	S%	xERA	Ctl	Dom	Cmd	hr/9	BPV
2011	Rk	GCL Mets	0	0	1	13	8	4.15	1.31	7.7	290	33	69	4.18	1.4	5.5	4.0	0.7	80
2012	Rk	Kingsport	1	3	0	43	33	3.96	1.39	16.5	256	31	72	3.83	3.8	6.9	1.8	0.6	41
2013	A-	Brooklyn	3	3	0	70	64	2.06	1.01	22.4	230	30	80	2.18	1.5	8.2	5.3	0.3	124
2013	A	Savannah	2	3	0	29	14	3.72	1.41	24.6	300	33	74	4.54	1.9	4.3	2.3	0.6	46

Athletic framed pitcher, but has yet to learn to leverage height for strikeouts. Low effort delivery that he repeats well. Excellent command (1.6 Ctl in '13) and does a good job of keeping arm speed on secondary pitches. Throws across his body with a good bit of deception. Good feel for secondary pitches.

Gueller,Mitch — SP — Philadelphia — EXP MLB DEBUT: 2017 — POTENTIAL: #3 starter — 7C

Thrws R Age 20
2012 (1) HS (WA)

Velo	Pitch	Grade
90-93	FB	+++
80-83	CB	++
	CU	++

Year	Lev	Team	W	L	Sv	IP	K	ERA	WHIP	BF/G	OBA	H%	S%	xERA	Ctl	Dom	Cmd	hr/9	BPV
2012	Rk	GCL Phillies	1	5	0	27	19	5.31	1.40	14.3	254	31	58	3.25	4.0	6.3	1.6	0.0	24
2013	A-	Williamsport	3	8	0	58	35	5.89	1.88	19.5	336	38	68	6.28	4.0	5.4	1.3	0.6	7

High pick that has not yet justified his selection. Lack of FB command has hampered him so far and he's still learning the nuance and feel of his breaking pitch. As a northern high-schooler, needs more reps, along with consistency and confidence in his stuff. Developing slowly.

Guerrieri,Taylor — SP — Tampa Bay — EXP MLB DEBUT: 2016 — POTENTIAL: #2 starter — 9C

Thrws R Age 21
2011 (1) HS (SC)

Velo	Pitch	Grade
90-95	FB	++++
77-81	CB	++++
80-83	CU	+++

Year	Lev	Team	W	L	Sv	IP	K	ERA	WHIP	BF/G	OBA	H%	S%	xERA	Ctl	Dom	Cmd	hr/9	BPV
2012	A-	Hudson Valley	1	2	0	52	45	1.04	0.77	15.6	193	26	85	0.88	0.9	7.8	9.0	0.0	135
2013	A	Bowling Green	6	2	0	67	51	2.01	0.99	18.2	222	26	84	2.42	1.6	6.9	4.3	0.7	98

Long, lean SP who underwent TJ surgery in July and will concurrently serve 50-game drug suspension. Has incredible polish along with 2 plus offerings in FB and sharp CB. Locates with precision and can wipe out hitters with CB. CU has potential to be third top pitch. Keeps ball on ground and is tough to hit.

Guillon,Ismael — SP — Cincinnati — EXP MLB DEBUT: 2016 — POTENTIAL: #3 starter — 7D

Thrws L Age 22
2008 FA (Venezuela)

Velo	Pitch	Grade
88-92	FB	+++
	CU	+++
	CB	++

Year	Lev	Team	W	L	Sv	IP	K	ERA	WHIP	BF/G	OBA	H%	S%	xERA	Ctl	Dom	Cmd	hr/9	BPV
2010	Rk	AZL Reds	3	3	0	57	73	3.32	1.09	18.6	195	30	67	1.82	3.6	11.5	3.2	0.2	127
2011	Rk	Billings	3	6	0	63	61	6.57	1.97	20.1	305	36	69	6.87	6.6	8.7	1.3	1.6	-3
2012	Rk	Billings	4	1	0	51	63	2.29	1.24	18.8	213	32	81	2.43	4.2	11.1	2.6	0.2	104
2012	A	Dayton	2	0	0	24	27	2.60	1.20	24.3	244	33	81	3.26	2.6	10.0	3.9	0.7	128
2013	A	Dayton	7	8	0	121	134	4.76	1.57	19.7	218	28	72	4.14	7.1	10.0	1.4	1.0	7

Command issues kept Guillon from repeating '12 breakout. But all was not lost as CB improved and could give him three above-average pitches by time he reaches majors. Continues to strike out more than a batter an inning with good FB and plus CU. With lots of reps, could become nice mid-rotation starter.

Guilmet,Preston — RP — Cleveland — EXP MLB DEBUT: 2013 — POTENTIAL: Middle reliever — 6C

Thrws R Age 26
2009 (9) Arizona

Velo	Pitch	Grade
88-92	FB	+++
80-82	SL	+++
81-84	CU	++

Year	Lev	Team	W	L	Sv	IP	K	ERA	WHIP	BF/G	OBA	H%	S%	xERA	Ctl	Dom	Cmd	hr/9	BPV
2010	A	Lake County	4	1	11	52	79	2.25	0.87	6.4	193	32	76	1.55	1.7	13.7	7.9	0.5	217
2011	A+	Kinston	1	1	35	58	60	2.17	0.93	4.2	208	27	80	2.03	1.7	9.3	5.5	0.6	139
2012	AA	Akron	2	2	24	52	51	2.41	1.03	4.0	218	28	80	2.48	2.2	8.8	3.9	0.7	116
2013	AAA	Columbus	5	4	20	64	72	1.68	0.89	4.9	192	26	85	1.68	2.0	10.1	5.1	0.6	147
2013	MLB	CLE	0	0	0	5	1	10.19	2.08	6.5	349	36	45	6.45	5.1	1.7	0.3	0.0	-89

Poised, durable RP who served as closer in AAA. Succeeds with unusual arm action and uses height to throw on downhill plane. Spots FB within strike zone to get ahead of hitters and uses SL and CU with splitter-action to keep them guessing. Subject to flyballs as he can leave pitches up, but HR haven't been issue.

Gurka,Jason — RP — Baltimore — EXP MLB DEBUT: 2014 — POTENTIAL: Situational reliever — 6B

Thrws L Age 26
2008 (15) Angelina JC

Velo	Pitch	Grade
86-92	FB	+++
81-83	SL	++
	CU	+++

Year	Lev	Team	W	L	Sv	IP	K	ERA	WHIP	BF/G	OBA	H%	S%	xERA	Ctl	Dom	Cmd	hr/9	BPV
2011	A	Delmarva	2	0	0	25	33	2.52	1.20	7.7	284	39	88	4.46	0.7	11.9	16.5	1.4	212
2011	A+	Frederick	1	1	1	28	34	3.20	1.00	5.4	193	27	69	2.03	2.9	10.9	3.8	0.6	136
2012	A+	Frederick	1	2	1	45	43	2.20	0.93	8.5	191	26	76	1.44	2.4	8.6	3.6	0.2	108
2012	AA	Bowie	2	3	1	20	22	3.60	1.55	7.3	252	32	82	4.83	5.4	9.9	1.8	1.4	50
2013	AA	Bowie	2	2	4	39	46	2.98	1.35	8.2	240	34	78	3.33	4.1	10.6	2.6	0.5	97

Short lefty who has spent entire career in pen. Has chance to become situational RP due to ability to handle LHH. Posts high K rate with effective sinker and sharp SL. FB sits in 86-92 mph range and is spotted low in zone. Had bouts of wildness as he doesn't command offspeed pitches, but throws with little effort.

Hader,Josh — SP — Houston — EXP MLB DEBUT: 2016 — POTENTIAL: #4 starter — 7C

Thrws L Age 20
2012 (19) HS (MD)

Velo	Pitch	Grade
89-94	FB	+++
80-82	SL	+++
83-85	CU	++

Year	Lev	Team	W	L	Sv	IP	K	ERA	WHIP	BF/G	OBA	H%	S%	xERA	Ctl	Dom	Cmd	hr/9	BPV
2012	Rk	GCL Orioles	2	0	2	20	35	2.69	0.95	6.3	175	32	76	1.88	3.1	15.7	5.0	0.9	215
2012	A-	Aberdeen	0	0	0	8	13	0.00	0.49	5.4	81	17	100	0.00	2.2	14.4	6.5	0.0	218
2013	A	Delmarva	3	6	0	85	79	2.65	1.28	20.5	218	28	80	2.87	4.4	8.4	1.9	0.4	48
2013	A	Quad Cities	2	0	0	22	16	3.26	1.18	17.7	183	23	69	1.81	4.9	6.5	1.3	0.0	3

Long, lanky SP who was consistently good and added strength for stamina. Throws from deceptive, low ¾ slot, but can vary angle for different looks. Command can be issue due to mechanics, though can place strong FB into zone. SL projects to average and CU has chance for more if he repeats arm speed.

Hahn,Jesse — SP — Tampa Bay

EXP MLB DEBUT: 2015 | POTENTIAL: #3 SP / Setup RP | **8D**

Thrws R Age 24
2010 (6) Virginia Tech

Velo	Pitch	Grade
91-98	FB	++++
76-82	CB	+++
82-86	CU	++

Year	Lev	Team	W	L	Sv	IP	K	ERA	WHIP	BF/G	OBA	H%	S%	xERA	Ctl	Dom	Cmd	hr/9	BPV
2009	NCAA	Virginia Tech	1	2	1	24	23	6.00	1.96	6.7	334	42	69	6.55	4.9	8.6	1.8	0.8	42
2010	NCAA	Virginia Tech	5	4	0	73	76	3.70	1.25	22.8	256	33	72	3.56	2.5	9.4	3.8	0.7	120
2012	A-	Hudson Valley	2	2	0	52	55	2.77	1.02	14.3	206	29	70	1.64	2.6	9.5	3.7	0.0	119
2013	Rk	GCL Rays	0	0	0	2	4	0.00	2.00	9.6	415	71	100	7.40	0.0	18.0		0.0	342
2013	A+	Charlotte	2	1	0	67	63	2.15	1.09	13.8	225	30	79	2.20	2.4	8.5	3.5	0.1	105

Lean SP who bypassed Low-A, but had no trouble in High-A. Tough on hitters from both sides and is extreme GB guy. Has arm strength and pitch mix to post high K rates. Uses height to make angle difficult on batters. Plus FB is best offering and uses hard, overhand CB as solid complement. Injury history gives pause.

Hale,David — SP — Atlanta

EXP MLB DEBUT: 2013 | POTENTIAL: #4 starter | **7C**

Thrws R Age 26
2009 (3) Princeton

Velo	Pitch	Grade
92-94	FB	+++
80-83	SL	+++
80-83	CU	+++

Year	Lev	Team	W	L	Sv	IP	K	ERA	WHIP	BF/G	OBA	H%	S%	xERA	Ctl	Dom	Cmd	hr/9	BPV
2010	A	Rome	5	8	5	93	69	4.15	1.51	14.4	270	33	70	3.83	4.2	6.7	1.6	0.1	23
2011	A+	Lynchburg	4	6	0	101	86	4.10	1.35	15.0	271	33	71	4.09	2.7	7.7	2.9	0.8	84
2012	AA	Mississippi	8	4	0	145	124	3.78	1.29	22.1	228	28	72	3.27	4.2	7.7	1.9	0.7	44
2013	AAA	Gwinnett	6	9	0	114	77	3.23	1.39	21.9	276	32	78	4.13	2.8	6.1	2.1	0.6	51
2013	MLB	ATL	1	0	0	11	14	0.82	1.09	21.5	262	39	92	2.52	0.8	11.5	14.0	0.0	202

Athletic RH flies under the radar. Another solid season and pitched effectively in MLB. Plus arm strength and easy velocity on 92-94 mph FB. Complements FB with a plus SL and an avg CU. Drop in Dom, but could carve out a role at the back of a rotation.

Haley,Justin — SP — Boston

EXP MLB DEBUT: 2016 | POTENTIAL: #5 starter | **7C**

Thrws R Age 23
2012 (6) Fresno State

Velo	Pitch	Grade
87-94	FB	+++
77-81	CB	+++
82-84	CU	++

Year	Lev	Team	W	L	Sv	IP	K	ERA	WHIP	BF/G	OBA	H%	S%	xERA	Ctl	Dom	Cmd	hr/9	BPV
2011	NCAA	Fresno St.	1	0	0	32	28	2.52	1.40	15.1	267	33	84	3.94	3.4	7.9	2.3	0.6	68
2012	NCAA	Fresno St.	7	4	0	93	94	3.19	1.45	18.1	268	36	76	3.62	3.8	9.1	2.4	0.1	80
2012	A-	Lowell	0	1	0	33	33	1.90	1.18	10.2	198	27	84	2.21	4.4	9.0	2.1	0.3	62
2013	A	Greenville	7	11	0	124	124	3.70	1.38	20.0	217	28	75	3.36	5.4	9.0	1.7	0.7	35

Tall, durable SP who got better as season progressed. Pitches downhill with heavy FB that features excellent late action. Secondary pitches have potential to become solid-average, though has trouble commanding plate. Has posted decent K rate while limiting RHH. Could be sleeper if he throws more strikes.

Haley,Trey — RP — Cleveland

EXP MLB DEBUT: 2014 | POTENTIAL: Setup reliever | **7D**

Thrws R Age 24
2008 (2) HS (TX)

Velo	Pitch	Grade
92-99	FB	++++
80-83	CB	++
82-84	CU	++

Year	Lev	Team	W	L	Sv	IP	K	ERA	WHIP	BF/G	OBA	H%	S%	xERA	Ctl	Dom	Cmd	hr/9	BPV
2011	A+	Kinston	1	1	1	28	27	3.83	1.49	6.4	239	31	73	3.55	5.4	8.6	1.6	0.3	27
2012	Rk	AZL Indians	1	0	0	6	10	7.50	1.67	6.7	321	54	50	4.82	3.0	15.0	5.0	0.0	207
2012	A+	Carolina	0	0	2	17	16	1.05	0.82	5.2	142	20	86	0.45	3.2	8.4	2.7	0.0	84
2012	AA	Akron	3	1	0	15	23	1.79	1.39	7.1	190	34	86	2.36	6.6	13.7	2.1	0.0	88
2013	AA	Akron	1	4	7	44	46	4.70	1.73	5.1	230	32	70	3.72	8.0	9.4	1.2	0.0	-28

Max-effort RHP who has been reliever since '11. Has command issues due to violent delivery. Offers hint of deception and pitches aggressively off of plus FB. Patient hitters can lay off heavy FB and wait for inconsistent CB and CU. Very rarely allows HR and induces tons of GB. Big frame can be intimidating.

Harvey,Hunter — SP — Baltimore

EXP MLB DEBUT: 2017 | POTENTIAL: #2 starter | **8C**

Thrws R Age 19
2013 (1) HS (NC)

Velo	Pitch	Grade
89-94	FB	++++
80-83	CB	+++
81-84	CU	++

Year	Lev	Team	W	L	Sv	IP	K	ERA	WHIP	BF/G	OBA	H%	S%	xERA	Ctl	Dom	Cmd	hr/9	BPV
2013	Rk	GCL Orioles	0	0	0	13	18	1.37	0.92	9.8	213	35	83	1.44	1.4	12.4	9.0	0.0	203
2013	A-	Aberdeen	0	1	0	12	15	2.25	1.25	16.3	245	37	80	2.70	3.0	11.3	3.8	0.0	140

Tall, lean first round pick who is all about projection. Uses fast arm and clean delivery to pepper strike zone with quality FB and can keep ball down. Has potential for three above average offerings with big-breaking CB key to success. Can get hitters to chase breaking ball and needs CU to battle LHH.

Hassebrock,Blake — RP — Oakland

EXP MLB DEBUT: 2015 | POTENTIAL: Setup reliever | **7D**

Thrws R Age 24
2010 (8) UNC-Greensboro

Velo	Pitch	Grade
90-96	FB	+++
81-83	SL	+++
80-84	CU	+

Year	Lev	Team	W	L	Sv	IP	K	ERA	WHIP	BF/G	OBA	H%	S%	xERA	Ctl	Dom	Cmd	hr/9	BPV
2011	A	Burlington	7	8	0	139	110	2.65	1.29	22.0	253	31	81	3.48	3.0	7.1	2.4	0.6	66
2012	A	Burlington	2	2	0	27	20	4.00	1.59	23.8	302	35	78	5.36	3.3	6.7	2.0	1.0	48
2012	A+	Stockton	2	6	0	50	44	8.25	2.07	17.5	372	44	59	7.83	3.6	7.9	2.2	1.1	63
2013	A+	Stockton	2	4	1	61	68	4.28	1.41	9.9	249	34	70	3.72	4.3	10.0	2.3	0.6	83
2013	AA	Midland	0	2	0	16	5	6.71	1.55	5.9	284	30	54	4.61	3.9	2.8	0.7	0.6	-37

Tall, athletic pitcher who is versatile enough to perform in any role. Mostly RP in '13 and likely found niche. Has choppy mechanics, though repeats delivery which enhances solid-average FB that he locates well. SL can be decent and exhibit nice break, but CU is distant third pitch. Can be hittable and has limited upside.

Heaney,Andrew — SP — Miami

EXP MLB DEBUT: 2014 | POTENTIAL: #2 starter | **9C**

Thrws L Age 23
2012 (1) Oklahoma State

Velo	Pitch	Grade
91-97	FB	++++
	SL	++++
	CU	++++

Year	Lev	Team	W	L	Sv	IP	K	ERA	WHIP	BF/G	OBA	H%	S%	xERA	Ctl	Dom	Cmd	hr/9	BPV
2012	NCAA	Oklahoma St.	8	2	0	118	140	1.60	0.81	28.6	182	27	82	1.12	1.7	10.7	6.4	0.3	165
2012	Rk	GCL Marlins	0	0	0	7	9	2.57	1.29	14.4	262	39	78	3.01	2.6	11.6	4.5	0.0	157
2012	A	Greensboro	1	2	0	20	21	4.95	1.45	21.4	307	41	62	4.11	1.8	9.5	5.3	0.0	140
2013	A+	Jupiter	5	2	0	61	66	0.88	1.01	18.0	207	29	93	1.91	2.5	9.7	3.9	0.3	125
2013	AA	Jacksonville	4	1	0	33	23	2.98	1.20	22.3	249	29	76	3.19	2.4	6.2	2.6	0.5	64

Polished, advanced LHP put everything together in '13. Comes at hitters with a low-90s FB up to 97, hard SL, and CU that freezes RHH. Commands all pitches with ease and improved his pitch sequencing and in-AB adjustments. Easy, clean arm action with repeatable mechanics.

Heckathorn,Kyle — RP — Milwaukee

EXP MLB DEBUT: 2014 | POTENTIAL: Reliever | **6B**

Thrws R Age 26
2009 (1) Kennesaw State

Velo	Pitch	Grade
88-93	FB	+++
83-85	SL	+++
	CU	++

Year	Lev	Team	W	L	Sv	IP	K	ERA	WHIP	BF/G	OBA	H%	S%	xERA	Ctl	Dom	Cmd	hr/9	BPV
2010	A+	Brevard County	4	0	0	39	23	3.00	1.28	20.0	267	31	76	3.35	2.3	5.3	2.3	0.2	51
2011	A+	Brevard County	5	6	0	79	65	3.98	1.30	21.8	269	32	72	4.04	2.4	7.4	3.1	0.9	87
2011	AA	Huntsville	0	4	0	36	24	7.23	1.72	23.4	307	33	60	6.45	4.2	6.0	1.4	1.7	11
2012	AA	Huntsville	5	11	0	119	88	4.76	1.39	14.3	274	33	65	3.98	2.9	6.6	2.3	0.5	60
2013	AAA	Nashville	8	3	1	65	46	3.60	1.25	5.5	214	25	72	3.00	4.3	6.4	1.5	0.7	17

Tall, big-bodied RP officially moved to the pen in 2013 with better results. No longer reaches upper 90 with the FB, but uses hard SL and below average CU. Despite solid offerings, fails to finish hitters. Poor mechanics and erratic control of FB have led to command issues in the past and forced the move to the bullpen.

Hellweg,Johnny — SP — Milwaukee

EXP MLB DEBUT: 2013 | POTENTIAL: #3 starter/ Reliever | **8E**

Thrws R Age 25
2008 (16) Florida CC

Velo	Pitch	Grade
93-97	FB	++++
	CB	+++
	CU	++

Year	Lev	Team	W	L	Sv	IP	K	ERA	WHIP	BF/G	OBA	H%	S%	xERA	Ctl	Dom	Cmd	hr/9	BPV
2012	AA	Arkansas	5	10	0	119	88	3.40	1.38	23.9	238	28	76	3.56	4.5	6.6	1.5	0.6	15
2012	AA	Huntsville	2	1	0	20	17	2.70	1.55	12.5	221	29	81	3.18	6.8	7.7	1.1	0.0	-27
2013	A	Wisconsin	1	0	0	6	4	3.00	1.17	23.9	228	28	71	2.32	3.0	6.0	2.0	0.0	45
2013	AAA	Nashville	12	5	0	125	89	3.16	1.47	23.4	226	27	79	3.46	5.8	6.4	1.1	0.4	-24
2013	MLB	MIL	1	4	0	31	9	6.74	2.15	19.1	316	32	68	6.91	7.6	2.6	0.3	0.9	-140

Tall, skinny RH continues to be affected by inconsistent mechanics. Mid-90s FB up to 98 at times, complemented with an average CB and below average CU. Works downhill to get good ground ball rates while pounding his FB to generate swing-and-misses. Has dominant stuff, but future may be as a power RP.

Hembree,Heath — RP — San Francisco

EXP MLB DEBUT: 2013 | POTENTIAL: Setup reliever | **8C**

Thrws R Age 25
2010 (5) College of Charleston

Velo	Pitch	Grade
93-96	FB	++++
82-86	SL	++++
	CU	++

Year	Lev	Team	W	L	Sv	IP	K	ERA	WHIP	BF/G	OBA	H%	S%	xERA	Ctl	Dom	Cmd	hr/9	BPV
2011	AA	Richmond	1	1	17	28	34	2.87	1.17	4.0	201	29	75	2.25	4.1	10.9	2.6	0.3	101
2012	A+	San Jose	0	0	0	5	7	0.00	0.20	3.0	0	0	100	0.00	1.8	12.6	7.0	0.0	196
2012	AAA	Fresno	1	1	15	38	36	4.74	1.29	4.0	213	28	62	2.87	4.7	8.5	1.8	0.5	44
2013	AAA	Fresno	1	4	31	55	63	4.08	1.27	4.2	258	34	71	4.01	2.6	10.3	3.9	1.1	133
2013	MLB	SF	0	0	0	8	12	0.00	0.78	3.1	156	29	100	0.43	2.3	14.0	6.0	0.0	207

Strong-armed RP took a leap forward in 2013 and showed he has the potential to be a late-inning weapon. Pitches in the mid-90s up to 99 with the FB and pairs it with a plus, power SL that generates good swing-and-miss results. Improved mechanics have led to more elite Cmd numbers when paired with his plus Dom.

Hendricks,Kyle — SP — Chicago (N)

EXP MLB DEBUT: 2014 | POTENTIAL: #5 starter | **6B**

Thrws R Age 24
2011 (8) Dartmouth

Velo	Pitch	Grade
87-91	FB	++
	CB	+++
	CU	+++

Year	Lev	Team	W	L	Sv	IP	K	ERA	WHIP	BF/G	OBA	H%	S%	xERA	Ctl	Dom	Cmd	hr/9	BPV
2011	AA	Frisco	0	0	0	3	2	3.00	2.00	14.5	321	38	83	5.75	6.0	6.0	1.0	0.0	-36
2012	A+	Daytona	1	0	0	17	11	4.24	1.18	13.6	262	27	71	4.28	1.6	5.8	3.7	1.6	80
2012	A+	Myrtle Beach	5	8	0	130	112	2.83	1.06	25.3	251	31	75	2.85	1.0	7.7	7.5	0.6	129
2013	AA	Tennessee	10	3	0	126	101	1.86	1.05	23.3	231	29	82	2.27	1.9	7.2	3.9	0.2	98
2013	AAA	Iowa	3	1	0	40	27	2.48	1.08	26.0	237	28	78	2.62	1.8	6.1	3.4	0.5	79

Finesse, control artist continues to put up eye-popping numbers. FB rarely breaks 90 mph, but CB and CU are above-average and he understands how to keep hitters off-balance.Now has a career 4.9 Cmd rate and the pitching-thin Cubs can use the help.

Hensley,Ty — SP — New York (A)

EXP MLB DEBUT: 2016 | POTENTIAL: #2 starter | 9D

Thrws R Age 21
2012 (1) HS (OK)

Velo	Pitch	Grade
91-97	FB	++++
77-79	CB	+++
78-81	CU	++

Year	Lev	Team	W	L	Sv	IP	K	ERA	WHIP	BF/G	OBA	H%	S%	xERA	Ctl	Dom	Cmd	hr/9	BPV
2012	Rk	GCL Yankees	1	2	0	12	14	3.00	1.25	9.8	191	26	79	2.75	5.3	10.5	2.0	0.8	65

Tall, raw SP who did not pitch due to hip surgery. Shows high upside due to arm strength and FB/CB combo. Maintains velocity when healthy. Has tendency to slow arm speed on CU and can be erratic with arm slot. Ingredients are there for frontline starter, but needs time to develop and add polish.

Heredia,Luis — SP — Pittsburgh

EXP MLB DEBUT: 2016 | POTENTIAL: #2 starter | 8D

Thrws R Age 19
2010 FA (Mexico)

Velo	Pitch	Grade
90-93	FB	++++
	CB	++
83-85	CU	++
	SL	++

Year	Lev	Team	W	L	Sv	IP	K	ERA	WHIP	BF/G	OBA	H%	S%	xERA	Ctl	Dom	Cmd	hr/9	BPV
2011	Rk	GCL Pirates	1	2	0	30	23	4.78	1.56	11.0	248	29	70	4.41	5.7	6.9	1.2	0.9	-12
2012	A-	State College	4	2	0	66	40	2.72	1.10	18.5	221	26	75	2.34	2.7	5.4	2.0	0.3	43
2013	A	West Virginia	7	3	0	65	55	3.05	1.37	19.5	221	27	80	3.38	5.1	7.6	1.5	0.7	17

Tall, strong-armed hurler added weight—but not good weight—and velocity has topped out. Has a good 90-93 mph FB that can hit 95. CB, SL, and CU are avg or below and has yet to log more than 67 IP. Mechanics have become inconsistent, but is still just 19.

Heston,Chris — SP — San Francisco

EXP MLB DEBUT: 2014 | POTENTIAL: #5 starter | 7D

Thrws R Age 26
2009 (12) East Carolina

Velo	Pitch	Grade
87-89	FB	++
	CB	+++
	SL	++
	CU	+++

Year	Lev	Team	W	L	Sv	IP	K	ERA	WHIP	BF/G	OBA	H%	S%	xERA	Ctl	Dom	Cmd	hr/9	BPV
2009	Rk	AZL Giants	1	5	0	35	34	4.11	1.14	12.6	233	32	60	2.30	2.6	8.7	3.4	0.0	106
2010	A	Augusta	5	13	0	148	124	3.77	1.31	23.5	278	35	70	3.68	2.0	7.5	3.8	0.4	99
2011	A+	San Jose	12	4	0	151	131	3.16	1.22	25.4	253	31	75	3.31	2.4	7.8	3.3	0.6	94
2012	AA	Richmond	9	8	0	148	135	2.25	1.11	23.3	229	30	78	2.27	2.4	8.2	3.4	0.1	100
2013	AAA	Fresno	7	6	0	108	97	5.82	1.62	25.3	297	36	65	5.49	3.8	8.1	2.1	1.2	60

Finesse RH stalled at AAA where hitters got the best of him. Continues to do what he does best: pound upper-80s sinker down in the zone to generate ground balls. Mixes in a CB and CU, both of which flash average, and a below average SL. Uses height well to get good downhill plane and repeats his delivery.

Hillis,Andy — RP — Milwaukee

EXP MLB DEBUT: 2016 | POTENTIAL: Reliever | 7D

Thrws R Age 23
2013 (11) Lee (TN)

Velo	Pitch	Grade
93-98	FB	++++
	SL	++

Year	Lev	Team	W	L	Sv	IP	K	ERA	WHIP	BF/G	OBA	H%	S%	xERA	Ctl	Dom	Cmd	hr/9	BPV
2013	NCAA	Lee	3	0	9	37	66	0.97	0.92	4.6	125	27	91	0.68	4.6	16.0	3.5	0.2	182
2013	Rk	Helena	3	1	5	20	23	0.45	1.29	4.9	197	29	96	2.21	5.3	10.2	1.9	0.0	58

Big, strong RP chose college over pros in 2009 and has come a long way since. Upper-80s in HS turned in mid-90s up to 98 now. Works with a good downhill plane, pounding the zone with his FB and pairing it with a SL that flashes average. All-out delivery hinders his command and lead to questions about his future role in the pen.

Hoffman,Matt — RP — Minnesota

EXP MLB DEBUT: 2014 | POTENTIAL: Situational reliever | 6B

Thrws L Age 25
2007 (26) HS (OK)

Velo	Pitch	Grade
90-95	FB	+++
80-82	SL	++
82-83	CU	+++

Year	Lev	Team	W	L	Sv	IP	K	ERA	WHIP	BF/G	OBA	H%	S%	xERA	Ctl	Dom	Cmd	hr/9	BPV
2010	AAA	Toledo	0	0	0	4	4	10.98	3.17	8.2	438	51	67	13.02	8.8	8.8	1.0	2.2	-61
2011	AA	Erie	0	0	0	0	0			2.3							0.0		
2011	AAA	Toledo	2	5	0	62	46	3.19	1.34	5.3	255	31	76	3.51	3.3	6.7	2.0	0.4	48
2012	AAA	Toledo	1	2	0	46	32	3.71	1.54	4.7	297	34	78	4.95	3.1	6.2	2.0	0.8	46
2013	AAA	Toledo	4	3	0	35	35	2.06	1.37	3.7	245	32	87	3.51	4.1	9.0	2.2	0.5	69

Lefty RP who spent third year in AAA and increased K rate. Likely profiles as situational guy due to success against LHH. Throws across body, but generates good velocity with clean arm from low ¾ slot. SL has regressed, but CU has been effective. Control going backwards, though is OK trade-off for K rate.

Holland,Neil — RP — Washington

EXP MLB DEBUT: 2014 | POTENTIAL: Reliever | 7C

Thrws R Age 25
2010 (11) Louisville

Velo	Pitch	Grade
90-95	FB	+++
	CB	++
	CU	++

Year	Lev	Team	W	L	Sv	IP	K	ERA	WHIP	BF/G	OBA	H%	S%	xERA	Ctl	Dom	Cmd	hr/9	BPV
2011	A	Hagerstown	1	0	1	24	22	1.13	0.92	5.6	237	29	95	2.49	0.4	8.3	22.0	0.8	156
2011	A+	Potomac	4	0	1	29	20	2.77	1.03	5.6	203	24	72	1.96	2.8	6.2	2.2	0.3	54
2012	A+	Potomac	7	1	4	60	44	1.65	0.97	5.8	206	25	85	1.96	2.1	6.6	3.1	0.4	80
2012	AAA	Syracuse	0	0	0	1	0	0.00	0.00	2.8	0	0	100	0.00	0.0	0.0		0.0	18
2013	AA	Harrisburg	1	4	1	50	63	2.87	1.18	4.9	253	36	77	3.12	2.0	11.3	5.7	0.5	168

Side-armed throwing righty can hit 95 with his FB and complements it with a hard breaking CB and below-average CU. Progressing steadily through system, he's posted excellent ERA at each stop; Dom saw a nice bump at Double-A. Because of arm angle, can be equally effective against LH and RH hitters.

Hollon,Clinton — SP — Toronto

EXP MLB DEBUT: 2017 | POTENTIAL: #3 starter | 8D

Thrws R Age 19
2013 (2) HS (KY)

Velo	Pitch	Grade
90-95	FB	+++
81-84	SL	+++
80-83	CU	++

Year	Lev	Team	W	L	Sv	IP	K	ERA	WHIP	BF/G	OBA	H%	S%	xERA	Ctl	Dom	Cmd	hr/9	BPV
2013	Rk	Bluefield	0	1	0	5	5	10.59	1.76	11.7	294	35	38	6.37	5.3	8.8	1.7	1.8	34
2013	Rk	GCL Blue Jays	1	0	0	12	10	0.00	0.42	9.7	56	8	100	0.00	2.3	7.5	3.3	0.0	92

Quick-armed starter who throws with overhand slot. Gets good movement to pitches, especially FB that features late sinking action. Sharp SL is developing nicely while CU lags behind. CU could be average in due time as he has some feel. Has effort in delivery, but generally throws strikes and maintains velocity.

Holmberg,David — SP — Cincinnati

EXP MLB DEBUT: 2013 | POTENTIAL: #3 starter | 8B

Thrws L Age 22
2009 (2) HS (FL)

Velo	Pitch	Grade
88-92	FB	+++
	SL	++
80-83	CU	++++

Year	Lev	Team	W	L	Sv	IP	K	ERA	WHIP	BF/G	OBA	H%	S%	xERA	Ctl	Dom	Cmd	hr/9	BPV
2011	A+	Visalia	4	6	0	71	76	4.68	1.52	23.7	267	35	69	4.28	4.4	9.6	2.2	0.6	72
2012	A+	Visalia	6	3	0	78	86	3.00	0.97	24.7	220	29	71	2.34	1.6	9.9	6.1	0.7	153
2012	AA	Mobile	5	5	0	95	67	3.60	1.34	26.3	280	32	75	4.15	2.2	6.3	2.9	0.8	73
2013	AA	Mobile	5	8	0	157	116	2.75	1.20	24.3	238	28	80	3.16	2.9	6.6	2.3	0.7	60
2013	MLB	ARI	0	0	0	4	0	7.30	2.43	19.4	365	37	67	7.67	7.3	0.0	0.0	0.0	-179

Came to CIN from ARI in offseason trade and is close to major league ready. Locates well with excellent command; helps average arsenal play up. In addition to low 90s sinking FB, pounds the strike zone with average SL and plus CU. Uses height to get good downward action on pitches and repeats mechanics well.

Holmes,Clay — SP — Pittsburgh

EXP MLB DEBUT: 2016 | POTENTIAL: #3 starter | 8D

Thrws R Age 21
2011 (9) HS (AL)

Velo	Pitch	Grade
90-93	FB	++++
	SL	++
	CU	++

Year	Lev	Team	W	L	Sv	IP	K	ERA	WHIP	BF/G	OBA	H%	S%	xERA	Ctl	Dom	Cmd	hr/9	BPV
2012	A-	State College	5	3	0	59	34	2.28	1.08	17.7	174	20	78	1.62	4.4	5.2	1.2	0.2	-8
2013	A	West Virginia	5	6	0	119	90	4.08	1.47	19.6	240	29	72	3.73	5.2	6.8	1.3	0.5	0

RHP got off to a slow start, but turned things around in the 2nd half - 3.20 ERA. Has a good 90-93 mph FB that he throws downhill, getting GB outs - 3.1 GB/FB. Also has a good SL. CU and overall command need to be better, but has nice potential.

Hope,Mason — SP — Miami

EXP MLB DEBUT: 2016 | POTENTIAL: #3 starter | 8E

Thrws R Age 22
2011 (5) HS (OK)

Velo	Pitch	Grade
90-93	FB	++++
73-76	CB	++++
70-72	CU	++++

Year	Lev	Team	W	L	Sv	IP	K	ERA	WHIP	BF/G	OBA	H%	S%	xERA	Ctl	Dom	Cmd	hr/9	BPV
2011	Rk	GCL Marlins	2	0	0	27	31	3.32	1.25	15.8	261	37	71	2.93	2.3	10.3	4.4	0.0	141
2012	A-	Jamestown	3	4	0	71	53	2.91	1.39	21.4	264	32	78	3.48	3.4	6.7	2.0	0.1	46
2013	A	Greensboro	6	6	1	98	73	4.95	1.56	16.5	266	30	70	4.83	4.9	6.7	1.4	1.1	7

Former HS teammate of Archie Bradley continued to make a name for himself. Features a low-90s FB with solid down action, an above average CB that henerates swings and misses, and an ineffective CU. Quick arm and athleticism work in his favor, but delivery has led to control issues.

House,T.J. — SP — Cleveland

EXP MLB DEBUT: 2013 | POTENTIAL: #5 starter | 6B

Thrws L Age 24
2008 (16) HS (MS)

Velo	Pitch	Grade
87-92	FB	+++
79-84	SL	++
82-83	CU	+++

Year	Lev	Team	W	L	Sv	IP	K	ERA	WHIP	BF/G	OBA	H%	S%	xERA	Ctl	Dom	Cmd	hr/9	BPV
2011	A+	Kinston	6	12	0	130	89	5.19	1.53	22.6	266	30	66	4.52	4.6	6.2	1.3	0.8	6
2012	A+	Carolina	2	0	0	25	26	1.44	0.92	23.4	194	26	86	1.60	2.2	9.4	4.3	0.4	128
2012	AA	Akron	8	5	0	124	90	3.99	1.27	22.1	246	29	68	3.29	3.2	6.5	2.0	0.5	49
2013	AA	Akron	2	1	0	22	27	3.26	1.04	21.3	243	35	68	2.53	1.2	11.0	9.0	0.4	183
2013	AAA	Columbus	7	10	0	141	110	4.33	1.54	25.6	290	35	72	4.76	3.4	7.0	2.0	0.7	51

Athletic, durable LHP who leveraged feel and control in successful year. Doesn't have great upside as he lacks plus pitch, but he gets ahead of hitters with average FB. Changes speeds, though SL rarely misses bats. Has to continue to keep balls low. Can hang SL from time to time, but is generally a GB pitcher.

Houser,Adrian — SP — Houston

Thrws R Age 21 | 2011 (2) HS (OK) | EXP MLB DEBUT: 2017 | POTENTIAL: #3 starter | 8E

Velo	Pitch	Grade
90-95	FB	+++
76-78	CB	+++
79-83	CU	++

Year	Lev	Team	W	L	Sv	IP	K	ERA	WHIP	BF/G	OBA	H%	S%	xERA	Ctl	Dom	Cmd	hr/9	BPV
2011	Rk	Greeneville	1	2	0	25	19	4.64	1.59	18.5	260	32	69	4.13	5.4	6.8	1.3	0.4	-5
2011	Rk	GCL Astros	1	2	0	22	25	4.07	1.54	16.1	278	39	71	3.89	4.1	10.2	2.5	0.0	91
2012	Rk	Greeneville	3	4	0	58	54	4.19	1.31	21.8	245	32	65	3.02	3.6	8.4	2.3	0.2	72
2013	A-	Tri City	0	4	0	50	39	3.42	1.34	14.9	288	35	73	3.73	1.8	7.0	3.9	0.2	96

Slow developing SP who hasn't pitched above short-season. Has nice pitch mix and clean delivery while showcasing control. Drastically reduced walk rate and kept ball on ground, though K rate dropping. Hasn't found pitch to retire LHH as he telegraphs CB and CU. Can cut FB and throws on downhill plane.

Huijer,Lars — SP — Seattle

Thrws R Age 20 | 2011 FA (Netherlands) | EXP MLB DEBUT: 2017 | POTENTIAL: #4 starter | 7E

Velo	Pitch	Grade
85-90	FB	+++
72-75	CB	+++
77-79	CU	+++

Year	Lev	Team	W	L	Sv	IP	K	ERA	WHIP	BF/G	OBA	H%	S%	xERA	Ctl	Dom	Cmd	hr/9	BPV
2011	Rk	AZL Mariners	0	1	0	15	9	5.40	1.40	12.7	310	34	63	5.20	1.2	5.4	4.5	1.2	83
2012	Rk	Pulaski	1	2	2	32	21	3.91	1.65	7.2	300	35	75	4.80	3.9	5.9	1.5	0.3	18
2013	A-	Everett	8	2	0	71	61	3.04	1.13	20.0	221	28	72	2.35	2.9	7.7	2.7	0.3	78

Tall and young starter who lacks velocity at present, but gets quality pitch movement with nice two-seam FB. Best present pitch is solid-average CU that features late, tumbling action. Throws with good angle to plate and induces lots of groundballs. Slow CB exhibits nice break, but doesn't miss many bats.

Hultzen,Danny — SP — Seattle

Thrws L Age 24 | 2011 (1) Virginia | EXP MLB DEBUT: 2015 | POTENTIAL: #3 starter | 8C

Velo	Pitch	Grade
90-95	FB	++++
80-84	SL	+++
83-87	CU	++++

Year	Lev	Team	W	L	Sv	IP	K	ERA	WHIP	BF/G	OBA	H%	S%	xERA	Ctl	Dom	Cmd	hr/9	BPV
2011	NCAA	Virginia	12	3	0	118	165	1.37	0.84	24.0	186	30	84	1.14	1.8	12.6	7.2	0.2	197
2012	AA	Jackson	8	3	0	75	79	1.20	0.93	21.7	152	21	88	1.05	3.8	9.5	2.5	0.2	85
2012	AAA	Tacoma	1	4	0	48	57	5.98	1.91	19.0	265	37	67	4.98	8.0	10.6	1.3	0.4	-7
2013	Rk	AZL Mariners	1	0	0	5	8	1.80	0.60	17.1	175	33	67	0.19	0.0	14.4		0.0	277
2013	AAA	Tacoma	4	1	0	30	34	2.09	0.86	18.5	182	26	76	1.25	2.1	10.1	4.9	0.3	144

Polished LHP who will likely miss 2014 season after labrum surgery in Sept. When healthy, showcases instincts and pitchability with three pitch mix. Dominates LHH with sinking FB and above average CU is ideal for combatting RHH. Hides ball which enhances repertoire and keeps ball down. Can overthrow at times.

Hursh,Jason — SP — Atlanta

Thrws R Age 22 | 2013 (1) Oklahoma State | EXP MLB DEBUT: 2016 | POTENTIAL: #2 starter | 9D

Velo	Pitch	Grade
92-95	FB	++++
84-88	SL	+++
	CU	++

Year	Lev	Team	W	L	Sv	IP	K	ERA	WHIP	BF/G	OBA	H%	S%	xERA	Ctl	Dom	Cmd	hr/9	BPV
2011	NCAA	Oklahoma St.	1	1	0	29	10	2.77	1.61	12.9	298	33	81	4.44	3.7	3.1	0.8	0.0	-26
2013	NCAA	Oklahoma St.	6	5	0	106	86	2.80	1.25	27.0	260	32	78	3.26	2.4	7.3	3.1	0.3	85
2013	A	Rome	1	1	0	27	15	0.67	1.11	11.8	208	24	97	2.26	3.3	5.0	1.5	0.3	18

Strong-armed RHP had TJS, but was healthy in 2013. Nice three-pitch mix that includes a 92-95 FB that tops out a 99 mph, a SL, and an average CU. Solid frame, decent mechanics, and good stuff give him the potential to be a #2-#3 starter.

Hyatt,Nathan — RP — Atlanta

Thrws R Age 23 | 2012 (13) Appalachian State | EXP MLB DEBUT: 2015 | POTENTIAL: Power reliever | 7C

Velo	Pitch	Grade
92-95	FB	++++
83-85	SL	++++

Year	Lev	Team	W	L	Sv	IP	K	ERA	WHIP	BF/G	OBA	H%	S%	xERA	Ctl	Dom	Cmd	hr/9	BPV
2011	NCAA	Appalachian St.	6	5	0	88	70	4.29	1.59	24.3	252	31	73	4.17	5.7	7.1	1.3	0.5	-8
2012	NCAA	Appalachian St.	1	0	16	27	29	4.32	1.70	4.4	224	32	72	3.57	8.0	9.6	1.2	0.0	-24
2012	Rk	Danville	2	0	3	10	14	1.80	0.60	4.9	96	17	67	0.00	2.7	12.6	4.7	0.0	172
2012	A	Rome	0	0	3	14	23	1.27	1.06	5.0	200	37	87	1.62	3.2	14.6	4.6	0.0	195
2013	A+	Lynchburg	2	4	12	46	55	3.90	1.67	4.8	265	38	75	4.21	5.8	10.7	1.8	0.2	53

Short, strong-armed reliever logged 12 SV with a hefty Dom. Has a good 92-95 mph FB that hits 97. Complements FB with a plus SL that is a swing-and-miss offering. Struggles with control will need to be corrected if he is to have continued success.

Jackson,Luke — SP — Texas

Thrws R Age 22 | 2010 (1-S) HS (FL) | EXP MLB DEBUT: 2015 | POTENTIAL: #2 starter | 8B

Velo	Pitch	Grade
91-97	FB	++++
79-83	CB	+++
83-85	CU	++

Year	Lev	Team	W	L	Sv	IP	K	ERA	WHIP	BF/G	OBA	H%	S%	xERA	Ctl	Dom	Cmd	hr/9	BPV
2011	A	Hickory	5	6	0	75	78	5.64	1.75	18.0	282	36	69	5.49	5.8	9.4	1.6	1.1	31
2012	A	Hickory	5	5	0	64	72	4.92	1.50	21.3	259	35	66	4.05	4.6	10.1	2.2	0.6	75
2012	A+	Myrtle Beach	5	2	0	65	74	4.42	1.52	21.8	267	37	69	3.94	4.4	10.2	2.3	0.3	83
2013	A+	Myrtle Beach	9	4	0	101	104	2.41	1.25	21.6	217	29	83	2.86	4.2	9.3	2.2	0.5	72
2013	AA	Frisco	2	0	0	27	30	0.67	0.93	16.9	146	22	92	0.74	4.0	10.0	2.5	0.0	90

Aggressive, consistent SP who improved across board in breakout. Overall stuff is impressive, highlighted by plus FB and power CB. Struggles to throw consistent strikes, but has good feel and maintains velocity. Plane to plate makes him tough to hit, though will need better CU in upper levels. Rarely allows HR.

Jaime,Juan — RP — Atlanta

Thrws R Age 26 | 2005 FA (DR) | EXP MLB DEBUT: 2014 | POTENTIAL: Power reliever | 8E

Velo	Pitch	Grade
95-98	FB	++++
	SL	+
	CU	+

Year	Lev	Team	W	L	Sv	IP	K	ERA	WHIP	BF/G	OBA	H%	S%	xERA	Ctl	Dom	Cmd	hr/9	BPV
2009	A-	Vermont	2	1	0	24	36	1.88	1.25	16.3	181	32	83	1.90	5.6	13.5	2.4	0.0	109
2009	A	Hagerstown	3	1	0	31	40	2.31	1.22	15.7	200	29	83	2.60	4.6	11.5	2.5	0.6	101
2012	A+	Lynchburg	1	3	18	51	73	3.17	1.25	5.0	177	28	77	2.53	5.8	12.9	2.2	0.7	93
2013	AA	Mississippi	2	5	0	42	70	4.07	1.38	5.0	202	37	68	2.66	6.0	15.0	2.5	0.2	126

Strong-armed reliever might have the best velocity in the system and touched 99 mph in the AFL. Struck out 70 in 41 IP, but also walked 28. Also throws a below-average SL and CU. With some refinement he could develop into a reliever, but has work to do.

James,Chad — SP — Miami

Thrws L Age 23 | 2009 (1) HS (OK) | EXP MLB DEBUT: 2015 | POTENTIAL: #3 starter | 8E

Velo	Pitch	Grade
90-93	FB	++++
80-82	SL	++
78-80	CU	+++

Year	Lev	Team	W	L	Sv	IP	K	ERA	WHIP	BF/G	OBA	H%	S%	xERA	Ctl	Dom	Cmd	hr/9	BPV
2010	A	Greensboro	5	10	0	114	105	5.13	1.59	20.9	265	34	65	4.07	5.1	8.3	1.6	0.2	29
2011	A+	Jupiter	5	15	0	149	124	3.80	1.50	23.9	292	35	76	4.70	3.1	7.5	2.4	0.7	70
2012	A+	Jupiter	6	10	0	114	80	4.89	1.65	21.3	300	35	70	5.19	3.9	6.3	1.6	0.7	25
2013	A	Greensboro	2	6	0	53	57	5.76	1.60	18.1	276	35	65	4.97	4.7	9.7	2.0	1.0	64

Former 1st rd pick took another step back in '13. Continued to have erratic Cmd and mechanics. No longer up to 95, James sits 90-93 with good movement. SL and CU flash potential, but remain inconsistent. James has the stuff to be a mid-rotation starter, but a lot of question marks in his pitches and delivery are concerning.

Jenkins,Tyrell — SP — St. Louis

Thrws R Age 21 | 2010 (1) HS (TX) | EXP MLB DEBUT: 2015 | POTENTIAL: #2 starter | 8D

Velo	Pitch	Grade
93-96	FB	++++
	CB	++
74-76	CU	++

Year	Lev	Team	W	L	Sv	IP	K	ERA	WHIP	BF/G	OBA	H%	S%	xERA	Ctl	Dom	Cmd	hr/9	BPV
2010	Rk	Johnson City	0	0	0	3	2	0.00	1.33	6.2	191	24	100	2.30	6.0	6.0	1.0	0.0	-36
2011	Rk	Johnson City	4	2	0	56	55	3.86	1.36	21.3	285	37	71	4.00	2.1	8.8	4.2	0.5	121
2012	A	Quad Cities	4	4	0	82	80	5.15	1.46	18.5	266	34	63	4.06	3.9	8.8	2.2	0.5	69
2013	A	Peoria	4	4	0	49	34	4.77	1.53	21.3	269	31	69	4.46	4.4	6.2	1.4	0.7	11
2013	A+	Palm Beach	0	0	0	10	6	4.50	1.40	14.1	316	37	64	4.16	0.9	5.4	6.0	0.0	91

Shoulder injury limited him to 59.1 IP. When healthy he competes well with a 92-94 mph FB that hits 96. Also throws a good 1-7 CB and a nice CU. Has loose arm action, which leads to easy velocity. Comes at hitters with a low 3/4 slot and good movement.

Jensen,Chris — SP — Oakland

Thrws R Age 23 | 2011 (6) San Diego | EXP MLB DEBUT: 2016 | POTENTIAL: #4 starter/reliever | 6C

Velo	Pitch	Grade
92-94	FB	+++
76-79	CB	++
	CU	+

Year	Lev	Team	W	L	Sv	IP	K	ERA	WHIP	BF/G	OBA	H%	S%	xERA	Ctl	Dom	Cmd	hr/9	BPV
2010	NCAA	San Diego	2	0	0	47	33	3.25	1.19	8.2	231	26	76	3.32	3.1	6.3	2.1	1.0	49
2011	NCAA	San Diego	3	7	2	82	73	3.95	1.41	19.3	257	33	70	3.41	4.0	8.0	2.0	0.1	56
2011	A-	Tri-City	2	1	0	37	28	2.67	1.00	17.7	205	25	72	1.84	2.4	6.8	2.8	0.2	75
2012	A	Asheville	12	3	0	145	95	4.28	1.37	24.3	266	30	70	4.14	3.1	5.9	1.9	0.9	40
2013	A+	Modesto	5	8	0	152	136	4.56	1.31	22.5	273	33	66	4.11	2.3	8.0	3.5	0.9	101

Tall, durable SP who was obtained from COL in offseason. Advancing one level per year and could eventually move to pen to harness arm strength. Possesses average velocity, but can tick up at times. Throws strikes thanks to clean, repeatable mechanics and SL shows promise. Lacks dependable offspeed pitch.

Jimenez,Joe — SP — Detroit

Thrws R Age 19 | 2013 NDFA HS (PR) | EXP MLB DEBUT: 2018 | POTENTIAL: #4 starter | 7D

Velo	Pitch	Grade
88-94	FB	+++
79-82	SL	+++
74-78	CB	++
81-82	CU	++

Year	Lev	Team	W	L	Sv	IP	K	ERA	WHIP	BF/G	OBA	H%	S%	xERA	Ctl	Dom	Cmd	hr/9	BPV
2013	Rk	GCL Tigers	3	0	1	18	24	0.50	0.83	8.2	151	25	93	0.54	3.0	12.0	4.0	0.0	153

Big and aggressive pitcher who throws with clean mechanics and has twinge of projection with loose arm and strength. FB is most dependable offering as he commands well despite terrific movement. Throws two breaking balls and SL is best of them. Exhibits big break, but tough to keep in zone for strikes.

Johansen,Jacob — SP — Washington

EXP MLB DEBUT: 2015 | POTENTIAL: #3 starter/closer | 8E

Thrws R Age 23
2013 (2) Dallas Baptist

Velo	Pitch	Grade
95-96	FB	+ + + +
77-83	CB	+ +
86-90	SL	+ + +
	CU	+ +

Year	Lev	Team	W	L	Sv	IP	K	ERA	WHIP	BF/G	OBA	H%	S%	xERA	Ctl	Dom	Cmd	hr/9	BPV
2011	NCAA	Dallas Baptist	3	0	0	13	12	12.37	2.44	6.3	302	39	44	6.55	11.0	8.2	0.8	0.0	-130
2012	NCAA	Dallas Baptist	3	1	1	46	40	5.48	1.72	10.4	266	32	69	5.11	6.3	7.8	1.3	1.0	-10
2013	NCAA	Dallas Baptist	7	6	0	88	75	5.41	1.53	25.6	305	38	62	4.59	2.7	7.7	2.9	0.3	84
2013	A-	Auburn	1	1	0	42	44	1.07	0.95	15.9	156	22	90	1.12	3.8	9.4	2.4	0.2	83
2013	A	Hagerstown	0	2	0	9	7	5.93	1.98	21.8	336	39	71	6.87	4.9	6.9	1.4	1.0	9

Tall, athletic power pitcher with high upside. FB shows good downward angle and heavy sink. Dominated hitters at Low-A with FB and showed nice improvement on CB. All his pitches flash plus at times. Has closer stuff but WAS hopes can become mid-rotation starter.

John,Jordan — SP — Detroit

EXP MLB DEBUT: 2016 | POTENTIAL: #4 starter | 7E

Thrws L Age 23
2012 (6) Oklahoma

Velo	Pitch	Grade
85-90	FB	+ + +
74-77	CB	+ +
80-82	SL	+ +
83-85	CU	+ +

Year	Lev	Team	W	L	Sv	IP	K	ERA	WHIP	BF/G	OBA	H%	S%	xERA	Ctl	Dom	Cmd	hr/9	BPV
2011	NCAA	Oklahoma	4	2	0	61	54	2.36	1.19	12.3	242	31	79	2.69	2.7	8.0	3.0	0.1	90
2012	NCAA	Oklahoma	8	8	4	121	106	2.45	1.12	17.7	233	30	76	2.33	2.4	7.9	3.3	0.1	96
2012	Rk	GCL Tigers	0	0	0	3	5	0.00	0.31	3.3	100	20	100	0.00	0.0	14.1		0.0	271
2013	A	West Michigan	9	4	0	111	89	2.92	1.25	19.7	255	32	75	3.03	2.6	7.2	2.8	0.2	78

Command-oriented LHP with good size and durability. Throws with quick arm and clean delivery to pepper zone with strikes. Has extreme GB tendency with vicious sink on lively FB. Velocity isn't much, but sequences well and can throw all pitches for strikes. Lacks out pitch and could move to bullpen.

Johnson,Brian — SP — Boston

EXP MLB DEBUT: 2015 | POTENTIAL: #4 starter | 7C

Thrws L Age 23
2012 (1) Florida

Velo	Pitch	Grade
88-93	FB	+ + +
80-83	SL	+ + +
73-78	CB	+ +
83-86	CU	+ +

Year	Lev	Team	W	L	Sv	IP	K	ERA	WHIP	BF/G	OBA	H%	S%	xERA	Ctl	Dom	Cmd	hr/9	BPV
2012	NCAA	Florida	8	5	0	90	73	3.90	1.17	21.1	255	30	68	3.42	1.8	7.3	4.1	0.8	101
2012	A-	Lowell	0	0	0	5	4	0.00	0.58	4.4	120	16	100	0.00	1.7	6.9	4.0	0.0	96
2013	Rk	GCL Red Sox	0	0	0	5	7	0.00	0.60	8.6	66	12	100	0.00	3.6	12.6	3.5	0.0	148
2013	A	Greenville	1	6	0	69	69	2.87	1.13	18.2	204	27	76	2.40	3.7	9.0	2.5	0.5	81
2013	A+	Salem	1	0	0	11	8	1.64	1.27	22.5	225	28	86	2.54	4.1	6.5	1.6	0.0	25

Tall, strong LHP who missed time with shoulder issue. Extreme GB tendency with positive, sinking FB. Has posted reverse splits and is more about command and deception than stuff. Hides ball in repeatable delivery and changes speeds well. Can cut FB and mix in average CB and occasional SL.

Johnson,Chase — RP — San Francisco

EXP MLB DEBUT: 2016 | POTENTIAL: #4 starter | 7C

Thrws R Age 22
2013 (3) Cal Poly

Velo	Pitch	Grade
92-94	FB	+ + + +
	CB	+ +
	CU	+ +

Year	Lev	Team	W	L	Sv	IP	K	ERA	WHIP	BF/G	OBA	H%	S%	xERA	Ctl	Dom	Cmd	hr/9	BPV
2011	NCAA	Cal Poly	2	5	0	49	34	3.67	1.43	11.6	262	32	72	3.60	3.9	6.2	1.6	0.2	26
2012	NCAA	Cal Poly	3	4	8	35	31	3.34	1.20	5.6	227	30	69	2.37	3.3	8.0	2.4	0.0	71
2013	NCAA	Cal Poly	0	0	0	23	21	2.34	1.26	6.3	235	31	79	2.61	3.5	8.2	2.3	0.0	71
2013	Rk	AZL Giants	1	0	0	5	7	1.76	1.18	6.8	258	40	83	2.67	1.8	12.4	7.0	0.0	193
2013	A-	Salem-Keizer	3	2	0	41	37	4.17	1.17	16.4	237	30	64	3.05	2.6	8.1	3.1	0.7	93

Tall, athletic RH carried over college success to pros. Sits 92-94 with the FB, up to 97 at times with good sink to generate ground balls. No dependable secondary pitch, though CU flashes average. Ptiched primarily out of the stretch in college; SF will work him as a starter where his clean arm action and delivery works.

Johnson,Chris — SP — San Francisco

EXP MLB DEBUT: 2016 | POTENTIAL: #4 starter | 7C

Thrws R Age 22
2012 (17) Portland

Velo	Pitch	Grade
89-91	FB	+ +
72-74	CB	+ + +
80-82	SL	+ +
79-81	CU	+ +

Year	Lev	Team	W	L	Sv	IP	K	ERA	WHIP	BF/G	OBA	H%	S%	xERA	Ctl	Dom	Cmd	hr/9	BPV
2011	NCAA	Portland	3	5	0	83	58	3.57	1.23	24.0	254	30	71	3.33	2.4	6.3	2.6	0.5	67
2012	NCAA	Portland	4	4	0	76	57	3.08	1.34	21.1	274	33	78	3.82	2.5	6.8	2.7	0.5	72
2012	A-	Salem-Keizer	2	4	0	48	47	6.91	1.39	12.7	292	36	50	4.96	2.1	8.8	4.3	1.3	121
2013	A-	Salem-Keizer	6	3	0	83	78	2.49	0.88	20.5	217	29	69	1.54	0.9	8.5	9.8	0.1	147

Tall, durable SP repeated Low-A and found promising results. He has a clean, deceptive delivery that allows his four-pitch mix to play up. Sits in the upper-80s, low-90s with the sinking FB, complementing it with an average CB and a below average SL and CU. He mixes his pitches and rarely walks batters.

Johnson,Erik — SP — Chicago (A)

EXP MLB DEBUT: 2013 | POTENTIAL: #3 starter | 8C

Thrws R Age 24
2011 (2) California

Velo	Pitch	Grade
89-95	FB	+ + +
85-87	SL	+ + + +
73-75	CB	+ + +
80-83	CU	+ + +

Year	Lev	Team	W	L	Sv	IP	K	ERA	WHIP	BF/G	OBA	H%	S%	xERA	Ctl	Dom	Cmd	hr/9	BPV
2012	A	Kannapolis	2	2	0	43	39	2.30	1.35	19.9	243	30	85	3.55	4.0	8.2	2.1	0.6	58
2012	A+	Winston-Salem	4	3	0	49	48	2.75	1.08	23.9	237	32	72	2.19	1.8	8.8	4.8	0.0	127
2013	AA	Birmingham	8	2	0	84	74	2.24	0.93	22.5	194	24	79	1.89	2.2	7.9	3.5	0.6	100
2013	AAA	Charlotte	4	1	0	57	57	1.58	1.09	22.3	211	29	85	2.02	3.0	9.0	3.0	0.2	99
2013	MLB	CHW	3	2	0	28	18	3.25	1.55	24.2	291	31	87	5.68	3.6	5.8	1.6	1.6	27

Big, strong SP who cleaned up mechanics and threw with much improved control. Repeats smooth delivery effectively and owns four pitch mix. FB has good velocity and plays up due to downhill plane. Hard SL serves as K pitch, but will need to add polish to CU. Very tough on RHH and rarely allows HR.

Johnson,Pierce — SP — Chicago (N)

EXP MLB DEBUT: 2016 | POTENTIAL: #3 starter | 8D

Thrws R Age 23
2012 (1-S) Missouri State

Velo	Pitch	Grade
91-93	FB	+ + + +
86-88	CT	+ +
82-84	CU	+ +
80-83	CB	+ + +

Year	Lev	Team	W	L	Sv	IP	K	ERA	WHIP	BF/G	OBA	H%	S%	xERA	Ctl	Dom	Cmd	hr/9	BPV
2012	NCAA	Missouri St.	4	6	0	99	119	2.54	1.14	28.1	233	34	76	2.35	2.5	10.8	4.3	0.1	144
2012	Rk	AZL Cubs	0	0	0	3	2	0.00	1.33	6.2	321	38	100	4.07	0.0	6.0		0.0	126
2012	A-	Boise	0	0	0	8	12	4.50	1.63	8.9	307	49	69	4.51	3.4	13.5	4.0	0.0	170
2013	A	Kane County	5	5	0	69	74	3.12	1.30	21.9	258	35	77	3.51	2.9	9.6	3.4	0.5	114
2013	A+	Daytona	6	1	0	48	50	2.24	1.29	19.8	232	32	82	2.81	3.9	9.3	2.4	0.2	80

Tall RH had a solid full-season debut. Comes after hitters with a 91-93 mph FB with late life. Also has a plus CB that gets swings and misses, but CU is inconsistent. Does throw across his body and had health issues in the past, so durablity is an issue.

Johnson,Stephen — RP — San Francisco

EXP MLB DEBUT: 2015 | POTENTIAL: Power reliever | 7C

Thrws R Age 23
2012 (6) St. Edward's

Velo	Pitch	Grade
95-98	FB	+ + + +
	SL	+ +

Year	Lev	Team	W	L	Sv	IP	K	ERA	WHIP	BF/G	OBA	H%	S%	xERA	Ctl	Dom	Cmd	hr/9	BPV
2012	Rk	AZL Giants	0	0	0	2	2	4.50	1.50	4.3	151	22	67	2.25	9.0	9.0	1.0	0.0	-63
2012	A-	Salem-Keizer	0	2	2	19	19	4.71	1.62	5.0	261	33	72	4.76	5.7	9.0	1.6	0.9	26
2013	A	Augusta	5	1	8	52	71	3.63	1.36	4.8	218	34	72	2.96	5.2	12.3	2.4	0.3	99

Tall fireballer comes at hitters with upper-90s FB that has topped out at 101. Pairs it with a below average, slurvy SL. Funky arm action hinders his ability to command his pitches, leading to less than stellar Ctl. Gets a lot of swing-and-miss with the FB, but ability to throw strikes is a concern going forward.

Jones,Devin — SP — Baltimore

EXP MLB DEBUT: 2015 | POTENTIAL: #5 starter | 7D

Thrws R Age 23
2011 (9) Mississippi State

Velo	Pitch	Grade
89-94	FB	+ + +
80-84	SL	+ + +
81-83	CU	+ +

Year	Lev	Team	W	L	Sv	IP	K	ERA	WHIP	BF/G	OBA	H%	S%	xERA	Ctl	Dom	Cmd	hr/9	BPV
2011	A-	Aberdeen	2	4	2	23	21	6.21	1.81	7.7	307	38	65	5.76	5.0	8.1	1.6	0.8	28
2012	A	Delmarva	1	6	3	54	51	2.66	1.11	11.2	243	32	75	2.50	1.8	8.5	4.6	0.2	121
2012	A+	Frederick	7	1	0	54	29	2.82	1.20	24.2	257	28	80	3.58	2.0	4.8	2.4	0.8	51
2013	A+	Frederick	1	0	0	6	3	1.50	0.67	20.9	151	18	75	0.19	1.5	4.5	3.0	0.0	59
2013	AA	Bowie	4	7	0	123	108	5.85	1.58	22.5	296	35	64	5.44	3.5	7.9	2.3	1.2	65

Tall, lean RHP who posted much higher K rate, though still not dominant. Moved to rotation in mid-2012 and has value with durability and solid sinker. Throws downhill with FB that features tumbling action. Needs to hone secondary pitches and LHH can tee off on him (.350 oppBA). Can be hittable and control is erratic.

Jones,Tyler — RP — Minnesota

EXP MLB DEBUT: 2015 | POTENTIAL: Setup reliever | 6B

Thrws R Age 24
2011 (11) Louisiana State

Velo	Pitch	Grade
90-96	FB	+ + + +
82-84	SL	+ + +
75-79	CB	+ +
81-83	CU	+ +

Year	Lev	Team	W	L	Sv	IP	K	ERA	WHIP	BF/G	OBA	H%	S%	xERA	Ctl	Dom	Cmd	hr/9	BPV
2011	NCAA	Louisiana St.	4	0	0	39	37	5.28	1.51	12.1	246	33	61	3.38	5.3	8.5	1.6	0.0	28
2011	Rk	Elizabethton	0	0	0	7	8	12.86	2.57	9.4	448	54	50	12.09	2.6	10.3	4.0	2.6	134
2012	A	Beloit	5	5	0	86	102	4.70	1.45	20.4	270	38	67	4.04	3.7	10.6	2.9	0.5	111
2013	A	Cedar Rapids	4	3	9	37	44	1.94	0.94	5.8	154	24	77	0.86	3.9	10.7	2.8	0.0	105
2013	A+	Fort Myers	1	3	4	15	22	4.20	1.47	5.4	299	47	68	3.98	2.4	13.2	5.5	0.0	191

Big-bodied RP who dominated Low-A en route to promotion to High-A. Throws heavy FB with good life and late sink. Commands FB, though doesn't locate secondary offerings. Has spent time as closer and has right mentality and demeanor. Uses four pitches with FB and SL missing bats. CB and CU are inconsistent.

Jones,Zach — RP — Minnesota

EXP MLB DEBUT: 2015 | POTENTIAL: Setup reliever / Closer | 7C

Thrws R Age 23
2012 (4) San Jose State

Velo	Pitch	Grade
91-97	FB	+ + + +
82-85	SL	+ + +
	CU	+

Year	Lev	Team	W	L	Sv	IP	K	ERA	WHIP	BF/G	OBA	H%	S%	xERA	Ctl	Dom	Cmd	hr/9	BPV
2012	Rk	Elizabethton	0	0	0	6	9	0.00	1.00	3.8	106	20	100	0.50	6.0	13.5	2.3	0.0	99
2012	A	Beloit	0	0	4	14	25	3.21	1.14	4.6	186	36	73	2.26	4.5	16.1	3.6	0.6	186
2013	A+	Fort Myers	4	3	14	48	70	1.87	1.16	4.9	171	28	85	1.92	5.2	13.1	2.5	0.4	112

Athletic, aggressive RP who is very tough to hit (.172 oppBA) while racking up Ks and keeping ball on ground. Explosive FB is well above average, though can be straight at higher velocities. Can pitch up effectively. Hard SL is solid offering, but rarely changes speeds. Could use firmer mechanics.

Jorge, Felix — SP — Minnesota

Thrws R Age 20
2011 FA (DR)
89-95 FB +++
78-82 CB ++
81-84 CU ++

EXP MLB DEBUT: 2017 POTENTIAL: #3 starter 8D

Year	Lev	Team	W	L	Sv	IP	K	ERA	WHIP	BF/G	OBA	H%	S%	xERA	Ctl	Dom	Cmd	hr/9	BPV
2012	Rk	GCL Twins	0	3	1	34	37	2.37	1.23	11.5	237	34	79	2.56	3.2	9.7	3.1	0.0	108
2013	Rk	Elizabethton	2	2	0	61	72	2.95	1.21	20.5	246	35	75	2.90	2.7	10.6	4.0	0.3	138

Loose-armed RHP who shows advanced skills. Keeps walks to a minimum by spotting FB to both sides of plate. Lives in bottom half of zone with sinker and complements with erratic CB and CU. Secondary pitches have potential, but he needs strength and durability. Long-term project, but reward could be high.

Joseph, Donnie — RP — Kansas City

Thrws L Age 26
2009 (3) Houston
91-96 FB +++
82-85 SL ++++
CU +

EXP MLB DEBUT: 2013 POTENTIAL: Setup reliever 7A

Year	Lev	Team	W	L	Sv	IP	K	ERA	WHIP	BF/G	OBA	H%	S%	xERA	Ctl	Dom	Cmd	hr/9	BPV
2012	AA	Pensacola	4	2	13	30	46	0.90	0.70	4.1	133	24	90	0.28	2.4	13.8	5.8	0.3	201
2012	AAA	Louisville	4	1	5	22	22	2.86	1.41	5.2	262	35	77	3.35	3.7	9.0	2.4	0.0	81
2012	AAA	Omaha	1	0	2	17	19	4.21	1.99	7.5	303	41	79	5.90	6.8	10.0	1.5	0.5	13
2013	AAA	Omaha	4	3	6	54	84	3.99	1.46	4.9	203	33	74	3.45	6.6	13.9	2.1	0.8	90
2013	MLB	KC	0	0	0	6	7	0.00	1.40	4.0	199	31	100	2.52	6.3	11.1	1.8	0.0	46

Quick-armed RP who is lethal against LHH (.165 oppBA). Has potential to be more than situational guy because of high K rate. Has fine velocity, but plus SL is go-to pitch. Dominates LHH with SL, but will need to enhance below average command. Has tendency to overthrow which increases walk rate.

Julio, Erick — SP — Colorado

Thrws R Age 17
2013 FA (Colombia)
87-90 FB +++
CB +++
CU ++

EXP MLB DEBUT: 2018 POTENTIAL: #3 starter 7D

Year	Lev	Team	W	L	Sv	IP	K	ERA	WHIP	BF/G	OBA	H%	S%	xERA	Ctl	Dom	Cmd	hr/9	BPV
2013		Did not pitch in the US																	

Short Colombian hurler was one of the better international prospects in 2013. FB sits at 87-90 but projects to add more as he fills out. Backs up the FB with a plus CB and shows feel for CU. If velo tops here, he is more of a back-end arm, but still young.

Jungmann, Taylor — SP — Milwaukee

Thrws R Age 24
2011 (1) Texas
89-92 FB +++
76-81 SL +++
CU ++

EXP MLB DEBUT: 2014 POTENTIAL: #3 starter 8D

Year	Lev	Team	W	L	Sv	IP	K	ERA	WHIP	BF/G	OBA	H%	S%	xERA	Ctl	Dom	Cmd	hr/9	BPV
2009	NCAA	Texas	11	3	0	94	101	2.01	1.06	14.6	197	28	80	1.73	3.3	9.6	2.9	0.1	101
2010	NCAA	Texas	8	3	0	120	129	2.03	1.08	27.5	206	28	84	2.35	3.1	9.7	3.1	0.6	109
2011	NCAA	Texas	13	3	0	141	126	1.60	0.83	27.1	169	22	81	1.01	2.3	8.0	3.5	0.3	101
2012	A+	Brevard County	11	6	0	153	99	3.53	1.34	24.5	269	31	73	3.69	2.7	5.8	2.2	0.4	50
2013	AA	Huntsville	10	10	0	139	82	4.34	1.37	22.4	230	25	69	3.52	4.7	5.3	1.1	0.7	-14

Back in college he sat in the mid-90s with good command of his pitches, generating swing-and-misses with ease. Now his game features a low-90s FB, or sinker, with inconsistent secondary pitches and sporatic command and control. He works downhill well, but needs to refine his mechanics to get back to his college days.

Kahnle, Tommy — RP — Colorado

Thrws R Age 24
2010 (5) Lynn
92-98 FB ++++
82-84 SL ++
83-86 CU ++

EXP MLB DEBUT: 2014 POTENTIAL: Setup reliever 7D

Year	Lev	Team	W	L	Sv	IP	K	ERA	WHIP	BF/G	OBA	H%	S%	xERA	Ctl	Dom	Cmd	hr/9	BPV
2010	A-	Staten Island	0	0	3	16	25	0.56	0.50	4.8	62	13	88	0.00	2.8	14.1	5.0	0.0	195
2011	A	Charleston (Sc)	3	5	2	81	112	4.22	1.46	8.7	232	37	68	3.14	5.4	12.4	2.3	0.1	95
2012	A+	Tampa	2	1	6	55	72	2.45	0.98	7.0	162	25	76	1.50	3.9	11.8	3.0	0.5	124
2012	AA	Trenton	0	0	0	2	2	0.00	1.00	7.6	262	35	100	2.32	0.0	9.0	0.0	0.0	180
2013	AA	Trenton	1	3	15	60	74	2.85	1.38	5.5	183	26	81	2.85	6.8	11.1	1.6	0.6	36

Durable RP who served as closer in '13 and selected in Rule 5 draft by COL. Owns arm strength that pumps FB into mid-to-high 90s. Has effort in delivery which negatively impacts command. Needs to harness strength to throw more strikes. Can also elevate pitches. Tough to hit, but needs consistency in SL and CU.

Kaminsky, Rob — SP — St. Louis

Thrws L Age 19
2013 (1) HS (NJ)
88-92 FB +++
76-79 CB ++++
80-83 CU +++

EXP MLB DEBUT: 2016 POTENTIAL: #3 starter 7C

Year	Lev	Team	W	L	Sv	IP	K	ERA	WHIP	BF/G	OBA	H%	S%	xERA	Ctl	Dom	Cmd	hr/9	BPV
2013	Rk	GCL Cardinals	0	3	0	22	28	3.68	1.45	11.8	270	39	74	3.94	3.7	11.5	3.1	0.4	125

Short LH was the 28th pick in 2013. Has a good, lively FB that sits at 88-92. Had the best CB in the draft and an average CU. Repeats mechanics easily and throws strikes. At 5-11, 191 he lacks the size typical of most starters, but has good stuff.

Karns, Nate — SP — Washington

Thrws R Age 26
2009 (12) Texas Tech
90-93 FB +++
82-85 CB ++++
SL ++
83-85 CU +++

EXP MLB DEBUT: 2013 POTENTIAL: #4 starter 7C

Year	Lev	Team	W	L	Sv	IP	K	ERA	WHIP	BF/G	OBA	H%	S%	xERA	Ctl	Dom	Cmd	hr/9	BPV
2011	A-	Auburn	3	2	0	36	33	3.48	1.49	19.5	209	27	75	3.12	6.7	8.2	1.2	0.2	-16
2012	A	Hagerstown	3	0	2	44	61	2.04	1.00	15.3	156	26	79	1.20	4.3	12.4	2.9	0.2	126
2012	A+	Potomac	8	4	0	71	87	2.28	1.03	21.1	190	29	76	1.58	3.3	11.0	3.3	0.1	127
2013	AA	Harrisburg	10	6	0	132	155	3.27	1.19	23.0	226	30	76	3.20	3.3	10.6	3.2	1.0	120
2013	MLB	WAS	0	1	0	12	11	7.50	1.92	18.9	334	34	72	9.26	4.5	8.3	1.8	3.8	45

Very solid back-to-back seasons at High-A and Double-A. Posts excellent Dom for pitcher without elite velocity by utilizing secondary pitches well. Pounds zone with strikes, inducing weak contact, and get hitters to chase off-speed pitches out of the zone. Some questions remain regarding durability.

Kela, Keone — RP — Texas

Thrws R Age 21
2012 (12) Everett CC
91-99 FB ++++
82-86 SL +++

EXP MLB DEBUT: 2015 POTENTIAL: Setup reliever 7D

Year	Lev	Team	W	L	Sv	IP	K	ERA	WHIP	BF/G	OBA	H%	S%	xERA	Ctl	Dom	Cmd	hr/9	BPV
2012	Rk	AZL Rangers	0	1	0	11	15	1.62	0.72	4.4	113	20	75	0.00	3.2	12.2	3.8	0.0	149
2013	Rk	AZL Rangers	2	0	0	3	6	8.44	3.44	6.7	470	73	73	12.36	8.4	16.9	2.0	0.0	94
2013	A-	Spokane	1	2	2	16	26	3.89	1.42	5.7	271	45	73	3.97	3.3	14.4	4.3	0.6	188
2013	A	Hickory	2	2	1	18	20	2.47	1.32	6.3	260	36	79	3.08	3.0	9.9	3.3	0.0	116

Aggressive, strong RP who can reach triple-digits on gun with pure arm strength. Uses clean delivery and smooth arm action to pop velocity and showed improved control. Hard SL flashes above average, but doesn't command it well. Relies too much on FB and lacks any touch and feel for changing speeds.

Keller, Brad — SP — Arizona

Thrws R Age 18
2013 (8) HS (GA)
90-93 FB +++
SL +++
CU ++

EXP MLB DEBUT: 2016 POTENTIAL: #4 starter 7D

Year	Lev	Team	W	L	Sv	IP	K	ERA	WHIP	BF/G	OBA	H%	S%	xERA	Ctl	Dom	Cmd	hr/9	BPV
2013	Rk	AZL D'backs	7	3	0	56	61	2.24	1.41	18.3	251	34	84	3.48	4.2	9.8	2.3	0.3	81
2013	Rk	Missoula	0	0	0	6	4	4.50	1.67	13.5	262	32	70	4.03	6.0	6.0	1.0	0.0	-36

At 6'5", 230 has good size and a decent low-90s FB. Also has a good hard SL and a CU. Didn't get a lot of attention leading up to the draft, but worked hard and had an impressive pro debut, going 7-3 with a 2.44 ERA and striking out 9.3 per nine innings.

Kelly, Casey — SP — San Diego

Thrws R Age 24
2008 (1) HS (FL)
90-94 FB ++++
76-79 CB ++++
80-84 CU +++

EXP MLB DEBUT: 2012 POTENTIAL: #3 starter 8C

Year	Lev	Team	W	L	Sv	IP	K	ERA	WHIP	BF/G	OBA	H%	S%	xERA	Ctl	Dom	Cmd	hr/9	BPV
2011	AA	San Antonio	11	6	0	142	105	3.99	1.40	22.2	276	33	71	4.03	2.9	6.7	2.3	0.5	59
2012	Rk	AZL Padres	0	1	0	9	7	4.00	1.11	11.8	283	35	60	2.91	0.0	7.0	0.0	0.0	144
2012	A	San Antonio	0	1	0	16	18	3.89	0.86	9.3	194	27	54	1.63	1.7	10.0	6.0	0.0	153
2012	AAA	Tucson	0	0	0	12	14	2.25	1.00	22.9	262	38	75	2.30	0.0	10.5	0.0	0.6	207
2012	MLB	SD	2	3	0	29	26	6.21	1.69	21.8	323	38	66	6.44	3.1	8.1	2.6	1.6	79

Tall and very athletic SP who missed season after TJS in April. Thrives with impeccable FB location despite late, sinking action. Induces ton of GB and has shown increased K rate due to excellent, consistent CB. CU is good pitch, but needs polish to overall arsenal. Shouldn't take long for him to return to normal.

Kickham, Mike — SP — San Francisco

Thrws L Age 25
2010 (6) Missouri State
90-92 FB +++
80-83 SL +++
80-82 CU ++

EXP MLB DEBUT: 2013 POTENTIAL: #5 starter/Reliever 7D

Year	Lev	Team	W	L	Sv	IP	K	ERA	WHIP	BF/G	OBA	H%	S%	xERA	Ctl	Dom	Cmd	hr/9	BPV
2010	Rk	AZL Giants	0	0	0	2	3	12.86	2.86	8.9	403	58	50	9.36	8.6	12.9	1.5	0.0	18
2011	A	Augusta	5	10	0	111	103	4.13	1.34	22.0	263	33	70	3.88	3.0	8.3	2.8	0.7	87
2012	AA	Richmond	11	10	0	150	137	3.06	1.29	22.1	219	28	77	2.96	4.5	8.2	1.8	0.5	44
2013	AAA	Fresno	7	7	0	110	90	4.33	1.40	23.2	253	30	70	3.90	4.0	7.4	1.8	0.7	42
2013	MLB	SF	3	3	0	28	29	10.18	1.98	11.3	366	43	50	8.83	3.2	9.2	2.9	2.5	98

Physical LH has good low-90s FB that induces lots of groundballs, average SL, and a below average CU that has improved. Uses height to get good downhill plane and keep the ball down, though struggles to repeat his delivery and has Ctl issues. Got knocked around in limitied look in '13, but has backend starter upside.

Kime,Dace — SP — Cleveland

EXP MLB DEBUT: 2016 | POTENTIAL: #3 starter | 8D

Thrws R Age 22
2013 (3) Louisville

Velo	Pitch	Grade
90-94	FB	+++
78-82	CB	++++
	CU	++

Year	Lev	Team	W	L	Sv	IP	K	ERA	WHIP	BF/G	OBA	H%	S%	xERA	Ctl	Dom	Cmd	hr/9	BPV
2011	NCAA	Louisville	1	2	0	25	25	3.96	1.40	7.0	246	33	71	3.45	4.3	9.0	2.1	0.4	63
2012	NCAA	Louisville	1	0	0	40	42	4.93	1.37	6.2	225	31	61	2.97	4.9	9.4	1.9	0.2	54
2013	NCAA	Louisville	6	1	1	69	83	3.00	1.22	10.3	247	36	73	2.77	2.6	10.8	4.2	0.1	142
2013	A-	Mahoning Val	0	2	0	24	26	2.98	1.45	11.5	218	31	77	2.86	6.0	9.7	1.6	0.0	31

Big, durable RHP who thrives with lively FB and excellent CB. Can effectively add and subtract from FB with cutting action to give hitters variety of looks. Uses height and arm angle to keep ball down and CB serves as swing-and-miss pitch. Can have difficulty repeating complicated delivery.

Kingham,Nick — SP — Pittsburgh

EXP MLB DEBUT: 2015 | POTENTIAL: #3 starter | 8D

Thrws R Age 22
2010 (4) HS (TX)

Velo	Pitch	Grade
90-93	FB	++++
	CB	+++
	CU	+++

Year	Lev	Team	W	L	Sv	IP	K	ERA	WHIP	BF/G	OBA	H%	S%	xERA	Ctl	Dom	Cmd	hr/9	BPV
2010	Rk	GCL Pirates	0	0	0	3	2	0.00	1.00	5.7	262	32	100	2.35	0.0	6.0		0.0	126
2011	A-	State College	6	2	0	71	47	2.15	1.10	18.5	239	27	84	2.89	1.9	6.0	3.1	0.6	74
2012	A	West Virginia	6	8	0	127	117	4.39	1.19	18.9	243	29	65	3.55	2.6	8.3	3.3	1.1	98
2013	A+	Bradenton	6	3	0	70	75	3.09	0.99	20.5	218	29	71	2.43	1.8	9.6	5.4	0.8	143
2013	AA	Altoona	3	3	0	73	69	2.71	1.37	21.9	253	33	79	3.25	3.7	8.5	2.3	0.1	71

RH had an impressive breakout. FB sits at 90-93 and CB has some swing-and-miss. CU continues to improve, giving him three solid offerings. Wasn't as dominant when moved up to Double-A, but plus command of his FB keep hitters off-balance.

Kline,Branden — SP — Baltimore

EXP MLB DEBUT: 2015 | POTENTIAL: #3 SP / Setup RP | 8E

Thrws R Age 22
2012 (2) Virginia

Velo	Pitch	Grade
89-95	FB	+++
81-84	SL	+++
80-83	CB	++
80-82	CU	++

Year	Lev	Team	W	L	Sv	IP	K	ERA	WHIP	BF/G	OBA	H%	S%	xERA	Ctl	Dom	Cmd	hr/9	BPV
2010	NCAA	Virginia	5	1	3	64	56	3.64	1.15	11.6	230	27	73	3.34	2.8	7.9	2.8	1.1	84
2011	NCAA	Virginia	4	1	18	43	56	1.88	1.21	5.4	198	31	83	2.01	4.6	11.7	2.5	0.0	105
2012	NCAA	Virginia	7	3	0	93	94	3.57	1.37	24.4	244	32	73	3.38	4.2	9.1	2.2	0.4	69
2012	A-	Aberdeen	0	0	0	12	12	4.50	1.33	12.5	262	33	67	3.86	3.0	9.0	3.0	0.8	99
2013	A	Delmarva	1	2	0	35	32	5.90	1.57	22.0	293	36	63	5.16	3.6	8.2	2.3	1.0	69

Athletic RHP who fractured ankle in May, but pitched well upon return to AFL. Uses quick arm and high slot to keep ball down and induce high amount of GB. Has 2 solid pitches in FB and big-breaking SL. FB can be too flat and will need better CU. Sequences well, though could move to bullpen.

Knebel,Corey — RP — Detroit

EXP MLB DEBUT: 2015 | POTENTIAL: Closer | 7A

Thrws R Age 22
2013 (1-S) Texas

Velo	Pitch	Grade
91-98	FB	++++
79-82	CB	+++
84-86	CU	++

Year	Lev	Team	W	L	Sv	IP	K	ERA	WHIP	BF/G	OBA	H%	S%	xERA	Ctl	Dom	Cmd	hr/9	BPV
2011	NCAA	Texas	3	2	19	55	61	1.14	0.72	5.1	152	23	83	0.30	2.0	9.9	5.1	0.0	144
2012	NCAA	Texas	4	5	9	73	68	2.09	0.96	10.2	195	26	77	1.49	2.5	8.4	3.4	0.1	102
2013	NCAA	Texas	3	4	9	40	51	3.38	1.08	6.0	181	28	67	1.70	4.1	11.5	2.8	0.2	115
2013	A	West Michigan	2	1	15	31	41	0.87	0.77	3.6	138	23	88	0.26	2.9	11.9	4.1	0.0	154

Powerful RP who was college closer. Carried success over to pros where RHH couldn't hit him (.098 oppBA). Explosive FB plays up due to arm action and delivery. Pitch movement is above average and can throw three pitches for strikes. Shows some feel for CU and will need to improve if he wants to become starter.

Kukuk,Cody — SP — Boston

EXP MLB DEBUT: 2016 | POTENTIAL: #3 starter | 8E

Thrws L Age 21
2011 (7) HS (KS)

Velo	Pitch	Grade
88-94	FB	+++
81-83	SL	+++
80-83	CU	++

Year	Lev	Team	W	L	Sv	IP	K	ERA	WHIP	BF/G	OBA	H%	S%	xERA	Ctl	Dom	Cmd	hr/9	BPV
2012	Rk	GCL Red Sox	2	0	0	10	16	0.90	0.60	6.8	96	20	83	0.00	2.7	14.4	5.3	0.0	204
2013	A	Greenville	4	13	1	107	113	4.63	1.48	17.7	203	28	67	3.16	6.8	9.5	1.4	0.4	5

Tall, strong LHP who is very tough to make hard contact against, but lack of command limits upside. LHH only hit .165 against him, but walk rate elevated due to inability to repeat delivery. Hard SL can miss bats and CU shows glimpses. Needs lot of work to put everything together, especially delivery.

Labourt,Jairo — SP — Toronto

EXP MLB DEBUT: 2017 | POTENTIAL: #3 starter | 8D

Thrws L Age 20
2011 FA (DR)

Velo	Pitch	Grade
90-94	FB	+++
82-85	SL	++
81-83	CU	+++

Year	Lev	Team	W	L	Sv	IP	K	ERA	WHIP	BF/G	OBA	H%	S%	xERA	Ctl	Dom	Cmd	hr/9	BPV
2012	Rk	GCL Blue Jays	0	3	0	38	39	3.79	1.61	14.0	262	35	76	4.28	5.4	9.2	1.7	0.5	37
2013	Rk	Bluefield	2	2	0	51	45	1.93	1.04	16.4	213	27	84	2.28	2.5	7.9	3.2	0.5	94

Projectable SP with big frame and fast arm. Tweaked delivery and arm action leads to pitch movement. Dominates LHH with FB and solid-average CU. Can go to FB too often and needs more consistency in SL. Threw more strikes, but could use better FB command. Has sleeper potential and could move to bullpen.

Lamb,John — SP — Kansas City

EXP MLB DEBUT: 2014 | POTENTIAL: #3 starter | 8E

Thrws L Age 24
2008 (5) HS (CA)

Velo	Pitch	Grade
87-94	FB	+++
77-79	CB	+++
78-81	CU	+++

Year	Lev	Team	W	L	Sv	IP	K	ERA	WHIP	BF/G	OBA	H%	S%	xERA	Ctl	Dom	Cmd	hr/9	BPV
2011	AA	NW Arkansas	1	2	0	35	22	3.09	1.31	18.1	251	28	79	3.71	3.3	5.7	1.7	0.8	30
2012	Rk	AZL Royals	0	0	0	5	6	6.92	1.54	5.7	290	41	50	4.07	3.5	10.4	3.0	0.0	111
2012	Rk	Idaho Falls	0	1	0	7	8	7.61	1.55	15.5	310	37	56	6.78	2.5	10.1	4.0	2.5	132
2013	A+	Wilmington	4	12	0	92	76	5.66	1.39	20.4	295	34	61	4.99	1.9	7.4	4.0	1.3	101
2013	AAA	Omaha	1	2	0	16	10	6.75	1.38	22.4	250	29	48	3.66	3.9	5.6	1.4	0.6	13

Tall LHP who is slowly working way back after missing most of 2011 and 2012 due to elbow. Velocity slowly returning, though CB isn't as good as before. Doesn't throw with as much arm speed, but still has impeccable command and control of offerings. Still young enough to realize upside and should get opportunity.

Lamm,Mark — RP — Atlanta

EXP MLB DEBUT: 2014 | POTENTIAL: Reliever | 6C

Thrws R Age 26
2011 (6) Vanderbilt

Velo	Pitch	Grade
90-94	FB	+++
83-85	SL	+++
	CU	++

Year	Lev	Team	W	L	Sv	IP	K	ERA	WHIP	BF/G	OBA	H%	S%	xERA	Ctl	Dom	Cmd	hr/9	BPV
2011	Rk	Danville	0	0	0	2	4	0.00	0.00	2.8	0	0	100	0.00	0.0	18.0		0.0	342
2011	A+	Lynchburg	1	2	1	25	19	3.21	1.15	6.7	193	22	74	2.52	4.3	6.8	1.6	0.7	24
2012	AA	Mississippi	2	7	10	59	53	3.95	1.42	5.0	277	35	72	4.02	3.0	8.1	2.7	0.5	81
2013	AA	Mississippi	3	3	10	45	48	2.59	1.33	5.4	234	32	81	3.14	4.2	9.6	2.3	0.4	77
2013	AAA	Gwinnett	3	3	0	22	22	3.67	1.67	5.5	261	35	76	4.00	6.1	9.0	1.5	0.0	14

Former Vanderbilt starter is a TJ survivor and has transformed into a nice relief prospect. Has a good, but not overpowering 92-94 mph FB and an average SL and CU. Can struggle with control at times, but did log 10 saves for AA Mississippi in 2013.

Langfield,Dan — SP — Cincinnati

EXP MLB DEBUT: 2016 | POTENTIAL: Setup reliever | 7C

Thrws R Age 23
2012 (3) Memphis

Velo	Pitch	Grade
92-95	FB	+++
	SL	+++
	CB	++
	CU	++

Year	Lev	Team	W	L	Sv	IP	K	ERA	WHIP	BF/G	OBA	H%	S%	xERA	Ctl	Dom	Cmd	hr/9	BPV
2010	NCAA	Memphis	4	4	1	39	47	4.62	1.67	10.3	313	41	76	6.03	3.5	10.8	3.1	1.4	120
2011	NCAA	Memphis	3	3	0	85	94	4.34	1.48	24.4	243	33	70	3.76	5.2	9.9	1.9	0.5	57
2012	NCAA	Memphis	7	6	0	93	111	2.80	1.26	25.3	210	31	77	2.55	4.5	10.7	2.4	0.3	88
2012	Rk	Billings	3	0	0	37	54	2.68	1.19	9.9	206	34	77	2.26	4.1	13.1	3.2	0.2	143

Missed 2013 season with shoulder injury. Began rehab in fall and should be ready for start of season. Throws heavy mid-90s FB, but it can get straight and hittable. Also throws a good hard SL, but CB and CU inconsistent. CIN trying him as a starter but profiles best as setup reliever with nice FB/SL combo.

Law,Derek — RP — San Francisco

EXP MLB DEBUT: 2015 | POTENTIAL: Setup reliever | 7C

Thrws R Age 23
2011 (9) Miami Dade JC

Velo	Pitch	Grade
89-93	FB	+++
	CB	++++

Year	Lev	Team	W	L	Sv	IP	K	ERA	WHIP	BF/G	OBA	H%	S%	xERA	Ctl	Dom	Cmd	hr/9	BPV
2011	Rk	AZL Giants	0	0	4	18	19	2.50	1.00	4.6	240	34	72	2.02	1.0	9.5	9.5	0.0	162
2012	A	Augusta	5	2	2	55	67	2.93	1.23	7.0	224	31	81	3.31	3.8	10.9	2.9	1.0	113
2013	Rk	AZL Giants	1	0	0	5	9	3.46	0.96	3.9	214	41	60	1.54	1.7	15.6	9.0	0.0	252
2013	A	Augusta	0	3	3	35	48	2.31	1.06	7.1	215	34	78	2.06	2.6	12.3	4.8	0.3	171
2013	A+	San Jose	4	0	11	25	45	2.14	0.83	4.2	220	42	75	1.61	0.4	16.1	45.0	0.4	298

Big, athletic RP dominated across three levels in '13, striking out 102 in 66.1 IP. Comes at hitters with low-90s FB paired with a plus, power CB and generates plus swing-and-miss results. Controls both pitches well and rarely walks anyone. Rough arm action and violent delivery are concerns, but FB/CB combo are exciting.

Leathersich,Jack — RP — New York (N)

EXP MLB DEBUT: 2014 | POTENTIAL: Reliever | 7C

Thrws L Age 23
2011 (5) U Mass - Lowell

Velo	Pitch	Grade
91-93	FB	+++
78-81	CB	+++
	CU	++

Year	Lev	Team	W	L	Sv	IP	K	ERA	WHIP	BF/G	OBA	H%	S%	xERA	Ctl	Dom	Cmd	hr/9	BPV
2011	A-	Brooklyn	0	0	1	12	26	0.74	0.74	4.8	149	42	89	0.20	2.2	19.2	8.7	0.0	303
2012	A	Savannah	0	1	1	24	37	0.75	0.75	7.1	129	25	89	0.09	3.0	13.9	4.6	0.0	187
2012	A+	St. Lucie	2	5	1	48	76	4.13	1.35	7.7	232	39	69	3.30	4.5	14.3	3.2	0.6	153
2013	AA	Binghamton	2	0	3	29	55	1.55	1.20	4.9	188	40	88	2.12	4.9	17.0	3.4	0.3	191
2013	AAA	Las Vegas	2	0	0	29	47	7.76	2.10	5.1	281	46	61	5.90	9.0	14.6	1.6	0.6	38

Has posted Dom above 14 past three seasons while progressing quickly through system. Had tough first go in PCL. Nice FB/CB mix; hitters have a hard time picking up ball out of his hand. Nibbles around plate too much instead of challenging hitters. Relies on deception for swing-and-misses, high-effort delivery.

Ledbetter,David — SP — Texas

EXP MLB DEBUT: 2017 | POTENTIAL: #4 starter | 6B

Thrws R Age 22
2013 (3) Cedarville

Velo	Pitch	Grade
89-94	FB	++++
79-84	CB	+++
81-83	CU	++

Year	Lev	Team	W	L	Sv	IP	K	ERA	WHIP	BF/G	OBA	H%	S%	xERA	Ctl	Dom	Cmd	hr/9	BPV
2013	A-	Spokane	3	3	0	58	51	2.94	1.24	18.1	244	31	77	3.13	2.9	7.9	2.7	0.5	81

Short, athletic RHP who features big FB and pure arm strength. Exhibits clean arm action, but lacks projection. Mechanics are repeatable, though doesn't have much deception. Hard CB is nice complement to solid FB and CU thrown with good arm speed. K rate doesn't project well due to lack of knockout pitch.

Lee,C.C. — RP — Cleveland

EXP MLB DEBUT: 2013 | POTENTIAL: Setup reliever | 7A

Thrws R Age 27
2009 FA (Taiwan)

Velo	Pitch	Grade
89-95	FB	+++
80-82	SL	+++
	CU	+

Year	Lev	Team	W	L	Sv	IP	K	ERA	WHIP	BF/G	OBA	H%	S%	xERA	Ctl	Dom	Cmd	hr/9	BPV
2012	AAA	Columbus	2	0	0	7	8	2.57	0.86	5.1	202	25	80	2.39	1.3	10.3	8.0	1.3	168
2013	A	Lake County	0	0	0	2	4	0.00	1.00	3.8	151	38	100	0.90	4.5	18.0	4.0	0.0	221
2013	AA	Akron	0	0	0	8	9	3.38	0.88	3.7	117	18	57	0.33	4.5	10.1	2.3	0.0	79
2013	AAA	Columbus	1	0	0	19	24	2.37	1.00	3.8	207	31	78	2.04	2.4	11.4	4.8	0.5	159
2013	MLB	CLE	0	0	0	4	4	4.19	1.63	2.4	248	33	71	3.72	6.3	8.4	1.3	0.0	-1

Short, deceptive RP who returned in late May after TJ surgery. Hasn't pitched much in last 2 seasons, but control and moxie didn't miss beats. Establishes excellent FB early in count and complements with wipeout SL for Ks. Stuff plays up due to delivery and arm slot. Command comes and goes, but needs innings.

Lee,Zach — SP — Los Angeles (N)

EXP MLB DEBUT: 2014 | POTENTIAL: #2 starter | 9D

Thrws R Age 22
2010 (1) HS (TX)

Velo	Pitch	Grade
89-93	FB	+++
75-78	CB	+++
81-84	SL	+++
	CU	+++

Year	Lev	Team	W	L	Sv	IP	K	ERA	WHIP	BF/G	OBA	H%	S%	xERA	Ctl	Dom	Cmd	hr/9	BPV
2011	A	Great Lakes	9	6	0	109	91	3.47	1.22	18.3	247	30	73	3.39	2.6	7.5	2.8	0.7	82
2012	A+	Rancho Cuca	2	3	0	55	52	4.57	1.27	18.8	279	33	69	4.62	1.6	8.5	5.2	1.5	127
2012	AA	Chattanooga	4	3	0	65	51	4.28	1.40	21.1	273	32	71	4.27	3.0	7.0	2.3	0.8	63
2013	AA	Chattanooga	10	10	0	142	131	3.23	1.17	20.3	248	31	75	3.34	2.2	8.3	3.7	0.8	107

Strong, athletic SP with low-90s FB up to 95. Solid across the board, he shows four average-or-better pitches. While none are plus, he is great at pitch sequencing and knowing what to throw in any situation. His improved approach has translated to better command and his sound mechanics make for frontline starter potential.

Leesman,Charles — RP — Chicago (A)

EXP MLB DEBUT: 2013 | POTENTIAL: Middle reliever | 6B

Thrws L Age 27
2008 (11) Xavier

Velo	Pitch	Grade
84-90	FB	++
75-78	CB	+++
75-79	CU	+++

Year	Lev	Team	W	L	Sv	IP	K	ERA	WHIP	BF/G	OBA	H%	S%	xERA	Ctl	Dom	Cmd	hr/9	BPV
2010	AA	Birmingham	5	2	0	63	51	2.71	1.06	22.3	209	27	73	1.94	2.8	7.3	2.6	0.1	72
2011	AA	Birmingham	10	7	0	152	113	4.03	1.53	24.5	259	32	72	3.87	4.9	6.7	1.4	0.2	6
2012	AAA	Charlotte	12	10	0	135	103	2.47	1.34	21.6	253	30	83	3.58	3.5	6.9	2.0	0.5	48
2013	AAA	Charlotte	4	3	0	88	78	3.88	1.49	23.7	266	32	78	4.67	4.2	8.0	1.9	1.1	48
2013	MLB	CHW	0	0	0	15	13	7.06	2.09	9.4	271	32	67	6.31	9.4	7.6	0.8	1.2	-98

Tall, angular LHP who has been career starter, but transitioning to bullpen. Sequences average pitches, though lacks ideal velocity. CU is best pitch and moves ball around plate. Slow CB can yield Ks when he sets it up properly. Often pitches backwards, but must improve command in order to earn prominent role.

Leon,Arnold — SP — Oakland

EXP MLB DEBUT: 2014 | POTENTIAL: #5 starter | 6A

Thrws R Age 25
2008 FA (Mexico)

Velo	Pitch	Grade
88-95	FB	+++
75-79	CB	++
79-83	CU	+++

Year	Lev	Team	W	L	Sv	IP	K	ERA	WHIP	BF/G	OBA	H%	S%	xERA	Ctl	Dom	Cmd	hr/9	BPV
2012	A+	Stockton	0	1	0	15	25	5.36	2.05	6.1	379	59	73	7.39	3.0	14.9	5.0	0.6	206
2012	AA	Midland	1	0	1	15	18	2.37	1.32	6.3	284	41	80	3.41	1.8	10.7	6.0	0.0	162
2012	AAA	Sacramento	3	0	0	35	31	1.79	1.16	6.4	208	24	92	3.01	3.8	7.9	2.1	1.0	57
2013	AA	Midland	4	5	0	72	48	3.86	1.36	23.2	299	33	75	4.84	1.4	6.0	4.4	1.1	89
2013	AAA	Sacramento	5	3	0	71	49	4.43	1.32	24.5	288	34	66	4.00	1.6	6.2	3.8	0.5	85

Advanced pitcher who was converted to starter and showed pitchability. Throws with clean delivery and easy arm action. Locates average FB in lower half of zone and complements with nice CU. Has injury history and doesn't have lots of mileage on arm. Needs to hone slow CB as it isn't impact offering.

Light,Pat — SP — Boston

EXP MLB DEBUT: 2015 | POTENTIAL: #4 starter | 7D

Thrws R Age 23
2012 (1-S) Monmouth

Velo	Pitch	Grade
88-96	FB	+++
84-86	SL	+++
79-82	CU	+

Year	Lev	Team	W	L	Sv	IP	K	ERA	WHIP	BF/G	OBA	H%	S%	xERA	Ctl	Dom	Cmd	hr/9	BPV
2011	NCAA	Monmouth	4	5	0	75	61	4.07	1.33	22.3	281	34	69	3.89	2.0	7.3	3.6	0.5	94
2012	NCAA	Monmouth	8	3	0	101	102	2.40	0.99	27.5	228	31	75	2.09	1.4	9.1	6.4	0.3	143
2012	A-	Lowell	0	2	0	30	30	2.39	1.06	9.7	241	32	77	2.48	1.5	9.0	6.0	0.3	139
2013	Rk	GCL Red Sox	0	0	0	6	3	0.00	1.00	7.6	191	22	100	1.48	3.0	4.5	1.5	0.0	18
2013	A	Greenville	1	4	0	28	28	8.97	2.06	13.7	357	44	56	7.70	4.5	9.0	2.0	1.3	58

Long, lean SP who missed most of season with hamstring tear. Induces GB with heavy FB that he spots in lower half. Generally throws strikes and has average command. Hard SL lacks consistent break while CU remains below average pitch. Could eventually move to pen where power FB/SL combo could be solid.

Littrell,Corey — SP — Boston

EXP MLB DEBUT: 2016 | POTENTIAL: #5 starter | 6B

Thrws L Age 22
2013 (5) Kentucky

Velo	Pitch	Grade
86-92	FB	++
80-82	SL	+++
75-78	CB	++
80-83	CU	+++

Year	Lev	Team	W	L	Sv	IP	K	ERA	WHIP	BF/G	OBA	H%	S%	xERA	Ctl	Dom	Cmd	hr/9	BPV
2011	NCAA	Kentucky	6	6	0	68	51	6.99	1.74	19.5	319	37	59	5.93	3.8	6.7	1.8	0.9	36
2012	NCAA	Kentucky	9	2	0	98	87	2.75	1.31	25.4	273	35	78	3.44	2.3	8.0	3.5	0.2	100
2013	NCAA	Kentucky	6	5	0	94	77	3.73	1.32	27.8	251	30	74	3.80	3.3	7.4	2.2	0.9	60
2013	A-	Lowell	0	3	0	31	30	1.74	1.23	10.5	243	33	84	2.63	2.9	8.7	3.0	0.0	96

Tall LHP with deep repertoire who knows how to pitch. Locates offerings precisely to all quadrants of strike zone and has ability to change speeds. Velocity is a bit short, so pitch sequencing is key. Can be slow to plate with funky mechanics, but has good command. Posted reverse splits in pro debut.

Lively,Ben — SP — Cincinnati

EXP MLB DEBUT: 2016 | POTENTIAL: #3 starter/closer | 7D

Thrws R Age 22
2013 (4) Central Florida

Velo	Pitch	Grade
92-93	FB	+++
	SL	+++
	CB	+++
	CU	++

Year	Lev	Team	W	L	Sv	IP	K	ERA	WHIP	BF/G	OBA	H%	S%	xERA	Ctl	Dom	Cmd	hr/9	BPV
2011	NCAA	Central Florida	5	1	0	57	41	5.05	1.54	15.5	251	29	68	4.46	5.4	6.5	1.2	0.9	-10
2012	NCAA	Central Florida	9	2	0	81	84	3.00	1.38	17.9	227	31	77	2.92	5.0	9.3	1.9	0.1	51
2013	NCAA	Central Florida	7	5	0	106	101	2.04	1.09	27.7	227	30	81	2.27	2.4	8.6	3.6	0.2	108
2013	Rk	Billings	0	3	0	37	49	0.73	0.89	11.4	168	28	91	0.87	2.9	11.9	4.1	0.0	154
2013	A	Dayton	0	1	0	4	7	2.25	0.75	14.3	151	32	67	0.29	2.3	15.8	7.0	0.0	241

Mature approach and deception help pitches play up. Commands all four pitches well, and each could become average or better. FB shows nice downward tilt. Knows how to mix pitches well. Will be stretched deeper into games in '14. Ability to earn Ks without elite velocity will be tested at higher levels.

Lo,Chia-Jen — RP — Houston

EXP MLB DEBUT: 2013 | POTENTIAL: Closer | 7A

Thrws R Age 28
2008 FA (Taiwan)

Velo	Pitch	Grade
90-96	FB	++++
77-80	CB	+++
	CU	+

Year	Lev	Team	W	L	Sv	IP	K	ERA	WHIP	BF/G	OBA	H%	S%	xERA	Ctl	Dom	Cmd	hr/9	BPV
2012	A+	Lancaster	0	0	0	19	20	1.42	0.95	6.5	207	28	88	1.92	1.9	9.5	5.0	0.5	137
2013	A-	Tri City	0	0	4	6	12	4.50	1.00	3.8	228	45	60	3.19	1.5	18.0	12.0	1.5	302
2013	A	Quad Cities	0	0	1	3	2	0.00	0.67	3.5	106	13	100	0.00	3.0	6.0	2.0	0.0	45
2013	AA	Corpus Christi	0	0	1	7	6	3.75	1.25	3.7	307	36	75	4.80	0.0	7.5		1.3	153
2013	MLB	HOU	0	3	2	19	16	4.20	1.40	4.3	205	24	72	3.48	6.1	7.5	1.2	0.9	-11

Short, lean RP who has extensive injury history, but has closer potential. Can struggle to throw consistent strikes, but heavy FB can be tough to control. Uses FB as K pitch while CB can be thrown with varying velocity. Not much potential in hittable CU, but is very effective with two pitches when healthy.

Lobstein,Kyle — SP — Detroit

EXP MLB DEBUT: 2014 | POTENTIAL: #5 starter | 7E

Thrws L Age 24
2008 (2) HS (AZ)

Velo	Pitch	Grade
86-90	FB	++
77-79	CB	+++
81-83	CU	+++

Year	Lev	Team	W	L	Sv	IP	K	ERA	WHIP	BF/G	OBA	H%	S%	xERA	Ctl	Dom	Cmd	hr/9	BPV
2011	A+	Charlotte	9	9	0	121	85	3.72	1.24	22.3	260	30	72	3.69	2.2	6.3	2.8	0.8	72
2011	AA	Montgomery	1	1	0	11	11	7.36	1.82	25.5	311	33	69	8.18	4.9	9.0	1.8	3.3	47
2012	AA	Montgomery	8	7	0	144	129	4.06	1.45	22.8	256	32	73	4.09	4.3	8.1	1.9	0.8	47
2013	AA	Erie	7	4	0	95	83	3.12	1.25	25.8	255	32	76	3.41	2.6	7.9	3.1	0.6	90
2013	AAA	Toledo	6	3	0	72	65	3.50	1.36	23.2	264	34	73	3.50	3.1	8.1	2.6	0.2	80

Tall, durable LHP who was solid in first season with DET. Velocity hasn't increased as hoped and FB remains below average, but he throws with quick, clean arm action and evolving into sinkerballer. Offers pitch movement and has deception in CU. CB features nice break, but not swing-and-miss pitch.

Lopez,Jorge — RP — Milwaukee

EXP MLB DEBUT: 2016 | POTENTIAL: #3 starter | 7C

Thrws R Age 21
2011 (2) HS (PR)

Velo	Pitch	Grade
88-92	FB	+++
	CB	++++
	CU	++

Year	Lev	Team	W	L	Sv	IP	K	ERA	WHIP	BF/G	OBA	H%	S%	xERA	Ctl	Dom	Cmd	hr/9	BPV
2012	Rk	AZL Brewers	1	3	2	25	20	5.38	1.55	15.7	276	33	65	4.60	4.3	7.2	1.7	0.7	31
2013	A	Wisconsin	7	8	2	117	92	5.23	1.44	19.9	267	31	65	4.44	3.7	7.1	1.9	1.0	46

Tall, lanky RHP who is still raw, but flashes two above average pitches. He throws low-90s FB that will likely gain velocity as he grows, a CB that flashes plus, and a below average CU with potential. He is showing positive signs and if given time to properly develop, Lopez could pay huge dividends.

Lorenzen,Michael — RP — Cincinnati

EXP MLB DEBUT: 2015 | POTENTIAL: #3 starter/closer | 8E

Thrws R Age 22
2013 (1) Cal State Fullerton

Velo	Pitch	Grade
95-99	FB	++++
81-83	CB	+++

Year	Lev	Team	W	L	Sv	IP	K	ERA	WHIP	BF/G	OBA	H%	S%	xERA	Ctl	Dom	Cmd	hr/9	BPV
2013	NCAA	Cal St. Fullerton	3	0	19	22	20	2.03	0.95	3.8	214	29	76	1.57	1.6	8.1	5.0	0.0	120
2013	Rk	AZL Reds	0	0	0	1	1	0.00	1.00	3.8	262	35	100	2.32	0.0	9.0		0.0	180
2013	A	Dayton	1	0	2	8	7	0.00	1.11	3.5	235	31	100	2.25	2.2	7.8	3.5	0.0	98
2013	A+	Bakersfield	0	1	2	5	6	6.92	2.12	5.1	290	37	70	7.15	8.7	10.4	1.2	1.7	-29
2013	AA	Pensacola	0	0	0	6	5	4.50	2.00	4.1	262	30	82	6.26	9.0	7.5	0.8	1.5	-90

CIN giving collegiate OF/RP a chance to become SP. Pounds strike zone with plus FB that reaches 99; CB above-average. CU needs lots of work. Needs lots of reps as starter. Learning to throw secondary pitches for strikes will help chances of sticking as SP. Command must improve.

Lotzkar,Kyle — RP — Texas

EXP MLB DEBUT: 2015 | POTENTIAL: Reliever | 7E

Thrws R Age 24
2007 (1) HS (Canada)

Velo	Pitch	Grade
88-93	FB	++++
79-82	CB	+++
79-83	CU	+

Year	Lev	Team	W	L	Sv	IP	K	ERA	WHIP	BF/G	OBA	H%	S%	xERA	Ctl	Dom	Cmd	hr/9	BPV
2011	A	Dayton	3	2	0	66	72	4.35	1.15	18.8	215	27	65	3.09	3.4	9.8	2.9	1.1	102
2012	A+	Bakersfield	3	0	0	26	27	2.41	1.23	21.1	230	30	83	3.11	3.4	9.3	2.7	0.7	92
2012	AA	Pensacola	4	6	0	86	96	5.23	1.51	20.7	241	31	68	4.49	5.5	10.0	1.8	1.3	49
2013	A+	Bakersfield	1	2	1	29	33	7.09	1.95	6.1	274	38	61	5.16	8.0	10.2	1.3	0.3	-15
2013	AA	Pensacola	0	1	0	8	8	12.22	3.33	5.0	412	52	59	10.79	12.2	8.9	0.7	0.0	-152

CIN moved him to bullpen in 2013 where he had a disaster season, unable to locate the strike zone. He was released by CIN and signed by TEX who believes he still has quality stuff. Quick arm action give plus movement to FB and SL. Mechanics are jerky and he throws across his body with some deception.

Loux,Barret — SP — Chicago (N)

EXP MLB DEBUT: 2014 | POTENTIAL: #4 starter | 7C

Thrws R Age 25
2010 (1) Texas A&M

Velo	Pitch	Grade
89-94	FB	+++
78-81	CB	++
82-84	SL	+++
	CU	+++

Year	Lev	Team	W	L	Sv	IP	K	ERA	WHIP	BF/G	OBA	H%	S%	xERA	Ctl	Dom	Cmd	hr/9	BPV
2009	NCAA	Texas A&M	3	3	0	48	62	4.13	1.33	16.6	241	36	68	3.20	3.9	11.6	3.0	0.4	121
2010	NCAA	Texas A&M	11	2	0	105	136	2.83	1.07	24.0	209	31	75	2.34	2.9	11.7	4.0	0.6	149
2011	A+	Myrtle Beach	8	5	0	109	127	3.80	1.28	21.3	256	36	70	3.41	2.8	10.5	3.7	0.5	131
2012	AA	Frisco	14	1	0	127	100	3.47	1.27	20.8	251	30	74	3.53	2.9	7.1	2.4	0.7	67
2013	AAA	Iowa	4	6	0	80	76	4.84	1.64	18.8	274	35	69	4.51	5.2	8.6	1.7	0.5	32

Tall righty has failed to live up to expectations since being taken 6th overall in '10. Loux didn't sign due to injury and has struggled to establish himself. FB now sits at 90-92 with a decent CU and avg SL and CB. Struggled with Ctl, but has potential.

Lovegrove,Kieran — SP — Cleveland

EXP MLB DEBUT: 2017 | POTENTIAL: #3 starter | 8E

Thrws R Age 19
2012 (3) HS (CA)

Velo	Pitch	Grade
87-93	FB	++
83-86	SL	+++
82-85	CU	++

Year	Lev	Team	W	L	Sv	IP	K	ERA	WHIP	BF/G	OBA	H%	S%	xERA	Ctl	Dom	Cmd	hr/9	BPV
2012	Rk	AZL Indians	0	2	0	21	18	6.00	1.76	12.0	321	40	64	5.54	3.9	7.7	2.0	0.4	53
2013	Rk	AZL Indians	1	7	0	58	51	5.27	1.62	19.8	278	34	67	4.69	4.8	7.9	1.6	0.6	31

Tall, lanky RHP who repeated Rookie ball, but is still raw. May take time to develop and repeat delivery as he has moving parts. FB is currently below average, but offers loads of projection. SL is best present offering and has potential to miss bats. CU in infancy stage and needs quicker arm action to make potent.

Lowell,Charlie — SP — Miami

EXP MLB DEBUT: 2015 | POTENTIAL: #5 starter | 6C

Thrws L Age 23
2011 (6) Wichita State

Velo	Pitch	Grade
89-93	FB	+++
	SL	+++
	CU	++

Year	Lev	Team	W	L	Sv	IP	K	ERA	WHIP	BF/G	OBA	H%	S%	xERA	Ctl	Dom	Cmd	hr/9	BPV
2011	NCAA	Wichita St.	10	5	0	103	124	2.79	1.20	24.4	224	33	75	2.40	3.5	10.8	3.1	0.1	119
2011	Rk	GCL Marlins	0	1	0	1	2	49.09	5.45	4.6	563	78	0	20.47	16.4	16.4	1.0	0.0	-129
2011	A-	Jamestown	0	0	0	2	4	0.00	1.50	4.3	151	38	100	2.16	9.0	18.0	2.0	0.0	99
2012	A	Greensboro	5	5	0	109	117	4.37	1.36	19.9	226	30	69	3.46	4.9	9.6	2.0	0.7	60
2012	A+	Jupiter	0	0	0	5	5	1.80	1.00	19.1	221	25	100	3.48	1.8	9.0	5.0	1.8	131

Suspended all season for attacking his girlfriend. Big, stocky LH uses his size well to get good downhill plane on his low-90s FB. He complements it with an average SL and a show-me CU. Good pitch sequencing allows him to miss bats, but poor command affects Ctl. Has size and arsenal for back end rotation spot.

Lugo,Luis — SP — Cleveland

EXP MLB DEBUT: 2017 | POTENTIAL: #3 starter | 8D

Thrws L Age 20
2011 FA (Venezuela)

Velo	Pitch	Grade
88-92	FB	+++
74-77	CB	++
79-82	CU	+++

Year	Lev	Team	W	L	Sv	IP	K	ERA	WHIP	BF/G	OBA	H%	S%	xERA	Ctl	Dom	Cmd	hr/9	BPV
2011	Rk	AZL Indians	0	2	0	7	8	6.34	2.54	12.7	333	43	76	8.45	10.1	10.1	1.0	1.3	-73
2012	Rk	AZL Indians	2	4	0	42	51	4.50	1.40	16.1	243	34	69	3.87	4.5	10.9	2.4	0.9	93
2013	A-	Mahoning Val	1	4	0	50	30	1.98	1.00	17.4	216	25	80	1.93	2.0	5.4	2.7	0.2	62
2013	A	Lake County	0	1	0	14	14	3.83	1.35	19.6	260	34	72	3.77	3.2	8.9	2.8	0.6	93

Projectable LHP with excellent arm action and stuff that should lead to Ks. Focused on improving command and succeeded. FB sits in 88-92 mph range with plenty more in tank. Changes speeds like veteran, but CB is substandard at present. Can leave too many balls up and will need to hone delivery.

Madrid,Roman — RP — San Diego

EXP MLB DEBUT: 2015 | POTENTIAL: Setup reliever | 7B

Thrws R Age 23
2012 (7) Central Florida

Velo	Pitch	Grade
90-95	FB	+++
85-87	SL	+++
	CU	++

Year	Lev	Team	W	L	Sv	IP	K	ERA	WHIP	BF/G	OBA	H%	S%	xERA	Ctl	Dom	Cmd	hr/9	BPV
2012	NCAA	Central Florida	5	2	3	45	46	1.00	1.18	5.6	221	30	92	2.42	3.4	9.2	2.7	0.2	92
2012	A-	Eugene	7	0	13	37	44	2.91	1.00	4.6	199	30	68	1.50	2.7	10.7	4.0	0.0	138
2013	A	Fort Wayne	6	4	22	56	56	2.73	1.32	4.6	221	31	77	2.59	4.7	9.0	1.9	0.0	54

Short and strong reliever with potent two-pitch mix. Possesses pure arm strength to pound lower half of zone with hard sinker and SL that serves as K pitch. Has yet to allow HR as pro, but doesn't change speeds well. Arm action can get long which negatively impacts command and walk rate.

Magill,Matt — SP — Los Angeles (N)

EXP MLB DEBUT: 2013 | POTENTIAL: #4 starter | 7C

Thrws R Age 24
2008 (31) HS (CA)

Velo	Pitch	Grade
90-93	FB	+++
	CB	++
	SL	+++
	CU	++

Year	Lev	Team	W	L	Sv	IP	K	ERA	WHIP	BF/G	OBA	H%	S%	xERA	Ctl	Dom	Cmd	hr/9	BPV
2011	A+	Rancho Cuca	11	5	0	139	126	4.34	1.50	23.1	285	35	73	4.81	3.4	8.2	2.4	1.0	74
2012	AA	Chattanooga	11	8	0	146	168	3.76	1.29	23.1	236	33	71	3.14	3.8	10.3	2.8	0.5	103
2013	Rk	AZL Dodgers	0	0	0	3	3	0.00	0.33	9.5	106	15	100	0.00	0.0	9.0		0.0	180
2013	AAA	Albuquerque	6	2	0	85	101	3.49	1.43	20.1	231	32	77	3.67	5.3	10.7	2.0	0.7	67
2013	MLB	LA	0	2	0	28	26	6.50	1.99	22.2	257	29	71	6.57	9.1	8.4	0.9	1.9	-76

Slow development finally has paid dividends for LA. Gets good downhill plane on his four pitch mix that features a low-90s FB up to 95, a wipeout SL, and a below average CU and CB. Very aggressive on the mound, showing good pitch sequencing and a smooth, repeatable delivery that has led to improved control.

Magnifico,Damien — SP — Milwaukee

EXP MLB DEBUT: 2015 | POTENTIAL: Setup reliever | 7C

Thrws R Age 23
2012 (5) Oklahoma

Velo	Pitch	Grade
95-99	FB	+++++
	SL	+++

Year	Lev	Team	W	L	Sv	IP	K	ERA	WHIP	BF/G	OBA	H%	S%	xERA	Ctl	Dom	Cmd	hr/9	BPV
2012	NCAA	Oklahoma	3	1	2	51	34	3.70	1.59	10.7	280	33	75	4.24	4.4	6.0	1.4	0.2	7
2012	Rk	Helena	0	3	0	21	25	5.94	1.70	10.6	260	35	65	4.83	6.4	10.6	1.7	0.8	37
2013	A	Wisconsin	5	1	0	54	46	3.83	1.39	20.7	251	31	73	3.79	4.0	7.7	1.9	0.7	48
2013	A+	Brevard County	0	2	0	26	17	6.18	1.87	12.3	302	35	66	5.77	5.8	5.8	1.0	0.7	-35

Small fireballer struggled in first full season, failing to locate his plus-plus FB that reaches 100 mph. Mixes in the occasional average SL that has decent tilt. Max-effort delivery has his FB all over the place and elbow issues in the past make him a risk. Used as a starter now, his future is likely in the late innings as a RP.

Manaea,Sean — SP — Kansas City

EXP MLB DEBUT: 2015 | POTENTIAL: #2 starter | 8D

Thrws L Age 22
2013 (1-S) Indiana State

Velo	Pitch	Grade
88-95	FB	++++
82-85	SL	+++
84-87	CU	++

Year	Lev	Team	W	L	Sv	IP	K	ERA	WHIP	BF/G	OBA	H%	S%	xERA	Ctl	Dom	Cmd	hr/9	BPV
2011	NCAA	Indiana St.	5	5	0	83	82	4.33	1.42	23.5	230	30	70	3.57	5.2	8.9	1.7	0.6	37
2012	NCAA	Indiana St.	5	3	0	105	115	3.34	1.25	25.1	241	33	74	3.14	3.2	9.9	3.1	0.5	110
2013	NCAA	Indiana St.	5	4	0	73	93	1.48	1.04	21.7	192	29	88	1.86	3.3	11.5	3.4	0.4	134
2013		Did not pitch in the pros																	

Strong LHP who did not pitch due to hip surgery. When healthy, possesses lively FB with potential to add more ticks. Dom has potential to be high due to FB/SL combo. Low ¾ slot conducive to quality SL and generates Ks. Command regressed in 2013 and could use more consistent offspeed offering.

Maples,Dillon — SP — Chicago (N)

EXP MLB DEBUT: 2016 | POTENTIAL: #3 starter/reliever | 8D

Thrws R Age 22
2011 (14) HS (NC)

Velo	Pitch	Grade
93-95	FB	++++
75-78	CB	+++
80-83	CU	+++

Year	Lev	Team	W	L	Sv	IP	K	ERA	WHIP	BF/G	OBA	H%	S%	xERA	Ctl	Dom	Cmd	hr/9	BPV
2012	Rk	AZL Cubs	0	1	0	10	12	4.46	1.58	7.4	174	27	69	2.69	8.9	10.7	1.2	0.0	-30
2013	A-	Boise	5	2	0	42	41	2.14	1.33	17.4	238	32	82	2.84	4.1	8.8	2.2	0.0	66
2013	A	Kane County	0	2	1	34	34	8.42	1.87	14.6	255	34	51	4.67	8.2	8.9	1.1	0.3	-41

Signed for $2.5 million in '11 and has seen limited action since. Still has a plus mid-90s FB with good late movement and a plus CB. Mechanics remain a work in progress, but has nice athleticism. A move to relief could be the solution.

Marinez,Jhan — RP — Detroit

EXP MLB DEBUT: 2010 | POTENTIAL: Closer | 8E

Thrws R Age 25 — 2006 FA (DR)

- 92-98 FB +++
- 83-87 SL +++
- 84-88 CU +

Year	Lev	Team	W	L	Sv	IP	K	ERA	WHIP	BF/G	OBA	H%	S%	xERA	Ctl	Dom	Cmd	hr/9	BPV
2011	AA	Jacksonville	3	8	3	58	74	3.57	1.53	4.5	223	31	80	4.15	6.5	11.5	1.8	1.1	49
2012	AAA	Charlotte	4	2	4	63	65	2.86	1.10	6.2	180	23	77	2.21	4.3	9.3	2.2	0.7	69
2012	MLB	CHW	0	0	0	3	1	0.00	1.48	5.8	208	23	100	2.90	6.7	3.3	0.5	0.0	-102
2013	Rk	Bristol	0	0	0	2	7	8.18	1.82	5.1	244	166	50	3.94	8.2	28.6	3.5	0.0	313
2013	AAA	Charlotte	2	4	2	28	26	6.11	1.50	6.0	248	26	66	5.51	5.1	8.4	1.6	2.3	30

Live-armed RP who regressed and missed much of season due to injury. Slings ball from low slot with excellent velocity and movement. Can leave ball up and allow flyballs and HR. Lacks feel for pitching, but can succeed with FB/SL combo. Doesn't possess true offspeed pitch. Still has upside due to arm strength.

Marlowe,Christopher — RP — San Francisco

EXP MLB DEBUT: 2015 | POTENTIAL: #4 SP / Setup RP | 7B

Thrws R Age 24 — 2011 (5) Oklahoma State

- 92-95 FB ++++
- 81-84 CB ++++

Year	Lev	Team	W	L	Sv	IP	K	ERA	WHIP	BF/G	OBA	H%	S%	xERA	Ctl	Dom	Cmd	hr/9	BPV
2011	NCAA	Oklahoma St.	3	3	4	41	71	5.05	1.44	7.3	178	33	64	2.94	7.5	15.6	2.1	0.7	97
2011	Rk	AZL Giants	1	0	0	3	5	0.00	1.33	4.2	262	46	100	3.10	3.0	15.0	5.0	0.0	207
2012	A	Augusta	1	9	2	83	86	4.22	1.50	12.0	220	29	72	3.54	6.4	9.3	1.5	0.5	13
2013	A-	Salem-Keizer	0	0	0	8	6	1.11	0.74	4.1	180	23	83	0.67	1.1	6.7	6.0	0.0	108
2013	A+	San Jose	3	2	0	70	55	3.98	1.51	11.7	264	32	74	4.14	4.5	7.1	1.6	0.5	24

Undersized, athletic RP continues to impress with his low-to-mid-90s FB and power CB that flashes plus. Saw time as a SP, but small frame and well below average CU point to pen long term. Struggles with overall control of his pitches and needs to refine his command in order to live up to hype.

Maronde,Nick — RP — Los Angeles (A)

EXP MLB DEBUT: 2012 | POTENTIAL: Setup reliever | 7B

Thrws L Age 24 — 2011 (3) Florida

- 87-95 FB ++++
- 80-85 SL +++
- 80-82 CU ++

Year	Lev	Team	W	L	Sv	IP	K	ERA	WHIP	BF/G	OBA	H%	S%	xERA	Ctl	Dom	Cmd	hr/9	BPV
2012	A+	Inland Empire	3	1	0	59	60	1.83	0.91	22.1	194	25	84	1.81	2.1	9.1	4.3	0.6	125
2012	AA	Arkansas	3	2	0	32	21	3.36	1.31	18.9	301	35	73	3.96	0.8	5.9	7.0	0.3	101
2012	MLB	LAA	0	0	0	6	7	1.50	1.50	2.2	262	38	89	3.56	4.5	10.5	2.3	0.0	86
2013	AA	Arkansas	2	4	0	56	63	3.53	1.39	5.8	206	28	76	3.18	5.9	10.1	1.7	0.6	40
2013	MLB	LAA	0	0	0	5	5	6.79	2.26	2.7	211	23	73	6.45	13.6	8.5	0.6	1.7	-196

Strong, athletic LHP whose future role still up in air. Can start or relieve, but increasing walk rate needs attention. Arm action may be best served in pen, but still generates plus FB that he locates to both sides. Sharp SL can be stingy against LHH, but can be flat. Command is paramount to future success.

Marshall,Brett — SP — Chicago (N)

EXP MLB DEBUT: 2013 | POTENTIAL: #4 starter | 7B

Thrws R Age 24 — 2008 (6) HS (TX)

- 90-94 FB +++
- 82-85 SL +++
- 75-77 CB ++
- 78-81 CU +++

Year	Lev	Team	W	L	Sv	IP	K	ERA	WHIP	BF/G	OBA	H%	S%	xERA	Ctl	Dom	Cmd	hr/9	BPV
2010	A+	Tampa	0	0	0	4	6	4.50	1.25	16.3	307	49	60	3.56	0.0	13.5		0.0	261
2011	A+	Tampa	9	7	0	140	114	3.79	1.36	21.7	264	33	71	3.63	3.1	7.3	2.4	0.4	67
2012	AA	Trenton	13	7	0	158	120	3.53	1.29	24.1	253	29	75	3.75	3.0	6.8	2.3	0.9	59
2013	AAA	Scranton/W-B	7	10	0	138	120	5.14	1.53	24.1	270	32	68	4.82	4.4	7.8	1.8	1.1	39
2013	MLB	NYY	0	0	0	12	7	4.50	1.67	17.9	278	27	82	6.37	5.3	5.3	1.0	2.3	-29

Athletic and durable, he uses average FB with plus sinking action to keep ball on ground. Also uses high ¾ slot for downhill plane. Has found consistent release point, but still struggled to limit walks. K rate increased, though lacks true swing-and-miss pitch. Not much upside here, but has value as innings eater.

Martin,Cody — SP — Atlanta

EXP MLB DEBUT: 2014 | POTENTIAL: #3 starter | 8D

Thrws R Age 24 — 2011 (7) Gonzaga

- 90-94 FB +++
- 83-85 SL +++
- CB ++
- CU ++

Year	Lev	Team	W	L	Sv	IP	K	ERA	WHIP	BF/G	OBA	H%	S%	xERA	Ctl	Dom	Cmd	hr/9	BPV
2011	Rk	Danville	0	0	3	9	14	0.00	0.33	3.5	73	15	100	0.00	1.0	14.0	14.0	0.0	243
2011	A	Rome	1	0	6	24	35	1.49	0.91	6.4	209	33	90	2.08	1.5	13.1	8.8	0.7	213
2012	A+	Lynchburg	12	7	0	107	123	2.94	1.19	19.5	235	32	77	2.97	2.9	10.3	3.6	0.6	127
2013	AA	Mississippi	3	3	0	67	71	2.82	1.34	17.4	250	34	79	3.40	3.6	9.5	2.6	0.4	92
2013	AAA	Gwinnett	3	4	1	69	66	3.51	1.30	21.9	232	29	75	3.42	4.0	8.6	2.1	0.8	64

Another strong season has him on the verge of making his MLB debut. Features a good 91-94 mph FB with late life and a swing-and-miss SL. Also has a CB and CU, both of which could develop into avg offerings. Remains a starter for now.

Martin,Ethan — SP — Philadelphia

EXP MLB DEBUT: 2013 | POTENTIAL: Setup RP / Closer | 8C

Thrws R Age 25 — 2008 (1) HS (GA)

- 93-95 FB ++++
- 85-88 SL ++++
- 72-75 CB +++
- 80-83 CU +

Year	Lev	Team	W	L	Sv	IP	K	ERA	WHIP	BF/G	OBA	H%	S%	xERA	Ctl	Dom	Cmd	hr/9	BPV
2011	AA	Chattanooga	5	3	2	40	43	4.04	1.50	8.2	215	29	74	3.59	6.5	9.7	1.5	0.7	16
2012	AA	Chattanooga	8	6	0	118	112	3.58	1.27	24.1	211	28	71	2.71	4.7	8.5	1.8	0.4	46
2012	AA	Reading	5	0	0	39	35	3.21	1.20	22.5	208	26	75	2.78	4.1	8.0	1.9	0.7	51
2013	AAA	Lehigh Valley	11	5	0	115	107	4.14	1.40	23.1	224	28	72	3.64	5.2	8.4	1.6	0.9	27
2013	MLB	PHI	2	5	0	40	47	6.08	1.70	12.1	271	33	69	6.10	5.9	10.6	1.8	2.0	50

Has raw stuff to succeed, including lively mid-90s fastball and a hard curve and plus slider. Struggles to repeat mechanics, which leads to walks and high pitch counts. A reliever earlier in his career, his success in that role with PHI in 2013 in a tiny sample (7 IP; 11 K, 4 BB) hints that might be his future.

Martinez,Carlos — SP — St. Louis

EXP MLB DEBUT: 2013 | POTENTIAL: #2 starter/closer | 9C

Thrws R Age 22 — 2009 FA (DR)

- 94-98 FB +++++
- 78-81 CB ++
- CU ++

Year	Lev	Team	W	L	Sv	IP	K	ERA	WHIP	BF/G	OBA	H%	S%	xERA	Ctl	Dom	Cmd	hr/9	BPV
2012	A+	Palm Beach	2	2	0	33	34	3.00	1.18	18.9	238	33	72	2.45	2.7	9.3	3.4	0.0	111
2012	AA	Springfield	4	3	0	71	58	2.91	1.18	19.0	236	28	78	3.16	2.8	7.3	2.6	0.8	75
2013	AA	Springfield	1	0	0	11	9	2.41	1.07	14.5	258	31	82	3.22	0.8	7.2	9.0	0.8	126
2013	AAA	Memphis	5	3	0	68	63	2.51	1.19	21.0	220	28	79	2.63	3.6	8.3	2.3	0.4	72
2013	MLB	STL	2	1	1	28	24	5.09	1.41	5.7	280	35	62	3.92	2.9	7.6	2.7	0.3	78

Excellent breakout, dominating in the minors and then in a set-up role in the majors. Plus 100 mph in relief. He complements the heater with a good hard SL that at times is devastating. His change-up and curveball remain below average. Could start in 2014.

Martinez,Jonathan — SP — Los Angeles (N)

EXP MLB DEBUT: 2016 | POTENTIAL: #4 starter | 7D

Thrws R Age 20 — 2011 FA (Venezuela)

- 93-94 FB ++++
- SL ++
- CU ++

Year	Lev	Team	W	L	Sv	IP	K	ERA	WHIP	BF/G	OBA	H%	S%	xERA	Ctl	Dom	Cmd	hr/9	BPV
2012	Rk	AZL Dodgers	3	0	0	59	59	3.05	1.27	18.6	262	34	76	3.43	2.4	9.0	3.7	0.5	114
2012	Rk	Ogden	0	1	0	9	9	6.00	1.78	20.7	339	40	71	7.34	3.0	9.0	3.0	2.0	99
2013	Rk	Ogden	3	1	0	32	11	5.03	1.34	22.3	300	32	61	4.31	1.1	3.1	2.8	0.6	43
2013	A	Great Lakes	3	4	0	66	42	3.53	1.22	17.8	258	30	71	3.25	2.2	5.7	2.6	0.4	62

Short, strong RHP had an up-and-down season through two levels in 2013. Has good command and control of his three-pitch mix, but failed to miss bats like he did in 2012. FB sits in the low-90s up to 95 at times and he complements it with a SL and CU, both of which flash average. He has a clean arm and repeatable mechanics.

Martinez,Jose — SP — Arizona

EXP MLB DEBUT: 2017 | POTENTIAL: #2 starter/reliever | 8D

Thrws R Age 20 — 2012 FA (DR)

- 92-95 FB ++++
- 76-79 CB +++
- 81-84 SL +
- 78-81 CU +

Year	Lev	Team	W	L	Sv	IP	K	ERA	WHIP	BF/G	OBA	H%	S%	xERA	Ctl	Dom	Cmd	hr/9	BPV
2012	A-	Yakima	0	1	0	10	8	4.41	1.37	21.4	218	25	69	3.53	5.3	7.1	1.3	0.9	2
2013	A-	Hillsboro	2	3	0	38	30	4.03	1.18	15.2	157	18	67	2.21	5.9	7.1	1.2	0.7	-14

Athletic hurler from the D.R. has an electric arm and a 93-95 mph FB. Uses plus arm-speed to generate easy velocity. Mechanics and release point are inconsistent. Currently relies heavily on FB, but also has a plus hard CB, a SL, and a seldom used CU.

Martinez,Nick — SP — Texas

EXP MLB DEBUT: 2016 | POTENTIAL: #4 starter | 7C

Thrws R Age 23 — 2011 (18) Fordham

- 88-94 FB +++
- 77-80 CB +++
- 82-83 CU ++

Year	Lev	Team	W	L	Sv	IP	K	ERA	WHIP	BF/G	OBA	H%	S%	xERA	Ctl	Dom	Cmd	hr/9	BPV
2011	Rk	AZL Rangers	2	1	0	19	19	1.88	1.20	12.9	279	37	83	3.06	0.9	8.9	9.5	0.0	153
2011	A-	Spokane	1	2	0	39	37	2.54	1.36	18.1	252	34	79	3.09	3.7	8.5	2.3	0.0	72
2012	A	Hickory	8	6	1	117	109	4.84	1.35	15.7	268	34	63	3.87	2.8	8.4	2.9	0.6	92
2013	A+	Myrtle Beach	10	7	0	119	105	2.87	1.21	21.8	240	30	76	2.92	2.9	7.9	2.8	0.4	83
2013	AA	Frisco	2	0	0	32	23	1.13	0.56	21.6	109	13	82	0.00	2.0	6.5	3.3	0.3	81

Fast-armed, athletic RHP who finished 3rd in CAR in ERA. Was consistently good all season by locating solid-average FB to all quadrants of strike zone. Repeats athletic delivery and sets up secondary pitches well. CB has developed into dependable offering and next step is to polish CU.

Mateo,Luis — RP — New York (N)

EXP MLB DEBUT: 2015 | POTENTIAL: #2 starter | 9D

Thrws R Age 24 — 2011 FA (DR)

- 92-95 FB +++
- 86-89 SL ++++
- CU +

Year	Lev	Team	W	L	Sv	IP	K	ERA	WHIP	BF/G	OBA	H%	S%	xERA	Ctl	Dom	Cmd	hr/9	BPV
2012	A-	Brooklyn	4	5	0	73	85	2.46	0.90	22.7	217	31	72	1.70	1.1	10.5	9.4	0.2	176
2013	A+	St. Lucie	1	1	0	8	11	4.39	1.59	12.0	302	43	75	5.37	3.3	12.1	3.7	1.1	146
2013	AA	Binghamton	0	1	0	3	2	12.00	3.00	17.5	415	44	63	12.86	9.0	6.0	0.7	3.0	-117

Appeared four times before being shut down for TJ surgery. Has great stuff but 24 y/o with just 3 IP above A ball. Complements 92-95 FB with a plus hard SL. CU needs a lot of work, but has potential. Overpowered hitters at Brooklyn. Throws with plus command and could post elite Dom if returns to form post-surgery.

Matz,Steven — SP — New York (N)

EXP MLB DEBUT: 2016 | POTENTIAL: #4 starter | 7C

Thrws L Age 23
2009 (2) HS (NY)

- 92-95 FB ++++
- 83-85 CB +++
- 73-75 CU ++

Year	Lev	Team	W	L	Sv	IP	K	ERA	WHIP	BF/G	OBA	H%	S%	xERA	Ctl	Dom	Cmd	hr/9	BPV
2012	Rk	Kingsport	2	1	0	29	34	1.55	1.14	19.1	164	24	88	1.75	5.3	10.6	2.0	0.3	65
2013	A	Savannah	5	6	0	106	121	2.63	1.17	20.2	223	32	78	2.54	3.2	10.3	3.2	0.3	116

Finally completed first full season after significant injury delay. Has the stuff to be #4 starter if he can stay healthy. Works off plus FB that can hit 98 with movement. Complements FB with decent CB and CU that have potential to become above-average.

Matzek,Tyler — SP — Colorado

EXP MLB DEBUT: 2014 | POTENTIAL: #4 starter/reliever | 7D

Thrws L Age 23
2009 (1) HS (CA)

- 90-93 FB +++
- 80-83 SL ++++
- 74-76 CB +++
- CU ++

Year	Lev	Team	W	L	Sv	IP	K	ERA	WHIP	BF/G	OBA	H%	S%	xERA	Ctl	Dom	Cmd	hr/9	BPV
2010	A	Asheville	5	1	0	89	88	2.93	1.39	20.8	198	26	81	3.07	6.3	8.9	1.4	0.6	9
2011	A	Asheville	5	4	0	64	74	4.36	1.48	23.0	200	28	70	3.13	7.0	10.4	1.5	0.4	15
2011	A+	Modesto	0	3	0	33	37	9.82	2.42	17.3	268	34	59	7.26	12.5	10.1	0.8	1.4	-139
2012	A+	Modesto	6	8	0	142	153	4.62	1.61	22.5	251	34	70	4.11	6.0	9.7	1.6	0.4	30
2013	AA	Tulsa	8	9	0	142	95	3.80	1.57	24.0	268	30	78	4.65	4.8	6.0	1.3	0.8	-4

Ctl rate dropped to 4.8 in 2013, but Dom also plunged to 6.0. Continues to have good stuff, but the clock is ticking. Throws a 90-93 mph FB, a hard SL, a CB, and a CU. Tends to vary his release point and gets under the ball. Could move to relief.

May,Trevor — SP — Minnesota

EXP MLB DEBUT: 2014 | POTENTIAL: #3 starter | 8D

Thrws R Age 24
2008 (4) HS (WA)

- 90-95 FB +++
- 76-79 CB +++
- 82-85 SL ++
- 81-84 CU +++

Year	Lev	Team	W	L	Sv	IP	K	ERA	WHIP	BF/G	OBA	H%	S%	xERA	Ctl	Dom	Cmd	hr/9	BPV
2010	A	Lakewood	7	3	0	65	92	2.91	1.09	23.1	218	34	74	2.33	2.8	12.7	4.6	0.4	173
2010	A+	Clearwater	5	5	0	70	90	5.01	1.63	19.5	212	30	70	4.07	7.8	11.6	1.5	0.9	15
2011	A+	Clearwater	10	8	0	151	208	3.63	1.24	22.7	221	34	71	2.82	4.0	12.4	3.1	0.5	133
2012	AA	Reading	10	13	0	149	151	4.89	1.45	22.8	248	30	70	4.53	4.7	9.1	1.9	1.3	55
2013	AA	New Britain	9	9	0	151	159	4.52	1.43	23.8	259	34	69	4.14	4.0	9.5	2.4	0.8	81

Tall, strong RHP who repeated AA and still struggled to find consistency. Needs to stay tall in delivery and throw downhill. FB can be heavy with late, sinking action while he has two K pitches in CB and SL. Hard SL not thrown for strikes enough and may scrap. Average CU rounds out arsenal.

Mayers,Mike — SP — St. Louis

EXP MLB DEBUT: 2016 | POTENTIAL: #3 starter | 7C

Thrws R Age 22
2013 (3) Mississippi

- 90-93 FB +++
- 82-84 SL +++
- 78-81 CU ++

Year	Lev	Team	W	L	Sv	IP	K	ERA	WHIP	BF/G	OBA	H%	S%	xERA	Ctl	Dom	Cmd	hr/9	BPV
2011	NCAA	Mississippi	1	0	0	30	27	5.10	1.53	6.5	304	38	66	4.85	2.7	8.1	3.0	0.6	91
2012	NCAA	Mississippi	6	3	0	92	71	3.51	1.14	21.5	224	27	69	2.65	2.9	6.9	2.4	0.5	64
2013	NCAA	Mississippi	5	6	0	92	73	2.83	1.24	23.4	229	28	79	3.05	3.6	7.1	2.0	0.6	49
2013	Rk	GCL Cardinals	1	0	0	12	13	1.50	1.00	9.2	151	19	91	1.69	4.5	9.8	2.2	0.8	72
2013	A	Peoria	0	3	0	24	14	3.73	1.41	20.4	299	33	75	4.63	1.9	5.2	2.8	0.7	62

Third-round pick out of Mississippi. Has three average to above-average offerings including a good 90-93 mph FB. Lack of overpowering FB is compensated by an ability to throw strikes and a good SL. CU will need to improve as he moves up.

Mazzoni,Cory — SP — New York (N)

EXP MLB DEBUT: 2015 | POTENTIAL: #4 starter | 7D

Thrws R Age 24
2011 (2) North Carolina State

- 90-94 FB ++++
- 72-75 CB +++
- CU ++

Year	Lev	Team	W	L	Sv	IP	K	ERA	WHIP	BF/G	OBA	H%	S%	xERA	Ctl	Dom	Cmd	hr/9	BPV
2011	A-	Brooklyn	1	0	0	6	10	0.00	1.17	4.0	228	42	100	2.23	3.0	15.0	5.0	0.0	207
2011	A+	St. Lucie	1	1	0	7	8	2.57	1.14	4.6	262	34	86	3.87	1.3	10.3	8.0	1.3	168
2012	A+	St. Lucie	5	1	0	63	48	3.28	1.27	21.5	264	32	74	3.44	2.3	6.8	3.0	0.4	80
2012	AA	Binghamton	5	5	0	80	56	4.49	1.37	24.0	285	32	69	4.55	2.2	6.3	2.8	1.0	71
2013	AA	Binghamton	5	3	0	66	74	4.36	1.35	21.2	273	37	67	3.86	2.6	10.1	3.9	0.5	130

Injury limited him to 66 IP and clouds future role. Has above-average control, but FB can get a bit flat, and lots of effort in his delivery. Throws strikes but needs to improve and trust secondary pitches more. Lack of three solid pitches and stuff weakening in later innings could signal move to bullpen coming.

McCullers,Lance — SP — Houston

EXP MLB DEBUT: 2016 | POTENTIAL: #2 starter / Closer | 9D

Thrws R Age 20
2012 (1-S) HS (FL)

- 92-99 FB ++++
- 84-88 CB ++++
- 81-84 CU +

Year	Lev	Team	W	L	Sv	IP	K	ERA	WHIP	BF/G	OBA	H%	S%	xERA	Ctl	Dom	Cmd	hr/9	BPV
2012	Rk	Greeneville	0	3	0	15	17	4.80	1.33	15.6	191	24	67	3.39	6.0	10.2	1.7	1.2	40
2012	Rk	GCL Astros	0	1	0	11	12	1.64	1.09	10.8	244	34	83	2.29	1.6	9.8	6.0	0.0	151
2013	A	Quad Cities	6	5	0	104	117	3.20	1.35	17.4	238	33	75	3.13	4.2	10.1	2.4	0.3	86

Big, strong SP who may have best arm strength in org. Generates plus velocity with electric arm speed. FB is best current pitch and owns very hard CB that he can drop in for strikes or use as chase pitch. CU remains distant third. Effort in delivery results in lack of command, but posts high K and GB rates.

McGough,Scott — RP — Miami

EXP MLB DEBUT: 2014 | POTENTIAL: Reliever | 7E

Thrws R Age 24
2011 (5) Oregon

- 90-94 FB ++++
- 77-80 CB ++++
- CU ++

Year	Lev	Team	W	L	Sv	IP	K	ERA	WHIP	BF/G	OBA	H%	S%	xERA	Ctl	Dom	Cmd	hr/9	BPV
2011	A	Great Lakes	0	4	8	20	25	2.24	1.19	4.0	241	35	83	2.93	2.7	11.2	4.2	0.4	147
2012	A+	Jupiter	2	1	1	16	8	3.33	1.42	4.6	294	34	74	3.88	2.2	4.4	2.0	0.0	38
2012	A+	Rancho Cuca	3	5	5	47	48	4.01	1.51	5.8	253	33	74	4.01	5.0	9.2	1.8	0.6	49
2013	AA	Jacksonville	4	3	1	61	56	2.65	1.08	6.6	218	27	77	2.50	2.6	8.2	3.1	0.6	95
2013	AAA	New Orleans	0	1	0	5	3	5.29	1.96	12.2	357	38	78	7.94	3.5	5.3	1.5	1.8	18

Small, lanky RP has a low-to-mid-90s FB with a power CB and show-me CU. Attacks the strike zone with all three, though command has been spotty at times. Plus arm speed makes FB hard to pick up and he generates good swing-and-misses with the FB/CB combo. Should continue to move quickly.

McGuire,Deck — SP — Toronto

EXP MLB DEBUT: 2014 | POTENTIAL: #4 starter | 7C

Thrws R Age 25
2010 (1) Georgia Tech

- 88-94 FB +++
- 80-83 SL +++
- 77-80 CB ++
- CU ++

Year	Lev	Team	W	L	Sv	IP	K	ERA	WHIP	BF/G	OBA	H%	S%	xERA	Ctl	Dom	Cmd	hr/9	BPV
2010	NCAA	Georgia Tech	9	4	0	112	118	2.97	1.13	27.7	229	29	79	3.19	2.6	9.5	3.6	1.0	117
2011	A+	Dunedin	7	4	0	104	102	2.76	1.22	22.1	232	29	81	3.21	3.3	8.8	2.7	0.8	88
2011	AA	New Hampshire	2	1	0	20	22	4.46	1.34	21.0	260	31	74	4.80	3.1	9.8	3.1	1.8	110
2012	AA	New Hampshire	5	15	0	144	97	5.88	1.56	22.5	285	31	64	5.37	3.9	6.1	1.6	1.4	23
2013	AA	New Hampshire	9	10	0	157	143	4.87	1.32	24.1	250	31	63	3.62	3.4	8.2	2.4	0.7	74

Tall, durable SP who repeated AA and improved across board. Posted lower ERA, walk rate, and oppBA while increasing K rate. Has added more sink to average FB while SL thrown with more confidence. Can miss bats with FB and SL and generally works down in zone. Fringy CU could lead to bullpen role.

McNutt,Trey — RP — Chicago (N)

EXP MLB DEBUT: 2014 | POTENTIAL: Reliever | 7C

Thrws R Age 24
2009 (32) Shelton St. CC

- 93-95 FB +++
- CB +++
- CB ++

Year	Lev	Team	W	L	Sv	IP	K	ERA	WHIP	BF/G	OBA	H%	S%	xERA	Ctl	Dom	Cmd	hr/9	BPV
2010	AA	Tennessee	0	1	0	15	13	5.92	1.64	22.6	329	39	65	6.08	2.4	7.7	3.3	1.2	93
2011	AA	Tennessee	5	6	0	95	65	4.55	1.67	18.6	309	36	72	5.19	3.7	6.2	1.7	0.5	29
2012	AA	Tennessee	9	8	0	95	66	4.26	1.45	11.9	258	29	74	4.50	4.3	6.3	1.5	1.1	15
2013	Rk	AZL Cubs	0	0	0	2	3	0.00	1.50	4.3	347	53	100	4.86	0.0	13.5		0.0	261
2013	AA	Tennessee	2	5	2	31	23	4.63	1.35	4.8	242	28	67	3.77	4.1	6.7	1.6	0.9	28

Big, physical RH continues to underperform. Inconsistent mechanics and release point cause him to struggle with command. Mid-90s FB can be overthrown, causing it to flatten with poor command. Power CB can also be plus, but CU remains below average.

McPherson,Kyle — RP — Pittsburgh

EXP MLB DEBUT: 2012 | POTENTIAL: #4 starter | 7C

Thrws R Age 26
2007 (14) Mobile

- 88-92 FB +++
- 73-75 CB +++
- 80-83 CU +++

Year	Lev	Team	W	L	Sv	IP	K	ERA	WHIP	BF/G	OBA	H%	S%	xERA	Ctl	Dom	Cmd	hr/9	BPV
2011	AA	Altoona	8	5	0	89	82	3.03	1.08	21.7	230	29	74	2.76	2.1	8.3	3.9	0.7	110
2012	AA	Altoona	3	5	0	48	46	4.11	1.22	21.7	284	35	69	4.08	0.9	8.6	9.2	0.9	147
2012	AAA	Indianapolis	0	1	0	18	17	0.99	0.83	22.0	177	23	93	1.31	2.0	8.5	4.3	0.5	116
2012	MLB	PIT	0	2	0	26	21	2.74	1.18	10.5	244	28	82	3.52	2.4	7.2	3.0	1.0	83
2013	AAA	Indianapolis	0	1	0	4	2	21.43	3.57	13.4	482	53	33	13.14	8.6	4.3	0.5	0.0	-136

Tall, athletic RHP had TJS and logged just 4.2 IP. Prior to the injury showed a good 87-92 mph FB. Also had a good 11-5 CB and an effective CU. Real value is that he locates well. Could develop into a reliable, workhorse who keeps runners off base.

Meisner,Casey — SP — New York (N)

EXP MLB DEBUT: 2018 | POTENTIAL: #4 starter | 7E

Thrws R Age 19
2013 (3) HS (TX)

- 92-94 FB ++++
- 75-76 CB +++
- 80-82 CU +

Year	Lev	Team	W	L	Sv	IP	K	ERA	WHIP	BF/G	OBA	H%	S%	xERA	Ctl	Dom	Cmd	hr/9	BPV
2013	Rk	GCL Mets	1	3	0	35	28	3.08	1.17	14.0	238	30	71	2.45	2.6	7.2	2.8	0.0	78

Tall, lanky righty has tons of projection. Pounds the zone with a plus FB with good downward plane. Battles inconsistent mechanics and secondary pitches. Easy arm action, but delivery takes effort and lacks deception. CU a work in progress but shows promise. High upside but lots of work ahead.

Mejia,Adalberto — RP — San Francisco

EXP MLB DEBUT: 2015 | POTENTIAL: #4 Starter | 7B

Thrws L Age 21
2011 FA (DR)

Velo	Pitch	Grade
89-93	FB	+++
	SL	+++
	CU	++

Year	Lev	Team	W	L	Sv	IP	K	ERA	WHIP	BF/G	OBA	H%	S%	xERA	Ctl	Dom	Cmd	hr/9	BPV
2012	A	Augusta	10	7	0	106	79	3.98	1.35	14.7	289	35	69	3.92	1.8	6.7	3.8	0.3	90
2013	A+	San Jose	7	4	0	87	89	3.31	1.13	21.5	234	29	76	3.34	2.4	9.2	3.9	1.1	119
2013	AAA	Fresno	0	0	0	5	2	3.60	1.40	21.1	262	20	100	6.76	3.6	3.6	1.0	3.6	-14

Lanky, advanced LHP impressed in 2013, showing further development of his CU and smoother mechanics. FB sits in the low-90s with good cut and sink complemented by a solid SL and the CU. Doesn't overpower hitters, but continues to rack up Ks due to his pitchability and advanced command of the strike zone.

Mejia,Jefferson — SP — Chicago (N)

EXP MLB DEBUT: 2018 | POTENTIAL: #2 Starter | 8D

Thrws R Age 19
2013 FA (DR)

Velo	Pitch	Grade
90-93	FB	+++
73-75	CB	++
	CU	+++

Year	Lev	Team	W	L	Sv	IP	K	ERA	WHIP	BF/G	OBA	H%	S%	xERA	Ctl	Dom	Cmd	hr/9	BPV
2013		0 Did not pitch in the US																	

Tall, lanky RHP from the Dominican Republic. At 6-7, 190 he has some projectability left and already has a 90-93 mph FB. Also has a good CU and a CB with potential. Needs to figure out mechanics and learn to throw strikes, but has a ton of potential.

Mella,Keury — SP — San Francisco

EXP MLB DEBUT: 2017 | POTENTIAL: #3 Starter | 8E

Thrws R Age 20
2012 FA (DR)

Velo	Pitch	Grade
91-95	FB	++++
	CB	+++
	CU	+

Year	Lev	Team	W	L	Sv	IP	K	ERA	WHIP	BF/G	OBA	H%	S%	xERA	Ctl	Dom	Cmd	hr/9	BPV
2013	Rk	AZL Giants	3	2	0	36	41	2.25	1.25	14.7	251	36	80	2.79	2.8	10.3	3.7	0.0	128

Strong RH impressed in his second season. His body matured some and added velocity followed. His three-pitch mix features a low- to mid-90s FB, a CB that flashes plus, and a CU that is well below average. Some see a RP in the future but he continues to show a better feel for mixing his pitches.

Melotakis,Mason — SP — Minnesota

EXP MLB DEBUT: 2015 | POTENTIAL: Setup reliever | 7B

Thrws L Age 23
2012 (2) Northwestern State

Velo	Pitch	Grade
90-96	FB	++++
81-83	SL	+++
80-83	CU	+

Year	Lev	Team	W	L	Sv	IP	K	ERA	WHIP	BF/G	OBA	H%	S%	xERA	Ctl	Dom	Cmd	hr/9	BPV
2011	NCAA	Northw'stn St.	1	3	5	40	45	4.03	1.59	7.4	289	39	74	4.60	4.0	10.1	2.5	0.4	91
2012	NCAA	Northw'stn St.	4	4	7	62	70	3.63	1.05	10.4	212	29	67	2.47	2.6	10.2	3.9	0.7	130
2012	Rk	Elizabethton	1	1	0	6	10	1.45	0.65	3.1	103	21	75	0.00	2.9	14.5	5.0	0.0	201
2012	A	Beloit	3	1	1	17	24	2.11	1.11	5.2	237	33	94	3.72	2.1	12.6	6.0	1.6	189
2013	A	Cedar Rapids	11	4	1	111	84	3.16	1.31	19.1	253	30	76	3.45	3.2	6.8	2.2	0.5	55

Intimidating lefty who moved to rotation to start season and ended in pen. Likely future role is as RP due to power stuff and demeanor. Uses short arm that may not be pretty, but has plus FB that is swing-and-miss pitch. Power SL shows good break and depth, but rarely commands it. K rate should increase as RP.

Mendez,Roman — RP — Texas

EXP MLB DEBUT: 2015 | POTENTIAL: Setup reliever | 7D

Thrws R Age 23
2007 FA (DR)

Velo	Pitch	Grade
92-99	FB	++++
82-87	SL	+++
82-84	CU	++

Year	Lev	Team	W	L	Sv	IP	K	ERA	WHIP	BF/G	OBA	H%	S%	xERA	Ctl	Dom	Cmd	hr/9	BPV
2011	A	Hickory	9	1	1	117	130	3.31	1.38	18.9	262	35	77	3.78	3.5	10.0	2.9	0.5	105
2012	Rk	AZL Rangers	0	1	0	9	7	3.00	0.89	11.1	216	25	71	2.41	1.0	7.0	7.0	1.0	117
2012	A+	Myrtle Beach	4	6	1	70	71	5.14	1.34	16.2	259	33	62	3.99	3.2	9.1	2.8	0.9	96
2012	AA	Frisco	2	0	1	12	9	1.49	0.99	9.2	190	19	100	2.82	3.0	6.7	2.3	1.5	58
2013	AA	Frisco	2	0	2	24	24	1.86	0.95	5.7	150	20	82	1.20	4.1	8.9	2.2	0.4	68

Lean and athletic pitcher who incurred stress fracture in elbow and ended season in May. Throws with strong, quick arm from low slot to generate excellent velocity that touches upper 90s. Pitched out of bullpen and may be ideal role. All pitches exhibit heat and movement, though location leaves lots to be desired.

Meo,Anthony — SP — Arizona

EXP MLB DEBUT: 2014 | POTENTIAL: #3 starter/setup reliever | 8D

Thrws R Age 24
2011 (2) Coastal Carolina

Velo	Pitch	Grade
92-95	FB	+++
86-88	SL	+++
81-83	CB	++
83-85	CU	++

Year	Lev	Team	W	L	Sv	IP	K	ERA	WHIP	BF/G	OBA	H%	S%	xERA	Ctl	Dom	Cmd	hr/9	BPV
2011	Rk	AZL D'backs	0	0	0	1	2	0.00	0.00	2.8	0	0	100	0.00	0.0	18.0		0.0	342
2011	Rk	Missoula	0	0	0	2	1	0.00	0.00	5.6	0	0	100	0.00	0.0	4.5		0.0	99
2012	A+	Visalia	9	8	0	140	153	4.11	1.46	23.1	253	33	74	4.27	4.6	9.8	2.2	1.0	72
2013	A+	Visalia	1	1	0	22	22	7.70	2.12	5.2	285	36	62	6.23	8.9	8.9	1.0	0.8	-62
2013	AA	Mobile	0	4	0	35	17	6.41	1.60	19.4	238	23	62	5.00	6.4	4.4	0.7	1.5	-77

RH got hammered, going 1-5 with a 6.83 ERA. Has a good 92-94 mph FB, but struggled with control all year, walking 47 in 58 IP. Also throws a plus SL that can be swing-and-miss and a decent CU. CB remains below average and move to relief looks permanent.

Mercedes,Melvin — RP — Detroit

EXP MLB DEBUT: 2015 | POTENTIAL: Setup reliever | 7B

Thrws R Age 23
2008 FA (DR)

Velo	Pitch	Grade
93-98	FB	++++
85-88	SL	+++
	CU	+

Year	Lev	Team	W	L	Sv	IP	K	ERA	WHIP	BF/G	OBA	H%	S%	xERA	Ctl	Dom	Cmd	hr/9	BPV
2011	A	West Michigan	0	0	0	1	1	15.00	3.33	3.7	470	56	50	12.19	7.5	7.5	1.0	0.0	-50
2012	A	West Michigan	0	3	9	64	43	2.81	1.20	7.0	230	27	77	2.83	3.2	6.0	1.9	0.4	39
2012	A+	Lakeland	0	0	0	1	0	0.00	2.00	4.8	262	26	100	4.93	9.0	0.0	0.0	0.0	-225
2013	A+	Lakeland	3	1	11	28	17	0.96	1.00	4.5	226	26	93	2.18	1.6	5.5	3.4	0.3	73
2013	AA	Erie	2	1	12	25	19	1.44	1.28	3.9	246	28	97	3.85	3.2	6.8	2.1	1.1	54

Very aggressive RP who had breakout in first season above Low-A. Posted low K rate despite hard, effective stuff. Exhibited drastic improvement in control while commanding plus sinking FB. Can pitch up in zone and SL can register Ks. Lacks offspeed pitch to battle LHH, but FB/SL combo good enough for late innings.

Mercedes,Simon — SP — Boston

EXP MLB DEBUT: 2017 | POTENTIAL: #4 starter / Setup reliever | 7C

Thrws R Age 22
2012 FA (DR)

Velo	Pitch	Grade
90-95	FB	++++
78-83	SL	++
82-83	CU	+

Year	Lev	Team	W	L	Sv	IP	K	ERA	WHIP	BF/G	OBA	H%	S%	xERA	Ctl	Dom	Cmd	hr/9	BPV
2013	A-	Lowell	2	2	1	63	57	3.14	1.25	19.8	258	33	74	3.18	2.4	8.1	3.4	0.3	99

Durable SP who uses quick arm action to produce plus FB with heavy, late movement. Produces lots of GB and has power arsenal to register Ks. Lacks deception in delivery and needs to find consistency with both SL and CU. Slows arm speed on CU and will need more than FB to succeed at upper levels.

Merejo,Luis — RP — Atlanta

EXP MLB DEBUT: 2017 | POTENTIAL: #3 starter | 8D

Thrws L Age 19
2012 FA (DR)

Velo	Pitch	Grade
90-93	FB	+++
	CB	+
	CU	+

Year	Lev	Team	W	L	Sv	IP	K	ERA	WHIP	BF/G	OBA	H%	S%	xERA	Ctl	Dom	Cmd	hr/9	BPV
2012	Rk	GCL Braves	0	5	0	41	53	4.61	1.15	16.3	247	37	57	2.67	2.0	11.6	5.9	0.2	174
2013	Rk	Danville	1	0	0	10	11	0.00	1.30	13.7	221	32	100	2.53	4.5	9.9	2.2	0.0	75
2013	Rk	GCL Braves	0	0	0	6	1	0.00	1.33	12.5	191	20	100	2.35	6.0	1.5	0.3	0.0	-117

Undersized lefty from the Dominican Republic saw limited action, logging just 16 IP. FB sits at 90-93 mph. Also shows good feel for CU, but breaking ball is inconsistent. Showed good command in his pro debut, but needs to regroup in 2014.

Meyer,Alex — SP — Minnesota

EXP MLB DEBUT: 2014 | POTENTIAL: #2 starter | 9C

Thrws R Age 24
2011 (1) Kentucky

Velo	Pitch	Grade
91-98	FB	++++
83-87	SL	++++
81-83	CU	++

Year	Lev	Team	W	L	Sv	IP	K	ERA	WHIP	BF/G	OBA	H%	S%	xERA	Ctl	Dom	Cmd	hr/9	BPV
2011	NCAA	Kentucky	7	5	0	101	110	2.94	1.23	29.2	215	30	75	2.44	4.1	9.8	2.4	0.2	84
2012	A	Hagerstown	7	4	0	90	107	3.10	1.13	19.8	211	30	72	2.36	3.4	10.7	3.1	0.4	119
2012	A+	Potomac	3	2	0	39	32	2.31	1.03	21.4	209	26	79	2.15	2.5	7.4	2.9	0.5	82
2013	Rk	GCL Twins	0	0	0	8	16	1.11	1.23	10.9	235	51	90	2.46	3.3	17.8	5.3	0.0	248
2013	AA	New Britain	4	3	0	70	84	3.21	1.27	22.0	233	33	74	2.96	3.7	10.8	2.9	0.4	112

Tall, angular RHP who missed time with sore shoulder, but rebounded with strong AFL. Has high K ability along with GB tendencies. Pitches on downhill plane due to 6'9" height and can devastate hitters with FB and power SL. Improved command, but long levers result in difficulty repeating delivery.

Mirowski,Ritchie — RP — Washington

EXP MLB DEBUT: 2014 | POTENTIAL: Reliever | 7B

Thrws R Age 25
2011 (45) Oklahoma Baptist

Velo	Pitch	Grade
87-91	FB	++
75-79	CB	++
	CU	++

Year	Lev	Team	W	L	Sv	IP	K	ERA	WHIP	BF/G	OBA	H%	S%	xERA	Ctl	Dom	Cmd	hr/9	BPV
2011	A-	Auburn	1	2	0	24	20	2.61	1.45	7.4	261	33	80	3.46	4.1	7.5	1.8	0.0	42
2012	A-	Auburn	1	0	1	7	8	1.29	1.29	7.2	262	37	89	3.02	2.6	10.3	4.0	0.0	134
2012	A	Hagerstown	4	0	3	27	28	2.00	1.26	6.9	200	27	85	2.49	5.0	9.3	1.9	0.3	51
2013	A+	Potomac	8	3	6	48	59	1.50	0.90	5.6	191	25	95	2.20	2.1	11.1	5.4	1.1	161
2013	AA	Harrisburg	2	0	1	20	29	2.67	0.94	5.8	208	35	68	1.44	1.8	12.9	7.3	0.0	202

Has strung together three really nice seasons to start his pro career despite lack of a true plus offering. Throws from 3/4 arm slot and locates all of his pitches well. Worked through some control issues and posted career best 2.0 Ctl. After strong AFL showing, could find himself in a middle relief role for WAS soon.

Mitchell,Bryan

SP | New York (A) | EXP MLB DEBUT: 2014 | POTENTIAL: #4 starter | **7C**

Thrws R Age 23
2009 (16) HS (NC)

Velo	Pitch	Grade
88-94	FB	++++
79-81	CB	+++
84-85	CU	+

Year	Lev	Team	W	L	Sv	IP	K	ERA	WHIP	BF/G	OBA	H%	S%	xERA	Ctl	Dom	Cmd	hr/9	BPV
2010	A-	Staten Island	0	1	0	4	3	6.75	2.00	19.3	383	46	63	6.85	2.3	6.8	3.0	0.0	79
2011	A-	Staten Island	1	3	0	61	59	4.12	1.57	19.2	274	35	75	4.61	4.6	8.7	1.9	0.7	51
2012	A	Charleston (Sc)	9	11	0	120	121	4.58	1.49	19.2	240	32	69	3.76	5.4	9.1	1.7	0.5	36
2013	A+	Tampa	4	11	0	126	104	5.13	1.56	23.0	288	36	65	4.45	3.8	7.4	2.0	0.4	49
2013	AA	Trenton	0	0	0	18	16	1.98	1.04	23.4	214	28	79	1.82	2.5	7.9	3.2	0.0	94

Quick-armed SP who drastically improved control and continued to keep ball low. Falling K rate is a concern and has hittable stuff. Needs to mix offerings more efficiently and set up solid CB. Has tendency to overthrow which straightens FB. CU is distant third pitch, but FB and CB can flash plus.

Moll,Sam

RP | Colorado | EXP MLB DEBUT: 2016 | POTENTIAL: Reliever | **7C**

Thrws L Age 22
2013 (3) Memphis

Velo	Pitch	Grade
92-95	FB	+++
	CB	+++
	SL	++

Year	Lev	Team	W	L	Sv	IP	K	ERA	WHIP	BF/G	OBA	H%	S%	xERA	Ctl	Dom	Cmd	hr/9	BPV
2011	NCAA	Memphis	3	1	1	40	48	2.69	1.22	14.7	226	34	76	2.39	3.6	10.8	3.0	0.0	115
2012	NCAA	Memphis	5	5	1	95	59	3.50	1.42	25.2	253	30	74	3.55	4.2	5.6	1.3	0.3	6
2013	NCAA	Memphis	9	3	0	94	106	2.30	1.04	24.2	199	29	76	1.62	3.1	10.1	3.3	0.0	118
2013	A-	Tri-City	3	1	0	30	29	1.80	1.00	11.5	191	26	80	1.43	3.0	8.7	2.9	0.0	94

Short lefty was 3rd round pick out of Memphis. Worked both as a starter and relief with a good 94-96 mph FB and a power CB. Mechanics can be inconsistent, leading to struggles with control and making a relief role more likely.

Montas,Francellis

SP | Chicago (A) | EXP MLB DEBUT: 2016 | POTENTIAL: #2 starter | **8E**

Thrws R Age 21
2009 FA (DR)

Velo	Pitch	Grade
92-99	FB	++++
83-87	SL	++
84-88	CU	+

Year	Lev	Team	W	L	Sv	IP	K	ERA	WHIP	BF/G	OBA	H%	S%	xERA	Ctl	Dom	Cmd	hr/9	BPV
2012	Rk	GCL Red Sox	1	5	0	40	41	4.03	1.14	13.3	231	32	61	2.27	2.7	9.2	3.4	0.0	111
2012	A-	Lowell	0	0	0	3	4	0.00	1.88	15.0	357	50	100	5.99	2.8	11.3	4.0	0.0	145
2013	A	Greenville	2	9	0	85	96	5.71	1.48	19.3	281	37	62	4.79	3.4	10.2	3.0	1.1	109
2013	A	Kannapolis	3	2	0	25	31	4.64	1.51	21.8	220	32	68	3.36	6.4	11.1	1.7	0.4	44

Quick-armed pitcher who impressed with plus FB and solid SL. FB features armside run and can be tough to elevate. Has tendency to overthrow which leaves pitch flat. Has been hittable despite natural stuff and FB needs more separation from CU. Has ingredients to be very good, but still raw in development.

Montero,Rafael

SP | New York (N) | EXP MLB DEBUT: 2014 | POTENTIAL: #3 starter | **8B**

Thrws R Age 23
2011 FA (DR)

Velo	Pitch	Grade
91-93	FB	+++
80-83	SL	+++
	CU	++

Year	Lev	Team	W	L	Sv	IP	K	ERA	WHIP	BF/G	OBA	H%	S%	xERA	Ctl	Dom	Cmd	hr/9	BPV
2011	A-	Brooklyn	1	0	0	5	5	3.60	0.80	9.1	175	18	67	2.44	1.8	9.0	5.0	1.8	131
2012	A	Savannah	6	3	0	71	54	2.53	0.97	22.5	233	28	75	2.36	1.0	6.8	6.8	0.5	114
2012	A+	St. Lucie	5	2	0	50	56	2.15	0.92	23.4	198	28	77	1.63	2.0	10.0	5.1	0.4	145
2013	AA	Binghamton	7	3	0	66	72	2.45	0.92	22.5	215	30	73	1.76	1.4	9.8	7.2	0.3	157
2013	AAA	Las Vegas	5	4	0	88	78	3.06	1.25	22.4	255	32	75	3.24	2.6	8.0	3.1	0.4	92

Continues to exceed expectations of a short pitcher lacking dominant FB. Plus-plus control is his calling card. FB has nasty movement from 3/4 arm slot. Keeps hitters off-balance with plus SL and solid-average CU. Great work ethic, mound presence and pitch selection bode well for future.

Montgomery,Mark

RP | New York (A) | EXP MLB DEBUT: 2014 | POTENTIAL: Closer | **7A**

Thrws R Age 23
2011 (11) Longwood

Velo	Pitch	Grade
90-93	FB	+++
82-85	SL	++++
81-83	CU	+

Year	Lev	Team	W	L	Sv	IP	K	ERA	WHIP	BF/G	OBA	H%	S%	xERA	Ctl	Dom	Cmd	hr/9	BPV
2012	A+	Tampa	4	1	14	40	61	1.35	0.97	4.9	169	31	85	1.07	3.6	13.7	3.8	0.0	167
2012	AA	Trenton	3	1	1	24	38	1.88	0.75	5.7	151	27	76	0.66	2.3	14.3	6.3	0.4	214
2013	Rk	GCL Yankees	0	0	0	3	8	5.81	1.29	6.4	314	84	50	3.68	0.0	23.2		0.0	436
2013	Rk	GCL Yankees 2	0	0	0	2	2	0.00	0.50	3.3	151	22	100	0.00	0.0	9.0		0.0	180
2013	AAA	Scranton/W-B	2	3	0	40	49	3.38	1.53	7.0	242	33	81	4.20	5.6	11.0	2.0	0.9	65

Strong RP who took step back in '13, but still has potent FB/SL combo to be ideal late-innings guy. Walk rate regressed as he has tendency to overthrow. Delivery is a bit funky and deceptive which allows FB to play up. SL remains best pitch and can be thrown for strikes or as chaser. Lacks suitable CU.

Montgomery,Mike

SP | Tampa Bay | EXP MLB DEBUT: 2014 | POTENTIAL: #4 starter | **7D**

Thrws L Age 25
2008 (1-S) HS (CA)

Velo	Pitch	Grade
87-93	FB	+++
74-78	CB	++
81-83	CU	++++

Year	Lev	Team	W	L	Sv	IP	K	ERA	WHIP	BF/G	OBA	H%	S%	xERA	Ctl	Dom	Cmd	hr/9	BPV
2011	AAA	Omaha	5	11	0	150	129	5.33	1.50	23.2	270	33	65	4.56	4.1	7.7	1.9	0.9	46
2012	AA	NW Arkansas	2	6	0	58	44	6.67	1.55	25.4	297	32	60	5.98	3.3	6.8	2.1	1.9	53
2012	AAA	Omaha	3	6	0	91	67	5.72	1.68	24.1	300	34	67	5.71	4.2	6.6	1.6	1.2	22
2013	A+	Charlotte	0	1	0	8	10	6.59	1.46	17.6	280	41	50	3.72	3.3	11.0	3.3	0.0	127
2013	AAA	Durham	7	8	0	108	77	4.74	1.47	23.2	267	31	68	4.30	4.0	6.4	1.6	0.7	25

Tall LHP who has spent last 3 years in AAA and hasn't performed up to expectations. CU remains plus offering as he repeats arm speed. Declining K rate a concern, partly due to velocity that is taking step back. Can aim ball too much instead of letting ball fly. Still hope that he can regain FB and find consistent CB.

Mooneyham,Brett

SP | Washington | EXP MLB DEBUT: 2016 | POTENTIAL: #3 starter | **7D**

Thrws L Age 24
2012 (3) Stanford

Velo	Pitch	Grade
90-93	FB	+++
	SL	++
	CU	++

Year	Lev	Team	W	L	Sv	IP	K	ERA	WHIP	BF/G	OBA	H%	S%	xERA	Ctl	Dom	Cmd	hr/9	BPV
2010	NCAA	Stanford	3	7	0	87	99	5.07	1.59	22.5	237	32	68	4.22	6.4	10.2	1.6	0.8	29
2012	NCAA	Stanford	7	6	0	83	90	4.77	1.42	23.5	252	34	66	3.85	4.2	9.7	2.3	0.6	79
2012	A-	Auburn	2	2	0	42	29	2.57	1.24	17.1	233	27	80	2.95	3.4	6.2	1.8	0.4	37
2013	A	Hagerstown	10	3	0	93	79	1.94	0.98	20.8	160	20	83	1.50	4.0	7.6	1.9	0.5	48
2013	A+	Potomac	0	3	0	11	6	13.78	2.70	20.4	352	37	46	9.58	10.5	4.9	0.5	1.6	-179

Polished collegiate pitcher improved upon his solid debut in 2013. Comes after hitters with a solid, if not overpowering, arsenal. Needs to gain consistency with delivery and secondary pitches. Doesn't strike out a lot of hitters, but could become solid mid-rotation starter if he limits walks.

Moore,Navery

SP | Atlanta | EXP MLB DEBUT: 2015 | POTENTIAL: Reliever | **7C**

Thrws R Age 23
2011 (14) Vanderbilt

Velo	Pitch	Grade
92-96	FB	+++
	CB	+
	CU	+

Year	Lev	Team	W	L	Sv	IP	K	ERA	WHIP	BF/G	OBA	H%	S%	xERA	Ctl	Dom	Cmd	hr/9	BPV
2009	NCAA	Vanderbilt	0	0	0	5	2	7.20	2.00	8.0	262	25	67	6.58	9.0	3.6	0.4	1.8	-160
2010	NCAA	Vanderbilt	2	0	0	12	16	9.59	2.21	6.1	304	45	52	5.95	8.9	11.8	1.3	0.0	-9
2011	NCAA	Vanderbilt	4	2	11	29	25	1.23	1.03	4.0	179	22	93	1.96	3.7	7.7	2.1	0.6	57
2012	A	Rome	8	3	0	102	84	3.87	1.25	16.0	224	28	67	2.72	4.0	7.4	1.9	0.3	44
2013	A+	Lynchburg	7	7	0	87	60	6.19	1.63	21.6	311	36	61	5.43	3.2	6.2	1.9	0.8	43

Took a step back, posting a 6.16 ERA and getting hit at a .308 clip. Still has a good 92-96 mph FB, but doesn't get many swings and misses. Also has as below-average CB and a CU. Given his injury history and plus fastball, he profiles better as a reliever.

Moran,Brian

RP | Los Angeles (A) | EXP MLB DEBUT: 2014 | POTENTIAL: Situational reliever | **6A**

Thrws L Age 25
2009 (7) North Carolina

Velo	Pitch	Grade
84-90	FB	+++
77-80	SL	++
81-84	CU	++

Year	Lev	Team	W	L	Sv	IP	K	ERA	WHIP	BF/G	OBA	H%	S%	xERA	Ctl	Dom	Cmd	hr/9	BPV
2010	AA	West Tennessee	0	0	0	2	1	13.50	2.50	5.3	415	46	40	8.80	4.5	4.5	1.0	0.0	-23
2011	AA	Jackson	5	3	0	60	63	4.63	1.36	5.6	261	32	70	4.48	3.3	9.4	2.9	1.3	99
2012	AA	Jackson	1	2	0	31	29	1.15	1.15	5.2	254	33	91	2.88	1.7	8.4	4.8	0.3	122
2012	AAA	Tacoma	3	3	2	37	53	3.89	0.95	6.1	181	25	66	2.51	2.9	12.9	4.4	1.5	171
2013	AAA	Tacoma	2	5	4	62	85	3.47	1.45	5.5	285	42	77	4.29	2.9	12.3	4.3	0.6	161

Deceptive RP who was selected in Rule 5 by LAA and has good chance to stick. Rarely touches 90 on gun, but tough to square up FB due to delivery and angle to plate. FB rarely comes out straight and keeps LHH at bay. Not very effective against RHH due to lack of offspeed pitch and may be lefty specialist.

Moreno,Erling

SP | Chicago (N) | EXP MLB DEBUT: 2018 | POTENTIAL: #3 starter | **7D**

Thrws R Age 17
2013 FA (Colombia)

Velo	Pitch	Grade
87-91	FB	++
	CB	++
	CU	++

Year	Lev	Team	W	L	Sv	IP	K	ERA	WHIP	BF/G	OBA	H%	S%	xERA	Ctl	Dom	Cmd	hr/9	BPV
2013		Did not pitch in the US																	

Tall RH from Colombia signed for $650,000. FB currently sits at 87-91, but could add velocity as he matures. Already has a good CU and a CB that has potential. Shows good feel for pitching and will make his debut in 2014.

Morgan,Adam

RP | Philadelphia | EXP MLB DEBUT: 2014 | POTENTIAL: #3 starter | **7C**

Thrws L Age 24
2011 (3) Alabama

Velo	Pitch	Grade
90-93	FB	++++
84-86	SL	++++
75-78	CB	+++
80-82	CU	++

Year	Lev	Team	W	L	Sv	IP	K	ERA	WHIP	BF/G	OBA	H%	S%	xERA	Ctl	Dom	Cmd	hr/9	BPV
2011	A-	Williamsport	3	3	0	53	43	2.03	1.05	18.7	219	27	81	2.22	2.4	7.3	3.1	0.3	85
2012	A+	Clearwater	4	10	0	123	140	3.29	1.07	22.8	229	32	69	2.52	2.0	10.2	5.0	0.5	147
2012	AA	Reading	4	1	0	35	29	3.58	1.28	24.0	255	31	72	3.42	2.8	7.4	2.6	0.5	76
2013	Rk	GCL Phillies	0	1	0	7	8	2.57	0.86	12.9	233	34	67	1.56	0.0	10.3		0.0	203
2013	AAA	Lehigh Valley	2	7	0	71	49	4.05	1.55	19.4	295	33	78	5.39	3.3	6.2	1.9	1.3	41

Smooth, compact delivery leads to above average command of four pitches including swing-and-miss slider, sharp curve, and decent change-up. Was poised to make 2013 debut, but shoulder trouble limited his innings. Though surgery wasn't required, he'll need to prove his health in 2014.

Morin,Michael

RP | Los Angeles (A) | EXP MLB DEBUT: 2014 | POTENTIAL: Setup reliever | 6A

Thrws R Age 23
2012 (13) North Carolina

Velo	Pitch	Grade
90-94	FB	+ + +
79-83	SL	+ +
77-82	CU	+ + + +

Year	Lev	Team	W	L	Sv	IP	K	ERA	WHIP	BF/G	OBA	H%	S%	xERA	Ctl	Dom	Cmd	hr/9	BPV
2011	NCAA	North Carolina	4	2	10	64	66	4.64	1.27	8.2	259	35	59	2.94	2.5	9.3	3.7	0.0	117
2012	NCAA	North Carolina	6	4	19	58	55	1.40	0.98	5.8	189	24	89	1.80	2.9	8.5	2.9	0.5	92
2012	Rk	Orem	2	2	4	34	29	5.00	1.40	6.0	261	32	63	3.82	3.7	7.6	2.1	0.5	56
2013	A+	Inland Empire	3	1	13	39	43	1.85	0.90	4.8	214	29	82	1.87	1.2	9.9	8.6	0.5	165
2013	AA	Arkansas	0	2	10	31	33	2.03	1.00	4.6	229	31	83	2.43	1.5	9.6	6.6	0.6	151

Tall, unheralded RP who performed equally well on two levels as closer. May not have FB velocity to serve as stopper in big leagues, but locates all pitches effectively to all parts of strike zone. Owns excellent CU that features movement and drop. RHH rarely elevate ball, though LHH hit over .300 against him.

Mujica,Jose

SP | Tampa Bay | EXP MLB DEBUT: 2018 | POTENTIAL: #2 starter | 9E

Thrws R Age 18
2012 FA (Venezuela)

Velo	Pitch	Grade
87-93	FB	+ + +
77-80	CB	+ +
82-83	CU	+ + +

Year	Lev	Team	W	L	Sv	IP	K	ERA	WHIP	BF/G	OBA	H%	S%	xERA	Ctl	Dom	Cmd	hr/9	BPV
2013	Rk	GCL Rays	3	2	1	32	20	3.09	1.09	10.4	262	31	69	2.59	0.8	5.6	6.7	0.0	96

Strong, durable RHP who thrived in first pro season in U.S. Fresh arm generates heavy FB that hitters bury into ground. Throws lively FB with exceptional command while CU has sinking action. Doesn't have consistent breaking ball and will need to upgrade CB. Low K rate isn't indicative of potential.

Munson,Kevin

RP | Philadelphia | EXP MLB DEBUT: 2014 | POTENTIAL: Reliever | 6C

Thrws R Age 25
2010 (4) James Madison

Velo	Pitch	Grade
90-94	FB	+ + +
	SL	+ + +

Year	Lev	Team	W	L	Sv	IP	K	ERA	WHIP	BF/G	OBA	H%	S%	xERA	Ctl	Dom	Cmd	hr/9	BPV
2011	A+	Visalia	4	3	0	53	76	4.06	1.60	5.6	227	35	75	3.96	6.9	12.9	1.9	0.7	62
2011	AA	Mobile	0	0	0	3	2	0.00	1.33	6.2	262	32	100	3.19	3.0	6.0	2.0	0.0	45
2012	AA	Mobile	3	5	3	53	64	6.28	1.55	5.3	269	38	57	4.25	4.6	10.9	2.4	0.5	90
2013	AA	Mobile	2	2	13	31	39	3.46	1.03	4.1	162	20	74	2.50	4.3	11.3	2.6	1.4	104
2013	AAA	Reno	0	2	1	23	27	5.09	1.39	4.0	278	39	61	3.88	2.7	10.6	3.9	0.4	134

Short, RH reliever remains inconsistent. Has a nice two-pitch FB/SL mix. FB sits in the 90-94 range and can top out at 95 MPH. SL has nice swing and miss potential and good late depth. Has the ability to dominate, but gives up too many walks.

Murphy,Griffin

RP | Toronto | EXP MLB DEBUT: 2015 | POTENTIAL: Setup reliever | 6B

Thrws L Age 23
2010 (2) HS (CA)

Velo	Pitch	Grade
89-93	FB	+ + +
73-76	CB	+ +
80-83	CU	+ + +

Year	Lev	Team	W	L	Sv	IP	K	ERA	WHIP	BF/G	OBA	H%	S%	xERA	Ctl	Dom	Cmd	hr/9	BPV
2011	Rk	GCL Blue Jays	2	2	0	41	39	4.39	1.56	16.3	293	35	76	5.42	3.5	8.6	2.4	1.3	77
2012	Rk	Bluefield	1	2	1	37	42	1.70	1.00	9.4	187	27	83	1.60	3.2	10.2	3.2	0.2	117
2012	A-	Vancouver	0	0	0	2	2	4.29	0.95	4.0	252	34	50	2.07	0.0	8.6		0.0	172
2013	A	Lansing	1	3	1	71	60	4.18	1.56	8.6	285	35	74	4.80	3.9	7.6	1.9	0.8	49

Big, strong pitcher who converted to RP in '13. May not have more velocity to add due to arm action and delivery, but commands FB to both sides of plate. Can cut and sink FB to keep ball on ground while CU thrown with quality arm speed. Needs to refine CB to have dependable breaking ball at disposal.

Nelson,Jimmy

SP | Milwaukee | EXP MLB DEBUT: 2013 | POTENTIAL: #3 starter | 8D

Thrws R Age 25
2010 (2) Alabama

Velo	Pitch	Grade
92-96	FB	+ + + +
84-86	SL	+ + + +
	CU	+ +

Year	Lev	Team	W	L	Sv	IP	K	ERA	WHIP	BF/G	OBA	H%	S%	xERA	Ctl	Dom	Cmd	hr/9	BPV
2010	Rk	Helena	2	0	3	26	33	3.78	1.64	9.7	289	41	78	4.94	4.5	11.3	2.5	0.7	101
2011	A	Wisconsin	8	9	0	146	120	4.38	1.45	24.0	262	32	69	3.97	4.0	7.4	1.8	0.6	43
2012	A+	Brevard County	4	4	0	81	77	2.22	1.09	24.4	216	28	80	2.25	2.8	8.5	3.1	0.3	97
2012	AA	Huntsville	2	4	0	46	42	3.91	1.54	20.1	208	27	74	3.37	7.2	8.2	1.1	0.4	-30
2013	MLB	MIL	0	0	0	10	8	0.90	0.70	8.8	66	9	86	0.00	4.5	7.2	1.6	0.0	26

Big, strong SP uses size to generate plus velocity and pound the strike zone with mid-90s FB and plus SL. With his size he can struggle to repeat, causing his command and control to suffer. With clean arm action and two plus pitches, Nelson's future in the middle of a rotation seems bright.

Nicolino,Justin

SP | Miami | EXP MLB DEBUT: 2015 | POTENTIAL: #2 starter | 8B

Thrws L Age 22
2010 (2) HS (FL)

Velo	Pitch	Grade
88-94	FB	+ + + +
	CU	+ + + +
75-78	CB	+ + + +

Year	Lev	Team	W	L	Sv	IP	K	ERA	WHIP	BF/G	OBA	H%	S%	xERA	Ctl	Dom	Cmd	hr/9	BPV
2011	A-	Vancouver	5	1	0	52	64	1.04	0.75	15.5	160	25	85	0.43	1.9	11.1	5.8	0.0	166
2011	A	Lansing	1	1	0	8	9	3.29	1.59	12.0	322	44	77	4.69	2.2	9.9	4.5	0.0	137
2012	A	Lansing	10	4	0	124	119	2.47	1.07	17.2	242	31	78	2.65	1.5	8.6	5.7	0.4	132
2013	A+	Jupiter	5	2	0	96	64	2.25	1.11	21.0	247	29	81	2.78	1.7	6.0	3.6	0.4	80
2013	AA	Jacksonville	3	2	0	45	31	4.99	1.66	22.5	331	39	68	5.44	2.4	6.2	2.6	0.4	65

Tall, polished LHP who locates his upper-80s, low-90s FB and solid secondary pitches for strikes. Keeps the ball down and locates to both sides of the plate and effectively sequences his pitches. Dom won't be big part of his game, but his pitchability and good secondary offerings should take him far.

Nolin,Sean

SP | Toronto | EXP MLB DEBUT: 2013 | POTENTIAL: #4 starter | 7C

Thrws L Age 24
2010 (6) San Jacinto JC

Velo	Pitch	Grade
88-94	FB	+ + +
79-82	CB	+ +
81-84	SL	+ + +
80-82	CU	+ + +

Year	Lev	Team	W	L	Sv	IP	K	ERA	WHIP	BF/G	OBA	H%	S%	xERA	Ctl	Dom	Cmd	hr/9	BPV
2012	A+	Dunedin	9	0	0	86	90	2.20	1.08	19.8	229	30	84	2.77	2.2	9.4	4.3	0.7	128
2012	AA	New Hampshire	1	0	0	15	18	1.20	1.00	19.1	175	27	87	1.24	3.6	10.8	3.0	0.0	115
2013	AA	New Hampshire	8	3	0	92	103	3.03	1.24	22.0	255	35	77	3.36	2.4	10.1	4.1	0.6	133
2013	AAA	Buffalo	1	1	0	17	13	1.57	1.34	23.8	211	25	91	3.03	5.2	6.8	1.3	0.5	-1
2013	MLB	TOR	0	1	0	1	0	41.54	6.15	11.7	656	62	29	33.54	6.9	0.0	0.0	6.9	-169

Big, durable LHP who lacks projection due to frame and arm action, but present stuff is sufficient to succeed. Gets ahead of hitters with average FB and has feel for secondary stuff. Doesn't have out pitch, but sequences well and can vary arm slot to his advantage. Low ceiling guy, but good chance to stick.

Norris,Daniel

SP | Toronto | EXP MLB DEBUT: 2016 | POTENTIAL: #3 starter | 8E

Thrws L Age 21
2011 (2) HS (TN)

Velo	Pitch	Grade
90-96	FB	+ + +
75-78	CB	+ + +
81-83	CU	+ + +

Year	Lev	Team	W	L	Sv	IP	K	ERA	WHIP	BF/G	OBA	H%	S%	xERA	Ctl	Dom	Cmd	hr/9	BPV
2012	Rk	Bluefield	2	3	0	35	38	7.97	1.63	14.2	308	40	49	5.54	3.3	9.8	2.9	1.0	104
2012	A-	Vancouver	0	1	0	7	5	11.25	2.64	19.7	408	48	53	8.98	6.3	6.3	1.0	0.0	-38
2013	A	Lansing	1	7	0	85	99	4.23	1.50	16.0	259	36	72	4.12	4.6	10.5	2.3	0.6	81
2013	A+	Dunedin	1	0	0	5	1	0.00	0.60	17.1	66	7	100	0.00	3.6	1.8	0.5	0.0	-47

Very athletic pitcher who rebounded from poor debut in 2012. Regaining prospect status with variety of quality offerings. FB has potential to become plus with good velocity and movement. Has confidence to use CB and CU in any count and both could become above average. Lack of FB command hinders upside.

Northcraft,Aaron

SP | Atlanta | EXP MLB DEBUT: 2014 | POTENTIAL: #4 starter | 7B

Thrws R Age 24
2009 (10) HS (CA)

Velo	Pitch	Grade
88-92	FB	+ + +
73-75	CB	+ + +
80-83	CU	+ + +

Year	Lev	Team	W	L	Sv	IP	K	ERA	WHIP	BF/G	OBA	H%	S%	xERA	Ctl	Dom	Cmd	hr/9	BPV
2010	Rk	Danville	6	1	0	52	38	2.76	1.02	20.0	230	28	71	2.12	1.6	6.6	4.2	0.2	94
2010	A	Rome	1	3	0	14	8	8.30	2.55	18.9	346	39	66	8.17	9.6	5.1	0.5	0.6	-149
2011	A	Rome	7	8	0	113	88	3.34	1.32	20.3	253	30	76	3.61	3.3	7.0	2.1	0.6	56
2012	A+	Lynchburg	10	11	0	151	160	3.99	1.30	23.1	251	34	67	3.14	3.2	9.5	3.0	0.2	104
2013	AA	Mississippi	8	8	0	137	121	3.42	1.28	21.6	243	31	73	3.20	3.4	7.9	2.4	0.5	71

Finesse righty continues to exceed expectations. Has a decent 87-92 sinking FB that he locates well. Also has a good CU and an avg CB. Keeps the ball down in the zone and gave up just 11 HR in the past two seasons.

Nuno,Vidal

SP | New York (A) | EXP MLB DEBUT: 2013 | POTENTIAL: #5 starter | 6B

Thrws L Age 26
2009 (48) Baker

Velo	Pitch	Grade
85-91	FB	+ +
74-77	CB	+ + +
79-83	SL	+ + +
80-82	CU	+ +

Year	Lev	Team	W	L	Sv	IP	K	ERA	WHIP	BF/G	OBA	H%	S%	xERA	Ctl	Dom	Cmd	hr/9	BPV
2011	A	Charleston (Sc)	2	1	0	40	37	1.80	0.98	21.7	247	30	89	2.91	0.5	8.3	18.5	0.9	156
2012	A+	Tampa	1	1	0	24	26	2.99	1.16	8.7	245	32	77	3.19	2.2	9.7	4.3	0.7	132
2012	AA	Trenton	9	5	0	114	100	2.45	1.19	22.9	253	31	83	3.44	2.1	7.9	3.7	0.8	103
2013	AAA	Scranton/W-B	2	0	0	25	30	1.44	0.64	17.3	166	23	86	0.90	0.7	10.8	15.0	0.7	193
2013	MLB	NYY	1	2	0	20	9	2.25	1.10	15.7	221	23	85	2.93	2.7	4.1	1.5	0.9	18

Deceptive SP who reached NYY, but ended season in June due to groin injury. Lacks frontline velocity and stuff. Has impeccable ability to locate 4 pitches and near sidearm delivery messes with hitters' timing. Uses two breaking balls with varying velocities, but K rate doesn't project well in big leagues.

Oberg,Scott

RP | Colorado | EXP MLB DEBUT: 2015 | POTENTIAL: Reliever | 7B

Thrws R Age 24
2012 (15) Connecticut

Velo	Pitch	Grade
90-94	FB	+ + +
	CB	+ + +
	CU	+ +

Year	Lev	Team	W	L	Sv	IP	K	ERA	WHIP	BF/G	OBA	H%	S%	xERA	Ctl	Dom	Cmd	hr/9	BPV
2009	NCAA	Connecticut	4	0	1	30	11	1.79	1.03	6.1	248	27	81	2.26	0.9	3.3	3.7	0.0	53
2010	NCAA	Connecticut	5	2	1	46	30	1.95	1.04	5.9	235	29	79	2.10	1.6	5.9	3.8	0.0	81
2012	NCAA	Connecticut	5	0	9	36	36	1.00	0.89	6.1	157	22	88	0.77	3.2	9.0	2.8	0.0	92
2012	Rk	Grand Junction	0	2	13	27	29	2.33	0.96	4.1	208	28	79	2.15	2.0	9.7	4.8	0.7	138
2013	A+	Modesto	1	6	33	53	61	1.86	1.15	3.8	185	25	88	2.36	4.6	10.3	2.3	0.7	81

15th rounder is developing into a solid relief prospect, notching 33 SV in '13. Low-90s FB can hit 95 mph and has late arm-side run. Also has a swing-and-miss CB and a decent CU. Ctl could be better, but now has 10.8 Dom in two years.

Odorizzi, Jake — SP — Tampa Bay — EXP MLB DEBUT: 2012 — POTENTIAL: #3 starter — 8C

Thrws R Age 24
2008 (1-S) HS (IL)
88-94 FB +++
78-81 SL +++
73-76 CB +++
80-84 CU +++

Year	Lev	Team	W	L	Sv	IP	K	ERA	WHIP	BF/G	OBA	H%	S%	xERA	Ctl	Dom	Cmd	hr/9	BPV
2012	AA	NW Arkansas	4	2	0	38	47	3.32	0.97	20.6	201	29	66	1.90	2.4	11.1	4.7	0.5	154
2012	AAA	Omaha	11	3	0	107	88	2.94	1.35	23.5	258	30	83	4.12	3.4	7.4	2.2	1.0	60
2012	MLB	KC	0	1	0	7	4	4.93	1.64	16.3	280	30	73	5.39	4.9	4.9	1.0	1.2	-26
2013	AAA	Durham	9	6	0	124	124	3.34	1.14	22.3	224	28	74	2.98	2.9	9.0	3.1	0.9	102
2013	MLB	TAM	0	1	1	30	22	3.94	1.21	17.1	251	29	70	3.58	2.4	6.7	2.8	0.9	73

Athletic, command-oriented SP who finished 3rd in IL in K. Throws 4 pitches for strikes, and though he lacks an "out" pitch, stays ahead in count and keeps hitters off-balance. Commands FB to both sides and works to all corners of strike zone. Repeats delivery, making sinking CU best offering.

Okert, Steven — RP — San Francisco — EXP MLB DEBUT: 2015 — POTENTIAL: Power reliever — 7C

Thrws L Age 22
2012 (4) Oklahoma
90-96 FB ++++
SL +++
CU +

Year	Lev	Team	W	L	Sv	IP	K	ERA	WHIP	BF/G	OBA	H%	S%	xERA	Ctl	Dom	Cmd	hr/9	BPV
2012	Rk	AZL Giants	0	0	0	2	6	0.00	1.50	4.3	262	122	100	3.40	4.5	27.0	6.0	0.0	383
2012	A-	Salem-Keizer	2	0	0	26	22	2.40	1.41	7.4	260	33	81	3.35	3.8	7.6	2.0	0.0	52
2013	A	Augusta	2	2	2	60	59	2.99	1.31	5.7	245	32	78	3.30	3.6	8.8	2.5	0.4	80

Athletic LH comes at hitters with plus FB up to 97 at times, and complements it with an average SL that flashes potential. Controls both pitches well but his overall command is a work in progress. Works with good, clean arm action and effortless delivery that had many scouts believe he could be a SP if given that chance.

Oliver, Andy — SP — Pittsburgh — EXP MLB DEBUT: 2010 — POTENTIAL: #5 starter / Reliever — 7D

Thrws L Age 26
2009 (2) Oklahoma State
90-96 FB ++++
82-84 SL ++
81-84 CU +++

Year	Lev	Team	W	L	Sv	IP	K	ERA	WHIP	BF/G	OBA	H%	S%	xERA	Ctl	Dom	Cmd	hr/9	BPV
2010	AAA	Toledo	3	4	0	53	49	3.23	1.28	24.2	223	27	79	3.49	4.2	8.3	2.0	1.0	53
2011	AAA	Toledo	8	12	0	147	143	4.71	1.56	24.8	264	33	71	4.62	4.9	8.8	1.8	0.9	43
2011	MLB	DET	0	1	0	9	5	6.85	2.07	9.0	298	28	75	8.32	7.8	4.9	0.6	2.9	-105
2012	AAA	Toledo	5	9	0	118	112	4.88	1.62	18.7	236	30	69	4.04	6.7	8.5	1.3	0.5	-9
2013	AAA	Indianapolis	5	4	0	124	138	4.06	1.70	19.3	221	30	76	3.94	8.1	10.0	1.2	0.5	-21

Continues to struggle with control, walking 112, but also strikes out plenty. Has a plus mid-90s FB and an inconsistent CU. He sometimes throws a SL and at other times a CB. Mechanics remain a mess and a move to relief seems the only option.

Olmos, Edgar — RP — Miami — EXP MLB DEBUT: 2013 — POTENTIAL: Reliever — 6C

Thrws L Age 24
2008 (3) HS (CA)
92-97 FB ++++
SL +++
CU ++

Year	Lev	Team	W	L	Sv	IP	K	ERA	WHIP	BF/G	OBA	H%	S%	xERA	Ctl	Dom	Cmd	hr/9	BPV
2011	A+	Jupiter	4	17	0	127	101	6.65	1.95	21.7	318	37	66	6.42	5.7	7.1	1.2	0.9	-8
2012	A+	Jupiter	1	5	0	89	78	4.34	1.47	15.9	248	31	70	3.80	4.8	7.9	1.6	0.5	29
2012	AA	Jacksonville	0	1	0	16	13	0.56	1.48	7.7	149	20	96	2.20	8.9	7.2	0.8	0.0	-92
2013	AA	Jacksonville	4	2	1	50	41	2.51	1.48	5.7	250	31	82	3.54	4.9	7.4	1.5	0.2	20
2013	MLB	MIA	0	1	0	5	2	7.20	2.00	4.8	332	29	75	9.34	5.4	3.6	0.7	3.6	-63

Big, strong RP moved to the pen officially in 2013 and found instant success. Sat in the upper-80s in the rotation, but now throws 92-95 in relief. He pairs his FB with a mid-80s SL, both of which generate swings and misses. His all-out delivery leads to erratic Ctl and Cmd, but with a plus FB he should fair well in the pen.

Oramas, Juan — RP — San Diego — EXP MLB DEBUT: 2014 — POTENTIAL: #4 starter — 7C

Thrws L Age 24
2007 FA (Mexico)
89-92 FB +++
CB ++
CU ++

Year	Lev	Team	W	L	Sv	IP	K	ERA	WHIP	BF/G	OBA	H%	S%	xERA	Ctl	Dom	Cmd	hr/9	BPV
2011	AA	San Antonio	10	5	0	104	102	3.11	1.22	22.1	252	32	78	3.55	2.4	8.8	3.6	0.9	111
2011	AAA	Tucson	0	1	0	3	4	16.88	2.50	17.0	437	44	40	17.16	2.8	11.3	4.0	8.4	145
2012	AA	San Antonio	3	4	0	35	33	6.41	1.57	19.2	283	34	60	5.25	4.1	8.5	2.1	1.3	60
2013	Rk	AZL Padres	0	0	0	7	15	1.29	1.14	13.9	233	56	88	2.19	2.6	19.3	7.5	0.0	296
2013	AA	San Antonio	3	2	0	55	64	3.10	1.23	18.6	250	34	77	3.34	2.6	10.4	4.0	0.7	135

Short and aggressive starter who returned in June after TJ surgery in 2012. Spent third year in AA and showed progress with command and control. Works both sides of plate with nice FB and has been able to post high Dom despite lack of true out pitch. Has tendency to leave balls up and could be subject to HR.

Ortega, Jose — RP — Detroit — EXP MLB DEBUT: 2012 — POTENTIAL: Setup reliever — 7D

Thrws R Age 25
2006 FA (Venezuela)
92-97 FB ++++
82-86 SL ++
82-84 CU ++

Year	Lev	Team	W	L	Sv	IP	K	ERA	WHIP	BF/G	OBA	H%	S%	xERA	Ctl	Dom	Cmd	hr/9	BPV
2011	AAA	Toledo	1	3	0	50	44	6.30	1.76	6.9	302	36	65	6.01	4.9	7.9	1.6	1.3	29
2012	AAA	Toledo	5	8	1	62	68	5.79	2.04	6.7	302	40	71	6.07	7.4	9.8	1.3	0.6	-4
2012	MLB	DET	0	0	0	3	4	3.33	1.48	5.8	283	36	100	6.91	3.3	13.3	4.0	3.3	168
2013	AAA	Toledo	4	3	4	48	56	1.87	1.27	4.9	171	25	86	2.22	6.2	10.5	1.7	0.4	40
2013	MLB	DET	0	2	0	12	10	3.85	1.37	4.5	233	26	79	4.31	4.6	7.7	1.7	1.5	32

Thin and wiry-strong RP who had excellent year in repeat of AAA. Keeps ball down with plus-plus FB that features outstanding, late movement. Dominates RHH and will mix in occasional SL that shows flashes of being very good. Command is well below average and has plenty of effort in delivery.

Osich, Josh — RP — San Francisco — EXP MLB DEBUT: 2014 — POTENTIAL: Power reliever — 7C

Thrws L Age 25
2011 (6) Oregon State
93-95 FB ++++
SL +++
CU ++

Year	Lev	Team	W	L	Sv	IP	K	ERA	WHIP	BF/G	OBA	H%	S%	xERA	Ctl	Dom	Cmd	hr/9	BPV
2009	NCAA	Oregon St.	0	0	1	26	34	2.07	1.23	6.2	169	25	87	2.38	5.9	11.7	2.0	0.7	71
2011	NCAA	Oregon St.	6	4	0	76	79	3.66	1.26	19.4	224	30	71	2.92	4.0	9.3	2.3	0.5	78
2012	A+	San Jose	0	2	1	32	34	3.64	1.40	5.0	273	37	73	3.74	3.1	9.5	3.1	0.3	106
2013	A+	San Jose	3	1	12	40	48	2.47	1.05	4.6	221	32	76	2.09	2.2	10.8	4.8	0.2	151
2013	AA	Richmond	2	3	3	29	28	4.93	1.30	5.5	240	31	61	3.37	3.7	8.6	2.3	0.6	73

Strong LH struggled in AA, though power arsenal continued to miss bats. FB sits in mid-to-upper-90s, paired with an average SL. Shows a CU but is well behind the other two. Needs to refine command as he can struggle with his location at times. Would have been intriguing to see as a SP, but has long injury history.

Osuna, Roberto — SP — Toronto — EXP MLB DEBUT: 2017 — POTENTIAL: #3 starter — 8C

Thrws R Age 19
2011 FA (Mexico)
90-96 FB +++
80-82 SL ++
84-85 CU ++++

Year	Lev	Team	W	L	Sv	IP	K	ERA	WHIP	BF/G	OBA	H%	S%	xERA	Ctl	Dom	Cmd	hr/9	BPV
2012	Rk	Bluefield	1	0	0	24	24	1.50	1.00	13.1	210	28	87	2.00	2.3	9.0	4.0	0.4	119
2012	A-	Vancouver	1	0	0	19	25	3.28	1.20	15.4	205	31	73	2.51	4.2	11.7	2.8	0.5	115
2013	A	Lansing	3	5	0	42	51	5.56	1.19	16.9	247	33	55	3.78	2.4	10.9	4.6	1.3	151

Strong righty who only started 10 games before succumbing to TJ surgery in July. Has youth and time on side as he was only 18 in full-season ball. When healthy, has excellent velocity and puts hitters away with fringe-average SL and plus CU. Frame doesn't have much projection, but still has upside with quality stuff.

Overton, Dillon — SP — Oakland — EXP MLB DEBUT: 2016 — POTENTIAL: #4 starter — 7B

Thrws L Age 22
2013 (2) Oklahoma
87-94 FB +++
81-83 SL +++
81-84 CU +++

Year	Lev	Team	W	L	Sv	IP	K	ERA	WHIP	BF/G	OBA	H%	S%	xERA	Ctl	Dom	Cmd	hr/9	BPV
2011	NCAA	Oklahoma	8	4	0	74	59	2.31	1.42	13.7	256	32	83	3.42	4.0	7.2	1.8	0.1	39
2012	NCAA	Oklahoma	6	3	0	122	126	3.17	1.24	22.5	269	36	74	3.43	1.8	9.3	5.3	0.4	137
2013	NCAA	Oklahoma	9	3	0	92	79	3.03	1.24	23.4	259	33	74	3.08	2.2	7.7	3.4	0.2	96
2013		Did not pitch as a pro	0																

Tall, thin lefty who underwent TJ surgery after draft and expected back in late 2014. Lacks high ceiling and needs to add strength for stamina. Solid FB exhibits late action and plays up due to deceptive delivery. Both SL and CU can generate Ks and has feel for sequencing and changing speeds.

Owens, Henry — SP — Boston — EXP MLB DEBUT: 2015 — POTENTIAL: #3 starter — 8C

Thrws L Age 21
2011 (1-S) HS (CA)
88-94 FB +++
73-80 CB +++
80-82 CU +++

Year	Lev	Team	W	L	Sv	IP	K	ERA	WHIP	BF/G	OBA	H%	S%	xERA	Ctl	Dom	Cmd	hr/9	BPV
2012	A	Greenville	12	5	0	101	130	4.89	1.45	18.8	259	37	67	4.23	4.2	11.6	2.8	0.9	113
2013	A+	Salem	8	5	0	104	123	2.94	1.14	20.6	183	26	75	2.17	4.6	10.6	2.3	0.5	86
2013	AA	Portland	3	1	0	30	46	1.79	1.10	19.6	175	28	90	2.29	4.5	13.8	3.1	0.9	144

Tall SP who finished 2nd in minors in Ks. CU has been key for recent success and has been difficult to make hard contact against. Still struggles with walks and could add more strength to frame. Can register Ks with 3 pitches, including FB and CB. Has been a flyball pitcher, but hasn't been victim of HR rate.

Paniagua, Juan — RP — Chicago (N) — EXP MLB DEBUT: 2017 — POTENTIAL: #3 starter — 8E

Thrws R Age 24
2012 FA (DR)
94-98 FB ++++
SL ++
82-84 CU ++

Year	Lev	Team	W	L	Sv	IP	K	ERA	WHIP	BF/G	OBA	H%	S%	xERA	Ctl	Dom	Cmd	hr/9	BPV
2012	Rk	AZL Cubs	1	0	0	3	4	0.00	0.31	5.0	0	0	100	0.00	2.8	11.3	4.0	0.0	145
2013	Rk	AZL Cubs	0	0	0	3	4	0.00	0.67	10.5	191	31	100	0.56	0.0	12.0	0.0	0.0	234
2013	A-	Boise	0	0	0	14	18	11.57	3.06	13.6	432	57	59	10.97	7.7	11.6	1.5	0.6	18
2013	A	Kane County	0	2	0	7	6	8.75	3.06	14.1	330	41	68	8.54	15.0	7.5	0.5	0.0	-252

Short Dominican hurler has a checkered history. Originial contract was voided due to fake birthday and has been an enigma since signing with the Cubs. Has a good upper-90s FB and a nasty slider, but walked 24 in 21.2 IP. Much work to be done.

Parra,Geordy — RP — Arizona

EXP MLB DEBUT: 2015 | POTENTIAL: Reliever | 6C

Thrws R Age 20
2011 FA (Venezuela)

Velo	Pitch	Grade
91-95	FB	++
	SL	++

Year	Lev	Team	W	L	Sv	IP	K	ERA	WHIP	BF/G	OBA	H%	S%	xERA	Ctl	Dom	Cmd	hr/9	BPV
2012	Rk	AZL D'backs	1	4	0	39	37	5.51	1.81	15.1	320	40	69	5.88	4.4	8.5	1.9	0.7	53
2013	Rk	Missoula	4	1	0	22	35	0.41	1.13	4.6	183	34	96	1.60	4.5	14.2	3.2	0.0	153
2013	A	South Bend	0	0	0	4	4	0.00	0.98	3.9	206	28	100	1.54	2.2	8.8	4.0	0.0	117

Skinny RH reliever was lights-out in 2013, going 4-1 with a 0.33 ERA in 27 IP. FB hits upper 90s in relief and mixes in a nice SL. FB hitting 99 mph in the AZL and does a good job keeping hitters off balance. Under the radar prospect.

Paxton,James — SP — Seattle

EXP MLB DEBUT: 2013 | POTENTIAL: #2 starter | 8B

Thrws L Age 25
2010 (4) Kentucky

Velo	Pitch	Grade
90-97	FB	++++
76-79	CB	++++
82-84	CU	+++

Year	Lev	Team	W	L	Sv	IP	K	ERA	WHIP	BF/G	OBA	H%	S%	xERA	Ctl	Dom	Cmd	hr/9	BPV
2011	A	Clinton	3	3	0	56	80	2.73	1.34	23.3	222	36	78	2.76	4.8	12.9	2.7	0.2	119
2011	AA	Jackson	3	0	0	39	51	1.85	1.05	21.6	203	31	85	2.10	3.0	11.8	3.9	0.5	149
2012	AA	Jackson	9	4	0	106	110	3.05	1.41	21.4	243	32	79	3.50	4.6	9.3	2.0	0.4	62
2013	AAA	Tacoma	8	11	0	145	131	4.46	1.49	22.3	278	35	70	4.37	3.6	8.1	2.3	0.6	67
2013	MLB	SEA	3	0	0	24	21	1.50	0.92	22.4	181	22	90	1.83	2.6	7.9	3.0	0.8	89

Tall, deceptive LHP who attacks hitters with terrific FB/CB combo and either gets Ks or induces GB. K rate has fallen at each level, but sequencing better and polishing CU. Control issues arise and length in delivery leads to fringy command. Destroys LHH with arm slot and big-breaking CB.

Payano,Victor — SP — Texas

EXP MLB DEBUT: 2017 | POTENTIAL: #3 starter | 8E

Thrws L Age 21
2010 FA (DR)

Velo	Pitch	Grade
88-95	FB	+++
72-75	CB	++
80-82	CU	++

Year	Lev	Team	W	L	Sv	IP	K	ERA	WHIP	BF/G	OBA	H%	S%	xERA	Ctl	Dom	Cmd	hr/9	BPV
2011	A-	Spokane	2	5	0	48	43	5.44	1.67	14.4	281	33	70	5.51	5.1	8.1	1.6	1.3	26
2012	A	Hickory	6	8	1	105	97	4.63	1.51	18.2	247	31	70	4.06	5.3	8.3	1.6	0.7	24
2013	A+	Myrtle Beach	5	7	0	87	96	6.30	1.63	17.6	257	33	62	4.90	5.9	9.9	1.7	1.1	38

Lanky LHP who has raw skills and delivery along with desirable upside. Regressed throughout year and ended season in July. Throws from high slot and features FB that can be electric. Slot is good for slow, overhand CB and has some feel for changing speeds. Allows HR when pitches are flat.

Pena,Ariel — SP — Milwaukee

EXP MLB DEBUT: 2014 | POTENTIAL: #4 Starter/Power Reliever | 7C

Thrws R Age 25
2007 FA (DR)

Velo	Pitch	Grade
92-95	FB	++++
84-86	SL	+++
	CU	+

Year	Lev	Team	W	L	Sv	IP	K	ERA	WHIP	BF/G	OBA	H%	S%	xERA	Ctl	Dom	Cmd	hr/9	BPV
2011	A+	Inland Empire	10	6	0	151	180	4.46	1.55	24.5	265	37	71	4.30	4.8	10.7	2.2	0.6	81
2011	AAA	Salt Lake	0	0	0	4	3	2.25	2.75	22.3	383	46	91	8.74	9.0	6.8	0.8	0.0	-104
2012	AA	Arkansas	6	6	0	114	111	3.00	1.20	24.1	228	28	80	3.42	3.3	8.8	2.6	1.1	86
2012	AA	Huntsville	0	2	0	32	29	7.29	1.96	21.9	306	36	64	6.72	6.4	8.1	1.3	1.4	-10
2013	AA	Huntsville	8	9	0	142	131	3.74	1.37	22.0	223	27	76	3.75	5.0	8.3	1.7	1.1	32

Short, strong SP attacks hitters with a low- to mid-90s FB and a power SL, both of which get swings and misses. His CU is well below average and lacks deception. Command is erratic and he struggles to throw strikes. To remain a starter he needs to imrpove his Cmd or else a power reliever is his future.

Perez,Carlos — RP — Atlanta

EXP MLB DEBUT: 2015 | POTENTIAL: Reliever | 7D

Thrws L Age 22
2008 FA (DR)

Velo	Pitch	Grade
91-95	FB	+++
	CB	++
	CU	+

Year	Lev	Team	W	L	Sv	IP	K	ERA	WHIP	BF/G	OBA	H%	S%	xERA	Ctl	Dom	Cmd	hr/9	BPV
2011	A	Rome	4	10	1	125	109	4.82	1.63	19.9	281	35	70	4.67	4.8	7.8	1.7	0.5	31
2012	Rk	Danville	3	2	0	30	50	2.09	1.16	7.5	190	36	80	1.76	4.5	14.9	3.3	0.0	166
2012	A	Rome	0	3	0	19	12	12.79	2.74	15.1	381	42	51	10.02	9.0	5.7	0.6	1.4	-123
2013	A	Rome	3	0	2	32	37	2.25	0.88	5.9	181	26	74	1.25	2.3	10.4	4.6	0.3	145
2013	A+	Lynchburg	0	0	1	13	15	4.09	1.29	6.0	139	18	69	2.22	7.5	10.2	1.4	0.7	0

Made a successful transition from starting to relief and has been good in that role, putting up solid numbers at Low and High-A. Has a good 91-93 mph FB that can go as high as 95 mph and an improved CB. CU remains below avg and is seldom used in relief.

Perez,Mayky — SP — San Diego

EXP MLB DEBUT: 2018 | POTENTIAL: #3 starter | 8E

Thrws R Age 17
2013 FA (DR)

Velo	Pitch	Grade
88-92	FB	+++
77-79	SL	++
	CU	++

Year	Lev	Team	W	L	Sv	IP	K	ERA	WHIP	BF/G	OBA	H%	S%	xERA	Ctl	Dom	Cmd	hr/9	BPV
2013		Did not pitch in the US																	

Tall, lean, and projectable pitcher who needs polish after signing as 16-year-old. Owns ideal frame to increase pedestrian velocity. FB features late movement and can induce GB. Delivery needs to be smoother, but has deception. SL and CU both show flashes of becoming average offerings.

Peters,Tanner — SP — Oakland

EXP MLB DEBUT: 2015 | POTENTIAL: #5 starter | 6B

Thrws R Age 23
2011 (16) Nevada-Las Vegas

Velo	Pitch	Grade
88-93	FB	++
78-80	CB	+++
80-83	CU	+++

Year	Lev	Team	W	L	Sv	IP	K	ERA	WHIP	BF/G	OBA	H%	S%	xERA	Ctl	Dom	Cmd	hr/9	BPV
2011	NCAA	UNLV	9	4	0	120	105	1.50	0.97	30.3	214	28	84	1.76	1.8	7.9	4.4	0.1	111
2011	A-	Vermont	1	1	11	26	33	1.37	0.76	4.5	140	21	84	0.58	2.7	11.3	4.1	0.3	148
2012	A-	Vermont	0	0	0	3	7	6.00	1.33	6.2	191	58	50	2.15	6.0	21.0	3.5	0.0	234
2012	A	Burlington	2	6	0	68	66	3.17	1.12	19.1	232	28	76	3.21	2.4	8.7	3.7	1.1	111
2013	A+	Stockton	12	8	0	165	159	4.09	1.17	23.6	264	32	70	4.02	1.5	8.7	5.9	1.3	134

Short and lean starter who has low ceiling, but solid chance to reach it. Has pinpoint control with mediocre FB that doesn't exhibit much movement. Best pitches are CB and CU. CB isn't much of a K offering, though CU is deceptive and leaves hitters befuddled. Allows lots of HR due to poor angle to plate.

Petricka,Jake — RP — Chicago (A)

EXP MLB DEBUT: 2013 | POTENTIAL: Setup reliever | 8D

Thrws R Age 26
2010 (2) Indiana State

Velo	Pitch	Grade
91-97	FB	++++
80-83	CB	++
82-84	CU	+++

Year	Lev	Team	W	L	Sv	IP	K	ERA	WHIP	BF/G	OBA	H%	S%	xERA	Ctl	Dom	Cmd	hr/9	BPV
2012	A+	Winston-Salem	5	5	0	82	84	5.36	1.69	19.5	286	38	66	4.61	5.0	9.2	1.8	0.2	48
2012	AA	Birmingham	3	3	0	57	27	5.51	1.71	25.9	281	29	69	5.46	5.5	4.2	0.8	1.1	-54
2013	AA	Birmingham	3	0	0	39	41	2.07	1.38	7.8	246	34	85	3.28	4.1	9.4	2.3	0.2	76
2013	AAA	Charlotte	2	0	1	15	17	1.19	1.06	5.9	174	26	88	1.38	4.2	10.1	2.4	0.0	88
2013	MLB	CHW	1	1	0	19	10	3.26	1.55	5.3	269	31	77	3.85	4.7	4.7	1.0	0.0	-24

Tall, angular RHP who converted to RP in 2013 and reached CHW. Uses height to throw on downhill plane and induce high GB rate. Does not allow many HR and can register Ks with FB and CU. CB is too erratic to be effective and walk rate continues to be issue. If FB command improves, he should have major role in pen.

Pike,Tyler — SP — Seattle

EXP MLB DEBUT: 2017 | POTENTIAL: #4 starter | 7B

Thrws L Age 20
2012 (3) HS (FL)

Velo	Pitch	Grade
88-93	FB	+++
73-78	CB	+++
80-83	CU	++

Year	Lev	Team	W	L	Sv	IP	K	ERA	WHIP	BF/G	OBA	H%	S%	xERA	Ctl	Dom	Cmd	hr/9	BPV
2012	Rk	AZL Mariners	2	1	0	50	57	1.79	1.10	17.9	194	28	83	1.86	3.8	10.2	2.7	0.2	100
2013	A	Clinton	7	4	0	110	90	2.37	1.18	20.0	190	24	81	2.28	4.7	7.4	1.6	0.4	25

Crafty, consistent lefty who was excellent each month. Exhibits athletic delivery to generate decent velocity with pitch movement. Can nibble at corners which negatively impacts command, but can be stingy without high K rate. Slow CB freezes LHH and feel for CU should make it average offering in near-term.

Pimentel,Stolmy — SP — Pittsburgh

EXP MLB DEBUT: 2013 | POTENTIAL: #3 starter | 7C

Thrws R Age 24
2006 FA (DR)

Velo	Pitch	Grade
90-94	FB	+++
	SL	++
	CU	++++

Year	Lev	Team	W	L	Sv	IP	K	ERA	WHIP	BF/G	OBA	H%	S%	xERA	Ctl	Dom	Cmd	hr/9	BPV
2011	AA	Portland	0	9	0	50	30	9.16	1.96	16.0	347	38	52	7.43	4.1	5.4	1.3	1.4	3
2012	AA	Portland	6	7	0	115	86	4.61	1.36	21.9	261	31	66	3.91	3.3	6.7	2.0	0.7	50
2013	AA	Altoona	4	3	0	77	61	3.62	1.41	25.1	254	30	77	4.15	4.1	7.1	1.7	0.9	36
2013	AAA	Indianapolis	2	6	0	92	62	3.13	1.05	25.5	227	26	71	2.57	2.1	6.1	3.0	0.6	72
2013	MLB	PIT	0	0	0	9	9	1.94	0.86	6.8	186	26	75	1.02	1.9	8.7	4.5	0.0	123

Strong-armed hurler came over to the Pirates in the Hanrahan trade and made his MLB debut in 2013. Features a decent 92-94 four-seam FB that can hit 98 in relief. Also has a plus CU. Control has been better in relief and has the stuff to succeed.

Pineyro,Ivan — SP — Chicago (N)

EXP MLB DEBUT: 2017 | POTENTIAL: #4 starter | 7D

Thrws R Age 22
2011 FA (DR)

Velo	Pitch	Grade
90-93	FB	+++
	CB	++
	CU	+++

Year	Lev	Team	W	L	Sv	IP	K	ERA	WHIP	BF/G	OBA	H%	S%	xERA	Ctl	Dom	Cmd	hr/9	BPV
2012	Rk	GCL Nationals	0	0	0	22	23	2.43	0.90	16.5	172	22	78	1.72	2.8	9.3	3.3	0.8	109
2012	A-	Auburn	3	2	0	34	27	5.54	1.67	19.1	338	40	65	5.68	2.1	7.1	3.4	0.5	89
2013	A	Hagerstown	5	3	0	66	65	3.14	1.12	20.0	234	30	73	2.77	2.3	8.9	3.8	0.5	115
2013	A+	Daytona	3	1	0	45	38	3.40	1.18	22.5	257	32	71	3.09	1.8	7.6	4.2	0.4	106
2013	A+	Potomac	1	0	0	14	8	3.80	1.34	19.7	259	29	72	3.76	3.2	5.1	1.6	0.6	24

Came over to the Cubs in the Scott Hairston trade and had an impressive breakout in 2013, going 9-4 with a 3.29 ERA. FB sits at 90-94 and shows a potentially plus CU. CB remains a work in progress. Good command gives him a chance.

Pivetta,Nic — SP — Washington

EXP MLB DEBUT: 2017 | POTENTIAL: #3 starter/reliever | 7D

Thrws R Age 21
2013 (4) New Mexico JC

- 90-93 FB + + +
- CB + + +
- CU + +

Year	Lev	Team	W	L	Sv	IP	K	ERA	WHIP	BF/G	OBA	H%	S%	xERA	Ctl	Dom	Cmd	hr/9	BPV
2013	Rk	GCL Nationals	1	0	0	12	8	2.21	1.07	11.9	242	29	77	2.25	1.5	5.9	4.0	0.0	84
2013	A-	Auburn	0	1	0	21	17	3.41	1.42	17.9	242	30	76	3.53	4.7	7.3	1.5	0.4	22

At 6'5" with a FB that can hit mid 90s, there's definitely projection here. Late bloomer who's quickly put together repeatable mechanics and smooth, clean arm action. Throws from 3/4 arm slot; secondary pitches show promise of becoming average or better in the future.

Portillo,Adys — SP — San Diego

EXP MLB DEBUT: 2015 | POTENTIAL: #3 starter | 7D

Thrws R Age 22
2008 FA (Venezuela)

- 92-97 FB + + + +
- CB + +
- CU + +

Year	Lev	Team	W	L	Sv	IP	K	ERA	WHIP	BF/G	OBA	H%	S%	xERA	Ctl	Dom	Cmd	hr/9	BPV
2010	A	Fort Wayne	0	0	0	2	1	4.50	1.50	8.6	262	18	100	7.85	4.5	4.5	1.0	4.5	-23
2011	A	Fort Wayne	3	11	0	82	97	7.13	1.75	16.3	278	37	59	5.45	6.0	10.6	1.8	1.1	47
2012	A	Fort Wayne	6	6	0	91	81	1.88	1.09	19.8	174	22	83	1.74	4.4	8.0	1.8	0.3	42
2012	AA	San Antonio	2	5	0	35	26	7.20	1.69	19.7	256	29	56	4.96	6.4	6.7	1.0	1.0	-35
2013	A	Fort Wayne	0	1	0	9	10	4.95	1.98	14.6	353	47	72	6.20	4.0	9.9	2.5	0.0	89

Big-framed starter who missed most of season with strained lat. Owns big and heavy FB that is thrown with incredible arm speed. Has tidied up delivery to throw from more consistent slot, but has trouble repeating mechanics and throwing strikes. FB is among best in org, but lacks dependable secondary pitch.

Pounders,Brooks — SP — Kansas City

EXP MLB DEBUT: 2015 | POTENTIAL: #5 starter | 6B

Thrws R Age 23
2009 (2) HS (CA)

- 86-93 FB + + +
- 74-79 CB + +
- 78-82 CU + + +

Year	Lev	Team	W	L	Sv	IP	K	ERA	WHIP	BF/G	OBA	H%	S%	xERA	Ctl	Dom	Cmd	hr/9	BPV
2010	A-	State College	3	3	1	42	29	4.49	1.31	10.9	252	28	68	3.99	3.2	6.2	1.9	1.1	43
2011	A	West Virginia	5	5	3	66	72	3.68	1.14	7.3	247	31	73	3.60	1.9	9.8	5.1	1.2	143
2012	A	Kane County	3	2	0	50	57	3.41	1.41	17.7	269	37	75	3.78	3.4	10.2	3.0	0.4	110
2012	A+	Wilmington	6	4	0	83	75	4.33	1.35	21.6	271	34	67	3.83	2.7	8.1	3.0	0.5	91
2013	AA	NW Arkansas	5	7	1	116	100	4.50	1.28	17.6	246	29	66	3.71	3.3	7.8	2.4	0.9	70

Large-framed, durable pitcher who threw no-hitter in 2013. Commands 3 offerings well and pitches to contact with efficiency. Doesn't miss many bats with ordinary stuff and can be flyball pitcher. Lacks projection with arm action, though has some deception by using FB arm speed with CU. Could be solid option as RP.

Purke,Matt — SP — Washington

EXP MLB DEBUT: 2015 | POTENTIAL: #3 starter | 8D

Thrws L Age 24
2011 (3) Texas Christian

- 91-93 FB + + + +
- 78-81 SL + + +
- 76-78 CU + + +

Year	Lev	Team	W	L	Sv	IP	K	ERA	WHIP	BF/G	OBA	H%	S%	xERA	Ctl	Dom	Cmd	hr/9	BPV
2010	NCAA	Texas Christian	16	0	0	116	142	3.02	1.08	22.6	217	31	72	2.35	2.6	11.0	4.2	0.5	145
2011	NCAA	Texas Christian	5	1	0	52	61	1.72	1.07	18.5	197	28	85	1.98	3.4	10.5	3.1	0.3	114
2012	A	Hagerstown	0	2	0	15	14	5.96	1.79	23.2	260	33	65	4.85	7.2	8.3	1.2	0.6	-25
2013	A	Hagerstown	1	1	0	29	41	2.48	1.10	19.0	234	35	83	3.05	2.2	12.7	5.9	0.9	188
2013	A+	Potomac	5	3	0	61	41	4.43	1.39	21.4	280	33	67	4.01	2.7	6.0	2.3	0.4	55

Health is biggest question mark. Owns great pitch mix and works hard. Has missed lots of time to injury, but surgery seems to have corrected command issues. Also cleaned up delivery and got velocity back on FB. Can command FB to both sides of plate and CU is out pitch. Needs to build endurance in 2014.

Quackenbush,Kevin — RP — San Diego

EXP MLB DEBUT: 2014 | POTENTIAL: Reliever | 7B

Thrws R Age 25
2011 (8) South Florida

- 87-92 FB + + + +
- SL + +
- CU + +

Year	Lev	Team	W	L	Sv	IP	K	ERA	WHIP	BF/G	OBA	H%	S%	xERA	Ctl	Dom	Cmd	hr/9	BPV
2011	A-	Eugene	1	0	9	20	33	0.45	0.94	4.5	186	35	95	1.16	2.7	14.7	5.5	0.0	210
2011	A	Fort Wayne	1	1	9	21	38	0.85	0.85	4.3	168	36	89	0.73	2.6	16.2	6.3	0.0	241
2012	A+	Lake Elsinore	3	2	27	57	70	0.94	1.12	4.3	207	31	92	2.04	3.5	11.0	3.2	0.2	123
2013	AA	San Antonio	2	0	13	31	46	0.29	0.84	3.9	155	27	100	0.85	2.9	13.4	4.6	0.3	180
2013	AAA	Tucson	8	2	4	34	38	2.91	1.53	5.3	256	36	79	3.56	5.0	10.1	2.0	0.0	63

Tall and very deceptive RP who has posted crazy stats despite lack of pure stuff. Has spent entire career in pen and has closing experience. Primarily uses sneaky FB that appears quicker due to ability to hide ball in delivery. Throws with good angle to plate and rarely allows HR. SL and CU are fringy at best.

Ramirez,Jose — SP — New York (A)

EXP MLB DEBUT: 2014 | POTENTIAL: #3 starter | 8D

Thrws R Age 24
2007 FA (DR)

- 91-96 FB + + +
- 82-85 SL + +
- 83-85 CU + + +

Year	Lev	Team	W	L	Sv	IP	K	ERA	WHIP	BF/G	OBA	H%	S%	xERA	Ctl	Dom	Cmd	hr/9	BPV
2011	A	Charleston (Sc)	5	7	0	79	74	4.90	1.47	22.6	274	34	68	4.63	3.6	8.4	2.3	1.0	71
2011	A+	Tampa	0	5	0	24	25	8.22	1.91	19.0	340	43	56	6.86	4.1	9.3	2.3	1.1	75
2012	A+	Tampa	7	6	0	98	94	3.21	1.24	19.0	249	32	76	3.37	2.7	8.6	3.1	0.6	99
2013	AA	Trenton	1	3	1	42	50	2.78	1.02	18.0	191	23	83	2.87	3.2	10.7	3.3	1.5	124
2013	AAA	Scranton/W-B	1	3	0	31	28	4.92	1.61	17.2	248	30	70	4.49	6.1	8.1	1.3	0.9	0

Tall, strong RHP whose season ended in July. Struggled in initial taste of AAA, though has the pitch mix and tenacity. FB exhibits excellent, late life and hard SL misses bats. CU can be his go-to offering at times. FB location comes and goes and has tendency to leave ball up. Delivery lacks deception and can be hittable.

Ramirez,Neil — SP — Chicago (N)

EXP MLB DEBUT: 2014 | POTENTIAL: #4 starter/reliever | 6B

Thrws R Age 25
2007 (1) HS (VA)

- 92-95 FB + + + +
- SL + +
- 85-86 CU + + +
- CB +

Year	Lev	Team	W	L	Sv	IP	K	ERA	WHIP	BF/G	OBA	H%	S%	xERA	Ctl	Dom	Cmd	hr/9	BPV
2011	AAA	Round Rock	4	3	0	74	86	3.64	1.32	17.1	232	32	74	3.40	4.3	10.4	2.5	0.7	91
2012	AA	Frisco	2	5	0	49	45	4.22	1.28	15.5	253	30	70	3.96	2.9	8.2	2.8	1.1	87
2012	AAA	Round Rock	6	8	0	74	63	7.66	1.47	21.2	272	31	47	5.04	3.8	7.7	2.0	1.5	54
2013	AA	Frisco	9	3	0	103	127	3.84	1.16	19.5	210	30	68	2.67	3.7	11.1	3.0	0.7	119
2013	AA	Tennessee	0	0	0	4	5	0.00	0.71	14.8	78	13	100	0.00	4.3	10.7	2.5	0.0	95

Claimed off waivers by CHC in August, despite having a decent season at Double-A. Still has a good 90-94 mph FB, a solid CU, a CB, and a SL, but secondary offerings are inconsistent. Limited upside at 25 years old, but career 9.5 Dom says he'll continue to get chances.

Ramirez,Noe — RP — Boston

EXP MLB DEBUT: 2014 | POTENTIAL: Middle reliever | 6A

Thrws R Age 24
2011 (4) Cal St Fullerton

- 89-94 FB + + +
- 80-85 SL + +
- 81-84 CU + + + +

Year	Lev	Team	W	L	Sv	IP	K	ERA	WHIP	BF/G	OBA	H%	S%	xERA	Ctl	Dom	Cmd	hr/9	BPV
2010	NCAA	Cal St. Fullerton	12	1	0	106	119	2.54	1.05	25.6	235	32	79	2.79	1.6	10.1	6.3	0.8	156
2011	NCAA	Cal St. Fullerton	8	3	0	82	91	1.75	0.85	23.2	183	27	77	0.96	2.0	10.0	5.1	0.0	144
2012	A	Greenville	2	7	0	84	82	4.17	1.28	21.6	273	33	72	4.39	2.0	8.8	4.3	1.3	121
2013	A+	Salem	2	1	1	47	44	2.11	1.06	8.7	236	32	78	2.14	1.7	8.4	4.9	0.0	123
2013	AA	Portland	1	1	5	28	31	2.87	1.06	7.3	217	27	81	3.08	2.6	9.9	3.9	1.3	127

Wiry strong righty who has flown under radar despite posting solid numbers. Spent season in pen and focused on FB command. Hides ball well in deceptive delivery and can fire FB to lower half. Hitters rarely elevate ball and bury in ground. Repeats arm speed on CU that is best offering, but has below average SL.

Ranaudo,Anthony — SP — Boston

EXP MLB DEBUT: 2014 | POTENTIAL: #3 starter | 8C

Thrws R Age 24
2010 (1-S) LSU

- 88-96 FB + + +
- 78-82 CB + + +
- 81-83 CU + + +

Year	Lev	Team	W	L	Sv	IP	K	ERA	WHIP	BF/G	OBA	H%	S%	xERA	Ctl	Dom	Cmd	hr/9	BPV
2011	A	Greenville	4	1	0	46	50	3.33	1.11	18.1	212	28	72	2.68	3.1	9.8	3.1	0.8	110
2011	A+	Salem	5	5	0	81	67	4.33	1.36	21.2	259	31	68	3.83	3.3	7.4	2.2	0.7	62
2012	AA	Portland	1	3	0	37	27	6.77	1.83	19.2	281	32	63	5.61	6.5	6.5	1.0	1.0	-41
2013	AA	Portland	8	4	0	109	106	2.97	1.10	22.5	206	26	76	2.55	3.3	8.7	2.7	0.7	86
2013	AAA	Pawtucket	3	1	0	30	21	2.99	1.30	20.6	274	33	76	3.54	2.1	6.3	3.0	0.3	75

Tall, strong SP who followed up disastrous 2012 season with dominant effort. Selected for Futures Game due to consistency in 3 solid-average offerings. Lively FB has some pep from downhill angle while CB and CU are effective against RHH and LHH. Can nibble at times which impacts Dom, but projects well.

Rasmus,Cory — RP — Los Angeles (A)

EXP MLB DEBUT: 2013 | POTENTIAL: Setup reliever | 7D

Thrws R Age 26
2006 (1-S) HS (AL)

- 90-95 FB + + +
- 80-83 CB + + +
- 84-87 CU + + +

Year	Lev	Team	W	L	Sv	IP	K	ERA	WHIP	BF/G	OBA	H%	S%	xERA	Ctl	Dom	Cmd	hr/9	BPV
2011	A+	Lynchburg	1	5	0	26	40	7.21	1.53	16.3	275	40	54	5.39	4.1	13.7	3.3	1.7	154
2012	AA	Mississippi	3	5	7	58	62	3.71	1.32	4.8	215	29	72	2.96	4.9	9.6	1.9	0.5	57
2013	AAA	Gwinnett	3	1	14	36	48	1.74	1.16	3.9	164	25	88	1.97	5.5	11.9	2.2	0.5	85
2013	AAA	Salt Lake	1	1	3	9	8	2.93	1.20	4.1	188	25	73	1.90	4.9	7.8	1.6	0.0	27
2013	MLB	LAA	1	1	0	22	20	5.39	1.71	5.2	282	30	77	6.72	5.4	8.3	1.5	2.5	22

Power RP who is regaining velocity after multiple surgeries. Was on shuttle between minors and majors and can be menace to LHH and RHH. Pitches aggressively early in count with quality FB and has big-sweeping CB to mess with timing. CU may be best offering and uses for success against LHH.

Rasmussen,Rob — SP — Toronto

EXP MLB DEBUT: 2014 | POTENTIAL: #5 starter / Middle RP | 6B

Thrws L Age 25
2010 (2) UCLA

- 87-93 FB + + +
- 76-79 CB + + +
- 81-84 SL + + +
- 81-83 CU + +

Year	Lev	Team	W	L	Sv	IP	K	ERA	WHIP	BF/G	OBA	H%	S%	xERA	Ctl	Dom	Cmd	hr/9	BPV
2011	A+	Jupiter	12	10	0	148	118	3.65	1.42	22.5	251	30	75	3.83	4.3	7.2	1.7	0.6	31
2012	A+	Jupiter	4	7	0	87	75	3.92	1.36	22.8	252	31	72	3.70	3.7	7.7	2.1	0.6	57
2012	AA	Corpus Christi	4	4	0	54	44	4.82	1.40	20.8	275	32	67	4.48	3.0	7.3	2.4	1.0	69
2013	AA	Chattanooga	3	4	0	81	76	2.55	1.09	19.8	208	26	78	2.37	3.1	8.4	2.7	0.6	86
2013	AAA	Albuquerque	0	7	0	54	37	6.49	1.77	20.7	296	32	66	6.34	5.3	6.2	1.2	1.7	-15

Small-bodied pitcher who is now in fifth org. Began season in AA before promotion to AAA in June where he struggled mightily. Command and control issues limit effectiveness, but flashes 4 decent offerings. None are plus and can mix well. FB is flat while both breaking balls can be good with varying velocity.

Ray, Robbie — SP — Detroit

EXP MLB DEBUT: 2014 | POTENTIAL: #4 starter | 7C

Thrws L Age 22
2010 (12) HS (TN)

Velo	Pitch	Grade
90-95	FB	+++
80-84	SL	+++
	CU	+++

Year	Lev	Team	W	L	Sv	IP	K	ERA	WHIP	BF/G	OBA	H%	S%	xERA	Ctl	Dom	Cmd	hr/9	BPV
2011	A	Hagerstown	2	3	0	89	95	3.13	1.22	18.0	221	30	74	2.62	3.8	9.6	2.5	0.3	87
2012	A+	Potomac	4	12	0	105	86	6.59	1.63	21.3	291	34	60	5.46	4.2	7.4	1.8	1.2	37
2013	A+	Potomac	6	3	0	84	100	3.11	1.20	21.1	202	27	78	2.96	4.4	10.7	2.4	1.0	92
2013	AA	Harrisburg	5	2	0	58	60	3.72	1.33	21.9	255	33	73	3.63	3.3	9.3	2.9	0.6	98

Very nice bounce-back season after rough 2012. Turnaround was in large part due to cleaning up and adding deception to his delivery. FB velo has inched up to 90-95, but can take something off and add movement. Plus SL and much-improved CU round out arsenal. Needs to work on repeating mechanics.

Reed,Chris — SP — Los Angeles (N)

EXP MLB DEBUT: 2014 | POTENTIAL: #3 starter | 8D

Thrws L Age 24
2011 (1) Stanford

Velo	Pitch	Grade
89-95	FB	++++
	SL	+++
	CU	++

Year	Lev	Team	W	L	Sv	IP	K	ERA	WHIP	BF/G	OBA	H%	S%	xERA	Ctl	Dom	Cmd	hr/9	BPV
2011	NCAA	Stanford	6	2	9	49	48	2.56	1.02	6.7	201	27	73	1.76	2.7	8.8	3.2	0.2	102
2011	A+	Rancho Cuca	0	1	0	7	9	7.71	1.86	10.9	313	43	58	6.42	5.1	11.6	2.3	1.3	87
2012	A+	Rancho Cuca	1	4	0	35	38	3.09	1.11	19.7	202	28	71	2.08	3.6	9.8	2.7	0.3	97
2012	AA	Chattanooga	0	4	0	35	29	4.87	1.45	12.5	238	29	65	3.64	5.1	7.4	1.5	0.5	13
2013	AA	Chattanooga	4	11	0	137	106	3.87	1.39	19.9	249	30	73	3.70	4.1	7.0	1.7	0.6	32

Tall, thin LHP continues to thrive as a SP since being converted from a closer in college. Funk in his delivery creates deception, and low-90s FB with good sink make him one of the best GB pitchers in the minors. Induces weak contact with good sequencing, though inconsistent release point hinder Cmd and Ctl.

Reed,Cody — SP — Kansas City

EXP MLB DEBUT: 2017 | POTENTIAL: #3 starter | 8D

Thrws L Age 21
2013 (2) NW Mississippi CC

Velo	Pitch	Grade
88-94	FB	++++
82-84	SL	+++
80-83	CU	++

Year	Lev	Team	W	L	Sv	IP	K	ERA	WHIP	BF/G	OBA	H%	S%	xERA	Ctl	Dom	Cmd	hr/9	BPV
2013	Rk	Idaho Falls	0	1	0	29	25	6.16	1.85	9.1	274	35	63	4.63	7.1	7.7	1.1	0.0	-35

Projectable lefty who has high upside predicated on GB-inducing sinker. Owns arm strength and throws with clean action and mechanics. Uses height well to throw downhill and has athleticism to increase velocity. Secondary offerings lack consistency, though SL has plus potential. Deep sleeper in solid org.

Reed,Evan — RP — Detroit

EXP MLB DEBUT: 2013 | POTENTIAL: Middle reliever | 6B

Thrws R Age 28
2007 (3) Cal Poly

Velo	Pitch	Grade
91-97	FB	+++
85-87	SL	+++
	CU	++

Year	Lev	Team	W	L	Sv	IP	K	ERA	WHIP	BF/G	OBA	H%	S%	xERA	Ctl	Dom	Cmd	hr/9	BPV
2011	A+	Jupiter	0	1	0	15	13	4.14	1.25	5.6	174	23	63	1.88	5.9	7.7	1.3	0.0	-3
2012	AA	Jacksonville	3	1	12	34	43	2.37	1.02	4.9	199	30	76	1.81	2.9	11.3	3.9	0.3	144
2012	AAA	New Orleans	2	3	1	32	27	7.27	1.83	6.5	321	39	58	5.84	4.5	7.5	1.7	0.6	33
2013	AAA	Toledo	1	4	1	49	49	2.56	1.18	6.1	215	29	77	2.33	3.7	9.0	2.5	0.2	81
2013	MLB	DET	0	1	0	23	17	4.25	1.55	6.4	299	35	74	4.97	3.1	6.6	2.1	0.8	53

Large-framed RP who was on shuttle between minors and DET. Lively FB can be electric and when he throws for strikes, can knock out hitters with hard SL. Has tendency to slow arm and aim ball which negatively impacts command. Generally keeps ball down, though can leave SL up when he gets around it.

Reininger,Zach — RP — Detroit

EXP MLB DEBUT: 2016 | POTENTIAL: Setup reliever | 7C

Thrws R Age 21
2013 (8) Hill JC

Velo	Pitch	Grade
88-93	FB	+++
78-80	SL	+++
74-78	CB	++
	CU	++

Year	Lev	Team	W	L	Sv	IP	K	ERA	WHIP	BF/G	OBA	H%	S%	xERA	Ctl	Dom	Cmd	hr/9	BPV
2013	A-	Connecticut	1	2	10	27	32	1.00	0.85	4.5	183	28	87	0.94	2.0	10.7	5.3	0.0	156

Tall, athletic pitcher who served as closer and is still new to pitching. Owns athletic delivery that he repeats; has some projection to add velocity to active FB. Sequences 4 pitches and could move to rotation. May lack out pitch, but throws quality strikes with advanced command and moxie.

Reyes,Alexander — SP — St. Louis

EXP MLB DEBUT: 2017 | POTENTIAL: #2 starter | 9D

Thrws R Age 19
2012 FA (DR)

Velo	Pitch	Grade
92-95	FB	++++
	CB	++
	CU	+++

Year	Lev	Team	W	L	Sv	IP	K	ERA	WHIP	BF/G	OBA	H%	S%	xERA	Ctl	Dom	Cmd	hr/9	BPV
2013	Rk	Johnson City	6	4	0	58	68	3.41	1.41	20.5	248	36	74	3.29	4.3	10.5	2.4	0.2	90

Cardinals signed for $950,000, and he looked very impressive in his debut. Has a plus 92-95 mph FB that hits 97. Also has a good hard CB and a CU that has plus potential. Is still raw and inconsistent with his mechanics, but has long-term potential.

Rhee,Dae-Eun — RP — Chicago (N)

EXP MLB DEBUT: 2014 | POTENTIAL: #5 starter/reliever | 6C

Thrws R Age 25
2007 FA (South Korea)

Velo	Pitch	Grade
88-92	FB	++
	CB	+++
	CU	+++

Year	Lev	Team	W	L	Sv	IP	K	ERA	WHIP	BF/G	OBA	H%	S%	xERA	Ctl	Dom	Cmd	hr/9	BPV
2011	A+	Daytona	8	7	0	127	117	4.03	1.37	21.3	268	33	71	3.99	3.0	8.3	2.7	0.7	85
2012	AA	Tennessee	9	8	0	142	78	4.81	1.54	23.0	295	32	71	5.27	3.2	4.9	1.5	1.1	20
2013	Rk	AZL Cubs	0	0	0	4	0	2.25	1.50	8.6	307	31	83	4.33	2.3	0.0	0.0	0.0	-43
2013	A-	Boise	1	0	0	8	8	0.00	0.50	13.3	151	22	100	0.00	0.0	9.0		0.0	180
2013	AA	Tennessee	5	1	0	59	35	3.35	1.12	21.2	216	23	73	2.92	3.0	5.3	1.8	0.9	32

Was once again limited to just 15 starts. Had good results, but Dom continues to decline as he moves up. Heater is now in the 88-92 range, though he does have a good breaking ball and a good CU. A move to relief seems a logical progression.

Riefenhauser,C.J. — RP — Tampa Bay

EXP MLB DEBUT: 2014 | POTENTIAL: Setup reliever | 7B

Thrws L Age 24
2010 (20) Chipola JC

Velo	Pitch	Grade
88-94	FB	+++
82-85	SL	+++
80-83	CU	+++

Year	Lev	Team	W	L	Sv	IP	K	ERA	WHIP	BF/G	OBA	H%	S%	xERA	Ctl	Dom	Cmd	hr/9	BPV
2011	A+	Charlotte	1	3	0	37	24	4.14	1.24	18.8	251	28	67	3.50	2.7	5.8	2.2	0.7	51
2012	A+	Charlotte	7	8	1	96	103	4.78	1.35	17.4	266	34	66	4.22	3.0	9.6	3.2	1.0	111
2012	AA	Montgomery	1	1	0	18	15	3.48	1.27	8.2	227	23	84	4.43	4.0	7.5	1.9	2.0	45
2013	AA	Montgomery	4	0	11	53	48	0.51	0.74	5.5	158	20	100	0.88	1.9	8.2	4.4	0.5	114
2013	AAA	Durham	2	1	0	20	22	3.12	1.09	4.6	197	26	75	2.55	3.6	9.8	2.8	0.9	98

Short and aggressive RP who has been lethal against LHH (under .100 oppBA). Works and lives down in strike zone and throws easy strikes with quality, natural stuff. FB sits in low 90s and mixes in hard SL and nice CU. Pitches play up due to deception, though size and arm angle could be problem in big leagues.

Rivero,Felipe — SP — Tampa Bay

EXP MLB DEBUT: 2015 | POTENTIAL: #3 starter | 8D

Thrws L Age 22
2008 FA (Venezuela)

Velo	Pitch	Grade
88-95	FB	+++
75-78	CB	+++
81-83	CU	++

Year	Lev	Team	W	L	Sv	IP	K	ERA	WHIP	BF/G	OBA	H%	S%	xERA	Ctl	Dom	Cmd	hr/9	BPV
2011	Rk	Princeton	3	3	0	60	57	4.64	1.28	17.6	274	34	66	4.19	1.9	8.5	4.4	1.0	119
2012	A	Bowling Green	8	8	0	113	98	3.42	1.27	17.1	265	33	73	3.43	2.3	7.8	3.4	0.4	96
2013	A+	Charlotte	9	7	0	127	91	3.40	1.37	21.3	254	30	75	3.63	3.7	6.4	1.8	0.5	35

Short, light-framed lefty with very fast arm and advanced feel. Declining K rate is concern, but induces weak contact with three pitch mix. FB features late movement and CB exhibits big breaking action. CU has average potential due to deceptive arm speed. Has tendency to leave balls up in zone and needs better FB command.

Roach,Donn — SP — San Diego

EXP MLB DEBUT: 2015 | POTENTIAL: #4 starter/reliever | 7B

Thrws R Age 24
2010 (3) Arizona

Velo	Pitch	Grade
87-92	FB	+++
	SP	++
73-75	CB	+

Year	Lev	Team	W	L	Sv	IP	K	ERA	WHIP	BF/G	OBA	H%	S%	xERA	Ctl	Dom	Cmd	hr/9	BPV
2011	A	Cedar Rapids	5	5	2	70	68	3.47	1.33	6.5	270	36	72	3.37	2.6	8.7	3.4	0.1	106
2012	A+	Inland Empire	5	0	0	41	29	2.18	0.95	25.9	237	29	76	2.08	0.7	6.3	9.7	0.2	114
2012	A+	Lake Elsinore	5	1	0	46	44	1.75	1.13	22.8	239	32	84	2.52	2.1	8.6	4.0	0.2	114
2012	AA	San Antonio	1	1	0	17	5	1.59	1.00	16.2	158	17	82	1.13	4.2	2.6	0.6	0.0	-49
2013	AA	San Antonio	8	12	0	142	77	3.54	1.25	20.7	256	29	71	3.33	2.5	4.9	1.9	0.4	37

Durable and athletic sinkerballer who succeeds by pitching to contact. Clean, quick arm produces plenty of sink to pitches and is extreme groundball guy. Throws a lot of strikes with all pitches, including splitter and CB. Rarely misses bats, but works efficiently and offerings work well late in games.

Robson,Thomas — SP — Toronto

EXP MLB DEBUT: 2016 | POTENTIAL: #4 starter | 7C

Thrws R Age 21
2011 (4) HS (CAN)

Velo	Pitch	Grade
88-94	FB	++++
74-78	CB	+++
81-82	CU	++

Year	Lev	Team	W	L	Sv	IP	K	ERA	WHIP	BF/G	OBA	H%	S%	xERA	Ctl	Dom	Cmd	hr/9	BPV
2012	Rk	Bluefield	0	2	0	11	7	4.09	0.91	13.7	244	25	63	3.42	0.0	5.7		1.6	121
2013	Rk	Bluefield	3	0	0	26	18	1.38	0.77	15.6	170	20	84	0.96	1.7	6.2	3.6	0.3	83
2013	A-	Vancouver	3	0	0	38	29	0.94	1.02	20.9	207	26	90	1.69	2.6	6.9	2.6	0.0	71

Big-framed starter who has nice feel for pitching. Shows in repeatable delivery and easy arm action. Generates good velocity and movement with plus FB and effectively moves ball around plate. Doesn't allow much hard contact, but will need to refine both CB and CU to have success at upper levels.

Pitchers / 2014 Minor League Baseball Analyst

Rodgers,Brady — SP — Houston

EXP MLB DEBUT: 2015 | POTENTIAL: #4 starter | 7E

Thrws R Age 23
2012 (3) Arizona State

Velo	Pitch	Grade
88-92	FB	+++
75-78	CB	++
82-84	SL	+++
	CU	++

Year	Lev	Team	W	L	Sv	IP	K	ERA	WHIP	BF/G	OBA	H%	S%	xERA	Ctl	Dom	Cmd	hr/9	BPV
2012	NCAA	Arizona St.	10	2	0	106	75	2.37	0.98	28.8	229	28	75	2.10	1.3	6.4	5.0	0.3	98
2012	A-	Tri City	7	2	0	62	49	2.90	1.14	20.5	255	30	77	3.29	1.6	7.1	4.5	0.7	103
2013	A+	Lancaster	10	8	1	112	104	5.38	1.41	17.5	299	36	63	4.96	1.8	8.4	4.5	1.1	119
2013	AA	Corpus Christi	1	0	0	5	6	0.00	1.00	19.1	262	38	100	2.30	0.0	10.8		0.0	212
2013	AAA	Oklahoma City	0	0	0	5	4	1.80	1.00	19.1	262	33	80	2.33	0.0	7.2		0.0	148

Athletic, durable SP who was victim of hitter's park in 2013, but showed progress with pitch mix. Doesn't waste pitches, works quickly and locates FB. Lacks out pitch and will need to polish CU to stick as SP. Could be factor in pen where velocity could increase and SL more effective in short stints.

Rodgers,Colin — SP — Kansas City

EXP MLB DEBUT: 2017 | POTENTIAL: #4 starter | 7D

Thrws L Age 20
2012 (3) HS (LA)

Velo	Pitch	Grade
85-93	FB	+++
75-80	CB	+++
79-83	CU	+++

Year	Lev	Team	W	L	Sv	IP	K	ERA	WHIP	BF/G	OBA	H%	S%	xERA	Ctl	Dom	Cmd	hr/9	BPV
2012	Rk	Burlington	3	1	0	48	25	2.06	1.16	17.4	228	26	83	2.68	3.0	4.7	1.6	0.4	21
2013	A	Lexington	3	3	0	44	33	3.27	1.43	20.8	253	29	80	4.07	4.3	6.8	1.6	0.8	24

Short, advanced LHP whose season cut short in May. Exhibits polished repertoire and adds and subtracts well. Gives hitters different looks with easy, deceptive delivery. May not have a knockout pitch, but CB can be tough and CU has average potential. Size may limit him in terms of durability, but maintains velocity.

Rodriguez,Eduardo — SP — Baltimore

EXP MLB DEBUT: 2014 | POTENTIAL: #3 starter | 8C

Thrws L Age 21
2010 FA (Venezuela)

Velo	Pitch	Grade
88-94	FB	+++
80-84	SL	+++
82-84	CU	++++

Year	Lev	Team	W	L	Sv	IP	K	ERA	WHIP	BF/G	OBA	H%	S%	xERA	Ctl	Dom	Cmd	hr/9	BPV
2011	Rk	GCL Orioles	1	1	1	44	46	1.83	1.02	15.4	183	26	80	1.38	3.5	9.4	2.7	0.0	93
2011	A-	Aberdeen	0	0	0	4	4	6.75	1.75	18.3	347	41	67	7.65	2.3	9.0	4.0	2.3	119
2012	A	Delmarva	5	7	0	107	73	3.70	1.24	19.8	254	30	69	3.17	2.5	6.1	2.4	0.3	60
2013	A+	Frederick	6	4	0	85	66	2.86	1.21	24.5	245	30	77	3.04	2.6	7.0	2.6	0.4	72
2013	AA	Bowie	4	3	0	59	59	4.26	1.30	22.2	241	31	68	3.51	3.6	9.0	2.5	0.8	81

Durable starter who was youngest pitcher in CAR and eventually promoted to AA. Developing quickly due to polish and ability to keep hitters guessing. FB ticked up in velocity while CU remains best offering. Commands pitches well despite above average movement. Dom rate increased, but still doesn't project well.

Rodriguez,Santos — RP — Chicago (A)

EXP MLB DEBUT: 2014 | POTENTIAL: Setup reliever | 7C

Thrws L Age 26
2006 FA (DR)

Velo	Pitch	Grade
91-98	FB	++++
79-82	SL	+++
84-85	CU	++

Year	Lev	Team	W	L	Sv	IP	K	ERA	WHIP	BF/G	OBA	H%	S%	xERA	Ctl	Dom	Cmd	hr/9	BPV
2011	A+	Winston-Salem	2	3	2	62	49	3.77	1.66	6.9	286	34	78	4.89	4.8	7.1	1.5	0.6	17
2012	AA	Birmingham	2	4	8	64	60	2.81	1.03	6.7	155	18	77	1.91	4.6	8.4	1.8	0.8	45
2012	AAA	Charlotte	0	0	0	7	9	3.80	1.27	5.8	259	39	67	2.93	2.5	11.4	4.5	0.0	155
2013	AA	Birmingham	1	0	0	23	25	2.35	1.17	6.1	167	23	81	1.96	5.5	9.8	1.8	0.4	46
2013	AAA	Charlotte	1	0	0	24	36	7.44	1.98	6.5	235	36	62	5.45	10.0	13.4	1.3	1.1	-12

Live-armed RP who fell apart upon promotion to AAA in June. Mechanics are very erratic and has violent delivery that is difficult to repeat. Has trouble locating FB in strike zone and walk rate much too high. When on, can be unhittable with very high K rate. Has worked on smoother arm action in order to tame lively FB.

Rogers,Taylor — SP — Minnesota

EXP MLB DEBUT: 2016 | POTENTIAL: #5 starter | 6B

Thrws L Age 23
2012 (11) Kentucky

Velo	Pitch	Grade
87-91	FB	+++
75-79	CB	+++
79-83	CU	++

Year	Lev	Team	W	L	Sv	IP	K	ERA	WHIP	BF/G	OBA	H%	S%	xERA	Ctl	Dom	Cmd	hr/9	BPV
2012	NCAA	Kentucky	6	4	1	89	84	4.55	1.39	22.1	291	37	67	4.29	2.1	8.5	4.0	0.6	113
2012	Rk	Elizabethton	2	1	0	30	39	1.80	0.83	18.3	191	28	83	1.55	1.5	11.7	7.8	0.6	188
2012	A	Beloit	2	2	0	33	35	2.72	1.36	15.4	261	32	88	4.49	3.3	9.5	2.9	1.4	101
2013	A	Cedar Rapids	0	1	0	10	10	7.20	1.80	15.4	332	42	59	6.24	3.6	9.0	2.5	0.9	83
2013	A+	Fort Myers	11	6	0	130	83	2.56	1.16	23.6	245	29	78	2.85	2.2	5.7	2.6	0.3	62

Thin, athletic pitcher who may not have swing-and-miss stuff, but throws strikes and offers plus command. Repeats delivery and uses two-seamer to keep ball down. Rarely allows HR and toys with LHH (.203 oppBA) by mixing effective CB and CU. Profiles as back-end starter who can eat innings.

Romano,Sal — SP — Cincinnati

EXP MLB DEBUT: 2016 | POTENTIAL: #5 starter/reliever | 7C

Thrws R Age 20
2011 (23) HS (CT)

Velo	Pitch	Grade
89-92	FB	+++
	CB	++
	CU	++

Year	Lev	Team	W	L	Sv	IP	K	ERA	WHIP	BF/G	OBA	H%	S%	xERA	Ctl	Dom	Cmd	hr/9	BPV
2012	Rk	Billings	5	6	0	64	52	5.34	1.51	18.5	290	36	61	4.17	3.2	7.3	2.3	0.1	62
2013	A	Dayton	7	11	0	120	89	4.87	1.59	21.2	283	33	70	4.84	4.3	6.7	1.6	0.7	23

Extreme groundball pitcher who uses height for downward tilt on FB with nice tailing action. CB and CU both inconsistent but could become above-average. CB shows good late bite, and maintains arm speed on CU. Control is hurdle to cross to becoming mid-rotation starter.

Romero,Enny — SP — Tampa Bay

EXP MLB DEBUT: 2013 | POTENTIAL: #3 starter | 8C

Thrws L Age 23
2008 FA (DR)

Velo	Pitch	Grade
88-96	FB	++++
82-86	SL	+++
80-83	CU	+++

Year	Lev	Team	W	L	Sv	IP	K	ERA	WHIP	BF/G	OBA	H%	S%	xERA	Ctl	Dom	Cmd	hr/9	BPV
2011	A	Bowling Green	5	5	0	114	140	4.26	1.51	19.0	244	34	72	4.01	5.4	11.1	2.1	0.7	72
2012	A+	Charlotte	5	7	0	126	107	3.93	1.31	20.8	200	25	69	2.66	5.4	7.6	1.4	0.4	9
2013	AA	Montgomery	11	7	0	140	110	2.76	1.31	21.4	218	26	80	3.08	4.7	7.1	1.5	0.6	19
2013	AAA	Durham	0	0	0	8	2	0.00	0.75	28.6	151	16	100	0.43	2.3	2.3	1.0	0.0	-2
2013	MLB	TAM	0	0	0	5	0	0.00	1.06	18.3	70	7	100	0.48	7.7	0.0	0.0	0.0	-189

Projectable pitcher who is coming along quickly. Has proven tough to hit with impressive arm. Likes to use FB as get-ahead pitch and hard SL serves as finishing offering. Posted reverse splits in 2013 and succeeded against RHH, but needs more consistent slot and better CU. Has yet to solve control issues.

Rosin,Seth — SP — Los Angeles (N)

EXP MLB DEBUT: 2014 | POTENTIAL: Reliever | 7C

Thrws R Age 25
2010 (4) Minnesota

Velo	Pitch	Grade
91-93	FB	+++
	CB	++
	CU	++

Year	Lev	Team	W	L	Sv	IP	K	ERA	WHIP	BF/G	OBA	H%	S%	xERA	Ctl	Dom	Cmd	hr/9	BPV
2010	A-	Salem-Keizer	1	1	0	11	9	4.91	0.91	6.8	225	29	40	1.62	0.8	7.4	9.0	0.0	128
2011	A	Augusta	2	3	2	89	93	3.34	1.25	9.3	244	33	72	2.98	3.0	9.4	3.1	0.3	105
2012	A+	Clearwater	0	1	0	12	7	3.00	0.92	14.9	171	21	64	1.04	3.0	5.3	1.8	0.0	32
2012	A+	San Jose	2	1	10	56	68	4.33	1.19	6.6	236	32	66	3.35	2.9	10.9	3.8	1.0	136
2013	AA	Reading	9	6	0	126	96	4.35	1.23	19.6	252	29	66	3.65	2.5	6.8	2.7	0.9	74

Though he spent 2013 as a starter, lack of reliable secondary pitches likely to push him to the bullpen long-term. Blessed with great size (6-6, 250), he is able to repeat his delivery, but FB only clocks in at average. A Rule 5 selection who ended up in LA.

Ross,Joe — SP — San Diego

EXP MLB DEBUT: 2016 | POTENTIAL: #3 starter | 9D

Thrws R Age 21
2011 (1) HS (CA)

Velo	Pitch	Grade
91-97	FB	++++
78-82	SL	++
	CU	++

Year	Lev	Team	W	L	Sv	IP	K	ERA	WHIP	BF/G	OBA	H%	S%	xERA	Ctl	Dom	Cmd	hr/9	BPV
2011	Rk	AZL Padres	0	0	0	1	0	0.00	2.00	4.8	415	41	100	7.58	0.0	0.0		0.0	18
2012	Rk	AZL Padres	0	0	0	0	1			4.6							0.5		
2012	A-	Eugene	0	2	0	26	28	2.06	0.95	12.4	178	25	79	1.48	3.1	9.6	3.1	0.3	108
2012	A	Fort Wayne	0	2	0	27	27	6.31	1.62	20.1	302	39	60	5.09	3.7	9.0	2.5	0.7	81
2013	A	Fort Wayne	5	8	0	122	79	3.76	1.34	22.1	265	31	72	3.74	2.9	5.8	2.0	0.5	43

Very athletic starter who has stuff that should result in higher K rate in future. Works with very quick arm action that produces late movement to electric FB. Keeps ball in lower half of zone and hitters bury into ground. SL can be flat while CU still in infancy stage. Could move to pen as he loses steam in later innings.

Roth,Michael — SP — Los Angeles (A)

EXP MLB DEBUT: 2013 | POTENTIAL: #5 starter | 6B

Thrws L Age 24
2012 (9) South Carolina

Velo	Pitch	Grade
83-89	FB	++
77-79	SL	++
74-77	CB	++
79-82	CU	+++

Year	Lev	Team	W	L	Sv	IP	K	ERA	WHIP	BF/G	OBA	H%	S%	xERA	Ctl	Dom	Cmd	hr/9	BPV
2011	NCAA	South Carolina	14	3	0	145	112	1.06	1.03	26.6	209	26	90	1.90	2.5	7.0	2.7	0.2	74
2012	NCAA	South Carolina	9	1	0	137	93	2.43	1.04	26.4	207	25	77	2.05	2.7	6.1	2.3	0.3	55
2012	Rk	Orem	0	2	0	22	21	4.91	1.55	8.7	270	34	69	4.58	4.5	8.6	1.9	0.8	51
2013	AA	Arkansas	6	3	0	79	51	4.21	1.43	19.8	257	29	72	4.21	4.1	5.8	1.4	0.9	12
2013	MLB	LAA	1	1	0	20	17	7.20	1.50	5.8	299	38	47	4.12	2.7	7.7	2.8	0.0	83

Savvy LHP who was starter in minors and used out of pen with LAA. Does not throw hard, but hides ball with sneaky delivery. Varies arm slots and angles to trick hitters. CU is best pitch and features late tumbling action. Induces loads of gb, but struggles to command plate. Walk rate a concern for pitch-to-contact.

Ruffin,Chance — RP — Seattle

EXP MLB DEBUT: 2011 | POTENTIAL: Setup reliever | 7D

Thrws R Age 25
2010 (1-S) Texas

Velo	Pitch	Grade
89-95	FB	+++
81-83	SL	+++
76-78	CB	++
80-82	CU	++

Year	Lev	Team	W	L	Sv	IP	K	ERA	WHIP	BF/G	OBA	H%	S%	xERA	Ctl	Dom	Cmd	hr/9	BPV
2011	AAA	Toledo	0	0	9	14	17	1.90	1.41	4.6	259	36	89	3.88	3.8	10.8	2.8	0.6	109
2012	AAA	Tacoma	0	5	1	70	54	6.03	1.57	6.2	275	32	62	4.91	4.5	6.9	1.5	1.0	21
2013	AA	Jackson	4	4	0	83	57	3.90	1.27	21.2	259	29	73	4.10	2.5	6.2	2.5	1.2	62
2013	AAA	Tacoma	1	2	0	29	25	4.01	1.16	7.8	254	30	68	3.50	1.8	7.7	4.2	0.9	107
2013	MLB	SEA	0	2	0	10	15	8.35	1.96	5.2	339	47	63	8.48	4.6	13.9	3.0	2.8	143

Short, aggressive pitcher who began season in rotation, but moved back to pen later. Control and command returned, though still throws across body. Quick arm action adds pitch movement and low slot enhances SL that hasn't been as solid as years past. Often uses SL to set up FB, though needs CU for LHH.

BaseballHQ.com — 100

Rutledge,Lex
RP | **Baltimore** | EXP MLB DEBUT: 2015 | POTENTIAL: Setup reliever | **7D**

Thrws L Age 23
2012 (6) Samford

Velo	Pitch	Grade
89-96	FB	++++
80-82	CB	+++
	CU	+

Year	Lev	Team	W	L	Sv	IP	K	ERA	WHIP	BF/G	OBA	H%	S%	xERA	Ctl	Dom	Cmd	hr/9	BPV
2012	NCAA	Samford	1	4	2	35	52	6.90	1.56	6.2	238	40	51	3.37	6.1	13.3	2.2	0.0	92
2012	Rk	GCL Orioles	0	1	0	11	13	1.64	1.09	7.2	225	33	83	2.05	2.5	10.6	4.3	0.0	143
2012	A-	Aberdeen	0	3	0	12	12	9.67	2.40	10.5	319	40	57	7.39	9.7	8.9	0.9	0.7	-82
2013	A	Delmarva	4	3	1	43	45	1.46	1.02	9.2	187	26	86	1.63	3.3	9.4	2.8	0.2	97
2013	A+	Frederick	1	0	0	12	15	8.11	2.05	6.6	343	47	58	6.89	5.2	11.1	2.1	0.7	78

Power RP who has solid FB/CB combo for late innings role. Uses very high slot to offer deception and can knock out hitters with big-bending CB. Owns natural arm strength and can pump FB into zone. Delivery has been difficult to maintain and sometimes loses command. Lacks feel for changing speeds.

Sadzeck,Connor
SP | **Texas** | EXP MLB DEBUT: 2016 | POTENTIAL: #3 starter | **8D**

Thrws R Age 22
2011 (11) Howard JC

Velo	Pitch	Grade
88-94	FB	+++
79-83	SL	+++
79-84	CU	++

Year	Lev	Team	W	L	Sv	IP	K	ERA	WHIP	BF/G	OBA	H%	S%	xERA	Ctl	Dom	Cmd	hr/9	BPV
2012	A-	Spokane	1	4	0	62	58	4.06	1.47	17.7	201	26	71	3.00	6.8	8.4	1.2	0.3	-15
2013	A	Hickory	12	4	0	132	78	2.25	1.16	21.9	215	25	81	2.41	3.5	5.3	1.5	0.3	20

Tall, projectable RHP who led SAL in ERA despite low K rate. Doesn't use height to advantage with delivery, but throws with velocity and has average secondaries. Lack of swing-and-miss is concern for higher levels and hope is that he continues to command plate and mix pitches effectively.

Salazar,Carlos
SP | **Atlanta** | EXP MLB DEBUT: 2018 | POTENTIAL: #3 SP / Power RP | **8D**

Thrws R Age 19
2013 (3) HS (CA)

Velo	Pitch	Grade
91-96	FB	++++
81-84	CU	++
80-83	CB	+

Year	Lev	Team	W	L	Sv	IP	K	ERA	WHIP	BF/G	OBA	H%	S%	xERA	Ctl	Dom	Cmd	hr/9	BPV
2013	Rk	GCL Braves	0	3	0	13	14	6.92	1.77	7.5	329	44	57	5.27	3.5	9.7	2.8	0.0	99

Third round pick struggled in his debut. Has a good live FB that sits at 91-96 and can hit 98 mph. Also has a decent CU, but his CB is below-avg and he lacks confidence. Will need to show improvement to remain a starter, but has a live arm.

Salcedo,Adrian
RP | **Minnesota** | EXP MLB DEBUT: 2015 | POTENTIAL: Setup reliever | **7C**

Thrws R Age 23
2007 FA (DR)

Velo	Pitch	Grade
89-95	FB	+++
80-83	SL	++
77-79	CB	++
81-82	CU	+++

Year	Lev	Team	W	L	Sv	IP	K	ERA	WHIP	BF/G	OBA	H%	S%	xERA	Ctl	Dom	Cmd	hr/9	BPV
2010	A+	Fort Myers	1	3	0	27	16	6.31	1.85	21.1	355	39	66	6.88	2.7	5.3	2.0	1.0	42
2011	A	Beloit	6	6	0	135	92	2.93	1.17	18.6	256	31	74	2.95	1.8	6.1	3.4	0.3	80
2012	Rk	GCL Twins	0	1	0	5	4	3.53	1.57	7.5	327	40	75	4.76	1.8	7.1	4.0	0.0	97
2012	A+	Fort Myers	0	1	0	25	14	6.45	1.91	14.8	318	36	64	5.83	5.4	5.0	0.9	0.4	-37
2013	A+	Fort Myers	6	3	2	58	54	3.72	1.17	6.8	244	30	71	3.39	2.3	8.4	3.6	0.9	106

Tall, loose-armed RHP who missed most of 2012 and returned as RP. Dom much higher out of pen and has shown consistently higher velocity in short stints. Pitches lack movement despite quick arm, but uses height to pitch on downward angle. Sinker and CU are best pitches while SL and CB are erratic at best.

Sampson,Adrian
SP | **Pittsburgh** | EXP MLB DEBUT: 2016 | POTENTIAL: #4 starter | **7D**

Thrws R Age 22
2012 (5) Bellevue CC

Velo	Pitch	Grade
88-92	FB	+++
	CB	+++
	CU	++

Year	Lev	Team	W	L	Sv	IP	K	ERA	WHIP	BF/G	OBA	H%	S%	xERA	Ctl	Dom	Cmd	hr/9	BPV
2011	NCAA	Bellevue CC	6	2	0	62	82	1.88	0.88	23.0	186	n/a	n/a	n/a	2.2	11.9	5.5	n/a	173
2012	NCAA	Bellevue CC	11	0	0	79	107	1.37	0.94	22.9	174	28	86	1.26	3.1	12.2	4.0	0.2	154
2012	A-	State College	0	1	0	42	44	2.99	1.30	15.8	242	32	77	3.21	3.6	9.4	2.6	0.4	89
2013	A+	Bradenton	5	8	0	140	85	5.14	1.42	23.8	310	34	66	5.20	1.4	5.5	3.9	1.2	78

Compact, strong-armed starter was a 5th round pick struggled in his full-season debut, Has a decent 88-92 mph FB, a good CB, and an inconsistent CU. Shows good control, but doesn't miss many bats and will need to show better results in 2014.

Sampson,Keyvius
SP | **San Diego** | EXP MLB DEBUT: 2014 | POTENTIAL: #3 starter | **8C**

Thrws R Age 23
2009 (4) HS (FL)

Velo	Pitch	Grade
89-95	FB	++++
82-84	SL	+++
	CU	+++

Year	Lev	Team	W	L	Sv	IP	K	ERA	WHIP	BF/G	OBA	H%	S%	xERA	Ctl	Dom	Cmd	hr/9	BPV
2010	A-	Eugene	3	3	0	43	58	3.56	1.21	17.3	224	33	73	3.10	3.6	12.1	3.4	0.8	140
2011	A	Fort Wayne	12	3	0	118	143	2.90	1.10	19.3	196	28	75	2.29	3.7	10.9	2.9	0.6	113
2012	AA	San Antonio	8	11	0	122	122	5.01	1.35	19.6	239	30	63	3.66	4.2	9.0	2.1	0.8	66
2013	AA	San Antonio	10	4	0	103	110	2.27	1.04	20.9	203	26	83	2.39	2.9	9.6	3.3	0.8	113
2013	AAA	Tucson	2	3	0	38	25	7.11	1.92	20.0	291	32	63	6.20	6.9	5.9	0.9	1.2	-61

Short and aggressive pitcher who began in AAA, but dominated AA upon demotion. Velocity increased throughout year and ditched CB in favor of hard SL that misses bats. Tough on RHH and has decent CU to combat LHH. Command still needs polish, but learning how to sequence and hold velocity deep into games.

Sanburn,Nolan
SP | **Oakland** | EXP MLB DEBUT: 2015 | POTENTIAL: #3 SP / Setup RP | **8D**

Thrws R Age 22
2012 (2) Arkansas

Velo	Pitch	Grade
90-97	FB	++++
83-85	SL	+++
80-82	CB	+++
81-82	CU	+

Year	Lev	Team	W	L	Sv	IP	K	ERA	WHIP	BF/G	OBA	H%	S%	xERA	Ctl	Dom	Cmd	hr/9	BPV
2011	NCAA	Arkansas	2	4	8	32	35	3.64	1.34	5.6	236	32	73	3.35	4.2	9.8	2.3	0.6	81
2012	NCAA	Arkansas	4	1	0	40	49	2.46	1.27	7.5	204	31	78	2.23	4.9	11.0	2.2	0.0	82
2012	A-	Vermont	0	1	0	18	19	3.96	1.59	11.5	309	39	78	5.44	3.0	9.4	3.2	1.0	107
2013	Rk	AZL Athletics	0	0	0	4	6	2.25	1.00	7.6	210	36	75	1.61	2.3	13.5	6.0	0.0	200
2013	A	Beloit	1	3	0	26	20	1.38	1.00	7.1	188	23	88	1.74	3.1	6.9	2.2	0.3	59

Aggressive, diminutive RHP who missed bulk of season due to shoulder problem. Should be healthy for 2014, but future role uncertain. Can be dynamic SP due to deep arsenal, though FB could be dominant offering in late innings. Spots FB low and works both sides of plate. Two breaking balls are solid-average.

Sanchez,Aaron
SP | **Toronto** | EXP MLB DEBUT: 2015 | POTENTIAL: #2 starter | **9B**

Thrws R Age 22
2010 (1-S) HS (CA)

Velo	Pitch	Grade
92-98	FB	++++
78-83	CB	++++
81-84	CU	++

Year	Lev	Team	W	L	Sv	IP	K	ERA	WHIP	BF/G	OBA	H%	S%	xERA	Ctl	Dom	Cmd	hr/9	BPV
2010	A-	Auburn	0	1	0	6	9	4.50	1.50	13.0	191	34	67	2.65	7.5	13.5	1.8	0.0	59
2011	Rk	Bluefield	3	2	1	42	43	5.55	1.49	16.5	274	35	63	4.53	3.8	9.2	2.4	0.9	79
2011	A-	Vancouver	0	1	0	11	13	4.82	1.43	15.9	202	30	63	2.62	6.4	10.4	1.6	0.0	32
2012	A	Lansing	8	5	0	90	97	2.50	1.28	14.8	201	28	80	2.52	5.1	9.7	1.9	0.3	55
2013	A+	Dunedin	4	5	0	86	75	3.34	1.20	15.7	206	26	72	2.50	4.2	7.8	1.9	0.4	46

Very projectable RHP with outstanding stuff and clean, effortless delivery. Dom wasn't as high as years past, but induced high amount of GB. Quick arm generates velocity and movement. Sharp CB has speed and break and is used as strikeout pitch. Needs to improve command and CU while holding velocity deep.

Sanchez,Angel
SP | **Miami** | EXP MLB DEBUT: 2015 | POTENTIAL: #3 starter | **8E**

Thrws R Age 24
2010 FA (DR)

Velo	Pitch	Grade
90-95	FB	++++
	SL	++++
80-83	CU	+++

Year	Lev	Team	W	L	Sv	IP	K	ERA	WHIP	BF/G	OBA	H%	S%	xERA	Ctl	Dom	Cmd	hr/9	BPV
2011	A	Great Lakes	8	4	0	99	84	2.82	1.12	19.5	205	26	75	2.34	3.5	7.6	2.2	0.5	60
2012	A+	Rancho Cuca	6	12	0	130	103	6.58	1.60	21.3	300	33	62	6.09	3.5	7.1	2.0	1.8	51
2013	A	Great Lakes	2	7	0	72	70	4.88	1.50	22.2	283	36	68	4.58	3.5	8.8	2.5	0.8	81
2013	A+	Jupiter	4	3	0	50	42	3.23	1.32	20.7	242	29	79	3.70	3.8	7.5	2.0	0.9	52
2013	A+	Rancho Cuca	0	0	0	9	12	3.00	1.11	17.7	240	37	70	2.27	2.0	12.0	6.0	0.0	180

Part of the Nolasco deal, he had a quality rebound season in 2013, showing the size and stuff of a front line starter. FB sits in the low-90s up to 95 with good movement. SL flashes plus with good tilt and CU has average potential. Plus arm speed with clean arm action and delivery. Needs to refine command to take the next step.

Sanchez,Jesus
RP | **Milwaukee** | EXP MLB DEBUT: 2014 | POTENTIAL: Reliever | **6B**

Thrws R Age 26
2004 FA (Venezuela)

Velo	Pitch	Grade
90-93	FB	+++
	SL	++
	CU	+

Year	Lev	Team	W	L	Sv	IP	K	ERA	WHIP	BF/G	OBA	H%	S%	xERA	Ctl	Dom	Cmd	hr/9	BPV
2011	AA	Huntsville	4	7	1	99	66	4.91	1.53	14.3	271	30	70	4.91	4.3	6.0	1.4	1.2	11
2012	AA	Huntsville	3	2	11	45	41	1.60	1.04	5.4	211	27	87	2.15	2.6	8.2	3.2	0.4	95
2012	AAA	Nashville	4	1	0	26	23	1.72	1.23	5.3	238	31	84	2.58	3.1	7.9	2.6	0.0	77
2013	AAA	Nashville	4	3	7	70	50	2.83	1.24	5.9	259	30	79	3.52	2.3	6.4	2.8	0.6	71

Short, stocky RP continues to succeed since being converted from a C. Sits in the low-90s and offers a below average SL and CU. Commands all three pitches well and keeps the ball down in the zone. He does not overpower his opponent, but throws strikes and knows how to get outs.

Sanchez,Victor
SP | **Seattle** | EXP MLB DEBUT: 2017 | POTENTIAL: #3 starter | **8C**

Thrws R Age 19
2011 FA (Venezuela)

Velo	Pitch	Grade
90-94	FB	++++
82-84	SL	++
77-79	CB	++
81-83	CU	+++

Year	Lev	Team	W	L	Sv	IP	K	ERA	WHIP	BF/G	OBA	H%	S%	xERA	Ctl	Dom	Cmd	hr/9	BPV
2012	A-	Everett	6	2	0	85	69	3.18	1.13	22.4	224	27	73	2.66	2.9	7.3	2.6	0.5	72
2013	A	Clinton	6	6	0	113	79	2.79	1.10	22.1	249	30	74	2.72	1.4	6.3	4.4	0.3	92

Big-bodied RHP who finished 2nd in MWL in ERA. Possesses advanced skills, especially pitch mixing and throwing breaking balls for strikes. Doesn't post high K rate as he pitches to contact, but changes speeds and can locate plus FB to both sides of plate. Doesn't repeat arm speed or slot, but exhibits deception.

Pitchers / 2014 Minor League Baseball Analyst

Sappington,Mark | SP | Los Angeles (A) | EXP MLB DEBUT: 2015 | POTENTIAL: #3 starter | 8C

Thrws R Age 23
2012 (5) Rockhurst

Velo	Pitch	Grade
91-97	FB	++++
80-83	SL	+++
81-84	CU	++

Year	Lev	Team	W	L	Sv	IP	K	ERA	WHIP	BF/G	OBA	H%	S%	xERA	Ctl	Dom	Cmd	hr/9	BPV
2012	Rk	Orem	1	1	0	36	34	5.22	1.30	9.9	233	29	59	3.39	4.0	8.5	2.1	0.7	63
2013	A+	Inland Empire	11	4	0	130	110	3.39	1.27	24.2	219	27	75	3.10	4.3	7.6	1.8	0.7	39
2013	AA	Arkansas	1	1	0	25	26	3.93	1.71	22.8	245	33	76	4.20	7.1	9.3	1.3	0.4	-8

Tall, deceptive SP who finished 3rd in CAL in ERA. Tough to make hard contact against due to height and angle to plate. Could post higher K rate by being more aggressive with hard SL. Plus FB is best pitch and induces GB. Needs to command plate better and get ahead in count.

Sawyer,Nick | RP | Tampa Bay | EXP MLB DEBUT: 2016 | POTENTIAL: Setup reliever | 7C

Thrws R Age 22
2012 (40) Howard JC

Velo	Pitch	Grade
90-96	FB	+++
81-83	CB	+++
	CU	+

Year	Lev	Team	W	L	Sv	IP	K	ERA	WHIP	BF/G	OBA	H%	S%	xERA	Ctl	Dom	Cmd	hr/9	BPV
2012	Rk	GCL Rays	1	0	0	4	6	0.00	1.19	5.6	202	34	100	2.00	4.3	12.9	3.0	0.0	134
2012	Rk	Princeton	2	1	5	24	50	0.37	0.66	5.6	81	25	94	0.00	3.7	18.7	5.0	0.0	253
2012	A	Bowling Green	1	0	0	3	3	0.00	1.00	5.7	106	15	100	0.55	6.0	9.0	1.5	0.0	18
2013	A	Bowling Green	2	5	5	59	80	4.26	1.55	7.2	165	26	72	2.93	9.0	12.2	1.4	0.5	-5

Aggressive reliever who can't find plate on consistent basis, but has been very tough to hit with deceptive, short arm action and sneaky fast FB. Hitters only batted .160 against him, but walks hurt. Short stature doesn't allow him to keep ball down and max-effort delivery has been tough to repeat. CB shows plus at times.

Schlosser,Gus | SP | Atlanta | EXP MLB DEBUT: 2015 | POTENTIAL: #5 starter | 6B

Thrws R Age 25
2011 (17) Florida Southern

Velo	Pitch	Grade
90-92	FB	++
	SL	+++
	CU	+

Year	Lev	Team	W	L	Sv	IP	K	ERA	WHIP	BF/G	OBA	H%	S%	xERA	Ctl	Dom	Cmd	hr/9	BPV
2011	Rk	Danville	0	0	0	5	8	0.00	0.40	8.1	66	14	100	0.00	1.8	14.4	8.0	0.0	229
2011	A	Rome	2	0	8	29	34	1.85	0.89	5.7	211	31	77	1.37	1.2	10.5	8.5	0.0	173
2012	A+	Lynchburg	13	7	0	165	139	3.38	1.14	24.2	251	31	71	3.01	1.8	7.6	4.2	0.5	106
2013	AA	Mississippi	7	6	0	135	101	2.40	1.20	21.7	236	29	80	2.82	2.9	6.7	2.3	0.3	60

24-year-old finesse RH dominates despte less than overpowering stuff. FB sits at 90-92 mph, but has good cutting action and gets tons of GB outs. Mixes in a good SL and a show-me CU. For career is now 22-13 with a 2.79 ERA, but gets no attention.

Schrader,Clay | RP | Baltimore | EXP MLB DEBUT: 2014 | POTENTIAL: Setup reliever | 7D

Thrws R Age 24
2010 (10) San Jacinto JC

Velo	Pitch	Grade
90-95	FB	++++
79-82	SL	++
82-83	CU	++

Year	Lev	Team	W	L	Sv	IP	K	ERA	WHIP	BF/G	OBA	H%	S%	xERA	Ctl	Dom	Cmd	hr/9	BPV
2011	A	Delmarva	1	1	2	22	38	2.05	1.09	7.2	151	29	83	1.54	5.3	15.5	2.9	0.4	154
2011	A+	Frederick	1	1	3	24	35	1.13	1.13	6.3	106	18	92	1.17	7.1	13.1	1.8	0.4	62
2012	A+	Frederick	1	1	4	35	51	1.29	1.34	6.3	168	30	89	2.00	6.9	13.1	1.9	0.0	67
2012	AA	Bowie	1	0	1	23	17	2.74	1.70	5.5	188	23	84	3.54	9.4	6.7	0.7	0.4	-116
2013	AA	Bowie	5	4	0	56	62	4.34	1.52	6.9	240	31	73	4.23	5.6	10.0	1.8	1.0	45

Short, stocky RP who has spent entire career in pen. Has been better against LHP than RHP and may be result of violent, aggressive delivery. Throws across body which impacts command and doesn't throw consistent strikes. When on, he can dominate with plus FB. SL shows nice bite, but much too inconsistent.

Schugel,A.J. | SP | Arizona | EXP MLB DEBUT: 2014 | POTENTIAL: #5 starter | 6B

Thrws R Age 25
2010 (25) Central Arizona JC

Velo	Pitch	Grade
89-93	FB	++++
77-81	SL	++
80-82	CU	+++

Year	Lev	Team	W	L	Sv	IP	K	ERA	WHIP	BF/G	OBA	H%	S%	xERA	Ctl	Dom	Cmd	hr/9	BPV
2010	Rk	Orem	2	2	1	7	9	8.87	1.97	5.7	285	42	50	5.08	7.6	11.4	1.5	0.0	18
2011	A	Cedar Rapids	4	3	1	90	80	2.60	1.24	14.6	223	29	78	2.62	3.9	8.0	2.1	0.2	57
2011	A+	Inland Empire	1	2	0	19	15	5.16	1.46	20.5	289	35	63	4.32	2.8	7.0	2.5	0.5	69
2012	AA	Arkansas	6	8	0	140	109	2.89	1.23	21.0	228	27	78	3.01	3.5	7.0	2.0	0.6	49
2013	AAA	Salt Lake	4	6	0	89	76	7.07	1.73	21.3	325	38	59	6.25	3.3	7.7	2.3	1.2	66

Short SP who saw season end in July with foot injury. Suffered thru miserable campaign as oppBA and ERA soared despite similar Ctl and Dom from 2012. Throws from ¾ slot to generate late-sinking FB with nice tail. Average CU can register Ks, though SL hasn't developed as much as hoped.

Scoggins,Reid | SP | Los Angeles (A) | EXP MLB DEBUT: 2015 | POTENTIAL: #4 starter / Closer | 7E

Thrws R Age 23
2012 (15) Howard JC

Velo	Pitch	Grade
91-98	FB	++++
83-86	SL	++
	CU	+

Year	Lev	Team	W	L	Sv	IP	K	ERA	WHIP	BF/G	OBA	H%	S%	xERA	Ctl	Dom	Cmd	hr/9	BPV
2012	Rk	AZL Angels	1	0	0	17	34	4.24	1.59	5.0	213	48	70	3.08	7.4	18.0	2.4	0.0	142
2012	A	Cedar Rapids	0	0	0	3	7	5.81	2.26	5.2	255	63	71	5.29	11.6	20.3	1.8	0.0	70
2013	A	Burlington	1	4	0	65	76	3.46	1.35	12.9	224	33	72	2.83	4.8	10.5	2.2	0.1	77

Tall, aggressive pitcher who may be best served in pen long-term as he has plus FB and no offspeed pitch. Velocity all the way back from TJ surgery in 2011 and posts high K rate. Misses bats with FB and SL that can stymie hitters from both sides. Lacks feel and trust for below average CU and can be inefficient.

Selman,Sam | SP | Kansas City | EXP MLB DEBUT: 2015 | POTENTIAL: #3 starter | 8C

Thrws L Age 23
2012 (2) Vanderbilt

Velo	Pitch	Grade
90-96	FB	++++
82-86	SL	+++
78-81	CB	+++
82-84	CU	++

Year	Lev	Team	W	L	Sv	IP	K	ERA	WHIP	BF/G	OBA	H%	S%	xERA	Ctl	Dom	Cmd	hr/9	BPV
2010	NCAA	Vanderbilt	0	0	0	6	8	9.00	2.33	7.7	371	50	62	8.83	6.0	12.0	2.0	1.5	72
2011	NCAA	Vanderbilt	0	0	0	6	6	1.48	1.31	3.6	225	31	88	2.62	4.4	8.9	2.0	0.0	58
2012	NCAA	Vanderbilt	9	3	0	76	80	3.55	1.43	19.0	235	32	74	3.28	5.1	9.5	1.9	0.2	51
2012	Rk	Idaho Falls	5	4	0	60	89	2.10	1.11	18.2	210	35	80	2.03	3.3	13.3	4.0	0.1	169
2013	A+	Wilmington	11	9	0	125	128	3.38	1.38	19.5	200	27	74	2.69	6.1	9.2	1.5	0.2	19

Lean SP who finished 3rd in CAR in Ks, but also led league in walks. Pitches off plus FB that hitters have tough time elevating. Throws from high slot and hides ball in deceptive delivery. Nasty SL is best secondary pitch, but needs to improve CU. Held LHH to .186 oppBA, but also tough on RHH. Walk rate needs attention.

Severino,Luis | SP | New York (A) | EXP MLB DEBUT: 2017 | POTENTIAL: #3 starter | 8D

Thrws R Age 20
2011 FA (DR)

Velo	Pitch	Grade
91-96	FB	++++
82-84	SL	++
83-85	CU	++

Year	Lev	Team	W	L	Sv	IP	K	ERA	WHIP	BF/G	OBA	H%	S%	xERA	Ctl	Dom	Cmd	hr/9	BPV
2013	Rk	GCL Yankees	3	1	0	26	32	1.38	0.84	15.9	179	28	82	0.87	2.1	11.0	5.3	0.0	161
2013	A	Charleston (Sc)	1	1	0	17	21	4.19	1.45	18.4	302	42	71	4.52	2.1	11.0	5.3	0.5	159

Quick-armed SP who thrived in first year in U.S. Induces tons of GB with hard, sinking FB. Generates velocity with easy, athletic delivery and can miss bats with inconsistent SL. CU is developing nicely as he is learning to repeat arm speed and slot. Can overthrow and lose command at times. Has high ceiling.

Sherfy,Jimmie | RP | Arizona | EXP MLB DEBUT: 2015 | POTENTIAL: Setup reliever | 7C

Thrws R Age 22
2013 (13) Oregon

Velo	Pitch	Grade
94-96	FB	++++
	SL	++

Year	Lev	Team	W	L	Sv	IP	K	ERA	WHIP	BF/G	OBA	H%	S%	xERA	Ctl	Dom	Cmd	hr/9	BPV
2011	NCAA	Oregon	0	0	0	1	0	40.91	7.27	5.6	721	69	43	42.56	0.0	0.0		8.2	18
2012	NCAA	Oregon	5	3	19	61	93	2.21	1.15	6.7	173	30	81	1.82	5.0	13.7	2.7	0.3	129
2013	NCAA	Oregon	2	0	21	40	55	2.25	1.18	4.2	226	36	79	2.26	3.2	12.4	3.9	0.0	156
2013	A-	Hillsboro	0	0	5	9	17	0.00	0.44	3.3	106	26	100	0.00	1.0	17.0	17.0	0.0	297
2013	A	South Bend	1	1	2	8	12	2.22	1.60	4.0	304	48	85	4.42	3.3	13.3	4.0	0.0	168

RH was one of the better college closers for Oregon. Has a good 94-96 mph FB and a swing-and-miss SL. Had an impressive pro debut, going 1-1 with a 1.04 ERA, 4 BB/29 K. Given his plus two-pitch mix and collegiate experience, he could move up quickly.

Shipers,Jordan | SP | Seattle | EXP MLB DEBUT: 2016 | POTENTIAL: #4 starter | 7D

Thrws L Age 23
2010 (16) HS (MO)

Velo	Pitch	Grade
88-94	FB	+++
81-85	SL	++
80-82	CU	+++

Year	Lev	Team	W	L	Sv	IP	K	ERA	WHIP	BF/G	OBA	H%	S%	xERA	Ctl	Dom	Cmd	hr/9	BPV
2011	A-	Everett	1	5	0	49	47	4.76	1.54	21.5	265	33	69	4.42	4.8	8.6	1.8	0.7	44
2012	A	Clinton	4	5	0	118	64	3.89	1.31	21.2	270	30	71	3.88	2.4	4.9	2.1	0.7	42
2013	Rk	AZL Mariners	1	0	0	14	12	3.86	1.14	13.9	218	27	67	2.72	3.2	7.7	2.4	0.6	70
2013	A+	High Desert	4	3	0	54	33	6.50	1.48	21.1	269	30	55	4.60	4.0	5.5	1.4	1.0	9

Short, very athletic LHP who is better than numbers suggest. Has pitchability and moxie that allows average arsenal to play up. Can rear back and pitch with greater power, but sits in low-90s most of time. Likes to use CU with splitter action early in count against RHH. K rate doesn't project well.

Shipley,Braden | SP | Arizona | EXP MLB DEBUT: 2016 | POTENTIAL: #2 starter | 9D

Thrws R Age 22
2013 (1) Nevada

Velo	Pitch	Grade
93-96	FB	++++
78-80	CB	+++
83-86	CU	+++

Year	Lev	Team	W	L	Sv	IP	K	ERA	WHIP	BF/G	OBA	H%	S%	xERA	Ctl	Dom	Cmd	hr/9	BPV
2011	NCAA	Nevada	1	0	0	10	13	8.91	2.67	11.1	387	54	63	8.58	8.0	11.6	1.4	0.0	10
2012	NCAA	Nevada	9	4	0	98	88	2.20	1.15	26.0	209	27	81	2.29	3.7	8.1	2.2	0.3	64
2013	NCAA	Nevada	7	3	0	107	102	2.77	1.10	28.0	218	29	75	2.32	2.9	8.6	3.0	0.3	95
2013	A-	Hillsboro	0	2	0	19	24	7.58	1.89	11.2	359	50	57	6.53	2.8	11.4	4.0	0.5	146
2013	A	South Bend	0	1	0	20	16	2.67	1.09	19.7	197	23	80	2.58	3.6	7.1	2.0	0.9	50

Strong RH from Nevada was pick 15 in 2013 draft. Converted from SS to SP due to power arm. FB sits at 93-96 mph and hits 99. Also has a good hard CB and a CU with potential. Remains raw on the mound, but ARI is excited about his raw potential.

BaseballHQ.com — 102

Shoemaker,Matt — SP — Los Angeles (A)

EXP MLB DEBUT: 2013 | POTENTIAL: #5 starter | 6C

Thrws R Age 27
2008 NDFA Eastern Michigan

Velo	Pitch	Grade
88-93	FB	+ + +
80-82	SL	+ + +
81-84	CU	+ + +

Year	Lev	Team	W	L	Sv	IP	K	ERA	WHIP	BF/G	OBA	H%	S%	xERA	Ctl	Dom	Cmd	hr/9	BPV
2010	AAA	Salt Lake	2	1	0	15	9	5.96	1.85	23.5	320	37	64	5.37	4.8	5.4	1.1	0.0	-14
2011	AA	Arkansas	12	5	0	156	129	2.48	1.07	26.4	231	27	83	3.02	2.0	7.4	3.7	1.0	97
2011	AAA	Salt Lake	0	2	0	21	12	8.14	1.90	24.8	321	35	57	6.73	5.1	5.1	1.0	1.3	-28
2012	AAA	Salt Lake	11	10	0	176	124	5.67	1.56	26.6	315	35	65	5.74	2.3	6.3	2.8	1.3	70
2013	AAA	Salt Lake	11	13	0	184	160	4.64	1.31	26.2	290	34	68	4.75	1.4	7.8	5.5	1.3	121

Control-oriented starter who repeated Triple-A and had better results second time around. Has hittable stuff and subject to flyballs and HR. Lively FB features late action and can be thrown for strikes early in count. Lacks power breaking ball as suitable complement, but adds and subtracts well. CU exhibits splitter action.

Simmons,Shae — RP — Atlanta

EXP MLB DEBUT: 2014 | POTENTIAL: Setup reliever | 8D

Thrws R Age 23
2012 (22) SE Missouri State

Velo	Pitch	Grade
90-94	FB	+ + + +
	SL	+ + +
	CU	+ +

Year	Lev	Team	W	L	Sv	IP	K	ERA	WHIP	BF/G	OBA	H%	S%	xERA	Ctl	Dom	Cmd	hr/9	BPV
2012	NCAA	SE Missouri St.	7	4	0	82	89	4.50	1.71	24.7	276	38	72	4.49	5.7	9.8	1.7	0.2	40
2012	Rk	Danville	0	2	2	10	21	3.56	1.88	5.3	279	60	79	4.68	7.1	18.7	2.6	0.0	162
2012	Rk	GCL Braves	2	0	0	14	15	0.00	0.92	7.5	112	17	100	0.40	5.1	9.6	1.9	0.0	52
2013	A	Rome	1	1	24	42	66	1.50	0.97	4.1	180	33	83	1.18	3.2	14.1	4.4	0.0	185
2013	AA	Mississippi	0	0	0	11	16	2.45	1.09	3.9	139	25	75	1.06	5.7	13.1	2.3	0.0	99

Short, RH relief prospect was dominate at two levels, logging 24 saves and striking out 82 in 53.1 IP. Has a good 90-94 mph FB that tops out at 97 mph, a plus hard SL, and a decent CU. Jumped from Low-A to AA and profiles as a nice back end arm.

Sims,Lucas — SP — Atlanta

EXP MLB DEBUT: 2016 | POTENTIAL: #2 starter | 9C

Thrws R Age 20
2012 (1) HS (GA)

Velo	Pitch	Grade
92-95	FB	+ + + +
73-75	CB	+ + +
	CU	+ +

Year	Lev	Team	W	L	Sv	IP	K	ERA	WHIP	BF/G	OBA	H%	S%	xERA	Ctl	Dom	Cmd	hr/9	BPV
2012	Rk	Danville	2	4	0	27	29	4.33	1.41	14.3	255	34	69	3.86	4.0	9.7	2.4	0.7	84
2012	Rk	GCL Braves	0	0	0	7	10	1.29	0.43	7.6	92	9	100	0.15	1.3	12.9	10.0	1.3	215
2013	A	Rome	12	4	0	116	134	2.63	1.11	16.3	202	29	75	2.04	3.6	10.4	2.9	0.2	109

Athletic RHP had a breakout year in full-season debut. FB tops out a 94 mph with good late life to go along with plus three-quarters CB. CU remains below-avg, but FB command allows him to dominate. Limited SAL hitters to a .203 BAA and gave up just 3 HR.

Slegers,Aaron — SP — Minnesota

EXP MLB DEBUT: 2016 | POTENTIAL: Setup reliever | 7D

Thrws R Age 21
2013 (5) Indiana

Velo	Pitch	Grade
87-93	FB	+ + +
80-82	SL	+ + +
80-82	CU	+ +

Year	Lev	Team	W	L	Sv	IP	K	ERA	WHIP	BF/G	OBA	H%	S%	xERA	Ctl	Dom	Cmd	hr/9	BPV
2011	NCAA	Indiana	0	0	0	1	0	0.00	0.00	2.8	0	0	100	0.00	0.0	0.0		0.0	18
2012	NCAA	Indiana	0	1	1	7	5	6.34	1.83	6.6	310	37	62	5.15	5.1	6.3	1.3	0.0	-5
2013	NCAA	Indiana	9	2	0	106	59	2.04	1.18	23.6	265	31	81	2.94	1.4	5.0	3.5	0.1	69
2013	Rk	Elizabethton	0	0	3	19	18	0.47	0.95	8.0	230	31	94	1.77	0.9	8.5	9.0	0.0	146

Towering pitcher who repeats delivery despite plenty of moving limbs. FB velocity is average at best, but long arms make heater look sneaky quick. SL exhibits decent, late break and can miss bats. Doesn't have much deception in delivery and can slow arm speed and change slots on below average CU.

Smith,Burch — SP — San Diego

EXP MLB DEBUT: 2013 | POTENTIAL: #4 starter | 7C

Thrws R Age 24
2011 (14) Oklahoma

Velo	Pitch	Grade
90-97	FB	+ + + +
81-83	CU	+ + +
75-77	CB	+ +

Year	Lev	Team	W	L	Sv	IP	K	ERA	WHIP	BF/G	OBA	H%	S%	xERA	Ctl	Dom	Cmd	hr/9	BPV
2011	Rk	AZL Padres	0	0	1	2	4	4.50	2.00	4.8	347	65	75	6.07	4.5	18.0	4.0	0.0	221
2012	A+	Lake Elsinore	9	6	0	128	137	3.86	1.20	19.8	260	34	69	3.52	1.9	9.6	5.1	0.8	140
2013	AA	San Antonio	1	2	0	31	37	1.16	0.74	18.5	162	24	86	0.71	1.7	10.7	6.2	0.3	164
2013	AAA	Tucson	5	1	0	61	65	3.39	1.20	20.4	246	33	72	3.14	2.5	9.6	3.8	0.6	123
2013	MLB	SD	1	3	0	36	46	6.45	1.65	16.2	276	35	67	6.23	5.2	11.4	2.2	2.2	83

Tall, physical RHP who had breakout season and culminated with big league role. Tough to hit with plus FB that is difficult to elevate due to plus movement. Establishes plate with FB and counters with impressive, deceptive CU. Can register Ks with either offering. CB is far from polished and needs to stick as SP.

Smith,Carson — RP — Seattle

EXP MLB DEBUT: 2014 | POTENTIAL: Setup RP / Closer | 7A

Thrws R Age 24
2011 (8) Texas State

Velo	Pitch	Grade
90-96	FB	+ + + +
84-87	SL	+ + + +

Year	Lev	Team	W	L	Sv	IP	K	ERA	WHIP	BF/G	OBA	H%	S%	xERA	Ctl	Dom	Cmd	hr/9	BPV
2010	NCAA	Texas St.	10	4	3	104	94	3.11	1.12	17.1	240	31	72	2.67	2.1	8.1	3.9	0.3	108
2011	NCAA	Texas St.	9	3	0	113	129	1.99	1.22	26.9	220	32	83	2.46	3.8	10.3	2.7	0.2	100
2012	A+	High Desert	5	1	15	62	77	2.90	1.32	5.2	236	35	78	3.04	4.1	11.2	2.8	0.3	109
2013	AA	Jackson	1	3	15	50	71	1.80	1.00	4.3	190	31	82	1.54	3.1	12.8	4.2	0.2	165

Physical RP with exceptional GB and K rates. Very tough to make hard contact against due to low ¾ angle and FB/SL combo. Possesses violent delivery which keeps him in bullpen and rarely adds and subtracts, but thrives with two offerings. FB exhibits heavy sink while hard SL is impact pitch at any level.

Smith,Kyle — SP — Houston

EXP MLB DEBUT: 2016 | POTENTIAL: #4 starter | 7D

Thrws R Age 21
2011 (4) HS (FL)

Velo	Pitch	Grade
87-93	FB	+ + +
77-80	CB	+ + +
79-82	CU	+ +

Year	Lev	Team	W	L	Sv	IP	K	ERA	WHIP	BF/G	OBA	H%	S%	xERA	Ctl	Dom	Cmd	hr/9	BPV
2012	Rk	Idaho Falls	1	0	0	5	11	1.80	0.80	18.1	175	49	75	0.64	1.8	19.8	11.0	0.0	326
2012	A	Kane County	4	3	0	67	87	2.95	1.22	20.9	247	37	76	3.02	2.7	11.7	4.4	0.4	156
2013	A+	Lancaster	1	1	0	23	21	7.40	1.52	20.0	285	33	52	5.42	3.5	8.2	2.3	1.6	71
2013	A+	Wilmington	5	4	0	104	96	2.85	1.17	21.9	241	30	79	3.20	2.5	8.3	3.3	0.8	100

Advanced SP who combines polished arsenal with clean arm. Repeats delivery which is asset for pitch location and command. FB may lack premium velocity, but he uses it to set up excellent CB. Doesn't carry much size or strength in frame and declining K rate a concern. Has tendency to pitch up.

Smoral,Matt — SP — Toronto

EXP MLB DEBUT: 2017 | POTENTIAL: #3 starter | 8E

Thrws L Age 20
2012 (1-S) HS (OH)

Velo	Pitch	Grade
91-96	FB	+ + +
80-85	SL	+ + + +
82-84	CU	+

Year	Lev	Team	W	L	Sv	IP	K	ERA	WHIP	BF/G	OBA	H%	S%	xERA	Ctl	Dom	Cmd	hr/9	BPV
2013	Rk	GCL Blue Jays	0	2	0	25	27	7.14	1.90	7.9	236	32	60	4.59	9.3	9.6	1.0	0.4	-59

Tall, lanky, and athletic SP who returned after missing all 2012 with broken foot. Has difficulty maintaining delivery due to long levers. Control and command well below average, but has natural pitch mix. Best present pitch is hard SL that has plus break. Uses low ¾ slot to sling ball to plate with good velocity.

Snell,Blake — SP — Tampa Bay

EXP MLB DEBUT: 2016 | POTENTIAL: #3 starter | 8D

Thrws L Age 21
2011 (1-S) HS (WA)

Velo	Pitch	Grade
88-94	FB	+ + + +
80-83	SL	+ + +
77-80	CB	+ +
82-85	CU	+ +

Year	Lev	Team	W	L	Sv	IP	K	ERA	WHIP	BF/G	OBA	H%	S%	xERA	Ctl	Dom	Cmd	hr/9	BPV
2011	Rk	GCL Rays	1	2	0	26	26	3.10	1.57	10.4	290	39	78	4.15	3.8	9.0	2.4	0.0	77
2012	Rk	Princeton	5	1	0	47	53	2.10	1.08	16.7	204	27	85	2.49	3.2	10.1	3.1	0.8	113
2013	A	Bowling Green	4	9	0	99	106	4.27	1.65	19.2	244	32	75	4.38	6.6	9.6	1.5	0.7	12

Tall, thin LHP who can dominate hitters, particularly LHH, with sinking FB and wipeout SL. Gets outs with Ks or GB due to heavy FB and pitch movement. Velocity could increase with added strength. Can be inefficient due to poor control and command. Rarely throws breaking balls for strikes.

Snodgress,Scott — SP — Chicago (A)

EXP MLB DEBUT: 2014 | POTENTIAL: #4 starter | 7C

Thrws L Age 24
2011 (5) Stanford

Velo	Pitch	Grade
89-95	FB	+ + +
80-82	CB	+ + +
81-85	CU	+ +

Year	Lev	Team	W	L	Sv	IP	K	ERA	WHIP	BF/G	OBA	H%	S%	xERA	Ctl	Dom	Cmd	hr/9	BPV
2011	NCAA	Stanford	2	2	2	31	38	4.65	1.77	5.7	236	34	72	4.18	8.1	11.0	1.4	0.3	-3
2011	Rk	Great Falls	3	3	0	59	68	3.35	1.32	15.3	268	36	77	3.91	2.6	10.4	4.0	0.8	134
2012	A	Kannapolis	3	3	0	99	84	3.64	1.36	21.8	236	30	73	3.24	4.5	7.6	1.7	0.4	35
2012	A+	Winston-Salem	4	0	0	42	44	1.50	0.98	19.9	180	24	87	1.64	3.2	9.4	2.9	0.4	101
2013	AA	Birmingham	11	11	0	143	90	4.71	1.43	23.4	266	30	66	4.02	3.7	5.7	1.5	0.6	20

Tall, durable SP who has arm strength and deception. Tweaked delivery to be quicker to plate, but hasn't dominated as size or stuff suggest. Needs to throw secondary pitches for strikes more consistently, but FB can be good when spotted in lower half. Can rely on FB and must polish CB to give him K pitch.

Snow,Forrest — RP — Seattle

EXP MLB DEBUT: 2014 | POTENTIAL: Setup reliever | 7D

Thrws R Age 25
2010 (36) Washington

Velo	Pitch	Grade
90-95	FB	+ + +
74-77	CB	+ +
84-86	SL	+ +
82-86	CU	+ + +

Year	Lev	Team	W	L	Sv	IP	K	ERA	WHIP	BF/G	OBA	H%	S%	xERA	Ctl	Dom	Cmd	hr/9	BPV
2011	AAA	Tacoma	1	2	0	35	36	5.38	1.25	15.9	256	32	58	3.83	2.6	9.2	3.6	1.0	115
2012	AA	Jackson	4	5	0	61	43	4.43	1.48	13.8	262	31	68	3.82	4.3	6.3	1.5	0.3	17
2012	AAA	Tacoma	1	4	0	56	56	8.49	1.90	20.4	303	37	55	6.40	6.1	9.0	1.5	1.3	15
2013	AA	Jackson	1	5	0	42	41	3.00	0.90	6.8	186	24	67	1.53	2.4	8.8	3.7	0.4	113
2013	AAA	Tacoma	4	0	0	40	43	2.93	1.28	8.6	232	29	83	3.66	3.8	9.7	2.5	1.1	89

Tall pitcher who moved back to pen in 2013. Will serve 50-game suspension for drug of abuse to begin season. Has posted much better stats as RP and has more consistent velocity. Still uses four pitches, though neither breaking ball is swing-and-miss offering. Best pitch is deceptive CU thrown with excellent arm speed.

Solis,Sammy — RP — Washington

EXP MLB DEBUT: 2015 | POTENTIAL: #3 starter | 8D

Thrws L Age 25
2010 (2) San Diego

Velo	Pitch	Grade
92-94	FB	++++
78-80	CB	++++
80-82	CU	++

Year	Lev	Team	W	L	Sv	IP	K	ERA	WHIP	BF/G	OBA	H%	S%	xERA	Ctl	Dom	Cmd	hr/9	BPV
2010	A	Hagerstown	0	0	0	4	3	0.00	0.50	6.6	151	19	100	0.00	0.0	6.8		0.0	140
2011	A	Hagerstown	2	1	0	40	40	4.04	1.27	23.4	256	33	69	3.56	2.7	9.0	3.3	0.7	107
2011	A+	Potomac	6	2	0	56	53	2.73	1.28	23.0	278	35	82	4.02	1.8	8.5	4.8	0.8	123
2013	Rk	GCL Nationals	0	0	0	2	3	0.00	0.50	6.6	151	27	100	0.00	0.0	13.5		0.0	261
2013	A+	Potomac	2	1	0	57	40	3.46	1.35	18.3	264	31	74	3.70	3.0	6.3	2.1	0.5	51

Positive return from TJ surgery in 2013, leading AFL in Ks. Good size, mechanics, and stuff. FB shows good natural movement, and he commands it well. Will go to improved CU on any count, but CB is out pitch. Good makeup and throws a lot of strikes.

Spruill,Zeke — SP — Arizona

EXP MLB DEBUT: 2013 | POTENTIAL: #4 starter | 6C

Thrws R Age 24
2008 (2) HS (GA)

Velo	Pitch	Grade
92-93	FB	+++
76-83	SL	+++
79-82	CU	++

Year	Lev	Team	W	L	Sv	IP	K	ERA	WHIP	BF/G	OBA	H%	S%	xERA	Ctl	Dom	Cmd	hr/9	BPV
2011	AA	Mississippi	3	2	0	45	16	3.20	1.38	27.0	262	27	78	3.89	3.4	3.2	0.9	0.6	-16
2012	AA	Mississippi	9	11	0	161	106	3.68	1.27	24.4	258	30	70	3.38	2.6	5.9	2.3	0.4	55
2013	AA	Mobile	0	3	0	31	20	1.44	1.15	24.8	214	26	86	2.12	3.5	5.8	1.7	0.0	28
2013	AAA	Reno	6	5	0	92	48	4.21	1.42	24.4	274	30	72	4.34	3.2	4.7	1.5	0.8	15
2013	MLB	Arizona	0	2	0	11	9	5.56	1.94	9.2	354	38	79	4.94	4.0	7.1	1.8	2.4	38

Tall, lanky RH had mixed results. Started off well AA and ended the year in the majors, but Ctl and Dom headed in the wrong direction. Competes well with a 92-93 mph FB, but CB and CU are inconsistent. Now profiles as a back-end starter or middle relief.

Stanek,Ryne — SP — Tampa Bay

EXP MLB DEBUT: 2016 | POTENTIAL: #2 starter | 8D

Thrws R Age 22
2013 (1) Arkansas

Velo	Pitch	Grade
90-97	FB	++++
82-86	SL	+++
75-78	CB	++
83-88	CU	++

Year	Lev	Team	W	L	Sv	IP	K	ERA	WHIP	BF/G	OBA	H%	S%	xERA	Ctl	Dom	Cmd	hr/9	BPV
2011	NCAA	Arkansas	4	2	1	64	41	3.94	1.19	17.1	217	24	69	3.03	3.7	5.8	1.6	0.8	23
2012	NCAA	Arkansas	8	4	0	92	83	2.83	1.20	21.8	224	29	75	2.53	3.5	8.1	2.3	0.2	69
2013	NCAA	Arkansas	10	2	0	97	79	1.39	1.16	24.2	208	26	91	2.49	3.8	7.3	1.9	0.5	47
2013		Did not pitch as a pro																	

Athletic SP who didn't pitch upon signing and will likely miss half of 2014 due to hip surgery. Mechanics need tweaking and delivery can be rough, but mix is deep and strong. FB is best present offering and is able to mix in two breaking balls and improving CU. Lack of deception results in low K rates.

Stankiewicz,Teddy — SP — Boston

EXP MLB DEBUT: 2017 | POTENTIAL: #3 starter | 8E

Thrws R Age 20
2013 (2) Seminole State JC

Velo	Pitch	Grade
89-94	FB	+++
80-85	SL	+++
75-78	CB	+++
81-83	CU	+

Year	Lev	Team	W	L	Sv	IP	K	ERA	WHIP	BF/G	OBA	H%	S%	xERA	Ctl	Dom	Cmd	hr/9	BPV
2013	A-	Lowell	0	0	0	19	15	2.34	0.99	8.1	239	29	78	2.44	0.9	7.0	7.5	0.5	119

Tall SP with impressive arm action and feel. Needs to add more strength in order to maintain velocity deep into games, but has solid present velocity with potential for more. Commands plate with FB and mixes in decent CB and hard SL. Development of CU and more consistent mechanics paramount for future success.

Stephenson,Robert — SP — Cincinnati

EXP MLB DEBUT: 2015 | POTENTIAL: #2 starter | 9C

Thrws R Age 21
2011 (1) HS (CA)

Velo	Pitch	Grade
94-97	FB	++++
73-75	CB	+++
78-80	CU	++++

Year	Lev	Team	W	L	Sv	IP	K	ERA	WHIP	BF/G	OBA	H%	S%	xERA	Ctl	Dom	Cmd	hr/9	BPV
2013	A	Dayton	5	3	0	77	96	2.57	0.99	20.9	205	30	76	2.09	2.3	11.2	4.8	0.6	157
2013	AA	Pensacola	0	2	0	16	18	5.00	1.85	18.9	271	35	75	5.63	7.2	10.0	1.4	1.1	3

Got back on track after rough April. Has size, mound demeanor, and stuff to be impact pitcher in very near future. Toned down max-effort delivery, but FB still hits upper 90s. Saw nice development in CB, which gives him close to three plus pitches that he can command.

Stewart,Kohl — SP — Minnesota

EXP MLB DEBUT: 2017 | POTENTIAL: #2 starter | 9D

Thrws R Age 19
2013 (1) HS (TX)

Velo	Pitch	Grade
90-96	FB	++++
83-87	SL	++++
75-79	CB	++
	CU	++

Year	Lev	Team	W	L	Sv	IP	K	ERA	WHIP	BF/G	OBA	H%	S%	xERA	Ctl	Dom	Cmd	hr/9	BPV
2013	Rk	Elizabethton	0	0	0	4	8	0.00	0.50	13.3	81	23	100	0.00	2.3	18.0	8.0	0.0	281
2013	Rk	GCL Twins	0	0	0	16	16	1.69	0.94	10.0	210	29	80	1.49	1.7	9.0	5.3	0.0	134

Very athletic SP who combines power stuff with clean delivery to give him high upside. Uses quick arm to generate plus FB and hard-breaking SL. Has deep arsenal for age and includes potential average CB and CU. Needs to improve command of breaking balls and should add strength with more pro experience.

Stilson,John — RP — Toronto

EXP MLB DEBUT: 2014 | POTENTIAL: Setup reliever | 7B

Thrws R Age 23
2011 (3) Texas A&M

Velo	Pitch	Grade
91-96	FB	++++
84-87	SL	++
80-82	CU	+++

Year	Lev	Team	W	L	Sv	IP	K	ERA	WHIP	BF/G	OBA	H%	S%	xERA	Ctl	Dom	Cmd	hr/9	BPV
2011	NCAA	Texas A&M	5	2	1	91	92	1.68	1.14	24.1	226	31	84	2.29	2.9	9.1	3.2	0.1	104
2012	A+	Dunedin	3	0	0	54	47	2.83	1.39	17.5	269	34	79	3.71	3.2	7.8	2.5	0.3	73
2012	AA	New Hampshire	2	4	1	50	44	5.04	1.54	12.8	277	33	69	4.91	4.1	7.9	1.9	1.1	49
2013	AA	New Hampshire	0	0	1	2	6	4.29	1.43	4.5	336	103	67	4.37	0.0	25.7		0.0	481
2013	AAA	Buffalo	6	2	4	47	47	2.10	1.08	5.6	213	28	83	2.44	2.9	9.0	3.1	0.6	102

Deceptive pitcher who converted to RP in 2013. Found his niche as he can blow FB by hitters and keep ball on ground with both FB and vicious CU. Has hard SL that he uses as chase pitch, but can be flat. Effort in delivery deters return to SP role, but adds deception that enhances repertoire.

Stites,Matt — RP — Arizona

EXP MLB DEBUT: 2014 | POTENTIAL: Closer | 7B

Thrws R Age 24
2011 (17) Missouri

Velo	Pitch	Grade
92-96	FB	++++
80-83	SL	++++
	CU	++

Year	Lev	Team	W	L	Sv	IP	K	ERA	WHIP	BF/G	OBA	H%	S%	xERA	Ctl	Dom	Cmd	hr/9	BPV
2011	NCAA	Missouri	0	0	0	10	6	6.18	1.67	22.9	311	36	59	4.76	3.5	5.3	1.5	0.0	18
2011	A-	Eugene	4	0	5	32	36	1.96	0.68	4.7	134	19	71	0.27	2.2	10.1	4.5	0.3	139
2012	A	Fort Wayne	2	0	13	48	60	0.75	0.58	3.9	155	22	100	0.66	0.6	11.2	20.0	0.7	205
2013	AA	San Antonio	2	2	14	52	51	2.08	0.87	4.2	201	24	85	2.19	1.4	8.8	6.4	1.0	140

Short RH was converted to relief and has been dominant. Came over in Kennedy trade and has a plus 92-96 mph FB. Also has a plus hard SL and a below-average CU. Aggressive on the mound and has excellent control. Now has a career 1.53 ERA in 135.1 IP.

Stratton,Chris — SP — San Francisco

EXP MLB DEBUT: 2015 | POTENTIAL: #3 starter | 8D

Thrws R Age 23
2012 (1) Mississippi State

Velo	Pitch	Grade
89-95	FB	++++
	SL	+++
	CU	++

Year	Lev	Team	W	L	Sv	IP	K	ERA	WHIP	BF/G	OBA	H%	S%	xERA	Ctl	Dom	Cmd	hr/9	BPV
2010	NCAA	Mississippi St.	5	3	0	78	76	5.30	1.61	24.7	276	34	68	5.04	4.8	8.8	1.8	1.0	45
2011	NCAA	Mississippi St.	5	7	0	74	74	5.22	1.44	21.1	279	36	63	4.37	3.2	9.0	2.8	0.7	95
2012	NCAA	Mississippi St.	11	2	1	109	127	2.39	1.00	24.5	214	30	78	2.23	2.1	10.5	5.1	0.6	151
2012	A-	Salem-Keizer	0	1	0	16	16	2.80	1.49	8.7	236	31	83	3.73	5.6	8.9	1.6	0.6	28
2013	A	Augusta	9	3	0	132	123	3.27	1.33	24.9	256	33	75	3.38	3.2	8.4	2.6	0.3	82

Athletic righty with ideal pitcher's frame uses size well to work down in the zone mixing in three-pitch mix. Fastball sits in the low 90s up to 95, mixing in a slider that flashes plus, and a change that will be an average offering. He has good command of the strike zone, using his effortless delivery to repeat his mechanics.

Streich,Seth — SP — Oakland

EXP MLB DEBUT: 2015 | POTENTIAL: #3 starter | 8E

Thrws R Age 23
2012 (6) Ohio

Velo	Pitch	Grade
89-95	FB	+++
76-79	CB	++
81-83	SL	++
81-84	CU	+++

Year	Lev	Team	W	L	Sv	IP	K	ERA	WHIP	BF/G	OBA	H%	S%	xERA	Ctl	Dom	Cmd	hr/9	BPV
2011	NCAA	Ohio	3	6	0	96	80	4.02	1.38	28.9	259	32	71	3.88	3.6	7.5	2.1	0.7	57
2012	NCAA	Ohio	4	7	0	75	62	4.43	1.56	25.3	277	34	70	4.28	4.3	7.4	1.7	0.4	35
2012	Rk	AZL Athletics	0	0	0	2	6	4.09	0.91	4.1	139	83	50	0.48	4.1	24.5	6.0	0.0	349
2012	A-	Vermont	4	1	0	34	42	2.63	1.26	9.3	212	31	79	2.55	4.5	11.1	2.5	0.3	96
2013	A	Beloit	10	6	0	110	82	3.84	1.41	22.2	268	33	71	3.61	3.3	6.7	2.0	0.2	48

Big and strong SP whose season ended in July due to forearm problem. Pounds bottom half of zone with FB and keeps walks to minimum. Battles LHH with excellent CU that features dynamite movement. Uses both CB and SL, though both below average. RHH can tee off on secondary pitches, but he rarely allows HR.

Stripling,Ross — SP — Los Angeles (N)

EXP MLB DEBUT: 2014 | POTENTIAL: #4 starter | 7C

Thrws R Age 24
2012 (5) Texas A&M

Velo	Pitch	Grade
88-94	FB	+++
73-75	CB	+++
	SL	+++
	CU	++

Year	Lev	Team	W	L	Sv	IP	K	ERA	WHIP	BF/G	OBA	H%	S%	xERA	Ctl	Dom	Cmd	hr/9	BPV
2011	NCAA	Texas A&M	14	2	4	125	113	2.30	0.87	19.3	205	26	74	1.61	1.3	8.1	6.3	0.4	129
2012	NCAA	Texas A&M	10	4	0	125	120	3.09	0.99	29.8	229	30	69	2.34	1.4	8.6	6.3	0.5	136
2012	Rk	Ogden	1	0	0	36	37	1.25	0.89	9.6	203	29	84	1.28	1.5	9.2	6.2	0.0	144
2013	A+	Rancho Cuca	2	0	0	33	34	2.98	1.05	21.4	204	28	71	1.97	3.0	9.2	3.1	0.3	103
2013	AA	Chattanooga	6	4	1	94	83	2.78	1.17	17.9	256	32	76	3.03	1.8	7.9	4.4	0.4	112

Polished RH has combination of pure stuff and pitchability. With clean arm action and repeatable mechanics, he pounds the zone with low-90s FB and solid off-speed. His 12-6 CB and tight SL both get high praise and have swing-and-miss potential. Plus Cmd and Ctl will allow him to make an impact sooner than later.

Stroman,Marcus — SP — Toronto

EXP MLB DEBUT: 2014 | POTENTIAL: #3 starter / Closer | 8B

Thrws R Age 23
2012 (1) Duke

Velo	Pitch	Grade
90-96	FB	+++
88-90	CT	+++
84-88	SL	++++
	CU	+++

Year	Lev	Team	W	L	Sv	IP	K	ERA	WHIP	BF/G	OBA	H%	S%	xERA	Ctl	Dom	Cmd	hr/9	BPV
2011	NCAA	Duke	3	4	4	64	90	2.81	1.25	15.3	246	39	76	2.82	2.9	12.6	4.3	0.1	166
2012	NCAA	Duke	6	5	0	98	136	2.39	1.11	27.5	231	36	80	2.59	2.4	12.5	5.2	0.5	178
2012	A-	Vancouver	1	0	0	11	15	3.24	0.99	6.0	204	33	64	1.52	2.4	12.2	5.0	0.0	171
2012	AA	New Hampshire	2	0	0	8	8	3.38	1.75	4.6	262	32	85	5.26	6.8	9.0	1.3	1.1	-2
2013	AA	New Hampshire	9	5	0	111	129	3.32	1.13	22.0	240	32	75	3.33	2.2	10.4	4.8	1.1	147

Short, athletic RHP who began season late due to PED suspension. Moved to starter in 2013 and future role unclear. Has excellent stuff, highlighted by plus-plus SL. Cuts FB and can blow it by hitters. LHH hit only .171 against him due to solid, deceptive CU. FB can be straight, but has excellent command and control.

Stumpf,Daniel — SP — Kansas City

EXP MLB DEBUT: 2016 | POTENTIAL: #4 starter | 7D

Thrws L Age 23
2012 (9) San Jacinto JC

Velo	Pitch	Grade
88-94	FB	+++
80-85	SL	++
80-82	CU	++

Year	Lev	Team	W	L	Sv	IP	K	ERA	WHIP	BF/G	OBA	H%	S%	xERA	Ctl	Dom	Cmd	hr/9	BPV
2012	Rk	Burlington	2	1	5	29	34	1.55	0.97	5.8	197	28	85	1.68	2.5	10.6	4.3	0.3	141
2013	A	Lexington	10	10	0	137	117	3.08	1.12	21.6	210	26	74	2.57	3.3	7.7	2.3	0.7	68

Unheralded pitcher who held hitters to .210 BA in 2013 and did a nice job of pitch sequencing. Doesn't wow with pure, hard stuff, but keeps ball in lower part of zone. Commands secondary pitches well, including SL and CU that have average potential. SL can be flat at times which limits ability to miss bats.

Suero,Wander — SP — Washington

EXP MLB DEBUT: 2016 | POTENTIAL: Reliever | 6B

Thrws R Age 22
2010 FA (DR)

Velo	Pitch	Grade
	FB	++
	CB	++

Year	Lev	Team	W	L	Sv	IP	K	ERA	WHIP	BF/G	OBA	H%	S%	xERA	Ctl	Dom	Cmd	hr/9	BPV
2013	Rk	GCL Nationals	8	1	0	49	46	1.65	0.82	13.7	163	21	82	1.01	2.4	8.4	3.5	0.4	106

Athletic righty from the Dominican Republic doesn't appear to have the arsenal to remain as starter long-term. Primarily throws FB and CB, will occasionally mix in CU. Put together a really nice GCL season overpowering hitters with his two-pitch mix. WAS hopes he can develop into a productive long-reliever.

Suggs,Colby — RP — Miami

EXP MLB DEBUT: 2015 | POTENTIAL: Setup reliever | 7B

Thrws R Age 22
2013 (3) Arkansas

Velo	Pitch	Grade
93-98	FB	++++
78-83	CB	++++

Year	Lev	Team	W	L	Sv	IP	K	ERA	WHIP	BF/G	OBA	H%	S%	xERA	Ctl	Dom	Cmd	hr/9	BPV
2012	NCAA	Arkansas	7	1	0	39	36	1.38	1.15	5.2	191	24	91	2.26	4.4	8.3	1.9	0.5	49
2013	NCAA	Arkansas	0	0	13	20	29	1.78	1.34	3.7	149	26	85	1.78	7.6	12.9	1.7	0.0	46
2013	Rk	GCL Marlins	0	0	0	1	1	9.00	3.00	5.8	262	35	67	7.36	18.0	9.0	0.5	0.0	-306
2013	A-	Batavia	1	0	3	8	11	1.13	0.88	4.2	181	30	86	0.97	2.3	12.4	5.5	0.0	180
2013	A+	Jupiter	1	3	0	18	26	3.98	1.27	5.3	150	26	65	1.62	7.0	12.9	1.9	0.0	63

Short, big-bodied RP uses lower half to generate mid-90s FB up to 98. Pairs it with a power CB with tight spin and sharp downward action. The combo generates plus Dom results, though his max effort delivery has led to huge Ctl and Cmd issues. His arsenal has closer potential, but he need smoother mechanics to reach that ceiling.

Sulbaran,Miguel — SP — Minnesota

EXP MLB DEBUT: 2017 | POTENTIAL: #4 starter | 7D

Thrws L Age 20
2011 FA (Venezuela)

Velo	Pitch	Grade
87-92	FB	+++
75-79	CB	++
78-82	SL	+++
81-82	CU	++

Year	Lev	Team	W	L	Sv	IP	K	ERA	WHIP	BF/G	OBA	H%	S%	xERA	Ctl	Dom	Cmd	hr/9	BPV
2012	Rk	AZL Dodgers	6	3	0	57	62	2.52	1.16	20.6	261	36	78	2.99	1.4	9.8	6.9	0.3	156
2012	Rk	Ogden	0	1	0	5	4	5.40	1.20	20.1	262	28	60	4.53	1.8	7.2	4.0	1.8	99
2012	A	Great Lakes	0	1	0	6	3	15.00	2.83	17.0	434	44	47	12.90	6.0	4.5	0.8	3.0	-63
2013	A	Cedar Rapids	3	0	0	20	16	2.70	1.30	20.6	271	34	77	3.22	2.3	7.2	3.2	0.0	87
2013	A	Great Lakes	6	4	1	92	85	3.03	1.26	16.3	255	33	75	3.16	2.6	8.3	3.1	0.3	96

Short, polished SP who owns deep arsenal of pitches and throws all for strikes. May not have true swing-and-miss offering, but he relies on command and pitch location. Had more success against RHH despite limited CU. Lively, sinking FB induces GB while SL is better of two breaking balls. Size mutes any projection.

Surkamp,Eric — SP — Chicago (A)

EXP MLB DEBUT: 2011 | POTENTIAL: #5 starter | 6B

Thrws L Age 26
2008 (6) North Carolina State

Velo	Pitch	Grade
87-90	FB	++
75-78	CB	+++
	CT	++
	CU	++

Year	Lev	Team	W	L	Sv	IP	K	ERA	WHIP	BF/G	OBA	H%	S%	xERA	Ctl	Dom	Cmd	hr/9	BPV
2011	A+	San Jose	1	0	0	6	5	0.00	0.83	21.9	191	25	100	1.03	1.5	7.5	5.0	0.0	113
2011	AA	Richmond	10	4	0	142	165	2.03	1.08	24.1	215	31	82	2.21	2.8	10.5	3.8	0.3	131
2013	A+	San Jose	0	0	0	15	17	2.98	0.73	10.7	158	19	67	1.49	1.8	10.1	5.7	1.2	152
2013	AAA	Fresno	7	1	0	71	54	2.78	1.07	25.1	218	26	75	2.42	2.5	6.8	2.7	0.5	73
2013	MLB	SF	0	1	0	3	0	23.33	3.33	16.6	542	48	29	20.75	0.0	0.0		6.7	18

First season back from TJS showed promising results. FB sits in the upper-80s with good sink, complemented by a below average CT, CU, and CB that flashes plus at times. Proven strike thrower limits walks and has proven he can miss bats. Has aptitude and mix of pitches to hold down a backend starter spot.

Swagerty,Jordan — RP — St. Louis

EXP MLB DEBUT: 2015 | POTENTIAL: #4 SP/Reliever | 7C

Thrws R Age 24
2010 (2) Arizona State

Velo	Pitch	Grade
88-95	FB	++++
83-85	CU	++
	CB	+++

Year	Lev	Team	W	L	Sv	IP	K	ERA	WHIP	BF/G	OBA	H%	S%	xERA	Ctl	Dom	Cmd	hr/9	BPV
2011	A	Quad Cities	3	1	0	30	30	1.50	0.67	20.9	175	23	83	0.98	0.6	9.0	15.0	0.6	164
2011	A+	Palm Beach	2	2	5	54	52	1.83	1.07	9.6	216	29	82	2.06	2.7	8.7	3.3	0.2	102
2011	AA	Springfield	0	0	3	9	7	2.97	1.43	4.3	238	27	83	4.02	4.9	6.9	1.4	1.0	9
2013	Rk	GCL Cardinals	0	0	0	4	5	0.00	0.50	4.4	151	24	100	0.00	0.0	11.3		0.0	221
2013	A+	Palm Beach	0	1	0	6	4	14.52	3.06	6.1	386	45	47	9.61	11.6	5.8	0.5	0.0	-191

Missed all of 2012 with TJS saw only 10.2 IP in 2013. Prior to the injury featured an 90-94 mph FB. Best pitch is a plus slurve that has late break. Also has a nice CU. Solid three-pitch mix gives him a chance to start once he reaches the majors.

Syndergaard,Noah — SP — New York (N)

EXP MLB DEBUT: 2014 | POTENTIAL: #2 starter | 9C

Thrws R Age 21
2010 (1) HS (TX)

Velo	Pitch	Grade
92-98	FB	++++
82-85	SL	++++
80-82	CB	+++
81-85	CU	+++

Year	Lev	Team	W	L	Sv	IP	K	ERA	WHIP	BF/G	OBA	H%	S%	xERA	Ctl	Dom	Cmd	hr/9	BPV
2011	A-	Vancouver	1	2	0	18	22	2.00	1.11	17.7	228	34	80	2.13	2.5	11.0	4.4	0.0	149
2011	A	Lansing	0	0	0	9	9	3.00	1.11	17.7	240	33	70	2.30	2.0	9.0	4.5	0.0	126
2012	A	Lansing	8	5	1	103	122	2.62	1.09	14.9	218	32	75	2.19	2.7	10.6	3.9	0.3	137
2013	A+	St. Lucie	3	3	0	63	64	3.13	1.22	21.3	255	34	74	3.17	2.3	9.1	4.0	0.4	121
2013	AA	Binghamton	6	1	0	54	69	3.00	1.07	19.1	232	31	80	3.34	2.0	11.5	5.8	1.3	171

Tall, athletic starter collects lots of Ks and groundballs. FB can be dominant and SL developed into a plus pitch in 2013. Hitters will chase CU out of the zone. Exhibits mound presence, repeatable mechanics, and command of all four pitches. Has makings of innings-eater with high Dom and Cmd.

Taillon,Jameson — SP — Pittsburgh

EXP MLB DEBUT: 2014 | POTENTIAL: #1 starter | 9C

Thrws R Age 22
2010 (1) HS (TX)

Velo	Pitch	Grade
93-97	FB	++++
83-85	CB	++++
83-86	CU	+++
	SL	++

Year	Lev	Team	W	L	Sv	IP	K	ERA	WHIP	BF/G	OBA	H%	S%	xERA	Ctl	Dom	Cmd	hr/9	BPV
2011	A	West Virginia	2	3	0	92	97	4.00	1.20	16.1	255	33	69	3.56	2.1	9.5	4.4	0.9	130
2012	A+	Bradenton	6	8	0	125	98	3.82	1.17	21.7	236	28	68	3.09	2.7	7.1	2.6	0.7	73
2012	AA	Altoona	3	0	0	17	18	1.59	0.71	20.0	187	27	75	0.63	0.5	9.5	18.0	0.0	175
2013	AA	Altoona	4	7	0	110	106	3.68	1.34	22.9	265	34	74	3.85	2.9	8.7	2.9	0.7	95
2013	AAA	Indianapolis	1	3	0	37	37	3.89	1.27	25.2	229	31	67	2.79	3.9	9.0	2.3	0.2	75

Tall RH has a plus 93-97 mph sinking FB that hits 99. Also has a good CB that has become his go-to breaking ball. Also working on developing a change-up, but it is still a work in progress, lacking consistency. Has the size and power to dominate.

Tapia,Domingo — SP — New York (N)

EXP MLB DEBUT: 2015 | POTENTIAL: #3 starter/setup reliever | 7C

Thrws R Age 22
2009 FA (DR)

Velo	Pitch	Grade
95-98	FB	++++
	CB	++
	CU	+

Year	Lev	Team	W	L	Sv	IP	K	ERA	WHIP	BF/G	OBA	H%	S%	xERA	Ctl	Dom	Cmd	hr/9	BPV
2010	Rk	GCL Mets	4	3	0	47	29	3.45	1.26	19.2	270	32	69	3.11	1.9	5.6	2.9	0.0	66
2011	Rk	Kingsport	5	5	0	50	30	3.78	1.32	18.8	262	30	71	3.67	2.9	5.4	1.9	0.5	37
2011	A-	Brooklyn	1	0	0	6	6	0.00	0.83	21.9	228	31	100	1.45	0.0	9.0		0.0	180
2012	A	Savannah	6	5	0	108	101	3.99	1.15	21.5	232	31	62	2.45	2.7	8.4	3.2	0.2	97
2013	A+	St. Lucie	3	9	0	101	89	4.63	1.48	18.9	234	30	67	3.43	5.6	7.9	1.4	0.3	9

Control issues surfaced for first time as he had trouble repeating mechanics. CB improved and close to being solid-average. Throws plus two-seam FB from a 3/4 arm slot. Whip-like arm action generates good movement, but poor follow through. If mechanics and Ctl don't improve, move to pen may be imminent.

Tarpley,Stephen — SP — Baltimore

EXP MLB DEBUT: 2016 | POTENTIAL: #3 starter | 8D

Thrws L Age 21
2013 (3) Scottsdale CC

Velo	Pitch	Grade
88-95	FB	+++
78-80	CB	+++
82-84	SL	++
	CU	+++

Year	Lev	Team	W	L	Sv	IP	K	ERA	WHIP	BF/G	OBA	H%	S%	xERA	Ctl	Dom	Cmd	hr/9	BPV
2013	Rk	GCL Orioles	0	1	0	21	25	2.14	1.10	11.7	252	37	78	2.41	1.3	10.7	8.3	0.0	176

Athletic, raw SP who has room to grow into lean frame. Loose arm produces above average velocity and can uncork nice CB and CU. Also uses SL, but slot more conducive to CB. Has high ceiling and raw pitch mix, but throws strikes. Gets ahead of hitters with FB and limits HR by keeping ball down.

Taylor, Blake — SP — Pittsburgh — EXP MLB DEBUT: 2017 — POTENTIAL: #3 starter — 7C

Thrws L Age 18
2013 (2) HS (CA)
88-94 FB +++
76-78 CB ++++
84-86 CU ++

Year	Lev	Team	W	L	Sv	IP	K	ERA	WHIP	BF/G	OBA	H%	S%	xERA	Ctl	Dom	Cmd	hr/9	BPV
2013	Rk	GCL Pirates	0	2	0	21	13	2.57	0.76	9.4	106	13	63	0.00	3.9	5.6	1.4	0.0	14

Tall, projectable lefty was the Pirates 2nd round pick. Already has a good 88-92 mph FB that hits 94. Also has a good CB, but did not use his CU much in HS. Limited opposing batters to a .104 BA in 21 IP. Will make his full-season debut in 2014.

Tejeda, Enosil — RP — Cleveland — EXP MLB DEBUT: 2014 — POTENTIAL: Middle reliever — 6A

Thrws R Age 25
2010 FA (DR)
86-90 FB +++
75-79 CB ++
80-82 CU +++

Year	Lev	Team	W	L	Sv	IP	K	ERA	WHIP	BF/G	OBA	H%	S%	xERA	Ctl	Dom	Cmd	hr/9	BPV
2011	A-	Mahoning Val	2	2	12	34	57	2.91	1.06	4.7	180	35	69	1.39	4.0	15.1	3.8	0.0	182
2012	A-	Mahoning Val	2	0	3	10	10	1.78	1.19	5.1	219	30	83	2.24	3.6	8.9	2.5	0.0	82
2012	A	Lake County	3	1	8	22	15	1.23	0.86	4.5	173	22	84	0.91	2.5	6.1	2.5	0.0	62
2013	A+	Carolina	1	2	2	17	30	2.09	1.16	4.9	185	37	80	1.70	4.7	15.7	3.3	0.0	173
2013	AA	Akron	1	1	0	40	36	0.90	0.90	4.5	169	23	89	0.93	2.9	8.1	2.8	0.0	84

Very deceptive RP who has still not allowed HR in 3 seasons. Stats much better than stuff suggests. Uses short arm action and funky release point to deliver FB with minimal velocity. FB exhibits movement and hitters bury it into ground. Secondary pitches are fringy, but K rate may continue despite lack of true out pitch.

Thomas, Ian — SP — Atlanta — EXP MLB DEBUT: 2015 — POTENTIAL: #5 SP / Long RP — 7D

Thrws L Age 27
2012 FA (VCU)
90-92 FB +++
CU +++
CB ++

Year	Lev	Team	W	L	Sv	IP	K	ERA	WHIP	BF/G	OBA	H%	S%	xERA	Ctl	Dom	Cmd	hr/9	BPV
2009	NCAA	VCU	4	4	0	71	58	4.30	1.45	27.6	280	32	74	4.90	3.2	7.3	2.3	1.3	65
2012	A	Rome	5	0	6	45	58	3.19	1.33	7.2	261	37	79	3.85	3.0	11.5	3.9	0.8	145
2013	AA	Mississippi	7	8	1	104	123	2.77	1.05	10.3	197	28	75	2.17	3.2	10.6	3.3	0.6	123

Former indy league hurler has made a nice transition as a pro and more than held his own at AA. Lefty has a decent 90-92 mph FB and a plus CU. Showed advanced ability to throw strikes consistently and proved difficult to hit, with 37 BB/123 K.

Thompson, Jake — SP — Detroit — EXP MLB DEBUT: 2017 — POTENTIAL: #3 starter — 8C

Thrws R Age 20
2012 (2) HS (TX)
88-94 FB +++
82-84 SL +++
80-83 CU +++

Year	Lev	Team	W	L	Sv	IP	K	ERA	WHIP	BF/G	OBA	H%	S%	xERA	Ctl	Dom	Cmd	hr/9	BPV
2012	Rk	GCL Tigers	1	2	0	28	31	1.92	0.85	14.7	150	21	78	0.91	3.2	9.9	3.1	0.3	110
2013	A	West Michigan	3	3	0	83	91	3.14	1.34	20.3	252	34	77	3.43	3.5	9.9	2.8	0.4	102

Tall, physical RHP with monitored workload. Can pepper strike zone with quality FB that features heavy life. Has ability to blow by hitters up in zone or bury it low. Throws on downhill plane which enhances SL and CU, though SL can be flat. Profiles as mid-rotation option, but needs innings to prove durability.

Thompson, Jeff — SP — Detroit — EXP MLB DEBUT: 2016 — POTENTIAL: #4 starter — 7C

Thrws R Age 22
2013 (3) Louisville
89-94 FB +++
84-86 SL +++
80-84 CU ++

Year	Lev	Team	W	L	Sv	IP	K	ERA	WHIP	BF/G	OBA	H%	S%	xERA	Ctl	Dom	Cmd	hr/9	BPV
2011	NCAA	Louisville	2	1	1	39	43	2.76	1.48	9.3	266	35	84	4.23	4.1	9.9	2.4	0.7	84
2012	NCAA	Louisville	9	4	0	78	73	4.03	1.47	22.4	259	34	71	3.68	4.4	8.4	1.9	0.2	51
2013	NCAA	Louisville	11	2	0	107	113	2.19	0.94	23.7	182	24	80	1.73	2.9	9.5	3.3	0.6	112
2013	A	West Michigan	2	2	1	45	42	3.80	1.33	13.4	244	31	72	3.49	3.8	8.4	2.2	0.6	67

Tall, big-bodied SP who throws with excellent angle to plate to induce high amount of GB. Showed improvement with FB and can mess with hitters timing with solid-average SL. Needs to upgrade CU to have chance for future success. Slows down arm speed and telegraphs it. Rarely allows HR.

Thorpe, Lewis — SP — Minnesota — EXP MLB DEBUT: 2017 — POTENTIAL: #3 starter — 8C

Thrws L Age 18
2012 FA (Australia)
88-95 FB ++++
78-80 CB +++
81-82 CU ++

Year	Lev	Team	W	L	Sv	IP	K	ERA	WHIP	BF/G	OBA	H%	S%	xERA	Ctl	Dom	Cmd	hr/9	BPV
2013	Rk	GCL Twins	4	1	0	44	64	2.05	0.86	13.5	205	33	78	1.59	1.2	13.1	10.7	0.4	221

Lean, projectable LHP who led GCL in Ks. FB may not have plus velocity but has explosive late movement that is tough to hit. Has deception in clean, repeatable delivery. Changes speeds well, but secondary pitches need time to develop. Fits Twins mold by limiting walks. LHH hit .071 against him.

Thurman, Andrew — SP — Houston — EXP MLB DEBUT: 2015 — POTENTIAL: #4 starter — 7C

Thrws R Age 22
2013 (2) UC-Irvine
90-94 FB +++
78-81 SL +++
73-76 CB ++
81-83 CU +++

Year	Lev	Team	W	L	Sv	IP	K	ERA	WHIP	BF/G	OBA	H%	S%	xERA	Ctl	Dom	Cmd	hr/9	BPV
2011	NCAA	California-Irvine	3	3	1	66	58	3.82	1.32	13.0	276	35	69	3.59	2.2	7.9	3.6	0.3	101
2012	NCAA	California-Irvine	8	3	0	98	69	2.66	0.93	24.5	197	24	70	1.52	2.1	6.3	3.0	0.2	75
2013	NCAA	California-Irvine	6	4	0	100	91	3.24	1.04	27.6	231	31	66	2.11	1.7	8.2	4.8	0.1	119
2013	A-	Tri City	4	2	1	39	43	3.90	1.38	13.7	280	36	76	4.59	2.5	9.9	3.9	1.1	128

Tall, strong SP who is safe and solid bet to pitch in big leagues. Has deep repertoire and knows how to sequence. Pitches off solid-average FB and uses 2 breaking balls. Neither is true out pitch, though SL can be used as chaser. CU is best secondary. Pitches up in zone and can be hittable when FB arrives flat.

Tillman, Daniel — RP — Los Angeles (A) — EXP MLB DEBUT: 2015 — POTENTIAL: Closer — 7D

Thrws R Age 25
2010 (2) Florida Southern
91-97 FB ++++
78-84 SL ++
80-82 CU ++

Year	Lev	Team	W	L	Sv	IP	K	ERA	WHIP	BF/G	OBA	H%	S%	xERA	Ctl	Dom	Cmd	hr/9	BPV
2012	A+	Inland Empire	1	1	8	24	31	1.88	1.00	4.2	129	21	79	0.74	5.3	11.6	2.2	0.0	86
2012	AA	Arkansas	1	5	0	19	21	12.25	2.20	4.8	299	38	41	7.20	9.0	9.9	1.1	1.4	-46
2013	Rk	AZL Angels	0	0	0	4	5	0.00	0.00	3.8	0	0	100	0.00		11.3		0.0	221
2013	A+	Inland Empire	1	2	0	13	13	6.92	1.77	4.6	247	32	59	4.70	7.6	9.0	1.2	0.7	-26
2013	AA	Arkansas	0	0	0	8	6	8.89	1.60	4.5	116	15	38	2.19	11.1	6.7	0.6	0.0	-162

Max-effort RP who is seemingly running in place and can't get past High-A. Was horrendous in AA in 2012 and 2013 and misses innings. Can be a GB guy and tough to make hard contact against. Problems stem from lack of control and release point. FB is plus pitch, but secondaries lag far behind.

Tirado, Alberto — SP — Toronto — EXP MLB DEBUT: 2017 — POTENTIAL: #2 starter — 9E

Thrws R Age 19
2011 FA (DR)
88-95 FB ++++
83-88 SL +++
81-82 CU +++

Year	Lev	Team	W	L	Sv	IP	K	ERA	WHIP	BF/G	OBA	H%	S%	xERA	Ctl	Dom	Cmd	hr/9	BPV
2012	Rk	Bluefield	2	0	0	11	11	2.45	0.82	13.3	114	13	67	0.22	4.1	4.1	1.0	0.0	-19
2012	Rk	GCL Blue Jays	1	2	0	37	34	2.68	1.08	13.1	212	28	73	1.88	2.9	8.3	2.8	0.0	88
2013	Rk	Bluefield	3	0	0	48	44	1.68	1.27	16.4	232	30	87	2.78	3.7	8.2	2.2	0.2	65

Thin, projectable SP with very high ceiling. Locates FB in lower half to induce GB. Has nice present FB with more ticks coming. Shows advanced CU with repeatable delivery, though hard SL needs polish. Can overthrow at times and delivery needs to be smoother to tap into electric arm.

Tonkin, Mike — RP — Minnesota — EXP MLB DEBUT: 2013 — POTENTIAL: Closer — 7C

Thrws R Age 24
2008 (30) HS (CA)
91-96 FB ++++
80-83 SL +++
81-83 CU ++

Year	Lev	Team	W	L	Sv	IP	K	ERA	WHIP	BF/G	OBA	H%	S%	xERA	Ctl	Dom	Cmd	hr/9	BPV
2012	A	Beloit	3	0	6	39	53	1.38	0.97	6.7	209	33	86	1.75	2.1	12.2	5.9	0.2	182
2012	A+	Fort Myers	1	1	6	30	44	2.99	1.16	5.4	220	35	76	2.71	3.3	13.2	4.0	0.0	166
2013	AA	New Britain	1	2	7	24	30	2.24	1.20	4.4	236	36	79	2.46	3.0	11.2	3.8	0.0	139
2013	AAA	Rochester	1	2	14	32	36	4.47	1.27	4.4	267	35	66	3.85	2.2	10.1	4.5	0.8	139
2013	MLB	MIN	0	0	0	11	10	0.82	1.09	4.8	225	30	92	2.07	0.8	8.2	3.3	0.0	99

Tall, aggressive RP who served as closer in minors and reached MIN late. Made slight revision to delivery and ended up with more consistent, hard heat. FB can be explosive, but relies on it too much and can overthrow. Powerful SL can be good and will need to use more against RHH. Lacks feel for CU.

Torres, Yeralf — SP — Atlanta — EXP MLB DEBUT: 2017 — POTENTIAL: #3 Starter — 7D

Thrws R Age 18
2012 FA (DR)
90-93 FB ++++
73-75 CB +
CU +

Year	Lev	Team	W	L	Sv	IP	K	ERA	WHIP	BF/G	OBA	H%	S%	xERA	Ctl	Dom	Cmd	hr/9	BPV
2013		Did not pitch in the US																		

17-year-old Dominican hurler was signed for $550,000. Already has a 90-93 mph FB, a mid-70s CB that is inconsistent, but has potential, and a below-average CU. Inconsistent mechanics and release point lead to struggles with control.

Travieso,Nick — SP — Cincinnati

EXP MLB DEBUT: 2016 | POTENTIAL: #3 starter | 8D

Thrws R Age 20
2012 (1) HS (FL)

Velo	Pitch	Grade
91-94	FB	++++
82-85	SL	+++
	CU	+++

Year	Lev	Team	W	L	Sv	IP	K	ERA	WHIP	BF/G	OBA	H%	S%	xERA	Ctl	Dom	Cmd	hr/9	BPV
2012	Rk	AZL Reds	0	2	0	21	14	4.71	1.19	10.5	252	27	64	3.91	2.1	6.0	2.8	1.3	68
2013	A	Dayton	7	4	0	81	61	4.66	1.35	19.9	266	31	66	4.02	3.0	6.8	2.3	0.8	59

Advanced command and feel for pitching. Plus 94 mph FB with nice tilt, mid 80s hard SL and improving CU. Simple, repeatable mechanics with clean, easy arm action. Progressing nicely for pitcher entering 3rd season as starter. Improved follow-through and more confidence throwing CU all that's lacking.

Treinen,Blake — RP — Washington

EXP MLB DEBUT: 2015 | POTENTIAL: #3 starter | 8E

Thrws R Age 26
2011 (7) South Dakota State

Velo	Pitch	Grade
90-97	FB	+++
82-86	SL	+++
82-85	CU	++

Year	Lev	Team	W	L	Sv	IP	K	ERA	WHIP	BF/G	OBA	H%	S%	xERA	Ctl	Dom	Cmd	hr/9	BPV
2011	Rk	AZL Athletics	0	0	0	3	7	0.00	1.33	4.2	262	67	100	3.04	3.0	21.0	7.0	0.0	315
2011	A	Burlington	1	1	2	27	29	3.67	1.00	5.7	208	29	62	1.93	2.3	9.7	4.1	0.3	129
2012	A+	Stockton	7	7	0	103	92	4.37	1.35	17.9	285	35	70	4.44	2.0	8.0	4.0	1.0	108
2013	A-	Auburn	0	0	0	6	7	0.00	0.17	9.0	56	9	100	0.00	0.0	10.5		0.0	207
2013	AA	Harrisburg	6	7	0	118	86	3.65	1.34	23.4	273	32	74	3.98	2.5	6.5	2.6	0.7	68

Has bounced back and forth between starter and reliever; put together some nice starts at Double-A. Owns arm strength and excellent heavy FB, but continues struggling getting LHH out (.295 oppBA). Can drop velo on FB to get more movement. SL a nice second pitch, CU needs work. Gets lots of groundball outs.

Tropeano,Nick — SP — Houston

EXP MLB DEBUT: 2014 | POTENTIAL: #3 starter | 8D

Thrws R Age 23
2011 (5) Stony Brook

Velo	Pitch	Grade
90-95	FB	+++
81-83	SL	++
81-85	CU	++++

Year	Lev	Team	W	L	Sv	IP	K	ERA	WHIP	BF/G	OBA	H%	S%	xERA	Ctl	Dom	Cmd	hr/9	BPV
2011	NCAA	Stony Brook	12	1	0	93	119	1.84	0.94	24.9	194	30	81	1.54	2.3	11.5	5.0	0.3	163
2011	A-	Tri City	3	2	0	53	63	2.37	1.19	17.7	219	32	79	2.37	3.6	10.7	3.0	0.2	114
2012	A	Lexington	6	4	0	87	97	2.79	1.18	23.2	239	33	76	2.75	2.7	10.0	3.7	0.3	126
2012	A+	Lancaster	6	3	0	70	69	3.33	1.32	24.2	267	33	79	4.17	2.7	8.8	3.3	1.0	105
2013	AA	Corpus Christi	7	10	5	133	130	4.12	1.34	19.8	272	34	72	4.27	2.6	8.8	3.3	1.0	105

Strike-throwing SP who led TL in Ks. Exhibits solid control and uses FB to effectively set up secondary offerings, particularly plus CU. Throws CU with impressive arm speed and offers sink and fade. Velocity increasing, but SL hasn't developed much. Can give up HR and needs to focus on keeping ball down.

Tseng,Jen-Ho — SP — Chicago (N)

EXP MLB DEBUT: 2017 | POTENTIAL: #3 starter | 8D

Thrws R Age 19
2013 FA (Taiwan)

Velo	Pitch	Grade
90-93	FB	+++
85-88	SL	+++
	CB	+++
	CU	+++

Year	Lev	Team	W	L	Sv	IP	K	ERA	WHIP	BF/G	OBA	H%	S%	xERA	Ctl	Dom	Cmd	hr/9	BPV
2013		Did not pitch in the US																	

18-year-old Tiawanese RH signed with the Cubs for $1.625 million. Has a good low-90s FB that can hit 95 mph with some movement, a hard SL that has potential, and a good over-hand knuckle curve. Hesitation in delivery causes deception and he locates his FB well. Does throw with some effort.

Tuivailala,Samuel — RP — St. Louis

EXP MLB DEBUT: 2016 | POTENTIAL: Closer | 7D

Thrws R Age 21
2010 (3) HS (CA)

Velo	Pitch	Grade
93-96	FB	++++
	CB	++
	CU	++

Year	Lev	Team	W	L	Sv	IP	K	ERA	WHIP	BF/G	OBA	H%	S%	xERA	Ctl	Dom	Cmd	hr/9	BPV
2012	Rk	Johnson City	0	0	0	13	23	4.15	1.92	5.6	247	45	79	5.02	9.0	15.9	1.8	0.7	62
2013	A	Peoria	0	3	1	35	50	5.38	1.45	5.4	238	39	59	3.11	5.1	12.8	2.5	0.0	110

Cards tried this athletic 3rd rounder as a position player when drafted, but moved him to the mound in 2012. Has an upper-90s FB when working in relief. Dominated at times with 12.8 K/9, but also struggled with control. CB and CU remain raw, but he has a big arm and good size.

Turley,Nik — SP — New York (A)

EXP MLB DEBUT: 2014 | POTENTIAL: #4 starter | 7C

Thrws L Age 24
2008 (50) HS (CA)

Velo	Pitch	Grade
87-92	FB	+++
75-77	CB	+++
79-83	CU	++

Year	Lev	Team	W	L	Sv	IP	K	ERA	WHIP	BF/G	OBA	H%	S%	xERA	Ctl	Dom	Cmd	hr/9	BPV
2011	A+	Tampa	0	0	0	7	5	6.34	1.69	16.0	355	40	64	6.73	1.3	6.3	5.0	1.3	98
2012	A+	Tampa	9	5	0	112	116	2.89	1.26	19.9	235	31	78	3.14	3.5	9.3	2.6	0.6	90
2012	AA	Trenton	1	0	0	5	1	5.40	1.80	23.1	362	38	67	6.00	1.8	1.8	1.0	0.0	2
2013	AA	Trenton	11	8	0	139	137	3.88	1.38	21.6	233	30	73	3.56	4.7	8.9	1.9	0.7	50
2013	AAA	Scranton/W-B	0	0	0	6	4	1.50	0.83	21.9	106	13	80	0.16	4.5	6.0	1.3	0.0	5

Big, physical LHP who knows how to pitch. Velocity is subpar and seems to lose steam late. Succeeds by cutting and sinking FB and sequencing pitches. Control regressed, but CB improved to point where he could miss more bats. CU can be OK, but still inconsistent. Back-end profile with limited upside.

Turnbull,Kylin — SP — Washington

EXP MLB DEBUT: 2015 | POTENTIAL: #5 starter/reliever | 6D

Thrws L Age 24
2011 (4) Santa Barbara CC

Velo	Pitch	Grade
88-92	FB	++
80-84	SL	++
	CU	+

Year	Lev	Team	W	L	Sv	IP	K	ERA	WHIP	BF/G	OBA	H%	S%	xERA	Ctl	Dom	Cmd	hr/9	BPV
2012	Rk	GCL Nationals	0	1	0	9	9	2.97	1.21	9.2	300	40	73	3.40	0.0	8.9		0.0	178
2012	A	Hagerstown	4	5	0	89	51	5.16	1.51	21.4	293	33	65	4.65	3.0	5.2	1.7	0.6	29
2013	A-	Auburn	2	0	0	18	15	1.99	1.05	17.5	239	29	83	2.62	1.5	7.5	5.0	0.5	112
2013	A	Hagerstown	6	5	0	83	67	3.58	1.36	21.7	293	34	78	4.71	1.7	7.3	4.2	1.1	102
2013	A+	Potomac	0	3	0	10	3	15.15	2.77	18.8	413	43	41	10.28	7.1	2.7	0.4	0.9	-126

The 4th round pick in 2011 was sent down a level after a rough start at Potomac. He made some mechanical adjustments and put together a nice season. Works downhill with his low 90s FB, and also throws inconsistent SL. CU not much to speak of at this point. Made progress with control, but still a ways to go.

Underwood,Duane — SP — Chicago (N)

EXP MLB DEBUT: 2016 | POTENTIAL: #3 starter | 7D

Thrws R Age 19
2012 (2) HS (GA)

Velo	Pitch	Grade
91-94	FB	++++
73-75	CB	++
	CU	++

Year	Lev	Team	W	L	Sv	IP	K	ERA	WHIP	BF/G	OBA	H%	S%	xERA	Ctl	Dom	Cmd	hr/9	BPV
2012	Rk	AZL Cubs	0	1	0	8	7	5.49	1.59	7.2	232	27	67	4.45	6.6	7.7	1.2	1.1	-22
2013	A-	Boise	3	4	0	54	36	4.99	1.65	17.3	289	33	69	4.98	4.5	6.0	1.3	0.7	5

Strong-armed RH had a pedestrian year in rookie ball, striking out 6 per 9. FB sits at 91-94 and can hit 97 but can be straight. CB has plus potential along with an avg CU, but both remain inconsistent. Does have good athleticism but needs to repeat his mechanics and smooth out the rough edges.

Urena,Jose — SP — Miami

EXP MLB DEBUT: 2015 | POTENTIAL: #3 starter | 8D

Thrws R Age 22
2008 FA (DR)

Velo	Pitch	Grade
92-97	FB	++++
	CU	++++
	SL	++++

Year	Lev	Team	W	L	Sv	IP	K	ERA	WHIP	BF/G	OBA	H%	S%	xERA	Ctl	Dom	Cmd	hr/9	BPV
2011	A-	Jamestown	4	7	0	72	48	4.36	1.43	20.4	267	31	69	3.96	3.6	6.0	1.7	0.5	28
2012	A	Greensboro	9	6	2	138	101	3.39	1.25	20.8	269	31	75	3.85	1.9	6.6	3.5	0.8	85
2013	A+	Jupiter	10	7	0	149	107	3.74	1.19	22.1	260	31	68	3.24	1.7	6.5	3.7	0.5	87

Lean, projectable SP with live arm improved his Ctl and Cmd for second consecutive year. Plus arm strength generates plus FB, a good splitter-like SL and inconsistent CU that has potential. Pure stuff is electric, but he doesn't have high Dom. Throws strikes, but needs to refine overall command to remain a SP.

Urias,Julio — SP — Los Angeles (N)

EXP MLB DEBUT: 2016 | POTENTIAL: #2 starter | 9D

Thrws L Age 17
2012 FA (Mexico)

Velo	Pitch	Grade
91-96	FB	++++
77-82	CB	+++
	CU	++

Year	Lev	Team	W	L	Sv	IP	K	ERA	WHIP	BF/G	OBA	H%	S%	xERA	Ctl	Dom	Cmd	hr/9	BPV
2013	A	Great Lakes	2	0	0	54	67	2.50	1.11	11.8	224	31	82	2.85	2.7	11.1	4.2	0.8	147

Small, projectable LH made huge impact in 2013, pitching at 16/17 years old. Turned heads with pitchability, using quality sinking and cutting FB. CB flashes plus and inconsistent CU has chance to be above average. He has good mechanics and great command of his pitches, limiting walks and racking up the strikeouts.

Vance,Kevin — RP — Chicago (A)

EXP MLB DEBUT: 2014 | POTENTIAL: Setup reliever | 6A

Thrws R Age 23
2011 (19) Connecticut

Velo	Pitch	Grade
87-94	FB	+++
78-82	CB	++++
81-82	CU	++

Year	Lev	Team	W	L	Sv	IP	K	ERA	WHIP	BF/G	OBA	H%	S%	xERA	Ctl	Dom	Cmd	hr/9	BPV
2011	NCAA	Connecticut	1	0	13	28	31	1.60	0.67	3.8	141	21	74	0.05	1.9	9.9	5.2	0.0	144
2011	Rk	Great Falls	2	1	1	35	58	4.60	1.56	7.0	312	50	71	5.13	2.6	14.8	5.8	0.8	216
2012	A	Kannapolis	4	2	0	79	70	3.07	1.24	16.9	239	30	76	3.04	3.2	8.0	2.5	0.5	75
2012	A+	Winston-Salem	1	0	0	21	29	1.70	1.13	7.6	241	34	95	3.54	2.1	12.3	5.8	1.3	182
2013	AA	Birmingham	2	6	7	69	84	3.91	1.32	7.1	220	32	70	3.05	4.7	11.0	2.3	0.5	88

Aggressive RP who has flown under radar, but could be option in CHW pen. Doesn't have ideal frame, but induces weak contact with average FB and terrific CB. Breaker is go-to pitch and can use to set up FB. Struggles to repeat delivery and slot, impacting command. Owns fringy CU, but won't use often.

Vasquez,Kelvin — SP — Texas

EXP MLB DEBUT: 2017 | POTENTIAL: #3 starter | 8D

Thrws R Age 21
2011 FA (DR)

Velo	Pitch	Grade
89-94	FB	+++
81-84	SL	+++
78-82	CU	++

Year	Lev	Team	W	L	Sv	IP	K	ERA	WHIP	BF/G	OBA	H%	S%	xERA	Ctl	Dom	Cmd	hr/9	BPV
2013	A-	Spokane	2	2	0	63	72	2.14	1.27	18.4	205	29	84	2.66	4.8	10.3	2.1	0.4	72
2013	A	Hickory	2	2	0	26	19	6.55	1.88	15.3	296	33	67	6.35	6.2	6.6	1.1	1.4	-32

Tall, lanky SP who led NWL in ERA upon demotion from Low-A. Plenty of velocity left in tank as he grows into lean frame. FB features movement and induces high amount of GB. Struggles with LHH and improved CU could be recipe for success. FB sets up effective SL and throws with deceptive arm speed.

Velasquez, Vincent — SP — Houston

EXP MLB DEBUT: 2016 | POTENTIAL: #3 starter | 8B

Thrws R Age 22
2010 (2) HS (CA)

Velo	Pitch	Grade
91-95	FB	++++
75-78	CB	+++
81-84	CU	+++

Year	Lev	Team	W	L	Sv	IP	K	ERA	WHIP	BF/G	OBA	H%	S%	xERA	Ctl	Dom	Cmd	hr/9	BPV
2010	Rk	Greeneville	2	2	0	29	25	3.09	1.00	13.9	226	26	76	3.02	1.5	7.7	5.0	1.2	115
2012	A-	Tri City	4	1	0	45	51	3.38	1.19	20.2	225	31	71	2.69	3.4	10.2	3.0	0.4	109
2013	A	Quad Cities	9	4	3	110	123	3.19	1.12	17.3	225	31	72	2.66	2.7	10.1	3.7	0.6	126
2013	A+	Lancaster	0	2	0	14	19	6.34	1.55	20.7	259	36	60	4.82	5.1	12.0	2.4	1.3	98

Athletic SP who is regaining feel after missing all 2011 with elbow surgery. Finished 2nd in MWL in Ks, thanks to plus FB and sharp CB. Repeats arm speed on CU which gives him third solid offering. Limits BA due to movement and pitches downhill for GB. Has impressive upside, but needs experience and polish.

Ventura,Yordano — SP — Kansas City

EXP MLB DEBUT: 2013 | POTENTIAL: #1 starter | 9B

Thrws R Age 23
2008 FA (DR)

Velo	Pitch	Grade
93-98	FB	++++
79-83	CB	++++
82-85	CU	+++

Year	Lev	Team	W	L	Sv	IP	K	ERA	WHIP	BF/G	OBA	H%	S%	xERA	Ctl	Dom	Cmd	hr/9	BPV
2012	A+	Wilmington	3	5	0	76	98	3.31	1.24	19.3	235	34	76	3.31	3.3	11.6	3.5	0.8	137
2012	AA	NW Arkansas	1	2	0	29	25	4.64	1.24	19.7	219	28	60	2.66	4.0	7.7	1.9	0.3	49
2013	AA	NW Arkansas	3	2	0	57	74	2.36	1.03	20.0	195	29	79	1.97	3.1	11.6	3.7	0.5	143
2013	AAA	Omaha	5	4	0	77	81	3.74	1.47	22.0	269	36	74	4.03	3.9	9.5	2.5	0.5	84
2013	MLB	KC	0	1	0	15	11	3.53	1.24	20.7	232	24	81	4.21	3.5	6.5	1.8	1.8	39

Short, explosive SP who dominated AA en route to big league trial. Can tantalize with amazing FB and swing-and-miss CB. Has learned to set up CB by locating FB well and has the arm speed for potential plus CU. Size can be hindrance and is inefficient at times, but can dominate with aggressive style.

Verbitsky,Bryan — SP — San Diego

EXP MLB DEBUT: 2016 | POTENTIAL: #5 starter/reliever | 7D

Thrws R Age 22
2013 (3) Hofstra

Velo	Pitch	Grade
88-94	FB	+++
	CU	++
	SL	++

Year	Lev	Team	W	L	Sv	IP	K	ERA	WHIP	BF/G	OBA	H%	S%	xERA	Ctl	Dom	Cmd	hr/9	BPV
2011	NCAA	Hofstra	0	0	3	16	16	3.35	1.24	3.8	209	27	74	2.78	4.5	8.9	2.0	0.6	58
2012	NCAA	Hofstra	1	3	5	26	20	6.21	1.88	5.8	335	39	67	6.63	4.1	6.9	1.7	1.0	30
2013	NCAA	Hofstra	3	4	3	44	51	2.66	0.84	8.5	179	25	69	1.26	2.0	10.4	5.1	0.4	151
2013	A-	Eugene	0	6	0	49	47	4.03	1.63	15.6	233	30	74	3.87	7.0	8.6	1.2	0.4	-15

Short, strong RHP who doesn't have much pitching experience, yet has upside. Works quickly with solid-average FB that could increase in velocity with tweaks to arm action. Likes to keep ball low and induce weak contact. Secondary pitches need improvement, especially CU. Could move to pen in long-term.

VerHagen,Drew — SP — Detroit

EXP MLB DEBUT: 2015 | POTENTIAL: #4 starter | 7C

Thrws R Age 23
2012 (4) Vanderbilt

Velo	Pitch	Grade
90-95	FB	+++
77-80	CB	+++
80-83	CU	++

Year	Lev	Team	W	L	Sv	IP	K	ERA	WHIP	BF/G	OBA	H%	S%	xERA	Ctl	Dom	Cmd	hr/9	BPV
2012	NCAA	Vanderbilt	6	3	2	69	37	3.52	1.33	10.6	247	28	72	3.24	3.6	4.8	1.3	0.3	6
2012	Rk	GCL Tigers	0	0	0	4	2	2.25	1.25	8.1	307	35	80	3.65	0.0	4.5		0.0	99
2012	A+	Lakeland	0	3	0	27	17	3.67	1.26	13.8	208	25	68	2.31	4.7	5.7	1.2	0.0	-6
2013	A+	Lakeland	5	3	0	67	35	2.82	1.13	22.1	206	24	73	2.10	3.6	4.7	1.3	0.1	5
2013	AA	Erie	2	5	0	60	40	3.00	1.17	19.9	239	28	75	2.88	2.6	6.0	2.4	0.5	57

Big, strong SP who was equally good on two levels. Has pitchability and amazing feel for craft. Sets up hitters by sequencing average offerings and throws on downhill angle. FB can be good, but arm action limits movement. Average CB exhibits nice break, though CU remains work in progress.

Vizcaino,Arodys — SP — Chicago (N)

EXP MLB DEBUT: 2011 | POTENTIAL: #3 starter/Setup Reliever | 8D

Thrws R Age 23
2007 FA (DR)

Velo	Pitch	Grade
89-96	FB	++++
80-83	CB	++++
83-85	CU	++

Year	Lev	Team	W	L	Sv	IP	K	ERA	WHIP	BF/G	OBA	H%	S%	xERA	Ctl	Dom	Cmd	hr/9	BPV
2010	A	Rome	9	4	0	71	68	2.40	1.01	19.5	239	32	75	2.16	1.1	8.6	7.6	0.1	142
2010	A+	Myrtle Beach	0	0	0	13	11	4.77	1.44	18.7	301	36	67	4.64	2.0	7.5	3.7	0.7	98
2011	A+	Lynchburg	2	2	0	40	37	2.47	1.02	17.1	215	27	79	2.41	2.2	8.3	3.7	0.7	107
2011	AA	Mississippi	2	3	0	49	55	3.84	1.26	18.2	241	33	69	3.20	3.3	10.1	3.1	0.5	110
2011	AAA	Gwinnett	1	0	0	7	8	1.29	1.00	4.5	262	34	100	3.51	0.0	10.3		1.3	203

Missed all of 2012-13 recovering from TJS. Prior to injury, featured plus 92-95 mph FB that topped out at 97 mph, an above-average CB, and an inconsistent CU. When used in relief, FB was 94-97 mph and the FB/CB proved highly effective. Whether in relief or as a starter, has the potential to be an impact arm.

von Schamann,Duke — SP — Los Angeles (N)

EXP MLB DEBUT: 2014 | POTENTIAL: #5 starter | 6C

Thrws R Age 23
2012 (15) Texas Tech

Velo	Pitch	Grade
87-90	FB	++
	SL	++
	CU	++

Year	Lev	Team	W	L	Sv	IP	K	ERA	WHIP	BF/G	OBA	H%	S%	xERA	Ctl	Dom	Cmd	hr/9	BPV
2012	Rk	Ogden	1	0	0	3	2	0.00	0.33	4.7	106	13	100	0.00	0.0	6.0		0.0	126
2012	A	Great Lakes	4	4	0	67	42	3.22	1.07	21.7	238	28	70	2.60	1.7	5.6	3.2	0.4	72
2012	AA	Chattanooga	1	0	0	5	0	1.80	0.80	18.1	175	18	75	0.84	1.8	0.0	0.0	0.0	-31
2013	A+	Rancho Cuca	8	2	0	64	50	4.35	1.28	23.9	261	30	69	4.09	2.5	7.0	2.8	1.1	76
2013	AA	Chattanooga	3	5	0	66	50	5.03	1.54	18.0	305	35	68	5.23	2.7	6.8	2.5	1.0	67

Tall, strong SP works downhill with ease, pounding sinker to generate ground balls. Has good control, and while nothing is average or better, he does well sequencing and setting up sinker. Arm works well and repeats delivery for a big guy. Will never dominate his opponent, but works in the back end of the rotation.

Voth,Austin — SP — Washington

EXP MLB DEBUT: 2016 | POTENTIAL: #3 starter | 7D

Thrws R Age 22
2013 (5) Washington

Velo	Pitch	Grade
92-95	FB	+++
72-74	SL	+++
	CU	++

Year	Lev	Team	W	L	Sv	IP	K	ERA	WHIP	BF/G	OBA	H%	S%	xERA	Ctl	Dom	Cmd	hr/9	BPV
2012	NCAA	Washington	7	1	1	67	62	4.16	1.16	12.1	228	29	64	2.80	3.0	8.3	2.8	0.5	88
2013	NCAA	Washington	7	6	1	105	98	3.00	1.30	25.5	250	32	78	3.41	3.3	8.4	2.6	0.5	81
2013	Rk	GCL Nationals	0	0	0	5	4	0.00	0.80	9.1	221	28	100	1.30	0.0	7.2		0.0	148
2013	A-	Auburn	2	0	0	30	42	1.49	0.83	15.7	198	33	80	1.04	1.2	12.5	10.5	0.0	211
2013	A	Hagerstown	1	0	0	10	9	3.53	0.98	19.4	218	29	60	1.70	1.8	7.9	4.5	0.0	113

Earned two promotions during debut season by showing good stuff, pitch mix, and durability. Repeats delivery well with good arm action and throws lots of strikes. CU shows promise of becoming third average or better pitch. Works downhill with his FB that reaches 95, and commands it to both sides of the plate.

Wagner,Tyler — SP — Milwaukee

EXP MLB DEBUT: 2016 | POTENTIAL: #4 starter | 7C

Thrws R Age 23
2012 (4) Utah

Velo	Pitch	Grade
92-97	FB	++++
	SL	++
	CU	+++

Year	Lev	Team	W	L	Sv	IP	K	ERA	WHIP	BF/G	OBA	H%	S%	xERA	Ctl	Dom	Cmd	hr/9	BPV
2010	NCAA	Utah	0	1	3	21	23	2.13	0.90	7.9	144	20	78	1.06	3.8	9.8	2.6	0.4	91
2011	NCAA	Utah	4	3	12	35	33	2.05	1.25	5.7	214	28	84	2.59	4.4	8.5	1.9	0.3	53
2012	NCAA	Utah	2	6	2	42	34	3.63	1.78	8.8	287	36	78	4.86	5.8	7.3	1.3	0.2	-7
2012	Rk	Helena	1	4	0	48	47	7.84	1.76	15.8	317	39	54	6.11	4.1	8.8	2.1	1.1	65
2013	A	Wisconsin	10	8	0	148	116	3.22	1.25	22.3	236	28	75	3.19	3.4	7.0	2.1	0.6	53

Tall, athletic SP throws his low-to-mid-90s FB with good sink to produce ground balls. His secondaries include a SL and CU, both which have average potential. He commands the FB well, but needs to refine his secondaries. With a clean arm and decent arsenal he has a good chance to be a quality backend starter.

Wahl,Bobby — SP — Oakland

EXP MLB DEBUT: 2015 | POTENTIAL: #3 starter | 8C

Thrws R Age 22
2013 (5) Mississippi

Velo	Pitch	Grade
88-95	FB	+++
82-84	SL	++++
80-82	CU	+++

Year	Lev	Team	W	L	Sv	IP	K	ERA	WHIP	BF/G	OBA	H%	S%	xERA	Ctl	Dom	Cmd	hr/9	BPV
2011	NCAA	Mississippi	0	2	4	30	26	4.50	1.47	7.1	281	35	67	4.05	3.3	7.8	2.4	0.3	69
2012	NCAA	Mississippi	7	4	0	99	104	2.55	1.09	22.8	214	29	78	2.44	2.9	9.5	3.3	0.5	110
2013	NCAA	Mississippi	10	0	0	97	78	2.04	1.16	24.2	201	25	83	2.23	4.1	7.2	1.8	0.3	38
2013	Rk	AZL Athletics	0	0	0	1	1	9.00	2.00	4.8	0	0	50	2.18	18.0	9.0	0.5	0.0	-306
2013	A-	Vermont	0	0	2	20	27	4.01	1.29	9.2	260	36	74	4.24	2.7	12.0	4.5	1.3	162

Strong, stocky SP who dropped in draft due to inconsistency, but has terrific upside. Can dominate in stretches with FB/SL combo. Pitches with good angle to plate which enhances FB. Plus, hard SL is best offering, but can use too much. Exhibits some effort in delivery, but has sinking CU to remain starter.

Walker,Taijuan — SP — Seattle

EXP MLB DEBUT: 2013 | POTENTIAL: #1 starter | 9A

Thrws R Age 21
2010 (1-S) HS (CA)

Velo	Pitch	Grade
92-98	FB	+++++
73-78	CB	+++
86-89	SL	++++
85-87	CU	+++

Year	Lev	Team	W	L	Sv	IP	K	ERA	WHIP	BF/G	OBA	H%	S%	xERA	Ctl	Dom	Cmd	hr/9	BPV
2011	A	Clinton	6	5	0	96	113	2.90	1.12	21.1	203	29	74	2.21	3.6	10.6	2.9	0.4	110
2012	AA	Jackson	7	10	0	126	118	4.71	1.38	21.2	258	32	67	4.03	3.6	8.4	2.4	0.9	73
2013	AA	Jackson	4	7	0	84	96	2.46	1.05	23.2	197	27	79	2.20	3.2	10.3	3.2	0.6	116
2013	AAA	Tacoma	5	3	0	57	64	3.63	1.42	22.0	251	34	76	3.96	4.3	10.1	2.4	0.8	85
2013	MLB	SEA	1	0	0	15	12	3.60	1.00	19.1	206	27	60	1.63	2.4	7.2	3.0	0.0	83

Extremely athletic SP who returned to AA to start season and dominated en route to SEA. Possesses all tools to be future ace. Improving FB command makes heater plus-plus while featuring explosive life. Can register Ks with all pitches, especially FB and SL. Holds velocity well and CU can be deceptive.

Walters,Jeffrey — RP — New York (N)

EXP MLB DEBUT: 2014 | POTENTIAL: Reliever | 7C

Thrws R Age 26
2010 (7) Georgia

91-95	FB	+++
83-85	SL	+++

Year	Lev	Team	W	L	Sv	IP	K	ERA	WHIP	BF/G	OBA	H%	S%	xERA	Ctl	Dom	Cmd	hr/9	BPV
2010	Rk	Kingsport	0	2	0	10	9	8.10	1.90	15.7	316	36	59	7.08	5.4	8.1	1.5	1.8	18
2011	A-	Brooklyn	4	6	0	65	48	3.32	1.32	19.2	253	30	75	3.42	3.3	6.6	2.0	0.4	48
2012	A	Savannah	3	2	4	28	30	0.96	0.85	6.1	202	29	88	1.18	1.3	9.6	7.5	0.0	156
2012	A+	St. Lucie	1	3	0	26	19	3.79	1.34	5.7	268	32	71	3.61	2.8	6.6	2.4	0.3	61
2013	AA	Binghamton	4	3	38	56	60	2.09	1.11	4.1	226	31	82	2.41	2.6	9.6	3.8	0.3	122

Move to bullpen in 2012 revitalized prospect status. Throws from 3/4 arm slot and can change velocity and amount of movement on his above-average FB. Follows FB with nice power SL. Nice arm action and mechanics along with mound demeanor. Has periods of iffy command, but solid most of the time.

Warner,Ryan — SP — Colorado

EXP MLB DEBUT: 2017 | POTENTIAL: #5 starter | 7D

Thrws R Age 20
2012 (3) HS (CO)

88-91	FB	+++
	CB	+++
	CU	++

Year	Lev	Team	W	L	Sv	IP	K	ERA	WHIP	BF/G	OBA	H%	S%	xERA	Ctl	Dom	Cmd	hr/9	BPV
2012	Rk	Grand Junction	3	0	0	45	36	7.00	1.69	14.5	332	37	61	6.82	2.6	7.2	2.8	1.8	77
2013	A-	Tri-City	3	4	0	88	46	3.37	1.16	23.4	241	27	70	2.87	2.3	4.7	2.0	0.4	39

Projectable righty has room to add velocity as he fills out his lanky 6-7, 195 frame. Currently has a FB that sits at 88-91 mph, topping out at 93 mph. CB has potential and good deception on his CU, but both need to be more consistent. Held his own in rookie ball, but 4.7 Dom is a red flag.

Watson,Shane — SP — Philadelphia

EXP MLB DEBUT: 2016 | POTENTIAL: #4 starter | 7D

Thrws R Age 20
2012 (1) HS (CA)

92-94	FB	+++
75-77	CB	++
80-82	CU	++

Year	Lev	Team	W	L	Sv	IP	K	ERA	WHIP	BF/G	OBA	H%	S%	xERA	Ctl	Dom	Cmd	hr/9	BPV
2012	Rk	GCL Phillies	0	1	0	7	8	1.29	0.86	5.1	202	30	83	1.18	1.3	10.3	8.0	0.0	168
2013	A	Lakewood	4	6	0	72	53	4.75	1.26	18.4	237	25	67	4.08	3.5	6.6	1.9	1.5	43

Shoulder fatigue limited him to just 16 starts in 2013, with mixed results. Features a plus fastball that sits 92-94 that he pounds inside, though command of it comes and goes. Has a big-breaking curve and fringy change-up. Athletic and fields position well. Shoulder trouble re-surfaced in the fall; a health risk at present.

Webb,Daniel — RP — Chicago (A)

EXP MLB DEBUT: 2013 | POTENTIAL: Setup reliever | 7B

Thrws R Age 24
2009 (18) NW Florida State JC

91-98	FB	++++
83-86	SL	+++
85-87	CU	+

Year	Lev	Team	W	L	Sv	IP	K	ERA	WHIP	BF/G	OBA	H%	S%	xERA	Ctl	Dom	Cmd	hr/9	BPV
2012	A	Kannapolis	1	8	3	62	50	5.81	1.61	8.9	295	36	61	4.62	3.9	7.3	1.9	0.3	43
2013	A+	Winston-Salem	1	0	2	15	19	0.00	1.00	7.2	191	30	100	1.41	3.0	11.4	3.8	0.0	142
2013	AA	Birmingham	0	0	4	20	21	1.79	0.80	5.6	163	24	75	0.59	2.2	9.4	4.2	0.0	127
2013	AAA	Charlotte	1	1	4	27	38	2.99	1.51	5.6	239	37	80	3.58	5.6	12.6	2.2	0.3	93
2013	MLB	CHW	0	0	0	11	10	3.19	1.15	5.0	220	29	69	2.16	3.2	8.0	2.5	0.0	75

Power-armed RP who pitched on four levels. Moved to bullpen in 2012 and seems to have found role. Velocity and stuff play up in short stints and has demeanor of late innings guy. Can fire FB into zone and counters with hard SL—both are out pitches. Lacks feel for changing speeds and needs to throw strikes.

Webster,Allen — SP — Boston

EXP MLB DEBUT: 2013 | POTENTIAL: #2 starter | 9D

Thrws R Age 24
2008 (18) HS (NC)

91-97	FB	++++
83-87	SL	++
73-77	CB	+++
82-84	CU	++++

Year	Lev	Team	W	L	Sv	IP	K	ERA	WHIP	BF/G	OBA	H%	S%	xERA	Ctl	Dom	Cmd	hr/9	BPV
2011	AA	Chattanooga	6	3	0	91	73	5.04	1.51	21.9	282	34	66	4.55	3.6	7.2	2.0	0.7	52
2012	AA	Chattanooga	6	8	0	121	117	3.56	1.46	19.2	260	35	73	3.52	4.2	8.7	2.1	0.1	60
2012	AA	Portland	0	1	0	9	12	8.00	1.89	21.2	339	47	56	6.65	4.0	12.0	3.0	1.0	126
2013	AAA	Pawtucket	8	4	0	105	116	3.60	1.09	19.5	193	26	69	2.39	3.7	9.9	2.7	0.8	97
2013	MLB	BOS	1	2	0	30	23	8.61	1.82	17.6	302	32	54	6.93	5.3	6.8	1.3	2.1	-3

Athletic, durable RHP who fared well in minors but had horrendous time with BOS in 7 starts. Overall stuff is impressive, led by plus FB and sinking CU. Both breaking balls have moments, though hard SL is inconsistent. Despite CU, has trouble with LHH. When on, can be tough to hit and can post high K rates.

Weickel,Walker — SP — San Diego

EXP MLB DEBUT: 2016 | POTENTIAL: #3 starter | 8D

Thrws R Age 20
2012 (1) HS (FL)

89-95	FB	+++
	CB	+++
	CU	++

Year	Lev	Team	W	L	Sv	IP	K	ERA	WHIP	BF/G	OBA	H%	S%	xERA	Ctl	Dom	Cmd	hr/9	BPV
2012	Rk	AZL Padres	1	3	0	14	12	4.50	1.57	6.8	288	37	68	4.15	3.9	7.7	2.0	0.0	53
2013	A	Fort Wayne	3	6	0	110	82	5.06	1.52	19.9	287	34	66	4.63	3.5	6.7	1.9	0.7	44

Tall and lean starter who uses height well. Has been too hittable, but has upside and projection. Pitches downhill with sinking FB and keeps ball on ground. Could grow into three average to above-average offerings, but needs polish and fine-tuning. Lacks deception in delivery and can be inconsistent.

Welker,Duke — RP — Pittsburgh

EXP MLB DEBUT: 2013 | POTENTIAL: Setup reliever | 7D

Thrws R Age 28
2007 (2) Arkansas

92-96	FB	+++
83-85	SL	+++
81-84	CU	+

Year	Lev	Team	W	L	Sv	IP	K	ERA	WHIP	BF/G	OBA	H%	S%	xERA	Ctl	Dom	Cmd	hr/9	BPV
2011	AA	Altoona	1	0	0	10	9	5.40	1.20	5.0	281	36	50	3.09	0.9	8.1	9.0	0.0	140
2012	AA	Altoona	2	1	5	23	19	2.34	1.13	6.1	226	29	77	2.18	2.7	7.4	2.7	0.0	78
2012	AAA	Indianapolis	0	1	0	31	30	2.31	1.35	5.0	214	28	83	2.85	5.2	8.7	1.7	0.3	34
2013	AAA	Indianapolis	3	4	9	63	65	3.57	1.33	5.5	230	31	73	3.13	4.4	9.3	2.1	0.4	66
2013	MLB	PIT	0	0	0	1	1	0.00	0.00	1.8	0	0	100	0.00	0.0	6.9		0.0	143

Tall, durable RHP who has been RP since 2009. Establishes plate with hard, heavy FB and complements with hard SL that features late bite. Mostly two-pitch guy, but has increased K rate and becoming more effective against LHH. Keeps ball down and has been tough to hit. Needs to address control problems.

Wells,Benjamin — SP — Chicago (N)

EXP MLB DEBUT: 2015 | POTENTIAL: #4 starter | 6C

Thrws R Age 21
2010 (7) HS (AR)

88-92	FB	+++
	CB	++
	CU	++

Year	Lev	Team	W	L	Sv	IP	K	ERA	WHIP	BF/G	OBA	H%	S%	xERA	Ctl	Dom	Cmd	hr/9	BPV
2011	A-	Boise	4	4	0	77	53	4.67	1.32	20.0	276	32	63	3.80	2.2	6.2	2.8	0.5	69
2012	Rk	AZL Cubs	0	0	0	1	3	0.00	1.00	3.8	0	0	100	0.00	9.0	27.0	3.0	0.0	261
2012	A	Peoria	3	2	1	44	36	3.27	1.36	15.3	279	35	73	3.49	2.5	7.4	3.0	0.0	84
2013	A+	Daytona	9	6	0	112	69	3.29	1.21	19.7	233	26	74	3.03	3.2	5.5	1.7	0.6	31

Strong RH uses heavy 90-93 mph sinking FB that tops out at 94. Logged a career high in IP and held up well. Drop in Dom makes success at the big league level a question. Secondary offerings are not advanced. CB and CU both need work, but has clean, repeatable mechanics. Could be moved to relief.

West,Aaron — SP — Houston

EXP MLB DEBUT: 2015 | POTENTIAL: #5 starter | 6B

Thrws R Age 24
2012 (17) Washington

89-95	FB	+++
80-82	SL	++
79-82	CU	+++

Year	Lev	Team	W	L	Sv	IP	K	ERA	WHIP	BF/G	OBA	H%	S%	xERA	Ctl	Dom	Cmd	hr/9	BPV
2010	NCAA	Washington	0	1	0	9	7	9.00	2.44	11.8	371	35	76	12.45	7.0	7.0	1.0	5.0	-45
2011	NCAA	Washington	1	8	0	73	44	5.18	1.48	19.6	304	34	65	4.87	2.2	5.4	2.4	0.7	56
2012	NCAA	Washington	7	5	1	96	65	2.53	1.11	22.2	247	30	76	2.62	1.7	6.1	3.6	0.2	82
2012	A-	Tri City	6	2	0	61	59	2.06	0.96	19.3	225	29	80	2.16	1.3	8.7	6.6	0.4	138
2013	A+	Lancaster	10	8	0	108	112	5.24	1.40	17.5	305	40	61	4.49	1.4	9.3	6.6	0.6	148

Durable SP who possesses clean delivery and ability to locate FB. Induces fair share of GB and keeps hitters off-balance with solid CU. Repeats arm speed which gives him hint of deception, but can be guilty of sitting in middle of plate. K rate not likely to last without better SL, but maintains and holds velocity.

Whalen,Bob — SP — New York (N)

EXP MLB DEBUT: 2017 | POTENTIAL: #5 starter/reliever | 6C

Thrws R Age 20
2012 (12) HS (FL)

91-93	FB	+++
77-79	CB	++
	SL	++
	CU	++

Year	Lev	Team	W	L	Sv	IP	K	ERA	WHIP	BF/G	OBA	H%	S%	xERA	Ctl	Dom	Cmd	hr/9	BPV
2013	Rk	Kingsport	3	2	0	72	76	1.87	0.93	22.5	197	28	79	1.44	2.1	9.5	4.5	0.1	131

Strong-framed pitcher throws lots of strikes and gets lots of groundball outs. Excellent debut after fixing mechanical flaws. Everything works off his sinking FB with plus movement. Comfortable throwing any pitch in any count, but not much projection left, and won't strike out as many hitters at higher levels.

Whiting,Boone — SP — St. Louis

EXP MLB DEBUT: 2014 | POTENTIAL: #4 starter/reliever | 7D

Thrws R Age 24
2010 (18) Centenary

86-91	FB	++
81-83	SL	++
	CU	++

Year	Lev	Team	W	L	Sv	IP	K	ERA	WHIP	BF/G	OBA	H%	S%	xERA	Ctl	Dom	Cmd	hr/9	BPV
2012	Rk	GCL Cardinals	0	0	0	7	11	7.71	1.57	7.7	336	51	50	6.05	1.3	14.1	11.0	1.3	238
2012	A	Quad Cities	1	0	0	16	14	0.56	0.50	17.7	134	18	88	0.00	0.6	7.9	14.0	0.0	145
2012	AA	Springfield	0	0	0	12	9	1.50	1.17	23.9	245	31	86	2.54	2.3	6.8	3.0	0.0	79
2013	AA	Springfield	3	2	0	30	34	2.98	1.16	20.0	247	34	76	3.07	2.1	10.1	4.9	0.6	144
2013	AAA	Memphis	5	5	0	105	99	4.11	1.40	21.1	265	33	73	4.25	3.4	8.5	2.5	0.9	78

Short RH competes well even without an overpowering FB. High 3/4 delivery and features a 87-91 mph FB that tops out at 92. Also has a decent 81-83 mph SL and a good CU that gives him a chance to succeed. Best weapon is that he throws tons of strikes and could help out at the back end of a rotation.

Wieland,Joe
SP | **San Diego** | EXP MLB DEBUT: 2012 | POTENTIAL: #3 starter | **8B**

Thrws R Age 24
2008 (4) HS (NV)

88-93	FB	+++
80-83	CB	+++
79-82	CU	+++

Year	Lev	Team	W	L	Sv	IP	K	ERA	WHIP	BF/G	OBA	H%	S%	xERA	Ctl	Dom	Cmd	hr/9	BPV
2011	A+	Myrtle Beach	6	3	0	85	96	2.11	0.96	23.0	245	33	83	2.68	0.4	10.1	24.0	0.7	189
2011	AA	Frisco	4	0	0	44	36	1.23	1.05	24.3	220	27	91	2.29	2.3	7.4	3.3	0.4	90
2011	AA	San Antonio	3	1	0	26	18	2.77	1.12	20.5	239	29	72	2.33	2.1	6.2	3.0	0.0	74
2012	AAA	Tucson	0	1	0	7	11	3.75	1.67	16.2	330	52	75	4.98	2.5	13.8	5.5	0.0	198
2012	MLB	SD	0	4	0	28	24	4.55	1.26	22.6	250	28	70	4.36	2.9	7.8	2.7	1.6	79

Tall and command-oriented starter who missed entire season due to TJ surgery and setbacks. Reached SD in 2012 based upon polished pitch sequencing and control. Sets up secondary pitches well with quality FB that he locates to all quadrants. Big CB can register Ks while CU can be good.

Williams,Devin
SP | **Milwaukee** | EXP MLB DEBUT: 2016 | POTENTIAL: #2 starter | **8E**

Thrws R Age 19
2013 (2) HS (MO)

88-95	FB	++++
	CB	+++
	CU	+++

Year	Lev	Team	W	L	Sv	IP	K	ERA	WHIP	BF/G	OBA	H%	S%	xERA	Ctl	Dom	Cmd	hr/9	BPV
2013	Rk	AZL Brewers	1	3	1	34	39	3.42	1.46	11.3	225	33	74	2.99	5.8	10.3	1.8	0.0	46

Tall, lanky RH with raw pitching ability. Uses a four-seam and two-seam that ranges from 88-95 with the potential for more as he grows into his small frame. Complements it with a CB and CU that both flash plus, but remain inconsistent. Mechanics have led to less than stellar Cmd and Ctl, but remain a work in progress.

Williams,Trevor
SP | **Miami** | EXP MLB DEBUT: 2016 | POTENTIAL: #4 starter | **7C**

Thrws R Age 22
2013 (2) Arizona State

90-95	FB	++++
77-80	CU	++++
83-85	SL	+++
	CB	+++

Year	Lev	Team	W	L	Sv	IP	K	ERA	WHIP	BF/G	OBA	H%	S%	xERA	Ctl	Dom	Cmd	hr/9	BPV
2012	NCAA	Arizona St.	11	2	0	101	55	1.87	0.90	25.1	219	24	83	2.13	1.0	4.9	5.0	0.6	80
2013	NCAA	Arizona St.	6	6	0	111	81	4.13	1.35	29.0	284	34	67	3.68	2.1	6.6	3.1	0.2	79
2013	Rk	GCL Marlins	0	0	0	2	1	4.50	1.50	8.6	347	39	67	4.95	0.0	4.5		0.0	99
2013	A-	Batavia	0	2	0	29	20	2.48	1.17	11.6	241	30	76	2.50	2.5	6.2	2.5	0.0	63
2013	A	Greensboro	0	0	0	3	3	0.00	0.67	10.5	191	27	100	0.59	0.0	9.0		0.0	180

Big, durable SP with good four-pitch arsenal. FB sits in the low-90s and he complements it with a plus CU with great fading action, a SL and a CB both of which flash average. Has good control of pitches and commands them. He is not a big strikeout pitcher, but with good pitchability he knows how to get hitters out.

Wilson,Tyler
SP | **Baltimore** | EXP MLB DEBUT: 2015 | POTENTIAL: #5 starter | **6B**

Thrws R Age 24
2011 (10) Virginia

87-91	FB	+++
80-82	SL	+++
81-83	CU	++

Year	Lev	Team	W	L	Sv	IP	K	ERA	WHIP	BF/G	OBA	H%	S%	xERA	Ctl	Dom	Cmd	hr/9	BPV
2011	A-	Aberdeen	0	0	0	30	24	2.10	0.77	17.9	183	20	84	1.90	1.2	7.2	6.0	1.2	115
2012	A	Delmarva	3	3	0	32	29	5.06	1.28	21.9	250	30	62	3.92	3.1	8.2	2.6	1.1	81
2012	A+	Frederick	7	7	0	111	114	3.49	1.03	22.5	233	29	70	2.91	1.5	9.2	6.0	1.0	143
2013	A+	Frederick	1	1	0	62	48	4.49	1.32	23.4	246	29	65	3.47	3.6	7.0	1.9	0.6	45
2013	AA	Bowie	7	5	0	89	70	3.84	1.20	22.4	253	28	73	3.95	2.2	7.1	3.2	1.3	85

Athletic RHP who is developing quickly and finding success thanks to excellent command. FB velocity is a little short and lacks upside, but spots pitches and repeats delivery and slot. Inconsistent CU limits effectiveness against LHH and has more of #5 profile. Keeps ball down and has durability and stamina.

Windle,Tom
SP | **Los Angeles (N)** | EXP MLB DEBUT: 2016 | POTENTIAL: #4 starter | **7C**

Thrws L Age 22
2013 (2) Minnesota

90-92	FB	+++
81-84	SL	++
80-82	CU	+++

Year	Lev	Team	W	L	Sv	IP	K	ERA	WHIP	BF/G	OBA	H%	S%	xERA	Ctl	Dom	Cmd	hr/9	BPV
2011	NCAA	Minnesota	6	2	2	41	35	1.53	1.12	8.5	232	30	87	2.44	2.4	7.7	3.2	0.2	91
2012	NCAA	Minnesota	3	5	1	41	37	3.28	1.29	9.4	237	29	76	3.34	3.7	8.1	2.2	0.7	63
2013	NCAA	Minnesota	6	4	0	92	86	2.15	1.12	25.9	212	28	80	2.16	3.2	8.4	2.6	0.2	82
2013	A	Great Lakes	5	1	0	53	51	2.71	1.32	16.9	250	33	79	3.27	3.4	8.6	2.6	0.3	82

Tall, slender LHP shows plus command and strong pitchability, generating lots of ground balls. Generates good downhill plane, pounding the zone with his low-90s FB, inconsistent SL, and solid CU. Stiffness in delivery lead to speculation of a RP role, but solid Ctl and Cmd will keep in the rotation for now.

Winiarski,Cody
RP | **Chicago (A)** | EXP MLB DEBUT: 2015 | POTENTIAL: Middle reliever | **6B**

Thrws R Age 24
2011 (36) Virginia

87-91	FB	+++
80-85	SL	++
81-83	CU	++++

Year	Lev	Team	W	L	Sv	IP	K	ERA	WHIP	BF/G	OBA	H%	S%	xERA	Ctl	Dom	Cmd	hr/9	BPV
2010	NCAA	Virginia	5	0	0	75	44	4.68	1.45	18.9	279	29	72	5.10	3.2	5.3	1.6	1.4	26
2011	NCAA	Virginia	6	4	1	77	58	2.92	1.08	15.8	216	27	71	2.06	2.7	6.8	2.5	0.1	67
2011	Rk	Great Falls	1	1	2	20	29	1.80	1.05	4.6	232	38	81	2.00	1.8	13.1	7.3	0.0	204
2013	A+	Winston-Salem	0	2	10	55	67	2.93	1.34	6.4	239	34	79	3.32	4.1	10.9	2.7	0.5	105
2013	AA	Birmingham	1	0	3	11	18	0.00	0.64	4.8	139	28	100	0.00	1.6	14.7	9.0	0.0	239

Lean RP who didn't allow ER after promotion to AA. Relies more on command and pitchability as he lacks natural stuff. CU can be good at times and keeps hitters at bay. Has deception and throws across body, but spots ball well. FB is average at best and lack of breaking ball keeps him out of future late innings role.

Winkler,Danny
SP | **Colorado** | EXP MLB DEBUT: 2015 | POTENTIAL: #3 starter | **7C**

Thrws R Age 24
2011 (20) Central Florida

89-93	FB	+++
80-82	SL	++++
	CU	++

Year	Lev	Team	W	L	Sv	IP	K	ERA	WHIP	BF/G	OBA	H%	S%	xERA	Ctl	Dom	Cmd	hr/9	BPV
2011	NCAA	Central Florida	3	4	0	82	92	4.71	1.33	18.9	269	37	62	3.53	2.6	10.1	3.8	0.3	128
2011	Rk	Casper	4	3	0	57	65	3.94	1.45	20.3	284	38	75	4.66	3.0	10.2	3.4	0.9	122
2012	A	Asheville	11	10	0	145	136	4.47	1.37	24.3	271	33	69	4.32	2.9	8.4	2.9	1.0	91
2013	A+	Modesto	12	5	0	130	152	2.97	0.93	22.2	186	24	74	2.16	2.6	10.5	4.1	1.0	138
2013	AA	Tulsa	1	2	0	26	23	3.09	1.26	21.4	237	28	80	3.62	3.4	7.9	2.3	1.0	67

Short righty attacks hitters with a 91-93 mph FB and a plus SL. Keeps the ball down in the zone and gets swings and misses with SL. Thrived in the hitter-friendly CAL with a 2.97 ERA and 4.1 Cmd. Production raises his profile to a mid-rotation candidate with good control and the ability to mss bats.

Wiper,Cole
SP | **Texas** | EXP MLB DEBUT: 2017 | POTENTIAL: #4 starter | **7C**

Thrws R Age 22
2013 (10) Oregon

89-95	FB	+++
77-80	CB	+++
80-83	SL	++
82-84	CU	++

Year	Lev	Team	W	L	Sv	IP	K	ERA	WHIP	BF/G	OBA	H%	S%	xERA	Ctl	Dom	Cmd	hr/9	BPV
2013	NCAA	Oregon	2	1	0	12	4	7.38	2.38	9.1	356	37	68	8.02	7.4	3.0	0.4	0.7	-128
2013	Rk	AZL Rangers	3	1	0	25	26	2.15	1.16	10.0	229	32	79	2.27	2.9	9.3	3.3	0.0	108

Tall, thin SP who was potent with command of four pitches. Throws consistent strikes with good angle to plate. FB sets tone early in count and can effectively mix in 2 breaking balls and CU that has potential to be solid. Has tendency to slow arm speed and lower slot for CU. Velocity could increase with cleaner arm.

Wisler,Matt
SP | **San Diego** | EXP MLB DEBUT: 2015 | POTENTIAL: #3 starter | **8C**

Thrws R Age 21
2011 (7) HS (OH)

90-95	FB	+++
82-85	SL	+++
74-76	CB	+++
	CU	++

Year	Lev	Team	W	L	Sv	IP	K	ERA	WHIP	BF/G	OBA	H%	S%	xERA	Ctl	Dom	Cmd	hr/9	BPV
2011	Rk	AZL Padres	0	0	0	0	0			4.0							0.0		
2012	A	Fort Wayne	5	4	0	114	113	2.53	1.08	18.5	228	31	75	2.15	2.2	8.9	4.0	0.1	119
2013	A+	Lake Elsinore	2	1	0	31	28	2.03	0.90	19.2	201	26	78	1.58	1.7	8.1	4.7	0.3	117
2013	AA	San Antonio	8	5	0	105	103	3.00	1.07	20.4	223	29	73	2.54	2.3	8.8	3.8	0.6	114

Tall and athletic starter who continues to evolve into top prospect. Has feel for pitching by spotting FB impeccably and using two breaking balls to keep hitters off-guard. SL misses bats on any level and CU improving steadily. Throws easy strikes despite pitch movement, but hasn't fared well against LHH.

Wittgren,Nick
RP | **Miami** | EXP MLB DEBUT: 2015 | POTENTIAL: Setup reliever | **7B**

Thrws R Age 23
2012 (9) Purdue

89-93	FB	++++
	CB	+++

Year	Lev	Team	W	L	Sv	IP	K	ERA	WHIP	BF/G	OBA	H%	S%	xERA	Ctl	Dom	Cmd	hr/9	BPV
2012	NCAA	Purdue	3	0	10	41	39	1.76	1.15	6.3	232	31	83	2.30	2.6	8.6	3.3	0.0	101
2012	A-	Jamestown	0	2	11	24	34	1.49	1.16	5.7	260	41	86	2.65	1.5	12.6	8.5	0.0	205
2012	A	Greensboro	0	0	2	6	13	0.00	0.33	3.2	56	20	100	0.00	1.5	19.5	13.0	0.0	329
2013	A+	Jupiter	2	1	25	54	59	0.83	0.96	4.3	216	30	92	1.77	1.7	9.8	5.9	0.2	150
2013	AA	Jacksonville	0	0	1	4	4	0.00	0.00	2.8	0	0	100	0.00	0.0	9.0		0.0	180

Big, athletic RP continues to display plus Cmd and Ctl in CL role. Lacks plus velocity, but attacks hitters with deceptive, low-90s FB and good power CB. Commands both pitches with ease and while he does not overpower hitters, his deceptive, repeatable mechanics have allowed him to be elite in Dom, Ctl, and Cmd.

Wojciechowski,Asher
SP | **Houston** | EXP MLB DEBUT: 2014 | POTENTIAL: #4 starter | **7C**

Thrws R Age 25
2010 (1-S) The Citadel

89-94	FB	+++
80-85	SL	+++
81-84	CB	+++
	CU	++

Year	Lev	Team	W	L	Sv	IP	K	ERA	WHIP	BF/G	OBA	H%	S%	xERA	Ctl	Dom	Cmd	hr/9	BPV
2011	A+	Dunedin	11	9	0	130	96	4.70	1.44	22.2	298	34	69	4.94	2.1	6.6	3.1	1.0	80
2012	A+	Dunedin	7	3	0	93	76	3.58	1.21	20.9	257	32	69	3.08	2.1	7.3	3.5	0.3	93
2012	AA	Corpus Christi	2	2	0	43	34	2.08	1.02	20.7	198	25	77	1.57	2.9	7.1	2.4	0.0	67
2013	AA	Corpus Christi	2	1	1	26	27	2.08	0.92	16.2	188	26	78	1.52	2.4	9.3	3.9	0.3	121
2013	AAA	Oklahoma City	9	7	0	134	104	3.56	1.19	24.4	235	28	71	3.10	3.0	7.0	2.4	0.7	64

Tall, durable SP who can be tough to hit with excellent FB with natural cutting action. K rate has fallen last few seasons and is learning to become more efficient by inducing weak contact. Likes to power ball by hitters and has nasty SL at times. Developing feel for below average CU and is key to future success.

Wood,Austin — SP — Los Angeles (A)

EXP MLB DEBUT: 2015 | POTENTIAL: #3 starter | **8E**

Thrws R Age 23 | 2011 (6) USC

Velo	Pitch	Grade
91-97	FB	++++
81-83	SL	+++
80-82	CU	++

Year	Lev	Team	W	L	Sv	IP	K	ERA	WHIP	BF/G	OBA	H%	S%	xERA	Ctl	Dom	Cmd	hr/9	BPV
2011	NCAA	USC	5	7	0	77	50	5.61	1.61	21.3	293	34	62	4.55	4.0	5.8	1.5	0.2	16
2011	Rk	Orem	0	0	0	1	1	24.55	3.64	3.6	563	59	33	23.66	0.0	8.2		8.2	165
2012	A	Cedar Rapids	5	12	0	127	109	4.32	1.55	21.4	258	33	70	3.93	5.1	7.7	1.5	0.3	19
2013	Rk	AZL Angels	0	0	0	4	4	2.20	1.95	9.8	257	35	88	4.65	8.8	8.8	1.0	0.0	-61
2013	A+	Inland Empire	0	3	0	21	18	4.25	1.75	19.4	295	36	75	5.08	5.1	7.6	1.5	0.4	18

Tall, athletic SP who missed most of season with arm ailment. Attempted to return in July, but quickly shelved again. Has quality stuff, highlighted by plus FB. Power SL can act as out pitch and has some feel for CU. FB can be flat at higher velocities and often pitches behind in count. Needs pitch for LHH.

Wright,Austin — SP — Philadelphia

EXP MLB DEBUT: 2014 | POTENTIAL: Reliever | **6B**

Thrws L Age 24 | 2011 (8) Mississippi

Velo	Pitch	Grade
91-93	FB	+++
75-77	CB	++
82-83	CU	++

Year	Lev	Team	W	L	Sv	IP	K	ERA	WHIP	BF/G	OBA	H%	S%	xERA	Ctl	Dom	Cmd	hr/9	BPV
2011	NCAA	Mississippi	5	4	0	70	67	4.75	1.48	21.5	286	36	68	4.48	3.2	8.6	2.7	0.6	86
2011	A-	Williamsport	3	1	0	34	44	3.42	1.26	17.4	237	36	71	2.86	3.4	11.6	3.4	0.3	134
2011	A	Lakewood	1	2	0	33	41	2.71	1.14	18.8	236	34	78	2.83	2.4	11.1	4.6	0.5	152
2012	A+	Clearwater	11	5	0	147	133	3.49	1.41	23.0	262	33	77	3.98	3.7	8.1	2.2	0.7	65
2013	AA	Reading	6	5	0	94	77	5.93	1.59	15.4	255	29	64	4.91	5.6	7.4	1.3	1.2	-2

Quick rise was slowed by shoulder problems in 2013, but seemed to take well to a mid-season switch to relief work. Gets good number of strikeouts, in part due to quirky delivery that looks rushed. Could be a multi-inning reliever if he's able to keep walks in check.

Wright,Mike — SP — Baltimore

EXP MLB DEBUT: 2015 | POTENTIAL: #3 starter | **8D**

Thrws R Age 24 | 2011 (3) East Carolina

Velo	Pitch	Grade
89-94	FB	+++
82-85	SL	+++
	CU	++

Year	Lev	Team	W	L	Sv	IP	K	ERA	WHIP	BF/G	OBA	H%	S%	xERA	Ctl	Dom	Cmd	hr/9	BPV
2011	A	Delmarva	1	1	0	13	12	10.91	1.89	15.6	361	42	41	8.07	2.7	8.2	3.0	2.0	92
2012	A+	Frederick	5	2	0	46	35	2.93	1.13	22.8	266	32	76	3.26	1.0	6.8	7.0	0.6	115
2012	AA	Bowie	5	3	0	62	45	4.93	1.42	21.9	288	33	67	4.72	2.5	6.5	2.6	1.0	69
2013	AA	Bowie	11	3	0	143	136	3.27	1.33	22.9	273	35	76	3.86	2.5	8.5	3.5	0.6	106
2013	AAA	Norfolk	0	0	0	6	2	0.00	0.97	23.5	255	28	100	2.21	0.0	2.9		0.0	70

Tall, durable starter who led EL in ERA. Had breakout in last 2 months and continues to show improvement with K rate and control. Lacks true out pitch, but sequences pitches while maintaining velocity. SL can be solid and consistent, and CU has potential. Throws strikes and profiles as mid-rotation guy.

Yambati,Robinson — RP — Kansas City

EXP MLB DEBUT: 2016 | POTENTIAL: Setup reliever | **7E**

Thrws R Age 23 | 2008 FA (DR)

Velo	Pitch	Grade
90-96	FB	++++
80-82	SL	++
	CU	++

Year	Lev	Team	W	L	Sv	IP	K	ERA	WHIP	BF/G	OBA	H%	S%	xERA	Ctl	Dom	Cmd	hr/9	BPV
2010	Rk	AZL Royals	8	2	0	66	64	2.72	1.16	18.8	259	35	74	2.69	1.6	8.7	5.3	0.0	131
2011	Rk	Burlington	0	5	0	17	9	19.36	3.20	12.9	476	49	37	14.98	5.8	4.7	0.8	3.1	-53
2012	A	Kane County	2	1	2	44	33	3.26	1.29	11.4	243	30	73	3.01	3.5	6.7	1.9	0.2	45
2012	A+	Wilmington	2	1	5	25	31	2.16	1.28	6.0	238	36	81	2.68	3.6	11.2	3.1	0.0	122
2013	A+	Wilmington	0	1	3	35	42	3.85	1.45	6.0	250	35	73	3.76	4.6	10.8	2.3	0.5	87

Tall, lean RHP whose season ended in July due to elbow injury. Converted to RP in 2012 and saw K rate increase. Pitches off explosive FB, but hasn't mastered reliable secondary. SL can be average and can be very tough against RHH (.174 oppBA). Inconsistent delivery hinders command and needs to throw more strikes.

Ybarra,Tyler — RP — Toronto

EXP MLB DEBUT: 2014 | POTENTIAL: Setup reliever | **6A**

Thrws L Age 24 | 2008 (43) HS (KS)

Velo	Pitch	Grade
90-95	FB	++++
81-83	SL	+++
80-82	CU	+

Year	Lev	Team	W	L	Sv	IP	K	ERA	WHIP	BF/G	OBA	H%	S%	xERA	Ctl	Dom	Cmd	hr/9	BPV
2009	Rk	GCL Blue Jays	2	4	0	20	11	6.72	1.94	6.0	338	38	63	6.32	4.5	4.9	1.1	0.4	-14
2011	Rk	Bluefield	2	0	0	46	54	2.15	1.09	12.8	208	30	81	2.19	3.1	10.6	3.4	0.4	124
2012	A	Lansing	3	2	2	43	57	2.29	1.48	7.1	238	36	85	3.57	5.4	11.9	2.2	0.4	86
2013	A+	Dunedin	2	3	2	55	65	1.96	1.14	5.6	162	25	81	1.45	5.4	10.6	2.0	0.0	64

Underpublicized lefty RP who rarely allows HR and induces ton of GB. LHH hit only .133 against him and he has arm slot and lively FB to be effective against RHH as well. Must throw strikes in order to be trusted in late innings and has potential to have potent FB/SL combo. Deceptive delivery adds to intrigue.

Ynoa,Gabriel — SP — New York (N)

EXP MLB DEBUT: 2016 | POTENTIAL: #3 starter | **7C**

Thrws R Age 21 | 2010 FA (DR)

Velo	Pitch	Grade
91-92	FB	+++
80-82	CB	++
	CU	++++

Year	Lev	Team	W	L	Sv	IP	K	ERA	WHIP	BF/G	OBA	H%	S%	xERA	Ctl	Dom	Cmd	hr/9	BPV
2011	Rk	GCL Mets	2	3	0	48	21	3.00	1.15	19.0	274	30	72	3.08	0.8	3.9	5.3	0.2	69
2011	Rk	Kingsport	0	0	1	8	6	4.50	0.75	14.3	210	11	100	5.27	0.0	6.8		4.5	140
2012	A-	Brooklyn	5	2	0	76	64	2.24	0.93	22.0	221	28	74	1.74	1.2	7.6	6.4	0.1	122
2013	A	Savannah	15	4	0	135	106	2.73	1.03	23.6	244	29	75	2.73	1.1	7.1	6.6	0.6	116

SAL Pitcher of the Year walked only 16 batters in 135.2 IP at Low-A. Exhibits nice poise and mound demeanor. Excellent plus CU and throws lots of strikes with a smooth delivery. Success at higher levels may be challenging without elite velo on FB and below-average breaking ball.

Ynoa,Michael — SP — Oakland

EXP MLB DEBUT: 2016 | POTENTIAL: #3 starter | **8D**

Thrws R Age 22 | 2008 FA (DR)

Velo	Pitch	Grade
90-95	FB	++++
79-82	CB	+++
81-83	CU	++

Year	Lev	Team	W	L	Sv	IP	K	ERA	WHIP	BF/G	OBA	H%	S%	xERA	Ctl	Dom	Cmd	hr/9	BPV
2010	Rk	AZL Athletics	0	1	0	9	11	5.00	1.11	11.8	191	26	56	2.63	4.0	11.0	2.8	1.0	108
2012	Rk	AZL Athletics	0	1	0	10	6	5.40	2.00	8.0	281	31	74	5.98	8.1	5.4	0.7	0.9	-104
2012	A-	Vermont	1	3	0	20	19	7.13	1.78	11.6	260	32	59	5.10	7.1	8.5	1.2	0.9	-22
2013	A	Beloit	2	1	0	54	48	2.16	1.16	14.4	227	29	83	2.75	3.0	8.0	2.7	0.5	81
2013	A+	Stockton	1	2	1	21	20	7.71	1.90	14.2	280	35	58	5.66	7.3	8.6	1.2	0.9	-24

Thin, projectable SP who appeared in Futures Game, but fell apart in High-A. Smooth arm could lead to more velocity and present FB is plus pitch already. Throws downhill and mixes in sharp CB. Has trouble repeating mechanics and arm slot varies. FB command needs attention along with subpar CU.

Zastryzny,Rob — SP — Chicago (N)

EXP MLB DEBUT: 2016 | POTENTIAL: #3 starter | **7C**

Thrws L Age 22 | 2013 (2) Missouri

Velo	Pitch	Grade
90-93	FB	+++
80-83	SL	+++
	CB	++

Year	Lev	Team	W	L	Sv	IP	K	ERA	WHIP	BF/G	OBA	H%	S%	xERA	Ctl	Dom	Cmd	hr/9	BPV
2011	NCAA	Missouri	0	1	0	10	6	3.53	1.47	21.9	277	33	73	3.75	3.5	5.3	1.5	0.0	18
2012	NCAA	Missouri	5	5	0	109	76	3.80	1.28	26.3	262	31	69	3.37	2.6	6.3	2.5	0.3	62
2013	NCAA	Missouri	2	9	0	90	82	3.39	1.30	28.6	268	33	78	4.09	2.4	8.2	3.4	1.0	101
2013	A-	Boise	0	0	0	14	16	3.19	1.35	7.3	274	39	74	3.35	2.6	10.2	4.0	0.0	133
2013	A	Kane County	1	0	0	9	6	0.98	1.41	13.0	258	31	92	3.33	3.9	5.9	1.5	0.0	18

Polished collegiate lefty was 2nd round pick. Lacks premium velocity and FB sits at 88-92 mph with good sink. Also has a good CU and a usable breaking ball. Tends to locate all three offerings and showed good control in college. He's athletic, works quickly, and has simple and repeatable mechanics.

Zimmer,Kyle — SP — Kansas City

EXP MLB DEBUT: 2014 | POTENTIAL: #1 starter | **9B**

Thrws R Age 22 | 2012 (1) San Francisco

Velo	Pitch	Grade
92-97	FB	++++
80-81	CB	++++
82-84	SL	+++
83-85	CU	+++

Year	Lev	Team	W	L	Sv	IP	K	ERA	WHIP	BF/G	OBA	H%	S%	xERA	Ctl	Dom	Cmd	hr/9	BPV
2012	NCAA	San Francisco	5	3	0	88	104	2.86	1.04	26.2	232	33	72	2.30	1.7	10.6	6.1	0.3	162
2012	Rk	AZL Royals	1	0	0	10	13	0.90	0.50	11.1	151	25	80	0.00	0.0	11.7		0.0	229
2012	A	Kane County	2	3	0	29	29	2.47	1.44	20.7	292	38	83	4.15	2.5	8.9	3.6	0.3	112
2013	A+	Wilmington	4	8	0	89	113	4.84	1.24	20.1	241	34	62	3.49	3.1	11.4	3.6	0.9	139
2013	AA	NW Arkansas	2	1	0	18	27	1.98	0.88	16.8	176	27	86	1.85	2.5	13.4	5.4	1.0	192

Powerful hurler who has #1 starter potential. Ended season on hot streak and has arsenal to be dominant. FB provides velocity and movement while knockout SL and big-breaking CB are potent offerings. Still learning to sequence pitches, but does good job of repeating athletic delivery and arm slot.

Ziomek,Kevin — SP — Detroit

EXP MLB DEBUT: 2016 | POTENTIAL: #4 starter | **7D**

Thrws L Age 22 | 2013 (2) Vanderbilt

Velo	Pitch	Grade
89-94	FB	+++
78-83	SL	+++
	CU	++

Year	Lev	Team	W	L	Sv	IP	K	ERA	WHIP	BF/G	OBA	H%	S%	xERA	Ctl	Dom	Cmd	hr/9	BPV
2011	NCAA	Vanderbilt	3	0	1	45	47	1.60	1.09	6.5	206	29	85	2.00	3.2	9.4	2.9	0.2	101
2012	NCAA	Vanderbilt	5	6	0	79	79	5.23	1.49	18.0	262	33	65	4.30	4.4	9.0	2.0	0.8	60
2013	NCAA	Vanderbilt	11	3	0	119	115	2.12	1.00	26.7	191	26	78	1.64	3.0	8.7	2.9	0.2	93
2013	A-	Connecticut	0	1	0	8	3	4.50	1.25	8.1	181	20	60	2.01	5.6	3.4	0.6	0.0	-73

Advanced and athletic lefty who throws with clean arm action and deceptive mechanics. FB looks quicker than velocity shows and hitters have trouble picking up out of hand. Throws strikes with all pitches despite throwing across body. CU developing into average offering, but lacks out pitch against RHH.

Zych,Tony — RP — Chicago (N)

EXP MLB DEBUT: 2014 | POTENTIAL: Possible closer | **7C**

Thrws R Age 23 | 2011 (4) Louisville

Velo	Pitch	Grade
94-97	FB	++++
83-85	SL	+++

Year	Lev	Team	W	L	Sv	IP	K	ERA	WHIP	BF/G	OBA	H%	S%	xERA	Ctl	Dom	Cmd	hr/9	BPV
2011	Rk	AZL Cubs	0	0	0	2	3	4.50	1.50	4.3	262	43	67	3.53	4.5	13.5	3.0	0.0	140
2011	A-	Boise	0	0	0	2	2	0.00	0.50	3.3	0	0	100	0.00	4.5	9.0	2.0	0.0	59
2012	A+	Daytona	3	3	6	36	36	3.23	1.08	5.2	239	33	67	2.20	1.7	9.0	5.1	0.0	132
2012	AA	Tennessee	2	1	0	24	28	4.46	1.57	5.3	276	38	70	4.28	4.5	10.4	2.3	0.4	85
2013	AA	Tennessee	5	5	3	56	40	3.05	1.29	4.9	244	29	76	3.13	3.4	6.4	1.9	0.3	43

Tall, athletic reliever has a plus 94-97 mph FB and a good SL. Throws from a low 3/4 slot adding some deception and good movement. Held his own in repeat of Double-A, but dominance drop is a slight concern. Still has the stuff and velo to move into a closer role down the road.

MAJOR LEAGUE EQUIVALENTS

In his 1985 *Baseball Abstract,* Bill James introduced the concept of major league equivalencies. His assertion was that, with the proper adjustments, a minor leaguer's statistics could be converted to an equivalent major league level performance with a great deal of accuracy.

Because of wide variations in the level of play among different minor leagues, it is difficult to get a true reading on a player's potential. For instance, a .300 batting average achieved in the high-offense Pacific Coast League is not nearly as much of an accomplishment as a similar level in the Eastern League. MLEs normalize these types of variances, for all statistical categories.

The actual MLEs are not projections. They represent how a player's previous performance might look at the major league level. However, the MLE stat line can be used in forecasting future performance in just the same way as a major league stat line would.

The model we use contains a few variations to James' version and updates all of the minor league and ballpark factors. In addition, we designed a module to convert pitching statistics, which is something James did not originally do.

Do MLEs really work?

Used correctly, MLEs are excellent indicators of potential. But just like we cannot take traditional major league statistics at face value, the same goes for MLEs. The underlying measures of base skill—batting eye ratios, pitching command ratios, etc.—are far more accurate in evaluating future talent than raw home runs, batting averages or ERAs.

The charts we present here also provide the unique perspective of looking at up to five years' worth of data. Ironically, the longer the history, the less likely the player is a legitimate prospect—he should have made it to the majors before compiling a long history in AA and/or AAA ball. Of course, the shorter trends

are more difficult to read despite them often belonging to players with higher ceilings. But even here we can find small indications of players improving their skills, or struggling, as they rise through more difficult levels of competition. Since players—especially those with any talent—are promoted rapidly through major league systems, a two or three-year scan is often all we get to spot any trends.

Here are some things to look for as you scan these charts:

Target players who...
- spent a full year in AA and then a full year in AAA
- had consistent playing time from one year to the next
- improved their base skills as they were promoted

Raise the warning flag for players who...
- were stuck at a level for multiple seasons, or regressed
- displayed marked changes in playing time from one year to the next
- showed large drops in BPIs from one year to the next

Players are listed on the charts if they spent at least part of 2009-2013 in Triple-A or Double-A and had at least 100 AB or 30 IP within those two levels. Each is listed with the organization with which they finished the season.

Only statistics accumulated in Triple-A and Double-A ball are included (players who split a season are indicated as a/a); Single-A stats are excluded.

Each player's actual AB and IP totals are used as the base for the conversion. However, it is more useful to compare performances using common levels, so rely on the ratios and sabermetric gauges. Complete explanations of these formulas appear in the Glossary.

BATTER	B	Yr	Age	Pos	Lvl	Tm	AB	R	H	D	T	HR	RBI	BB	K	SB	CS	BA	OB	Slg	OPS	bb%	ct%	Eye	PX	SX	RC/G	BPV
Adames,Cristhian	B	13	22	SS	aa	COL	389	36	101	19	2	3	29	27	78	10	7	259	306	340	646	6%	80%	0.34	63	86	2.86	11
Adrianza,Ehire	B	12	23	SS	aa	SF	451	46	91	21	4	2	28	35	99	14	4	203	261	285	546	7%	78%	0.35	61	116	1.88	12
		13	24	SS	a/a	SF	395	38	86	16	4	1	24	37	89	12	9	217	285	286	571	9%	78%	0.42	54	107	2.02	5
Aguilar,Jesus	R	13	23	1B	aa	CLE	499	49	116	25	0	12	78	41	122	0	1	233	291	353	644	8%	76%	0.34	91	24	2.90	-1
Ahmed,Nick	R	13	23	SS	aa	ARI	487	49	109	20	5	4	39	27	78	22	8	223	264	309	573	5%	84%	0.35	59	134	2.16	36
Alberto,Hanser	R	13	21	SS	aa	TEX	356	32	74	6	4	4	34	14	42	11	5	208	237	278	515	4%	88%	0.32	40	115	1.81	29
Alcantara,Arismendy	B	13	22	SS	aa	CHC	494	55	120	33	3	12	55	51	138	25	7	243	314	395	709	9%	72%	0.37	120	116	3.43	40
Aliotti,Anthony	L	12	25	1B	aa	OAK	455	53	109	24	1	7	56	51	155	0	0	238	315	339	654	10%	66%	0.33	88	37	2.98	-33
		13	26	1B	aa	OAK	494	46	126	26	1	9	50	59	155	2	2	256	335	366	701	11%	69%	0.38	95	41	3.51	-14
Almanzar,Michael	R	13	23	3B	aa	BOS	507	51	124	29	2	12	62	32	109	10	3	245	290	382	671	6%	79%	0.29	99	91	3.10	34
Almonte,Abraham	B	12	23	OF	aa	NYY	319	38	78	15	3	4	20	30	65	24	6	246	311	344	655	9%	80%	0.47	68	129	3.14	31
		13	24	CF	a/a	SEA	440	63	112	19	4	11	53	54	114	20	9	255	336	393	729	11%	74%	0.47	98	124	3.77	36
Almonte,Zoilo	B	11	22	OF	aa	NYY	175	18	40	10	1	3	18	11	49	3	1	226	273	336	610	6%	72%	0.24	77	83	3.17	-10
		12	23	OF	aa	NYY	419	51	105	20	1	19	56	20	113	12	4	250	285	439	724	5%	73%	0.18	129	88	3.72	33
		13	24	LF	aaa	NYY	259	25	70	11	1	6	31	25	52	3	1	269	335	384	718	9%	80%	0.49	79	58	3.94	20
Asencio,Yeison	R	13	24	RF	aa	SD	291	20	67	13	3	2	26	11	34	2	2	230	257	308	566	4%	88%	0.32	54	71	2.05	27
Austin,Tyler	R	13	22	RF	aa	NYY	319	36	76	16	1	6	34	35	85	3	0	237	311	344	656	10%	73%	0.41	85	70	3.09	4
Avery,Xavier	L	10	21	OF	aa	BAL	107	8	24	5	0	3	14	5	25	8	0	221	257	356	613	5%	76%	0.20	87	91	3.44	14
		11	21	OF	aa	BAL	557	63	137	29	2	4	23	42	163	32	15	245	298	324	622	7%	71%	0.26	60	107	3.32	-21
		12	22	OF	aaa	BAL	390	51	88	12	4	8	31	45	111	20	7	226	306	338	644	10%	72%	0.41	78	124	2.91	9
		13	23	CF	a/a	SEA	467	59	107	19	3	3	30	45	139	24	9	230	297	302	599	9%	70%	0.32	63	125	2.50	-11
Baez,Javier	R	13	21	SS	aa	CHC	218	31	58	14	0	16	43	16	76	6	2	266	315	550	866	7%	65%	0.21	223	74	5.27	77
Barnhart,Tucker	B	12	21	C	aa	CIN	130	9	25	4	1	2	11	10	24	1	1	190	247	278	524	7%	82%	0.41	55	60	1.79	5
		13	22	C	aa	CIN	339	28	83	17	1	3	40	40	62	1	0	244	324	328	653	11%	82%	0.64	65	40	2.99	13
Beckham,Tim	R	12	22	SS	aaa	TAM	285	33	65	9	1	5	23	24	79	5	0	227	286	315	602	8%	72%	0.30	64	87	2.72	-17
		13	23	SS	aaa	TAM	460	58	111	22	6	3	42	36	123	14	8	242	296	335	631	7%	73%	0.29	74	127	2.57	7
Belnome,Vince	L	11	23	2B	aa	SD	267	42	72	15	1	11	46	37	72	0	6	269	359	458	817	12%	73%	0.51	118	41	5.68	25
		12	24	DH	aaa	SD	258	19	55	8	1	3	22	31	89	3	1	211	296	285	581	11%	65%	0.35	62	58	2.39	-48
		13	25	1B	aaa	TAM	444	61	111	29	3	6	53	66	130	0	2	250	348	368	715	13%	71%	0.51	101	55	3.37	8
Beltre,Engel	L	10	21	OF	aa	TEX	181	12	45	4	4	1	12	8	19	7	2	250	283	336	619	4%	89%	0.42	49	150	3.36	52
		11	22	OF	aa	TEX	437	49	92	14	6	1	21	21	109	12	6	210	247	272	519	5%	75%	0.20	42	145	2.20	-12
		12	23	OF	aa	TEX	564	63	137	16	16	12	43	21	124	28	11	244	270	390	660	4%	78%	0.17	85	146	2.76	33
		13	24	CF	aaa	TEX	394	43	102	17	1	6	25	21	92	11	14	259	295	351	647	5%	77%	0.22	71	79	2.75	-1
Bethancourt,Christian	R	12	21	C	aa	ATL	268	26	60	5	1	2	23	10	50	7	6	224	251	266	518	3%	81%	0.19	28	82	1.87	-18
		13	22	C	aa	ATL	358	37	93	20	0	10	39	14	63	10	8	259	287	402	689	4%	82%	0.22	98	69	3.21	38
Bogaerts,Xander	R	13	20	SS	a/a	BOS	444	57	125	24	5	11	53	50	101	6	3	281	353	434	787	10%	77%	0.49	107	92	4.45	45
Bradley,Jackie	L	12	22	OF	aa	BOS	229	31	60	17	2	5	24	29	52	7	3	260	343	412	755	11%	77%	0.56	110	94	3.80	50
		13	23	CF	aaa	BOS	320	44	81	26	2	7	27	31	81	5	8	254	321	420	741	9%	75%	0.38	131	89	3.30	50
Brentz,Bryce	R	12	24	OF	a/a	BOS	473	51	126	31	1	13	62	33	150	6	6	267	314	419	734	6%	68%	0.22	123	58	3.71	4
		13	25	RF	aaa	BOS	326	27	75	16	1	12	42	15	98	1	0	231	264	395	658	4%	70%	0.15	124	38	3.00	1
Brett,Ryan	R	13	22	2B	aa	TAM	105	16	22	5	1	2	13	7	16	3	0	209	255	342	597	6%	85%	0.42	86	128	2.41	61
Brown,Gary	R	12	24	OF	aa	SF	538	64	135	31	2	6	37	34	99	29	20	250	295	345	640	6%	82%	0.34	70	104	2.61	28
		13	25	CF	aaa	SF	558	52	100	23	4	7	33	22	161	11	13	179	210	273	482	4%	71%	0.13	75	106	1.29	-14
Burns,Andy	R	13	23	3B	aa	TOR	265	30	59	17	2	6	24	17	61	9	6	224	270	365	635	6%	77%	0.27	106	111	2.45	40
Burns,Billy	B	13	24	CF	aa	WAS	114	21	33	4	0	0	6	15	19	16	2	289	372	321	692	12%	84%	0.80	29	124	4.52	20
Buss,Nick	L	12	26	OF	aa	LA	492	53	110	20	6	6	43	28	85	14	15	223	265	325	590	5%	83%	0.33	65	109	2.05	29
		13	27	RF	aaa	LA	459	54	105	22	5	11	64	27	114	14	3	229	271	372	644	5%	75%	0.23	102	130	2.78	35
Cabrera,Ramon	B	12	23	C	a/a	PIT	389	40	98	21	2	2	42	32	46	0	3	251	308	333	640	8%	88%	0.69	57	40	2.72	28
		13	24	DH	a/a	DET	461	45	116	27	3	1	55	44	59	3	1	251	317	328	644	9%	87%	0.75	59	71	2.78	37
Calixte,Orlando	R	13	21	SS	aa	KC	484	48	111	23	4	6	29	34	136	11	12	229	280	332	611	7%	72%	0.25	82	97	2.30	-3
Casali,Curt	R	13	25	C	aa	TAM	120	20	39	9	0	4	25	17	22	0	0	322	404	493	897	12%	82%	0.75	121	30	6.31	59
Castellanos,Nick	R	12	20	OF	aa	DET	322	29	78	13	1	6	21	11	77	4	4	244	269	344	614	3%	76%	0.15	71	67	2.59	-10
		13	21	LF	aaa	DET	533	69	137	34	1	15	65	44	102	3	1	257	314	410	724	8%	81%	0.43	108	68	3.69	48
Cecchini,Garin	L	13	22	3B	aa	BOS	240	28	67	14	2	2	22	39	56	6	2	278	380	376	756	14%	77%	0.71	79	93	4.04	29
Centeno,Juan	L	12	23	C	aa	NYM	281	23	65	9	1	0	28	18	48	1	1	230	276	274	550	6%	83%	0.38	34	56	2.08	-10
		13	24	C	a/a	NYM	236	20	56	8	2	0	21	8	35	1	1	237	263	287	549	3%	85%	0.23	38	67	2.05	-1
Choi,Ji-Man	L	13	22	1B	a/a	SEA	243	24	56	10	2	8	36	30	40	2	2	231	315	395	711	11%	83%	0.74	101	64	3.42	57
Choice,Michael	R	12	23	OF	aa	OAK	359	45	87	13	2	7	43	26	101	4	1	242	292	345	637	7%	72%	0.25	75	84	2.96	-13
		13	24	LF	aaa	OAK	510	63	124	24	1	9	62	50	135	1	2	244	311	344	655	9%	74%	0.37	80	41	3.04	-10
Collier,Zach	L	13	23	CF	aa	PHI	446	42	84	12	6	6	27	35	145	13	7	188	247	284	531	7%	67%	0.24	73	126	1.76	-18
Collins,Tyler	L	13	23	LF	aa	DET	466	53	99	25	0	16	63	39	129	3	6	212	272	372	644	8%	72%	0.30	121	47	2.67	18
Colon,Christian	R	11	22	SS	aa	KC	491	51	111	13	2	5	45	33	54	12	8	226	275	291	566	6%	89%	0.62	43	87	2.70	31
		12	23	SS	a/a	KC	290	27	75	9	2	4	24	25	30	9	7	260	318	345	663	8%	90%	0.81	50	79	3.15	40
		13	24	2B	aaa	KC	512	57	123	11	3	9	46	32	63	12	5	240	285	325	610	6%	88%	0.51	49	99	2.80	34
Cowart,Kaleb	B	13	21	3B	aa	LAA	498	42	99	18	1	5	37	32	136	12	5	199	247	266	513	6%	73%	0.23	56	81	1.79	-26

BATTER	B	Yr	Age	Pos	Lvl	Tm	AB	R	H	D	T	HR	RBI	BB	K	SB	CS	BA	OB	Slg	OPS	bb%	ct%	Eye	PX	SX	RC/G	BPV
Cox,Zack	L	11	22	3B	aa	STL	352	35	83	15	0	6	31	19	78	0	1	236	275	331	606	5%	78%	0.25	65	31	3.12	-14
		12	23	3B	a/a	MIA	394	32	86	25	1	7	34	18	101	1	0	219	253	340	593	4%	74%	0.18	94	45	2.26	-3
		13	24	3B	a/a	MIA	288	26	67	14	2	2	24	34	82	2	0	234	315	317	632	11%	72%	0.42	71	62	2.74	-15
Cron,C.J.	R	13	23	1B	aa	LAA	519	48	124	32	1	11	71	19	95	7	4	240	266	366	632	4%	82%	0.20	91	66	2.65	29
Cunningham,Todd	B	12	23	OF	aa	ATL	466	65	130	21	5	2	43	33	58	20	9	279	326	360	686	7%	87%	0.56	53	121	3.39	44
		13	24	CF	aaa	ATL	427	47	99	12	4	2	30	32	72	16	8	231	284	286	570	7%	83%	0.44	38	111	2.26	12
Curry,Matt	L	11	23	1B	aa	PIT	302	30	65	15	2	5	31	26	95	1	1	214	277	323	600	8%	69%	0.27	73	75	3.07	-27
		12	24	1B	a/a	PIT	401	44	102	31	4	8	64	36	115	3	6	254	315	414	730	8%	71%	0.31	125	75	3.27	26
		13	25	1B	aa	PIT	105	8	22	4	0	3	12	4	39	2	0	205	231	315	547	3%	63%	0.09	94	53	2.15	-48
Cuthbert,Cheslor	R	13	21	3B	aa	KC	237	20	46	15	0	5	23	16	53	4	2	194	245	314	559	6%	78%	0.30	93	63	1.93	18
D'Arnaud,Travis	R	11	22	C	aa	TOR	424	61	121	31	1	18	66	28	113	3	2	285	330	493	823	6%	73%	0.25	134	66	5.93	35
		12	23	C	aaa	TOR	279	31	79	18	2	12	36	13	69	1	1	284	316	489	805	4%	75%	0.19	140	50	4.56	39
Darnell,James	R	10	24	3B	aa	SD	373	39	83	18	1	8	43	39	60	2	0	223	297	339	636	10%	84%	0.65	77	57	3.60	35
		11	24	3B	a/a	SD	422	54	99	21	1	13	52	47	99	1	2	234	311	383	693	10%	77%	0.48	95	48	4.22	19
		12	25	3B	aaa	SD	116	15	23	4	0	4	14	11	32	1	1	199	270	347	617	9%	73%	0.36	101	50	2.55	6
Davidson,Matthew	R	12	21	3B	aa	ARI	486	65	119	28	2	19	62	54	133	2	4	245	320	428	748	10%	73%	0.40	129	59	3.81	33
		13	22	3B	aaa	ARI	443	58	104	28	2	11	47	28	150	1	0	235	281	385	666	6%	66%	0.19	129	51	2.93	-3
Davis,Kentrail	L	12	24	OF	aa	MIL	438	43	105	21	5	6	32	44	141	15	12	241	309	354	663	9%	68%	0.31	89	104	2.75	-6
		13	25	RF	a/a	MIL	500	57	113	22	5	6	35	51	150	19	13	226	298	327	625	9%	70%	0.34	81	117	2.48	1
Decker,Jaff	L	11	21	OF	aa	SD	496	67	95	23	1	13	69	82	168	11	6	192	306	321	627	14%	66%	0.49	83	88	3.46	-12
		12	22	OF	aa	SD	147	23	23	2	2	2	7	33	42	5	2	154	309	236	546	18%	71%	0.78	54	116	1.89	1
		13	23	CF	aaa	SD	350	43	82	19	1	6	27	38	112	3	7	233	309	346	655	10%	68%	0.34	97	56	2.76	-12
DeJesus,Ivan	R	10	23	2B	aaa	LA	533	54	122	25	1	4	42	19	53	4	1	228	254	302	556	3%	90%	0.35	55	73	2.61	35
		11	24	2B	aaa	LA	387	35	90	14	1	5	34	25	84	2	1	232	278	309	587	6%	78%	0.30	53	56	2.99	-13
		12	25	2B	aaa	BOS	250	30	69	13	2	2	27	13	63	2	1	276	311	374	685	5%	75%	0.20	75	81	3.29	-5
		13	26	2B	aaa	PIT	304	27	81	24	2	2	24	21	74	4	2	267	315	380	694	6%	76%	0.29	97	77	3.11	19
Dickerson,Alex	L	13	23	RF	aa	PIT	451	48	114	34	2	12	54	20	95	3	8	252	285	416	701	4%	79%	0.22	120	84	3.05	48
Dugan,Kelly	L	13	23	RF	aa	PHI	212	19	48	11	1	8	17	4	61	0	1	226	240	392	632	2%	71%	0.06	124	44	2.58	2
Duvall,Adam	R	13	25	3B	aa	SF	385	43	77	19	3	10	41	25	86	1	1	200	248	343	591	6%	78%	0.29	100	79	2.20	29
Eibner,Brett	R	13	25	CF	aa	KC	441	56	92	15	9	13	31	40	166	5	3	209	274	372	645	8%	62%	0.24	128	118	2.60	5
Fields,Daniel	L	12	21	OF	aa	DET	106	11	26	4	0	2	6	10	22	7	1	241	309	322	631	9%	80%	0.48	56	83	3.24	8
		13	22	CF	aa	DET	457	57	119	24	6	8	47	35	134	19	8	261	313	392	706	7%	71%	0.26	103	137	3.38	22
Fletcher,Brian	R	12	24	OF	aa	KC	254	24	56	10	2	7	26	11	104	5	3	222	255	356	611	4%	59%	0.11	114	95	2.43	-34
		13	25	LF	a/a	KC	315	39	78	12	1	12	42	14	84	5	2	249	280	410	690	4%	73%	0.16	113	88	3.43	21
Flores,Ramon	L	13	21	LF	aa	NYY	534	67	129	23	4	6	47	66	104	6	6	242	325	334	659	11%	81%	0.63	66	80	2.91	23
Flores,Wilmer	R	12	21	3B	aa	NYM	251	31	66	15	2	7	28	16	33	0	0	261	306	412	718	6%	87%	0.50	92	49	3.61	50
		13	22	2B	aaa	NYM	424	45	108	27	2	10	56	16	75	1	3	255	282	402	684	4%	82%	0.22	103	55	3.05	38
Franco,Maikel	R	13	21	3B	aa	PHI	277	37	84	12	1	12	40	8	35	1	2	303	322	488	810	3%	88%	0.23	108	60	4.95	62
Freitas,David	R	13	24	C	a/a	OAK	321	34	60	11	0	6	22	23	61	0	0	186	240	282	522	7%	81%	0.38	66	36	1.85	3
Fuentes,Reymond	L	12	21	OF	aa	SD	473	42	87	17	3	3	27	44	152	28	10	184	253	252	505	8%	68%	0.29	56	123	1.68	-28
		13	22	RF	a/a	SD	400	56	116	22	2	4	33	40	94	27	12	290	355	386	741	9%	77%	0.43	77	111	4.05	21
Galvez,Jonathan	R	12	21	2B	aa	SD	312	38	78	17	2	4	28	27	81	10	3	249	308	357	665	8%	74%	0.33	83	98	3.08	9
		13	22	2B	aaa	SD	410	46	95	20	1	4	35	24	121	15	8	232	275	313	587	6%	70%	0.20	72	100	2.33	-17
Garcia,Leury	B	12	21	2B	aa	TEX	377	45	105	12	11	2	24	18	81	25	7	280	313	381	694	5%	79%	0.22	62	149	3.35	20
		13	22	SS	aaa	CHW	223	28	54	8	3	4	16	14	68	12	4	243	287	359	646	6%	69%	0.20	88	146	2.87	6
Glaesmann,Todd	R	13	23	LF	aa	TAM	487	43	100	24	3	8	44	21	125	5	2	206	239	317	556	4%	74%	0.17	86	83	1.97	1
Goodwin,Brian	L	12	22	OF	aa	WAS	166	14	34	7	1	4	12	14	52	2	3	203	265	332	597	8%	68%	0.27	98	65	2.21	-11
		13	23	CF	aa	WAS	457	66	104	17	8	8	32	50	129	15	12	228	304	356	660	10%	72%	0.39	92	137	2.68	23
Green,Grant	R	11	24	SS	aa	OAK	530	53	124	27	1	6	43	27	140	4	9	234	271	321	592	5%	74%	0.19	63	53	2.80	-28
		12	25	OF	aaa	OAK	524	50	124	23	4	9	52	23	91	9	11	236	268	351	619	4%	83%	0.25	73	87	2.42	25
		13	26	2B	aaa	LAA	402	41	97	21	2	6	32	18	98	2	3	241	273	345	618	4%	76%	0.18	81	67	2.57	-3
Grichuk,Randal	R	13	22	RF	aa	LAA	500	74	114	24	6	17	56	23	101	8	5	228	262	403	666	4%	80%	0.23	114	124	2.79	58
Guyer,Brandon	R	09	24	OF	aa	CHC	189	18	32	12	1	1	12	8	30	6	6	171	204	259	463	4%	84%	0.26	68	115	1.48	36
		10	25	OF	aa	CHC	369	56	109	35	4	10	42	20	41	22	4	297	333	489	822	5%	89%	0.50	132	150	6.17	119
		11	25	OF	aaa	TAM	388	60	102	24	4	10	47	27	94	12	7	263	311	429	740	7%	76%	0.29	107	140	4.61	45
		13	27	RF	aaa	TAM	356	55	86	18	5	5	31	22	77	17	4	242	286	363	649	6%	78%	0.28	86	159	2.84	43
Ha,Jae-Hoon	R	11	21	OF	aa	CHC	226	24	57	15	1	2	19	8	30	5	10	254	281	357	637	4%	87%	0.27	76	76	2.90	39
		12	22	OF	aa	CHC	465	51	116	25	3	5	38	41	104	9	5	249	311	347	658	8%	78%	0.40	74	83	2.93	13
		13	23	CF	a/a	CHC	323	33	72	16	0	5	27	22	74	12	3	221	272	314	586	6%	77%	0.30	73	88	2.41	8
Hamilton,Billy	B	12	22	SS	aa	CIN	175	29	47	4	4	1	13	32	47	45	17	271	384	359	743	15%	73%	0.68	55	174	4.00	22
		13	23	CF	aaa	CIN	504	63	117	16	3	6	35	32	114	63	17	233	278	313	591	6%	77%	0.28	57	159	2.66	16
Hanson,Alen	B	13	21	SS	aa	PIT	137	10	32	4	4	1	8	6	27	5	2	232	265	331	596	4%	81%	0.23	61	123	2.17	19
Hazelbaker,Jeremy	L	11	24	OF	aa	BOS	354	42	81	18	2	8	29	30	117	25	9	229	289	360	649	8%	67%	0.25	85	130	3.55	-7
		12	25	OF	a/a	BOS	466	63	114	24	5	15	54	27	137	29	13	245	287	410	697	6%	71%	0.20	119	138	3.18	32
		13	26	LF	aaa	BOS	428	45	94	12	1	8	39	26	152	27	8	220	265	309	574	6%	64%	0.17	74	119	2.42	-34

BATTER	B	Yr	Age	Pos	Lvl	Tm	AB	R	H	D	T	HR	RBI	BB	K	SB	CS	BA	OB	Slg	OPS	bb%	ct%	Eye	PX	SX	RC/G	BPV
Head,Miles	R	12	21	3B	aa	OAK	213	20	51	8	2	4	22	13	84	0	1	239	282	343	625	6%	61%	0.15	89	61	2.67	-54
		13	22	3B	aa	OAK	148	10	25	3	0	1	6	10	46	0	1	168	219	219	438	6%	69%	0.21	43	32	1.26	-65
Heathcott,Slade	L	13	23	CF	aa	NYY	399	49	94	20	5	8	40	30	117	12	9	235	288	366	654	7%	71%	0.25	101	122	2.68	16
Hefflinger,Robby	R	13	23	LF	aa	ATL	188	16	29	8	1	5	21	13	72	2	1	155	209	288	496	6%	62%	0.18	117	77	1.46	-21
Hernandez,Cesar	B	12	22	2B	a/a	PHI	532	52	142	28	9	2	47	26	86	18	16	266	300	363	664	5%	84%	0.30	65	115	2.66	33
		13	23	2B	a/a	PHI	401	47	109	12	6	2	28	33	94	25	9	272	326	344	670	7%	77%	0.35	51	141	3.31	7
Herrera,Odubel	L	13	22	2B	aa	TEX	389	32	97	12	6	2	26	14	69	13	5	248	275	327	602	4%	82%	0.21	51	123	2.45	16
Hicks,John	R	13	24	C	aa	SEA	296	35	63	12	1	3	26	20	73	12	4	212	262	292	554	6%	75%	0.28	64	108	2.10	0
Holaday,Bryan	R	11	24	C	aa	DET	330	26	68	15	0	5	32	20	84	5	1	206	251	301	553	6%	75%	0.24	66	60	2.57	-18
		12	25	C	aaa	DET	250	14	51	10	1	2	19	16	48	2	0	205	254	271	526	6%	81%	0.35	49	49	1.85	-8
		13	26	C	aaa	DET	288	22	64	15	1	3	19	13	64	0	1	221	256	312	568	4%	78%	0.21	72	41	2.08	-8
Jackson,Brett	L	10	22	OF	aa	CHC	228	35	56	12	3	5	21	23	47	14	5	246	315	390	705	9%	79%	0.49	92	157	4.34	59
		11	23	OF	a/a	CHC	431	57	100	20	3	14	39	49	154	14	8	232	311	392	703	10%	64%	0.32	99	116	4.19	-7
		12	24	OF	aaa	CHC	407	47	89	18	9	11	34	34	180	19	6	219	279	391	670	8%	56%	0.19	149	142	2.79	3
		13	25	CF	a/a	CHC	310	25	56	9	4	4	20	26	133	7	8	182	245	280	524	8%	57%	0.19	89	111	1.57	-49
Jackson,Ryan	R	11	23	SS	aa	STL	533	41	117	27	2	6	46	28	104	1	0	219	258	312	571	5%	80%	0.27	67	52	2.76	3
		12	24	SS	aaa	STL	445	44	99	19	1	7	34	33	86	1	0	223	277	313	590	7%	81%	0.38	63	49	2.45	4
		13	25	SS	aaa	STL	442	36	101	16	1	2	25	39	106	1	0	229	291	282	573	8%	76%	0.37	45	71	2.42	-20
Jacobs,Brandon	R	13	23	LF	aa	CHW	164	12	36	8	1	2	18	10	59	2	3	221	266	316	582	6%	64%	0.17	89	63	2.07	-40
Jimenez,Luis	R	11	23	3B	aa	LAA	490	52	126	35	1	15	79	22	79	13	7	258	289	424	714	4%	84%	0.27	112	79	4.19	59
		12	24	3B	aaa	LAA	485	52	118	30	1	10	57	12	83	11	8	244	263	373	637	3%	83%	0.15	88	85	2.61	35
		13	25	3B	aaa	LAA	197	17	42	7	1	2	26	7	32	7	4	213	240	291	531	3%	84%	0.22	53	102	1.86	17
Jones,James	L	13	25	RF	a/a	SEA	378	35	87	13	7	4	35	33	91	21	11	231	293	335	628	8%	76%	0.36	71	136	2.54	19
Joseph,Corban	L	10	22	2B	aa	NYY	111	9	20	5	2	0	11	13	27	1	0	182	269	264	532	11%	76%	0.49	56	121	2.51	8
		11	23	2B	aa	NYY	499	59	121	33	5	5	46	48	116	3	3	243	309	356	665	9%	77%	0.41	81	93	3.89	19
		12	24	2B	a/a	NYY	413	47	100	25	1	14	49	55	78	0	1	243	332	409	741	12%	81%	0.70	108	34	3.79	46
		13	25	2B	aaa	NYY	188	25	40	8	0	6	16	17	44	2	0	212	279	344	623	8%	77%	0.39	93	62	2.77	18
Joseph,Tommy	R	12	21	C	aa	PHI	404	35	93	22	0	9	38	27	105	0	4	231	280	353	632	6%	74%	0.26	91	18	2.62	-11
Kelly,Ty	B	12	24	3B	a/a	BAL	208	22	56	11	1	2	24	20	34	2	0	271	335	362	697	9%	84%	0.58	64	69	3.53	25
		13	25	2B	a/a	SEA	480	65	119	22	2	3	49	80	111	5	11	248	356	320	676	14%	77%	0.72	59	61	3.02	4
Kiermaier,Kevin	L	13	23	CF	a/a	TAM	508	73	132	18	13	5	33	36	99	17	13	260	310	374	684	7%	80%	0.37	72	139	2.91	36
Kobernus,Jeff	R	12	24	2B	aa	WAS	330	33	82	9	1	1	15	14	63	33	12	247	279	291	570	4%	81%	0.23	32	121	2.42	-4
		13	25	LF	aaa	WAS	371	43	100	16	1	1	26	19	67	31	11	269	305	326	630	5%	82%	0.28	47	124	2.98	14
La Stella,Tommy	L	13	24	2B	aa	ATL	283	27	88	20	2	3	35	31	40	6	1	311	379	426	805	10%	86%	0.79	83	77	4.94	56
Lamarre,Ryan	R	12	24	OF	aa	CIN	482	58	115	20	2	5	27	51	136	26	11	238	311	318	630	10%	72%	0.38	63	108	2.80	-9
		13	25	CF	a/a	CIN	462	49	100	16	3	10	32	37	109	20	15	216	274	328	602	7%	76%	0.34	77	108	2.31	16
Lee,Hak-Ju	L	11	21	SS	aa	TAM	100	12	17	1	3	1	5	8	24	4	2	172	235	272	507	8%	76%	0.35	50	240	2.02	33
		12	22	SS	aa	TAM	475	55	111	13	9	3	30	41	114	30	10	233	294	318	612	8%	76%	0.36	55	147	2.57	10
Lennerton,Jordan	L	12	26	1B	aa	DET	495	55	111	28	1	15	62	58	160	2	5	223	304	378	683	10%	68%	0.36	122	39	3.06	3
		13	27	1B	aaa	DET	514	52	119	21	1	13	43	61	152	0	4	231	313	349	663	11%	70%	0.40	91	26	3.09	-14
Leon,Sandy	B	12	23	C	a/a	WAS	187	19	54	16	0	2	19	16	30	1	0	288	344	410	755	8%	84%	0.53	92	34	4.06	37
		13	24	C	aa	WAS	310	28	48	11	1	2	20	35	62	0	0	155	241	218	458	10%	80%	0.56	47	40	1.30	-8
Lindsey,Taylor	L	13	22	2B	aa	LAA	508	59	125	20	4	13	49	40	102	3	4	245	300	380	681	7%	80%	0.40	88	78	3.20	30
Liriano,Rymer	R	12	21	OF	aa	SD	183	19	39	8	2	2	16	17	58	8	1	214	281	314	595	8%	69%	0.29	80	119	2.42	-7
Mahtook,Mikie	R	12	23	OF	aa	TAM	153	14	33	9	1	3	20	9	35	3	3	215	257	343	600	5%	77%	0.25	92	79	2.14	18
		13	24	RF	aa	TAM	511	56	110	25	7	5	54	34	119	20	9	216	264	322	586	6%	77%	0.28	79	136	2.11	26
Marisnick,Jake	R	12	21	OF	aa	TOR	223	21	49	11	3	2	13	9	49	12	4	218	248	315	563	4%	78%	0.19	69	134	1.98	17
		13	22	CF	aa	MIA	265	37	72	12	2	10	40	16	79	9	7	272	313	451	764	6%	70%	0.20	131	118	3.98	34
Marte,Alfredo	R	12	23	OF	aa	ARI	398	53	107	24	3	16	59	26	79	5	7	269	313	466	779	6%	80%	0.33	125	77	4.03	58
		13	24	RF	aaa	ARI	311	23	70	20	1	4	29	13	73	1	1	225	256	337	593	4%	76%	0.18	91	46	2.23	2
Martinez,Francisco	R	11	21	3B	aa	SEA	477	68	124	19	5	8	57	19	118	8	11	259	288	369	656	4%	75%	0.16	69	124	3.44	4
		12	22	3B	aa	SEA	352	50	73	15	1	2	21	40	96	25	8	207	288	267	555	10%	73%	0.42	52	121	2.20	-9
		13	23	CF	aa	SEA	126	7	24	5	0	0	5	6	49	6	0	188	222	230	452	4%	61%	0.11	52	86	1.50	-79
Martinson,Jason	R	13	25	SS	aa	WAS	173	15	28	3	2	3	15	14	62	2	0	159	224	254	478	8%	64%	0.23	70	99	1.49	-40
Mattair,Travis	R	13	25	1B	aa	CIN	475	44	103	13	2	13	48	34	123	2	2	217	269	331	600	7%	74%	0.28	79	51	2.56	-10
McCann,James	R	12	22	C	aa	DET	220	12	39	11	0	2	15	6	46	2	2	179	202	250	452	3%	79%	0.14	56	43	1.21	-18
		13	23	C	aa	DET	441	40	108	26	1	6	43	23	90	2	3	246	283	353	636	5%	80%	0.25	82	51	2.69	11
McGuiness,Chris	L	12	24	1B	aa	TEX	456	50	110	23	0	20	60	54	115	0	1	242	322	426	748	11%	75%	0.47	124	17	4.03	27
		13	25	1B	aaa	TEX	362	38	77	26	1	9	45	49	96	1	0	213	306	363	670	12%	74%	0.51	120	43	2.87	29
Medica,Tommy	R	13	25	1B	aa	SD	280	38	71	17	3	13	46	23	81	3	2	254	310	477	788	8%	71%	0.29	164	94	4.13	61
Mitchell,Jared	L	12	24	OF	a/a	CHW	455	56	96	21	9	10	54	70	209	17	7	210	315	365	681	13%	54%	0.33	142	127	2.86	-4
		13	25	CF	a/a	CHW	300	23	43	7	1	5	18	44	144	13	7	144	253	222	474	13%	52%	0.30	79	99	1.44	-72
Morban,Julio	L	13	21	RF	aa	SEA	295	43	82	18	4	6	41	27	107	7	2	279	339	432	772	8%	64%	0.25	134	128	4.13	20
Morris,Hunter	L	12	24	1B	aa	MIL	522	61	140	37	5	24	89	32	137	2	1	268	311	491	802	6%	74%	0.24	154	65	4.35	52
		13	25	1B	aaa	MIL	497	42	102	22	2	19	51	31	146	2	1	205	252	372	624	6%	71%	0.21	123	57	2.58	12

BATTER	B	Yr	Age	Pos	Lvl	Tm	AB	R	H	D	T	HR	RBI	BB	K	SB	CS	BA	OB	Slg	OPS	bb%	ct%	Eye	PX	SX	RC/G	BPV
Muncy,Max	L	13	23	1B	aa	OAK	172	17	37	10	2	3	19	19	38	0	1	213	291	340	631	10%	78%	0.50	94	61	2.39	27
Murphy,J.R.	R	12	21	C	aa	NYY	147	19	31	11	1	4	13	13	34	0	0	212	277	371	649	8%	77%	0.39	115	55	2.59	35
		13	22	C	a/a	NYY	413	52	104	27	0	12	40	40	78	1	1	251	318	402	720	9%	81%	0.52	107	39	3.61	42
Navarro,Efren	L	10	24	1B	aa	LAA	453	36	106	22	1	5	38	23	39	5	5	233	270	318	588	5%	91%	0.60	61	55	2.87	43
		12	26	1B	aaa	LAA	528	50	117	26	0	4	47	23	86	2	2	222	253	297	551	4%	84%	0.26	56	51	2.01	5
		13	27	1B	aaa	LAA	513	49	121	28	2	4	48	39	129	5	6	236	290	318	608	7%	75%	0.30	71	64	2.40	-9
Ngoepe,Gift	B	13	23	SS	aa	PIT	220	23	34	9	1	2	12	21	86	8	3	154	227	237	464	9%	61%	0.24	80	124	1.27	-35
Odor,Rougned	L	13	19	2B	aa	TEX	134	18	42	8	2	6	17	8	24	4	2	313	351	540	891	6%	82%	0.34	143	110	5.71	90
Olt,Mike	R	12	24	3B	aa	TEX	354	50	93	16	1	25	64	48	109	3	0	262	350	521	872	12%	69%	0.44	176	61	5.78	62
		13	25	3B	a/a	CHC	373	36	62	17	1	11	31	42	154	0	0	167	251	305	556	10%	59%	0.27	127	34	1.97	-31
O'Neill,Mike	L	13	25	LF	a/a	STL	471	60	122	13	1	1	28	68	43	14	5	259	352	302	654	13%	91%	1.56	30	87	3.31	40
Oropesa,Ricky	L	13	24	1B	aa	SF	241	14	40	5	0	4	17	11	85	0	0	167	203	233	436	4%	65%	0.12	55	17	1.32	-82
Ortega,Rafael	L	13	22	CF	aa	COL	158	18	35	4	2	1	8	15	26	7	4	222	289	290	578	9%	84%	0.57	43	119	2.21	24
Owings,Chris	R	12	21	SS	aa	ARI	297	28	73	10	3	5	23	9	73	3	3	247	268	352	620	3%	75%	0.12	70	87	2.61	-9
		13	22	SS	aaa	ARI	546	67	153	27	6	8	52	14	112	13	8	280	298	398	696	2%	80%	0.12	83	117	3.33	26
Panik,Joe	L	13	23	2B	aa	SF	522	47	113	23	3	2	42	42	77	7	6	216	275	286	560	8%	85%	0.55	52	80	2.02	23
Parker,Kyle	R	13	24	LF	aa	COL	480	54	130	22	3	21	57	30	103	5	7	270	313	460	773	6%	79%	0.29	124	67	4.20	47
Pederson,Joc	L	13	21	CF	aa	LA	439	73	114	22	2	20	52	64	123	28	9	260	353	457	811	13%	72%	0.51	142	119	4.88	64
Peguero,Francisco	R	11	23	OF	aa	SF	285	29	81	11	6	4	31	4	49	7	1	285	296	407	703	1%	83%	0.08	75	151	4.39	41
		12	24	OF	aaa	SF	449	31	99	17	7	3	46	10	96	1	0	222	238	310	548	2%	79%	0.10	59	77	1.90	-9
		13	25	RF	aaa	SF	272	26	68	10	1	2	21	9	62	2	0	251	274	315	589	3%	77%	0.14	50	76	2.55	-20
Perez,Carlos	R	13	23	C	a/a	HOU	317	27	75	16	0	2	29	23	58	1	1	236	287	309	596	7%	82%	0.40	59	34	2.44	0
Perez,Eury	R	12	22	OF	a/a	WAS	510	45	144	17	2	0	33	12	84	38	16	283	299	325	624	2%	84%	0.14	32	107	2.95	-2
		13	22	CF	aaa	WAS	403	42	106	16	4	5	21	9	70	17	9	264	280	361	641	2%	83%	0.13	65	120	2.85	25
Perez,Hernan	R	13	22	2B	a/a	DET	429	40	119	28	2	3	32	14	57	24	8	277	299	375	674	3%	87%	0.24	73	110	3.20	46
Perio,Noah	L	13	22	2B	aa	MIA	177	17	38	7	0	1	12	15	31	2	0	213	273	265	538	8%	82%	0.47	42	56	2.06	-3
Pillar,Kevin	R	13	24	CF	a/a	TOR	505	56	137	35	5	7	43	23	80	17	15	271	302	405	707	4%	84%	0.29	94	109	3.07	56
Pinto,Josmil	R	13	24	C	a/a	MIN	456	49	121	28	1	10	56	51	95	0	2	264	338	398	736	10%	79%	0.54	98	30	3.82	26
Piscotty,Stephen	R	13	22	RF	aa	STL	184	13	48	8	0	4	18	15	21	5	3	259	314	372	687	7%	89%	0.71	71	50	3.45	43
Polanco,Gregory	L	13	22	CF	a/a	PIT	252	30	59	12	2	4	33	28	37	11	8	234	310	346	657	10%	85%	0.75	75	100	2.81	53
Puello,Cesar	R	13	22	RF	aa	NYM	331	50	94	17	1	13	57	22	95	19	8	283	327	462	789	6%	71%	0.23	133	114	4.54	41
Ramirez,Jose	B	13	21	2B	aa	CLE	482	60	114	15	4	2	29	29	45	29	18	237	281	297	577	6%	91%	0.65	39	129	2.23	46
Ramsey,James	L	13	24	CF	a/a	STL	350	45	72	9	1	10	32	40	124	6	5	206	287	328	615	10%	65%	0.32	96	87	2.64	-16
Realmuto,Jacob	R	13	22	C	aa	MIA	368	35	81	20	2	4	33	33	78	8	1	221	285	322	607	8%	79%	0.42	77	99	2.44	25
Robertson,Daniel	R	11	26	OF	aa	SD	438	67	94	17	3	3	30	40	66	14	7	214	280	289	570	8%	85%	0.61	52	128	2.77	39
		12	27	OF	aaa	SD	490	45	108	20	3	1	24	33	77	12	10	220	268	279	548	6%	84%	0.42	44	86	1.90	13
		13	28	RF	aaa	SD	484	55	103	18	6	1	32	38	83	14	8	212	269	280	549	7%	83%	0.45	48	123	1.89	23
Rodriguez,Ronny	R	13	21	SS	aa	CLE	468	48	108	23	4	4	40	12	84	9	3	231	250	320	570	3%	82%	0.14	65	111	2.13	21
Rodriguez,Yorman	R	13	21	RF	aa	CIN	262	27	67	14	2	4	28	23	82	4	0	255	314	370	684	8%	69%	0.27	97	86	3.34	-5
Rogers,Jason	R	13	25	1B	aa	MIL	481	54	114	22	2	20	68	47	102	5	2	236	305	411	715	9%	79%	0.47	115	69	3.63	48
Romero,Stefen	R	12	24	2B	aa	SEA	216	34	66	13	3	10	44	13	44	5	3	307	346	536	882	6%	79%	0.29	142	108	5.48	77
		13	25	LF	aaa	SEA	375	34	82	18	2	7	50	19	109	5	5	218	257	334	591	5%	71%	0.18	91	85	2.22	-6
Rosario,Eddie	L	13	22	2B	aa	MIN	289	31	73	17	3	3	30	17	73	5	4	254	295	362	657	5%	75%	0.23	87	97	2.76	11
Rupp,Cameron	R	13	25	C	a/a	PHI	325	26	69	14	0	11	33	18	107	1	1	213	254	354	608	5%	67%	0.16	112	28	2.53	-22
Saladino,Tyler	R	12	23	SS	a/a	CHW	467	66	99	15	3	4	37	72	123	32	9	211	317	281	598	13%	74%	0.59	52	127	2.59	3
		13	24	SS	aa	CHW	424	39	86	15	1	5	44	45	99	22	9	203	280	279	559	10%	77%	0.46	58	102	2.16	5
Salcedo,Edward	R	13	22	3B	aa	ATL	468	45	105	21	2	10	48	38	123	17	11	224	283	341	624	8%	74%	0.31	89	91	2.58	11
Sanchez,Carlos	B	12	20	SS	a/a	CHW	158	19	51	11	1	0	12	10	31	6	5	324	364	401	765	6%	80%	0.31	65	87	4.13	13
		13	21	2B	aaa	CHW	432	41	96	19	1	0	23	27	84	13	8	221	266	272	538	6%	81%	0.32	44	97	1.91	0
Sanchez,Tony	R	11	23	C	aa	PIT	402	37	86	13	1	4	35	37	80	4	6	214	280	278	558	8%	80%	0.46	44	54	2.62	-9
		12	24	C	a/a	PIT	347	35	77	24	1	6	35	33	84	1	1	221	288	347	635	9%	76%	0.39	96	45	2.56	13
		13	25	C	a/a	PIT	277	28	66	24	0	7	32	21	70	0	0	237	290	398	688	7%	75%	0.29	131	24	3.01	27
Sano,Miguel	R	13	20	3B	aa	MIN	233	28	50	14	3	14	44	29	85	2	1	213	301	476	777	11%	63%	0.34	210	85	3.79	72
Santana,Daniel	B	13	23	SS	aa	MIN	539	50	142	20	9	1	34	19	104	23	15	263	287	339	626	3%	81%	0.18	53	129	2.56	13
Santana,Domingo	R	13	21	RF	aa	HOU	416	58	95	21	2	21	51	38	155	10	5	228	292	436	728	8%	63%	0.24	170	97	3.54	35
Sardinas,Luis	B	13	20	SS	aa	TEX	135	11	35	4	0	1	13	3	21	4	2	256	274	308	582	3%	84%	0.16	39	67	2.57	-4
Schoop,Jonathan	R	12	21	2B	aa	BAL	485	54	109	22	1	12	45	39	108	4	3	224	282	348	630	7%	78%	0.36	84	57	2.74	12
		13	22	2B	aaa	BAL	270	25	64	10	0	8	28	11	59	1	2	237	266	366	632	4%	78%	0.18	88	33	2.81	3
Semien,Marcus	R	13	23	SS	a/a	CHW	518	89	134	30	4	18	54	88	102	19	6	259	367	440	807	15%	80%	0.86	120	120	4.68	84
Shaw,Travis	L	12	22	1B	aa	BOS	110	11	24	14	0	2	10	17	36	1	1	222	328	412	740	14%	68%	0.48	174	36	3.02	49
		13	23	1B	aa	BOS	444	43	89	21	3	12	38	59	127	5	3	201	294	341	635	12%	71%	0.46	106	76	2.61	19
Singleton,Jonathan	L	12	21	1B	aa	HOU	461	69	115	24	3	16	58	65	146	5	2	250	343	422	765	12%	68%	0.44	128	84	4.16	27
		13	22	1B	a/a	HOU	283	28	57	14	1	6	31	44	118	1	0	200	308	322	630	13%	58%	0.37	117	48	2.65	-29

BATTER	B	Yr	Age	Pos	Lvl	Tm	AB	R	H	D	T	HR	RBI	BB	K	SB	CS	BA	OB	Slg	OPS	bb%	ct%	Eye	PX	SX	RC/G	BPV
Soto,Neftali	R	11	22	1B	a/a	CIN	396	51	97	16	2	25	58	19	110	0	1	244	279	483	761	5%	72%	0.17	138	57	4.59	27
		12	23	1B	aaa	CIN	465	43	100	26	0	12	46	32	132	2	1	214	265	347	612	6%	72%	0.24	101	38	2.49	-6
		13	24	3B	aaa	CIN	461	45	112	18	0	14	51	21	118	2	1	243	277	376	653	4%	74%	0.18	95	45	3.13	-2
Souza,Steven	R	13	24	RF	aa	WAS	273	43	73	21	1	12	35	31	83	16	7	266	341	481	822	10%	69%	0.37	170	111	4.62	69
Spangenberg,Cory	L	13	22	2B	aa	SD	287	30	76	9	3	2	17	15	69	16	12	266	302	334	636	5%	76%	0.22	51	116	2.71	-9
Springer,George	R	13	24	CF	a/a	HOU	492	81	128	24	3	29	82	64	190	34	9	261	346	499	845	12%	61%	0.34	194	133	5.29	66
Stassi,Max	R	13	22	C	aa	HOU	289	32	72	18	1	14	48	15	77	1	1	248	286	462	748	5%	73%	0.20	155	50	3.76	45
Suarez,Eugenio	R	13	22	SS	aa	DET	442	43	102	21	4	7	36	36	101	7	12	231	288	346	634	7%	77%	0.35	84	82	2.43	17
Susac,Andrew	R	13	23	C	aa	SF	262	24	55	15	0	7	34	31	78	1	0	211	294	353	648	11%	70%	0.40	114	30	2.84	5
Szczur,Matt	R	12	23	OF	aa	CHC	143	19	27	6	3	2	5	11	32	3	2	189	248	314	562	7%	78%	0.35	80	134	1.70	32
		13	24	CF	aa	CHC	512	59	124	24	3	2	34	39	86	17	14	243	297	315	611	7%	83%	0.45	55	100	2.42	23
Taveras,Oscar	L	12	20	OF	aa	STL	477	67	137	33	5	17	76	35	60	8	1	287	336	484	820	7%	87%	0.59	117	104	4.79	90
		13	21	CF	aaa	STL	173	20	47	11	0	4	25	7	24	4	1	271	301	398	699	4%	86%	0.30	88	72	3.56	47
Taylor,Chris	R	13	23	SS	aa	SEA	256	42	69	11	3	1	15	37	64	16	3	270	363	347	710	13%	75%	0.59	60	143	3.81	19
Taylor,Michael D.	R	09	24	OF	a/a	PHI	428	61	124	25	3	19	70	39	61	18	6	291	350	495	845	8%	86%	0.64	126	110	6.43	95
		10	25	OF	aaa	OAK	464	54	99	20	4	4	53	35	67	11	7	213	268	298	566	7%	86%	0.52	59	111	2.66	39
		11	26	OF	aaa	OAK	349	33	72	12	0	10	42	30	98	9	6	207	269	327	596	8%	72%	0.30	75	65	2.89	-16
		12	27	OF	aaa	OAK	449	53	98	24	1	7	44	58	133	12	4	218	307	323	630	11%	70%	0.43	86	85	2.72	0
		13	28	RF	aaa	OAK	420	35	87	19	1	10	54	33	112	3	3	206	264	327	591	7%	73%	0.29	91	53	2.33	-2
Thompson,Trayce	R	13	22	CF	aa	CHW	507	65	108	23	4	15	61	55	154	21	9	213	291	359	651	10%	70%	0.36	111	122	2.83	26
Triunfel,Carlos	R	10	21	SS	aa	SEA	470	41	108	10	1	5	34	10	43	2	10	230	247	289	536	2%	91%	0.24	38	46	2.16	14
		11	21	SS	a/a	SEA	506	37	120	24	2	4	32	20	102	4	8	237	265	315	580	4%	80%	0.19	57	56	2.70	-8
		12	22	SS	aaa	SEA	496	54	107	26	1	7	46	17	104	2	2	215	242	313	555	3%	79%	0.17	72	67	1.99	2
		13	23	SS	aaa	SEA	383	39	89	18	2	3	22	12	91	4	5	232	256	314	569	3%	76%	0.13	65	83	2.11	-10
Tucker,Preston	L	13	23	LF	aa	HOU	237	28	54	13	1	8	23	21	53	0	1	229	293	390	683	8%	78%	0.41	112	47	3.14	33
Urrutia,Henry	L	13	26	RF	a/a	BAL	314	36	92	18	1	7	37	24	60	1	1	294	344	426	770	7%	81%	0.40	94	43	4.47	28
Urshela,Giovanny	R	13	22	3B	aa	CLE	445	32	104	21	1	6	33	10	54	1	1	233	251	325	576	2%	88%	0.19	63	41	2.25	21
Vaughn,Cory	R	13	24	LF	aa	NYM	262	30	58	7	1	8	37	18	93	7	1	220	270	341	611	6%	65%	0.19	95	91	2.80	-23
Vazquez,Christian	R	13	23	C	a/a	BOS	345	37	91	19	1	4	37	37	48	5	6	264	334	356	691	10%	86%	0.76	67	62	3.30	38
Villalona,Angel	R	13	23	1B	aa	SF	196	17	38	9	0	5	21	6	68	0	0	193	217	318	534	3%	65%	0.09	107	30	1.84	-37
Villanueva,Christian	R	13	22	3B	aa	CHC	490	48	114	37	2	15	57	28	129	4	8	233	275	408	683	5%	74%	0.22	136	59	2.79	34
Vitters,Josh	R	12	23	3B	aaa	CHC	415	40	109	28	2	13	50	23	87	4	3	263	301	431	732	5%	79%	0.26	114	60	3.65	38
Walker,Keenyn	B	13	23	RF	aa	CHW	462	63	84	15	4	3	26	63	173	31	16	181	279	248	527	12%	63%	0.36	61	138	1.75	-33
Walsh,Colin	B	13	24	2B	aa	STL	118	11	21	4	0	1	4	12	27	2	0	181	255	251	506	9%	77%	0.44	54	62	1.79	-10
Walters,Zach	B	12	23	SS	a/a	WAS	262	26	62	14	3	6	20	11	71	1	0	235	265	375	640	4%	73%	0.15	101	80	2.67	6
		13	24	SS	aaa	WAS	487	51	105	28	3	22	57	14	148	3	3	216	237	420	657	3%	70%	0.09	153	83	2.62	33
Wates,Austin	R	12	24	OF	aa	HOU	359	41	91	14	3	5	34	22	84	12	13	255	297	352	650	6%	77%	0.26	67	100	2.73	4
		13	25	LF	a/a	HOU	136	14	35	4	2	1	7	12	25	11	1	260	321	343	664	8%	81%	0.48	54	143	3.44	30
Wheeler,Tim	L	11	23	OF	aa	COL	561	73	144	25	5	26	60	40	148	15	13	257	306	459	765	7%	74%	0.27	120	112	4.63	39
		12	24	OF	aaa	COL	379	41	97	24	3	1	23	18	75	4	8	256	289	345	635	4%	80%	0.24	69	79	2.45	11
		13	25	RF	aaa	COL	397	34	84	13	2	3	24	19	96	7	8	212	247	282	530	4%	76%	0.19	54	82	1.78	-18
Wilkins,Andy	L	12	24	1B	aa	CHW	435	52	90	24	1	15	53	53	110	5	5	207	293	369	662	11%	75%	0.48	113	55	2.85	29
		13	25	1B	a/a	CHW	458	48	111	26	0	16	61	45	130	4	1	243	310	401	711	9%	72%	0.34	121	49	3.61	18
Williams,Everett	L	13	23	LF	aa	SD	331	31	76	10	1	2	26	24	93	8	4	230	282	279	560	7%	72%	0.26	42	80	2.25	-40
Witherspoon,Travis	R	12	23	OF	aa	LAA	208	25	38	8	1	5	19	21	59	8	4	181	256	307	563	9%	72%	0.35	89	109	1.99	10
		13	24	CF	aa	LAA	448	48	82	15	2	8	31	44	136	25	11	183	255	281	537	9%	70%	0.32	77	119	1.89	-4
Wong,Kolten	L	12	22	2B	aa	STL	523	62	130	20	4	6	41	36	81	16	12	249	297	339	637	6%	84%	0.44	58	100	2.75	29
		13	23	2B	aaa	STL	412	52	108	18	6	7	35	32	67	15	1	261	315	385	700	7%	84%	0.48	80	138	3.59	57

PITCHER	Th	Yr	Age	LvL	Org	W	L	G	Sv	IP	H	ER	HR	BB	K	ERA	WHIP	BF/G	OBA	bb/9	k/9	Cmd	hr/9	H%	S%	BPV
Adam,Jason	R	13	22	aa	KC	8	11	26	0	144	171	97	12	52	106	6.04	1.55	24.2	297	3.3	6.6	2.0	0.7	35%	60%	55
Adams,Austin	R	11	25	aa	CLE	11	10	26	0	136	176	71	6	67	106	4.72	1.79	24.6	307	4.5	7	1.6	0.4	38%	73%	57
		13	27	aa	CLE	3	2	45	4	55	52	18	3	29	60	3.02	1.47	5.2	250	4.8	9.8	2.0	0.5	34%	80%	91
Ames,Steven	R	11	23	aa	LA	2	2	28	5	33	34	9	3	10	35	2.47	1.32	4.9	260	2.6	9.8	3.7	0.7	35%	84%	117
		12	24	aa	LA	3	3	54	18	63	60	13	2	13	60	1.84	1.14	4.6	251	1.8	8.5	4.7	0.3	33%	85%	146
		13	25	aaa	MIA	3	2	39	8	46	73	25	7	20	30	4.92	2.00	5.7	358	3.9	5.7	1.5	1.4	39%	79%	8
Anderson,Chase	R	12	25	aa	ARI	5	4	21	0	104	111	43	11	26	78	3.73	1.32	20.5	275	2.2	6.7	3.0	0.9	32%	75%	75
		13	26	aaa	ARI	4	7	26	0	88	117	57	11	31	64	5.82	1.67	15.2	320	3.1	6.5	2.1	1.1	37%	66%	41
Andriese,Matt	R	13	24	a/a	SD	11	7	27	0	135	143	49	4	28	91	3.29	1.27	20.4	274	1.9	6.1	3.3	0.3	32%	73%	96
Armstrong,Shawn	R	13	23	aa	CLE	2	3	30	0	33	35	16	2	19	37	4.33	1.64	4.9	271	5.3	10	1.9	0.5	37%	73%	85
Banuelos,Manny	L	11	20	a/a	NYY	6	7	27	0	130	146	65	11	71	110	4.52	1.68	22.1	278	4.9	7.6	1.5	0.8	34%	74%	54
Barnes,Matt	R	13	23	a/a	BOS	6	10	25	0	113	135	65	12	49	119	5.15	1.62	20.1	297	3.9	9.4	2.4	1	38%	69%	75
Barrett,Aaron	R	13	25	aa	WAS	1	1	51	26	50	48	15	2	15	54	2.68	1.25	4	252	2.6	9.7	3.7	0.4	34%	79%	128
Bassitt,Chris	R	13	24	aa	CHW	4	2	8	0	48	43	16	3	20	32	3.04	1.33	24.7	242	3.8	6	1.6	0.5	28%	78%	59
Bauer,Trevor	R	12	21	a/a	ARI	12	2	22	0	130	113	37	9	55	136	2.54	1.29	24.3	236	3.8	9.4	2.5	0.6	31%	82%	98
		13	22	aaa	CLE	6	7	22	0	121	136	68	15	72	92	5.06	1.72	25	285	5.3	6.9	1.3	1.1	33%	73%	32
Belfiore,Mike	L	12	24	aa	BAL	5	1	28	2	47	50	18	2	21	41	3.43	1.50	7.3	273	4	7.7	1.9	0.5	34%	77%	74
		13	25	aaa	BAL	2	1	37	1	76	99	36	11	31	66	4.19	1.72	9.4	316	3.7	7.8	2.1	1.3	37%	79%	45
Bergman,Christian	R	13	25	aa	COL	8	7	27	0	171	214	97	42	26	85	5.11	1.40	26.7	307	1.4	4.5	3.3	2.2	30%	72%	23
Betances,Dellin	R	11	23	a/a	NYY	4	9	25	0	126	120	66	12	74	119	4.69	1.54	22.5	246	5.3	8.5	1.6	0.9	31%	70%	65
		12	24	NYY		6	9	27	0	131	172	120	17	106	102	8.20	2.12	24	317	7.2	7	1.0	1.2	37%	61%	18
		13	25	aaa	NYY	6	4	38	5	84	66	36	3	47	87	3.80	1.35	9.2	219	5	9.3	1.8	0.3	30%	70%	96
Bettis,Chad	R	13	24	aa	COL	3	4	12	0	63	78	39	15	14	53	5.52	1.46	22.5	304	2.1	7.6	3.7	2.1	34%	69%	54
Biddle,Jesse	L	13	22	aa	PHI	5	14	27	0	138	111	59	10	77	134	3.86	1.36	21.4	222	5	8.7	1.7	0.7	28%	72%	80
Black,Victor	R	12	24	aa	PIT	2	3	51	13	60	48	14	2	29	66	2.08	1.28	4.8	220	4.4	9.9	2.3	0.3	31%	84%	109
		13	25	aaa	PIT	5	3	38	17	47	33	15	2	21	49	2.97	1.14	4.9	199	4	9.4	2.4	0.4	27%	74%	110
Blair,Seth	R	13	24	aa	STL	3	9	24	0	130	164	79	17	47	96	5.47	1.63	24	310	3.3	6.7	2.0	1.1	35%	68%	41
Bochy,Brett	R	12	25	aa	SF	7	3	41	14	53	36	20	3	19	57	3.39	1.03	5	193	3.2	9.5	3.0	0.6	26%	67%	120
		13	26	aaa	SF	1	1	45	2	56	54	24	1	15	46	3.84	1.22	5.1	254	2.4	7.3	3.1	0.2	32%	67%	106
Bonilla,Lisalberto	R	12	22	aa	PHI	2	1	21	3	33	24	7	1	16	40	1.86	1.24	6.4	207	4.5	10.9	2.4	0.3	31%	86%	122
		13	23	a/a	TEX	7	5	47	6	73	82	52	11	35	87	6.34	1.59	6.9	284	4.2	10.7	2.5	1.3	37%	61%	75
Bradley,Archie	R	13	21	aa	ARI	12	5	21	0	123	111	36	6	60	104	2.62	1.38	24.7	242	4.4	7.6	1.7	0.5	30%	82%	75
Brasier,Ryan	R	10	23	aa	LAA	7	12	28	0	142	147	96	31	67	78	6.08	1.51	22.5	262	4.2	4.9	1.2	2	27%	65%	-2
		11	24	a/a	LAA	2	2	50	19	52	49	18	3	21	43	3.16	1.33	4.5	241	3.7	7.3	2.0	0.5	30%	77%	78
		12	25	aaa	LAA	7	3	55	13	60	69	28	1	22	44	4.21	1.53	4.7	292	3.3	6.6	2.0	0.1	36%	70%	75
		13	26	aaa	LAA	5	2	38	10	57	71	23	4	14	46	3.69	1.49	6.4	306	2.2	7.3	3.4	0.7	37%	76%	87
Britton,Drake	L	12	23	aa	BOS	4	7	16	0	85	104	46	3	39	64	4.94	1.69	23.9	303	4.2	6.8	1.6	0.4	36%	69%	58
		13	24	a/a	BOS	7	7	18	0	103	124	55	6	38	70	4.80	1.59	25.1	301	3.4	6.1	1.8	0.5	35%	69%	55
Buchanan,Jake	R	12	23	a/a	HOU	5	10	30	0	142	195	86	11	35	76	5.46	1.62	21	327	2.2	4.8	2.2	0.7	36%	66%	43
		13	24	a/a	HOU	12	7	30	1	158	172	59	11	22	85	3.38	1.23	21.4	278	1.3	4.8	3.8	0.6	31%	73%	90
Buckel,Cody	R	12	20	aa	TEX	5	5	13	0	69	64	36	9	23	58	4.72	1.26	21.7	247	3	7.6	2.5	1.2	29%	65%	68
Burgos,Hiram	R	12	25	a/a	MIL	8	3	21	0	130	128	41	8	46	94	2.86	1.34	25.7	259	3.2	6.5	2.0	0.6	31%	80%	67
		13	26	aaa	MIL	1	4	7	0	31	29	15	7	13	20	4.51	1.38	18.4	254	3.7	5.8	1.5	2.2	25%	77%	6
Cabrera,Alberto	R	10	22	aa	CHC	0	4	10	0	42	63	34	1	23	31	7.25	2.04	20.9	338	4.9	6.6	1.3	0.2	41%	61%	49
		11	23	a/a	CHC	9	8	28	0	137	192	99	15	70	85	6.50	1.91	23.7	324	4.6	5.5	1.2	1	37%	66%	19
		12	24	a/a	CHC	4	1	36	5	55	68	23	7	14	61	3.72	1.51	6.6	306	2.4	10	4.2	1.1	40%	79%	110
		13	25	a/a	CHC	10	6	33	0	133	151	68	15	54	103	4.61	1.55	17.6	287	3.7	7	1.9	1	33%	72%	48
Cabrera,Edwar	L	12	25	a/a	COL	11	5	21	0	130	111	57	28	37	92	3.99	1.15	24.5	234	2.6	6.4	2.5	2	23%	76%	40
Caminero,Arquimedes	R	13	26	a/a	MIA	6	2	43	5	54	43	29	5	25	59	4.76	1.26	5.1	219	4.2	9.7	2.3	0.8	29%	62%	94
Castro,Simon	R	10	22	a/a	SD	7	7	26	0	140	128	52	7	41	101	3.34	1.21	22.2	238	2.6	6.5	2.5	0.5	29%	72%	84
		11	23	a/a	SD	7	8	22	0	115	127	61	10	30	84	4.74	1.37	22.4	274	2.4	6.5	2.8	0.7	33%	65%	75
		12	24	a/a	CHW	7	5	20	0	115	147	64	8	31	76	5.01	1.55	25.1	311	2.5	5.9	2.4	0.6	36%	67%	60
		13	25	aaa	CHW	3	7	27	0	93	121	80	20	40	69	7.78	1.74	15.6	317	3.9	6.7	1.7	1.9	34%	57%	10
Chaffee,Ryan	R	12	24	aa	LAA	5	1	37	0	43	29	17	3	28	46	3.54	1.33	4.8	193	5.9	9.7	1.6	0.7	25%	75%	87
		13	25	aa	LAA	3	2	47	0	62	48	24	3	35	60	3.53	1.35	5.5	217	5.1	8.8	1.7	0.4	29%	73%	88
Chafin,Andrew	L	13	23	aa	ARI	10	7	21	0	126	145	55	7	43	74	3.91	1.49	25.9	289	3	5.2	1.7	0.5	33%	73%	51
Chapman,Kevin	L	11	23	aa	KC	1	2	25	3	40	40	24	4	20	41	5.34	1.50	7	257	4.4	9.2	2.1	1	33%	65%	73
		12	24	aa	HOU	6	3	49	2	58	53	18	2	30	50	2.76	1.44	5	245	4.7	7.7	1.6	0.3	31%	81%	78
		13	25	aaa	HOU	1	2	45	2	51	48	21	2	37	51	3.69	1.68	5.1	253	6.6	9.1	1.4	0.4	33%	78%	76
Clark,Tyler	R	13	24	aa	DET	1	0	22	0	33	43	16	1	21	26	4.39	1.96	7.1	320	5.7	7.2	1.3	0.3	39%	76%	51
Claudio,Alexander	L	13	21	aa	TEX	1	5	21	0	32	34	14	3	12	25	3.88	1.43	6.4	275	3.3	7	2.1	0.8	32%	75%	63

PITCHER	Th	Yr	Age	LvL	Org	W	L	G	Sv	IP	H	ER	HR	BB	K	ERA	WHIP	BF/G	OBA	bb/9	k/9	Cmd	hr/9	H%	S%	BPV
Cleto,Maikel	R	11	22	a/a	STL	7	5	20	0	106	97	45	6	49	87	3.86	1.38	22.7	239	4.2	7.4	1.8	0.5	30%	72%	73
		12	23	aaa	STL	3	2	45	2	54	55	33	3	21	55	5.61	1.42	5.1	266	3.6	9.3	2.6	0.6	35%	59%	94
		13	24	aaa	KC	3	5	35	1	91	99	69	5	76	72	6.84	1.91	12.4	278	7.5	7.1	0.9	0.5	34%	62%	46
Clinard,Will	R	13	24	aa	DET	2	3	22	1	34	43	26	7	20	20	6.75	1.84	7.3	310	5.2	5.4	1.0	1.7	33%	66%	-5
Cole,A.J.	R	13	21	aa	WAS	4	2	7	0	45	35	13	3	9	41	2.54	0.96	24.5	213	1.8	8.2	4.5	0.6	27%	76%	138
Colome,Alex	R	11	22	aa	TAM	3	4	9	0	52	43	25	5	26	27	4.25	1.33	24.5	221	4.5	4.7	1.1	0.8	24%	69%	38
		12	23	a/a	TAM	8	4	17	0	92	90	39	3	41	78	3.82	1.43	22.9	258	4	7.6	1.9	0.3	32%	72%	80
		13	24	aaa	TAM	4	6	14	0	70	71	27	5	28	61	3.50	1.42	21.3	264	3.6	7.8	2.1	0.6	33%	76%	75
Colvin,Brody	R	12	22	aa	PHI	1	4	7	0	33	48	45	6	22	14	12.50	2.14	23.1	341	6.1	3.8	0.6	1.7	35%	38%	-29
		13	23	aa	PHI	3	2	21	0	77	86	59	9	52	31	6.92	1.79	17	283	6.1	3.6	0.6	1.1	29%	61%	0
Conley,Adam	L	13	23	aa	MIA	11	7	26	0	139	149	65	8	42	117	4.19	1.38	22.4	276	2.7	7.6	2.8	0.5	34%	69%	89
Contreras,Carlos	R	13	22	aa	CIN	3	2	8	0	42	43	17	3	22	23	3.71	1.54	23.1	266	4.7	4.9	1.0	0.6	30%	77%	35
Cooney,Tim	L	13	23	aa	STL	7	10	20	0	118	142	53	7	17	105	4.02	1.35	24.7	299	1.3	8	6.0	0.5	37%	70%	153
Corcino,Daniel	R	12	22	aa	CIN	8	8	26	0	143	132	62	12	67	111	3.92	1.39	23.2	245	4.2	7	1.6	0.7	29%	73%	60
		13	23	aaa	CIN	7	14	28	0	129	169	110	23	76	78	7.65	1.90	21.7	317	5.3	5.4	1.0	1.6	34%	61%	-4
Crabbe,Timothy	R	12	24	aa	CIN	3	6	18	0	86	100	64	12	71	79	6.64	1.98	23	291	7.4	8.2	1.1	1.3	35%	68%	31
		13	25	a/a	CIN	7	9	27	0	153	191	72	18	47	90	4.26	1.56	24.8	307	2.8	5.3	1.9	1	34%	75%	34
Crosby,Casey	L	11	23	aa	DET	9	7	25	0	132	138	70	12	74	99	4.78	1.61	23.9	264	5.1	6.8	1.3	0.8	32%	71%	47
		12	24	aaa	DET	7	9	22	0	126	132	69	13	65	89	4.96	1.57	25.1	271	4.7	6.4	1.4	0.9	31%	70%	39
		13	25	aaa	DET	2	5	13	0	58	68	41	4	41	47	6.35	1.89	20.9	293	6.4	7.3	1.1	0.6	36%	65%	48
Cumpton,Brandon	R	12	24	aa	PIT	12	11	27	0	152	177	82	10	46	69	4.84	1.47	24.2	292	2.7	4.1	1.5	0.6	32%	66%	35
		13	25	a/a	PIT	6	8	23	0	132	146	62	6	48	75	4.24	1.47	24.6	283	3.3	5.1	1.6	0.4	32%	70%	50
Dayton,Grant	L	13	26	aa	MIA	4	4	30	1	38	42	14	5	14	48	3.26	1.48	5.4	281	3.4	11.3	3.3	1.1	38%	83%	101
Degrom,Jacob	R	13	25	a/a	NYM	6	7	24	0	136	165	68	9	40	89	4.52	1.51	24.5	301	2.7	5.9	2.2	0.6	35%	70%	59
DeSclafani,Anthony	R	13	23	aa	MIA	5	4	13	0	75	88	36	8	16	56	4.34	1.39	24.3	294	1.9	6.7	3.6	1	34%	71%	83
Drake,Oliver	R	11	24	a/a	BAL	3	5	13	0	66	94	48	11	26	40	6.51	1.81	24	328	3.5	5.4	1.6	1.4	36%	66%	12
		13	26	aa	BAL	3	0	19	8	31	23	8	1	14	30	2.18	1.19	6.5	208	4	8.7	2.1	0.4	27%	83%	99
Dwyer,Chris	L	11	23	aa	KC	8	10	27	0	140	135	94	12	73	102	6.04	1.48	22.8	247	4.7	6.6	1.4	0.8	29%	58%	51
		12	24	a/a	KC	8	12	26	0	136	172	101	21	67	83	6.70	1.76	23.9	309	4.5	5.5	1.2	1.4	33%	63%	10
		13	25	aaa	KC	10	11	29	0	160	169	80	16	75	88	4.50	1.53	23.9	273	4.2	5	1.2	0.9	30%	72%	28
Escobar,Edwin	L	13	21	aa	SF	5	4	10	0	54	44	15	1	11	47	2.52	1.03	20.8	225	1.9	7.8	4.1	0.2	29%	75%	136
Figueroa,Pedro	L	10	25	aa	OAK	1	6	13	0	71	95	48	6	28	48	6.13	1.73	25.4	313	3.6	6	1.7	0.8	37%	64%	40
		12	27	aaa	OAK	0	2	32	1	45	40	14	1	18	32	2.89	1.32	5.8	242	3.7	6.4	1.7	0.2	29%	77%	75
		13	28	aaa	OAK	3	4	46	2	59	66	30	8	35	37	4.54	1.70	5.8	284	5.3	5.6	1.1	1.2	31%	77%	18
Flynn,Brian	L	12	22	aa	MIA	3	1	9	0	50	63	28	4	15	30	5.01	1.56	24.3	308	2.8	5.4	2.0	0.7	35%	68%	47
		13	23	a/a	MIA	7	12	27	0	161	172	60	10	48	134	3.38	1.37	25	275	2.7	7.5	2.8	0.6	34%	76%	86
Foltynewicz,Mike	R	13	22	aa	HOU	5	3	23	3	103	82	37	8	51	85	3.18	1.28	18.4	220	4.4	7.4	1.7	0.7	26%	77%	69
Font,Wilmer	R	13	23	a/a	TEX	2	2	42	14	52	27	8	3	36	58	1.38	1.19	5	153	6.2	10.1	1.6	0.5	21%	91%	105
Fornataro,Eric	R	12	24	aa	STL	3	3	57	5	68	61	20	1	17	34	2.62	1.15	4.7	242	2.3	4.5	2.0	0.1	28%	76%	71
		13	25	aaa	STL	1	4	37	1	55	74	42	5	23	31	6.82	1.76	6.9	322	3.8	5.1	1.3	0.8	36%	60%	26
Freeman,Sam	L	12	25	a/a	STL	3	5	42	1	48	42	11	4	16	31	2.08	1.22	4.6	236	3.1	5.9	1.9	0.7	27%	86%	63
		13	26	aaa	STL	7	2	49	2	70	66	27	4	28	52	3.44	1.36	5.9	253	3.6	6.7	1.8	0.5	30%	75%	68
Gagnon,Drew	R	13	23	aa	MIL	4	9	16	0	84	111	66	16	45	51	7.05	1.85	24.5	319	4.8	5.4	1.1	1.7	34%	64%	-3
Garcia,Christian	R	12	27	a/a	WAS	2	1	45	21	52	39	6	0	18	50	1.11	1.07	4.5	207	3	8.6	2.8	0	28%	89%	124
Garcia,Onelki	L	13	24	a/a	LA	2	4	35	1	62	51	22	3	35	56	3.23	1.39	7.5	227	5	8.1	1.6	0.4	29%	77%	79
Garcia,Yimi	R	13	23	aa	LA	4	6	49	19	60	41	21	10	15	73	3.17	0.92	4.6	194	2.2	10.8	5.0	1.6	24%	76%	140
Gardner,Joe	R	11	23	aa	COL	10	11	25	0	134	157	74	8	53	65	4.98	1.57	24	287	3.5	4.4	1.2	0.6	32%	67%	33
		12	24	aa	COL	8	8	28	1	138	171	95	21	45	77	6.18	1.56	21.6	304	2.9	5	1.7	1.4	32%	62%	20
		13	25	aa	COL	6	4	35	2	55	69	52	10	20	46	8.39	1.61	7	305	3.3	7.4	2.2	1.6	35%	47%	37
Gast,John	L	11	22	aa	STL	4	4	13	0	79	77	31	7	28	46	3.52	1.33	25.9	250	3.2	5.2	1.6	0.7	28%	75%	48
		12	23	a/a	STL	13	7	28	0	161	175	77	13	54	106	4.33	1.42	24.4	278	3	6	2.0	0.7	32%	70%	55
		13	24	aaa	STL	3	1	7	0	39	31	6	0	13	29	1.29	1.14	21.9	223	3	6.7	2.2	0	28%	87%	97
Gausman,Kevin	R	13	22	a/a	BAL	3	6	16	0	82	91	38	5	14	70	4.19	1.28	21	282	1.5	7.7	5.0	0.5	35%	67%	134
Geltz,Steve	R	12	25	a/a	LAA	3	1	46	11	59	48	22	4	20	57	3.41	1.14	5.1	222	3	8.7	2.9	0.6	28%	71%	105
		13	26	aaa	TAM	5	3	41	3	67	41	25	8	25	65	3.36	0.98	6.2	180	3.3	8.7	2.6	1.1	21%	71%	94
Gilmartin,Sean	L	12	22	a/a	ATL	6	10	27	0	157	169	77	15	38	99	4.39	1.32	24.1	276	2.2	5.7	2.6	0.9	31%	68%	62
		13	23	aaa	ATL	3	8	17	0	91	128	69	13	33	57	6.78	1.77	24.5	332	3.3	5.6	1.7	1.2	37%	62%	21
Goforth,David	R	13	25	aa	MIL	4	3	20	5	47	39	22	1	20	30	4.33	1.27	9.5	230	3.9	5.8	1.5	0.3	27%	64%	67
Graham,J.R.	R	12	22	aa	ATL	3	1	9	0	45	40	19	2	17	37	3.85	1.26	20.6	238	3.4	7.4	2.2	0.4	30%	69%	85
		13	23	aa	ATL	1	3	8	0	36	46	21	0	10	24	5.20	1.59	19.7	316	2.6	6.2	2.3	0	38%	64%	78
Granier,Drew	R	13	25	aa	OAK	3	6	14	0	72	94	48	8	43	45	5.99	1.90	24.4	316	5.4	5.7	1.0	1	35%	69%	16

PITCHER	Th	Yr	Age	LvL	Org	W	L	G	Sv	IP	H	ER	HR	BB	K	ERA	WHIP	BF/G	OBA	bb/9	k/9	Cmd	hr/9	H%	S%	BPV
Guilmet,Preston	R	12	25	aa	CLE	2	2	50	24	53	52	19	5	14	41	3.31	1.25	4.3	258	2.4	7.1	2.9	0.8	30%	76%	83
		13	26	aaa	CLE	5	4	49	20	64	54	16	5	15	58	2.22	1.07	5.1	228	2.1	8.1	3.9	0.7	28%	82%	119
Gurka,Jason	L	13	25	aa	BAL	2	2	20	4	40	41	16	2	19	37	3.61	1.52	8.6	271	4.3	8.4	2.0	0.6	34%	77%	75
Hale,David	R	12	25	aa	ATL	8	4	27	0	146	147	79	13	72	104	4.86	1.50	23.3	264	4.5	6.4	1.4	0.8	30%	68%	48
		13	26	aaa	ATL	6	9	22	0	115	149	52	9	38	63	4.05	1.64	23.2	316	3	4.9	1.6	0.7	35%	76%	35
Haley,Trey	R	13	23	aa	CLE	1	4	39	7	44	40	24	0	36	39	4.98	1.73	5.1	243	7.4	8	1.1	0	32%	68%	77
Heaney,Andrew	L	13	22	aa	MIA	4	1	6	0	34	36	14	2	10	21	3.72	1.37	23.5	276	2.7	5.7	2.1	0.6	32%	73%	61
Heckathorn,Kyle	R	11	23	aa	MIL	0	4	7	0	36	50	33	8	17	21	8.08	1.85	24.7	321	4.2	5.2	1.2	1.9	34%	58%	-8
		12	24	aa	MIL	5	11	35	0	119	148	76	8	40	76	5.76	1.57	15	306	3	5.7	1.9	0.6	35%	62%	50
		13	25	aaa	MIL	8	3	48	1	65	58	30	6	32	38	4.17	1.38	5.7	239	4.5	5.3	1.2	0.8	26%	71%	39
Hellweg,Johnny	R	12	24	aa	MIL	7	11	28	0	140	141	62	9	78	90	3.99	1.57	21.9	264	5	5.8	1.1	0.6	30%	75%	43
		13	25	aaa	MIL	12	5	23	0	126	119	51	7	84	74	3.65	1.61	24.2	251	6	5.3	0.9	0.5	28%	78%	40
Hembree,Heath	R	12	23	aaa	SF	1	1	39	15	38	30	19	2	17	31	4.55	1.24	4	218	4.1	7.3	1.8	0.4	27%	61%	81
		13	24	aaa	SF	1	4	54	31	55	55	23	5	14	53	3.75	1.25	4.2	260	2.3	8.6	3.7	0.8	33%	72%	109
Hendricks,Kyle	R	13	24	a/a	CHC	13	4	27	0	166	164	44	5	35	107	2.39	1.20	24.8	259	1.9	5.8	3.0	0.3	31%	80%	93
Heston,Chris	R	12	24	aa	SF	9	8	25	0	149	151	49	2	41	113	2.94	1.29	24.4	264	2.5	6.8	2.7	0.1	33%	76%	97
		13	25	aaa	SF	7	6	19	0	109	134	66	10	41	80	5.46	1.61	25.4	304	3.4	6.6	1.9	0.8	35%	66%	49
Hoffman,Matt	L	10	22	a/a	DET	1	2	29	0	31	49	30	5	22	23	8.85	2.27	5.6	349	6.4	6.7	1.1	1.4	41%	61%	6
		11	23	a/a	DET	2	5	50	0	63	69	29	3	24	38	4.17	1.50	5.5	275	3.5	5.4	1.5	0.5	32%	72%	51
		12	24	aaa	DET	1	2	43	0	46	65	23	4	16	25	4.56	1.74	4.9	332	3.1	4.9	1.6	0.9	36%	75%	26
		13	25	aaa	DET	4	3	40	0	35	39	11	2	17	27	2.70	1.59	3.9	285	4.2	6.9	1.6	0.6	34%	85%	56
Holland,Neil	R	13	25	aa	WAS	1	4	41	1	51	58	20	3	11	50	3.56	1.35	5.2	287	1.9	8.8	4.6	0.6	37%	74%	128
Holmberg,David	L	12	21	aa	ARI	5	5	15	0	95	118	46	9	22	58	4.38	1.48	27.2	307	2.1	5.5	2.6	0.9	34%	72%	55
		13	22	aa	ARI	5	8	26	0	157	166	64	15	51	100	3.69	1.38	25.4	272	2.9	5.7	2.0	0.9	31%	76%	50
House,T.J.	L	12	23	aa	CLE	8	5	23	0	124	138	73	8	46	76	5.29	1.48	23.2	282	3.3	5.5	1.7	0.6	32%	63%	49
		13	24	a/a	CLE	9	11	28	0	164	210	89	12	56	115	4.87	1.62	26	312	3.1	6.3	2.0	0.7	36%	70%	53
Hultzen,Danny	L	12	23	a/a	SEA	9	7	25	0	124	95	46	4	74	121	3.33	1.37	20.8	214	5.4	8.8	1.6	0.3	29%	75%	91
		13	24	aaa	SEA	4	1	6	0	31	20	7	1	7	30	2.00	0.86	18.8	187	1.9	8.7	4.5	0.2	25%	77%	156
Jaime,Juan	R	13	26	a/a	ATL	2	5	35	0	42	38	26	1	31	57	5.59	1.65	5.4	243	6.7	12.3	1.8	0.3	38%	63%	111
Johnson,Erik	R	13	24	a/a	CHW	12	3	24	0	142	122	41	10	47	112	2.60	1.19	23.7	234	3	7.1	2.4	0.6	28%	80%	82
Jones,Devin	R	13	23	aa	BAL	4	7	24	0	123	166	94	20	48	90	6.86	1.74	23.4	323	3.5	6.6	1.9	1.5	36%	62%	25
Joseph,Donnie	L	11	24	aa	CIN	1	3	57	8	58	71	45	8	28	56	6.99	1.71	4.7	295	4.4	8.6	2.0	1.2	37%	59%	52
		12	25	a/a	KC	9	3	55	20	70	65	21	2	30	68	2.70	1.36	5.3	248	3.9	8.8	2.2	0.2	33%	80%	98
		13	26	aaa	KC	4	3	47	6	55	48	31	5	43	65	5.11	1.66	5.2	238	7	10.7	1.5	0.9	32%	70%	76
Jungmann,Taylor	R	13	24	aa	MIL	10	10	26	0	139	141	87	15	79	70	5.59	1.58	23.6	264	5.1	4.5	0.9	1	28%	65%	19
Kahnle,Tom	R	13	24	aa	NYY	1	3	46	15	60	46	25	5	48	61	3.77	1.57	5.7	215	7.2	9.1	1.3	0.8	27%	78%	69
Karns,Nate	R	13	26	aa	WAS	10	6	23	0	133	133	61	17	48	119	4.16	1.37	24.2	263	3.3	8.1	2.5	1.1	31%	73%	69
Kelly,Casey	R	10	21	aa	BOS	3	5	21	0	95	124	60	10	31	72	5.68	1.63	20.6	309	3	6.9	2.3	0.9	37%	65%	56
		11	22	aa	SD	11	6	27	0	142	153	58	6	43	95	3.70	1.38	22.6	269	2.7	6	2.2	0.4	32%	72%	73
Kickham,Mike	L	12	24	aa	SF	11	10	28	0	151	144	67	9	77	115	4.00	1.47	23.1	254	4.6	6.9	1.5	0.5	30%	73%	61
		13	25	aaa	SF	7	7	20	0	111	109	50	6	44	74	4.06	1.38	23.3	259	3.6	6	1.7	0.5	30%	70%	59
Kingham,Nick	R	13	22	aa	PIT	3	3	14	0	73	76	24	1	27	57	2.95	1.41	22.2	269	3.4	6.9	2.1	0.1	33%	77%	83
Lamb,John	L	10	20	aa	KC	2	1	7	0	33	38	21	2	11	24	5.71	1.50	20.8	283	3.1	6.6	2.1	0.5	34%	60%	67
		11	21	aa	KC	1	2	8	0	35	35	12	3	12	18	3.20	1.33	18.6	254	3	4.7	1.6	0.7	29%	77%	46
Lamm,Mark	R	12	24	aa	ATL	2	7	50	10	60	76	33	3	21	45	4.95	1.63	5.3	312	3.2	6.8	2.1	0.5	37%	69%	64
		13	25	a/a	ATL	6	6	53	10	68	74	28	2	38	59	3.74	1.65	5.7	279	5.1	7.7	1.5	0.3	35%	76%	69
Lee,Zach	R	12	21	aa	LA	4	3	13	0	66	75	35	6	20	44	4.74	1.46	21.6	289	2.8	6.1	2.2	0.8	33%	68%	55
		13	22	aa	LA	10	10	28	0	143	152	62	15	36	114	3.94	1.31	21.1	274	2.2	7.2	3.2	0.9	32%	72%	83
Leesman,Charles	L	10	24	aa	CHW	5	2	11	0	63	57	25	1	22	44	3.52	1.24	23.9	235	3.1	6.2	2.0	0.1	29%	69%	83
		11	24	aa	CHW	10	7	27	0	152	183	90	6	95	96	5.34	1.83	26.7	292	5.6	5.7	1.0	0.3	35%	69%	42
		12	25	aaa	CHW	12	10	26	0	135	165	53	12	64	87	3.53	1.70	23.5	303	4.3	5.8	1.4	0.8	34%	81%	34
		13	26	aaa	CHW	4	3	16	0	88	114	52	16	50	64	5.28	1.86	25.8	314	5.1	6.5	1.3	1.6	35%	76%	9
Leon,Arnold	R	12	24	a/a	OAK	4	0	32	1	51	47	12	4	18	41	2.07	1.26	6.5	246	3.1	7.3	2.3	0.6	30%	87%	80
		13	25	a/a	OAK	9	8	25	0	144	188	72	12	24	79	4.50	1.47	24.7	316	1.5	4.9	3.3	0.7	35%	70%	68
Lobstein,Kyle	L	12	23	aa	TAM	8	7	27	0	144	154	72	12	66	111	4.50	1.53	23.2	276	4.1	7	1.7	0.7	33%	71%	55
		13	24	a/a	DET	13	7	28	0	168	196	77	9	52	117	4.11	1.48	25.7	293	2.8	6.3	2.2	0.5	34%	72%	67
Lotzkar,Kyle	R	12	23	aa	CIN	4	6	18	0	86	93	66	16	56	83	6.92	1.73	21.8	277	5.8	8.6	1.5	1.7	32%	62%	32
Loux,Barret	R	12	23	aa	TEX	14	1	25	0	127	144	64	14	44	81	4.55	1.48	21.8	287	3.1	5.8	1.9	1	32%	71%	42
		13	24	aaa	CHC	4	6	19	0	80	98	51	4	48	64	5.74	1.83	19.6	303	5.4	7.2	1.3	0.5	37%	67%	51
Magill,Matt	R	12	23	aa	LA	11	8	26	0	146	143	70	8	58	142	4.32	1.37	23.6	257	3.6	8.7	2.4	0.5	33%	68%	92
		13	24	aaa	LA	6	2	18	0	86	76	33	6	47	85	3.42	1.43	20.2	239	4.9	8.9	1.8	0.7	31%	77%	78

PITCHER	Th	Yr	Age	LvL	Org	W	L	G	Sv	IP	H	ER	HR	BB	K	ERA	WHIP	BF/G	OBA	bb/9	k/9	Cmd	hr/9	H%	S%	BPV
Marinez,Jhan	R	11	23	aa	FLA	3	8	56	3	58	51	25	7	43	67	3.89	1.62	4.7	233	6.6	10.4	1.6	1	32%	79%	73
		12	24	aaa	CHW	4	2	40	4	63	49	28	7	36	56	4.01	1.35	6.6	216	5.2	8	1.5	1	26%	73%	61
Maronde,Nick	L	12	23	aa	LAA	3	2	7	0	32	46	15	1	3	18	4.26	1.52	20.1	336	0.9	4.9	5.8	0.3	38%	71%	129
		13	24	aa	LAA	2	4	41	0	56	47	26	4	36	53	4.16	1.48	5.9	229	5.7	8.5	1.5	0.6	29%	72%	73
Marshall,Brett	R	12	22	aa	NYY	13	7	27	0	158	173	75	19	54	103	4.27	1.43	24.9	279	3.1	5.8	1.9	1.1	31%	73%	41
		13	23	aaa	NYY	7	10	25	0	139	176	108	24	73	101	6.98	1.80	25.6	311	4.7	6.5	1.4	1.6	34%	63%	14
Martin,Cody	R	13	24	a/a	ATL	6	7	29	1	137	145	60	10	60	117	3.98	1.50	20.4	273	4	7.7	1.9	0.7	33%	74%	67
Martin,Ethan	R	11	22	aa	LA	5	3	21	2	40	32	18	3	25	38	3.92	1.40	8.3	213	5.5	8.5	1.5	0.6	28%	72%	78
		12	23	aa	PHI	13	6	27	0	158	133	71	9	78	126	4.03	1.34	24.3	231	4.5	7.2	1.6	0.5	28%	69%	71
		13	24	aaa	PHI	11	5	21	0	116	107	61	12	67	90	4.77	1.51	23.8	247	5.3	7	1.3	0.9	29%	70%	47
Martinez,Nick	R	13	23	aa	TEX	2	0	5	0	32	14	6	1	8	19	1.58	0.66	22.3	132	2.1	5.3	2.5	0.4	15%	79%	101
Matzek,Tyler	L	13	23	aa	COL	8	9	26	0	142	186	87	21	82	76	5.52	1.89	25.8	317	5.2	4.8	0.9	1.3	34%	73%	0
May,Trevor	R	12	23	aa	PHI	10	13	28	0	150	157	94	24	77	129	5.64	1.56	23.4	271	4.6	7.8	1.7	1.4	31%	67%	40
		13	24	aa	MIN	9	9	27	0	152	168	86	13	68	131	5.13	1.56	24.6	282	4	7.7	1.9	0.8	34%	67%	62
Mazzoni,Cory	R	12	23	aa	NYM	5	5	14	0	81	96	42	9	18	46	4.66	1.42	24.4	298	2	5.1	2.5	1	33%	69%	51
		13	24	aa	NYM	5	3	13	0	66	77	34	4	18	63	4.66	1.43	21.6	292	2.5	8.6	3.5	0.6	37%	67%	105
McGough,Scott	R	13	24	a/a	MIA	4	4	38	1	67	68	28	6	23	52	3.70	1.36	7.4	265	3.1	7	2.3	0.8	31%	74%	69
McGuire,Deck	R	12	23	aa	TOR	5	15	28	0	144	189	117	27	63	84	7.30	1.75	23.5	318	3.9	5.2	1.3	1.7	34%	60%	1
		13	24	aa	TOR	9	10	27	0	157	170	100	14	58	119	5.73	1.45	24.9	277	3.3	6.8	2.1	0.8	32%	60%	60
McNutt,Trey	R	11	22	aa	CHC	5	6	23	0	95	132	54	5	38	56	5.11	1.79	19.4	323	3.6	5.3	1.5	0.5	37%	70%	38
		12	23	aa	CHC	9	8	34	0	95	108	55	14	47	56	5.23	1.63	12.4	288	4.4	5.3	1.2	1.3	31%	71%	15
		13	24	aa	CHC	2	5	27	2	31	32	19	3	15	19	5.50	1.50	5	269	4.2	5.5	1.3	0.9	30%	64%	34
McPherson,Kyle	R	11	24	aa	PIT	8	5	16	0	89	87	36	7	21	65	3.65	1.21	23.1	251	2.1	6.5	3.1	0.7	30%	71%	86
		12	25	a/a	PIT	3	6	12	0	67	81	33	7	9	48	4.37	1.34	23.2	299	1.3	6.5	5.1	0.9	34%	69%	115
Meo,Anthony	R	13	23	aa	ARI	0	4	8	0	35	38	34	8	26	14	8.73	1.82	20.5	277	6.6	3.7	0.6	2	26%	53%	-26
Meyer,Alex	R	13	23	aa	MIN	4	3	13	0	70	66	28	3	29	70	3.58	1.36	22.5	252	3.7	9	2.5	0.4	33%	73%	100
Montero,Rafael	R	13	23	a/a	NYM	12	7	27	0	155	138	45	5	31	131	2.60	1.09	22.5	239	1.8	7.6	4.3	0.3	30%	76%	133
Montgomery,Mark	R	13	23	aaa	NYY	2	3	25	0	40	44	20	6	27	41	4.60	1.77	7.3	281	6	9.2	1.5	1.3	35%	77%	48
Montgomery,Mike	L	10	21	aa	KC	5	4	13	0	59	60	25	4	23	42	3.80	1.40	19.7	258	3.5	6.4	1.8	0.6	31%	73%	62
		11	22	aaa	KC	5	11	28	0	151	166	93	13	63	107	5.54	1.52	23.9	275	3.7	6.4	1.7	0.8	33%	63%	51
		12	23	a/a	KC	5	12	27	0	150	198	113	22	62	90	6.77	1.74	25.3	320	3.7	5.4	1.5	1.3	35%	62%	15
		13	24	aaa	TAM	7	8	20	0	109	126	65	9	47	65	5.38	1.59	24	291	3.9	5.4	1.4	0.7	33%	66%	36
Moran,Brian	L	11	23	aa	SEA	5	3	45	0	61	66	34	8	22	55	5.11	1.45	5.9	272	3.2	8.2	2.6	1.2	33%	67%	66
		12	24	a/a	SEA	4	5	47	2	69	59	22	7	18	71	2.92	1.13	5.8	234	2.4	9.4	3.9	0.9	30%	78%	120
		13	25	aaa	SEA	2	5	48	4	63	75	24	3	19	72	3.43	1.50	5.6	297	2.8	10.4	3.8	0.5	41%	77%	122
Morgan,Adam	L	12	22	aa	PHI	4	1	6	0	36	38	16	2	11	25	4.01	1.35	24.8	272	2.7	6.4	2.4	0.5	32%	70%	73
		13	23	aaa	PHI	2	7	16	0	71	94	36	11	26	42	4.57	1.67	20	318	3.2	5.3	1.6	1.4	34%	77%	17
Morin,Michael	R	13	22	aa	LAA	0	2	26	10	31	29	8	2	5	29	2.31	1.08	4.6	248	1.4	8.4	6.2	0.5	32%	81%	171
Munson,Kevin	R	12	23	aa	ARI	3	5	44	3	53	65	46	4	27	54	7.87	1.73	5.5	302	4.6	9.1	2.0	0.6	39%	51%	73
		13	24	a/a	ARI	2	4	53	14	55	48	29	7	21	55	4.73	1.26	4.2	236	3.5	9	2.6	1.1	29%	64%	84
Nelson,Jimmy	R	12	23	aa	MIL	2	4	10	0	46	39	24	2	38	37	4.65	1.67	20.6	231	7.4	7.2	1.0	0.5	28%	71%	59
		13	24	a/a	MIL	10	10	27	0	152	160	66	9	68	139	3.93	1.50	24.4	271	4	8.2	2.0	0.5	34%	74%	77
Nicolino,Justin	L	13	22	aa	MIA	3	2	9	0	45	74	32	2	13	29	6.28	1.92	23.9	365	2.6	5.7	2.2	0.4	42%	65%	48
Nolin,Sean	L	13	24	a/a	TOR	9	4	20	0	110	119	41	8	35	96	3.37	1.39	23.2	277	2.8	7.8	2.8	0.7	34%	77%	85
Northcraft,Aaron	R	13	23	aa	ATL	8	8	26	0	137	148	67	8	53	105	4.40	1.47	22.6	277	3.5	6.9	2.0	0.5	33%	69%	67
Nuno,Vidal	L	12	25	aa	NYY	9	5	20	0	114	133	40	14	29	80	3.16	1.42	24.2	292	2.3	6.3	2.7	1.1	33%	82%	60
Odorizzi,Jake	R	11	21	aa	KC	5	3	12	0	69	69	37	11	20	45	4.90	1.30	24.2	257	2.6	5.9	2.3	1.4	28%	66%	43
		12	22	a/a	KC	15	5	26	0	145	143	54	12	48	112	3.31	1.31	23.1	259	2.9	6.9	2.4	0.8	31%	77%	71
		13	23	aaa	TAM	9	6	22	0	124	112	51	12	38	107	3.72	1.21	22.8	242	2.8	7.7	2.8	0.8	29%	71%	87
Oliver,Andy	L	10	23	a/a	DET	9	8	23	0	130	132	59	15	48	102	4.08	1.38	24.3	258	3.3	7.1	2.1	1	31%	73%	59
Olmos,Edgar	L	13	23	aa	MIA	4	2	38	1	50	56	18	1	30	37	3.23	1.72	6	283	5.4	6.6	1.2	0.2	34%	80%	58
Oramas,Juan	L	11	21	a/a	SD	10	6	20	0	108	99	34	9	25	97	2.85	1.15	22	238	2.1	8.1	3.9	0.7	30%	78%	116
		12	22	aa	SD	3	4	8	0	35	41	25	4	15	30	6.43	1.59	19.5	290	3.9	7.6	1.9	1.1	34%	59%	52
		13	23	aa	SD	3	2	12	0	56	58	21	4	16	56	3.42	1.32	19.2	268	2.6	9.1	3.5	0.6	35%	75%	112
Ortega,Jose	R	11	23	aaa	DET	1	3	33	0	50	72	44	8	27	36	7.93	1.98	7.4	330	4.9	6.5	1.3	1.5	38%	60%	13
		12	24	aaa	DET	5	8	45	1	63	90	49	4	51	54	7.10	2.24	7.1	336	7.3	7.8	1.1	0.6	41%	67%	38
		13	25	aaa	DET	4	3	40	4	48	34	13	2	34	43	2.45	1.42	5.1	201	6.3	8	1.3	0.4	26%	84%	76
Owens,Henry	L	13	21	aa	BOS	3	1	6	0	30	20	7	3	15	40	2.14	1.16	20.1	193	4.4	11.8	2.7	0.9	27%	87%	116
Paxton,James	L	11	23	aa	SEA	3	0	7	0	39	31	9	2	13	45	2.05	1.12	22.5	214	3	10.4	3.5	0.4	31%	83%	135
		12	24	aa	SEA	9	4	21	0	106	115	46	5	58	96	3.88	1.63	22.5	277	4.9	8.1	1.6	0.5	35%	76%	69
		13	25	aaa	SEA	8	11	28	0	146	169	72	9	56	112	4.42	1.54	22.7	291	3.5	6.9	2.0	0.5	35%	71%	64

PITCHER	Th	Yr	Age	LvL	Org	W	L	G	Sv	IP	H	ER	HR	BB	K	ERA	WHIP	BF/G	OBA	bb/9	k/9	Cmd	hr/9	H%	S%	BPV
Pena,Ariel	R	12	23	aa	MIL	6	8	26	0	147	153	76	22	66	122	4.67	1.50	24.4	270	4.1	7.5	1.8	1.3	31%	73%	44
		13	24	aa	MIL	8	9	27	0	142	139	76	23	86	112	4.82	1.58	23.2	257	5.4	7.1	1.3	1.4	29%	74%	30
Petricka,Jake	R	12	24	aa	CHW	3	3	10	0	58	74	43	9	39	23	6.68	1.97	27.6	312	6.2	3.6	0.6	1.4	32%	68%	-15
		13	25	a/a	CHW	5	0	31	1	55	56	15	1	30	48	2.45	1.58	7.8	267	5	8	1.6	0.2	34%	84%	76
Pimentel,Stolmy	R	11	21	aa	BOS	0	9	15	0	50	80	55	7	22	26	9.81	2.03	16.6	354	3.9	4.6	1.2	1.3	39%	50%	-3
		12	22	aa	BOS	6	7	22	0	116	136	77	10	43	74	5.97	1.55	23	295	3.3	5.7	1.7	0.8	33%	61%	43
		13	23	a/a	PIT	6	9	27	0	169	167	71	13	52	99	3.77	1.30	25.8	259	2.8	5.3	1.9	0.7	29%	72%	54
Portillo,Adys	R	12	21	aa	SD	2	5	8	0	35	35	28	3	24	24	7.20	1.69	19.7	262	6.2	6.1	1.0	0.8	30%	56%	35
Pounders,Brooks	R	13	23	aa	KC	5	7	27	1	116	122	69	12	42	82	5.34	1.41	18.2	272	3.2	6.4	2.0	0.9	31%	63%	52
Quackenbush,Kevin	R	13	25	a/a	SD	10	2	57	17	65	53	12	1	28	71	1.70	1.25	4.6	225	3.9	9.8	2.5	0.1	32%	86%	118
Ramirez,Jose	R	13	23	a/a	NYY	2	6	17	1	74	69	40	14	38	65	4.87	1.45	18.5	249	4.7	8	1.7	1.7	28%	72%	39
Ramirez,Neil	R	11	22	a/a	TEX	5	3	24	0	93	82	36	7	41	93	3.50	1.31	16.5	230	3.9	9	2.3	0.7	30%	75%	89
		12	23	a/a	TEX	8	13	28	0	123	145	105	23	48	88	7.70	1.57	19.3	295	3.5	6.4	1.8	1.7	32%	52%	23
		13	24	aa	CHC	9	3	22	0	108	90	53	9	46	111	4.40	1.27	20	230	3.8	9.2	2.4	0.7	30%	66%	93
Ranaudo,Anthony	R	12	23	aa	BOS	1	3	9	0	38	50	37	5	28	23	8.88	2.06	20.4	318	6.7	5.4	0.8	1.1	35%	55%	8
		13	24	a/a	BOS	11	5	25	0	140	134	59	11	49	104	3.77	1.30	23.1	253	3.1	6.7	2.1	0.7	30%	72%	68
Rasmus,Cory	R	12	25	aa	ATL	3	5	50	7	59	55	31	3	34	52	4.75	1.52	5.1	249	5.3	8	1.5	0.5	31%	68%	69
		13	26	aaa	LAA	4	2	46	17	46	27	9	1	23	45	1.73	1.07	3.9	169	4.5	8.8	2.0	0.3	23%	85%	107
Rasmussen,Rob	L	12	23	aa	HOU	4	4	11	0	54	62	30	6	17	38	4.93	1.44	21.1	287	2.8	6.3	2.3	1	33%	67%	54
		13	24	a/a	LA	3	11	28	0	136	139	69	15	59	95	4.58	1.46	20.7	266	3.9	6.3	1.6	1	30%	71%	42
Ray,Robbie	L	13	22	aa	WAS	5	2	11	0	58	63	28	4	19	50	4.38	1.42	22.4	278	3	7.8	2.6	0.7	34%	69%	80
Reed,Chris	L	12	22	aa	LA	0	4	12	0	35	34	21	2	19	25	5.46	1.50	12.7	255	4.8	6.4	1.3	0.5	30%	62%	55
		13	23	aa	LA	4	11	29	0	138	150	74	10	65	91	4.82	1.57	20.8	279	4.3	5.9	1.4	0.7	32%	69%	43
Reed,Evan	R	10	25	a/a	FLA	2	1	32	5	42	42	9	1	15	33	1.98	1.37	5.7	255	3.3	7	2.1	0.2	32%	85%	84
		12	26	a/a	MIA	5	4	50	13	67	81	44	3	30	56	5.82	1.65	6	299	4	7.4	1.9	0.4	37%	62%	67
		13	27	aaa	DET	1	4	32	1	50	49	19	1	22	36	3.48	1.41	6.6	258	3.9	6.6	1.7	0.2	31%	74%	71
Rhee,Dae-Eun	R	12	23	aa	CHC	9	8	27	0	142	195	93	21	53	66	5.90	1.74	24.1	327	3.3	4.2	1.2	1.3	34%	68%	2
		13	24	aa	CHC	5	1	11	0	59	53	26	7	21	29	3.99	1.25	22	242	3.2	4.4	1.4	1	25%	71%	33
Riefenhauser,C.J.	L	13	23	a/a	TAM	6	1	51	11	74	46	11	5	18	60	1.35	0.88	5.3	182	2.2	7.4	3.3	0.6	22%	89%	115
Roach,Donn	R	13	24	aa	SD	8	12	28	0	143	156	64	7	41	66	4.01	1.38	21.4	279	2.6	4.2	1.6	0.4	31%	70%	46
Rodriguez,Eduardo	L	13	20	aa	BAL	4	3	11	0	60	57	31	6	23	52	4.72	1.35	22.6	254	3.5	7.8	2.3	0.9	31%	66%	73
Rodriguez,Santos	L	12	24	a/a	CHW	2	4	42	8	71	48	30	8	41	59	3.79	1.25	6.9	194	5.2	7.5	1.5	1	22%	73%	61
		13	25	a/a	CHW	2	0	33	0	48	42	35	6	50	51	6.64	1.93	6.9	240	9.4	9.6	1.0	1.1	30%	66%	54
Romero,Enny	L	13	22	a/a	TAM	11	7	28	0	148	123	47	8	70	99	2.83	1.31	21.9	228	4.3	6	1.4	0.5	26%	79%	60
Rosin,Seth	R	13	25	aa	PHI	9	6	26	0	127	136	69	14	35	79	4.88	1.35	20.3	276	2.5	5.6	2.2	1	31%	65%	51
Roth,Michael	L	13	23	aa	LAA	6	3	17	0	79	87	43	8	34	44	4.87	1.53	20.3	280	3.9	5	1.3	0.9	31%	69%	30
Ruffin,Chance	R	11	23	a/a	DET	3	3	44	19	49	43	13	3	22	49	2.46	1.32	4.7	231	4	9.1	2.3	0.6	31%	84%	93
		12	24	aaa	SEA	0	5	50	1	71	79	47	7	33	47	5.93	1.59	6.2	284	4.2	6	1.4	0.9	32%	62%	38
		13	25	a/a	SEA	5	6	31	0	113	126	56	14	30	70	4.46	1.38	15.3	284	2.4	5.6	2.3	1.1	31%	70%	48
Sampson,Keyvius	R	12	21	aa	SD	8	11	26	0	122	112	68	9	55	112	5.00	1.36	19.7	244	4	8.2	2.0	0.7	31%	63%	78
		13	22	a/a	SD	12	7	28	0	141	120	54	11	57	121	3.44	1.25	20.6	232	3.6	7.7	2.1	0.7	28%	74%	78
Sanchez,Jesus	R	11	24	aa	MIL	4	7	30	1	99	118	62	14	48	57	5.64	1.68	15.2	290	4.4	5.2	1.2	1.3	32%	69%	14
		12	25	a/a	MIL	7	3	52	11	72	68	16	2	24	54	2.04	1.28	5.6	252	3	6.7	2.3	0.3	31%	85%	84
		13	26	aaa	MIL	4	3	48	7	70	81	26	6	19	41	3.35	1.43	6.2	292	2.5	5.3	2.1	0.8	32%	79%	49
Schlosser,Gus	R	13	25	aa	ATL	7	6	25	0	135	146	48	6	48	84	3.22	1.44	23	277	3.2	5.6	1.8	0.4	32%	77%	58
Schrader,Clay	R	13	23	aa	BAL	5	4	35	0	56	57	32	7	35	52	5.10	1.64	7.1	265	5.7	8.3	1.5	1.1	32%	71%	49
Schugel,A.J.	R	12	23	aa	LAA	6	8	27	0	140	139	57	10	56	92	3.68	1.39	21.9	259	3.6	5.9	1.6	0.7	30%	74%	53
		13	24	aaa	LAA	4	6	19	0	89	119	60	8	27	64	6.03	1.63	20.9	320	2.7	6.5	2.4	0.8	37%	63%	54
Shoemaker,Matt	R	11	25	a/a	LAA	12	7	27	0	177	180	69	20	44	113	3.48	1.27	27.5	258	2.3	5.8	2.5	1	29%	76%	61
		12	26	aaa	LAA	11	10	29	0	177	247	111	22	42	99	5.67	1.64	27.1	332	2.1	5	2.4	1.1	36%	67%	35
		13	27	aaa	LAA	11	13	29	0	184	222	87	20	25	127	4.23	1.34	26.4	299	1.2	6.2	5.0	1	34%	71%	107
Smith,Burch	R	13	23	a/a	SD	6	3	18	0	92	76	27	4	22	90	2.59	1.06	19.9	226	2.1	8.8	4.2	0.4	30%	76%	138
Smith,Carson	R	13	24	aa	SEA	1	3	44	15	50	40	13	1	19	62	2.35	1.17	4.5	221	3.3	11.1	3.3	0.2	33%	79%	141
Snodgress,Scott	L	13	24	aa	CHW	11	11	26	0	144	179	101	13	70	77	6.31	1.74	25.2	307	4.4	4.8	1.1	0.8	34%	63%	21
Snow,Forrest	R	11	22	aaa	SEA	1	2	9	0	35	32	17	3	8	32	4.38	1.14	15.9	236	2.1	8.2	3.9	0.7	30%	62%	117
		12	24	a/a	SEA	5	9	32	0	118	145	93	10	68	86	7.08	1.81	17	305	5.2	6.6	1.3	0.7	36%	59%	38
		13	25	a/a	SEA	5	5	42	0	82	70	31	7	29	72	3.37	1.20	7.9	232	3.2	7.9	2.5	0.8	28%	74%	85
Spruill,Zeke	R	11	22	aa	ATL	3	2	7	0	45	48	17	3	16	14	3.39	1.43	27.9	268	3.2	2.8	0.9	0.6	29%	77%	20
		12	23	aa	ATL	9	11	27	0	162	184	82	9	47	92	4.54	1.43	25.5	288	2.6	5.1	1.9	0.5	33%	67%	55
		13	24	a/a	ARI	6	8	21	0	124	139	55	9	43	56	4.01	1.47	25.3	284	3.2	4.1	1.3	0.6	31%	73%	31
Stilson,John	R	12	22	aa	TOR	2	4	17	1	50	62	34	7	23	39	6.14	1.69	13.3	305	4.1	7	1.7	1.3	35%	65%	33
		13	23	a/a	TOR	6	2	35	5	50	45	14	3	15	45	2.59	1.19	5.7	242	2.6	8.1	3.1	0.6	30%	81%	101

PITCHER	Th	Yr	Age	LvL	Org	W	L	G	Sv	IP	H	ER	HR	BB	K	ERA	WHIP	BF/G	OBA	bb/9	k/9	Cmd	hr/9	H%	S%	BPV
Stites, Matt	R	13	23	aa	SD	2	2	46	14	52	41	13	6	8	45	2.31	0.94	4.3	218	1.4	7.8	5.6	1	26%	82%	147
Stripling, Ross	R	13	24	aa	LA	6	4	21	1	94	109	37	5	20	70	3.54	1.37	18.8	291	1.9	6.7	3.5	0.5	35%	74%	96
Stroman, Marcus	R	13	22	aa	TOR	9	5	20	0	112	109	46	14	25	111	3.74	1.21	22.5	258	2	9	4.4	1.2	32%	73%	115
Surkamp, Eric	L	11	24	aa	SF	10	4	23	0	142	133	42	6	46	135	2.63	1.26	25.8	242	2.9	8.6	2.9	0.4	32%	79%	109
		13	26	aaa	SF	7	1	11	0	71	59	21	3	18	43	2.67	1.09	25.4	228	2.3	5.5	2.4	0.4	26%	76%	81
Syndergaard, Noah	R	13	21	aa	NYM	6	1	11	0	54	48	18	8	11	62	3.04	1.09	19.2	239	1.8	10.3	5.7	1.3	31%	79%	151
Taillon, Jameson	R	13	22	a/a	PIT	5	10	26	0	147	156	67	8	48	117	4.12	1.38	23.8	273	2.9	7.2	2.5	0.5	33%	70%	80
Tejeda, Enosil	R	13	24	aa	CLE	1	1	33	0	41	25	4	0	12	30	0.96	0.93	4.6	181	2.7	6.7	2.5	0	23%	89%	110
Thomas, Ian	L	13	26	aa	ATL	7	8	39	1	104	91	44	9	41	101	3.79	1.27	10.9	237	3.5	8.7	2.5	0.7	30%	71%	89
Tonkin, Mike	R	13	24	a/a	MIN	2	4	52	21	57	61	25	3	16	54	3.94	1.35	4.6	275	2.5	8.6	3.4	0.4	35%	70%	108
Treinen, Blake	R	13	25	aa	WAS	6	7	21	0	119	150	60	10	33	68	4.55	1.54	24.6	309	2.5	5.1	2.1	0.8	34%	71%	44
Tropeano, Nick	R	13	23	aa	HOU	7	10	28	5	134	156	69	16	39	113	4.64	1.46	20.4	293	2.6	7.6	2.9	1.1	35%	70%	71
Turley, Nik	L	13	24	aa	NYY	11	8	28	0	145	149	83	15	82	116	5.13	1.60	22.9	268	5.1	7.2	1.4	1	31%	69%	45
Vance, Kevin	R	13	23	aa	CHW	2	6	40	7	69	66	39	6	42	73	5.15	1.57	7.6	254	5.5	9.6	1.7	0.7	33%	67%	76
Ventura, Yordano	R	13	22	a/a	KC	8	6	26	0	135	134	55	7	52	130	3.70	1.38	21.8	261	3.5	8.7	2.5	0.5	34%	73%	94
Verhagen, Drew	R	13	23	aa	DET	2	5	12	0	60	61	24	3	16	32	3.60	1.29	20.5	265	2.5	4.8	2.0	0.5	30%	72%	58
Vizcaino, Arodys	R	11	21	a/a	ATL	3	3	17	0	57	56	25	4	17	56	3.90	1.29	14	252	2.8	8.9	3.2	0.6	33%	70%	107
Von Schamann, Duke	R	13	22	aa	LA	3	5	16	0	67	94	45	8	20	44	6.12	1.72	18.9	334	2.7	5.9	2.1	1.1	37%	65%	36
Walker, Taijuan	R	12	20	aa	SEA	7	10	25	0	127	138	78	12	50	110	5.57	1.49	21.8	279	3.6	7.8	2.2	0.9	34%	62%	66
		13	21	a/a	SEA	9	10	25	0	141	119	49	10	55	147	3.10	1.23	22.9	230	3.5	9.3	2.7	0.6	30%	76%	102
Walters, Jeffrey	R	13	26	aa	NYM	4	3	53	38	56	53	14	2	16	49	2.33	1.22	4.3	250	2.5	7.9	3.1	0.3	32%	81%	107
Webster, Allen	R	11	21	aa	LA	6	3	18	0	91	103	49	6	30	65	4.88	1.46	22.2	279	3	6.4	2.1	0.6	34%	66%	65
		12	22	aa	BOS	6	9	29	0	131	158	73	2	62	110	5.02	1.68	20.3	299	4.3	7.6	1.8	0.2	38%	68%	73
		13	23	aaa	BOS	8	4	21	0	105	83	53	10	44	97	4.51	1.21	20.2	220	3.8	8.3	2.2	0.8	27%	64%	82
Welker, Duke	R	12	26	a/a	PIT	2	2	41	5	55	52	19	1	27	37	3.05	1.44	5.7	253	4.3	6	1.4	0.2	30%	78%	64
		13	27	aaa	PIT	3	4	48	9	63	65	31	3	32	48	4.42	1.53	5.7	267	4.5	6.9	1.5	0.4	32%	70%	62
Whiting, Boone	R	13	24	a/a	STL	8	7	27	0	136	150	63	12	47	109	4.19	1.44	21.5	280	3.1	7.2	2.3	0.8	33%	72%	68
Wieland, Joe	R	11	21	aa	SD	7	1	12	0	70	57	13	1	16	49	1.65	1.04	23.1	219	2	6.4	3.2	0.2	27%	84%	110
Wilson, Tyler	R	13	24	aa	BAL	7	5	16	0	89	99	46	16	23	57	4.59	1.36	23.3	281	2.3	5.8	2.5	1.6	30%	72%	39
Wisler, Matt	R	13	21	aa	SD	8	5	20	0	105	91	38	6	26	93	3.24	1.12	20.7	236	2.2	8	3.6	0.5	30%	72%	115
Wojciechowski, Asher	R	12	24	aa	HOU	2	2	8	0	44	33	12	0	13	29	2.38	1.05	21.1	209	2.7	5.9	2.2	0	26%	75%	94
		13	25	a/a	HOU	11	8	28	1	160	154	69	12	53	110	3.87	1.29	23.5	254	3	6.2	2.1	0.7	29%	71%	65
Wright, Austin	L	13	24	aa	PHI	6	5	27	0	94	101	68	14	58	64	6.53	1.69	15.8	276	5.5	6.2	1.1	1.3	30%	62%	21
Wright, Mike	R	12	22	aa	BAL	5	3	12	0	62	79	39	8	16	38	5.68	1.53	22.6	311	2.4	5.5	2.3	1.2	34%	64%	40
		13	23	a/a	BAL	11	3	27	0	150	183	63	11	40	116	3.79	1.48	24	301	2.4	6.9	2.9	0.7	36%	75%	77
Zych, Tony	R	13	23	aa	CHC	5	5	47	3	56	58	22	2	22	34	3.58	1.42	5.1	268	3.5	5.5	1.6	0.3	31%	74%	57

This section of the book may be the smallest as far as word count is concerned, but may be the most important, as this is where players' skills and potential are tied together and ranked against their peers. The rankings that follow are divided into long-term potential in the major leagues and shorter-term fantasy value.

HQ100: Lists the top 100 minor league prospects in terms of long-range potential in the major leagues. The overall list is the work of five minor-league analysts at BaseballHQ.com (Rob Gordon, Jeremy Deloney, Brent Hershey, Colby Garrapy and Chris Mallonee). Gordon and Deloney also provide their own personal lists.

ORGANIZATIONAL: Lists the top 15 minor league prospects within each organization in terms of long-range potential in the major leagues.

POSITIONAL: Lists the top 15 prospects, by position, in terms of long-range potential in the major leagues.

TOP POWER: Lists the top 25 prospects that have the potential to hit for power in the major leagues, combining raw power, plate discipline, and at the ability to make their power game-usable.

TOP BA: Lists the top 25 prospects that have the potential to hit for high batting average in the major leagues, combining contact ability, plate discipline, hitting mechanics and strength.

TOP SPEED: Lists the top 25 prospects that have the potential to steal bases in the major leagues, combining raw speed and base-running instincts.

TOP FASTBALL: Lists the top 25 pitchers that have the best fastball, combining velocity and pitch movement.

TOP BREAKING BALL: Lists the top 25 pitchers that have the best breaking ball, combining pitch movement, strikeout potential, and consistency.

2014 TOP FANTASY PROSPECTS: Lists the top 100 minor league prospects that will have the most value to their respective fantasy teams in 2014.

TOP 100 ARCHIVE: Takes a look back at the top 100 lists from the past eight years.

The rankings in this book are the creation of the minor league department at BaseballHQ.com. While several baseball personnel contributed player information to the book, no opinions were solicited or received in comparing players.

THE HQ100: TOP PROSPECTS OF 2014

1	Byron Buxton	OF	MIN		51	Alen Hanson	SS	PIT
2	Oscar Taveras	OF	STL		52	Marcus Stroman	RHP	TOR
3	Xander Bogaerts	SS	BOS		53	Kohl Stewart	RHP	MIN
4	Taijuan Walker	RHP	SEA		54	Max Fried	LHP	SD
5	Miguel Sano	3B	MIN		55	Jake Odorizzi	RHP	TAM
6	Francisco Lindor	SS	CLE		56	Michael Choice	OF	TEX
7	Javier Baez	SS	CHC		57	C.J. Edwards	RHP	CHC
8	Archie Bradley	RHP	ARI		58	Trevor Bauer	RHP	CLE
9	Carlos Correa	SS	HOU		59	Julio Urias	LHP	LA
10	Gregory Polanco	OF	PIT		60	Jake Marisnick	OF	MIA
11	Addison Russell	SS	OAK		61	Jesse Biddle	LHP	PHI
12	Jameson Taillon	RHP	PIT		62	Eddie Rosario	2B	MIN
13	Kris Bryant	3B	CHC		63	Lucas Sims	RHP	ATL
14	Dylan Bundy	RHP	BAL		64	Lance McCullers	RHP	HOU
15	George Springer	OF	HOU		65	A.J. Cole	RHP	WAS
16	Nick Castellanos	3B	DET		66	Rougned Odor	2B	TEX
17	Noah Syndergaard	RHP	NYM		67	Colin Moran	3B	MIA
18	Kevin Gausman	RHP	BAL		68	Mike Foltynewicz	RHP	HOU
19	Carlos Martinez	RHP	STL		69	Allen Webster	RHP	BOS
20	Robert Stephenson	RHP	CIN		70	Chris Owings	SS	ARI
21	Yordano Ventura	RHP	KC		71	Eduardo Rodriguez	LHP	BAL
22	Jonathan Gray	RHP	COL		72	Miguel Almonte	RHP	KC
23	Kyle Zimmer	RHP	KC		73	Blake Swihart	C	BOS
24	Albert Almora	OF	CHC		74	Jose Abreu	1B	CHW
25	Mark Appel	RHP	HOU		75	Zach Lee	RHP	LA
26	Aaron Sanchez	RHP	TOR		76	Danny Hultzen	LHP	SEA
27	Travis d'Arnaud	C	NYM		77	Matt Wisler	RHP	SD
28	Kyle Crick	RHP	SF		78	Matt Barnes	RHP	BOS
29	Joc Pederson	OF	LA		79	James Paxton	LHP	SEA
30	Alex Meyer	RHP	MIN		80	Rosell Herrera	SS	COL
31	Garin Cecchini	3B	BOS		81	Erik Johnson	RHP	CHW
32	Jorge Soler	OF	CHC		82	David Dahl	OF	COL
33	Jonathan Singleton	1B	HOU		83	Hak-Ju Lee	SS	TAM
34	Maikel Franco	3B	PHI		84	D.J. Peterson	3B	SEA
35	Lucas Giolito	RHP	WAS		85	Luke Jackson	RHP	TEX
36	Eddie Butler	RHP	COL		86	Delino DeShields	OF	HOU
37	Andrew Heaney	LHP	MIA		87	Brian Goodwin	OF	WAS
38	Jackie Bradley	OF	BOS		88	Hunter Dozier	SS	KC
39	Taylor Guerrieri	RHP	TAM		89	Matt Davidson	3B	CHW
40	Corey Seager	SS	LA		90	Anthony Ranaudo	RHP	BOS
41	Adalberto Mondesi	SS	KC		91	Jimmy Nelson	RHP	MIL
42	Billy Hamilton	OF	CIN		92	Bubba Starling	OF	KC
43	Clint Frazier	OF	CLE		93	Christian Bethancourt	C	ATL
44	Tyler Glasnow	RHP	PIT		94	Courtney Hawkins	OF	CHW
45	Kolten Wong	2B	STL		95	Domingo Santana	OF	HOU
46	Henry Owens	LHP	BOS		96	Kaleb Cowart	3B	LAA
47	Gary Sanchez	C	NYY		97	Jose Berrios	RHP	MIN
48	Jorge Alfaro	C	TEX		98	Braden Shipley	RHP	ARI
49	Austin Meadows	OF	PIT		99	Justin Nicolino	LHP	MIA
50	Austin Hedges	C	SD		100	Alex Colome	RHP	TAM

ROB GORDON'S TOP 100

#	Player	Pos	Team	#	Player	Pos	Team
1	Byron Buxton	OF	MIN	51	Alen Hanson	SS	PIT
2	Oscar Taveras	OF	STL	52	Lucas Giolito	RHP	WAS
3	Xander Bogaerts	SS	BOS	53	Aaron Sanchez	RHP	TOR
4	Francisco Lindor	SS	CLE	54	C.J. Edwards	RHP	CHC
5	Archie Bradley	RHP	ARI	55	Erik Johnson	RHP	CHW
6	Miguel Sano	3B	MIN	56	Miguel A. Gonzalez	RHP	PHI
7	Javier Baez	SS	CHC	57	Lance McCullers	RHP	HOU
8	Taijuan Walker	RHP	SEA	58	Lucas Sims	RHP	ATL
9	Carlos Correa	SS	HOU	59	Michael Choice	OF	TEX
10	Addison Russell	SS	OAK	60	Rosell Herrera	SS	COL
11	Gregory Polanco	OF	PIT	61	Gary Sanchez	C	NYY
12	Carlos Martinez	RHP	STL	62	Austin Hedges	C	SD
13	Kris Bryant	3B	CHC	63	Rougned Odor	2B	TEX
14	Albert Almora	OF	CHC	64	Julio Urias	LHP	LA
15	Robert Stephenson	RHP	CIN	65	David Dahl	OF	COL
16	Noah Syndergaard	RHP	NYM	66	Jake Marisnick	OF	MIA
17	Jameson Taillon	RHP	PIT	67	Marcus Stroman	RHP	TOR
18	George Springer	OF	HOU	68	Danny Hultzen	LHP	SEA
19	Nick Castellanos	3B	DET	69	Miguel Almonte	RHP	KC
20	Mark Appel	RHP	HOU	70	Trevor Bauer	RHP	CLE
21	Jonathan Gray	RHP	COL	71	Max Fried	LHP	SD
22	Dylan Bundy	RHP	BAL	72	Delino DeShields	OF	HOU
23	Kyle Zimmer	RHP	KC	73	Kohl Stewart	RHP	MIN
24	Billy Hamilton	OF	CIN	74	Eduardo Rodriguez	LHP	BAL
25	Kevin Gausman	RHP	BAL	75	Christian Bethancourt	C	ATL
26	Travis d'Arnaud	C	NYM	76	Matt Wisler	RHP	SD
27	Yordano Ventura	RHP	KC	77	Rafael De Paula	RHP	NYY
28	Jorge Soler	OF	CHC	78	Rafael Montero	RHP	NYM
29	Garin Cecchini	3B	BOS	79	Allen Webster	RHP	BOS
30	Kolten Wong	2B	STL	80	Blake Swihart	C	BOS
31	Maikel Franco	3B	PHI	81	A.J. Cole	RHP	WAS
32	Tyler Glasnow	RHP	PIT	82	Matt Barnes	RHP	BOS
33	Kyle Crick	RHP	SF	83	Zach Lee	RHP	LA
34	Corey Seager	SS	LA	84	Kyle Parker	OF	COL
35	Eddie Rosario	2B	MIN	85	Arismendy Alcantara	2B/SS	CHC
36	Jesse Biddle	LHP	PHI	86	Mike Foltynewicz	RHP	HOU
37	Eddie Butler	RHP	COL	87	Hunter Renfroe	OF	SD
38	Andrew Heaney	LHP	MIA	88	Stephen Piscotty	OF	STL
39	Joc Pederson	OF	LA	89	Matt Davidson	3B	CHW
40	Henry Owens	LHP	BOS	90	Colin Moran	3B	MIA
41	Alex Meyer	RHP	MIN	91	Anthony Ranaudo	RHP	BOS
42	Jorge Alfaro	C	TEX	92	Courtney Hawkins	OF	CHW
43	Jonathan Singleton	1B	HOU	93	Dorssys Paulino	SS	CLE
44	Jake Odorizzi	RHP	TAM	94	J.P. Crawford	SS	PHI
45	Taylor Guerrieri	RHP	TAM	95	Alex Reyes	RHP	STL
46	Adalberto Mondesi	SS	KC	96	Braden Shipley	RHP	ARI
47	Jackie Bradley	OF	BOS	97	Chris Stratton	RHP	SF
48	Clint Frazier	OF	CLE	98	J.R. Graham	RHP	ATL
49	Chris Owings	SS	ARI	99	Alex Colome	RHP	TAM
50	Austin Meadows	OF	PIT	100	C.J. Cron	1B	LAA

JEREMY DELONEY'S TOP 100

#	Player	Pos	Team	#	Player	Pos	Team
1	Byron Buxton	OF	MIN	51	Travis d'Arnaud	C	NYM
2	Taijuan Walker	RHP	SEA	52	Colin Moran	3B	MIA
3	Dylan Bundy	RHP	BAL	53	Jackie Bradley	OF	BOS
4	Miguel Sano	3B	MIN	54	Hak-Ju Lee	SS	TAM
5	Javier Baez	SS	CHC	55	Domingo Santana	OF	HOU
6	Oscar Taveras	OF	STL	56	Max Fried	LHP	SD
7	Carlos Correa	SS	HOU	57	Austin Meadows	OF	PIT
8	Francisco Lindor	SS	CLE	58	Braden Shipley	RHP	ARI
9	Kris Bryant	3B	CHC	59	Jose Abreu	1B	CHW
10	Kyle Zimmer	RHP	KC	60	Maikel Franco	3B	PHI
11	Xander Bogaerts	SS	BOS	61	James Paxton	LHP	SEA
12	Yordano Ventura	RHP	KC	62	Nick Kingham	RHP	PIT
13	Aaron Sanchez	RHP	TOR	63	Jose Berrios	RHP	MIN
14	Gregory Polanco	OF	PIT	64	Kaleb Cowart	3B	LAA
15	Archie Bradley	RHP	ARI	65	Henry Owens	LHP	BOS
16	Jonathan Gray	RHP	COL	66	Trevor Bauer	RHP	CLE
17	Mark Appel	RHP	HOU	67	Michael Choice	OF	TEX
18	George Springer	OF	HOU	68	D.J. Peterson	3B	SEA
19	Kevin Gausman	RHP	BAL	69	Alen Hanson	SS	PIT
20	Nick Castellanos	3B/OF	DET	70	Austin Hedges	C	SD
21	Addison Russell	SS	OAK	71	Anthony Ranaudo	RHP	BOS
22	Jameson Taillon	RHP	PIT	72	Alex Colome	RHP	TAM
23	Carlos Martinez	RHP	STL	73	Matt Wisler	RHP	SD
24	Andrew Heaney	LHP	MIA	74	Jake Marisnick	OF	MIA
25	Kyle Crick	RHP	SF	75	Lance McCullers	RHP	HOU
26	Taylor Guerrieri	RHP	TAM	76	Jorge Alfaro	C	TEX
27	Joc Pederson	OF	LA	77	Jorge Soler	OF	CHC
28	Lucas Giolito	RHP	WAS	78	Kolten Wong	2B	STL
29	Alex Meyer	RHP	MIN	79	Jake Odorizzi	RHP	TAM
30	Gary Sanchez	C	NYY	80	Miguel Almonte	RHP	KC
31	Clint Frazier	OF	CLE	81	Allen Webster	RHP	BOS
32	Robert Stephenson	RHP	CIN	82	A.J. Cole	RHP	WAS
33	Mike Foltynewicz	RHP	HOU	83	Billy Hamilton	OF	CIN
34	Tyler Glasnow	RHP	PIT	84	Alex Gonzalez	RHP	TEX
35	Jonathan Singleton	1B	HOU	85	J.R. Graham	RHP	ATL
36	Albert Almora	OF	CHC	86	Jimmy Nelson	RHP	MIL
37	Kohl Stewart	RHP	MIN	87	Zach Lee	RHP	LA
38	Corey Seager	SS	LA	88	Jonathan Schoop	2B	BAL
39	Luke Jackson	RHP	TEX	89	Courtney Hawkins	OF	CHW
40	Eddie Butler	RHP	COL	90	Jason Hursh	RHP	ATL
41	Garin Cecchini	3B	BOS	91	Brian Goodwin	OF	WAS
42	Noah Syndergaard	RHP	NYM	92	Eduardo Rodriguez	LHP	BAL
43	Hunter Dozier	SS	KC	93	Lewis Brinson	OF	TEX
44	Marcus Stroman	RHP	TOR	94	Erik Johnson	RHP	CHW
45	C.J. Edwards	RHP	CHC	95	Phil Ervin	OF	CIN
46	Blake Swihart	C	BOS	96	Edwin Escobar	LHP	SF
47	Vince Velasquez	RHP	HOU	97	Justin Nicolino	LHP	MIA
48	Julio Urias	LHP	LA	98	Stephen Piscotty	OF	STL
49	Adalberto Mondesi	SS	KC	99	Chris Owings	SS	ARI
50	Lucas Sims	RHP	ATL	100	Victor Sanchez	RHP	SEA

Top Prospects by Organization

AL EAST

BALTIMORE ORIOLES
1. Dylan Bundy, RHP
2. Kevin Gausman, RHP
3. Jonathan Schoop, 2B
4. Eduardo Rodriguez, LHP
5. Hunter Harvey, RHP
6. Mike Wright, RHP
7. Tim Berry, LHP
8. Christian Walker, 1B
9. Parker Bridwell, RHP
10. Michael Ohlman, C
11. Zach Davies, RHP
12. Stephen Tarpley, LHP
13. Henry Urrutia, OF
14. Adrian Marin, SS
15. Chance Sisco, C

BOSTON RED SOX
1. Xander Bogaerts, SS
2. Garin Cecchini, 3B
3. Blake Swihart, C
4. Jackie Bradley, OF
5. Henry Owens, LHP
6. Anthony Ranaudo, RHP
7. Allen Webster, RHP
8. Matt Barnes, RHP
9. Trey Ball, LHP
10. Mookie Betts, 2B
11. Drake Britton, LHP
12. Bryce Brentz, OF
13. Manuel Margot, OF
14. Brian Johnson, LHP
15. Deven Marrero, SS

NEW YORK YANKEES
1. Gary Sanchez, C
2. Eric Jagielo, 3B
3. Rafael De Paula, RHP
4. Tyler Austin, OF
5. Mason Williams, OF
6. Ty Hensley, RHP
7. Jose Campos, RHP
8. Manny Banuelos, LHP
9. Peter O'Brien, C
10. Jose Ramirez, RHP
11. Ian Clarkin, LHP
12. Mark Montgomery, RHP
13. Greg Bird, 1B
14. J.R. Murphy, C
15. Slade Heathcott, OF

TAMPA BAY RAYS
1. Taylor Guerrieri, RHP
2. Hak-Ju Lee, SS
3. Alex Colome, RHP
4. Jake Odorizzi, RHP
5. Enny Romero, LHP
6. Andrew Toles, OF
7. Jesse Hahn, RHP
8. Blake Snell, LHP
9. Ryan Brett, 2B
10. Felipe Rivero, LHP
11. Richie Shaffer, 3B
12. Ryne Stanek, RHP
13. Oscar Hernandez, C
14. Nick Ciuffo, C
15. Jose Mujica, RHP

TORONTO BLUE JAYS
1. Aaron Sanchez, RHP
2. Marcus Stroman, RHP
3. D.J. Davis, OF
4. Roberto Osuna, RHP
5. Alberto Tirado, RHP
6. Franklin Barreto, SS
7. Jairo Labourt, LHP
8. Andy Burns, SS/3B
9. Matt Dean, 1B
10. John Stilson, RHP
11. Chase DeJong, RHP
12. Kevin Pillar, OF
13. Mitch Nay, 3B
14. Adonys Cardona, RHP
15. Sean Nolin, LHP

AL CENTRAL

CHICAGO WHITE SOX
1. Jose Abreu, 1B
2. Courtney Hawkins, OF
3. Erik Johnson, RHP
4. Tim Anderson, SS
5. Matt Davidson, 3B
6. Marcus Semien, INF
7. Carlos Sanchez, 2B/SS
8. Adam Engel, OF
9. Tyler Danish, RHP
10. Daniel Webb, RHP
11. Trayce Thompson, OF
12. Leury Garcia, INF
13. Jacob Petricka, RHP
14. Chris Beck, RHP
15. Kevin Vance, RHP

CLEVELAND INDIANS
1. Francisco Lindor, SS
2. Clint Frazier, OF
3. Trevor Bauer, RHP
4. Dorssys Paulino, SS
5. Tyler Naquin, OF
6. Dace Kime, RHP
7. C.C. Lee, RHP
8. Cody Anderson, RHP
9. Jose Ramirez, 2B
10. Dylan Baker, RHP
11. Francisco Mejia, C
12. Luis Lugo, LHP
13. Sean Brady, LHP
14. Luigi Rodriguez, OF
15. Austin Adams, RHP

DETROIT TIGERS
1. Nick Castellanos, 3B
2. Jonathon Crawford, RHP
3. Jake Thompson, RHP
4. Devon Travis, 2B
5. Corey Knebel, RHP
6. James McCann, C
7. Eugenio Suarez, SS
8. Melvin Mercedes, RHP
9. Robbie Ray, LHP
10. Zac Reininger, RHP
11. Tyler Collins, OF
12. Daniel Fields, OF
13. Jeff Thompson, RHP
14. Casey Crosby, LHP
15. Austin Schotts, OF

KANSAS CITY ROYALS
1. Kyle Zimmer, RHP
2. Yordano Ventura, RHP
3. Hunter Dozier, SS/3B
4. Adalberto Mondesi, SS
5. Miguel Almonte, RHP
6. Jorge Bonifacio, OF
7. Bubba Starling, OF
8. Sam Selman, LHP
9. Sean Manaea, LHP
10. Elier Hernandez, OF
11. Jason Adam, RHP
12. Cheslor Cuthbert, 3B
13. Donnie Joseph, LHP
14. Orlando Calixte, SS
15. Cody Reed, LHP

MINNESOTA TWINS
1. Byron Buxton, OF
2. Miguel Sano, 3B
3. Alex Meyer, RHP
4. Kohl Stewart, RHP
5. Jose Berrios, RHP
6. Eddie Rosario, 2B
7. Lewis Thorpe, LHP
8. Travis Harrison, 3B
9. Jorge Polanco, 2B/SS
10. Josmil Pinto, C
11. Ryan Eades, RHP
12. Adam Brett Walker, OF
13. Felix Jorge, RHP
14. Trevor May, RHP
15. Mason Melotakis, LHP

AL WEST

HOUSTON ASTROS
1. Carlos Correa, SS
2. Mark Appel, RHP
3. George Springer, OF
4. Mike Foltynewicz, RHP
5. Jonathan Singleton, 1B
6. Vince Velasquez, RHP
7. Domingo Santana, OF
8. Lance McCullers, RHP
9. Rio Ruiz, 3B
10. Michael Feliz, RHP
11. Nick Tropeano, RHP
12. Delino DeShields, OF
13. Max Stassi, C
14. Chia-Jen Lo, RHP
15. Danry Vasquez, OF

LOS ANGELES ANGELS
1. Kaleb Cowart, 3B
2. Taylor Lindsey, 2B
3. C.J. Cron, 1B
4. Mark Sappington, RHP
5. R.J. Alvarez, RHP
6. Hunter Green, LHP
7. Alex Yarbrough, 2B
8. Natanael Delgado, OF
9. Nick Maronde, LHP
10. Jose Rondon, SS
11. Cam Bedrosian, RHP
12. Ryan Chaffee, RHP
13. Luis Jimenez, 3B
14. Mike Morin, RHP
15. Zach Borenstein, OF

OAKLAND ATHLETICS
1. Addison Russell, SS
2. Bobby Wahl, RHP
3. Billy McKinney, OF
4. Daniel Robertson, SS
5. Nolan Sanburn, RHP
6. Raul Alcantara, RHP
7. Matt Olson, 1B
8. Dillon Overton, LHP
9. Renato Nunez, 3B
10. Michael Ynoa, RHP
11. Max Muncy, 1B
12. B.J. Boyd, OF
13. Bruce Maxwell, C
14. Seth Streich, RHP
15. Chad Pinder, SS

SEATTLE MARINERS
1. Taijuan Walker, RHP
2. James Paxton, LHP
3. D.J. Peterson, 3B
4. Victor Sanchez, RHP
5. Edwin Diaz, RHP
6. Danny Hultzen, LHP
7. Austin Wilson, OF
8. Carson Smith, RHP
9. Stefen Romero, OF
10. Chris Taylor, 2B/SS
11. Luiz Gohara, LHP
12. Tyler Pike, LHP
13. Gabriel Guerrero, OF
14. Tyler Marlette, C
15. Tyler O'Neill, OF

TEXAS RANGERS
1. Luke Jackson, RHP
2. Michael Choice, OF
3. Jorge Alfaro, C
4. Alex Gonzalez, RHP
5. Lewis Brinson, OF
6. Rougned Odor, 2B
7. Luis Sardinas, SS
8. Nomar Mazara, OF
9. Nick Williams, OF
10. Joey Gallo, 3B
11. Wilmer Font, RHP
12. Ronald Guzman, 1B
13. Akeem Bostick, RHP
14. Jairo Beras, OF
15. Travis Demeritte, SS

TOP PROSPECTS BY ORGANIZATION

NL EAST

ATLANTA BRAVES
1. Lucas Sims, RHP
2. Christian Bethancourt, C
3. J.R. Graham, RHP
4. Jason Hursh, RHP
5. Mauricio Cabrera, RHP
6. Jose Peraza, SS
7. Tommy La Stella, 2B
8. Victor Caratini, 3B
9. Cody Martin, RHP
10. Victor Reyes, OF
11. Josh Elander, OF
12. David Hale, RHP
13. Todd Cunningham, OF
14. Luis Merejo, LHP
15. Shae Simmons, RHP

MIAMI MARLINS
1. Andrew Heaney, LHP
2. Colin Moran, 3B
3. Jake Marisnick, OF
4. Justin Nicolino, LHP
5. Adam Conley, LHP
6. Anthony DeSclafani, RHP
7. Jose Urena, RHP
8. Avery Romero, 2B
9. Brian Flynn, LHP
10. J.T. Realmuto, C
11. Mason Hope, RHP
12. Jesus Solorzano, OF
13. Nick Wittgren, RHP
14. Austin Brice, RHP
15. Brent Keys, OF

NEW YORK METS
1. Noah Syndergaard, RHP
2. Travis d'Arnaud, C
3. Rafael Montero, RHP
4. Dominic Smith, 1B
5. Wilmer Flores, INF
6. Brandon Nimmo, OF
7. Kevin Plawecki, C
8. Amed Rosario, SS
9. Cesar Puello, OF
10. Dilson Herrera, 2B
11. Michael Fulmer, RHP
12. Gavin Cecchini, SS
13. Jacob deGrom, RHP
14. Jeurys Familia, RHP
15. Cory Mazzoni, RHP

PHILADELPHIA PHILLIES
1. Maikel Franco, 3B
2. J.P. Crawford, SS
3. Jesse Biddle, LHP
4. Miguel Gonzalez, RHP
5. Carlos Tocci, OF
6. Aaron Altherr, OF
7. Roman Quinn, SS
8. Ethan Martin, RHP
9. Dylan Cozens, OF
10. Adam Morgan, LHP
11. Tommy Joseph, C
12. Kelly Dugan, OF
13. Severino Gonzalez, RHP
14. Zach Green, 3B
15. Cesar Hernandez, 2B

WASHINGTON NATIONALS
1. Lucas Giolito, RHP
2. A.J. Cole, RHP
3. Brian Goodwin, OF
4. Michael Taylor, OF
5. Nathan Karns, RHP
6. Matt Skole, 1B
7. Sammy Solis, LHP
8. Matt Purke, LHP
9. Jeff Kobernus, 2B
10. Eury Perez, OF
11. Steven Souza, OF
12. Jake Johansen, RHP
13. Tony Renda, 2B
14. Zach Walters, SS
15. Austin Voth, RHP

NL CENTRAL

CHICAGO CUBS
1. Javier Baez, SS
2. Kris Bryant, 3B
3. Albert Almora, OF
4. C.J. Edwards, RHP
5. Jorge Soler, OF
6. Arismendy Alcantara, SS
7. Dan Vogelbach, 1B
8. Pierce Johnson, RHP
9. Mike Olt, 3B
10. Arodys Vizcaino, RHP
11. Eloy Jimenez, OF
12. Gleyber Torres, SS
13. Rob Zastryzny, LHP
14. Christian Villanueva, 3B
15. Jeimer Candelario, 3B

CINCINNATI REDS
1. Robert Stephenson, RHP
2. Billy Hamilton, OF
3. Phillip Ervin, OF
4. Jesse Winker, OF
5. Nick Travieso, RHP
6. Yorman Rodriguez, OF
7. Michael Lorenzen, RHP
8. Daniel Corcino, RHP
9. Carlos Contreras, RHP
10. Ben Lively, RHP
11. Ryan Wright, 2B
12. Tanner Rahier, 3B
13. Neftali Soto, 3B
14. Amir Garrett, LHP
15. Gabriel Rosa, OF

MILWAUKEE BREWERS
1. Jimmy Nelson, RHP
2. Tyrone Taylor, OF
3. Victor Roache, OF
4. Devin Williams, RHP
5. Mitch Haniger, OF
6. Orlando Arcia, SS
7. Taylor Jungmann, RHP
8. Johnny Hellweg, RHP
9. Tucker Neuhaus, SS/3B
10. David Goforth, RHP
11. Jorge Lopez, RHP
12. Hunter Morris, 1B
13. Clint Coulter, C
14. Nick Delmonico, 3B
15. Jed Bradley, LHP

PITTSBURGH PIRATES
1. Gregory Polanco, OF
2. Jameson Taillon, RHP
3. Tyler Glasnow, RHP
4. Austin Meadows, OF
5. Alen Hanson, SS
6. Josh Bell, OF
7. Reese McGuire, C
8. Nick Kingham, RHP
9. Luis Heredia, RHP
10. Barrett Barnes, OF
11. Harold Ramirez, OF
12. Wyatt Mathisen, C
13. Jin-De Jhang, C
14. Tony Sanchez, C
15. Cody Dickson, LHP

ST. LOUIS CARDINALS
1. Oscar Taveras, OF
2. Carlos Martinez, RHP
3. Kolten Wong, 2B
4. Stephen Piscotty, OF
5. Alex Reyes, RHP
6. Marco Gonzales, LHP
7. Rob Kaminsky, LHP
8. Tyrell Jenkins, RHP
9. Tim Cooney, LHP
10. James Ramsey, OF
11. Randal Grichuk, OF
12. Charlie Tilson, OF
13. Carson Kelly, 3B/C
14. Patrick Wisdom, 3B
15. John Gast, LHP

NL WEST

ARIZONA DIAMONDBACKS
1. Archie Bradley, RHP
2. Chris Owings, SS
3. Braden Shipley, RHP
4. Jake Lamb, 3B
5. Aaron Blair, RHP
6. Stryker Trahan, C
7. Jake Barrett, RHP
8. Jose Martinez, RHP
9. Brandon Drury, 3B
10. Justin Williams, OF
11. Matt Stites, RHP
12. Sergio Alcantara, SS
13. Andrew Chafin, RHP
14. Brad Keller, RHP
15. Jamie Westbrook, 2B

COLORADO ROCKIES
1. Jonathan Gray, RHP
2. Eddie Butler, RHP
3. Rosell Herrera, SS
4. David Dahl, OF
5. Kyle Parker, OF
6. Chad Bettis, RHP
7. Ryan McMahon, 3B
8. Tom Murphy, C
9. Raimel Tapia, OF
10. Trevor Story, SS
11. Tyler Anderson, LHP
12. Jayson Aquino, LHP
13. Tyler Matzek, LHP
14. Tim Wheeler, OF
15. Emerson Jimenez, SS

LOS ANGELES DODGERS
1. Joc Pederson, OF
2. Zach Lee, RHP
3. Corey Seager, SS
4. Julio Urias, LHP
5. Chris Anderson, RHP
6. Alexander Guerrero, 2B
7. Chris Reed, LHP
8. Ross Stripling, RHP
9. Alex Santana, 3B
10. Onelki Garcia, LHP
11. Matt Magill, RHP
12. Zach Bird, RHP
13. Jose Dominguez, RHP
14. Noel Cuevas, OF
15. Tom Windle, LHP

SAN DIEGO PADRES
1. Austin Hedges, C
2. Max Fried, LHP
3. Matt Wisler, RHP
4. Hunter Renfroe, OF
5. Joe Ross, RHP
6. Casey Kelly, RHP
7. Rymer Liriano, OF
8. Jace Peterson, SS
9. Keyvius Sampson, RHP
10. Zach Eflin, RHP
11. Burch Smith, RHP
12. Matt Andriese, RHP
13. Walker Weickel, RHP
14. Joe Wieland, RHP
15. Cory Spangenberg, 2B

SAN FRANCISCO GIANTS
1. Kyle Crick, RHP
2. Edwin Escobar, LHP
3. Adalberto Mejia, LHP
4. Mac Williamson, OF
5. Christian Arroyo, SS
6. Clayton Blackburn, RHP
7. Joe Panik, 2B
8. Chris Stratton, RHP
9. Ty Blach, LHP
10. Heath Hembree, RHP
11. Martin Agosta, RHP
12. Ryder Jones, 3B
13. Keury Mella, RHP
14. Gustavo Cabrera, OF
15. Johneshwy Fargas, OF

TOP PROSPECTS BY POSITION

CATCHER
1. Travis d'Arnaud, NYM
2. Gary Sanchez, NYY
3. Jorge Alfaro, TEX
4. Austin Hedges, SD
5. Blake Swihart, BOS
6. Christian Bethancourt, ATL
7. Kevin Plawecki, NYM
8. Josmil Pinto, MIN
9. James McCann, DET
10. Reese McGuire, PIT
11. Tom Murphy, COL
12. Stryker Trahan, ARI
13. J.R. Murphy, NYY
14. Nick Ciuffo, TAM
15. Max Stassi, HOU

FIRST BASE
1. Jonathan Singleton, HOU
2. Jose Abreu, CHW
3. Dominic Smith, NYM
4. C.J. Cron, LAA
5. Dan Vogelbach, CHC
6. Matt Skole, WAS
7. Christian Walker, BAL
8. Greg Bird, NYY
9. Hunter Morris, MIL
10. Matt Olson, OAK
11. Max Muncy, OAK
12. Seth Mejias-Brean, CIN
13. Ronald Guzman, TEX
14. Matt Dean, TOR
15. Keon Barnum, CHW

SECOND BASE
1. Kolten Wong, STL
2. Eddie Rosario, MIN
3. Rougned Odor, TEX
4. Jonathan Schoop, BAL
5. Cory Spangenberg, SD
6. Taylor Lindsey, LAA
7. Mookie Betts, BOS
8. Wilmer Flores, NYM
9. Tommy La Stella, ATL
10. Alex Guerrero, LA
11. Avery Romero, MIA
12. Ryan Brett, TAM
13. Joe Panik, SF
14. Dilson Herrera, NYM
15. Devon Travis, DET

SHORTSTOP
1. Xander Bogaerts, BOS
2. Francisco Lindor, CLE
3. Javier Baez, CHC
4. Carlos Correa, HOU
5. Addison Russell, OAK
6. Corey Seager, LA
7. Adalberto Mondesi, KC
8. Alen Hanson, PIT
9. Chris Owings, ARI
10. Rosell Herrera, COL
11. Hak-Ju Lee, TAM
12. Hunter Dozier, KC
13. Arismendy Alcantara, CHC
14. Luis Sardinas, TEX
15. J.P. Crawford, PHI

THIRD BASE
1. Miguel Sano, MIN
2. Kris Bryant, CHC
3. Nick Castellanos, DET
4. Garin Cecchini, BOS
5. Maikel Franco, PHI
6. Colin Moran, MIA
7. D.J. Peterson, SEA
8. Matt Davidson, CHW
9. Kaleb Cowart, LAA
10. Rio Ruiz, HOU
11. Mike Olt, CHC
12. Joey Gallo, TEX
13. Jake Lamb, ARI
14. Brandon Drury, ARI
15. Ryan McMahon, COL

OUTFIELD
1. Byron Buxton, MIN
2. Oscar Taveras, STL
3. Gregory Polanco, PIT
4. George Springer, HOU
5. Albert Almora, CHC
6. Joc Pederson, LA
7. Jorge Soler, CHC
8. Jackie Bradley, BOS
9. Billy Hamilton, CIN
10. Clint Frazier, CLE
11. Austin Meadows, PIT
12. Michael Choice, TEX
13. Jake Marisnick, MIA
14. David Dahl, COL
15. Delino DeShields, HOU
16. Brian Goodwin, WAS
17. Bubba Starling, KC
18. Courtney Hawkins, CHW
19. Domingo Santana, HOU
20. Josh Bell, PIT
21. Jorge Bonifacio, KC
22. Stephen Piscotty, STL
23. Lewis Brinson, TEX
24. Kyle Parker, COL
25. Hunter Renfroe, SD
26. Tyrone Taylor, MIL
27. Phil Ervin, CIN
28. D.J. Davis, TOR
29. Mason Williams, NYY
30. Victor Roache, MIL
31. Rymer Liriano, SD
32. Jesse Winker, CIN
33. Andrew Toles, TAM
34. Randal Grichuk, STL
35. Carlos Tocci, PHI
36. Michael Taylor, WAS
37. Adam Brett Walker, MIN
38. Bryce Brentz, BOS
39. Harold Ramirez, PIT
40. Brandon Nimmo, NYM
41. Yorman Rodriguez, CIN
42. Nick Williams, TEX
43. Nomar Mazara, TEX
44. Mitch Haniger, MIL
45. Raimel Tapia, COL

STARTING PITCHER
1. Taijuan Walker, SEA
2. Archie Bradley, ARI
3. Jameson Taillon, PIT
4. Dylan Bundy, BAL
5. Noah Syndergaard, NYM
6. Kevin Gausman, BAL
7. Carlos Martinez, STL
8. Robert Stephenson, CIN
9. Yordano Ventura, KC
10. Jonathan Gray, COL
11. Kyle Zimmer, KC
12. Mark Appel, HOU
13. Aaron Sanchez, TOR
14. Kyle Crick, SF
15. Alex Meyer, MIN
16. Lucas Giolito, WAS
17. Eddie Butler, COL
18. Andrew Heaney, MIA
19. Taylor Guerrieri, TAM
20. Tyler Glasnow, PIT
21. Henry Owens, BOS
22. Marcus Stroman, TOR
23. Kohl Stewart, MIN
24. Max Fried, SD
25. Jake Odorizzi, TAM
26. C.J. Edwards, CHC
27. Trevor Bauer, CLE
28. Julio Urias, LA
29. Jesse Biddle, PHI
30. Lucas Sims, ATL
31. Lance McCullers, HOU
32. A.J. Cole, WAS
33. Mike Foltynewicz, HOU
34. Allen Webster, BOS
35. Eduardo Rodriguez, BAL
36. Miguel Almonte, KC
37. Zach Lee, LA
38. Danny Hultzen, SEA
39. Matt Wisler, SD
40. Matt Barnes, BOS
41. James Paxton, SEA
42. Erik Johnson, CHW
43. Luke Jackson, TEX
44. Anthony Ranaudo, BOS
45. Jimmy Nelson, MIL
46. Alex Colome, TAM
47. Justin Nicolino, MIA
48. Vince Velasquez, HOU
49. Hunter Harvey, BAL
50. Jose Berrios, MIN
51. Braden Shipley, ARI
52. Rafael Montero, NYM
53. Rafael De Paula, NYY
54. Nick Kingham, PIT
55. J.R. Graham, ATL
56. Trey Ball, BOS
57. Alex Gonzalez, TEX
58. Clayton Blackburn, SF
59. Trevor May, MIN
60. Jason Hursh, ATL

61. Daniel Norris, TOR
62. Alex Reyes, STL
63. Casey Kelly, SD
64. Edwin Escobar, SF
65. Chris Stratton, SF
66. Victor Sanchez, SEA
67. Miguel Gonzalez, PHI
68. Chad Bettis, COL
69. Luis Heredia, PIT
70. Sean Manaea, KC
71. Mark Sappington, LAA
72. Anthony DeSclafani, MIA
73. Mauricio Cabrera, ATL
74. Edwin Diaz, SEA
75. Jesse Hahn, TAM

RELIEF PITCHERS
1. Heath Hembree, SF
2. Chia-Jen Lo, HOU
3. Jake Barrett, ARI
4. Shae Simmons, ATL
5. Corey Knebel, DET
6. Carson Smith, SEA
7. Daniel Webb, CHW
8. Kevin Quackenbush, SD
9. Matt Stites, ARI
10. Scott Oberg, COL
11. Aaron Barrett, WAS
12. R.J. Alvarez, LAA
13. Vic Black, NYM
14. Sam Freeman, STL
15. Mark Montgomery, NYY

TOP PROSPECTS BY SKILLS

2014 TOP FANTASY IMPACT

TOP POWER

Joey Gallo, 3B, TEX
Miguel Sano, 3B, MIN
Javier Baez, SS, CHC
Oscar Taveras, OF, STL
Kris Bryant, 3B, CHC
George Springer, OF, HOU
Joc Pederson, OF, LA
Jose Abreu, 1B, CHW
Domingo Santana, OF, HOU
Dan Vogelbach, 1B, CHC
Gary Sanchez, C, NYY
Jonathan Singleton, 1B, HOU
Jesse Winker, OF, CIN
Jorge Alfaro, C, TEX
Mike Olt, 3B, CHC
Michael Choice, OF, TEX
Xander Bogaerts, SS, BOS
Kyle Parker, OF, COL
Adam Brett Walker, OF, MIN
Travis d'Arnaud, C, NYM
C.J. Cron, 1B, LAA
Victor Roache, OF, MIL
Robby Hefflinger, OF, ATL
Zach Walters, SS, WAS
Renato Nunez, 3B, OAK

TOP SPEED

Billy Hamilton, OF, CIN
Byron Buxton, OF, MIN
Delino DeShields, OF, HOU
Gregory Polanco, OF, PIT
Michael Taylor, OF, WAS
Rymer Liriano, OF, SD
Tim Anderson, SS, CHW
Jace Peterson, SS, SD
Andrew Toles, OF, TAM
Francisco Lindor, SS, CLE
George Springer, OF, HOU
Alen Hanson, SS, PIT
D.J. Davis, OF, TOR
Junior Arias, OF, CIN
Keenyn Walker, OF, CHW
Hak-Ju Lee, SS, TAM
Billy Burns, OF, OAK
Mookie Betts, 2B, BOS
Luis Sardinas, SS, TEX
Eury Perez, OF, WAS
Chris Taylor, SS, SEA
Micah Johnson, 2B, CHW
James Baldwin, OF, LA
Addison Russell, SS, OAK
Adalberto Mondesi, SS, KC

TOP BREAKING BALL

Mark Appel, RHP, HOU
Jonathan Gray, RHP, COL
Carlos Martinez, RHP, STL
Marcus Stroman, RHP, TOR
Yordano Ventura, RHP, KC
Aaron Sanchez, RHP, TOR
Kyle Zimmer, RHP, KC
Taijuan Walker, RHP, SEA
Kyle Crick, RHP, SF
Archie Bradley, RHP, ARI
Dylan Bundy, RHP, BAL
Noah Syndergaard, RHP, NYM
James Paxton, LHP, SEA

TOP BA

Byron Buxton, OF, MIN
Oscar Taveras, OF, STL
Kris Bryant, 3B, CHC
Jesse Winker, OF, CIN
D.J. Peterson, 3B, SEA
Albert Almora, OF, CHC
Francisco Lindor, SS, CLE
Nick Castellanos, 3B, DET
Colin Moran, 3B, MIA
Rosell Herrera, SS, COL
Carlos Correa, SS, HOU
Garin Cecchini, 3B, BOS
Phillip Ervin, OF, CIN
Eddie Rosario, 2B, MIN
Corey Seager, SS, LA
Travis d'Arnaud, C, NYM
Eric Jagielo, 3B, NYY
Dominic Smith, 1B, NYM
Mookie Betts, 2B, BOS
David Dahl, OF, COL
Miguel Sano, 3B, MIN
Joc Pederson, OF, LA
Addison Russell, SS, OAK
Devon Travis, 2B, DET
Christian Walker, 1B, BAL

TOP FASTBALL

Dylan Bundy, RHP, BAL
Taijuan Walker, RHP, SEA
Carlos Martinez, RHP, STL
Jonathan Gray, RHP, COL
Jameson Taillon, RHP, PIT
Lucas Giolito, RHP, WAS
Mike Foltynewicz, RHP, HOU
Mark Appel, RHP, HOU
Archie Bradley, RHP, ARI
Eddie Butler, RHP, COL
Kyle Crick, RHP, SF
Yordano Ventura, RHP, KC
Lance McCullers, RHP, HOU
Noah Syndergaard, RHP, NYM
C.J. Edwards, RHP, CHC
Kevin Gausman, RHP, BAL
Robert Stephenson, RHP, CIN
Aaron Sanchez, RHP, TOR
Max Fried, LHP, SD
Kyle Zimmer, RHP, KC
Alex Meyer, RHP, MIN
Tyler Glasnow, RHP, PIT
Braden Shipley, RHP, ARI
Andrew Heaney, LHP, MIA
Jose Dominguez, RHP, LA

Lucas Giolito, RHP, WAS
Andrew Heaney, LHP, MIA
Justin Nicolino, LHP, MIA
Jameson Taillon, RHP, PIT
C.J. Edwards, RHP, CHC
Carson Smith, RHP, SEA
Michael Fulmer, RHP, NYM
Taylor Guerrieri, RHP, TAM
Alex Gonzalez, RHP, TEX
Nate Karns, RHP, WAS
Erik Johnson, RHP, CHW
Trevor Bauer, RHP, CLE
Alex Meyer, RHP, MIN

1 Jose Abreu (1B, CHW)
2 Xander Bogaerts (INF, BOS)
3 Carlos Martinez (RHP, STL)
4 Billy Hamilton (OF, CIN)
5 Oscar Taveras (OF, STL)
6 Travis D'Arnaud (C, NYM)
7 Yordano Ventura (RHP, KC)
8 Jonathan Singleton (1B, HOU)
9 Nick Castellanos (3B, DET)
10 Matt Davidson (3B, CHW)

11 Trevor Bauer (RHP, CLE)
12 George Springer (OF, HOU)
13 Taijuan Walker (RHP, SEA)
14 Kevin Gausman (RHP, BAL)
15 Marcus Semien (INF, CHW)
16 Jake Marisnick (OF, MIA)
17 Archie Bradley (RHP, ARI)
18 Michael Choice (OF, TEX)
19 Jake Odorizzi (RHP, TAM)
20 Rafael Montero (RHP, NYM)

21 Chris Owings (SS, ARI)
22 Jimmy Nelson (RHP, MIL)
23 Jameson Taillon (RHP, PIT)
24 Kyle Zimmer (RHP, KC)
25 Erik Johnson (RHP, CHW)
26 Ethan Martin (RHP, PHI)
27 Kolten Wong (2B, STL)
28 Mike Olt (3B, CHC)
29 Max Stassi (C, HOU)
30 Marcus Stroman (RHP, TOR)

31 Jackie Bradley (OF, BOS)
32 Christian Bethancourt (C, ATL)
33 Andrew Heaney (LHP, MIA)
34 Henry Urrutia (OF, BAL)
35 Alex Meyer (RHP, MIN)
36 James Paxton (LHP, SEA)
37 Wilmer Flores (2B/3B, NYM)
38 Chi-Jen Lo (RHP, HOU)
39 Javier Baez (SS, CHC)
40 Josmil Pinto (C, MIN)

41 Allen Webster (RHP, BOS)
42 Joe Wieland (RHP, SD)
43 Zach Lee (RHP, LA)
44 Anthony Ranaudo (RHP, BOS)
45 Enny Romero (LHP, TAM)
46 Robert Stephenson (RHP, CIN)
47 Chad Bettis (RHP, COL)
48 Chris Dwyer (LHP, KC)
49 Tommy La Stella (2B, ATL)
50 Kevin Pillar (OF, TOR)

51 Tony Sanchez (C, PIT)
52 David Hale (RHP, ATL)
53 Kevin Chapman (LHP, HOU)
54 Luis Jimenez (3B, LAA)
55 Alex Colome (RHP, TAM)
56 Kris Bryant (3B, CHC)
57 Joc Pederson (OF, LA)
58 Brian Flynn (LHP, MIA)
59 Sean Gilmartin (LHP, MIN)
60 Nate Karns (RHP, WAS)

61 C.J. Cron (1B, LAA)
62 Jonathan Schoop (INF, BAL)
63 David Holmberg (RHP, CIN)
64 Reymond Fuentes (OF, SD)
65 Mark Montgomery (RHP, NYY)
66 Sean Nolin (LHP, TOR)
67 Leury Garcia (INF, CHW)
68 Miguel Sano (3B, MIN)
69 Matt Skole (1B, WAS)
70 Adam Morgan (LHP, PHI)

71 Daniel Corcino (RHP, CIN)
72 Nick Maronde (LHP, LAA)
73 Casey Kelly (RHP, SD)
74 Arodys Vizcaino (RHP, CHC)
75 Matt Barnes (RHP, BOS)
76 Brian Goodwin (OF, WAS)
77 Bryan Holaday (C, DET)
78 Kyle Parker (OF/1B, COL)
79 C.C. Lee (RHP, CLE)
80 Alex Guerrero (2B/SS, LA)

81 Maikel Franco (3B, PHI)
82 Hunter Morris (1B, MIL)
83 Jake Petricka (RHP, CHW)
84 Zeke Spruill (RHP, ARI)
85 Carson Smith (RHP, SEA)
86 Tim Wheeler (OF, COL)
87 Engel Beltre (OF, TEX)
88 Matt Magill (RHP, LA)
89 Kevin Kiermaier (OF, TAM)
90 Cody Martin (RHP, ATL)

91 Francisco Lindor (SS, CLE)
92 Johnny Hellweg (RHP, MIL)
93 Taylor Lindsey (2B, LAA)
94 Gary Brown (OF, SF)
95 Dylan Bundy (RHP, BAL)
96 Keyvius Sampson (RHP, SD)
97 Jeff Kobernus (2B, WAS)
98 Heath Hembree (RHP, SF)
99 J. R. Murphy (C, NYY)
100 Jesse Biddle (LHP, PHI)

TOP 100 PROSPECTS ARCHIVE

2013

1. Jurickson Profar (SS, TEX)
2. Dylan Bundy (RHP, BAL)
3. Wil Myers (OF, TAM)
4. Gerrit Cole (RHP, PIT)
5. Oscar Taveras (OF, STL)
6. Taijuan Walker (RHP, SEA)
7. Trevor Bauer (RHP, CLE)
8. Jose Fernandez (RHP, MIA)
9. Travis d'Arnaud (C, NYM)
10. Miguel Sano (3B, MIN)
11. Zack Wheeler (RHP, NYM)
12. Christian Yelich (OF, MIA)
13. Tyler Skaggs (LHP, ARI)
14. Francisco Lindor (SS, CLE)
15. Javier Baez (SS, CHC)
16. Shelby Miller (RHP, STL)
17. Nick Castellanos (OF, DET)
18. Xander Bogaerts (SS, BOS)
19. Jameson Taillon (RHP, PIT)
20. Danny Hultzen (LHP, SEA)
21. Jonathan Singleton (1B, HOU)
22. Mike Zunino (C, SEA)
23. Billy Hamilton (OF, CIN)
24. Anthony Rendon (3B, WAS)
25. Mike Olt (3B, TEX)
26. Byron Buxton (OF, MIN)
27. Nolan Arenado (3B, COL)
28. Carlos Correa (SS, HOU)
29. Archie Bradley (RHP, ARI)
30. Julio Teheran (RHP, ATL)
31. Matt Barnes (RHP, BOS)
32. Gary Sanchez (C, NYY)
33. Jackie Bradley (OF, BOS)
34. Carlos Martinez (RHP, STL)
35. Bubba Starling (OF, KC)
36. Jake Odorizzi (RHP, TAM)
37. Jedd Gyorko (3B, SD)
38. Alen Hanson (SS, PIT)
39. George Springer (OF, HOU)
40. Nick Franklin (2B, SEA)
41. Aaron Sanchez (RHP, TOR)
42. Albert Almora (OF, CHC)
43. Kaleb Cowart (3B, LAA)
44. Taylor Guerrieri (RHP, TAM)
45. Kyle Zimmer (RHP, KC)
46. Noah Syndergaard (RHP, NYM)
47. Kolten Wong (2B, STL)
48. Tyler Austin (OF, NYY)
49. James Paxton (LHP, SEA)
50. Rymer Liriano (OF, SD)

51. Jake Marisnick (OF, MIA)
52. Trevor Story (SS, COL)
53. Kevin Gausman (RHP, BAL)
54. Trevor Rosenthal (RHP, STL)
55. Alex Meyer (RHP, MIN)
56. Jorge Soler (OF, CHC)
57. Matt Davidson (3B, ARI)
58. Brett Jackson (OF, CHC)
59. Michael Choice (OF, OAK)
60. David Dahl (OF, COL)
61. Mason Williams (OF, NYY)
62. Robert Stephenson (RHP, CIN)
63. Chris Archer (RHP, TAM)
64. Oswaldo Arcia (OF, MIN)
65. Zach Lee (RHP, LA)
66. Tony Cingrani (LHP, CIN)
67. Jesse Biddle (LHP, PHI)
68. Gregory Polanco (OF, PIT)
69. Addison Russell (SS, OAK)
70. Robbie Erlin (RHP, SD)
71. Courtney Hawkins (OF, CHW)
72. Brian Goodwin (OF, WAS)
73. Martin Perez (LHP, TEX)
74. Luis Heredia (RHP, PIT)
75. Yasiel Puig (OF, LA)
76. Wilmer Flores (3B, NYM)
77. Justin Nicolino (LHP, MIA)
78. Max Fried (LHP, SD)
79. Adam Eaton (OF, ARI)
80. Gary Brown (OF, SF)
81. Casey Kelly (RHP, SD)
82. Lucas Giolito (RHP, WAS)
83. Wily Peralta (RHP, MIL)
84. Michael Wacha (RHP, STL)
85. Austin Hedges (C, SD)
86. Kyle Gibson (RHP, MIN)
87. Hak-Ju Lee (SS, TAM)
88. Dan Straily (RHP, OAK)
89. Kyle Crick (RHP, SF)
90. Avisail Garcia (OF, DET)
91. Cody Buckel (RHP, TEX)
92. Tyler Thornburg (RHP, MIL)
93. Allen Webster (RHP, BOS)
94. Jarred Cosart (RHP, HOU)
95. Bruce Rondon (RHP, DET)
96. Delino DeShields (2B, HOU)
97. A.J. Cole (RHP, OAK)
98. Manny Banuelos (LHP, NYY)
99. Yordano Ventura (RHP, KC)
100. Trevor May (RHP, MIN)

2012

1. Bryce Harper (OF, WAS)
2. Matt Moore (LHP, TAM)
3. Mike Trout (OF, LAA)
4. Julio Teheran (RHP, ATL)
5. Jesus Montero (C, NYY)
6. Jurickson Profar (SS, TEX)
7. Manny Machado (SS, BAL)
8. Gerrit Cole (RHP, PIT)
9. Devin Mesoraco (C, CIN)
10. Wil Myers (OF, KC)
11. Miguel Sano (3B, MIN)
12. Jacob Turner (RHP, DET)
13. Anthony Rendon (3B, WAS)
14. Trevor Bauer (RHP, ARI)
15. Nolan Arenado (3B , COL)
16. Jameson Taillon (RHP, PIT)
17. Shelby Miller (RHP, STL)
18. Dylan Bundy (RHP, BAL)
19. Brett Jackson (OF, CHC)
20. Drew Pomeranz (LHP, COL)
21. Martin Perez (LHP, TEX)
22. Yonder Alonso (1B, SD)
23. Taijuan Walker (RHP, SEA)
24. Danny Hultzen (LHP, SEA)
25. Gary Brown (OF, SF)
26. Anthony Rizzo (1B, CHC)
27. Bubba Starling (OF, KC)
28. Travis d'Arnaud (C, TOR)
29. Mike Montgomery (LHP, KC)
30. Jake Odorizzi (RHP, KC)
31. Hak-Ju Lee (SS, TAM)
32. Jonathan Singleton (1B, HOU)
33. Garrett Richards (RHP, LAA)
34. Manny Banuelos (LHP, NYY)
35. James Paxton (LHP, SEA)
36. Jarrod Parker (RHP, OAK)
37. Carlos Martinez (RHP, STL)
38. Jake Marisnick (OF, TOR)
39. Yasmani Grandal (C, SD)
40. Trevor May (RHP, PHI)
41. Gary Sanchez (C, NYY)
42. Mike Olt (3B, TEX)
43. Wilin Rosario (C, COL)
44. John Lamb (LHP, KC)
45. Francisco Lindor (SS, CLE)
46. Dellin Betances (RHP, NYY)
47. Michael Choice (OF, OAK)
48. Arodys Vizcaino (RHP, ATL)
49. Trayvon Robinson (OF, SEA)
50. Matt Harvey (RHP, NYM)

51. Will Middlebrooks (3B, BOS)
52. Jedd Gyorko (3B, SD)
53. Randall Delgado (RHP, ATL)
54. Zack Wheeler (RHP, NYM)
55. Zach Lee (RHP, LA)
56. Tyler Skaggs (LHP, ARI)
57. Nick Castellanos (3B, DET)
58. Robbie Erlin (LHP, SD)
59. Christian Yelich (OF, MIA)
60. Anthony Gose (OF, TOR)
61. Addison Reed (RHP, CHW)
62. Javier Baez (SS, CHC)
63. Starling Marte (OF, PIT)
64. Kaleb Cowart (3B, LAA)
65. George Springer (OF, HOU)
66. Jarred Cosart (RHP, HOU)
67. Jean Segura (2B, LAA)
68. Kolten Wong (2B, STL)
69. Nick Franklin (SS, SEA)
70. Alex Torres (RHP, TAM)
71. Rymer Liriano (OF, SD)
72. Josh Bell (OF, PIT)
73. Leonys Martin (OF, TEX)
74. Joe Wieland (RHP, SD)
75. Joe Benson (OF, MIN)
76. Wily Peralta (RHP, MIL)
77. Tim Wheeler (OF, COL)
78. Oscar Taveras (OF, STL)
79. Xander Bogaerts (SS, BOS)
80. Archie Bradley (RHP, ARI)
81. Kyle Gibson (RHP, MIN)
82. Allen Webster (RHP, LA)
83. C.J. Cron (1B, LAA)
84. Grant Green (OF, OAK)
85. Brad Peacock (RHP, OAK)
86. Chris Dwyer (LHP, KC)
87. Billy Hamilton (SS, CIN)
88. A.J. Cole (RHP, OAK)
89. Aaron Hicks (OF, MIN)
90. Noah Syndergaard (RHP, TOR)
91. Tyrell Jenkins (RHP, STL)
92. Anthony Ranaudo (RHP, BOS)
93. Jed Bradley (LHP, MIL)
94. Nathan Eovaldi (RHP, LA)
95. Andrelton Simmons (SS, ATL)
96. Taylor Guerrieri (RHP, TAM)
97. Cheslor Cuthbert (3B, KC)
98. Edward Salcedo (3B, ATL)
99. Domingo Santana, OF, HOU)
100. Jesse Biddle (LHP, PHI)

TOP 100 PROSPECTS ARCHIVE

2011

1. Bryce Harper (OF, WAS)
2. Domonic Brown (OF, PHI)
3. Jesus Montero (C, NYY)
4. Mike Trout (OF, LAA)
5. Jeremy Hellickson (RHP, TAM)
6. Aroldis Chapman (LHP, CIN)
7. Eric Hosmer (1B, KC)
8. Dustin Ackley (2B, SEA)
9. Desmond Jennings (OF, TAM)
10. Julio Teheran (RHP, ATL)

11. Mike Moustakas (3B, KC)
12. Brandon Belt (1B, SF)
13. Freddie Freeman (1B, ATL)
14. Michael Pineda (RHP, SEA)
15. Matt Moore (LHP, TAM)
16. Mike Montgomery (LHP, KC)
17. Brett Jackson (OF, CHC)
18. Nick Franklin (SS, SEA)
19. Jameson Taillon (RHP, PIT)
20. Jacob Turner (RHP, DET)

21. Shelby Miller (RHP, STL)
22. Martin Perez (LHP, TEX)
23. Wil Myers (C, KC)
24. Kyle Gibson (RHP, MIN)
25. Lonnie Chisenhall (3B, CLE)
26. Tyler Matzek (LHP, COL)
27. Brett Lawrie (2B, TOR)
28. Yonder Alonso (1B, CIN)
29. Jarrod Parker (RHP, ARI)
30. Jonathan Singleton (1B, PHI)

31. Tanner Scheppers (RHP,TEX)
32. Kyle Drabek (RHP, TOR)
33. Jason Knapp (RHP, CLE)
34. Manny Banuelos (LHP, NYY)
35. Alex White (RHP, CLE)
36. Jason Kipnis (2B, CLE)
37. Wilin Rosario (C, COL)
38. Manny Machado (SS, BAL)
39. Chris Sale (LHP, CHW)
40. Devin Mesoraco (C, CIN)

41. Tyler Chatwood (RHP, LAA)
42. John Lamb (LHP, KC)
43. Danny Duffy (LHP, KC)
44. Trevor May (RHP, PHI)
45. Mike Minor (LHP, ATL)
46. Jarred Cosart (RHP, PHI)
47. Tony Sanchez (C, PIT)
48. Brody Colvin (RHP, PHI)
49. Zach Britton (LHP, BAL)
50. Dee Gordon (SS, LA)

51. Miguel Sano (3B, MIN)
52. Grant Green (SS, OAK)
53. Danny Espinosa (SS, WAS)
54. Simon Castro (RHP, SD)
55. Derek Norris (C, WAS)
56. Chris Archer (RHP, CHC)
57. Jurickson Profar (SS, TEX)
58. Zack Cox (3B, STL)
59. Billy Hamilton (2B, CIN)
60. Gary Sanchez (C, NYY)

61. Zach Lee (RHP, LA)
62. Drew Pomeranz (LHP, CLE)
63. Randall Delgado (RHP, ATL)
64. Michael Choice (OF, OAK)
65. Nick Weglarz (OF, CLE)
66. Nolan Arenado (3B, COL)
67. Chris Carter (1B/OF, OAK)
68. Arodys Vizcaino (RHP, ATL)
69. Trey McNutt (RHP, CHC)
70. Dellin Betances (RHP, NYY)

71. Aaron Hicks (OF, MIN)
72. Aaron Crow (RHP, KC)
73. Jake McGee (LHP, TAM)
74. Lars Anderson (1B, BOS)
75. Fabio Martinez (RHP, LAA)
76. Ben Revere (OF, MIN)
77. Jordan Lyles (RHP, HOU)
78. Casey Kelly (RHP, SD)
79. Trayvon Robinson (OF, LA)
80. Craig Kimbrel (RHP, ATL)

81. Jose Iglesias (SS, BOS)
82. Garrett Richards (RHP, LAA)
83. Allen Webster (RHP, LA)
84. Chris Dwyer (LHP, KC)
85. Alex Colome (RHP, TAM)
86. Zack Wheeler (RHP, SF)
87. Andy Oliver (LHP, DET)
88. Andrew Brackman (RHP,NYY)
89. Wilmer Flores (SS, NYM)
90. Christian Friedrich (LHP, COL)

91. Anthony Ranaudo (RHP, BOS)
92. Aaron Miller (LHP, LA)
93. Matt Harvey (RHP, NYM)
94. Mark Rogers (RHP, MIL)
95. Jean Segura (2B, LAA)
96. Hank Conger (C, LAA)
97. J.P. Arencibia (C, TOR)
98. Matt Dominguez (3B, FLA)
99. Jerry Sands (1B, LA)
100. Nick Castellanos (3B, DET)

2010

1. Stephen Strasburg (RHP, WAS)
2. Jason Heyward (OF, ATL)
3. Jesus Montero (C, NYY)
4. Buster Posey (C, SF)
5. Justin Smoak (1B, TEX)
6. Pedro Alvarez (3B, PIT)
7. Carlos Santana (C, CLE)
8. Desmond Jennings (OF, TAM)
9. Brian Matusz (LHP, BAL)
10. Neftali Feliz (RHP, TEX)

11. Brett Wallace (3B, TOR)
12. Mike Stanton (OF. FLA)
13. M. Bumgarner (LHP, SF)
14. J. Hellickson (RHP, TAM)
15. Dustin Ackley (1B/OF, SEA)
16. Aroldis Chapman (LHP, CIN)
17. Yonder Alonso (1B, CIN)
18. Alcides Escobar (SS, MIL)
19. Brett Lawrie (2B, MIL)
20. Starlin Castro (SS, CHC)

21. Logan Morrison (1B, FLA)
22. Mike Montgomery (LHP, KC)
23. Domonic Brown (OF, PHI)
24. Josh Vitters (3B, CHC)
25. R. Westmoreland (OF, BOS)
26. Todd Frazier (3B/OF, CIN)
27. Eric Hosmer (1B, KC)
28. Freddie Freeman (1B, ATL)
29. Derek Norris (C, WAS)
30. Martin Perez (LHP, TEX)

31. Wade Davis (RHP, TAM)
32. Trevor Reckling (LHP, LAA)
33. Jordan Walden (RHP, LAA)
34. Mat Gamel (3B, MIL)
35. Tyler Flowers (C, CHW)
36. T. Scheppers (RHP, TEX)
37. Casey Crosby (LHP, DET)
38. Austin Jackson (OF, DET)
39. Devaris Gordon (SS, LA)
40. Kyle Drabek (RHP, TOR)

41. Ben Revere (OF, MIN)
42. Michael Taylor (OF, OAK)
43. Jacob Turner (RHP, DET)
44. Tim Beckham (SS, TAM)
45. Carlos Triunfel (SS, SEA)
46. Aaron Crow (RHP, KC)
47. Matt Moore (LHP, TAM)
48. Jarrod Parker (RHP, ARI)
49. F. Martinez (OF, NYM)
50. C. Friedrich (LHP, COL)

51. Jenrry Mejia (RHP, NYM)
52. Tyler Matzek (LHP, COL)
53. Brett Jackson (OF, CHC)
54. Aaron Hicks (OF, MIN)
55. Jhoulys Chacin (RHP, COL)
56. Josh Bell (3B, BAL)
57. Brandon Allen (1B, ARI)
58. Chris Carter (1B, OAK)
59. Jason Knapp (RHP, CLE)
60. Danny Duffy (LHP, KC)

61. Tim Alderson (RHP, PIT)
62. Matt Dominguez (3B, FLA)
63. Mike Moustakas (3B, KC)
64. Jake Arrieta (RHP, BAL)
65. Carlos Carrasco (RHP, CLE)
66. Wilmer Flores (SS, NYM)
67. Drew Storen (RHP, WAS)
68. Lonnie Chisenhall (3B, CLE)
69. Aaron Poreda (LHP, SD)
70. A. Cashner (RHP, CHC)

71. Tony Sanchez (C, PIT)
72. Julio Teheran (RHP, ATL)
73. Jose Tabata (OF, PIT)
74. Jason Castro (C, HOU)
75. Casey Kelly (RHP, BOS)
76. Alex White (RHP, CLE)
77. Jay Jackson (RHP, CHC)
78. Dan Hudson (RHP, CHW)
79. Brandon Erbe (RHP, BAL)
80. Zack Wheeler (RHP, SF)

81. Shelby Miller (RHP, STL)
82. Jordan Lyles (RHP, HOU)
83. Simon Castro (RHP, SD)
84. Aaron Miller (LHP, LA)
85. Michael Ynoa (RHP, OAK)
86. Ethan Martin (RHP, LA)
87. Scott Elbert (LHP, LA)
88. Nick Weglarz (OF, CLE)
89. Donavan Tate (OF, SD)
90. Jordan Danks (OF, CHW)

91. Hector Rondon (RHP, CLE)
92. Chris Heisey (OF, CIN)
93. Kyle Gibson (RHP, MIN)
94. Mike Leake (RHP, CIN)
95. Mike Trout (OF, LAA)
96. Jake McGee (LHP, TAM)
97. Chad James (LHP, FLA)
98. C. Bethancourt (C, NYY)
99. Miguel Sano (SS, MIN)
100. Noel Arguelles (LHP, KC)

TOP 100 PROSPECTS ARCHIVE

2009

1. Matt Wieters (C, BAL)
2. David Price (LHP, TAM)
3. Rick Porcello (RHP, DET)
4. Colby Rasmus (OF, STL)
5. Madison Bumgarner (LHP, SF)
6. Neftali Feliz (RHP, TEX)
7. Jason Heyward (OF, ATL)
8. Andrew McCutchen (OF, PIT)
9. Pedro Alvarez (3B, PIT)
10. Cameron Maybin (OF, FLA)

11. Trevor Cahill (RHP, OAK)
12. Mike Moustakas (3B/SS, KC)
13. Jordan Zimmermann (RHP, WAS)
14. Travis Snider (OF, TOR)
15. Tim Beckham (SS, TAM)
16. Eric Hosmer (1B, KC)
17. Tommy Hanson (RHP, ATL)
18. Dexter Fowler (OF, COL)
19. Brett Anderson (LHP, OAK)
20. Carlos Triunfel (SS/2B, SEA)

21. Buster Posey (C, SF)
22. Chris Tillman (RHP, BAL)
23. Brian Matusz (LHP, BAL)
24. Justin Smoak (1B, TEX)
25. Jarrod Parker (RHP, ARI)
26. Derek Holland (LHP, TEX)
27. Lars Anderson (1B, BOS)
28. Michael Inoa (RHP, OAK)
29. Mike Stanton (OF, FLA)
30. Taylor Teagarden (C, TEX)

31. Gordon Beckham (SS, CHW)
32. Brett Wallace (3B, STL)
33. Matt LaPorta (OF, CLE)
34. Jordan Schafer (OF, ATL)
35. Carlos Santana (C, CLE)
36. Aaron Hicks (OF, MIN)
37. Adam Miller (RHP, CLE)
38. Elvis Andrus (SS, TEX)
39. Alcides Escobar (SS, MIL)
40. Wade Davis (RHP, TAM)

41. Austin Jackson (OF, NYY)
42. Jesus Montero (C, NYY)
43. Tim Alderson (RHP, SF)
44. Jhoulys Chacin (RHP, COL)
45. Phillippe Aumont (RHP, SEA)
46. James McDonald (RHP, LA)
47. Reid Brignac (SS, TAM)
48. Desmond Jennings (OF, TAM)
49. Fernando Martinez (OF, NYM)
50. JP Arencibia (C, TOR)

51. Wilmer Flores (SS, NYM)
52. Brett Cecil (LHP, TOR)
53. Aaron Poreda (LHP, CHW)
54. Jeremy Jeffress (RHP, MIL)
55. Michael Main (RHP, TEX)
56. Josh Vitters (3B, CHC)
57. Mat Gamel (3B, MIL)
58. Yonder Alonso (1B, CIN)
59. Gio Gonzalez (LHP, OAK)
60. Michael Bowden (RHP, BOS)

61. Angel Villalona (1B, SF)
62. Carlos Carrasco (RHP, PHI)
63. Jake Arrieta (RHP, BAL)
64. Jordan Walden (RHP, LAA)
65. Freddie Freeman (1B, ATL)
66. Logan Morrison (1B, FLA)
67. Shooter Hunt (RHP, MIN)
68. Junichi Tazawa (RHP, BOS)
69. Nick Adenhart (RHP, LAA)
70. Jose Tabata (OF, PIT)

71. Adrian Cardenas (SS/2B, OAK)
72. Chris Carter (3B/OF, OAK)
73. Ben Revere (OF, MIN)
74. Josh Reddick (OF, BOS)
75. Jeremy Hellickson (RHP, TAM)
76. Justin Jackson (SS, TOR)
77. Wilson Ramos (C, MIN)
78. Jason Castro (C, HOU)
79. Julio Borbon (OF, TEX)
80. Tyler Flowers (C, CHW)

81. Gorkys Hernandez (OF, ATL)
82. Neftali Soto (3B, CIN)
83. Henry Rodriguez (RHP, OAK)
84. Dan Duffy (LHP, KC)
85. Daniel Cortes (RHP, KC)
86. Dayan Viciedo (3B, CHW)
87. Matt Dominguez (3B, FLA)
88. Jordan Danks (OF, CHW)
89. Chris Coghlan (2B, FLA)
90. Brian Bogusevic (OF, HOU)

91. Ryan Tucker (RHP, FLA)
92. Jonathon Niese (LHP, NYM)
93. Martin Perez (LHP, TEX)
94. James Simmons (RHP, OAK)
95. Nick Weglarz (OF/1B, CLE)
96. Daniel Bard (RHP, BOS)
97. Yamaico Navarro (SS, BOS)
98. Jose Ceda (RHP, FLA)
99. Jeff Samardzija (RHP, CHC)
100. Jason Donald (SS, PHI)

2008

1. Jay Bruce (OF, CIN)
2. Evan Longoria (3B, TAM)
3. Clay Buchholz (RHP, BOS)
4. Clayton Kershaw (LHP, LAD)
5. Joba Chamberlain (RHP, NYY)
6. Colby Rasmus (OF, STL)
7. Cameron Maybin (OF, FLA)
8. Homer Bailey (RHP, CIN)
9. David Price (LHP, TAM)
10. Andrew McCutchen (OF, PIT)

11. Brandon Wood (3B/SS, LAA)
12. Matt Wieters (C, BAL)
13. Jacoby Ellsbury (OF, BOS)
14. Travis Snider (OF, TOR)
15. Reid Brignac (SS, TAM)
16. Jacob McGee (LHP, TAM)
17. Wade Davis (RHP, TAM)
18. Adam Miller (RHP, CLE)
19. Rick Porcello (RHP, DET)
20. Franklin Morales (LHP, COL)

21. Carlos Triunfel (SS, SEA)
22. Andy LaRoche (3B/OF, LAD)
23. Jordan Schafer (OF, ATL)
24. Kosuke Fukodome (OF, CHC)
25. Jose Tabata (OF, NYY)
26. Carlos Gonzalez (OF, OAK)
27. Joey Votto (1B/OF, CIN)
28. Daric Barton (1B, OAK)
29. Angel Villalona (3B, SF)
30. Eric Hurley (RHP, TEX)

31. Nick Adenhart (RHP, LAA)
32. Fernando Martinez (OF, NYM)
33. Ross Detwiler (LHP, WAS)
34. Johnny Cueto (RHP, CIN)
35. Chris Marrero (OF, WAS)
36. Jason Heyward (OF, ATL)
37. Mike Moustakas (SS, KC)
38. Elvis Andrus (SS, TEX)
39. Taylor Teagarden (C, TEX)
40. Ian Kennedy (RHP, NYY)

41. Kasey Kiker (LHP, TEX)
42. Scott Elbert (LHP, LAD)
43. Justin Masterson (RHP, BOS)
44. Max Scherzer (RHP, ARI)
45. Brandon Jones (OF, ATL)
46. Josh Vitters (3B, CHC)
47. Jarrod Parker (RHP, ARI)
48. Matt Antonelli (2B, SD)
49. Gio Gonzalez (LHP, CHW)
50. Ian Stewart (3B, COL)

51. Chase Headley (3B, SD)
52. Anthony Swarzak (RHP, MIN)
53. Jair Jurrjens (RHP, DET)
54. Billy Rowell (3B, BAL)
55. Jeff Clement (C, SEA)
56. Tyler Colvin (OF, CHC)
57. Neil Walker (3B, PIT)
58. Geovany Soto (C/1B, CHC)
59. Steven Pearce (1B/OF, PIT)
60. Fautino de los Santos (RHP, CHW)

61. Manny Parra (LHP, MIL)
62. Matt LaPorta (OF, MIL)
63. Austin Jackson (OF, NYY)
64. Carlos Carrasco (RHP, PHI)
65. Jed Lowrie (SS/2B, BOS)
66. Deolis Guerra (RHP, NYM)
67. Jonathon Meloan (RHP, LAD)
68. Chin-Lung Hu (SS, LAD)
69. Blake Beaven (RHP, TEX)
70. Michael Main (RHP, TEX)

71. Gorkys Hernandez (OF, ATL)
72. Jeff Niemann (RHP, TAM)
73. Desmond Jennings (OF, TAM)
74. Radhames Liz (RHP, BAL)
75. Chuck Lofgren (LHP, CLE)
76. Luke Hochevar (RHP, KC)
77. Brent Lillibridge (SS, ATL)
78. Jaime Garcia (LHP, STL)
79. Bryan Anderson (C, STL)
80. Troy Patton (LHP, BAL)

81. Nolan Reimold (OF, BAL)
82. Matt Latos (RHP, SD)
83. Tommy Hanson (RHP, ATL)
84. Aaron Poreda (LHP, CHW)
85. Cole Rohrbough (LHP, ATL)
86. Lars Anderson (1B, BOS)
87. Chris Volstad (RHP, FLA)
88. Henry Sosa (RHP, SF)
89. Madison Bumgarner (LHP, SF)
90. Michael Bowden (RHP, BOS)

91. Hank Conger (C, LAA)
92. JR Towles (C, HOU)
93. Greg Reynolds (RHP, COL)
94. Adrian Cardenas (2B/SS, PHI)
95. Chris Nelson (SS, COL)
96. Ryan Kalish (OF, BOS)
97. Dexter Fowler (OF, COL)
98. James McDonald (RHP, LAD)
99. Beau Mills (3B/1B, CLE)
100. Michael Burgess (OF, WAS)

TOP 100 PROSPECTS ARCHIVE

2007

1. Delmon Young (OF, TAM)
2. Alex Gordon (3B, KC)
3. Daisuke Matsuzaka (RHP, BOS)
4. Justin Upton (OF, ARI)
5. Homer Bailey (RHP, CIN)
6. Philip Hughes (RHP, NYY)
7. Brandon Wood (SS, LAA)
8. Jay Bruce (OF, CIN)
9. Billy Butler (OF, KC)
10. Cameron Maybin (OF, DET)

11. Andrew McCutchen (OF, PIT)
12. Troy Tulowitzki (SS, COL)
13. Evan Longoria (3B, TAM)
14. Jose Tabata (OF, NYY)
15. Reid Brignac (SS, TAM)
16. Chris Young (OF, ARI)
17. Adam Miller (RHP, CLE)
18. Mike Pelfrey (RHP, NYM)
19. Carlos Gonzalez (OF, ARI)
20. Tim Lincecum (RHP, SF)

21. Andy LaRoche (3B, LAD)
22. Fernando Martinez (OF, NYM)
23. Yovani Gallardo (RHP, MIL)
24. Colby Rasmus (OF, STL)
25. Ryan Braun (3B, MIL)
26. Scott Elbert (LHP, LAD)
27. Nick Adenhart (RHP, LAA)
28. Andrew Miller (LHP, DET)
29. Billy Rowell (3B, BAL)
30. John Danks (LHP, CHW)

31. Luke Hochevar (RHP, KC)
32. Erick Aybar (SS, LAA)
33. Jacoby Ellsbury (OF, BOS)
34. Eric Hurley (RHP, TEX)
35. Ian Stewart (3B, COL)
36. Clay Buchholz (RHP, BOS)
37. Elvis Andrus (SS, ATL)
38. Jason Hirsh (RHP, COL)
39. Hunter Pence (OF, HOU)
40. Franklin Morales (LHP, COL)

41. Adam Lind (OF, TOR)
42. Travis Snider (OF, TOR)
43. Jeff Niemann (RHP, TAM)
44. Clayton Kershaw (LHP, LAD)
45. James Loney (1B, LAD)
46. Chris Iannetta (C, COL)
47. Elijah Dukes (OF, TAM)
48. Chuck Lofgren (LHP, CLE)
49. Joey Votto (1B, CIN)
50. Jacob McGee (LHP, TAM)

51. Adam Jones (OF, SEA)
52. Brad Lincoln (RHP, PIT)
53. Brian Barton (OF, CLE)
54. Will Inman (RHP, MIL)
55. Wade Davis (RHP, TAM)
56. Donald Veal (LHP, CHC)
57. Michael Bowden (RHP, BOS)
58. Ryan Sweeney (OF, CHW)
59. Josh Fields (3B, CHW)
60. Jarrod Saltalamacchia (C, ATL)

61. Felix Pie (OF, CHC)
62. Brandon Erbe (RHP, BAL)
63. Giovanny Gonzalez (LHP, CHW)
64. Trevor Crowe (OF, CLE)
65. Travis Buck (OF, OAK)
66. Daric Barton (1B, OAK)
67. Kevin Kouzmanoff (3B, SD)
68. Jeff Clement (C, SEA)
69. Neil Walker (C, PIT)
70. Troy Patton (LHP, HOU)

71. Brandon Morrow (RHP, SEA)
72. Dustin Pedroia (2B, BOS)
73. Blake DeWitt (2B, LAD)
74. Carlos Carrasco (RHP, PHI)
75. Jonathon Meloan (RHP, LAD)
76. Hank Conger (C, LAA)
77. Sean Rodriguez (SS, LAA)
78. Humberto Sanchez (RHP, NYY)
79. Phil Humber (RHP, NYM)
80. Edinson Volquez (RHP, TEX)

81. Dustin Nippert (RHP, ARI)
82. Anthony Swarzak (RHP, MIN)
83. Chris Parmalee (OF/1B, MIN)
84. Ubaldo Jimenez (RHP, COL)
85. Dexter Fowler (OF, COL)
86. Drew Stubbs (OF, CIN)
87. Miguel Montero (C, ARI)
88. Carlos Gomez (OF, NYM)
89. Kevin Slowey (RHP, MIN)
90. Nolan Reimold (OF, BAL)

91. Daniel Bard (RHP, BOS)
92. Chris Nelson (SS, COL)
93. Cedric Hunter (OF, SD)
94. Angel Villanoa (3B, SF)
95. Jamie Garcia (LHP, STL)
96. Travis Wood (LHP, CIN)
97. Cesar Carillo (RHP, SD)
98. Pedro Beato (RHP, BAL)
99. Joba Chamberlain (RHP, NYY)
100. Kei Igawa (LHP, NYY)

2006

1. Delmon Young (OF, TAM)
2. Justin Upton (OF/SS, ARI)
3. Brandon Wood (SS, LAA)
4. Ian Stewart (3B, COL)
5. Prince Fielder (1B, MIL)
6. Jeremy Hermida (OF, FLA)
7. Chad Billingsley (RHP, LAD)
8. Stephen Drew (SS, ARI)
9. Andy Marte (3B, BOS)
10. Francisco Liriano (LHP, MIN)

11. Alex Gordon (3B, KC)
12. Jarrod Saltalamacchia (C, ATL)
13. Carlos Quentin (OF, ARI)
14. Lastings Milledge (OF, NYM)
15. Conor Jackson (1B, ARI)
16. Joel Guzman (SS, LAD)
17. Nick Markakis (OF, BAL)
18. Adam Miller (RHP, CLE)
19. Matt Cain (RHP, SF)
20. Erick Aybar (SS, LAA)

21. Billy Butler (OF, KC)
22. Justin Verlander (RHP, DET)
23. Howie Kendrick (2B, LAA)
24. Andy LaRoche (3B, LAD)
25. Troy Tulowitski (SS, COL)
26. Jered Weaver (RHP, LAA)
27. Ryan Zimmerman (3B, WAS)
28. Chris Young (OF, ARI)
29. Elvis Andrus (SS, ATL)
30. Daric Barton (1B, OAK)

31. Scott Olson (LHP, FLA)
32. Jon Lester (LHP, BOS)
33. Cole Hamels (LHP, PHI)
34. Anthony Reyes (RHP, STL)
35. Mike Pelfrey (RHP, NYM)
36. Andrew McCutchen (OF, PIT)
37. Ryan Braun (3B, MIL)
38. Chris Nelson (SS, COL)
39. Kendry Morales (1B/OF, LAA)
40. Anibal Sanchez (RHP, FLA)

41. Hanley Ramirez (SS, FLA)
42. John Danks (LHP, TEX)
43. Edison Volquez (RHP, TEX)
44. Russell Martin (C, LAD)
45. Dustin Nippert (RHP, ARI)
46. Jon Papelbon (RHP, BOS)
47. Carlos Gonzales (OF, ARI)
48. Felix Pie (OF, CHC)
49. Yusmeiro Petit (RHP, FLA)
50. Dustin Pedroia (2B, BOS)

51. Joel Zumaya (RHP, DET)
52. Gio Gonzalez (LHP, PHI)
53. Hayden Penn (RHP, BAL)
54. Nolan Reimold (OF, BAL)
55. Homer Bailey (RHP, CIN)
56. Mark Pawelek (LHP, CHC)
57. Neil Walker (C, PIT)
58. Philip Hughes (RHP, NYY)
59. Jonathon Broxton (RHP, LAD)
60. Dustin McGowan (RHP, TOR)

61. Cameron Maybin (OF, DET)
62. Scott Elbert (LHP, LAD)
63. Andrew Lerew (RHP, ATL)
64. Yuniel Escobar (SS, ATL)
65. Jose Tabata (OF, NYY)
66. Craig Hansen (RHP, BOS)
67. Javier Herrera (OF, OAK)
68. James Loney (1B, LAD)
69. Matt Kemp (OF, LAD)
70. Jairo Garcia (RHP, OAK)

71. Ryan Sweeney (OF, CHW)
72. Thomas Diamond (RHP, TEX)
73. Cesar Carillo (RHP, SD)
74. Adam Loewen (LHP, BAL)
75. Chuck Tiffany (LHP, LAD)
76. Brian Anderson (OF, CHW)
77. Jeremy Sowers (LHP, CLE)
78. Matt Moses (3B, MIN)
79. Angel Guzman (RHP, CHC)
80. Jeff Clement (C, SEA)

81. Kenji Jojima (C, SEA)
82. Fernando Nieve (RHP, HOU)
83. Corey Hart (OF/3B, MIL)
84. Eric Duncan (3B, NYY)
85. Justin Huber (1B, KC)
86. Jeff Niemann (RHP, TAM)
87. Cliff Pennington (SS, OAK)
88. Jeff Mathis (C, LAA)
89. Troy Patton (LHP, HOU)
90. Jay Bruce (OF, CIN)

91. Colby Rasmus (OF, STL)
92. Jeff Bianchi (SS, KC)
93. Joaquin Arias (SS, TEX)
94. Eddy Martinez-Esteve (OF, SF)
95. Jason Kubel (OF, MIN)
96. Adam Jones (OF, SEA)
97. Ian Kinsler (2B, TEX)
98. Eric Hurley (RHP, TEX)
99. Anthony Swarzak (RHP, MIN)
100. Josh Barfield (2B, SD)

AVG: Batting Average (see also BA)

BA: Batting Average (see also AVG)

Base Performance Indicator (BPI): A statistical formula that measures an isolated aspect of a player's situation-independent raw skill or a gauge that helps capture the effects of random chance has on a skill. Although there are many such formulas, there are only a few that we are referring to when the term is used in this book. For pitchers, our BPI's are control (bb%), dominance (k/9), command (k/bb), opposition on base average (OOB), ground/line/fly ratios (G/L/F), and expected ERA (xERA). Random chance is measured witih the hit rate (H%) and strand rate (S%).

*Base Performance Value (BPV): A single value that describes a pitcher's overall raw skill level. This is more useful than any traditional statistical gauge to track performance trends and project future statistical output. The BPV formula combines and weights several BPIs:

(Dominance Rate x 6) + (Command ratio x 21) – Opposition HR Rate x 30) – ((Opp. Batting Average - .275) x 200)

The formula combines the individual raw skills of power, command, the ability to keep batters from reaching base, and the ability to prevent long hits, all characteristics that are unaffected by most external team factors. In tandem with a pitcher's strand rate, it provides a complete picture of the elements that contribute to a pitcher's ERA, and therefore serves as an accurate tool to project likely changes in ERA. BENCHMARKS: We generally consider a BPV of 50 to be the minimum level required for long-term success. The elite of bullpen aces will have BPV's in the excess of 100 and it is rare for these stoppers to enjoy long-term success with consistent levels under 75.

Batters Faced per Game *(Craig Wright)*

((IP x 2.82) + H + BB) / G

A measure of pitcher usage and one of the leading indicators for potential pitcher burnout.

Batting Average (BA, or AVG)

(H/AB)

Ratio of hits to at-bats, though it is a poor evaluative measure of hitting performance. It neglects the offensive value of the base on balls and assumes that all hits are created equal.

Batting Eye (Eye)

(Walks / Strikeouts)

A measure of a player's strike zone judgment, the raw ability to distinguish between balls and strikes. BENCHMARKS: The best hitters have eye ratios over 1.00 (indicating more walks than strikeouts) and are the most likely to be among a league's .300 hitters. At the other end of the scale are ratios

less than 0.50, which represent batters who likely also have lower BAs.

bb%: Walk rate (hitters)

bb/9: Opposition Walks per 9 IP

BF/Gm: Batters Faced Per Game

BPI: Base Performance Indicator

*BPV: Base Performance Value

Cmd: Command ratio

Command Ratio (Cmd)

(Strikeouts / Walks)

This is a measure of a pitcher's raw ability to get the ball over the plate. There is no more fundamental a skill than this, and so it is accurately used as a leading indicator to project future rises and falls in other gauges, such as ERA. Command is one of the best gauges to use to evaluate minor league performance. It is a prime component of a pitcher's base performance value. BENCHMARKS: Baseball's upper echelon of command pitchers will have ratios in excess of 3.0. Pitchers with ratios under 1.0 — indicating that they walk more batters than they strike out — have virtually no potential for long term success. If you make no other changes in your approach to drafting a pitching staff, limiting your focus to only pitchers with a command ratio of 2.0 or better will substantially improve your odds of success.

Contact Rate (ct%)

((AB - K) / AB)

Measures a batter's ability to get wood on the ball and hit it into the field of play. BENCHMARK: Those batters with the best contact skill will have levels of 90% or better. The hackers of society will have levels of 75% or less.

Control Rate (bb/9), or Opposition Walks per Game

BB Allowed x 9 / IP

Measures how many walks a pitcher allows per game equivalent. BENCHMARK: The best pitchers will have bb/9 levels of 3.0 or less.

ct%: Contact rate

Ctl: Control Rate

Dom: Dominance Rate

Dominance Rate (k/9), or Opposition Strikeouts per Game

(K Allowed x 9 / IP)

Measures how many strikeouts a pitcher allows per game equivalent. BENCHMARK: The best pitchers will have k/9 levels of 6.0 or higher.

*Expected Earned Run Average (*Gill and Reeve*)

(.575 x H [per 9 IP]) + (.94 x HR [per 9 IP]) + (.28 x BB [per 9 IP]) - (.01 x K [per 9 IP]) - Normalizing Factor

"xERA represents the expected ERA of the pitcher based on a normal distribution of his statistics. It is not influenced by situation-dependent factors." xERA erases the inequity between starters' and relievers' ERA's, eliminating the effect that a pitcher's success or failure has on another pitcher's ERA.

Similar to other gauges, the accuracy of this formula changes with the level of competition from one season to the next. The normalizing factor allows us to better approximate a pitcher's actual ERA. This value is usually somewhere around 2.77 and varies by league and year. **BENCHMARKS:** In general, xERA's should approximate a pitcher's ERA fairly closely. However, those pitchers who have large variances between the two gauges are candidates for further analysis.

Extra-Base Hit Rate (X/H)

(2B + 3B + HR) / Hits

X/H is a measure of power and can be used along with a player's slugging percentage and isolated power to gauge a player's ability to drive the ball. **BENCHMARKS:** Players with above average power will post X/H of greater than 38% and players with moderate power will post X/H of 30% or greater. Weak hitters with below average power will have a X/H level of less than 20%.

Eye: Batting Eye

h%: Hit rate (batters)

H%: Hits Allowed per Balls in Play (pitchers)

Hit Rate (h% or H%)

(H—HR) / (AB – HR - K)

The percent of balls hit into the field of play that fall for hits.

hr/9: Opposition Home Runs per 9 IP

ISO: Isolated Power

Isolated Power (ISO)

(Slugging Percentage - Batting Average)

Isolated Power is a measurement of power skill. Subtracting a player's BA from his SLG, we are essentially pulling out all the singles and single bases from the formula. What remains are the extra-base hits. ISO is not an absolute measurement as it assumes that two doubles is worth one home run, which certainly is not the case, but is another statistic that is a good measurement of raw power. **BENCHMARKS:** The game's top sluggers will tend to have ISO levels over .200. Weak hitters will be under .100.

k/9: Dominance rate (opposition strikeouts per 9 IP)

Major League Equivalency (*Bill James*)

A formula that converts a player's minor or foreign league statistics into a comparable performance in the major leagues. These are not projections, but conversions of current performance.

Contains adjustments for the level of play in individual leagues and teams. Works best with Triple-A stats, not quite as well with Double-A stats, and hardly at all with the lower levels. Foreign conversions are still a work in process. James' original formula only addressed batting. Our research has devised conversion formulas for pitchers, however, their best use comes when looking at BPI's, not traditional stats.

MLE: Major League Equivalency

OBP: On Base Percentage (batters)

OBA: Opposition Batting Average (pitchers)

On Base Percentage (OBP)

(H + BB) / (AB + BB)

Addressing one of the two deficiencies in BA, OBP gives value to those events that get batters on base, but are not hits. By adding walks (and often, hit batsmen) into the basic batting average formula, we have a better gauge of a batter's ability to reach base safely. An OBP of .350 can be read as "this batter gets on base 35% of the time."

Why this is a more important gauge than batting average? When a run is scored, there is no distinction made as to how that runner reached base. So, two thirds of the time—about how often a batter comes to the plate with the bases empty—a walk really is as good as a hit. **BENCHMARKS:** We all know what a .300 hitter is, but what represents "good" for OBP? That comparable level would likely be .400, with .275 representing the level of futility.

On Base Plus Slugging Percentage (OPS): A simple sum of the two gauges, it is considered as one of the better evaluators of overall performance. OPS combines the two basic elements of offensive production — the ability to get on base (OBP) and the ability to advance baserunners (SLG). **BENCHMARKS:** The game's top batters will have OPS levels over .900. The worst batters will have levels under .600.

Opposition Batting Average (OBA)

(Hits Allowed / ((IP x 2.82) + Hits Allowed))

A close approximation of the batting average achieved by opposing batters against a particular pitcher. **BENCHMARKS:** The converse of the benchmark for batters, the best pitchers will have levels under .250; the worst pitchers levels over .300.

Opposition Home Runs per Game (hr/9)

(HR Allowed x 9 / IP)

Measures how many home runs a pitcher allows per game equivalent. **BENCHMARK:** The best pitchers will have hr/9 levels of under 1.0.

Opposition On Base Average (OOB)

(Hits Allowed + BB) / ((IP x 2.82) + H + BB)

A close approximation of the on base average achieved by opposing batters against a particular pitcher. **BENCHMARK:** The best pitchers will have levels under .300; the worst pitchers levels over .375.

Opposition Strikeouts per Game: See Dominance Rate.

Opposition Walks per Game: See Control Rate.

OPS: On Base Plus Slugging Percentage

RC: Runs Created

RC/G: Runs Created Per Game

Runs Created *(Bill James)*

(H + BB - CS) x (Total bases + (.55 x SB)) / (AB + BB)

A formula that converts all offensive events into a total of runs scored. As calculated for individual teams, the result approximates a club's actual run total with great accuracy.

Runs Created Per Game *(Bill James)*

Runs Created / ((AB - H + CS) / 25.5)

RC expressed on a per-game basis might be considered the hypothetical ERA compiled against a particular batter. **BENCHMARKS:** Few players surpass the level of a 10.00 RC/G in any given season, but any level over 7.50 can still be considered very good. At the bottom are levels below 3.00.

S%: Strand Rate

Save: There are six events that need to occur in order for a pitcher to post a single save...

1. The starting pitcher and middle relievers must pitch well.
2. The offense must score enough runs.
3. It must be a reasonably close game.
4. The manager must choose to put the pitcher in for a save opportunity.
5. The pitcher must pitch well and hold the lead.
6. The manager must let him finish the game.

Of these six events, only one is within the control of the relief pitcher. As such, projecting saves for a reliever has little to do with skill and a lot to do with opportunity. However, pitchers with excellent skills sets may create opportunity for themselves.

Situation Independent: Describing a statistical gauge that measures performance apart from the context of team, ballpark, or other outside variables. Strikeouts and Walks, inasmuch as they are unaffected by the performance of a batter's surrounding team, are considered situation independent stats.

Conversely, RBIs are situation dependent because individual performance varies greatly by the performance of other batters on the team (you can't drive in runs if there is nobody on base). Similarly, pitching wins are as much a measure of the success of a pitcher as they are a measure of the success of the offense and defense performing behind that pitcher, and are therefore a poor measure of pitching performance alone.

Situation independent gauges are important for us to be able to separate a player's contribution to his team and isolate his performance so that we may judge it on its own merits.

Slg: Slugging Percentage

Slugging Percentage (Slg)

(Singles + (2 x Doubles) + (3 x Triples) + (4 x HR)) / AB

A measure of the total number of bases accumulated per at bat. It is a misnomer; it is not a true measure of a batter's slugging ability because it includes singles. SLG also assumes that each type of hit has proportionately increasing value (i.e. a double is twice as valuable as a single, etc.) which is not true. **BENCHMARKS:** The top batters will have levels over .500. The bottom batters will have levels under .300.

Strand Rate (S%)

(H + BB - ER) / (H + BB - HR)

Measures the percentage of allowed runners a pitcher strands, which incorporates both individual pitcher skill and bullpen effectiveness. **BENCHMARKS:** The most adept at stranding runners will have S% levels over 75%. Once a pitcher's S% starts dropping down below 65%, he's going to have problems with his ERA. Those pitchers with strand rates over 80% will have artificially low ERAs, which will be prone to relapse.

Strikeouts per Game: See Opposition Strikeouts per game.

Walks + Hits per Innings Pitched (WHIP): The number of baserunners a pitcher allows per inning. **BENCHMARKS:** Usually, a WHIP of under 1.20 is considered top level and over 1.50 is indicative of poor performance. Levels under 1.00 — allowing fewer runners than IP — represent extraordinary performance and are rarely maintained over time.

Walk rate (bb%)

(BB / (AB + BB))

A measure of a batter's eye and plate patience. BENCHMARKS: The best batters will have levels of over 10%. Those with the least plate patience will have levels of 5% or less.

Walks per Game: See Opposition Walks per Game.

WHIP: Walks + Hits per Innings Pitched

Wins: There are five events that need to occur in order for a pitcher to post a single win...

1. He must pitch well, allowing few runs.
2. The offense must score enough runs.
3. The defense must successfully field all batted balls.
4. The bullpen must hold the lead.
5. The manager must leave the pitcher in for 5 innings, and not remove him if the team is still behind.

X/H: Extra-base Hit Rate

*xERA: Expected ERA

---

* Asterisked formulas have updated versions in the Baseball Forecaster. *However, those updates include statistics like Ground Ball Rate, Fly Ball Rate or Line Drive Rate, for which we do not have reliable data for minor leaguers. So we use the previous version of those formulas, as listed here, for the players in this book.*

TEAM AFFILIATIONS

TEAM	ORG	LEAGUE	LEV	TEAM	ORG	LEAGUE	LEV
Aberdeen	BAL	New York-Penn League	SS	Connecticut	DET	New York-Penn League	SS
Akron	CLE	Eastern League	AA	Corpus Christi	HOU	Texas League	AA
Albuquerque	LAD	Pacific Coast League	AAA	Danville	ATL	Appalachian League	Rk
Altoona	PIT	Eastern League	AA	Dayton	CIN	Midwest League	A-
Arkansas	LAA	Texas League	AA	Daytona	CHC	Florida State League	A+
Asheville	COL	South Atlantic League	A-	Delmarva	BAL	South Atlantic League	A-
Auburn	WAS	New York-Penn League	SS	Dunedin	TOR	Florida State League	A+
Augusta	SF	South Atlantic League	A-	Durham	TAM	International League	AAA
AZL Angels	LAA	Arizona League	Rk	El Paso	SD	Pacific Coast League	AAA
AZL Athletics	OAK	Arizona League	Rk	Elizabethton	MIN	Appalachian League	Rk
AZL Brewers	MIL	Arizona League	Rk	Erie	DET	Eastern League	AA
AZL Cubs	CHC	Arizona League	Rk	Eugene	SD	Northwest League	SS
AZL Diamondbacks	ARI	Arizona League	Rk	Everett	SEA	Northwest League	SS
AZL Dodgers	LAD	Arizona League	Rk	Fort Myers	MIN	Florida State League	A+
AZL Giants	SF	Arizona League	Rk	Fort Wayne	SD	Midwest League	A-
AZL Indians	CLE	Arizona League	Rk	Frederick	BAL	Carolina League	A+
AZL Mariners	SEA	Arizona League	Rk	Fresno	SF	Pacific Coast League	AAA
AZL Padres	SD	Arizona League	Rk	Frisco	TEX	Texas League	AA
AZL Rangers	TEX	Arizona League	Rk	GCL Astros	HOU	Gulf Coast League	Rk
AZL Reds	CIN	Arizona League	Rk	GCL Blue Jays	TOR	Gulf Coast League	Rk
AZL Royals	KC	Arizona League	Rk	GCL Braves	ATL	Gulf Coast League	Rk
Bakersfield	CIN	California League	A+	GCL Cardinals	STL	Gulf Coast League	Rk
Batavia	MIA	New York-Penn League	SS	GCL Marlins	MIA	Gulf Coast League	Rk
Beloit	OAK	Midwest League	A-	GCL Mets	NYM	Gulf Coast League	Rk
Billings	CIN	Pioneer League	Rk	GCL Nationals	WAS	Gulf Coast League	Rk
Binghamton	NYM	Eastern League	AA	GCL Orioles	BAL	Gulf Coast League	Rk
Birmingham	CHW	Southern League	AA	GCL Phillies	PHI	Gulf Coast League	Rk
Bluefield	TOR	Appalachian League	Rk	GCL Pirates	PIT	Gulf Coast League	Rk
Boise	CHC	Northwest League	SS	GCL Rays	TAM	Gulf Coast League	Rk
Bowie	BAL	Eastern League	AA	GCL Red Sox	BOS	Gulf Coast League	Rk
Bowling Green	TAM	Midwest League	A-	GCL Tigers	DET	Gulf Coast League	Rk
Bradenton	PIT	Florida State League	A+	GCL Twins	MIN	Gulf Coast League	Rk
Brevard County	MIL	Florida State League	A+	GCL Yankees 1	NYY	Gulf Coast League	Rk
Bristol	PIT	Appalachian League	Rk	GCL Yankees 2	NYY	Gulf Coast League	Rk
Brooklyn	NYM	New York-Penn League	SS	Grand Junction	COL	Pioneer League	Rk
Buffalo	TOR	International League	AAA	Great Falls	CHW	Pioneer League	Rk
Burlington	KC	Appalachian League	Rk	Great Lakes	LAD	Midwest League	A-
Burlington	LAA	Midwest League	A-	Greeneville	HOU	Appalachian League	Rk
Carolina	CLE	Carolina League	A+	Greensboro	MIA	South Atlantic League	A-
Cedar Rapids	MIN	Midwest League	A-	Greenville	BOS	South Atlantic League	A-
Charleston	NYY	South Atlantic League	A-	Gwinnett	ATL	International League	AAA
Charlotte	CHW	International League	AAA	Hagerstown	WAS	South Atlantic League	A-
Charlotte	TAM	Florida State League	A+	Harrisburg	WAS	Eastern League	AA
Chattanooga	LAD	Southern League	AA	Helena	MIL	Pioneer League	Rk
Clearwater	PHI	Florida State League	A+	Hickory	TEX	South Atlantic League	A-
Clinton	SEA	Midwest League	A-	High Desert	SEA	California League	A+
Colorado Springs	COL	Pacific Coast League	AAA	Hillsboro	ARI	Northwest League	SS
Columbus	CLE	International League	AAA	Hudson Valley	TAM	New York-Penn League	SS

TEAM	ORG	LEAGUE	LEV
Huntsville	MIL	Southern League	AA
Idaho Falls	KC	Pioneer League	Rk
Indianapolis	PIT	International League	AAA
Inland Empire	LAA	California League	A+
Iowa	CHC	Pacific Coast League	AAA
Jackson	SEA	Southern League	AA
Jacksonville	MIA	Southern League	AA
Jamestown	PIT	New York-Penn League	SS
Johnson City	STL	Appalachian League	Rk
Jupiter	MIA	Florida State League	A+
Kane County	CHC	Midwest League	A-
Kannapolis	CHW	South Atlantic League	A-
Kingsport	NYM	Appalachian League	Rk
Lake County	CLE	Midwest League	A-
Lake Elsinore	SD	California League	A+
Lakeland	DET	Florida State League	A+
Lakewood	PHi	South Atlantic League	A-
Lancaster	HOU	California League	A+
Lansing	TOR	Midwest League	A-
Las Vegas	NYM	Pacific Coast League	AAA
Lehigh Valley	PHI	International League	AAA
Lexington	KC	South Atlantic League	A-
Louisville	CIN	International League	AAA
Lowell	BOS	New York-Penn League	SS
Lynchburg	ATL	Carolina League	A+
Mahoning Valley	CLE	New York-Penn League	SS
Memphis	STL	Pacific Coast League	AAA
Midland	OAK	Texas League	AA
Mississippi	ATL	Southern League	AA
Missoula	ARI	Pioneer League	Rk
Mobile	ARI	Southern League	AA
Modesto	COL	California League	A+
Montgomery	TAM	Southern League	AA
Myrtle Beach	TEX	Carolina League	A+
Nashville	MIL	Pacific Coast League	AAA
New Britain	MIN	Eastern League	AA
New Hampshire	TOR	Eastern League	AA
New Orleans	MIA	Pacific Coast League	AAA
Norfolk	BAL	International League	AAA
Northwest Arkansas	KC	Texas League	AA
Ogden	LAD	Pioneer League	Rk
Oklahoma City	HOU	Pacific Coast League	AAA
Omaha	KC	Pacific Coast League	AAA
Orem	LAA	Pioneer League	Rk
Palm Beach	STL	Florida State League	A+
Pawtucket	BOS	International League	AAA
Pensacola	CIN	Southern League	AA
Peoria	STL	Midwest League	A-
Portland	BOS	Eastern League	AA
Potomac	WAS	Carolina League	A+
Princeton	TAM	Appalachian League	Rk
Pulaski	SEA	Appalachian League	Rk
Quad Cities	HOU	Midwest League	A-
Rancho Cucamonga	LAD	California League	A+
Reading	PHI	Eastern League	AA
Reno	ARI	Pacific Coast League	AAA
Richmond	SF	Eastern League	AA
Rochester	MIN	International League	AAA
Rome	ATL	South Atlantic League	A-
Round Rock	TEX	Pacific Coast League	AAA
Sacramento	OAK	Pacific Coast League	AAA
Salem	BOS	Carolina League	A+
Salem-Keizer	SF	Northwest League	SS
Salt Lake	LAA	Pacific Coast League	AAA
San Antonio	SD	Texas League	AA
San Jose	SF	California League	A+
Savannah	NYM	South Atlantic League	A-
Scranton/Wilkes-Barre	NYY	International League	AAA
South Bend	ARI	Midwest League	A-
Spokane	TEX	Northwest League	SS
Springfield	STL	Texas League	AA
St. Lucie	NYM	Florida State League	A+
State College	STL	New York-Penn League	SS
Staten Island	NYY	New York-Penn League	SS
Stockton	OAK	California League	A+
Syracuse	WAS	International League	AAA
Tacoma	SEA	Pacific Coast League	AAA
Tampa	NYY	Florida State League	A+
Tennessee	CHC	Southern League	AA
Toledo	DET	International League	AAA
Trenton	NYY	Eastern League	AA
Tri-City	COL	Northwest League	SS
Tri-City	HOU	New York-Penn League	SS
Tulsa	COL	Texas League	AA
Vancouver	TOR	Northwest League	SS
Vermont	OAK	New York-Penn League	SS
Visalia	ARI	California League	A+
West Michigan	DET	Midwest League	A-
West Virginia	PIT	South Atlantic League	A-
Williamsport	PHI	New York-Penn League	SS
Wilmington	KC	Carolina League	A+
Winston-Salem	CHW	Carolina League	A+
Wisconsin	MIL	Midwest League	A-

2014 FANTASY BASEBALL WINNERS RESOURCE GUIDE

orders.baseballhq.com

10 REASONS

why winners rely on BASEBALL HQ PRODUCTS
for fantasy baseball information

1 **NO OTHER RESOURCE** provides you with more vital intelligence to help you win. Compare the depth of our offerings in these pages with any other information product or service.

2 **NO OTHER RESOURCE** provides more exclusive information, like cutting-edge component skills analyses, revolutionary strategies like the LIMA Plan, and innovative gaming formats like Rotisserie 500. *You won't find these anywhere else on the internet, guaranteed.*

3 **NO OTHER RESOURCE** has as long and consistent a track record of success in top national competitions... Our writers and readers have achieved 33 first place finishes, plus another 31 second and third place finishes since 1997. *No other resource comes remotely close.*

4 **NO OTHER RESOURCE** has as consistent a track record in projecting impact performances. In 2013, our readers had surprises like Domonic Brown, Chris Davis, Josh Donaldson, Stephen Drew, Adam Lind, Jonathan Lucroy, Starling Marte, Leonys Martin, Jean Segura, Andrew Cashner, Tyler Chatwood, Alex Cobb, Patrick Corbin, Ubaldo Jimenez, Corey Kluber, John Lackey, Ivan Nova, Anibal Sanchez and Max Scherzer on their teams, *and dozens more.*

5 **NO OTHER RESOURCE** is supported by more than 50 top writers and analysts — all paid professionals and proven winners, not weekend hobbyists or corporate staffers.

6 **NO OTHER RESOURCE** has a wider scope, providing valuable information not only for Rotisserie, but for alternative formats like simulations, salary cap contests, daily games, points, head-to-head, dynasty leagues and others.

7 **NO OTHER RESOURCE** is as highly regarded by its peers in the industry. Baseball HQ is the *only* three-time winner of the Fantasy Sports Trade Association's "Best Fantasy Baseball Online Content" award and Ron Shandler has won two lifetime achievement awards.

8 **NO OTHER RESOURCE** is as highly regarded *outside* of the fantasy industry. Many Major League general managers are regular customers. We were advisors to the St. Louis Cardinals in 2004 and our former Minor League Director is now a scout for the organization.

9 **NO OTHER RESOURCE** has been creating fantasy baseball winners for as long as we have. Our 28 years of stability *guarantees your investment*.

10 Year after year, more than 90% of our customers report that Baseball HQ products and services have helped them improve their performance in their fantasy leagues. That's the bottom line.

TO ORDER

MAIL check or money order to:
Baseball HQ/USA Today Sports Media Group, 1440 Broadway, 17th Floor, New York, NY 10018
PHONE 1-800-422-7820
FAX: 540-772-1969
ONLINE secure order form: *http://orders.baseballhq.com/*

SPRING 2014

FIRST PITCH
Fantasy Baseball Forums

Get a head start on the 2014 season with a unique opportunity to go one-on-one with some of the top writers and analysts in the fantasy baseball industry. First Pitch Forums bring the experts to some of the top cities in the USA for lively and informative symposium sessions.

These 3+ hour events combine player analysis with fantasy drafting, interactive activities and fun! You've never experienced anything so informative and entertaining! We've selected the top issues, topics, players and strategies that could make or break your fantasy season.

Our 2013 "Bold Statements" program identified many of last year's surprise players, such as Koji Uehara, Drew Smyly, Josh Donaldson, Anibal Sanchez, Evan Gattis, Stephen Drew, and John Lackey. The program addressed many relevant issues, from the riskiness of the Seattle pitching staff to the rise of Luke Hochevar. For 2014, we will once again be on the lookout for game-changing impact players, based on...

- Playing time opportunity
- Injury prognoses
- Bullpen volatility
- Minor league scouting
- Statistical analysis
- Breakout profile modeling
- and much more!

Ron Shandler and *Baseball Injury Report's* Rick Wilton chair the sessions, bringing a dynamic energy to every event. They are joined by guest experts from BaseballHQ.com and some of the leading sports media sources, like ESPN.com, MLB.com, USA Today Sports Weekly, Baseball America, Rotowire.com, Mastersball.com, KFFL.com and Sirius/XM Radio.

What you get for your registration

- 3+ hours of baseball talk with some of the baseball industry's top writers and analysts
- The chance to have *your* questions answered, 1-on-1 with the experts
- The opportunity to network with fellow fantasy leaguers from your area
- Freebies and discounts from leading industry vendors

Program description, forum sites and directions at
www.baseballhq.com/ seminars/index.shtml

2014 SITES

Saturday, February 22	**SAN FRANCISCO**
Saturday, February 22	**CHICAGO**
Sunday, February 23	**LOS ANGELES**
Friday, March 7	**WASHINGTON, DC**
Saturday, March 8	**NEW YORK**
Sunday, March 9	**BOSTON**
Saturday, March 15	**CINCINNATI**

NOTE: Schedule is preliminary and subject to change.

REGISTRATION: $39 per person in advance
$49 per person at the door

Don't forget - Oct. 31– Nov. 2 in Phoenix!